JESUS–
GOD AND MAN

WOLFHART PANNENBERG

JESUS–
GOD AND MAN

Translated by
LEWIS L. WILKINS
and
DUANE A. PRIEBE

SCM PRESS LTD
BLOOMSBURY STREET LONDON

1968

Translated from the German *Grundzüge der Christologie*
(Gütersloher Verlagshaus Gerd Mohn, Gütersloh, 1964)
by Lewis L. Wilkins and Duane A. Priebe

334 00773 9
First published in Great Britain 1968
by SCM Press Ltd
56 Bloomsbury Street London WC1
Second impression 1970
Third impression 1973
© The Westminster Press 1968
Printed in Great Britain by
Fletcher & Son Ltd, Norwich

CONTENTS

Part One: THE KNOWLEDGE OF
JESUS' DIVINITY

Part Two: JESUS THE MAN BEFORE GOD

Part Three: THE DIVINITY OF CHRIST AND THE MAN JESUS

ABBREVIATIONS

CCL   *Corpus Christianorum, series Latina.* Turnholti: Typographie Brepols Editores Pontificii, 1954.

CD   Karl Barth, *Church Dogmatics,* ed. by G. W. Bromiley and T. F. Torrance. 12 vols.; Edinburgh: T. & T. Clark, 1936-1962.

CR   *Corpus Reformatorum.*

EKL   *Evangelisches Kirchenlexikon. Kirchlich-theologisches Handwörter-buch,* ed. by H. Brunotte and O. Weber. Göttingen: Vandenhoeck & Ruprecht, 1956-1961.

EvTh   *Evangelische Theologie.*

GCS   *Die Griechischen Christlichen Schriftsteller.* Leipzig: J. C. Hinrichs'sche Buchhandlung; Berlin: Akademie-Verlag, 1897 ff.

CSEL   *Corpus Scriptorum Ecclesiasticorum Latinorum,* 79 vols. Vindobonae: C. Geroldi Filium, then F. Tempsky, 1866 ff.

GuV   Rudolf Bultmann, *Glauben und Verstehen: Gesammelte Aufsätze,* 3 vols. Tübingen: J. C. B. Mohr (Paul Siebeck), 1933, 1952, 1959.

KuD   *Kerygma und Dogma.*

LThK   *Lexikon für Theologie und Kirche.* 2d ed.; Freiburg: Verlag Herder, 1957-1967.

MPG   J. P. Migne, *Patrologiae cursus completus, series Graeca,* 161 vols. Paris, 1857-1866.

MPL   J. P. Migne, *Patrologiae cursus completus, series Latina,* 221 vols. Paris, 1884-1880.

NTS   *New Testament Studies.*

OaG   *Offenbarung als Geschichte,* ed. by Wolfhart Pannenberg (Beiheft 1 to *KuD*). Göttingen: Vandenhoeck & Ruprecht, 1961.

RE   *Realencyklopädie für protestantische Theologie und Kirche,* ed. by Albert Hauck. 3d ed.; Leipzig: J. C. Hinrichs'sche Buchhandlung, 1896-1913.

RGG   *Die Religion in Geschichte und Gegenwart,* ed. by K. Galling, 3d ed. Tübingen: J. C. B. Mohr (Paul Siebeck), 1957 ff.

SHA   *Sitzungsberichte der Heidelberger Akademie der Wissenschaften.*

9

SBA	*Sitzungsberichte der Deutschen Akademie der Wissenschaft zu Berlin.*
ThLZ	*Theologische Literaturzeitung.*
ThW	*Theologisches Wörterbuch zum Neuen Testament,* ed. by Gerhard Kittel and Gerhard Friedrich. Stuttgart: Verlag von W. Kohlhammer, 1933 ff.
ThD	*Theological Dictionary of the New Testament,* ed. by Gerhard Kittel, tr. and ed. by G. W. Bromiley. Wm. B. Eerdmans Publishing Company, 1964 ff.
ThZ	*Theologische Zeitschrift.*
WA	Martin Luther, *Werke: Kritische Gesamtausgabe.* Weimar: Herman Böhlau & Nachfolger, 1883 ff.
ZEE	*Zeitschrift für evangelische Ethik.*
ZKG	*Zeitschrift für Kirchengeschichte.*
ZNW	*Zeitschrift für die neutestamentliche Wissenschaft.*
ZsyTh	*Zeitschrift für systematische Theologie.*
ZThK	*Zeitschrift für Theologie und Kirche.*

FOREWORD TO THE FIRST GERMAN EDITION

To account theologically for faith in Jesus Christ is rendered difficult today by many problems. The great questions in the development of Christological doctrine have remained without effective solution since the time of the ancient church. Up to the present, the history of Christology has been dominated by the contrast between the Alexandrian fusion of Jesus with God and the Antiochene separation between Jesus and God, which emerges at constantly new stages. The difficulties that are present here, which will be treated extensively in the third part of this book, call for a new substantiation of Christology that goes behind those contrasting impulses, but also one that goes behind the question of an incarnational Christology in general, which is common to both of them. A sound basis for such a new substantiation of Christology, however, has not yet been found in spite of the Christological concerns of the nineteenth century and of the present.

In addition, since the Enlightenment the historical picture of Jesus has become farther and farther removed from dogmatic Christology in general. Since then it has appeared to be impossible to unite the God-man of Christological dogma with the historical reality of Jesus. The Christological thought of the nineteenth century and of the present also has been concerned with overcoming this growing cleft. However, it could not hinder the fact that the confessional statements about Jesus in the church's tradition either became strange and impossible for contemporary Christians to understand or sank into the undemonstrable subjectivity of so-called perceptions of faith.

Thus, dogmatic Christology is burdened by great difficulties, as much in its own realm as also with regard to its relation to the quest of the historical Jesus. However, the Christological task cannot be neglected and be made to wait until a time when these difficulties disappear by themselves. All theological statements win their Christian character only through their connection with Jesus. It is precisely Christology that discusses and establishes the justification and the appropriate form of theological reference to Jesus in a methodological way. Therefore, theology can clarify its Christian self-understanding only by a thematic and comprehensive involvement with the Christological problems.

11

This task seems to me to be particularly pressing with regard to the conception of the theology of history in the working circle to which I belong as well as in view of the criticisms that have been its lot. The theological justification of the approach of the theology of history depends decisively on the understanding of Christ that is connected with it. This has been characterized by the concept of the prehappening of the end of history in the activity and destiny of Jesus. This idea must be subjected to the question of its verification in terms of the entire range of Christological problems. Moreover, the thesis that God's revelation can be known from its historical manifestation in the history of Jesus can find the necessary clarification only by carrying out the interpretation of the Christological traditions as the development of the significance inherent in the activity and destiny of Jesus.

To be sure, I am far from supposing that this central problem would be sufficiently clarified by that. Rather, the Christological discussions in this book point at every step to ontological and epistemological implications that need their own comprehensive discussion. However, I hope that the theological relevance of such a theology of reason or eschatologically oriented ontology will become more readily apparent against the background of a Christology that is carried through at least in outline. Until then, may whoever finds enjoyment in it continue to measure my talk about knowledge and reality with the standard of a positivistic understanding of being and knowledge in order in this way to discover to his general surprise its inappropriateness.

Every contemporary Christology must confront both the inner tensions of the doctrinal tradition of Christology and the historical study of Jesus. If it would neglect the latter, it should look away from the historical reality of Jesus as it is accessible today. However, whoever would disdain the discussion with the tradition of Christological doctrine would deprive himself of the insight into the fact that and the way that the Christological models which have arisen in the history of theology and the conflict about them already stand in the service of the development of the significance of the history of Jesus, at least so far as the central issues are concerned. The neglect of the Christological tradition generally has as a consequence that one thinks he finds the present significance of Jesus in generalizations of certain aspects of his appearance that are astonishingly superficial and hasty. Absorption in the problems of the doctrinal tradition of Christology can guard against this kind of "hermeneutical" actualization. The lasting truth in this tradition, of course, only discloses itself to a critical appropriation that grasps and tests the individual Christological models and the process of the development of Christological doctrine itself as an interpretation of the appearance and history of Jesus.

Such a way of approaching the question presupposes that the history of Jesus carries its meaning in itself. That is true insofar as the universal meaning rooted in Jesus' claim to ultimate truth reaches out to all reality and all truth in general. For in this way the historical context in which the earthly history of Jesus took place does not come to this history as something external but is claimed by this history itself as its own horizon of meaning. The activity and destiny of Jesus naturally have their significance originally on the horizon of the history of Jewish traditions within whose context Jesus appeared. The original significance of Jesus' activity and destiny must be ascertained from this their nearest horizon. Only to the extent that the situation in the Jewish history of traditions out of which Jesus emerged with his message must be seen as determined by Jewish apocalyptic does it become necessary to describe the significance of the activity and destiny of Jesus in relation to the background of apocalyptic theology. This does not mean that the figure of Jesus melts into this background. Rather, it means primarily that his uniqueness is set off from this background. But constant reference to it is necessary precisely for the sake of making this uniqueness stand out.

The insights into the significance of the history of Jesus that may be attained in such a way do not at all form a final measuring rod against which every further interpretation would merely have to be checked. Much rather, the universal, eschatological claim of the appearance of Jesus and his history has driven the Christological tradition beyond the limits of the Jewish realm of tradition. It is with this in view that the motifs and the theological justification of the transition from the Hellenistic interpretation of the figure of Jesus to the ideas about the deity of Jesus, and to belief in the incarnation, are to be evaluated.

In this way a vision of the development of Christological doctrine emerges that sees it as a process in the history of traditions. It traces the formation of Christological statements as well as their continued transformation and reconstruction from the logic inherent in the activity and destiny of Jesus himself. The discovery of such material relationships forms a special task which has scarcely been noticed in the customary work on the history of doctrine, but which leads directly to the formation of systematic judgments. This is also true where the effectiveness of these material relationships has been mediated and concealed by other viewpoints. Therefore, they have not become a conscious motif in the thought of the theologians involved in the development of Christological doctrine, but they become apparent for the first time in our modern reflection on their relation to the historical Jesus in the history of traditions.

A comprehensive treatment of this task would have the character of a theory of the Christological tradition. This theory would be both historic and systematic at the same time, because the succession of interpretations belongs to the historic essence of the subject matter that is to be interpreted insofar as this leads to the inclusion of ever new points of view because of its universal meaning and thus constantly produces new interpretations. The presentation of the fundamentals of Christology in this book differs considerably from such a theory of the Christological tradition because it presents those material relationships between the history of Jesus and Christological interpretation only under special aspects of the subject matter, under the limitation of particular accentuated Christological conceptions or of typical tendencies in the development of Christological doctrine. However, it does not undertake a comprehensive interpretation of the whole process. At present such a theory of the Christological tradition is not yet possible because the "history of traditions" work on the Christological tradition is in its beginning stage. A theory of the Christological tradition can probably be expected sometime in the future as the result of the common work of many investigators. Fortunately, for such a project no common dogmatic presuppositions are required. On the contrary, it is to be hoped that a common basis for the formation of theological judgments will emerge from the discussion of these relationships in the history of traditions.

Nevertheless, it will be well because of this to abandon the conception that dogmatic statements must have the character of timelessly binding and unchanging truth. The history of dogmatics eliminates this opinion anyway. Perhaps the conscious abandonment of such claims for dogmatic work will render it possible for the first time to arrive at statements that are at least relatively binding. Thus, every Christological insight remains bound to a particular state of research and hence can become outmoded. In this it is to be distinguished from the truth of Jesus Christ himself, which sustains Christian faith, but which cannot be ultimately absorbed by any theological formulation.

The publication of this Christology would not have been possible without the manifold help of my reliable friend Hans-Reimer Leptihn in producing the manuscript. I thank my assistants Traugott Koch and Harald Ihmig as well as the theological student Bernd Steinseifer for their help with the corrections. I also wish to thank the first two named for the preparation of the index and for many suggestions with regard to the subject matter. In general I have received valuable comments from many sides. I acknowledge with special gratitude the assistance that I have received from Ulrich Wilckens during a long period of common work and through his criticism of the New Testament basis of the first draft of this book.

WOLFHART PANNENBERG

Mainz, August, 1964

FOREWORD TO THE SECOND GERMAN EDITION

For the new edition, in addition to formal corrections, a number of statements and formulations have been made more precise or corrected. Additions (pp. 51, 69, 136, 171, 262, 321) have been compensated for by condensations in order to preserve the pagination of the first edition.

WOLFHART PANNENBERG

Mainz, February, 1966

PREFACE TO THE ENGLISH EDITION

The gratitude the author owes to American theology and to American thought in general is but faintly indicated in the present book by the rare references to the scholarly work which has been done in the English language on problems of Christology. I regret that my time did not allow for a revision and extension of the German text which was completed in 1963 and only slightly revised in 1966. I hope the reader of this translation will be able to relate for himself what is said in this book to the work of such scholars as J. N. D. Kelly, G. L. Prestige, or R. V. Sellers, to mention only the patristic field of Christological research. As for the particular perspective of this book, R. A. Norris' investigation (1963) of the interrelation between anthropology and Christology in Appollinaris of Laodicea and Theodore of Mopsuestia is of special importance, but came to my attention only after the German text was completed. Similarly, I was not yet able to enter a discussion of constructive proposals such as Paul van Buren's attempt to reinterpret the Christological tradition.

Rev. Lewis L. Wilkins and his wife, Harriet, took over the enormous task of providing the first draft of the translation, part of which was used for my lectures at the University of Chicago in 1963. Dr. Duane A. Priebe established the final text of the translation. Mr. Karl Peters, besides his own graduate work at Union Theological Seminary, spent many hours verifying the references of the footnotes to German books or editions in corresponding English publications. He also rearranged all Scripture quotations according to the Revised Standard Version. Without the magnanimous help of all these people and especially the continuous efforts of Dr. Roland W. Tapp, who also contributed the English version of the indexes, this translation never would have been born. I am further indebted to Prof. Claude Welch for reading through a first stage of the English manuscript and providing me with helpful criticism and advice.

WOLFHART PANNENBERG

INTRODUCTION

Its teaching about Jesus Christ lies at the heart of every Christian theology. This involves what we as Christians have to say about Jesus in contrast to what one who is definitely a non-Christian or who provisionally abstains from a final, personal decision might say about Jesus.[1] In contrast to the non-Christian appraisals of Jesus and to well-intentioned people who see him as an especially noble man—but only that—the Christian is conscious of knowing Jesus' true significance by confessing him. A Christian's statements about Jesus must be for him, at least in their central content, more than simply one interpretation among other equally possible interpretations for the same set of facts. He knows and believes that only the Christian way of speaking about Jesus is appropriate to the facts, or better, to Jesus' person. Such a claim must, however, be accounted for; it must show itself to be true, not primarily in the face of others' doubts, but to the satisfaction of the believer's own concern for truth. Every Christian is asked whether his understanding of Jesus is also the true one that is appropriate to Jesus himself. The purpose of the Christological endeavor is to examine systematically this question and thus to account for the Christian teaching about Jesus, as well as to examine the teaching itself.

The distinctiveness of the Christological way of speaking about Jesus resides in its theological character. As Christians we know God only as he has been revealed in and through Jesus. All other talk about God can have, at most, provisional significance. In this sense it may be very meaningful and necessary, even a presupposition for the message of Christ.[2] But the way in which God is revealed through Jesus suspends even its own presupposition, so that one can only speak about God himself in that at the same time one

[1] Walter Künneth critically presents various "secular" evaluations of Jesus (Szczesny, Schoeps, Jaspers, Leist) in *Glauben an Jesus? Die Begegnung der Christologie mit der modernen Existenz* (Hamburg: F. Wittig, 1962), pp. 25 ff.

[2] It has been, in fact, the presupposition for the emergence of a Christology—and is in a certain sense inescapable—"to bring men first to faith in God as the prerequisite of a faith in Jesus Christ that is built up upon this." Gerhard Ebeling questions this in *Theology and Proclamation* (Fortress Press, 1966), p. 35.

talks about Jesus. Therefore, theology and Christology, the doctrine of God and the doctrine of Jesus as the Christ, are bound together. It is the goal of theology as well as of Christology to develop this connection.

Such development can take the idea of God as its guiding theme. It will then describe the suspension and assumption of the human question of God, its philosophical elaboration and its preliminary, inappropriate answer in the non-Christian religions and directions of thought, through the revelation in Christ. In this context one speaks about Jesus only from the point of view of his significance for the idea of God in the context of the history of that idea. What one might otherwise say about Jesus would have to be presupposed as already known. The procedure of Christology, on the contrary, begins with Jesus himself in order to find God in him. In this case, in turn, the idea of God must be presupposed historically and in substance.

CHAPTER

1

THE STARTING POINT

*Christology deals with Jesus as the basis of the confession and
the faith that he is the Christ of God.*

I. THE TASK OF CHRISTOLOGY

Even the apparently self-evident observation that Christology deals with
Jesus can be understood in very different ways. Does Christology involve the
Jesus who appeared in Palestine in the time of the emperor Tiberius and
who was crucified under the Roman procurator Pontius Pilate? Or does it
involve Jesus as he is proclaimed today and is present through the proclamation, whether it be in the hermeneutical achievement of the event of proclamation itself or as the one who is exalted to God's right hand and who thus
is also the living one who is present before all proclamation? For the moment
we are not concerned with the alternative offered in the second question as
to whether the presence of Christ is to be understood in the sense of the
event of proclamation or in the sense of the exalted Christ of the old dogmatics.[1] Our question goes behind this conflict: Does Christology have primarily to do with the Jesus of that past time or with the Jesus who is present
today? The two are certainly not mutually exclusive. The Jesus proclaimed
today is none other than the one who lived at that time in Palestine and
was crucified under Pilate—and vice versa. Nevertheless, it does make a
fundamental difference whether we seek to understand the present proclamation of who Jesus is and what he means for us in terms of what happened
at that time or whether, conversely, we speak of what happened then only
secondarily, that is, only in the light of what the proclamation says about it

[1] But Bultmann, also, says that in the kerygma "not the *historical* but the *exalted* Jesus"
says, "All authority has been given to me." Rudolf Bultmann, *Das Verhältnis der urchristlichen Christusbotschaft zum historischen Jesus* (Sitzungsberichte der Heidelberger
Akademie der Wissenschaften, Philosophisch-historische Klasse, 1930; 3d ed.; Heidelberg:
Carl Winter, 1962), p. 17.

today. The question is this: Must Christology begin with Jesus himself or with the kerygma of his community?

The idea that theology, when it deals with Jesus Christ, must take its starting point in the proclamation of his community has become very influential since Martin Kähler.[2] This idea was not completely original with Kähler. Albrecht Ritschl already had said this about the perception of Jesus: "One can attain the full extent of his historic reality only out of the faith which the Christian community has in him."[3] Such a point of view was suggested earlier by Schleiermacher and by the Erlangen school of theology.

Kähler advocated this idea especially in his famous book *The So-called Historical Jesus and the Historic, Biblical Christ* (1892).[4] In this book he attacked the theological claim of the quest for the historical Jesus which was at that time in full bloom. The quest for the historical Jesus sought to lay bare the man Jesus and his message from the later development of the piety and Christology of the Christian community as they are combined in the New Testament writings. The life of Jesus and his religion should have direct, exemplary meaning for Christians today. Jesus was set in opposition to Paul, who, as Harnack thought, had covered up the simple humanness of Jesus with his own bizarre Christology. Such a harsh contrast between Jesus and Paul has recently been advocated anew by Ethelbert Stauffer.[5] Kähler's work opposes that kind of quest for the historical Jesus which makes of him a mere man. Kähler rightly protested against the tendency to drive a cleft between Jesus and the apostles' preaching about Christ. In this sense his statement is correct: "The real Christ is the preached Christ."[6] It is based on the fact that, in general, "the personal effect which survives in a noticeable way for subsequent generations" (p. 19) belongs to the historical reality of any important figure. This personal effect in the case of Jesus is "the faith of his disciples, the conviction that one has in him the conqueror of guilt, sin, the Tempter, and death" (*ibid.*).

We repeat, Kähler is correct in these statements, insofar as he protests against setting the figure and message of Jesus in opposition to the apostolic preaching in such a way that no sort of continuity between the two would exist any longer. However, it does not follow from the rejection of such false antitheses either (1) that the effects of the person Jesus are to be found

[2] On Kähler, cf. Johannes Wirsching, *Gott in der Geschichte: Studien zur theologiegeschichtlichen Stellung und systematischen Grundlegung der Theologie Martin Kählers* (Munich: Chr. Kaiser Verlag, 1963), as well as Heinrich Leipold, *Offenbarung und Geschichte als Problem des Verstehens: Eine Untersuchung zur Theologie Martin Kählers* (Gütersloh: Gütersloher Verlagshaus Gerd Mohn, 1962).

[3] Albrecht Ritschl, *The Christian Doctrine of Justification and Reconciliation* (Edinburgh: T. & T. Clark, 1902), p. 3.

[4] Martin Kähler, *The So-called Historical Jesus and the Historic, Biblical Christ*, ed. and tr. by Carl E. Braaten (Fortress Press, 1964).

[5] Ethelbert Stauffer, *Jesus, Paulus und wir* (Hamburg: F. Wittig, 1961).

[6] Kähler, *The So-called Historical Jesus and the Historic, Biblical Christ*, p. 66.

only in the apostolic preaching or (2) that what is "truly historic" about Jesus is only his "personal effect." This effect radiated outward into definite and, already in early Christianity, varied historical situations. Therefore, something of the particular intellectual situation of the respective witness, of the questions that moved their times and to which they answered with their confession of Christ, also always adheres to the New Testament accounts of Jesus. This is the basis for the diversity of the New Testament witnesses to Jesus, which is not to be overlooked. Because the New Testament testimony to Christ so clearly bears the stamp of the particular contemporary problematic of the witnesses, one cannot simply equate Jesus himself with the apostles' witness to him, as Kähler expressed it in his formula about "the whole Biblical Christ."

In the sense of such an equation it is false to say that the real Christ is the preached Christ. One can and must get back to Jesus himself from the witness of the apostles by trying to recognize, and thus making allowance for, the relation of New Testament texts to their respective situations. It is quite possible to distinguish the figure of Jesus himself, as well as the outlines of his message, from the particular perspective in which it is transmitted through this or that New Testament witness. What is no longer "possible," according to the insights of the form-critical study of the Gospels, is really only the attempt to exploit the sequence of the presentation in our Gospels as a chronology of Jesus' life and ministry; for the sequence of presentation in all four Gospels has been proved to be determined by considerations of composition. This does not mean, however, that even the question of evidence in the Gospels for a chronology of Jesus' life is completely settled, not to speak of the question of a history of Jesus in general. Ultimately, Kähler is right on only one point: the historical reconstruction of the figure and proclamation of Jesus is always required to explain how the early Christian proclamation of Christ could emerge from the fate of Jesus. The assertion of an antithesis between Jesus and the primitive Christian kerygma about him remains unsatisfying also from a historical point of view. The continuity between the two must be made understandable.

Going back behind the apostolic kerygma to the historical Jesus is, therefore, possible. It is also necessary. Wilhelm Herrmann properly criticized Kähler at just this point: precisely because the New Testament witnesses proclaimed Jesus as he appeared to faith at that time, "this proclamation alone, if we leave it up to that, cannot protect us from the doubt that we want to base our faith on something that is perhaps not historical fact at all, but is itself a product of faith."[7] To be sure, Herrmann also shies away from basing faith on our historical knowledge about Jesus: "It is a fatal error to attempt to establish the basis of faith by means of historical investi-

[7] Wilhelm Herrmann, "Der geschichtliche Christus: Der Grund unseres Glaubens," *ZThK*, II (1892), 232-273; quotation, p. 253.

gation. The basis of faith must be something fixed; the results of historical study are continually changing. The basis of our faith must be grasped in the same independent fashion by learned and unlearned, by each for himself."[8] In this, Herrmann agrees with Kähler's demand that faith ought not to "depend on scholarly investigation."[9]

In the present revival of the quest of Jesus by Käsemann, Fuchs, Bornkamm, and others, this restriction has been overcome in principle. Whether Jesus himself or someone else was the real bearer of the message handed down by the writers of the Synoptic Gospels is no longer considered, with Bultmann, since it is an incidental question.[10] This position is possible for Bultmann because, for him, "the person of Jesus is absorbed in his word."[11] Over against that, it is recognized today that faith must have "support in the historical Jesus himself."[12] That means, certainly, in Jesus himself as he is accessible to our historical inquiry. One can agree completely with this assertion. The only question that remains is, What is really the decisive factor in Jesus' life and proclamation upon which faith is based? We will return at length to this question later.[13]

To go back behind the New Testament text to Jesus himself is unavoidable for another reason. Only in this way is it possible to see the unity that binds together the New Testament witnesses. As long as one only compares the varied witnesses, one will have to recognize the antitheses that appear even in passages that sound similar. The unity of Scripture will not be grasped in a comparison of the statements of the New Testament witnesses;

---

[8] Wilhelm Herrmann, *The Communion of the Christian with God* (G. P. Putnam's Sons, 1930), p. 76.

[9] Martin Kähler, *Der sogenannte historische Jesus und der geschichtliche, biblische Christus* (2d ed.; Leipzig: A. Deichert'sche Verlagsbuchhandlung Nachf. [Georg Böhme], 1896), p. 147. This part is not in the edition translated into English.

[10] Rudolf Bultmann, *Jesus and the Word* (Charles Scribner's Sons, 1958), pp. 13 f.

[11] Rudolf Bultmann, *GuV*, I, 274.

[12] Gerhard Ebeling, *The Nature of Faith* (Fortress Press, 1961), p. 46.

[13] On the renewal of scholarly concern about the historical Jesus in recent study, cf. James M. Robinson, *A New Quest of the Historical Jesus* (London: SCM Press, Ltd., 1959). Robinson's work is criticized by Van A. Harvey and Schubert M. Ogden in "How New Is the 'New Quest of the Historical Jesus'?" *The Historical Jesus and the Kerygmatic Christ: Essays on the New Quest of the Historical Jesus,* tr. and ed. by Carl E. Braaten and Roy A. Harrisville (Abingdon Press, 1964), pp. 197-242. Harvey and Ogden correctly show that the "new quest" of the historical Jesus is also determined by an interest in the *legitimation of the kerygma* through Jesus himself (esp. pp. 222 ff.), even though this expression is usually avoided with reference to themselves by those involved in the "new quest." The latter generally use this expression to characterize a period of research about Jesus that they think has been superseded. However, cf. Ebeling's statement that the situation qualified by Jesus "legitimates" the kerygma (*Theology and Proclamation,* pp. 74 f.; in the same sense also pp. 57 and 64). Ebeling means, however, that such legitimation is merely directed toward the demonstration of the relation of the kerygma to Jesus himself, but not toward a proof for the truth of the kerygma. The question about such proofs seems to him a perversion of the question of the basis for the kerygma (*ibid.,* p. 49; cf. pp. 57, 63, and esp. 70 f.).

it consists only in the one Jesus to whom they all refer, and will be recognizable, therefore, only when one has penetrated behind the kerygma of the apostles. The inner unity of the New Testament writings will be visible precisely when they are taken as a "historical source" and not only as a "preaching text." As a historical source they express not only "what was at once believed,"[14] but also permit something of Jesus himself, in whom the Christian believes, to be recognized.

Martin Kähler's main interest was to establish that the real Jesus is not the historian's picture of Jesus of Nazareth, but rather the Christ of faith who is experienced as contemporary reality. Therefore, Kähler said, "I can consider only that theology valid which helps to bring the facts of present, living Christianity to the most appropriate, clearest, and sharpest expression" (p. 26). Contemporary Christian experience was the pivotal point of his thought. On this point also Herrmann ultimately agreed with Kähler, although he saw this experience as grounded more in the experience that men can have today of Jesus than in the effect of the apostolic message.

The use of contemporary Christian experience as the point of departure for theology goes back, as we have already mentioned, to Schleiermacher and the Erlangen Lutheran theology of the nineteenth century. In his dogmatics[15] Schleiermacher constructed Christology by way of inference from contemporary Christian experience. The experience of redemption, of overcoming that which restricts the full consciousness of God, is for him that which is given. This experience is possible only within a "social totality," within a community of the redeemed, as it is to be found in the church. From the fact of a community of those who know themselves to be freed to a powerful consciousness of God, Schleiermacher reasons *a posteriori* to an originator, who must necessarily be presupposed, of such a "social totality" (§ 87,3) which, as something new, has taken the place of the social totality of sin. Everything else that is said about Christ in Schleiermacher's dogmatics concerns him merely as the founder of the social totality of the redeemed. It describes him as his image is presupposed in the corporate consciousness of redemption: "how, by virtue of this consciousness, the redeemer is postulated," to use a characteristic expression of Schleiermacher (§ 91,2). At this point the Erlangen new Lutheran theology of the nineteenth century followed Schleiermacher. Out of the contemporary Christian experience of redemption from sin, they inferred Jesus as its author. In distinction from Schleiermacher, those in Erlangen thought it possible to conjure up out of the Christian consciousness the entire Biblical Jesus tradition to the last detail, including the virgin birth.

The contemporary Christian experience of salvation as the point of depar-

[14] G. Ebeling, *The Nature of Faith*, p. 34.
[15] Friedrich Schleiermacher, *The Christian Faith* (2 vols.; Harper Torchbooks, The Cloister Library; Harper & Row, Publishers, Inc., 1963).

ture for theological thought also constituted the background of Kähler's position. In its modification produced by Kähler's Biblical theology this way of thinking is very much alive today. The contemporary experience of the truth of Christ is described in our day as identical with the confrontation by the proclamation and with the decision of faith for the proclamation. Bultmann, for example, speaks of "the confrontation with the proclaimed Christ" in the kerygma which meets me in my historical situation: "The *Kyrios Christos* encounters me in the kerygma of the church."[16] The Easter faith consists of the faith "that Jesus Christ is present in the kerygma."[17] Otto Weber also acknowledges a "confrontation with Jesus Christ which establishes and supports faith."[18] In his view the whole of Christology is theological reflection about this confrontation which occurs through the "message about Jesus Christ."

These ideas are also found in Paul Althaus. To be sure, he expressly differentiates himself from the Erlangen theology of experience.[19] Even as "experience," faith is not directed toward itself but toward its "ground and object."[20] Nevertheless, Althaus says that faith "does not have to do primarily with what Jesus *was,* but rather with what he is as he encounters us in the proclamation."[21] Certainly, Althaus also wants to maintain the importance of knowledge about the historical Jesus. "The revelatory character of the history of Jesus is not known by means of historical reflection or historical reasoning. But, on the other hand, it is not known *without these.* For the gospel deals with facts that, it is claimed, happened in this history of ours."[22] In opposition to Bultmann and Gogarten, Althaus observes that faith that is without security in the sense of the pure kerygmatic theology is "faith without foundation" (p. 32). On the other hand, he himself describes faith without reservation as a risk,[23] for Althaus also regards the character of what took place in Jesus as revelation to be founded in our contemporary experience of the proclaimed Christ, not in what we can know about Jesus of Nazareth. He is, thus, still in halfway agreement with his opponents. It is not without reason that Bultmann asked Althaus: If faith does not spring

[16] Rudolf Bultmann in *Kerygma and Myth: A Theological Debate,* ed. by Hans Werner Bartsch, tr. by Reginald H. Fuller, Vol. I (London: S.P.C.K., 1953), pp. 117 f.

[17] R. Bultmann, *Das Verhältnis der urchristlichen Christusbotschaft zum historischen Jesus,* p. 27.

[18] Otto Weber, *Grundlagen der Dogmatik* (2 vols.; Neukirchen Kreis Moers: Verlag der Buchhandlung des Erziehungsvereins, 1955 and 1962), Vol. II, p. 36.

[19] Paul Althaus, *Die christliche Wahrheit* (6th ed.; Gütersloh: C. Bertelsmann, 1962), pp. 426 f.

[20] *Ibid.,* p. 427.

[21] *Ibid.,* p. 423.

[22] Paul Althaus, *Fact and Faith in the Kerygma Today* (Muhlenberg Press, 1959), p. 34.

[23] Cf. P. Althaus, *Die christliche Wahrheit,* pp. 427, 601.

from the perception of historical facts, "what is the point, then, of legitimation through history?"[24]

However, Bultmann's own talk about an encounter with the proclaimed Christ in the kerygma cannot escape Herrmann's criticism of Kähler that the proclamation alone cannot protect us against the doubt as to whether we do not "want to base our faith on something that is perhaps not a historical fact at all, but is itself a product of faith." And if we—in distinction from Herrmann's opinion—cannot acquire substantiated knowledge of the "historical fact" designated Jesus in any way except through historical research, then the question about the history of Jesus is inescapable for the legitimation of the kerygma as a message that is derived from Jesus. If it cannot be shown that the proclamation about Christ has "support in the historical Jesus himself," then the proclamation must appear as a product of faith. "If the person to whom the kerygma refers is in no way concretely definable in his historicity, if the reference of the kerygma to Jesus consists exclusively in assertions for whose understanding Jesus himself is irrelevant, as merely a cipher that is accidental and in itself says nothing, then the kerygma—if it then could be kerygma at all—would be pure myth."[25]

How Jesus of Nazareth is the basis of the kerygma and of our faith still remains entirely open—whether only in the sense that the kerygma continues Jesus' own unprovable demand for faith or whether the truth upon which the Christian's trust in God is based can be shown in Jesus' destiny, beyond the mere claim of Jesus. One can make a decision on this question only after a more precise consideration of Jesus of Nazareth and the actual connection between him and the primitive Christian message. This much, however, is already clear: if we are supposed to speak about the foundation of our faith in him, then the one about whom we speak can be only Jesus of Nazareth. Admittedly, this basis of our faith stands the test and must stand the test of our present experience of reality, but it itself lies completely in what happened in the past.

Certainly, the believer knows very well that Jesus not only lived in the past but that as the risen and exalted Lord he is also alive today. However, one cannot achieve such knowledge about the living, present Lord through direct, present-day experience in association with the exalted Lord. Apparently, Gerhard Koch affirms something of the sort when he writes, "The Kyrios now reveals himself in the Easter meal."[26] Correspondingly, Koch says about the Christian community, "It experiences his presence in the Word

[24] R. Bultmann, Das Verhältnis der urchristlichen Christusbotschaft zum historischen Jesus, p. 13.

[25] G. Ebeling, Theology and Proclamation, p. 64.

[26] Gerhard Koch, Die Auferstehung Jesu Christi (Tübingen: J. C. B. Mohr [Paul Siebeck], 1959), p. 302.

and Sacrament."[27] The Lord's Supper, the word, but also history and Scripture are "signs" for Koch through which "the event of encounter" with the *Kyrios* can happen.[28] According to Koch, this encounter takes place in worship. "Recognition of the Lord, which means at the same time self-recognition, happens in the act of encounter. It occurs in worship."[29] "Worship is the Easter event."[30] Walter Künneth also speaks of an immediate experience of the exalted Lord. This experience establishes the certainty, not only of the reality of his resurrection, but also of his historical existence. "Because Jesus as the resurrected Lord shows himself to be effective in faith and because faith is certain that Jesus, the Lord, lives, faith knows as a consequence about the historical existence of Jesus of Nazareth."[31]

But who can be certain of such experiences? How can one distinguish them from self-delusion? Further, the New Testament testifies that through his exaltation Jesus has been removed from the earth and from his disciples. Only on the basis of what happened in the past, not because of present experiences, do we know that Jesus lives as the exalted Lord. Only in trust in the reliability of the report of Jesus' resurrection and exaltation are we able to turn in prayer to the one who is exalted and now lives, and thus to associate with him in the present. No one now has an experience of him as risen and exalted, at least not an experience that could be distinguished with certainty from illusion. In the Corinthian Gnosticism, Paul battled the illusion that one can *experience* the glory of the exalted Lord in the present. The *experience* of the presence of Christ is promised only for the end of time. Therefore, also, whatever concerns the certainty of the present life of the exalted Lord is based entirely on what happened in the past. Also, the character of the Christ event as revelation must be appropriate to what happened in Jesus of Nazareth as such if it is not to be simply a subjective addition to our interpretation.[32] In opposition to Althaus we must say, faith primarily has to do with what Jesus *was*. Only from that can we know what he is for us today and how proclamation about him is possible today.

Christology is concerned, therefore, not only with *unfolding* the Christian community's confession of Christ, but above all with *grounding* it in the activity and fate of Jesus in the past. The confession of Christ cannot be presupposed already and simply interpreted. Christology cannot take its point of departure from the confessions of the Reformation, for example, from the Christological statements of the Formula of Concord, or from the Christological formula of the Council of Chalcedon, nor can it simply develop the

---

[27] Gerhard Koch, *Die Gegenwart des Christus* (Berlin: Evang. Verlagsanstalt, 1949), p. 140.
[28] G. Koch, *Die Auferstehung Jesu Christi*, p. 305.
[29] *Ibid.*, p. 325.
[30] *Ibid.*, p. 330.
[31] W. Künneth, *Glauben an Jesus?*, pp. 286.
[32] Against P. Althaus, *Fact and Faith in the Kerygma Today*, pp. 33 f.

oldest primitive Christian confession, the sentence *Iēsous (Christos) Kyrios* ("Jesus is Lord," Rom. 1:4; 10:9; I Cor. 12:3). This confession itself must be grounded by Christology. The substantiation of the community's confession of Christ can be shown precisely in the New Testament, for Christology passed through a development in primitive Christianity, as Althaus also emphasizes.[33] It can be shown how faith in Jesus, the confession of him as Lord, originated. It can also be shown which questions gave rise to the growth of Christological concepts, for example, not only those about Jesus' death but also those about his birth.

Precisely in the Pauline epistles one can follow step by step the motives that led Paul to particular Christological formulations. In the Synoptic Gospels and with John this development is not so clear, since the Gospels do not contain explicit arguments; one can only draw conclusions from the present texts. A study of the history of the development of primitive Christian traditions would trace this whole process of the development of Christological concepts in detail. Beginnings in this direction can be found in Oscar Cullmann's *The Christology of the New Testament*.[34] The "history of traditions" approach is carried through more strictly in Ferdinand Hahn's dissertation *Christologische Hoheitstitel*.[35]

Althaus aptly characterized the dogmatic importance of the history of the Christological tradition in primitive Christianity: "Thought about Jesus drew conclusions from the first impulse. The notions of pre-existence, of incarnation, of the Trinity do not stand at the beginning. Dogmatics may not presuppose the historical result of this development as self-evident and use this as its basis. The religious confession of Jesus could simply be a particular case of the deification that often appears in the history of religions. Dogmatics has, therefore, the task of investigating the inner, material necessity of the Christological development in the New Testament and to make sure of it. Jesus' titles of honor and their history—the *Kyrios* title shows it most clearly— were influenced by the development of the history of religions prior to and in the environment of the young church. It is valid to determine the legitimate Christian sense of these titles, the essential Christological meaning that their use intended to express, but which is perhaps not bound to them. For this purpose dogmatic Christology must go behind the New Testament to the base to which it points and which supports faith in Jesus, that is, to the history of Jesus. Christology has to ask and show the extent to which this history substantiates faith in Jesus."[36]

33 P. Althaus, *Die christliche Wahrheit*, p. 424.

34 Oscar Cullmann, *The Christology of the New Testament,* tr. by Shirley C. Guthrie and Charles A. M. Hall (rev. ed., The New Testament Library; The Westminster Press, 1964).

35 Ferdinand Hahn, *Christologische Hoheitstitel: Ihre Geschichte im frühen Christentum* (Forschungen zur Religion und Literatur des Alten und Neuen Testaments, 83; Göttingen: Vandenhoeck & Ruprecht, 1963).

36 P. Althaus, *Die Christliche Wahrheit,* p. 424.

These excellent statements stand, certainly, in irreconcilable tension to Althaus' opinion that the character of the history of Jesus as revelation is "not known by means of historical reflection or historical reasoning."[37] Either the statement is valid that knowledge about the history as it happened, which is presupposed by faith, is "not yet knowledge of God's revelation in the events. This knowledge comes into existence first with faith itself"[38] or the final sentence of the paragraph quoted above is valid, that is, that Christology has to ask and show the extent to which the history of Jesus forms the basis of faith in him. How else is the history of Jesus supposed to substantiate faith in him except by showing itself to be the revelation of God? Only when its revelatory character is not something additional to the events but, rather, is inherent in them can the events form the basis of faith. Christology has to show just this.

Thus the task of Christology is to establish the true understanding of Jesus' significance from his history, which can be described comprehensively by saying that in this man God is revealed. The task has two sides: First, it involves the purely systematic derivation of particular insights with regard to Jesus from his history. Second, it must consider how the statements of primitive Christianity about Jesus came into existence in this way within a process of the formation of Christological tradition, even when the derivation of the Christological confessional statements in this process of the development and transmission of traditions is not reflected in primitive Christian literature. The same thing is true of the doctrinal development of Christology in the later church. All statements of this sort are to be tested in the light of Jesus' history and have value as examples for our task of forming Christological judgments. Even when it turns out that the form of traditional Christological formulations is bound to intellectual presuppositions of times that lie in the past for us, nevertheless, the effort to understand them as the expression of the significance belonging to the Christ event can help us find the way to the solution of the corresponding systematic task in our contemporary intellectual situation.

Excursus: Justification of the Title "Christology"

The thesis of this chapter is that Christology should show that Jesus "is the Christ of God." What does this mean? For us—as was true to a large extent for primitive Christianity—"Christ" has become a name, one part of the proper name "Jesus Christ." Originally, however, this word was not a proper name, but a title.[39] *Christos* is the Greek translation of the Hebrew

---

37 P. Althaus, *Fact and Faith in the Kerygma Today*, p. 34.

38 Paul Althaus, "Offenbarung als Geschichte und Glaube: Bemerkungen zu Wolfhart Pannenbergs Begriff der Offenbarung," *ThLZ*, LXXXVII (1962), 321 ff., 325.

39 See the chapter "Jesus the Messiah" in O. Cullmann, *The Christology of the New*

word for "Messiah," the "anointed one." In ancient Israel the king was in general the anointed one of God. After Zech. 6:13b one could also talk about a messianic high priest. The Qumran texts and the Testament of the Twelve Patriarchs especially emphasized the position of the priestly messiah beside the messianic king. Only occasionally was the messianic title connected with the concept of a Son of Man coming from heaven (Hahn, pp. 157 f.). There is, however, no unbroken line that leads from the Jewish messianic expectation to Jesus. Jesus himself probably expressly rejected the designation as Messiah (Cullmann, pp. 122 ff., on Mark 8:27 ff.; also, Hahn, pp. 226 ff.). Nevertheless, the messianic title emerged in the post-Easter community because of the inscription on the cross (Mark 15:26). At first it was applied to the Jesus who was expected to return in the future (Hahn, pp. 178, 179 ff.) and who as such was also identified with the Son of Man. The fact that the inscription on the cross was the origin of the transfer of the *Christos* title to Jesus also explains why shortly thereafter the title was linked with the passion tradition and the concept of suffering (Hahn, pp. 193 ff., esp. on Mark, ch. 15). Thus the earthly Jesus then was viewed as having already borne the title "Messiah."

Two other designations, "Son of David" and "Son of God," are closely related to the title *Christos*. Both refer materially to Jesus' messiahship, but in such a way that the Davidic sonship forms the basis of the candidacy for messianic honor, while Jesus is given the title "Son of God" in view of the inauguration into the messianic honor already accomplished through the resurrection (so esp. Rom. 1:3 f.; cf. further, Hahn, pp. 251 ff.). The title "Son of God" was connected in ancient Israel with the inauguration of the king, which occurred as adoption by Yahweh (Ps. 2:7). It implied there, as well as in the earliest Christian community, a clear subordination of the messiah to God. Only in Gentile Christianity did the title "Son of God" become a statement about the participation of Jesus in the divine essence.[40] Thus one may not simply relate the title *Christos* to the divinity of Jesus as Heinrich Vogel has recently done.[41] Rather, the material justification of the process in the history of traditions by which the man Jesus, who was designated as the Son of God, was recognized to be one with God himself is to be examined. This process in the history of traditions includes the central theme of Christology, namely, the task of understanding how this man is God. This involves the legitimacy of the transformation in the understanding of Jesus that took place in the transition from the Jewish into the Gentile

Testament, pp. 111-136; also esp. F. Hahn, *Christologische Hoheitstitel*, pp. 133-225, 280-333.

40 Rudolf Bultmann, *Theology of the New Testament* (2 vols.; Charles Scribner's Sons, 1951 and 1955), Vol. I, pp. 49 f.; Herbert Braun, "Der Sinn der neutestamentlichen Christologie," *ZThK*, LIV (1957), 341-377, esp. pp. 350 ff.

41 Heinrich Vogel, *Gott in Christo: Ein Erkenntnisgang durch die Grundprobleme der Dogmatik* (Berlin: Lettner-Verlag, 1951), pp. 165, 615 f.

sphere of tradition. It is to be asked whether motifs already implied in the Jewish Christian kerygma about Christ, in fact even in the activity and fate of Jesus himself, did not come to explicit expression in this process. The title *Christos,* together with the closely related title "Son of God," encompasses this whole process in the history of traditions as it developed from the recognition of Jesus as God's eschatological messenger to the recognition of his divinity.

The special significance of the title *Christos* lies in the breadth and capacity for change in its content, which, in addition, also could take up the entire tradition about Jesus, including the passion tradition. This significance seems to justify the fact that this title has become virtually Jesus' proper name and that the consideration of Jesus' significance attaches itself precisely to this early Christian title in calling itself "Christology." Other titles, such as the "New Moses" or the "Son of Man," have vanished with time, at the latest in the transition into the Gentile Christian sphere of tradition, because they could not assimilate the fullness of the aspects of Jesus' significance that evolved in the historical development of the traditions. Other titles, especially the concept of the *Kyrios* (Lord), certainly brought the divine position of Jesus to expression in a particular way for the Hellenistic mind. They could not, however, include the entire historical development of the message about Jesus' mission and fate as the title "Christ" did. (Fate designates what is sent, what happens to Jesus, in distinction from his work and activity. The mission of Jesus also belongs on the side of his work and activity insofar as it has been actively accomplished by him. Hence, it is set in contrast to the fate of Jesus as what is sent to him by God and is to be suffered and accepted by him.) Moreover, it is especially significant that the title "Christ," expresses the connection between Jesus' activity and fate and Israel's eschatological expectation (Cullmann correctly emphasizes this, p. 126). This connection remained constitutive for the Gentile Christian church as well. Jesus is what he is only in the context of Israel's expectation. Without the background of this tradition, Jesus would never have become the object of a Christology. Certainly this connection is also clear in other titles and generally throughout the New Testament, especially in Jesus' own message. His message can only be understood within the horizon of apocalyptic expectations, and the God whom Jesus called "Father" was none other than the God of the Old Testament. This context is concentrated in a most particular way in the title *Christos.* This title brings into view the whole arc of the suspenseful development of traditions from ancient Israel to the Gentile Christian church. This justifies the formulation of the content of the confession of Jesus at the beginning of this chapter: he is the Christ of God.

II. THE METHOD OF CHRISTOLOGY

It is clear from what has been said in the previous section about the task of Christology which of the two methods that are common in modern dogmatics is to be followed here. This involves the distinction between a Christology "from above" and a Christology "from below." For Christology that begins "from above," from the divinity of Jesus, the concept of the incarnation stands in the center. A Christology "from below," rising from the historical man Jesus to the recognition of his divinity, is concerned first of all with Jesus' message and fate and arrives only at the end at the concept of the incarnation.[42]

Christology "from above" was far more common in the ancient church, beginning with Ignatius of Antioch and the second-century Apologists. It became determinative for the further history of Christology, particularly in the form of the Alexandrian Christology of Athanasius in the fourth century and of Cyril in the fifth century. Some concepts that point in this direction occur already in the New Testament (e.g., Phil. 2:5 ff.; Rom. 8:3; Gal. 4:4). The structure of these concepts—the descent of the Son from the world above—is the opposite of what we can gather from the process of the development of primitive Christian traditions. The historical process of the development and transmission of traditions, in the course of which the unity of the man Jesus with God became recognized, runs counter to the kind of concepts that speak of God's becoming man.

The Christological procedure "from above to below" is followed in modern Protestant dogmatics by Karl Barth especially.[43] He speaks about a "history" of the incarnation: the Son of God goes into what is foreign, into humiliation, by becoming a man, uniting himself with the man Jesus (CD, IV/1, § 59). This connection means at the same time an inexpressible exaltation for the man Jesus to whose lot it fell (CD, IV/2, § 64: "the exaltation of the Son of Man"). Here, Barth has combined two doctrines which were distinguished in the orthodox Protestant dogmatics of the seventeenth century: on the one hand, the doctrine of Jesus as man and God, the so-called doctrine of the two natures, and on the other, the doctrine of the humiliation and exaltation of the incarnate Son of God as two consecutive stages along Jesus' path. By combining these two themes, Barth comes closer to the basic outline of the Gnostic

[42] The alternative between a Christology "from above" and one "from below" has recently been questioned by O. Weber, *Grundlagen der Dogmatik*, Vol. II, pp. 20 ff. Weber believes that he moves beyond this alternative by starting from the "encounter with Jesus Christ" (pp. 36 ff.). But the question remains whether in such an encounter one is concerned only with a man like other men or at the same time and in a unique way with God. The acuteness of the question as to the extent to which one has to do with God in Jesus cannot be avoided by means of the concept of encounter, which leaves everything unsettled.

[43] Karl Barth, *Church Dogmatics*, ed. by G. W. Bromiley and T. F. Torrance (12 vols.; Edinburgh: T. & T. Clark, 1936-1962).

redeemer myth than is necessarily characteristic of an incarnational Christology that is constructed "from above to below": the descent of the redeemer from heaven and his return there. This is also the basic concept of Barth's Christology. He thinks not only about an event of incarnation but about a circle consisting of descent and ascent. The difference in Barth, as in all of the church's Christology, is that the redeemer redeems not himself but man as a being essentially different from God. Further, Barth adds the feature that the humiliation of God is at the same time the exaltation of the man who is thereby united to him and conversely.

Before Barth, a Christology "from above" was undertaken in contemporary theology by Emil Brunner in *The Mediator*.[44] Brunner became the first of the "Dialectical Theologians" to present a draft of such a Christology. In his *Dogmatics*,[45] however, he used a different, inductive method. Heinrich Vogel also offers a Christology "from above," both in his Christology[46] and in his dogmatics *Gott in Christo*.

It is characteristic of all of these attempts to build a "Christology from above"[47] that the doctrine of the Trinity is presupposed and the question posed is: How has the Second Person of the Trinity (the Logos) assumed a human nature? There are three reasons why this method is not feasible for us:

1. A Christology from above presupposes the divinity of Jesus. The most important task of Christology is, however, precisely to present the reasons for the confession of Jesus' divinity. Instead of presupposing it, we must first inquire about how Jesus' appearance in history led to the recognition of his divinity.

2. A Christology that takes the divinity of the Logos as its point of departure and finds its problems only in the union of God and man in Jesus recognizes only with difficulty the determinative significance inherent in the distinctive features of the real, historical man, Jesus of Nazareth. The manifold relationships between Jesus and the Judaism of his time, which are essential to an understanding of his life and message, must appear as less important

44 The Macmillan Company, 1934.
45 Emil Brunner, *The Christian Doctrine of Creation and Redemption* (*Dogmatics,* Vol. II), tr. by Olive Wyon (The Westminster Press, 1952).
46 Heinrich Vogel, *Christologie,* I (1949).
47 Paul Tillich, *Systematic Theology* (3 vols.; The University of Chicago Press, 1951, 1957, 1963), Vol. II, presents a continuation of the Christology from above as it was conceived by the speculative theology of the nineteenth century in a unique way: the "New Being," which has become a historical reality in Jesus, is the essential nature of man himself, the eternal unity between God and man (p. 148). To that extent one could speak here materially of a Christology that begins from below with man (cf. pp. 78 ff.: "The Quest for the New Being and the Meaning of 'Christ' "; also, pp. 118 ff.). The fact that Tillich's Christology cannot be categorized by the alternative "from above" or "from below" is a consequence of his having conceived the "above" itself from the perspective of man. Therefore, it is characteristic that, according to Tillich, the essential nature of man, the eternal unity between God and man, not actually God himself, has appeared historically in Jesus and only in Jesus (p. 148).

to such a Christology, even when it discusses the offices of Christ as well as his humiliation and exaltation. Certainly if one knows from the beginning that Jesus Christ is the Son of God, then these relationships with the Judaism of Jesus' time are not so crucial for the basic Christological questions. Then only the participation of the Logos in everything that belongs to general human nature is important, since our human participation in divinity through Jesus depends upon that. But no determinative significance can accrue to the historical particularity of Jesus, unless it be to his death as a payment that atones for sins. However, in this perspective even the problem of Jesus' death can become to a certain extent something supplementary. The problem of Jesus' death then primarily involves the question, Why must the man who is engaged by God also be subjected to the universal human fate of death? These indications may for the present suffice to substantiate the assertion that the historical man Jesus in his historical singularity does not come properly into view in a Christology "from above." Let it be stressed once more that Jesus' relationship to Israel and to the Old Testament cannot be so fundamental for a Christology which takes its beginning point in the concept of the incarnation that such a Christology could not exist without it.

3. There remains one final reason why the method of a Christology "from above" is closed to us: one would have to stand in the position of God himself in order to follow the way of God's Son into the world. As a matter of fact, however, we always think from the context of a historically determined human situation. We can never leap over this limitation. Therefore, our starting point must lie in the question about the man Jesus; only in this way can we ask about his divinity. How the divine Logos, the Second Person of the Trinity, would be thought of apart from the incarnation and thus apart from the man Jesus completely escapes our imagination.

In spite of our rejection of a Christology "from above," we shall later show the relative justification for such a way of approaching the question, especially as it is to be seen in earlier periods of the church and of the history of theology. One cannot claim that the incarnational Christology which has ruled the history of the development of the Christological doctrine was simply a mistake. Nevertheless, the historical reality of Jesus, which has often been extremely restricted in this way, must be made fruitful today in its fullness.

The legitimacy of a Christology proceeding "from below," from the question about the historical reality of Jesus, has recently been disputed by Otto Weber.[48] Weber thinks that the presupposition for thinking "from below" is the openness of that "below" of historical existence in general to the divine "above" (Vol. II, p. 29). "No one can ascend from a 'below' which is somehow given toward an 'above' without holding this 'above' to be likewise at least potentially given in or with the 'below.' " (P. 35.) Weber here envisages

[48] O. Weber, *Grundlagen der Dogmatik,* Vol. II, pp. 26 ff. and 34 ff. The following quotations in the text are from this work.

the "below" as a generality, not with a view to the historical singularity of the man Jesus. Otherwise, he could not assert that in this way one would know "beforehand that which the believer knows only from the encounter with Jesus Christ and otherwise not at all" (p. 35). To be sure, an understanding of the word "God" and of the reality designated thereby is presupposed in a very particular sense by Jesus himself as well as by primitive Christianity and must in one way or another be likewise presupposed by us if we ask about Jesus. What is inherently new and contingent in a historical occurrence, and especially in Jesus' history, nevertheless radically qualifies all foreknowledge, even the foreknowledge about God that is unavoidably presupposed. Precisely for this reason, God has "met" men in Jesus in a way that is not the case otherwise, and one also cannot adequately grasp such differences of historical particularity as merely a matter of degree. A general idea of God and the word "God" related to this idea express only the human quest for God's reality. The particular way in which God's reality, about which one really has only the question in the general concept of God and in the word "God" that is related to this, confronts men historically through Jesus can only come into view in the light of the historical particularity of Jesus himself.

Thus, while Christology must begin with the man Jesus, its first question has to be that about his unity with God. Every statement about Jesus taken independently from his relationship to God could result only in a crass distortion of his historical reality. The modernistic presentation of Jesus at the height of the quest of the historical Jesus offers enough examples of this. In any case, if we are concerned not only with a description of the external circumstances of Jesus' life but with a total characterization of his appearance, the decisive point lies in his relationship to God, or more precisely, to the God of Israel. As has been said earlier, the specific element in the Christological question about Jesus is that it does not begin with some preliminary aspect of his deeds and words or of his effect on men, but with his relation to God as it is expressed in the whole of his activity on earth. Individual aspects of his work and his message as well as of his fate are then to be evaluated in this context.

We are not the first to employ the procedure of a Christology "from below," starting with the man Jesus in order to inquire simultaneously about his relationship to God. Impulses in this direction were made in the ancient church, in the Middle Ages, and by Luther, although the approach of the incarnational Christology was never successfully taken up into a more inclusive one. Rationalism, on the other hand, asked about the man Jesus, but no longer about his unity with God in the sense of Christological dogma. Schleiermacher thought of the unity of Jesus with God only in the sense of Jesus' God-consciousness.[49] In the nineteenth century, Albrecht Ritschl was the first to

[49] F. Schleiermacher, *The Christian Faith,* § 94: the continual strength of his conscious-

36

build his Christology on the question about the divinity of the historical man Jesus.[50] In this he has been followed not only by the narrower circle of the Ritschlian school up to Wilhelm Herrmann, but also by Werner Elert, Paul Althaus, Emil Brunner, Carl Heinz Ratschow and others among contemporary Protestant dogmaticians, and, of course, by Friedrich Gogarten and others, e.g., Gerhard Ebeling, who stand close to Bultmann. In starting a Christology "from below," we take the same direction as these theologians. Reservations toward their solutions will appear first in Chapter 3, when we shall ask how the divinity of the man Jesus is to be substantiated in detail. In any case, in the context of such a Christology "from below" it is clear that the confession of the divinity of the man Jesus requires substantiation, that it is not self-explanatory.

Before we come to the development of the basic Christological question about the divinity of Jesus, we must first clarify a further dimension of all Christological statements, namely, the relation between Christology and soteriology.

ness of God was "a veritable existence of God in Him." On this basis, Schleiermacher justifies the statement that in the Savior, God became man (§ 96, 3).

[50] A. Ritschl, *The Christian Doctrine of Justification and Reconciliation*, § 44-50.

CHAPTER

2

CHRISTOLOGY AND SOTERIOLOGY

The confession of faith in Jesus is not to be separated from Jesus' significance for us. The soteriological interest cannot, however, be the principle of Christological doctrine.

I. JESUS AS GOD AND SAVIOR

The two designations "God" and "Savior" form the content of the basic confession of the World Council of Churches, which was formulated at Amsterdam in 1948.[1] The divinity of Jesus and his freeing and redeeming significance for us are related in the closest possible way. To this extent, Melanchthon's famous sentence is appropriate: "Who Jesus Christ is becomes known in his saving action."[2] Nevertheless, the divinity of Jesus does not consist in his saving significance for us. Divinity and saving significance are interrelated as distinct things. The divinity of Jesus remains the *presupposition* for his saving significance for us and, conversely, the saving significance of his divinity is the reason why we take *interest* in the question of his divinity. Since Schleiermacher the close tie between Christology and soteriology has won general acceptance in theology. This is particularly to be seen in one characteristic feature of modern Christology. One no longer separates the divine-human person and the redemptive work of Jesus Christ, as was done in medieval Scholastic theology and, in its wake, in the dogmatics of sixteenth-

---

[1] On this, cf. E. Fincke, "Zur Geschichte der 'Basis' des Ökumenischen Rates der Kirchen," *EvTh*, XX (1960), 465-476. See also the critical discussion by Rudolf Bultmann, "The Christological Confession of the World Council of Churches," *Essays: Philosophical and Theological*, tr. by James C. G. Greig (London: SCM Press, Ltd., 1955), pp. 273-290. In the latter, the divinity of Christ is reduced to being "only an event at any given time" (p. 286); on this basis, the Chalcedonian formula is rejected (*ibid.*). The New Testament "pronouncements about Jesus' divinity or deity are not, in fact, pronouncements of his nature but seek to give expression to his significance" (p. 280). Here we already have the case of a reduction of Christology to soteriology, to the question of Jesus' existential significance.

[2] Philipp Melanchthon, Preface to the *Loci communes* (1521) (*CR* 21, p. 85).

and seventeenth-century Protestant orthodoxy, but, rather, with Schleiermacher both are conceived as two sides of the same thing.[3] From the relationship between Christology and soteriology Barth correctly concludes that Jesus' significance for us cannot be completely developed unless the question about his presence in his community is considered.

II. SOTERIOLOGICAL MOTIFS IN THE HISTORY OF CHRISTOLOGY[4]

Almost all Christological conceptions have had soteriological motifs. Changes in the soteriological interest, in man's understanding of salvation, explain, at least in part, the different forms Christology has taken at different times. In this section I will present only a few examples of this by indicating the soteriological motivations of important Christological theories. In order to contrast clearly the soteriological motifs that have often dominated the theological approach of entire epochs, we shall place them alongside one another as types. With such a procedure the reservation must be expressed that a more exact examination of the history of theology would have to break up these types again in order to make the whole variety of interrelated threads in the historical development apparent. This classification according to types is based on a summary of common basic tendencies within an entire field, neglecting the distinctions that exist and the connections with other features that are not relevant for the type. Nevertheless, such a classification is not without value for understanding. It has the advantage of focusing our attention on the content that is of interest for our immediate purpose.

1. Deification Through Incarnation

The motif of deification determined, as is well known, the whole history of Christology in the ancient church. In its main line of development, dei-

[3] F. Schleiermacher, *The Christian Faith*, § 92. Cf. Albrecht Ritschl, *Die christliche Lehre von Rechtfertigung und Versöhnung* (1st ed.; Bonn: Adolf Maritis, 1874), Vol. III, § 44, p. 343: It is false to distinguish between the doctrines of the person and the work of Jesus, since we perceive "the nature and attributes, i.e., the determination of being, only in the effect of a thing on us, and we think of the nature and extent of its effect on us as its essence"; Melanchthon's statement quoted above is cited to support this. Cf. also K. Barth, *CD*, IV/1, § 58, for an overview of the whole doctrine of reconciliation.

[4] Here see esp. Gustav Aulén, "Die drei Haupttypen des christlichen Versöhnungsgedankens," *ZsyTh*, VIII (1931), 501-538; on Aulén, cf. Karl Heim, *ZThK*, XIX (1938), 304-319. Further, Alois Grillmeier, "Die theologische und sprachliche Vorbereitung der christologischen Formel von Chalkedon," *Das Konzil von Chalkedon: Geschichte und Gegenwart*, ed. by Alois Grillmeier and Heinrich Bacht (3 vols.; Würzburg: Echter-Verlag, 1951-1954), Vol. I, pp. 5-202; *idem, LThK*, V (1960), 941-953. Also Arnold Gilg, *Weg und Bedeutung der altkirchlichen Christologie* (Munich: Chr. Kaiser Verlag, 1955); Wolfhart Pannenberg, art. "Christologie II," *RGG*, I (3d ed.), 1762-1777.

fication was thought of as the consequence of the incarnation, thus of the movement from God to man. The authoritative version of this concept was formulated toward the end of the second century by Irenaeus in his work against the heretics. The Son of God has become what we are in order that we might receive a share in his perfection.[5] Similarly, Athanasius in his writing about the incarnation of the Logos in the fourth century explained that man was originally created to participate in the divine Logos (*De incarnatione* I, 3) and how this destiny of his was fulfilled through Jesus Christ. Participation in the divine Logos has to do with the rationalness of man, corresponding to the old Greek definition of man as a creature that is involved with reason. Here the rationality of man is not understood simply as a natural quality, but as relatedness to God. However, through sin man has forfeited his participation in the divine Logos (I, 13). Redemption consists of imparting the divine Logos, and thus his rational essence, to man again (I, 14, 2). By this means death is conquered and immortality imparted. It was the concern for the deification of man that made it so important—against the Arians —that with the divine Logos God himself really became man in Jesus.

The same motif stands behind the formula that Gregory of Nazianzus used at the beginning of the Christological dispute in the fourth century: What has not been assumed has also not been saved. This formula is already to be found in Origen.[6] The whole man would not have been saved had not the Logos assumed the whole man. Therefore it was so ardently emphasized against Apollinaris of Laodicea in the fifth century that the divine Logos not only took on flesh but was a complete man with body, soul, and mind.

Also, with Cyril of Alexandria and the so-called Monophysites, who placed the unity of God and man realized in the incarnation at the center of their thought, the interest in the fact of redemption through union with God is apparent. In this line of patristic theology the primary concern was always that the Logos has assumed not only one man but human nature in general. Thus what is said about Jesus is potentially true about all other men insofar as they are bound to him in a common human nature.

2. Deification Through Assimilation to God (*homoiōsis theōi*)

The second, more ethically determined line of patristic Christology attached itself to the ethical ideal of the Platonic school. More exactly, this involved the so-called "middle Platonism" which flowered particularly in the second century. This ethical ideal is the striving toward the good, or rather, participation in the idea of the good achieved through such striving. However, ac-

[5] Irenaeus, *Adv. haer.* V, *praefatio: factus est quod sumus nos, uti nos perficeret esse quod est ipse* (MPG 7/2, 1120).
[6] Origen, *Dialogue with Heracleides, Sources Chret.*, 67 (1960), 70; Gregory of Nazianzus, *Ep.* 101 (*MPG* 37, 181C); cf. A. Grillmeier in *LThK*, VIII, 954 ff.

cording to Plato, the good is that which is truly divine.[7] Therefore, striving toward participation in the good means striving toward participation in that which is divine. That a participation of this sort really takes place is shown especially in the fact that the virtuous man becomes persistent in the good and thus becomes unchangeable like God.

In the patristic church, Jesus' unity with God was often understood in this sense as perfect *homoiōsis theōi*. Here Jesus appeared as the great example for man's ethical striving, and Jesus' saving significance was sought in that. This seems to have been the leading Christological idea in Origen.[8] The preexistent soul of Jesus was, in distinction to the souls of other men, completely surrendered to the Logos and thus united with it already before they were bound together in one body. In this sense a universal unification of the human with the divine begins with Jesus: through faith in the historically comprehensible man Jesus each Christian becomes drawn upward through everything bodily into the pure spirituality of the Logos to which Jesus was completely dedicated.

Origen's left-wing disciples went farther in this direction. In particular, Lucian of Antioch, at the beginning of the fourth century, interpreted the Logos as unchangeability in the virtuous life, which Jesus achieved through moral trial and which as such already means similarity to God. Such thoughts appear not only in this intellectual father of Arius but also in such a defender of orthodoxy as Gregory of Nyssa.[9] Later the Antiochene concept of the unity of God and man in Jesus Christ followed the idea of *homoiōsis theōi*. Theodore of Mopsuestia presented the matter in this way: Through the power of his free, human will, certainly with the support of God's grace, Jesus freed his soul from sinful drives. In this he is the example for all those who are called to freedom. In this manner Jesus made his soul unchangeable in the good and through this became ever more similar to the divine Logos. Thus the indwelling of the Logos in Jesus' soul constantly became more complete in the course of his moral development until the man Jesus was exalted through the resurrection to total unchangeableness and inability to suffer and became a participant in God's rule over the world.[10] According to this Antiochene concept, the incarnation had not taken place fully as early as the birth of Jesus, so that it was completed from then on, but it was accomplished increasingly in the course of Jesus' life. The unity of the man Jesus with God continuously be-

---

[7] Plato, *Republic* VI, 508b-509.

[8] Origen, *De princ.* II, 6,3 (*GCS* 22, pp. 141 f.); cf. Grillmeier, in *Chalkedon,* Vol. I, pp. 64 f.

[9] Gregory of Nyssa, *Adv. Apoll.* 32 (*MPG* 45, 1192D-1196A); see Grillmeier, *Chalkedon,* Vol. I, p. 157. See also Humbert Merki, *Homoiōsis Theōi von der platonischen Angleichung an Gott zur Gottähnlichkeit bei Gregor von Nyssa* (Fribourg, Switzerland: Paulus Verlag, 1952).

[10] References in Friedrich Loofs, *Leitfaden zum Studium der Dogmengeschichte,* ed. by Kurt Aland (6th ed.; Halle-Saale: Max Niemeyer, 1959), § 36, 4, p. 222. See esp. Theodore of Mopsuestia, *Homil. catech.* V, 11; also Grillmeier, in *Chalkedon,* Vol. I, p. 147.

came closer. His saving significance for us is essentially that of an ethical example. In the nineteenth century, I. A. Dorner still conceived of the unity of Jesus with God in this way.

The Christology of Vicarious Satisfaction

Anselm of Canterbury's writing *Cur Deus Homo* (1094/1098) reveals a different approach in contrast to patristic Christology. The penitential practice in the medieval church determined its intellectual horizon. Man is obligated to God to offer satisfaction for his sins (I, 11), for the offense through sin against God's right as Lord (I, 13), against his honor. The problem of sin now moves into the center of Christological thought in a way quite different from that, for example, of Athanasius.[11] According to Athanasius, sin could be removed through penance, but not morality. The latter is what really makes the incarnation of God necessary. With Anselm it is different. The sinner is held fast in the condition of sin by the duty to bring satisfaction. It is not enough for man to stop sinning, but over and beyond this he must offer satisfaction to God for the sin he has already committed. Such satisfaction can consist only of something that man does not already owe God. It can consist only in a work that goes beyond his obligation, that is, in a merit. The ordinary man cannot, however, accomplish such a thing (I, 20), because he already owes his Creator everything he has. Only the man Jesus, born without sin, can offer God a work of supererogation, the gift of his life. For, in distinction from all other men, Jesus as a man without sin was not condemned to death, he did not need to die (II, 11). Thus, the death of Jesus becomes the only conceivable work of supererogation that can be offered to God as satisfaction for men's sins. Anselm showed in the eleventh meditation "De redemptione humana" ("Concerning Human Redemption") that humanity in the person of Jesus offers God this satisfaction. Thus here also Jesus is the representative of men before God—however, not in their striving after the good, toward *homoiōsis theōi,* but in offering the satisfaction owed in penance for sin. This satisfaction, which is accomplished in the gift of Jesus' life, is universally effective because Jesus is at the same time God, and the life he offers has, therefore, infinite worth.[12] Only as the basis for the infinite value of Jesus' work of satisfaction does Anselm's theory require the dogma of Jesus' divinity in addition to that of his sinlessness. In this, one sees that the approach of Anselm's Christology was very different from that of the patristic church, for which the divinity of Jesus had direct saving significance. The interest in salvation now depended upon satisfaction, on penance for the sins of men, no

---

[11] Anselm, *Cur Deus Homo* I, 21 (*MPL* 158, 393 f.) with Athanasius, *De inc. verbi* 7 (*MPG* 25, 107).

[12] Anselm, II, 14; cf. II, 6: *Aliquid maius quam omne quod praeter Deum est.*

longer upon a deification of man as in the patristic church. Therefore, it no longer depended directly upon the divinity of Jesus.

Anselm's conception generally prevailed in the Middle Ages, particularly after the beginning of the thirteenth century. However, it was also taken over by the dogmatics of Protestant orthodoxy in the seventeenth century, although its primary concern is foreign to the authentically evangelical understanding of salvation. Even Luther could use traditional language in this matter. However, where he formulated things independently, another conception came to expression in him.

4. The Christology of God's Grace Alone[13]

Luther also saw in Jesus the representative of all men before God. For Luther, however, Jesus represents the rest of humanity neither in its striving for the good nor in the offering of works of satisfaction. Rather, Jesus is the representative of humanity before God by humbling himself under God's wrath against sin and thereby being righteous before God. This was, in any case, Luther's concept in the first lecture on the psalms from 1513 through 1515. The judgment of God stands in contrast to the judgments of men. God gives his grace to the one who is unrighteous in his own eyes and thereby shows himself to be humble before God. In this sense Christ is righteousness and so also faith in him is righteousness in a way that is derived from him (*fides Christi*).[14] In the cross of Christ this *judicium Dei,* which stands in contrast to human judgments, is apparent to us.[15] In the lecture on Romans of 1515 and 1516, Luther characterized Christ in the same sense as the pattern, the prototype, of all God's actions. Because God wanted to glorify Christ and install him as king, he permitted him on the contrary to die, to be broken, and to descend into hell. God deals in this way with all the saints.[16] Three sentences earlier Luther described the general rule of this divine action: The work of God must be hidden and is not recognized when it happens.[17] The

---

[13] On this, see esp. the excellent article by Yves M. J. Congar, "Regards et réflexions sur la christologie de Luther," in *Chalkedon,* Vol. III (1954), pp. 457-486; further, Erich Vogelsang, *Die Anfänge der Christologie Luthers nach der 1. Psalmenvorlesung* (Berlin: Walter de Gruyter & Co., 1929), and *idem, Der angefochtene Christus bei Luther* (Berlin: Walter de Gruyter & Co., 1932); Hans Joachim Iwand, *Rechtfertigungslehre und Christusglaube* (2d ed.; Munich: Chr. Kaiser Verlag, 1961), and H. Lanz, "Die Bedeutung Christi für die Rechtfertigungslehre in Luthers Römerbriefvorlesung," *Neue kirchliche Zeitschrift,* XXXIX (1928), 509-547. The literature mentioned relates only to the aspect of Luther's Christology accentuated here.

[14] Martin Luther, *WA* 3, pp. 462 f., 37 ff.: *Qui sibi iniustus est et ita coram deo humilis, huic dat deus gratiam suam. . . . Sic justitia tropologica est fides Christi.* On Christ as a prototype, cf. pp. 368 f. and 458, 4 ff.; on the relation between Christ and faith in Christ (*fides Christi*), *WA* 3, p. 458,8 ff.

[15] *WA* 3, p. 463, 17 f.: the *Judicium Dei* is *in cruce Christi nobis ostensum.*

[16] *WA* 56, p. 37, 4 ff.

[17] *WA* 56, p. 376, 31 f., cf. p. 392, 7 ff., 13.28 ff.

grace of God is hidden under its opposite. This is the root of Luther's *theologia crucis*.

Later, Luther emphasized not only this prototypal aspect but above all the vicarious character of Jesus' penal suffering. This is particularly clear in the well-known formula about the "happy exchange": because Christ bears our sins, we in turn receive a share in his righteousness.[18] But here as well Jesus is not thought of in an active role, as one who offers work to God but, rather, passively as the one whom God's judgment on sin has encountered in our place.

Thus the decisive root of Luther's theology of pure grace and pure faith is in his understanding of Christ. The tendency to understand Jesus from the standpoint of the work of God, of the gracious will of God, is also expressed in Luther's preference—as is also true later of other Reformers—for speaking about the office of Christ instead of about his work. We shall consider this idea in greater detail later.

5. The Prototype of the Religious Man

Schleiermacher sought man's salvation in the domination of the consciousness of God over all other knowledge and action. He found precisely this realized in a prototypal way in Jesus, and this concept determines all Christological statements in Schleiermacher's dogmatics (§ 93 ff.). Coming from Jesus, the impulses of his "sinless perfection" are effective in the Christian community and can still be experienced today (§ 99, 3). The prototypal "strength of his consciousness of God" constitutes for Schleiermacher the genuine content of the idea of Jesus' divinity (§ 94).

6. The Ideal of Moral Perfection

Kant's and later Ritschl's conception of the significance of Jesus as a prototype was somewhat different from that of Schleiermacher, namely, more in relation to the ethical task of man. Kant related Jesus to his "ideal of moral perfection" as the personification or the example of this idea, which is present for every man in his moral consciousness.[19] We cannot, however, think of a morally perfect man in any other way than as someone who not only lives morally himself but also spreads good in his environment and even sacrifices himself for it. Thus Kant says, "We cannot think about the ideal of a humanity that is pleasing to God (including moral perfection, as it is possible for a being in the world who is dependent upon needs and inclinations) other than by the idea of a man who would be willing not only to perform all

18 *De libertate christiana* (1520), c. 12. *WA* 7, pp. 25 f.
19 Immanuel Kant, *Religion Within the Limits of Reason Alone* (Harper & Row, Publishers, Inc., 1960), pp. 54 ff.

human duty himself and at the same time to spread good as widely as possible through teaching and example, but also, though tempted by the greatest enticements, to assume all suffering, even to the point of the most ignominious death, for the sake of the best in the world and even for his enemies."[20] Kant called the spreading of good by the morally perfect man, and thus the foundation of a community according to the laws of virtue, the "kingdom of God."[21]

Albrecht Ritschl followed Kant in emphasizing the central significance of a kingdom of God understood in this way as well as in the characterization of Jesus quoted above. However, Ritschl placed the concept of the spreading of good even more decidedly at the center of his thought than did Kant. He designated the spreading of good, with a word occasionally suggested by Schleiermacher (§ 100, 2), as the "vocation" of Jesus. Jesus' particular vocation consisted precisely in the "founding of a universal moral community of men";[22] he was the "founder of the Kingdom of God in the world."[23] Ritschl saw the perfect morality of Jesus in his complete devotion to this vocation. One perceives in the background of these ideas the impressive ideal of life of the bourgeoisie of the later nineteenth century. Jesus' suffering was looked upon as the highest expression of his faithfulness to his vocation.[24] The complete agreement of Jesus' will with God's will in working for the moral "Kingdom of God" substantiates for Ritschl the statement of the divinity of Christ in the sense that in him "the word of God is a human person."[25]

If one compares neo-Protestant Christology—whether in its purely religious form, as in Schleiermacher, or in the religious-ethical form of Ritschl—with the preceding types of soteriological motivation in Christology, one notices the modesty of its soteriological interest. The neo-Protestant theologians are concerned only with making possible the humanness of life on earth. They are no longer concerned with the conquest of death and with the theme of resurrection, and they deal with the question of the forgiveness of sins only in the sense that the possibility for every individual's overcoming sin derives from Jesus. Precisely because overcoming death through a transcendent being is not an issue here at all, one also cannot speak of a vicarious penal suffering of Jesus through which sin is overcome at a level that is inaccessible to us. One speaks as little about Jesus' vicarious suffering as about the resurrection life beyond death. The soteriological interest is limited here to the life on earth

20 *Ibid.*, p. 55.
21 *Ibid.*, pp. 85 ff.
22 A. Ritschl, *The Christian Doctrine of Justification and Reconciliation*, § 48, p. 449.
23 *Ibid.*, p. 451.
24 *Ibid.*, § 48, pp. 448 f. Cf. G. Ebeling, *The Nature of Faith*, pp. 56 f.: Jesus' existence as witness of faith includes "going his way to the end; it includes holding fast the witness of faith, in face of the charge of blasphemy and sedition; it includes the affirmation of God's nearness in the dereliction of the Cross."
25 A. Ritschl, *The Christian Doctrine of Justification and Reconciliation*, § 48, p. 451.

of which Paul has said: "If for this life only we have hoped in Christ, we are of all men most to be pitied" (I Cor. 15:19). This restriction of the soteriological interest is also true for the final type of Christology to be mentioned here.

7. The Christology of Pure Personality

Contemporary man, particularly in the first half of our century, has been largely concerned with saving his being as person from the tendencies of modern society toward the objectification of all relationships of life.[26] Christian faith is also very often interpreted in the sense of such personality, open to the future and to fellowmen. The concern is no longer for Schleiermacher's religious universality, and also the vocational ethos of the late nineteenth century continues to affect the personal thought of the present only in a changed form.

The attempt suggested by the present situation to answer the question of the possibility of being a person Christologically has been developed most completely by Friedrich Gogarten.[27] Gogarten's soteriological interest is devoted to the question about the possibility of being a genuine person as an "I" over against a "Thou" and from a "Thou," in contrast to the merely objective, technical involvement of the modern man with his world. The "Thou" from whom man as "I" exists is decisively the "Thou" of God. On this point this type is distinguished from the preceding ethical Christology for which Jesus' relationship to God was not a particular theme but only a function of his ethical effectiveness. Gogarten sees man's being as person fulfilled in Jesus, insofar as the latter exists entirely from God's "Thou." Gogarten calls this "sonship," with reference to Rom. 8:14 f.; Gal. 4:5 ff. In the sense that Jesus is the realization of personality as such, Gogarten can say that Jesus "is the Son of God precisely in his humanity" (p. 242) and "thus the being as person that is made accessible in him is not only human, but by being human it is divine" (p. 249). This is true of Jesus insofar as he is the one "whose being as person is the sonship that has no other knowledge of itself than the knowledge of the Fatherhood of God" (p. 274). This sonship is not only received from the Father, but the Father also requires it from man, namely, as responsibility for the world.[28]

---

[26] See also W. Pannenberg, art. "Person," *RGG*, V (3d ed.), 230-235; Gerhard Gloege, "Der theologische Personalismus als dogmatisches Problem," *KuD*, I (1955), 23-41; *idem*, *EKL*, III, 128 ff.

[27] Friedrich Gogarten, *Der Mensch zwischen Gott und Welt* (Stuttgart: Friedrich Vorwerk Verlag, 1952), esp. the chapter about "the word of God," pp. 234-274.

[28] *Ibid.*, cf. pp. 254 ff.; also, *Die Verkündigung Jesu Christi* (Heidelberg: Verlag Lambert Schneider, 1948), pp. 496 f. In the latter work Gogarten has emphasized the role of human togetherness, of love, as a constituent element of true being as person even more strongly than in his later book (Ch. 13, pp. 512 f.; Ch. 14, pp. 514 ff.).

With a slightly different nuance, but in connection with certain of Gogarten's ideas, a Christology of pure personality is also present in Gerhard Ebeling. Here the direction is provided by the concept of faith as trust in God's future, in God's power. Jesus is here essentially the witness of faith. He is this through his own certainty of God, as well as through opening the certainty of God to others by the call to faith. This call means to have from Jesus an "exemplary granting of participation in his way." "The freedom that Jesus took in full authority and the freedom that he gave in full authority hang inseparably together."[29]

III. THE PROBLEM OF THE SOTERIOLOGICAL APPROACH TO CHRISTOLOGY

In the first section it became clear that a separation between Christology and soteriology is not possible, because in general the soteriological interest, the interest in salvation, in the *beneficia Christi*, is what causes us to ask about the figure of Jesus. The second section has demonstrated how the history of Christology, with the changes in Christological patterns, has in fact been determined by particular soteriological interests. However, the danger that is involved in this connection between Christology and soteriology has emerged at the same time: Has one really spoken there about Jesus himself at all? Does it not perhaps rather involve projections onto Jesus' figure of the human desire for salvation and deification, of human striving after similarity to God, of the human duty to bring satisfaction for sins committed, of the human experience of bondage in failure, in the knowledge of one's own guilt, and, most clearly in neo-Protestantism, projections of the idea of perfect religiosity, of perfect morality, of pure personality, of radical trust? Do not the desires of men only become projected upon the figure of Jesus, personified in him? Kant expressly affirmed that Jesus is an example for the idea of moral perfection (cf. above n. 19). Such a statement is not far removed from Feuerbach's thesis that all religious concepts are only projections of human needs and wishes onto an imaginary transcendent world. The distinction between the Christ *principle* and its application to the historical *person* Jesus from A. E. Biedermann to Paul Tillich also lies along this line.[30]

The danger that Christology will be *constructed* out of the soteriological

29 G. Ebeling, *The Nature of Faith*, pp. 44-57: "The Witness of Faith." The two quotations are found on pp. 56 and 55. Cf. further, esp. on the catchword "certainty of God," the theses to Christology in Ebeling's book *Theology and Proclamation*, pp. 82 ff., as well as the important article "Jesus and Faith," *Word and Faith*, tr. by James W. Leitch (Fortress Press, 1963), pp. 201-246, where he also speaks of Jesus' own faith.

30 Alloys Emanuel Biedermann, *Christliche Dogmatik* (2d ed.; Berlin: Georg Reimer, 1885), Vol. II, § 790 f., § 814 ff.; Paul Tillich, *Systematic Theology*, Vol. II, pp. 93 ff., 107, 114. The quotation below in the text is from p. 150.

interest ought to be clear. Not everywhere is this so unreservedly expressed as by Tillich: "Christology is a function of soteriology." However, the tendency that is expressed here plays a part, more or less consciously and to a greater or lesser extent, in all the types of Christological thought considered here. The danger becomes acute when this procedure is elevated to a program, as by Melanchthon and later by Schleiermacher who constructed his Christology by inference from the experience of salvation. The same danger is apparent in Tillich and also becomes clear in Bultmann and his disciples as well when they say explicitly that the issue is not Jesus himself, the historical Jesus, but only his "significance" for us as opening up a new possibility of existence. Luther's *pro me* cannot properly be used to support such an argument.[31] Jesus possesses significance "for us" only to the extent that this significance is inherent in himself, in his history, and in his person constituted by this history. Only when this can be shown may we be sure that we are not merely attaching our questions, wishes, and thoughts to his figure.

Therefore, Christology, the question about Jesus himself, about his person, as he lived on earth in the time of Emperor Tiberius, must remain prior to all questions about his significance, to all soteriology. Soteriology must follow from Christology, not vice versa. Otherwise, faith in salvation itself loses any real foundation.

Thus we have been led by the consideration of the relation between Christology and soteriology to the same result that we came to in the previous chapter. Christology must start from Jesus of Nazareth, not from his significance for us as, for instance, the proclamation directly offers it. The significance of Jesus must be developed from what Jesus actually was then. This intention has been, by and large, at the basis of the Christological tradition. With the exception of Kant, Schleiermacher, Bultmann, and Tillich, one has not thought consciously from the perspective of a soteriological interest at the expense of the actual reality of Jesus of Nazareth. Even Ritschl did not want that. Thus one side of Jesus himself had its impact more or less clearly upon each of the various Christological conceptions described above. In the patristic, Alexandrian Christology it was the revelatory character of his existence and fate; for the Antiochene theologians and for Anselm, his human path in devo-

---

31 H. J. Iwand, "Wider den Missbrauch des pro me als methodisches Prinzip in der Theologie," *ThLZ*, LXXIX (1954), 453-456, has shown that in the appeal to Luther's *pro me* in contemporary theology, the Kantian subjectivity of experiential knowledge is often confused with Luther's idea of Jesus' dedication to us. In Luther the *per se* is always presupposed by the *pro me;* not until Kant's dualism of the things-in-themselves and appearance does the thing-in-itself become a mere limiting concept, the sphere of appearance become independent, but the thing-in-itself becomes inaccessible. Hegel's critique of Kant has made it clear that this contrast between "for us" and "in itself" involves a contrast of categories of reflection which cannot be set over against each other so abstractly because in the execution of reflection they are mutually conditioned, each by the other. Cf. Georg Wilhelm Friedrich Hegel, *The Logic of Hegel* (Oxford: The Clarendon Press, 1874), § 44 and § 60.

tion and obedience to the Father; and in Luther it was Jesus' conflict with Jewish law, which, nevertheless, was the law of God himself, and the vicarious character of his penal suffering. For Ritschl the proclamation of Jesus had come to life in its ethical aspect, which it also had in any case, as well as with regard to its unique nearness and intimacy to the fatherly God. Since Ritschl the uniqueness of Jesus' proclamation has come to the fore with increasing clarity, especially with regard to its eschatological character.

Thus, a presentation of Christology beginning with the past reality of Jesus does not necessarily need to break with the Christological tradition at every point. It must, however, examine the soteriological approach of the traditional Christologies in the light of the historical reality of Jesus. This is possible under the presupposition that a soteriological meaning is inherent in Jesus' history. The past reality of Jesus did not consist of brute facts in the positivistic sense, to which arbitrary interpretations, one as good as another, could be added. Rather, meaning already belongs to the activity and fate of Jesus in the original context in the history of traditions within which it occurred, from the perspective of which all subsequent, explicit interpretations can be judged. Thus, Christological research finds in the historical reality of Jesus the criterion for the critical examination of the Christological tradition and also the various soteriological concerns that have determined Christological presentations.

All soteriological motifs have one feature in common that is important for the formation of Christology. They bring to expression the fact that in Jesus the destiny of man in general has found its fulfillment, whether this be understood as deification in this or that way, as righteousness before God in the sense of the fulfillment of a legal requirement or of being declared righteous, as certainty of the relation to the world through pious self-consciousness, or as being freed for the ethical task or for being purely a person. It always involves the fact that the humanity of man in general is fulfilled through Jesus.

The establishment of the universal significance of Jesus, which is derived from God, cannot be replaced by talking about the fulfillment of the humanity of man through Jesus. Otherwise, both the universality of Jesus and his saving significance "for us" become mere assertions. Therefore, as we saw earlier, the relationship of Jesus to God must be discussed first, and only then can Jesus as man and as the fulfillment of human existence in general be discussed.

Hence, the first part of the Christological discussion presented here will deal with the knowledge of the divinity of Jesus Christ. Then a second part will be devoted to the fulfillment of human destiny through Jesus. The relationship of his divinity to his humanity, their compatibility and unity, will be the theme of the third part of this study.

Part One
The Knowledge of Jesus' Divinity

———————

JESUS' RESURRECTION AS THE GROUND OF HIS UNITY WITH GOD

Jesus' unity with God was not yet established by the claim implied in his pre-Easter appearance, but only by his resurrection from the dead.

I. THE PROLEPTIC ELEMENT IN JESUS' CLAIM TO AUTHORITY

Today when Christology is pursued "from below," from the investigation of the historical Jesus, Jesus' unity with God is substantiated in most cases by the claim to authority in his proclamation and work, not by his resurrection.

This is true, first, for a series of dogmatic Christologies. Dogmatics anticipated in many respects the theses of the New Testament scholars' study of Jesus, which has been renewed since 1950, with regard to a legitimation of the kerygma through the pre-Easter Jesus. Werner Elert[1] found the decisive argument for Jesus' divine Sonship in that even before the crisis caused by his crucifixion, Jesus claimed to be *the* Son of God. Elert supported this by the fact that when Jesus spoke of *his* Father, according to the tradition, he never included the disciples. For them it was always *your* Father.[2] Elert, in distinction from Albrecht Ritschl and Wilhelm Herrmann, placed great importance on Jesus' own claim. Ritschl was concerned, as we have already seen, with demonstrating why the disciples could designate Jesus as the Son of God, and he found the basis for this in the complete unity of Jesus' will with God's will in the establishment of an ethical "kingdom of God."[3] Elert rejected this approach, which asks why the "predicate" of divinity has been "conferred on" Jesus (p. 302), by pointing out that Jesus himself placed him-

---

[1] Werner Elert, *Der christliche Glaube: Grundlinien der lutherischen Dogmatik* (3d ed.; by Kinder, Hamburg: Furche Verlag, 1956), p. 303.

[2] Cf. Günther Bornkamm, *Jesus of Nazareth* (Harper & Row, Publishers, Inc., 1960), pp. 128 f.; in dogmatics Paul Althaus, *Die christliche Wahrheit*, p. 431.

[3] A. Ritschl, *The Christian Doctrine of Justification and Reconciliation*, § 48, pp. 451 f. On this point, see G. Bornkamm, *Jesus of Nazareth*, pp. 169 ff., esp. pp. 173 f.; so also Ernst Käsemann, "The Problem of the Historical Jesus," *Essays on New Testament*

self on God's side in his claim to authority. "It is decisive here, as said, that the testimony 'Christ the Son of God' is not primarily an attribution made by the apostles, but is contained in the whole of Christ's talk about God itself as witness to himself." (P. 303.) This formulation correctly makes clear that Jesus' claim need not have been made explicit through his own designation of himself as the Son of God. This question justifiably is not decisive for Elert. To that extent it is misleading when Elert says on p. 302: "This predicate [sic] is not a consequence of but rather the condition for the faith of the disciples." The more recent study of Jesus has shown, with general agreement, that the predicates, the Christological titles, are very probably consequences of faith, but that the claim of Jesus himself, which is implicitly contained not only in his message but in his whole work, precedes the faith of the disciples.[4]

Similarly to Elert, Paul Althaus says, "The authority that Jesus claims presupposes a nearness to God, a solidarity with him, that no other man has" (*Die christliche Wahrheit,* p. 431). "What Jesus does is blasphemy unless it comes from special authority. He claims this authority for himself. . . . For this reason God's forgiveness is a present event in his words of consolation in his eating with sinners" (p. 430). To be sure, Althaus does not stop with this indirect, implied claim to authority in the appearance, proclamation, and work of Jesus. He thinks that Jesus called himself the "Son of Man" and at least accepted the confession to him as the "Christ" (p. 430). But even if one allows this assumption to drop, together with the majority of contemporary critical exegetes, nothing is changed with regard to the fact of Jesus' claim. This is even more impressive in the implied form than if Jesus had attached his "self-consciousness," as it was formerly expressed, to one of the traditional titles.

More explicitly than Althaus, Emil Brunner sets forth in his dogmatics the "more indirect and suggestive way in which Jesus spoke of Himself."[5] "Jesus had to *be* the Christ, not to proclaim Him" (p. 247). The apostles did the latter for the first time, but they did it—as Brunner rightly emphasizes over against the liberal quest of Jesus—not in contrast to Jesus himself but as an expression of who Jesus himself is and what Jesus himself means for us (p. 252). Without the apostolic testimony, Brunner thinks, we could not catch sight of Jesus as the ground of faith, that is, this could not be done through

Themes (Studies in Biblical Theology, 41; London: SCM Press, Ltd., 1965), p. 44. As is well known, the starting point for this idea is to be found in Bultmann even as early as 1929. In his article "Kirche und Lehre im Neuen Testament," Bultmann says that in Jesus "a 'Christology' is implicitly contained in the call to decision in relation to his person" (*GuV*, I, 174). See also *idem, Theology of the New Testament,* Vol. I, p. 43.

4 Cf. G. Bornkamm, *Jesus of Nazareth,* pp. 169 ff., esp. pp. 173 f.; further, E. Käsemann, *Essays on New Testament Themes,* p. 44.

5 E. Brunner, *The Christian Doctrine of Creation and Redemption, Dogmatics:* Vol. II, p. 247. The following page numbers in the text refer to this work.

the study of the "historical Jesus" alone (pp. 253 ff.). At this point Brunner differs from Althaus and Elert. For the latter two theologians, as we have seen, the earthly Jesus' claim to authority is the basis of faith. For Brunner, it still requires supplementation in the apostolic witness, the vision of the "witnesses to the Resurrection" of Jesus (p. 252). "This twofold testimony is the objective basis of faith." (P. 251.)

Friedrich Gogarten also bases his Christology on Jesus' claim.[6] Jesus' claim that what was promised is present in him (p. 124) means "that *God* is present in him" (p. 125). Jesus could not legitimate himself to support this claim. He could only require men's decision (p. 126); for by interpreting the commandments of God, Jesus reveals God as the one who claims us completely, as "the God to whom man belongs" (p. 127). The word of Jesus is "God's direct claim on us" (p. 127). Therefore he cannot legitimate himself by means of appeal to another authority. The legitimating authority would have to be a higher one. Man would, in the end, belong to it and not to the God whom Jesus proclaims.[7]

In another way, Hermann Diem also starts with Jesus' claim to authority in his pre-Easter proclamation.[8] He maintains that "the history of Jesus is the history of the proclamation of himself" (p. 106). To be sure, Jesus' proclamation of himself is not supposed to become apparent through a "historical reconstruction of Jesus' proclamation" (p. 117), but rather through the "self-proclamation of Jesus Christ in the gospel" (p. 120). In this way, Diem characterizes "the fact that in the community's proclamation the history of Jesus Christ who proclaims himself is proclaimed as a history that has happened but does not lie in the past but occurs ever anew" (p. 127). Diem has since changed this position to the effect that one can inquire behind the Evangelists' testimony to Jesus himself, that is, "to that first phase in the history of the proclamation, the proclamation of the earthly Jesus himself."[9] With the question about the justification of such theses, we now turn to the exegetical research.

Jesus' pre-Easter claim to authority is at the center of the recently revived discussion about the historical Jesus.[10] This new quest for the historical Jesus

6 F. Gogarten, *Die Verkündigung Jesu Christi*, pp. 123-140. The page numbers are given in the text.

7 Also for Carl H. Ratschow, *Der angefochtene Glaube* (Gütersloh: Gütersloher Verlagshaus Gerd Mohn, 1957), the "man Jesus" in whom God "has occurred" stands in the center of attention (p. 25; cf. pp. 53 and 56).

8 Hermann Diem, *Dogmatics*, tr. by Harold Knight (The Westminster Press, 1959). The following quotations in the text are from this work.

9 Hermann Diem, *Der irdische Jesus und der Christus des Glaubens* (Tübingen: J. C. B. Mohr [Paul Siebeck], 1957), p. 12. In his *Dogmatics*, Diem still explicitly forbade going behind the kerygma in such a way (pp. 141 f.).

10 On this, see the detailed presentation of J. M. Robinson, *A New Quest of the Historical Jesus*.

was begun by Ernst Käsemann in 1953 with his lecture "The Problem of the Historical Jesus," which appeared in 1954 in *ZThK* (pp. 125-153). Käsemann's motif was "the question about the continuity of the gospel in the discontinuity of the times" (p. 152). In 1952, Käsemann had said: "Only if Jesus' proclamation decisively coincides with the proclamation about Jesus is it understandable, reasonable, and necessary that the Christian kerygma in the New Testament conceals the message of Jesus; only then is the resurrected Jesus the historical Jesus. From this perspective we are required, precisely as historians, to inquire behind Easter. . . . By this means we shall learn whether he stands behind the word of his church or not, whether the Christian kerygma is a myth that can be detached from his word and from himself or whether it binds us historically and insolubly to him."[11] Thus the motif of the new quest is formulated: it no longer involves—as did the liberal quest for the historical Jesus—the difference between Jesus and the apostolic kerygma, but it involves precisely the continuity between the kerygma and Jesus himself.

Käsemann has sought this continuity first of all in Jesus' message. He began with the antithesis of the Sermon on the Mount.[12] The "but I say to you," with which Jesus goes beyond the wording of the Torah, shows the authenticity of these words by their uniqueness. However, Jesus does not only set himself against the statement of another rabbi, in which case he would have to confirm his statement with Scriptural references. Rather, Jesus sets his *egō* against and above the authority of Moses himself, without any kind of justification. However, the authority above Moses himself, which Jesus here claims for himself, can be none other than the authority of God. Thus, through his "but I say to you," Jesus makes himself the spokesman for God himself.[13] Käsemann finds the same claim, "which surpasses that of every rabbi or prophet" (p. 145), in the position Jesus takes toward the law about the Sabbath and the laws concerning purification (pp. 145 f.). The "amen" with which Jesus introduces his sayings is to be understood as an answer to a voice of God that speaks to him, or, in any case, as an expression of a "highest and most immediate certainty, as it is given by inspiration" (p. 148). To be sure, Jesus probably never expressed his claim in the form of the traditional eschatological titles—Messiah, Son of Man, Son of God, etc. However, his community "testified to its having understood the uniqueness of his mission by answering his proclamation with its confession of him as the Mes-

[11] E. Käsemann, "Probleme neutestamentlicher Arbeit in Deutschland," in *Die Freiheit des Evangeliums und die Ordnung der Gesellschaft* (Munich: Chr. Kaiser Verlag, 1952), pp. 133-152, quotation on p. 151.

[12] Of these, at least the first, second, and fourth antitheses are to be attributed to Jesus himself: Matt. 5:21 f., 27 f., 33 ff. (So Käsemann, *ibid.*, p. 144.)

[13] E. Käsemann, "The Problem of the Historical Jesus," *Essays on New Testament Themes,* pp. 15-47, esp. pp. 37 f. The following page numbers in the text refer to this essay.

siah and the Son of God" (p. 150). Thus, the continuity between Jesus and the apostolic kerygma consists in the fact that Jesus' community designated and brought to expression the claim of Jesus in the only way possible at that time by its confession of him as Messiah and Son of God. Basically, Bultmann had already recognized this relation when he said, "Jesus' call to decision implies a Christology . . . which will unfold the implications of the positive answer to his demand for the decision, the obedient response that acknowledges God's revelation in Jesus."[14]

Käsemann's approach to the problem has since been extended by Ernst Fuchs, Günther Bornkamm, and Hans Conzelmann. "Käsemann's initial proposal of a new quest arose from the problem of the relation of Jesus' *message* to the Church's kerygma. This was soon followed from the Bultmannian side by a parallel proposal on the part of Ernst Fuchs, who concentrated upon Jesus' *conduct* as 'the real context of his preaching.' "[15] For Fuchs, Jesus' conduct came to expression especially in his celebration of the eschatological meal —which tradition had reserved for the future and for the righteous—with tax collectors and sinners already in the present (Matt. 11:19, and parallel). In turning toward sinners, Jesus maintained God's will as a merciful will, and, therefore, his community could later proclaim him as the Christ. In his parables, which according to Fuchs were spoken in connection with such eschatological meals (see Luke, ch. 15), Jesus made it understood that in his conduct of love for sinners the Kingdom of God was already present.[16]

If we return to the dogmatic attempts to base Christology on Jesus' claim, which were discussed at the beginning of this section, the basic agreement is striking. Dogmatics seems in this case to have preceded historical research.

[14] R. Bultmann, *Theology of the New Testament*, Vol. I, p. 43. Bultmann is distinguished from the "new quest of the historical Jesus" initiated by Käsemann in 1953 only by the fact that, unlike his pupils and also unlike Paul Althaus and Emil Brunner, he does not consider a legitimation of the kerygma by a recourse to the historical Jesus to be necessary. In this connection see Bultmann, *Das Verhältnis der urchristlichen Christusbotschaft zum historischen Jesus* (Sitzungsberichte der Heidelberger Akademie der Wissenschaften, Philosophisch-historische Klasse, 1960, 3. Abhandlung; Heidelberg: Carl Winter, 1961), and the justification of the quest of the historical Jesus, against Bultmann, by G. Ebeling, *Theology and Proclamation, passim.* Van A. Harvey and Schubert M. Ogden also emphasize that the idea of the legitimation of the kerygma by the historical Jesus is the decisive difference between Bultmann's own position and that of his pupils in their article "How New Is the 'New Quest of the Historical Jesus'?" in *The Historical Jesus and the Kerygmatic Christ: Essays on the New Quest of the Historical Jesus*, pp. 197-242.

[15] J. M. Robinson, *A New Quest of the Historical Jesus*, p. 14. On this, cf. esp. Ernst Fuchs, *Das Sakrament im Lichte der neueren Exegese* (1953); *Das urchristliche Sakramentsverständnis* (Schriftenreihe der kirchlichtheologischen Sozietät in Württemberg, 8; Bad Cannstatt: R. Müllerschön Verlag, 1958); "The Quest of the Historical Jesus," *Studies of the Historical Jesus*, tr. by Andrew Scobie (Alec R. Allenson, Inc., 1964), pp. 11-31.

[16] E. Fuchs, *Das urchristliche Sakramentsverständnis*, pp. 37 f. In 1953, Hans von Campenhausen wrote, "With the forgiveness of sins Jesus not only set himself against the law that was valid, . . . but he directly assumed the place in which only God can stand according to Jewish faith and knowledge" (*Kirchliches Amt und geistliche Vollmacht in den ersten drei Jahrhunderten* [1953], pp. 8 f.).

The idea that Jesus implicitly expressed the claim that God himself was at work in him not only in his proclamation but in his entire conduct has been carried farther by Günther Bornkamm and Hans Conzelmann. In Bornkamm this has been done by the idea that Jesus' claim results from the presence of the expected eschatological future in his activity. "To make the reality of God present, this is the essential mystery of Jesus."[17] While Bornkamm thus referred Jesus' claim to the apocalyptic horizon of his proclamation, Conzelmann interpreted it conversely as the abandonment of this horizon.[18] The interval of time before the end no longer played any role for Jesus. However, Conzelmann also must admit that Jesus stands "in the tradition of Jewish eschatology" (p. 641) and that one "cannot remove the future element" from his message (p. 642). Thus it remains questionable that in Conzelmann's interpretation the future aspect of Jesus' message is expressed only as a qualification of the present: "The future is now no longer a 'not yet,' but the positive qualification of this last time" (p. 644). As much as it is to be granted to Conzelmann that what is expected in the future in Jewish tradition has been "anticipated" in Jesus' activity, the reduction of Jesus' temporal statements to an existential meaning of immediate encounter with the Kingdom of God must be judged as a deactivation of the tension between the "already" and the "not yet" in Jesus' message.

Here it is preferable to follow Bornkamm's formulations, which admittedly only make the problem apparent. First, Jesus thought and spoke within the context of apocalyptic expectations. This is not denied by Conzelmann either. Thus one cannot remove Jesus' words from this context in the history of thought without eliminating their historical particularity. Second, the remarkable tension between the futurity of the end of the world and the presence of the final decision in the person of Jesus definitely leaves room for the question about the verification of Jesus' claim.[19] With Conzelmann this question about the verification of Jesus' claim is closed by the elimination of the temporal tension between future expectation and the presence of salvation in Jesus' person. Jesus' claim to be the presence of God is absolutized. In contrast, the tension between present and future in Jesus' proclamation makes the proleptic character of Jesus' claim apparent; that is, Jesus' claim means an anticipation of a confirmation that is to be expected only from the future. That can be shown in one of Jesus' sayings which possesses central significance in the context of his proclamation, in his word about the correspondence of the future judgment to the present attitude of men in relation to Jesus. "And I tell you, every one who acknowledges me before men, the Son of man also will ac-

---

17 G. Bornkamm, *Jesus of Nazareth*, p. 62.

18 Hans Conzelmann, "Gegenwart und Zukunft in der synoptischen Tradition," *ZThK*, LIV (1957), 277-296, esp. pp. 286 ff.; *idem*, art. "Jesus Christus," *RGG*, III (3d ed.), 619-653, to which the page numbers in the text refer.

19 See Ulrich Wilckens, "Das Offenbarungsverständnis in der Geschichte des Urchristentums," *OaG*, pp. 42-90, esp. pp. 58 ff.

knowledge before the angels of God."[20] This saying from Q is also found in Matthew (ch. 10:32 f.). To be sure, "Son of Man" here is replaced by "I." Further, there is a parallel tradition of the saying in Mark (ch. 8:38), which is also preserved by Luke (ch. 9:26).[21] All versions of the saying, with the exception of Matt. 10:32 f., have in common that Jesus distinguishes the Son of Man from himself as a different figure. This constitutes the most important argument for the age of the saying: after Easter such a distinction between Jesus and the judge at the end of the age would no longer have been formulated.[22] The substitution in Matthew's version of the "I" of Jesus for the "Son

---

20 Luke 12:8. The continuation in v. 9, "But he who denies me before men will be denied before the angels of God," is lacking in some of the old manuscripts and may be a later addition.

21 On the whole question of the authenticity of the "Son of Man" sayings and their role in the preaching of Jesus, see Heinz Eduard Tödt, *The Son of Man in the Synoptic Tradition*, tr. by Dorothea M. Barton (The New Testament Library; The Westminster Press, 1965).

22 So earlier R. Bultmann, *Theology of the New Testament*, Vol. I, pp. 28 ff. G. Bornkamm, also, holds the words about the coming Son of Man in the third person to be authentic, *Jesus of Nazareth*, p. 228. H. Braun, "Der Sinn der neutestamentlichen Christologie," *ZThK*, LIV (1957), 345, comes upon the "oldest layer" of the Synoptic tradition. Philipp Vielhauer has recently questioned whether the sayings about the coming Son of Man in the third person go back to Jesus himself, in "Gottesreich und Menschensohn in der Verkündigung Jesu," *Festschrift für Günter Dehn*, ed. by Wilhelm Schneemelcher (Neukirchen Kreis Moers: Verlag der Buchhandlung des Erziehungsvereins, 1957), pp. 51-79; he is followed by H. Conzelmann, *ZThK*, LIV (1957), 281 ff.; *ZThK*, LVI (1959), Beiheft 1, 9 f.; *RGG*, III (3d ed.), 631. Also, Eduard Schweizer, "Der Menschensohn," *ZNW*, L (1959), 185-209; and Ernst Käsemann, "Sätze heiligen Rechts im NT," *NTS*, I (1954/1955), 248-260; *idem*, "The Problem of the Historical Jesus," *Essays in New Testament Themes*, pp. 43 f. Vielhauer's arguments have been extensively and convincingly answered by Tödt (*The Son of Man in the Synoptic Tradition*, pp. 329-347). In his reply, "Jesus und der Menschensohn: Zur Diskussion mit Heinz Eduard Tödt und Eduard Schweizer," *ZThK*, LX (1963), 133-177, Vielhauer has not weakened Tödt's basic point of view; that is, he has not weakened either the argument that the "disconnected coexistence" of the Son of Man and the Kingdom of God could have arisen in Jesus' message as well as in Q (on that, see Vielhauer, *ibid.*, pp. 137 f.), or also the argument that the distinction of Jesus' "I" from the "Son of Man" in Luke 12:8 f. and parallels and Mark 8:38 and parallels would make the post-Easter emergence of this saying improbable (against this, Vielhauer, *ibid.*, pp. 141-147). That Jesus and the Son of Man could be distinguished by the post-Easter community to begin with as "two *states* of the same person" (Vielhauer, *ibid.*, p. 146) cannot be excluded, to be sure, in view of the analogy of the "two-stage Christology" (Rom. 1:3 f., etc.). Nevertheless, the assumption that this distinction would have been placed in the mouth of Jesus himself remains difficult. And in distinction from the "two-stage Christology," which set off the earthly Jesus as the Son of David Christologically from the exalted Son of God, wherever one's glance falls on the earthly Jesus from the perspective of the identity of the risen and returning Jesus with the Son of Man, the former also seems already to be included in the latter. However, that the post-Easter community had identified Jesus with the Son of Man can still best be understood through the fact that Jesus himself had spoken about the Son of Man. To be sure, it cannot be disputed that the saying in Luke 12:8 f. and parallels together with Mark 8:38 and parallels is unique in the Synoptic tradition about Jesus in terms of its type (Vielhauer, *ibid.*, p. 142; cf. E. Käsemann in *VF* (1962), p. 101), but by itself alone that is naturally still no argument against its genuineness. The forensic terminology, however, which according to Vielhauer indicates a post-Easter situation (so again *ZThK*, LX [1963],

59

of man" shows how the post-Easter community understood and transformed the saying of Jesus—how it by itself doubtless would have formed it. After Easter the eschatological judge would hardly have been distinguished from Jesus. The uniqueness of the original version of the saying consists only in distinguishing the future judge of the world from Jesus, but the saying aims at establishing a relation between the conduct of both. The community that men now have with Jesus will be valid before the forum of the Son of Man.[23] Men's present attitude toward Jesus is the criterion of their survival or destruction in the coming judgment. Here the same claim is apparent that is expressed by Jesus' "but I say to you" in the Sermon on the Mount, in the celebration of the eschatological meal with tax collectors and sinners, as well as in the emphasis on the presence of salvation in the whole of Jesus' message and action. This presence of salvation becomes apparent in its precise structure in the saying we have been considering, namely, as the anticipation of the future verdict. This is the proleptic structure of Jesus' claim.

Jesus' claim to authority through its proleptic structure corresponds to the

143 f.), can be adequately understood from the picture of the future judgment that takes place through the Son of Man, and from there it can have been extended to the attitude of men toward Jesus in the present (so F. Hahn, *Christologische Hoheitstitel,* p. 34.)

In reference to Käsemann, see Hahn, *ibid.,* pp. 34 f.: Even though "sacred law" may "in fact have played a decisive role for the life and order of the community, this does not by any means say that Jesus himself cannot also have made use of this form, just as he otherwise used traditional forms in his sayings. Perhaps not only the activity of the Spirit but, above all, the earthly Jesus himself caused the oldest community to use statements of sacred law to make clear to men the unconditionedness of their decision" (*ibid.,* p. 34).

Hahn stresses, against Schweizer, that the appearance side by side in Luke 12:8 f. of the Son of Man and a passive describing God's action is "no reason to doubt the authenticity of the statement. Rather, this only makes clear how little the Son of Man's own actions move into the foreground and compete with theocratic statements" (*ibid.,* pp. 35 f.).

When Willi N. Marxsen, *Anfangsprobleme der Christologie* (Gütersloh: Gütersloher Verlagshaus Gerd Mohn, 1960), pp. 20 ff., says that the earliest community *handed down* this saying, thus having distinguished between Jesus and the Son of Man (*ibid.,* p. 27), this is to be contested for the act of the tradition in contrast to the act of coining the saying. The word would certainly never have been *coined* as it is if Jesus had been intended as the Son of Man. But once *coined,* it could be interpreted without difficulty in the sense that the Son of Man, of whom it spoke, had now turned out to be identical with Jesus himself. The decisive argument—that the characteristic way of speaking of the Son of Man in the third person and thus in distinction from the first person of Jesus could no longer have arisen after Easter—remains valid in spite of all criticism. O. Weber, *Grundlagen der Dogmatik,* Vol. II, pp. 75 f., harmonizes when he considers the statement in the third person by Jesus himself to be possible in the sense of a self-prediction, following Otto, Holtzmann, and Schlatter.

23 W. Marxsen, *Anfangsprobleme der Christologie,* pp. 27 ff., agrees with Tödt, *The Son of Man in the Synoptic Tradition,* p. 66, and Hahn, *Christologische Hoheitstitel,* pp. 36 ff., in emphasizing correctly that the interest of the saying about the coming Son of Man is primarily directed toward a qualification of the present. Nonetheless, the meaning of this emphasis upon the present is understandable only against the background of the eschatological expectation. Therefore, one may not construe from this a contrast to the apocalyptic expectation as such, as if there did not exist, rather, an existential relation between them—though, to be sure, the specific turn to the present is scarcely as yet inherent in the general apocalyptic background.

apocalyptic vision's relation to history, which in turn goes back to the relation of the prophetic word of God to the future. The prophets received words that must be confirmed by their future fulfillment, and thereby must be shown to be Yahweh's words.[24] The apocalyptic's view of history, which also grasped future events before they occurred, required confirmation by the actual course of the events themselves. Therefore, in Dan. 11:1-39, the course of history described from the Persian empire to Antiochus IV provides the basis for confidence that the remainder of the prophecies will be fulfilled.

Jesus' activity is certainly profoundly different from that of the apocalyptic visionaries. In the first place, he does not hide his person under a pseudonym. He is conscious of what he brings as something new; this is presumably why he does not speak in the name of one of the canonical figures of the Old Testament tradition. Similar characteristics are to be found in John the Baptist and the Qumran community, to which both the Baptist, and through him Jesus, may have been connected in one way or another.[25] However, that Jesus presents his message in his own name and no longer in that of a canonical figure from *Heilsgeschichte* is, in the second place, perhaps connected with the fact that Jesus, like John the Baptist, had expected the end to be so imminent that he no longer described the path to it, but in view of it only issued a call to repentance. However, third, while in the Baptist's call to repentance only the judgment was present, in Jesus' activity eschatological salvation also had already made its appearance. Not merely the expectancy of ultimate salvation on the basis of repentance—that may also have been the case with John the Baptist—but salvation itself was present. For this reason, the future participation in salvation was decided by the attitude taken toward his person; for this reason, Jesus' own person, in distinction from the Baptist's, stands in the center. Thus, in the fourth place, with Jesus the end is not only—as in the apocalyptic writings—seen in advance, but it has happened in advance. These observations indicate profound differences between the activity of Jesus and that of the apocalyptic prophet, differences which also make it understandable why in Jesus, as probably earlier in John the Baptist, apocalyptic pictures of the end events recede into the background. Apocalyptic remains, nevertheless, the intellectual context of the Baptist's preaching of repentance as well as of the proleptic occurrence of God's rule through Jesus.[26]

This conclusion must be defended against the position recently expressed by Käsemann. In his article on "The Beginnings of Christian Theology,"[27] Käse-

---

[24] Deut. 18:21-22; I Kings 22:28. Cf. also Jer. 28:9.

[25] On this, see Conzelmann, *RGG*, III (3d ed.), 624 and 628.

[26] See U. Wilckens, "Das Offenbarungsverständnis in der Geschichte des Urchristentums," in *OaG*, esp. pp. 54 f.

[27] Ernst Käsemann, "Die Anfänge christlicher Theologie," *ZThK*, LVII (1960), 162-185. On the basis of the polemic against prophets in Matt. 7:22 f., Käsemann concludes that there was an early Christian prophetic movement of an apocalyptic character. He

mann has shown that the primitive Christian history of traditions bore an apocalyptic character from the very beginning. However, for Jesus himself, Käsemann thinks "that Jesus to be sure started from the apocalyptically determined message of the Baptist, but his own preaching was not constitutively (!)[28] stamped by apocalyptic; rather, he preached the immediacy of the near God. Whoever took this step cannot, I am convinced, have awaited the coming Son of Man . . . and the beginning of the parousia connected with that in order to experience the nearness of God. To have to unite both would mean for me not to be able to understand anything at all." Conzelmann says similarly "that statements about God's rule and those about the coming of his kingdom stand somewhat unrelated side by side."[29] Later we will discuss the connection between these two groups of sayings. Here we limit our argument to the question whether one would not make more progress if, instead of starting with the parables as an expression of the God who is "near" in his rule, one began from the eschatological nearness of God in order to understand the nearness of the Creator as well from this perspective. It should be said, against Käsemann's detachment of Jesus from the apocalyptic atmosphere that preceded and followed him, that such a postulate is historically not very probable. It must be considered more probable that in his own thought Jesus also had been connected with the apocalyptically determined message of the Baptist.[30]

Käsemann's special argument against the originality of Luke 12:8 f. and parallels is that here we are dealing with a statement of sacred law as it is otherwise found in the tradition of the primitive Christian community.[31] That such formulations by the community stand in contradiction to and not in continuity with Jesus himself is not established more precisely but is presupposed, even though the talk about the Son of Man in the third person makes a formulation by the community in this case very difficult to understand.

Hence, with Bultmann, Bornkamm, Tödt, and others against Vielhauer and

finds the forms of the preaching of such apocalyptic prophecy in statements of sacred law (pp. 171 ff.), in short maxims (pp. 173 f.), in apocalyptically grounded paraenetic statements (pp. 176 ff.), as well as in forms of cursing and blessing (pp. 178 f.). The quotation following in the text is found on pp. 179 f. After this was written, Käsemann published the article "Zum Thema der urchristlichen Apokalyptik," ZThK, LIX (1962), 257-284. This article sets forth the breadth of apocalyptic thought for primitive Christianity up to Paul.

28 With similar indefiniteness, it is asserted in ZThK, LIX (1962), 260, that apocalyptic does not come "strongly" to the fore in the somewhat certain Jesus tradition. Nevertheless, such a difference, which is only vaguely specified, is supposed, as it says in what immediately follows, to be "the constitutive difference from the preaching of the Baptist."

29 Hans Conzelmann, art. "Jesus Christus," RGG, III (3d ed.), 641.

30 The message of the Baptist is also characterized in this way by Käsemann (ZThK, LVII [1960], 179) and by Conzelmann (RGG, III [3d ed.], 624).

31 E. Käsemann, "The Problem of the Historical Jesus," Essays on New Testament Themes, p. 43.

Käsemann, I think that the oldest stratum of the sayings about the Son of Man comes from Jesus himself. The judgment, however, that Jesus' claim has proleptic character is supported, not only by this group of sayings, but by the convergence of their meaning with the total character of Jesus' activity as it is determined by the apocalyptic background.[32]

The claim of Jesus agrees—despite all the differences—with apocalyptic prophetic inspirations also in the fact that his claim requires future confirmation. It was valid on its own account as little as were prophetic words or apocalyptic visions.

The question about the confirmation of his claim to authority was also put to Jesus. We must think first here of the episode that is transmitted as the Pharisees' demand for a sign.[33] Here a divine confirmation of Jesus "from heaven" is demanded. Jesus rejects this demand. That does not mean, however, that he rejected every request for "legitimation," for a confirmation of his claim.[34] Rather, in response to John the Baptist's question whether he was the One who was to come, according to the report in Q, he pointed to his deeds: "The blind receive their sight and the lame walk, lepers are cleansed and the deaf hear, and the dead are raised up, and the poor have good news

32 U. Wilckens, "Das Offenbarungsverständnis in der Geschichte des Urchristentums," *OaG*, pp. 54 f. Käsemann also, admits that Jesus "began with the glowing imminent expectation of the Baptist" (*ZThK*, LIX [1962], 260). This makes it all the more remarkable that a message about the "distant" God is attributed to the Baptist (p. 261)—also that the "God who comes as judge" can still be near and apparently is so for John the Baptist—and that Jesus' message of the coming of the Kingdom, in contrast, is supposed to be "not exclusively or even primarily connected with a chronologically datable end of the world" (p. 261). It is certainly not exclusively, but probably, "primarily" so, if the specific presence of the Kingdom in Jesus' activity is to be understood from the perspective of the power of its future that makes everything else seem dim by comparison (as is to be shown in Part Two below). In any case, the converse is anything but "obvious" in the light of Jesus' beginning with the "glowing imminent expectation of the Baptist" (p. 261).

33 Mark 8:11 f.; Matt. 12:38-42; 16:1-4; Luke 11:16, 29-32; 12:54-56.

34 Thus F. Gogarten, *Die Verkündigung Jesu Christi*, pp. 125 f.; also, Ernst Lohmeyer, *Das Evangelium des Markus* (Kritisch-exegetischer Kommentar über das Neue Testament, begun by Heinrich August Wilhelm Meyer; 11th ed.; Göttingen: Vandenhoeck & Ruprecht, 1951), pp. 155 f. G. Bornkamm, *Jesus of Nazareth*, p. 133, says with respect to Mark 8:11 f. that the refusal to give a sign shows "that Jesus will not allow miracles to be considered a proof of God's working and power, which could be demanded as the prerequisite to faith." According to Julius Schniewind, *Das Evangelium nach Markus* (Das Neue Testament Deutsch: Neues Göttinger Bibelwerk; 6th ed.; Göttingen: Vandenhoeck & Ruprecht, 1952), p. 111, the reply to the demand for a sign reported in Mark, however, stands "absolutely in tension to Jesus' own evaluation of his miracles, as it is without doubt handed down to us in Matt. 11:5 f.; 12:28." In Matt. 12:38 ff., as in Luke, ch. 11, Jesus' answer to the demand for a sign is connected with the saying about Jonah, which, in any case, was interpreted by the Evangelists in terms of Jesus' death and resurrection corresponding to Jonah's miraculous rescue. Cf. Schniewind, *Das Evangelium nach Matthäus* (Das Neue Testament Deutsch: Neues Göttinger Bibelwerk; 5th ed.; Göttingen: Vandenhoeck & Ruprecht, 1950), p. 162. Accordingly, Jesus' resurrection is seen as the sign which had been demanded of him while he was alive but which then was given by God and confirmed his claim.

preached to them. And blessed is he who takes no offense at me" (Matt. 11: 5 f.). This saying possibly goes back to Jesus himself, although it may only later have been interpreted by the Christian community as a reply to the Baptist's inquiry.[35] The meaning of the saying consists in showing that the saving deeds of the end time are happening under Jesus' hands; they show who Jesus is. Therefore, it can be said, "Blessed is he who takes no offense at me." A saying transmitted by Luke (ch. 11:20) has a similar meaning: "But if it is by the finger of God that I cast out demons, then the kingdom of God has come upon you."[36] Thus, Jesus certainly was able to point to his mighty deeds as the verification and confirmation of his claim to authority. What meaning, then, did his refusal to produce the demanded "sign from heaven" have? In any case, it quite probably did not mean that Jesus had rejected any legitimation at all as a presupposition for recognizing his mission. Rather, one would have to say that the deeds of Jesus could authenticate his claim only to a certain extént, but not fully and completely.[37] Jesus' deeds could point to the beginning of the time of salvation, but they could not show unambiguously whether Jesus personally was the one in whom salvation or judgment are ultimately decided. It was, however, Jesus' claim that survival or destruction in the coming judgment by the Son of Man would be decided on the basis of one's relation to him. This claim by Jesus could be shown to be true only when the general resurrection of the dead occurred and the judgment of the Son of Man actually took place according to the standard of the relation of men to Jesus. Jesus could not give this "sign" on his own initiative; therefore, he re-

[35] Rudolf Bultmann, *The History of the Synoptic Tradition,* tr. by John Marsh (Oxford: Basil Blackwell & Mott, Ltd., 1963), p. 23. For the original meaning of the saying, see p. 129.

[36] Cf. R. Bultmann, *Theology of the New Testament,* Vol. I, p. 7. See also Mark 3:27 and parallels and Luke 10:18. This last saying could have preserved an apocalyptic vision of Jesus and would then be unique in the entire primitive Christian tradition. Bultmann conjectures that other visions of this sort could have been suppressed by the tradition (*The History of the Synoptic Tradition,* pp. 108 f.). In this connection, Bultmann notes, rightly of course, that Jesus had not been "an apocalyptist in the strict sense" (cf. also p. 161, n. 2). Jesus was not an apocalyptic because he had not written an apocalypse. Rather, he saw it as his task to call men to repentance and to proclaim salvation in view of the imminent Kingdom of God. However, Jesus' message about the imminence of the Kingdom of God is intrinsically related to the vision of the fall of Satan from heaven to earth; for with the fact that Satan has been defeated in heaven and has been cast down to earth the end time has begun (cf. also Rev. 12:9). The possibility cannot be excluded that the vision of the fall of Satan from heaven (cf. also Matt. 12:29) may have been the starting point of Jesus' message about the nearness of the Kingdom of God.

[37] On the following considerations, cf. U. Wilckens, *OaG,* pp. 59 ff. That the claim of Jesus regarding his own person could only be confirmed by his own fate (p. 60) requires a more precise justification. In the sense of Jesus' saying about the coming Son of Man, it would have to be said that the truth of his message must be confirmed at the arrival of the end events. It was confirmed in his own fate insofar as Jesus' resurrection must be understood as the beginning of the end event in his person. Jesus would hardly have expected that his own fate would be consummated by an act of God in him alone, without the arrival of the end events themselves (so, too, Wilckens, p. 61), if the imminent eschatological expectation was characteristic of his activity.

jected any inquiry about it. But even so this rejection also takes place in a particularly cautious way.[38] Thus the whole of Jesus' work remained aimed at the future verification of his claim to authority, at a confirmation that Jesus himself was unable to offer precisely because and insofar as it involved the legitimation of his own person, which is bound to the arrival of the announced end event. The question about such a future confirmation of Jesus' claim by God himself is held open by the temporal difference between the beginning of God's rule, which was already present in Jesus' activity, and its future fulfillment with the coming of the Son of Man on the clouds of heaven. Even the disciples of the pre-Easter Jesus could only follow his claim to authority in trust in its future confirmation by God himself, i.e., through the occurrence of the end of history.

Only when one sees that the question of the ultimate confirmation of Jesus' claim to authority stands over his entire path does one understand the point of the journey to Jerusalem. Jesus apparently was determined to bring about a decision.[39] That he virtually forced a decision seems to be suggested by the narrative of the cleansing of the Temple (Mark 11:15-19, and parallels), at least the kernel of which may be historical.[40]

From this point of view it would be very peculiar if Jesus had not reckoned at least with the possibility of his death in Jerusalem, though not in the sense of the predictions of the passion in the Gospels, which are certainly *vaticinia ex eventu*, as has been generally accepted since Wrede.[41] Nevertheless, his journey to Jerusalem was certainly no deed of despair. Jesus probably expected that God would, in one way or another, acknowledge him, even in the case of his own failure. This assumption is all the less to be rejected, since Jesus in any case reckoned with the imminent end of the world and the resurrection

[38] So, at least, if the reply to the demand for a sign was originally connected with the saying about the sign of Jonah (Q), as it is handed down by Matthew and Luke. On Mark 8:12, see the quotation from Schniewind in n. 34 above. On the question of authority (Mark 11:27-33) Jesus replies with the counterquestion about John the Baptist and his authority—he by no means rejects the question in principle, but rather avoids it. The reply, or deliberation, of the opponents in vs. 31 f. shows that Jesus' counterquestion was no longer understood by the early Christians who passed it on in the tradition, at least not by Mark. If it had been understood, the affirmation of the counterquestion put by Jesus as to the authority of John the Baptist would more probably have been followed by the challenge to accept Jesus' activity as authorized by God, analagous to that of John the Baptist, than by the question asking why they did not believe the Baptist (vs. 31 f.). This assumption is necessary because Jesus holds out the prospect of an answer to the question about his own authority.

[39] U. Wilckens, *OaG*, pp. 60 f.

[40] R. Bultmann, *History of the Synoptic Tradition*, p. 56. One also thinks of Jesus' saying about Herod, the "fox," Luke 13:31-33.

[41] The Synoptic predictions of Jesus' passion (Mark 8:31; 9:31; 10:33 f.) must be taken as *vaticinia ex eventu* because they "presume a detailed knowledge of the Passion and Easter story" (so G. Bornkamm, *Jesus of Nazareth*, p. 229). See also R. Bultmann, *The History of the Synoptic Tradition*, pp. 152 f., n. 1. J. Schniewind, *Das Evangelium nach Markus*, p. 117, is of a different opinion. On the question of its pre-Marcan origin, cf. H. E. Tödt, *The Son of Man in the Synoptic Tradition*, pp. 136-221, esp. p. 200.

of the dead and judgment of the Son of Man which were associated with that. Measured by the imminent nearness of these events of the end, it must have been of secondary significance for Jesus whether he himself would have to endure death before the end came. The truth of his proclamation did not need to depend on this. One way or the other the ultimate confirmation of his message through the imminent fulfillment of all history with the appearance of the Son of Man on the clouds of heaven was immediately at hand. This occurrence of the end, however, must bring the verification of his authority.

To summarize: There is no reason for the assumption that Jesus' claim to authority taken by itself justified faith in him. On the contrary, the pre-Easter Jesus' claim to authority stands from the beginning in relationship to the question of the future verification of his message through the occurrence of the future judgment of the Son of Man according to the attitude taken by men toward Jesus. Thus has been shown the proleptic structure of Jesus' claim to authority, which is analogous to that of the Old Testament prophetic sayings. This means, however, that Jesus' claim to authority by itself cannot be made the basis of a Christology, as though this only involved the "decision" in relation to him. Such Christology—and the preaching based upon it—would remain an empty assertion. Rather, everything depends upon the connection between Jesus' claim and its confirmation by God.

II. THE SIGNIFICANCE OF JESUS' RESURRECTION

As we have seen, in all probability the earthly Jesus' expectation was not directed toward, so to speak, a privately experienced resurrection from the dead but toward the imminent universal resurrection of the dead, which would, of course, include himself should his death precede it. Then when his disciples were confronted by the resurrected Jesus, they no doubt also understood this as the beginning of the universal resurrection of the dead, as the beginning of the events of the end of history. Twenty to thirty years after Jesus' death Paul still reckoned with the imminent, ultimate arrival of the resurrected Jesus for judgment, accompanied by the universal resurrection of the dead; this was still supposed to happen in his lifetime.[42] Only for the second generation of New Testament witnesses, for Mark, Matthew, Luke, John, for the authors of the Deutero-Pauline epistles and of Hebrews, did it become clear that the resurrection of Jesus was not yet the beginning of the immediately continuous sequence of the eschatological events but was a special event that happened to Jesus alone. Now the danger arose that the connection of Jesus' resurrection to the final occurrence of the universal resurrection of the dead and judgment would be lost from view. This danger is especially clear in Luke. Where the tension

[42] I Thess. 4:15,17; I Cor. 15:51. Only in Philippians does this become different for Paul.

between the present and the expectation for the future is lost, the occurrence of Jesus' resurrection loses the inherent significance that it originally had, that is, the significance that was inherent in it within its original context in the history of traditions, namely, in the horizon of the apocalyptic expectation for the future. For Jesus' Jewish contemporaries, insofar as they shared the apocalyptic expectation, the occurrence of the resurrection did not first need to be interpreted, but for them it spoke meaningfully in itself: If such a thing had happened, one could no longer doubt what it meant.

The following points summarize the most important elements that characterize the immediate inherent significance of Jesus' resurrection.

(a) If Jesus has been raised, then the end of the world has begun.

The universal resurrection of the dead and the judgment are imminent. This comes to expression in Paul's expectation that the resurrection of other men, especially of believers, will immediately follow that of Jesus.[43] Jesus is "the first-born among many brethren" (Rom. 8:29). Christ is raised as the first-fruits of those who have fallen asleep (I Cor. 15:20). Correspondingly, in Col. 1:18 Jesus is called the firstborn of the dead. The same expression is found in Rev. 1:5, indicating that this is a traditional, widely circulated formulation. The designation of Jesus as "Author of life," preserved by Luke in Acts 3:15, is to be understood as materially similar.

To the nearness of the end which began with Jesus' resurrection belongs, as well, the early Christian conviction that the same Spirit of God by which Jesus has been raised[44] now already dwells in the Christians.[45] In early Christianity the Spirit had eschatological significance. The word designated nothing else than the presence of the resurrection life in the Christians.

(b) If Jesus has been raised, this for a Jew can only mean that God himself has confirmed the pre-Easter activity of Jesus.

Jesus' claim to authority, through which he put himself in God's place, was, as we saw in the discussion of the antitheses in the Sermon on the Mount, blasphemous for Jewish ears. Because of this, Jesus was then also slandered by the Jews before the Roman governor as a rebel. If Jesus really has been raised, this claim has been visibly and unambiguously confirmed by the God of Israel, who was allegedly blasphemed by Jesus. This was done by Israel's God. A Jew —and for the moment we are speaking only of Jews—could certainly not take an event of this kind as one that came to be apart from the will of his God. That the primitive Christian proclamation in fact understood Jesus' resurrec-

[43] Rom. 5:12 ff.; I Cor. 15:45 ff.; but see also II Cor. 5:10. However, the judgment of the dead in the apocalyptic tradition in no sense always presupposes a resurrection of the wicked preceding their condemnation. On this, see below, pp. 78 ff.; for Paul, see also n. 64 below.

[44] Rom. 1:3; II Cor. 13:4; see also I Tim. 3:16; I Peter 3:18.

[45] Rom. 8:11, as well as the entire section ch. 8:1-11.

tion from the dead as the confirmation of his pre-Easter claim emerges above all in the speeches in Acts,[46] and perhaps also in the old expression that Jesus was shown to be justified in the Spirit.[47]

(c) *Through his resurrection from the dead, Jesus moved so close to the Son of Man that the insight became obvious: the Son of Man is none other than the man Jesus who will come again.*

In his previously mentioned book, H. E. Tödt has shown that the earliest community, to the extent that its theological thought comes to expression in Q, had already identified Jesus with the Son of Man, although in other respects it appears only to have continued the proclamation of Jesus himself. This assertion of the post-Easter community was not simply an arbitrary act.

It lets the question about the basis of such an identification of Jesus with the Son of Man be put in a meaningful way from the perspective of the event itself as it was experienced by the first Christians. To what extent was the presentation of Jesus' relation to the Son of Man different to his disciples after his resurrection from what it had been in his pre-Easter message?

The pre-Easter Jesus had already proclaimed a correspondence in function between his own attitude toward men and the future attitude of the Son of Man: the attitude of men toward Jesus and the community which he grants to others are valid before the forum of the Son of Man. The distinction between these two figures consists only in the fact that the pre-Easter Jesus walked visibly on the earth, whereas the Son of Man was to come only in the future on the clouds of heaven and was expected as a heavenly being. This difference disappeared, however, with Jesus' resurrection. As the one who has

[46] Acts 2:36; 3:15; 5:30 f.; *et al.* Recently Friedrich Mildenberger has asserted that Jesus' *death* must have been understood as the confirmation of his claim. "Jesus' death, which occurred on the basis of this claim, could, however, not be understood as its refutation; rather, it must have been understood as the confirmation of this claim in analogy to the typology of the fate of the prophet as it was known in that time." ("Auferstanden am dritten Tage nach den Schriften," in *EvTh,* XXIII [1963], 265-280, quotation p. 270.) The certainty established in this way had simply come to its ultimate success in the Easter visions (p. 271). In this it is correct that Jesus' death was understood in the light of the suffering of the prophets. However, the suffering in itself does not provide the necessary confirmation, but only the unavoidable fate of the prophet and the righteous man in general in this evil world. With this, however, misfortune and destruction are not unambiguous signs of righteousness, for normally in the divine ordering of events these are the reward of the evildoer. In contrast, the apocalyptic theology of suffering could maintain this much: that *contrary to appearances* earthly failure must not in all circumstances put the prophet in the wrong. Yet the confirmation of his message through its fulfillment remains to be expected without fail. What would a prophet be whose word was not fulfilled, even though he perished so miserably? Also, with regard to Messianic pretenders, things normally quieted down after their failure. According to Mildenberger's logic, the prophets would then have had to be proclaimed and believed in as Messiah more than ever precisely because of their failure.

[47] I Tim. 3:16b. Is this idea also perhaps in the background in Rom. 4:25? Admittedly, the text now reads, "put to death for *our* trespasses and raised for *our* justification."

been taken away to God, Jesus is a heavenly being. His coming from heaven, which was expected in the immediate future and was probably already initiated by the Easter appearances, will bring on the universal resurrection of the dead and judgment, just as the apocalyptic tradition had predicted of the appearance of the Son of Man on the clouds of heaven. Thus it is understandable that Jesus was no longer distinguished from the Son of Man, but was himself seen as the Son of Man whose coming was expected in the future, and the tradition about Jesus down to the details was connected with the expectation of the Son of Man. After Jesus' resurrection it must have become meaningless to expect a second figure in addition to him with the same function and the same mode of coming. By virtue of the resurrection, Jesus had moved into the role of the Son of Man.

(d) *If Jesus, having been raised from the dead, is ascended to God and if thereby the end of the world has begun, then God is ultimately revealed in Jesus.*

Only at the end of all events can God be revealed in his divinity, that is, as the one who works all things, who has power over everything. Only because in Jesus' resurrection the end of all things, which for us has not yet happened, has already occurred can it be said of Jesus that the ultimate already is present in him, and so also that God himself, his glory, has made its appearance in Jesus in a way that cannot be surpassed. Only because the end of the world is already present in Jesus' resurrection is God himself revealed in him.[48]

If these apocalyptic ideas are translated into Hellenistic terminology and conceptuality, their meaning is: in Jesus, God himself has appeared on earth. God himself—or God's revelatory figure, the Logos, the Son—has been among us as a man in the figure of Jesus. In this sense, in the transition of the Palestinian tradition into the Syrian sphere eschatology was translated throughout into epiphany. This Hellenistic concept of revelation prepared the basic pattern for the subsequent doctrine of incarnation.

The translation of the apocalyptic understanding of Jesus as the one in whom the glory of God is ultimately revealed, because in him the end event has already occurred in advance, into the Hellenistic concept of revelation as epiphany may also have been the path that led to the thesis of the true divinity of Jesus.[49] Jesus' divinity is already implied in some way in the conception of God's appearance in him, even though not with the later orthodox precision.

[48] On this, see my article in *OaG*, esp. pp. 95 ff., 103 ff.

[49] In terms of the history of traditions, the path to the perception of Jesus' divinity ran by way of the titles "Son of God" and "*Kyrios*," as has been suggested (cf. F. Hahn, *Christologische Hoheitstitel*). In this process the exegesis of Ps. 110:1 (LXX) played a decisive role. However, we are led to the driving forces behind the transformation in the history of traditions only by questioning the *motives* of such exegesis, and these motives may be related to Hellenistic ideas of epiphany.

*(e) The transition to the Gentile mission is motivated by the eschatological
resurrection of Jesus as resurrection of the crucified One.*

Israelite prophecy expected the self-demonstration of God, which it proclaimed, as an event that would take place before the eyes of all peoples. Not
just Israel but all nations were to recognize from this future event the exclusive
divinity of Israel's God. The exilic prophets Deutero-Isaiah and Ezekiel especially preached in this way. The same proclamation occurs repeatedly in the
psalms.[50] This expectation corresponds to the hope, rooted in the Jerusalem
tradition of the election of David and Zion, that in the end time all peoples
would submit themselves to the Lordship of Yahweh and his Anointed One.[51]

Also in postexilic Judaism the expectation remained alive that the nations
would one day be included in the eschatological salvation hoped for Israel.[52]
However, in contrast to this stood the dominant conception which regarded
the Gentiles simply as godless and which hoped for the time of God's vengeance on Israel's oppressors and their final annihilation at the arrival of the
Messianic Kingdom.[53]

Thus it is clear that the beginning of the end in Jesus' resurrection signified
the inclusion of the Gentiles into eschatological salvation only for those who
together with Jesus himself followed the universalistic line of Israelite tradition. However, even in this line of Jewish tradition and thus also in the
earliest Christian community, the consequence of a *mission* to the Gentiles
in the Pauline sense was not automatic. One sees that the significance of the
resurrection of Jesus in this point was less clear than in those previously
considered.

Jesus himself had stood in contrast to the Jewish propaganda of his time
and considered himself as sent only to the Israelites,[54] even though he also
seems on occasion to have recognized the faith of non-Jews as a valid acceptance of eschatological salvation, corresponding to the unconditionedness of his
assurance of salvation. Nonetheless, in contrast to apparently widely held conceptions of Jewish contemporaries, Jesus did not predict divine vengeance on
the Gentiles for the *eschaton,* but the participation of many of them in eschatological salvation,[55] while he threatened the impenitent Israelites with wrath-

[50] In greater detail in Rolf Rendtorff in *OaG*, pp. 38 f., 26 f.

[51] This Jerusalem tradition occurs in Ps. 2:8; Isa. 2:2 ff. (= Micah 4:1 ff.); cf. Zech.
9:10; also, the universalism of salvation in Deutero-Isaiah (like that of the Yahwist before him, Gen. 12:3 *et al.*) may be connected to this tradition. The previously mentioned
statements about Yahweh's universal revelation before all nations does not as such imply
such a universalism of salvation. Yahweh's divinity could also be revealed to the nations
not as the divinity of their God, but only of Israel's God.

[52] Paul Billerbeck, *Kommentar zum Neuen Testament aus Talmud und Midrash*
(Munich: C. H. Beck'sche Verlagsbuchhandlung, 1922 ff.), Vol. III, pp. 144, 150-152.

[53] References in Joachim Jeremias, *Jesus' Promise to the Nations* (Studies in Biblical
Theology, 24; Alec R. Allenson, Inc., 1958), p. 41.

[54] *Ibid.*, pp. 26 f. on Matt. 15:24.

[55] Matt. 25:34; cf. Matt. 8:11 f. and parallels; Luke 13:29. Jeremias, *ibid.*, pp. 47 f.

ful judgment. However, he expected the "incorporation of the Gentiles into the people of God as the result of God's eschatological act of power,"[56] as a consequence of the reestablishment of Zion to which the nations would then flock, not as the result of religious propaganda among the nations. In this sense the earliest community apparently restricted its mission to Israel, without for that reason condemning the Gentiles as excluded from eschatological salvation and without having to deny to those who occasionally came acceptance into the community. A Gentile *mission* seems to have arisen for the first time as a result of the conviction that the resurrected Jesus has now already been exalted to Lordship in heaven and consequently the news of his Lordship is to be carried to all nations.[57] However, even then it apparently still remained unclarified whether the evangelization of the Gentiles did not also have to aim at the acceptance of the law by them. A change in this apparently occurred only when Paul combined Jesus' crucifixion with the curse threatened by the law (Gal. 3:13). On this basis, he had to understand the law as abrogated in view of the Sonship that appeared in Jesus' resurrection, so that the rejection of Jesus by the Jews, which was completed in the cross, led to the inclusion of the Gentiles in salvation (v. 14) through faith in the message of salvation that is accessible now apart from the law (chs. 3:14 and 2:15 ff.). It is revealing that Paul did not originally justify the mission to the Gentiles by appealing

See also Ferdinand Hahn, *Mission in the New Testament*, tr. by Frank Clarke (London: SCM Press, Ltd., 1965), pp. 34 ff.

[56] J. Jeremias, *Jesus' Promise to the Nations*, p. 71; cf. in general pp. 59 ff. See also E. Käsemann, "Zum Thema der urchristlichen Apokalyptik," *ZThK*, LIX (1962), 257-284, esp. p. 267. Hahn supplements and corrects Jeremias by noting that the "acceptance of individual Gentiles" by Jesus must be seen together with his "promises for all nations" (*Mission in the New Testament*, p. 39; cf. pp. 31 ff.), so that also in this regard the eschatological future has already become present in Jesus' activity (*ibid.*, p. 33, n. 2). Jesus had, "by proclaiming to Israel the Kingdom of God, preached the claim and the salvation of God for everyone to hear, and even the Gentiles heard the news" (*ibid.*, p. 39). Only in this way is it understandable how Jesus' message could become the starting point also for the Gentile mission of his community (*ibid.*, pp. 39 f.; cf. p. 30). However, that is only convincing to the extent that it is maintained at the same time that Jesus regarded his mission as limited to Israel, so that the universal breadth of the communication of salvation to the Gentiles still remained for the future. A *direct* path to the Gentile *mission* did not lead from the message of Jesus but from his resurrection (and exaltation).

[57] F. Hahn, *ibid.*, pp. 63 ff., on Matt. 28:18-20. According to Hahn, however, the idea of a mission of the disciples did not first arise from faith in the exalted Lord, but a mission given by the pre-Easter Jesus (pp. 40 ff.) now became broadened to a universal mission in the conviction that with Jesus' exaltation "an essential step towards the final completion has already been taken and that therefore the bringing in of the Gentiles can now begin" (p. 68). That the tradition standing behind Matt. 28:18-20, however, appeals only to a task given by the resurrected Jesus, as the exalted one, without recalling a mission given by the earthly Jesus or the universal breadth of his message, shows that the decisive importance for the motivation falls here on the resurrection (as exaltation). The connection with the character of Jesus' earthly activity represents more a modern possibility of reflection in terms of the history of traditions, which, to be sure, accents a continuity that *actually* exists, not, however, an argument that becomes effective for the transition of Hellenistic Jewish Christianity to the Gentile mission.

to the universalistic promises of Old Testament prophets for the end time, but rather on the basis of the Christ event, specifically Christ's crucifixion (Gal. 3:13 f.)[58] as understood, certainly, in the light of the resurrection. Then Paul appeals to the fact that Abraham, whom Jewish propaganda had already presented as the father of the proselytes,[59] was justified by faith, as the Gentile Christians are now, so that it is the blessing of Abraham that has been carried through to the Gentiles through Jesus' cross with its removal of the curse of the law (Gal. 3:14; Rom., ch. 4). If the Gentile mission is thus at first related to Israelite covenant history through the figure of Abraham,[60] Paul can in Romans draw upon eschatological prophesies such as Isa. 11:10 (Rom. 15:12; see also Ps. 117:1; 18:49) and Hosea 2:23 (Rom. 9:25 f.; cf. I Peter 2:10) as proof from Scripture to justify the Gentile mission.[61] Still, Paul must have seen the correspondence of the eschatological meaning of the Gentiles' conversion to the eschatological character of the message about Christ which originated in Jesus' resurrection as the confirmation of his action.

Thus, even though the transition to the Gentile mission does not represent a direct consequence of the significance inherent in Jesus' resurrection by itself, it was inevitable as soon as Jesus' resurrection was understood in its connection with the crucifixion as the expression of his rejection by Israel (cf. Rom. 11:11 ff. and Acts 13:45). Certainly even in Paul's own case the report of Jesus' crucifixion alone did not effect his transformation from a persecutor of the Christian community to missionary to the Gentiles, but only his confrontation with the crucified as the resurrected Jesus. In this confrontation Paul's gospel of freedom from the law is immediately implied.

(f) *Particularly the last consequence throws light on the relationship between the* appearances *of the resurrected Jesus and the* words *spoken by him: what the early Christian tradition transmitted as the words of the risen Jesus is to be understood in terms of its content as the explication of the significance inherent in the resurrection itself.*

Word and event belong together in the appearances of the resurrected Jesus in such a way that they express the same content. The words of the risen Jesus add nothing new to the significance inherent in the event itself but, rather, state this significance. Only in this way can we understand Paul's claim, espe-

[58] Hahn in his arguments concerning Paul's understanding of mission (*Mission in the New Testament*, pp. 95-110) has not noticed this Pauline line of argumentation, so that he grasps the Pauline idea of the Gentile mission that is *independent of the law* only as an especially distinct understanding of the universal mission of the disciples implied in the concept of the exaltation of Jesus (pp. 100 f.).

[59] References in Jeremias, *Jesus' Promise to the Nations*, p. 14.

[60] As proof from Scripture, Paul cites Gen. 12:3 (Gal. 3:8) and Gen. 17:5 (Rom. 4:17).

[61] In this, for modern judgment, the reference to Hos. 2:23 is just as erroneous as that to Joel 2:32 (Rom. 10:13), since both refer to Israel. Nevertheless, Paul rightly claimed the universalism of eschatological salvation in the prophets for the mission to the Gentiles.

cially in Gal. 1:12, that he has received his gospel not from men but through the revelation of Jesus Christ. This happened in that it pleased God "to reveal his Son to me, in order that I might preach him among the Gentiles" (Gal. 1:16). Paul's gospel, one must understand, is the exegesis of the appearance of the resurrected Jesus that he experienced. The alternative, that Paul's gospel had been communicated in its completed form to him by way of audition, is to be excluded. Not the least thing speaking against it is the fact of a development in Pauline thought between the composition of First Thessalonians and Philippians.

In other cases, as for example the appearance of the resurrected Jesus to Peter, the relation between event and word is no longer accessible to us, especially since we can scarcely get a picture of the situation in which this appearance took place. To what extent the missionary command in Matt. 28:18 f. or the tradition standing behind John, ch. 21, reflect something of this situation or only concentrate on the later experience of the community cannot be decided here. However, one must consider the possibility that the differing situation in which the resurrection appearances were imparted to the various witnesses also conditioned a difference in the audition that was connected to the appearance.

The unity of event and word in the resurrection appearances is important for the question of how this event can establish faith. If the resurrection or the appearances of the resurrected Jesus were only brute facts without inherent significance, then, certainly, the origin of faith would not be understandable from this event. But that event had its own meaning within its sphere in the history of traditions: the beginning of the end, the confirmation and exaltation of Jesus by God himself, the ultimate demonstration of the divinity of Israel's God as the one God of all men. Only thus can Jesus' resurrection be the basis of faith without being supplemented by an external interpretation added to it.

Naturally, the same is not true of every event one might choose. Every man experiences in the area of his everyday life that the meaning of the various occurrences in the context of our life can be more or less clear in very different degrees. There are occurrences that contain such irresistible evidence that there can be no doubt about their meaning for us. But there are also events whose meaning remains obscure for us and which, when they are incisive, give cause for constantly new reflection over their significance. Within the horizon of Jewish tradition, the event of the Easter appearances experienced as the confrontation with the resurrected Jesus belonged, apparently, more to the first group of events which are to a great extent unambiguous. Jesus' crucifixion is different. This event was apparently experienced, in a quite different way, as obscure and enigmatic and had initiated very different interpretations, which must concern us later.

III. THE CONCEPTION OF RESURRECTION OF THE DEAD

Before tackling the historical problem of Jesus' resurrection, one should first explain the meaning of the expression "resurrection of the dead." Otherwise, one cannot possibly know what is at issue in the question about Jesus' rising or being raised.[62] With their expressions for the resurrection, the primitive Christian witnesses did not mean just a random miracle, but a very particular reality expected by postexilic Judaism in connection with the end of history. The conceptions aiming at this have their impulse already in the verbal construction "resurrection of the dead."

We must begin with a more formal observation, which, to be sure, is plain in the linguistic structure of the Jewish and New Testament statements about a future resurrection of the dead, but which apparently did not receive the basic attention it deserved from the Jewish apocalyptic and primitive Christianity. To speak about the resurrection of the dead is not comparable to speaking about any random circumstance that can be identified empirically at any time. Here we are dealing, rather, with a metaphor. This comes directly from the inner logic of the concept itself: in the same way that one is awakened from sleep and rises, so it will happen to the dead. Only the first part of the comparison, awakening from sleep, has a content that can be experienced in everyday life. The real purpose of the concept, however, does not lie here, but in speaking of another event that eludes everyday experience and can therefore only be expressed indirectly, that is, through the image of waking from sleep which is taken from ordinary experience. In this sense, speaking about a resurrection is metaphorical. The familiar experience of being awakened and rising from sleep serves as a parable for the completely unknown destiny expected for the dead.

The oldest Biblical evidence for a specific resurrection hope mentions resurrection and waking in parallel (Isa. 26:19). According to Dan. 12:2, many of those who "sleep" in the dust of the earth will "awake" at the end of the times. Ethiopian Enoch speaks wholly in picture language when it says (ch. 92:3): "The just man will arise from sleep." The same connection of the picture of death as sleep with the prospect of a future resurrection also appears in the Syriac Apocalypse of Baruch (ch. 30:1): "Then all those will arise who have gone to sleep hoping in him [the Messiah]." Again IV Ezra

---

[62] See Karl Heinrich Rengstorf, *Die Auferstehung Jesu: Form, Art und Sinn der urchristlichen Osterbotschaft* (4th ed.; Witten-Ruhr: Luther-Verlag, 1960), pp. 29 f.; also, E. Lichtenstein, "Die älteste christliche Glaubensformel," *ZKG*, LXIII (1950), 1-74, esp. pp. 28 ff. According to Ulrich Wilckens, *Die Missionsreden der Apostelgeschichte: Form- und traditionsgeschichtliche Untersuchungen* (Wissenschaftliche Monographien zum Alten und Neuen Testament, Vol. 5; 2d ed., 1963; Neukirchen Kreis Moers: Verlag der Buchhandlung des Erziehungsvereins, 1961), pp. 137 ff., *egeirein* is universal in early Christianity, while *anistanai* goes back to the "Son of Man" Christology of the passion summaries (see above, this chapter, n. 41).

says: "The dust releases those who sleep therein." In the New Testament, Paul speaks in I Thess. 4:13 ff. about "those who are asleep" in the context of the future resurrection. He also uses this imagery in other places when he refers to the dead (I Cor. 11:30; 15:6, 51). He calls the resurrected Jesus "the first fruits of those who have fallen asleep" (I Cor. 15:20).

An important material consequence follows immediately from the observation of the metaphorical structure of language about the resurrection of the dead: the intended reality and the mode in which it is expressed in language are essentially different. The intended reality is beyond the experience of the man who lives on this side of death. Thus the only possible mode of speaking about it is metaphorical, using images of this-worldly occurrences. Anyone who has become conscious of this structure involved in speaking about the resurrection of the dead can no longer fancy that he knows what is thus expressed in the same way that one knows an occurrence that has been investigated scientifically. Rather, this is a metaphorical way of speaking about an event that is still hidden to us in its true essence.

In primitive Christianity one was hardly so clearly aware of the limitation of speaking about a resurrection of the dead in a metaphorical form of expression as is unavoidably necessary today in order to distinguish our knowledge of the reality toward which the hope for resurrection is directed from the exact knowledge of the natural sciences and the understanding of reality induced by it. Nevertheless, in its own way, primitive Christianity knew how to express the qualitative difference between what was intended when it spoke of the resurrection of the dead and all this-worldly experience.

The notion of the resurrection of the dead that is most obvious on the basis of the analogy of sleeping and waking would be that of a revivification of the corpse in the sense of what has died standing up and walking around. It is, however, absolutely certain that the resurrection of the dead was not understood in this way in the primitive Christian and, in any case, in the oldest, the Pauline, concept. For Paul, resurrection means the new life of a new body, not the return of life into a dead but not yet decayed fleshly body. In one place Paul deals expressly with the question about the corporeality of those who are raised from the dead (I Cor. 15:35-56). It is self-evident for him that the future body will be a different one from the present body, not a fleshly body but—as he says—a "spiritual body." Just as in the present creation there are various kinds of bodies among earthly creatures themselves and as there is a difference between heavenly and earthly bodies, so also the resurrected will have a body; but it will be a different, special one (vs. 38-42), not perishable but imperishable in glory and power, not a fleshly body equipped with a soul but a spiritual body (vs. 43 f.).[63]

63 In reference to I Cor. 15:44, the comparison with Christ's glorious body in Phil. 3:21 in contrast to the lowly body is important. On the entire question, see E. Käsemann, *Leib und Leib Christi* (Tübingen: J. C. B. Mohr [Paul Siebeck], 1933). Especially con-

Paul describes the relationship of this spiritual body to the present perishable body as radical transformation: "I tell you this, brethren: flesh and blood cannot inherit the kingdom of God, nor does the perishable inherit the imperishable" (v. 50). According to Paul, the "transformation"[64] will, however, occur to the present mortal body. "For this perishable nature must put on the imperishable, and this mortal nature must put on immortality" (v. 53). On the one hand, the transformation of the perishable into a spiritual body will be so radical that nothing will remain unchanged. There is no substantial or structural continuity from the old to the new existence. On the other hand, however, the transformation will occur to the same earthly body that we are here: something different will not be produced in its place, but there is a historical continuity in the sense of continuous transition in the consummation of the transformation itself.[65] The expression "historical continuity" here means only that connection between the beginning and the end point which resides in the process of transformation itself, regardless of how radically this process may be conceived.

The explications in I Cor. 15:35-56 are not especially concerned with the resurrection of Jesus Christ, but with the resurrection that Christians expect of the future.[66] But Paul must have had the same conception of the resurrected Jesus, for he always and fully thought about Jesus' resurrection and that of

tested is whether it involves a body made of spirit instead of flesh, so that the difference affects only the material of the body (so Lietzmann, Bultmann), or whether it is a difference in the corporeality itself (so Werner Georg Kümmel in the Appendix to Hans Lietzmann, *An die Korinther I/II* [4th ed., Handbuch zum Neuen Testament, Vol. 9; Tübingen: J. C. B. Mohr (Paul Siebeck), 1949], pp. 194 f., in reference to Lietzmann, p. 84). The latter is probably more correct. Ingo Hermann, *Kyrios und Pneuma: Studien zur Christologie der paulinischen Hauptbriefe* (Munich: Kösel-Verlag, 1961), pp. 61 ff., makes the illuminating explanation that because of the eschatological significance of the idea of spirit, the *pneuma* designates the resurrection reality as such, and thus a spiritual body would be a body corresponding to the reality of the resurrection.

64 Paul speaks of *alassein*, not of *metamorphoun*.

65 So W. G. Kümmel, in Lietzmann, *An die Korinther I/II*, p. 195, against R. Bultmann, *Theology of the New Testament*, Vol. I, p. 198.

66 Paul does not speak here of the resurrection of all men in general. This follows from the fact that those who are damned in the judgment will hardly receive bodies of glory (cf. Syr. Baruch, ch. 51). Attention has rightly been called to the fact that Paul never speaks of a double resurrection to salvation *and* to damnation (see W. G. Kümmel, in Lietzmann, *An die Korinther I/II*, p. 193, in reference to p. 80, line 24, of Lietzmann's commentary on Corinthians). To be sure, II Cor. 5:10 says that all have to appear before Christ's judgment seat, but that as such does not necessarily mean a preceding resurrection of all. According to Enoch 22:13, at the end the judgment will go forth over the sinners without their previously having been raised. This is related to the fact that the resurrection from death is here the blessing of salvation as such, just as in Paul. In one passage, Paul says explicitly that in Christ *all* men are made alive (I Cor. 15:22; cf. the similar formulation in Rom. 5:18). Of course, this does not mean a universal resurrection in the sense of the double resurrection of some to salvation and others to judgment, but rather the participation of all men in salvation. The questions that arise here lead to the problem of whether or not Paul thought of a reconciliation of all things (cf. esp. Rom. 11:32).

Christians in essential parallel.[67] It is particularly significant that Paul understood the resurrection of the dead, and so also the resurrection of Jesus, not as mere resuscitation of a corpse but as radical transformation, because we have in Paul's statements the only report of a man who saw the resurrected Jesus himself. Apparently, no written accounts have been transmitted from the other witnesses of Jesus' resurrection. Hence the possibility suggests itself of taking what can be determined about the appearance Paul experienced as typical of the original character of all the Easter appearances. Without doubt Paul himself was of the opinion that he had been granted an appearance of the same sort as the other apostles before him. But the appearance of Christ to Paul must have been of such a sort that it could not be confused with a resuscitated corpse, but that it confronted him as a reality of an entirely different sort.[68]

This leads to the conclusion that one must sharply distinguish the resurrection of the dead in the Christian hope for the future from those resuscitations of corpses which are otherwise reported occasionally in ancient literature as especially marvelous miracles, even from the resuscitations accomplished by Jesus himself, according to the accounts of the Evangelists, such as the young man from Nain (Luke 7:11-17), the daughter of Jairus (Mark 5:35-43 and parallels), or Lazarus (John, ch. 11). Quite apart from the question of the credibility of such more or less late and legendary traditions, it is certain in any case that these narratives themselves have in mind an event of a different kind from that reported by the witnesses to Jesus' resurrection and that of the primitive Christian hope for the future. With Lazarus, the daughter of Jairus, and the young man from Nain, standing at the pinnacle of Jesus' miraculous healing activity, we have to do with the *temporary* return of a dead person into this life. The narrators themselves did not doubt, however, that those who had been reawakened to life in this way later died again. In contrast, Jesus' resurrection and the Christian hope of resurrection involve a life completely different from all life with which we are familiar, an imperishable life no longer limited by death, which at any rate, therefore, must be basically different from the organic form of life with which we are familiar.[69] The subsequent tradition of the church also maintained this profound substantial difference between the eschatological resurrection of the dead and the temporary revivification of a dead person.[70]

[67] Cf. Phil. 3:21; Rom. 6:8 f.; 8:29; *et al.* Cf. R. Bultmann, *Theology of the New Testament*, Vol. I, § 40; further, Hans von Campenhausen, *Der Ablauf der Osterereignisse und das leere Grab* (2d ed.; Heidelberg: Carl Winter, 1958), p. 20, n. 67.

[68] Also, Wilhelm Michaelis, *Die Erscheinungen des Auferstandenen* (Basel: H. Majer, 1944), p. 91, emphasizes that the corporeality of the Lord as he appeared to Paul is to be understood in the sense of the spiritual body of I Cor., ch. 15.

[69] K. H. Rengstorf, *Die Auferstehung Jesu*, p. 88, also calls attention to the difference in kind between Jesus' resurrection and the Christian's resurrection hope over against the raisings of the dead reported in the Gospels.

[70] Patristic theology consistently understood the resurrection of Christians as transfor-

If we return to Paul and ask where he actually derived his concept of the mode of the resurrection life, we cannot simply point to the appearance of the resurrected Jesus that happened to him. We must recognize that prior to Paul there already was a tradition in which the expectation of the resurrection of the dead was cultivated and within which Paul himself stood. This is the hope for the future in postexilic Judaism that was derived from apocalyptic.[71] The future resurrection of the dead was not always conceived in the same way, but was thought of in very different ways in the apocalyptic writings. These differences require, in many respects, more exact "history of traditions" investigation than they have yet received. For the present purposes we will focus our attention on two aspects: (1) the specific saving character of the hope in the resurrection, and (2) the concept of a transformation in connection with the resurrection.

For a long time the aspect of the saving significance of the resurrection has been discussed in scholarly circles under the alternatives of whether only the just or whether all men can expect a resurrection of the dead. We have already seen (n. 66 above) that Paul only speaks of resurrection with a view to believers. Thus, the resurrection as such already has saving character. Perhaps the same is to be affirmed about Jesus, for in his discussion with the Sadducees who denied the resurrection (Mark 12:26 f.) he justifies the hope of resurrection from the fact that the God of Abraham, Isaac, and Jacob is a God of the living, not of the dead. The picture of the Last Judgment (Matt. 25:31-46) says, to be sure, that "all the nations" will be assembled before the Son of

mation, not as a mere resuscitation. This is true not only of Origen (*De princ.* III, 6,6 [*GCS* 22, pp. 287 ff.]; cf. the study, which is still instructive, by George Scheurer, *Das Auferstehungsdogma der vornizänischen Zeit* [Würzburg: A. Gobel, 1896], pp. 64 ff. and 75). Also in Justin (*Apol.* I, 52, in E. J. Goodspeed, *Die ältesten Apologeten* [Göttingen: Vandenhoeck & Ruprecht, 1914], pp. 62 f.; *Dial.* 5 f., in *ibid.*, pp. 97 f.: *Dial.* 69,7, in *ibid.*, p. 180), Theophilus of Antioch (*Ad Autol.* 1,7, in *MPG* 6, 1033 f.), and Irenaeus (*Adv. haer.* V, 3,3, in *MPG* 7/2, 1131 f., *et al.;* cf. Thomas Christopher Dell, *Fiducia Christianorum: Studien zur Eschatologie der frühkatholischen Väter* [Dissertation, Heidelberg, 1959], pp. 49 ff.) the resurrection of the dead is expected as a transformation into an immortal nature. In the same way, Tertullian says that at the resurrection the *caro* will be transformed (*De resurr.* 55, in *MPL* 2, 875 ff.). Finally, Methodius of Olympus, who accused Origen of scarificing the material continuity of man in the resurrection of the dead (*MPG* 18, 317, n. 12), nevertheless maintained the concept of transformation. He even expressly emphasized the difference between the future resurrection and that of Christ, the firstborn from the dead, on the one hand, and the merely symbolic, transitory raising of Lazarus and others who later died again (*MPG* 18, 320, n. 14). Cf. G. Scheurer, *Das Auferstehungsdogma,* pp. 82-90.

71 See *RGG,* I (3d ed.), 694; Otto Plöger, *Theokratie und Eschatologie* (Neukirchen Kreis Moers: Verlag der Buchhandlung des Erziehungsvereins, 1959); Paul Volz, *Die Eschatologie der jüdischen Gemeinde im neutestamentlichen Zeitalter* (2d ed.; Tübingen: J. C. B. Mohr [Paul Siebeck], 1934), pp. 229 ff.; Aimo T. Nikolainen, *Der Auferstehungsglaube in der Bibel und in ihrer Umwelt* (2 vols.: Helsinki: Suomalainen Tiedeakatemia, 1944-1946); P. Billerbeck, *Kommentar,* Vol. IV/2, pp. 1166 ff. (32d Excursus, "Allgemeine oder teilweise Auferstehung der Toten"); R. Martin-Achard, *De la mort à la resurrection d'après l'Ancien Testament* (1956).

Man, who will make the separation between them. But this does not unconditionedly presuppose a resurrection any more than does II Cor. 5:10.

The understanding of the future resurrection as the content of salvation is already to be found in the oldest Biblical witness to this hope, Isa. 26:7 ff. Through the authoritative word of God in ch. 26:19 the righteous are promised that Yahweh will provide salvation for them through resurrection from death: "*Thy* dead shall live, their bodies shall rise. O dwellers of the dust, awake and sing for joy!" In Dan. 12:1-3, in contrast, the resurrection of the dead is not as such the saving event, since it means for some the entrance to eschatological salvation, for others, however, an awakening to "shame." Nevertheless, not all will thereby awaken from the dead. Still, this event is also not reserved for a few righteous people, but also will happen to those who are especially bad. The latter do not remain in the twilight condition of Sheol, but will be given over to punishment. The concept in the report of the second journey in the Apocalypse of Enoch (Enoch, ch. 22) is similar. Here those whose condition in their lifetime corresponded to their righteousness or unrighteousness remain in the twilight existence of Sheol. Only the martyrs (v. 12), on the one hand, and the wicked who had an easy life (v. 10), on the other, will face a further destiny. the martyrs, salvation; the wicked, destruction.[72] However, both groups of men are not, as in Dan., ch. 12, raised in order to receive their judgment then, but resurrection is imparted only to the just; as such it is already a share in salvation. The wicked receive their punishment without resurrection.

The concept of Enoch, ch. 51, in the second Similitude is different again. Here the idea of a double resurrection of the good and of the evil encountered in Daniel is extended to include all men in general. To be sure, it does not thereby talk about resurrection as such. It says only that the earth, Sheol, and hell will again surrender their contents and that the Son of Man will choose the righteous from among them. Also, here the interest is concentrated on the condition of the righteous: they will become angels in heaven. Beginning with Enoch, ch. 51, the idea of a universal resurrection apparently prevailed generally (cf. IV Ezra 7:29 ff.; Syr. Baruch 50:2 ff.). The older Tannaitic school of rabbis also taught a universal resurrection of the dead, while the later Pharisaic party, with the exception of Hillel and Shammai, expected only the resurrection of the righteous, according to Josephus.[73] The situation is similar in Syr. Baruch 30:1-5, corresponding to Enoch, ch. 22, as well as the Psalms of Solomon 3:12.

If the resurrection of the dead is to be understood as the entrance into the reality of salvation, then the question emerges about the relation of the new reality of life to the old, earthly existence. In marked contrast to Paul in I

[72] In the interpretation of the inconsistent ch. 22 of Enoch, I follow the form-critical analysis of Enoch by E. Rau (in preparation).
[73] Josephus, *De bello Jud.* II. viii.14; *Antiqu.* XVIII. i.3; *Contra Apionem* 2,30.

Cor., ch. 15, the older texts do not reflect upon this relation. Certainly Isa. 25:8 expected death to be destroyed forever (*'ad 'olam*); but this text does not enter into the transformation of the earthly form of life implied in such a statement. According to Dan. 12:3, the wise and those leading the people to righteousness will shine like the brightness of the firmament and like the stars; according to Enoch, ch. 51, the righteous are supposed to become angels in heaven. But here too there is no explicit reflection about the implicit transformation. Still, Enoch 50:1 does speak of a "transformation for the saints and the elect" that consists in the light that is over them as well as in the glory and honor that are given to them.

Nevertheless, in general the question as to what kind of transformation takes place in the transition from the old to the new life, from death to resurrection, seems to have become acute only in the first century of the Christian era. Syriac Baruch (chs. 50 to 51) for the first time describes a transformation in detail that, however, does not take place immediately with the resurrection, but the good are transformed to a better form and the bad to a worse only afterward with the judgment. The resurrection itself permits the dead to come forth as they were in life, so that mutual recognition can take place (ch. 50:2). Both events here distinguished, resurrection and transformation, are taken by Paul as a single event: the resurrection itself is understood as transformation. Jesus, too, so far as we can tell, understood the resurrection or, in any case, the condition of the resurrection life, as transformed in contrast to the present life. This is shown by the saying in Mark 12:25: They will be like the angels in heaven, neither marrying nor being given in marriage. Compare this with the apocalyptic passages that say that the resurrected will be transformed to the "radiance of the angels" (Dan. 12:3; Enoch 51:4; 104:2; IV Ezra 7:97; Syr. Baruch 51:5, 10). Thus the idea that a transformation is connected with the resurrection of the dead—whether in the act of the resurrection itself or in a subsequent, special event—is in no way a specifically primitive Christian or even Pauline understanding in contrast to the "orthodox" Jewish resurrection faith. It is a false generalization, although repeatedly asserted in exegetical literature,[74] that orthodox Jewish faith expected a mere resuscitation. Pre-

---

74 Therefore, it is not correct when Gerhard Kittel interprets the emphasis on the spiritual character of the corporeality of the resurrected as specifically Pauline in contrast to the "massively realistic" concept of Jewish faith in the resurrection ("Die Auferstehung Jesu," *Deutsche Theologie,* IV [1937], 133-168, citation from p. 139). K. H. Rengstorf also shares this error that the concept of a transformation of the present mortal body is something completely new in Paul. Therefore, he considers it to be "entirely excluded, that the New Testament kerygma is determined by the Jewish hope for the resurrection in its certainty that the resurrection will result in an entirely different kind of corporeality for the dead who are raised. In everything it says about the corporeality of those who are resurrected, the New Testament is independent of its Jewish origin" (*Die Auferstehung Jesu,* p. 88). Such a judgment is possible only because Rengstorf, like Kittel, has overlooked the fact that Paul's concept of a transformation of the body stands entirely within the context of the apocalyptic tradition.

cisely with regard to the concept of transformation, primitive Christianity and especially Paul thought traditionally; and that Paul identifies resurrection and transformation, in distinction from Syriac Baruch, derives meaningfully from his opinion that the resurrection would be given to the believers only, while Baruch had expected a double resurrection to salvation and judgment.

Thus Paul did not arrive at his concept of the resurrection as transformation for the first time because of the impression made by his encounter with the risen Jesus. Even the understanding of the qualitative difference between the resurrection life as imperishable and the present life as perishable has Jewish parallels.[75]

Only the traditional expectation of the end of history rooted in apocalyptic gave Paul the opportunity of designating the particular event that he experienced, as Jesus' other disciples had experienced it previously, as an event belonging to the category of resurrection life. Therefore, Paul called the expectation of a resurrection of the dead the presupposition for the recognition of Jesus' resurrection: "If the dead are not raised, then Christ has not been raised" (I Cor. 15:16). On the other hand, and Paul wants to move to this in his whole train of thought, the event of Jesus' resurrection in turn substantiates the truth of the expectation of a resurrection of the dead for believers, particularly for Gentile Christians who did not bring this expectation with them from their pre-Christian background (I Cor. 15:20). Admittedly, the general concept of the resurrection cannot altogether be established from Jesus' resurrection alone. Were that the meaning of Paul's argument, one would have to note critically that Paul wants to deduce more from the message of Jesus' resurrection for the truth of the general idea of resurrection than can be obtained from it. Such an argument would run in a circle. The expectation of resurrection must already be presupposed as a truth that is given by tradition or anthropologically or is established philosophically when one speaks about Jesus' resurrection. That this expectation has already become an event in Jesus can strengthen ex post facto the truth of the expectation, but cannot establish it for the first time. To be sure, only Jesus' resurrection guarantees to the individual his own future participation in salvation, and this is probably the real intention of Paul's argument. Understood in this way, Lichtenstein rightly says that when Paul "permits Christ's resurrection and the promised resurrection of the dead mutually to establish one another, . . . this circular argument can surprise only Greeks who deny the resurrection. For the presupposition of the event that thus has already happened is certainly that according to God's promise the dead shall rise."[76]

[75] Cf. the emphasis on the immortality of the resurrected in IV Ezra 7:75-99 and Psalms of Solomon 15:8: "I have taken on immortality through his name and have put off perishability through his goodness."

[76] E. Lichtenstein, "Die älteste christliche Glaubensformel," ZKG, LXIII (1950), 1-74; quotation, p. 31. One can therefore hardly agree with Walter Künneth that "the essential eschatology of the primitive Christian kerygma finds its legitimation in Jesus' resurrection,

The significance of the general expectation of the resurrection for the understanding of Jesus' resurrection corresponds to the fact that the primitive Christian missionary kerygma brought the apocalyptic expectation into the new Gentile Christian congregations. The freedom of the Gentile Christians from the Jewish law in no way meant that for them all Jewish traditions had become meaningless. By naming the resurrected Jesus as the one who will save us from the wrath to come, the summary of the Hellenistic missionary kerygma (I Thess. 1:10) already includes the apocalyptic expectation of the end of history. The second summary of the missionary kerygma (Heb. 6:1 f.) transmitted by the New Testament writings even explicitly calls the resurrection of the dead a component of the elementary doctrines taught to beginning Christians. This means that, even for the Gentile church, the apocalyptic expectation remained valid in its fundamental structure.

But can the apocalyptic conceptual world still be binding for us? In any case, one cannot deny this question without being clear about its importance. Although the apocalyptic concept of the end of the world may be untenable in many details, its fundamental elements, the expectation of a resurrection of the dead in connection with the end of the world and the Final Judgment, can still remain true even for us. At any rate the primitive Christian motivation for faith in Jesus as the Christ of God, in his exaltation, in his identification with the Son of Man, is essentially bound to the apocalyptic expectation for the end of history to such an extent that one must say that if the apocalyptic expectation should be totally excluded from the realm of possibility for us, then the early Christian faith in Christ is also excluded; then, however, the continuity would be broken between that which might still remain as Christianity after such a reduction and Jesus himself, together with the primitive Christian proclamation through Paul's time. One must be

and is not dependent on the imminent expectation of the parousia, nor is it done away with by the delay of the parousia" (*Glauben an Jesus?*, p. 227). The conclusion requires another basis because the eschatological expectation is already the presupposition of the kerygma of Jesus' own resurrection. To be sure, Künneth can claim support in the fact that Paul also in his argument with the church in Corinth tries to base the general hope of resurrection on the event of Jesus' resurrection. However, at the same time he still characterizes the general expectation of the resurrection as already the presupposition of the talk about the resurrection of Jesus himself. (I Cor. 15:16.) How can the two elements of Paul's argument be compatible? Ulrich Wilckens has recently called attention to the fact that for Paul the basis for the Christian's hope of resurrection in Jesus' resurrection is connected with the fact that the resurrection as such is the content of salvation, and salvation is mediated through Jesus. Thus the concept of the future resurrection of the dead may already be presupposed so that one can speak about Jesus' resurrection. However, "the event of Jesus' resurrection was understood as the basis for the occurrence of the future resurrection of the Christians as their participation in eschatological salvation" ("Der Ursprung der Überlieferung der Erscheinungen des Auferstandenen: Zur traditionsgeschichtlichen Analyse von I Kor. 15, 1-11," *Dogma und Denkstrukturen; Festschrift für E. Schlink*, ed. by Wilfried Joest and Wolfhart Pannenberg [Göttingen: Vandenhoeck & Ruprecht, 1963], pp. 56-95, esp. pp. 89 f.). Wilckens has also shown that the argument in I Cor., ch. 15, has as its prototype I Thess., ch. 4 (*ibid.*, pp. 59 ff.).

clear about the fact that when one discusses the truth of the apocalyptic expectation of a future judgment and a resurrection of the dead, one is dealing directly with the basis of the Christian faith. Why the man Jesus can be the ultimate revelation of God, why in him and only in him God is supposed to have appeared, remains incomprehensible apart from the horizon of the apocalyptic expectation.

The knowledge of Jesus obtained within this apocalyptic horizon of expectation certainly can subsequently be translated into different patterns of thought, for example, into Gnostic thought; but it cannot be established from the perspective of these other patterns of thought. Where such a new basis has been sought, Jesus again and again has become merely the example of a Gnostic or a philosophical idea whose truth is ultimately independent of the history of Jesus. The basis of the knowledge of Jesus' significance remains bound to the original apocalyptic horizon of Jesus' history, which at the same time has also been modified by this history. If this horizon is eliminated, the basis of faith is lost; then Christology becomes mythology and no longer has true continuity with Jesus himself and with the witness of the apostles.

Of course, such considerations in no way decide the question of the truth of the apocalyptic expectation. Only the seriousness of this question is intended to be made apparent.

Whether or not the apocalyptic expectation of a resurrection of the dead can still have binding validity as truth today may be decided by its relation to an understanding of man consistent with the approach and results of a way of thinking that is engaged with all presently accessible phenomena. Does a meaningful relation exist here—perhaps even a relation that is indispensable to a sober understanding of the human situation—or not? One may presumably characterize it as a generally demonstrable anthropological finding that the definition of the essence of man does not come to ultimate fulfillment in the finitude of his earthly life. Only if the individual man has his destiny exclusively in the community of humanity, if he thus finds the purpose of his existence not as an individual but only in his belonging to society, if he is thus completely absorbed as an individual in humanity as it is at hand in his concrete society, only then would the idea of a life beyond death be something to be relinquished. Therefore, also in Israel the idea of a future resurrection of the dead was not thought of as long as the individual was entirely absorbed in his people.

However, in spite of the truth of the statement that a man can realize his humanity only in community with others, one must affirm that the human destiny which every individual seeks is different from the particular community and society in which he lives. Even if sometime or other the ideal state could be realized, the question would remain as to the participation of individuals in earlier generations in the destiny of man in general, which is still the destiny of each individual. But if the destiny of the individual man is not absorbed in his relation to society, the question is inescapable whether the individual may expect a fulfillment of his destiny as man beyond death, or whether the question about man's humanity must simply be disregarded as meaningless. In the life of the individual the search for the definition of his humanity finds, as has been said, no final answer.

To be sure, modern man apparently lives surprisingly well without being disturbed by the question about death. But it is very doubtful whether this picture is not deceptive. Ernst Bloch has expressed the suspicion "that death (we do not know for how long) can only be suppressed so well because new life was once hidden behind it, that is, it was dreamed about and believed to be there. Thus it becomes improbable that the creaturely anxiety in the face of death has been removed by the late bourgeoisie merely by looking away. Superficiality alone is no emancipation. And suppression alone gives no feeling of victory. . . . The paltry confession to nothing (*Nichts*) would hardly be sufficient to keep the head high and to work as if there were no end. Rather, clear signs indicate that earlier and richer forms of wishful dreams continue and give support in the subconscious. Through what remains from these ideals, the so-called modern man does not feel the chasm that unceasingly surrounds him and that certainly will engulf him at last. Through these remnants he saves, quite unawares, his sense of self-identity. Through them the impression arises that man is not perishing, but only that one day the world has the whim no longer to appear to him. Thus, in its ability to suppress the anxiety of all earlier times, apparently this quite shallow courage feasts on a borrowed credit card. It lives from earlier hopes and the support that they once had provided."[77]

Whether or not hope is a meaningful attitude in life at all is decided for the individual in the final analysis in the question of whether there is anything to be hoped for beyond death. The meaning of all provisional images of hope is threatened by the inescapability of the fate of death. This harshest hindrance to hope, the knowledge of the inescapability of one's own death, is, just like hope itself, specifically human. If death is the end, then all hope for a coming fulfillment of existence seems to be foolish. For how foolish it is to long for a future that, first, always remains uncertain and, second, even at best —namely, when it is really fulfilled—only brings one nearer to the grave. In contrast, the proper art of living would indeed consist in enjoying the present day: "Let us eat and drink, for tomorrow we die" (I Cor. 15:32). But this, too, provides no exit. When knowledge of the inescapability of death has really seized a person, then everything that fills his days becomes stale and empty. Modern medicine has recognized that radical hopelessness has death as its consequence. On the other hand, through a hope which is directed without illusion toward the future, even the mortally ill, even with full knowledge

[77] Ernst Bloch, *Das Prinzip Hoffnung* (2d ed.; Frankfurt am Main: Suhrkamp Verlag, 1959), Vol. II, pp. 1360 f.

of their condition, can acquire strength to endure the end of their existence in a human way.[78]

The phenomenology of hope indicates that it belongs to the essence of conscious human existence to hope beyond death. This supposition is confirmed by consideration of that specific element in human existence summarily expressed in the language of modern anthropology by the concept of man's openness in relation to the world (*Weltoffenheit*) or his environmental freedom (*Umweltfreiheit*). More precisely, this concept involves an openness that goes beyond every finite situation. Man is not restricted in his behavior by definite environmental signs whose perception sets off instinctive reactions. Rather, he himself must first determine the direction of his impulses. In this he never achieves more than a temporary concretion of his striving. The whole of his impulses point beyond every given situation and press toward further, better fulfillment. Thus man must always seek further for that which could grant the fulfillment of the totality of his impulses, for his destiny, while animals live out their destiny without question. Now it belongs to the structure of human existence to press on, even beyond death, that search for one's own destiny, which never comes to an end. As has been mentioned, man is the only being who knows that he must die. Precisely this knowledge makes possible the question of what lies beyond death, just as one has already asked beyond each limit even by recognizing it as such. Just this is the characteristic feature of the human excess of initiative, which always asks beyond every concretion of its own striving and beyond every limit in general in search of the appropriate fulfillment of human destiny. The images formed by hope beyond death, to which the concept of the immortality of the soul as well as that of

[78] H. Plügge, "Über die Hoffnung," *Der leidende Mensch: Personale Psychotherapie in anthropologischer Sicht*, ed. by Arië Sborowitz and Ernst Michel (Darmstadt: Wissenschaftliche Buchgesellschaft, 1960), pp. 429-444, esp. p. 436, about sick people in a hopeless situation who create hope without "a well-defined object." "For them it involves the future, the certainty that somehow they enter into a future, and that they do not confront an end that is simply a pit, nothing." Such hope can arise precisely in incurable cases where even the sick person no longer has the illusion of getting well, a hope "in some sort of certain continued existence of the person, in a self-realization in the future, in an indefinable, but somehow ensured renewal." (*Ibid.*, p. 438.) Plügge stresses the constructive effect of such hope: "It makes it possible for the sick person to emerge from the previous egocentric attitude; it establishes new relationships and duties; it creates an inner independence and a freedom from the symptoms, a freedom from captivity to the illness that could not be achieved before the crisis. This elevation in dignity also becomes clear in the patience that can be made possible only by hope and that now takes the place of anxiety that has been overcome" (*ibid.*, p. 439). In this hope, which not only is born of despair (so *ibid.*, p. 440, against G. Marcel), the sick person lives in the light of a future "that certainly is undefined and unknown in its contours but is given in its substance as the salvation of the person" (*ibid.*, p. 443). Cf. also the article by A. Jores, "Der Tod des Menschen in psychologischer Sicht," in the same volume, pp. 417-428. There Jores describes how the so-called "profound" hopelessness leads to death, both in the voodoo death of primitive taboo offenders, in the death of pensioners, and in suicide because of hopelessness. By contrast, hope is a decisive factor in the process of recuperation (*ibid.*, pp. 426 f.).

a resurrection of the dead belong, are the expression of such unceasing questioning by man about himself. Thus, because of the structure of human existence, it is necessary for man in one way or another to conceive of the fulfillment of his destiny and indeed of the totality of his existence beyond death. Where such inquiry beyond death, in understood metaphors, does not happen or, perhaps more precisely, where it is suppressed—since the drive to such questioning in man is inalienable—the clarity of the accomplishment of existence is impaired; there the humanity of man as man is impaired, not only in a single element but in the very openness of questioning and seeking that characterizes man's behavior. This openness is lost when questioning beyond death does not take place. To surrender oneself to such questioning is the condition for man's full humanness; and, as has already been said, such a question remains empty when it does not involve definite conceptions. Without the formation of definite, even if only preliminary, metaphorical conceptions, the questioning beyond death cannot become certain of its own interest. Then even the question itself grows weak.

Admittedly, men can constitute such concepts of their destiny that goes out beyond death only from the standpoint of their present self-understanding. These concepts unavoidably remain, therefore, merely symbolic. They remain inadequate in comparison to that which they are intended to express, for any life on the other side of death is inaccessible to our experience in this world. That one may remain conscious of the inadequacy of every concept of destiny and not fall into false certainties belongs to the soberness of the question about what lies beyond death. But although every such concept remains inadequate, we as men are obliged to form such ideas in order to attain and to preserve the consciousness of our destiny that goes out beyond death in them.

In spite of all the unavoidable inadequacy of every concept that reaches out beyond death—because every such concept must take its content from our experience in this world—nevertheless, the particular content of such ideas is not simply left to an arbitrary decision. Even in this area there remains a possibility of distinguishing and testing. That is, one can and must ask to what extent the motives that drive us to devise such pictures in general find appropriate expression in the particular concept. One must also ask whether a picture of the human destiny beyond death is in accordance with the anthropological structure just described that furnished the justification of our construction of such concepts at all.

That well-founded distinctions can be made here will be made clear by contrasting the hope of resurrection with the concept of immortality. Until recently the Greek concept of the immortality of the soul has obstructed the question about the truth of the Biblical hope of resurrection in the Western history of ideas. One has long been persuaded about the immortality of the soul as about an assured, established fact. The hope of resurrection, in contrast, appeared to be a concept guaranteed only by a supernatural authority of revelation and, in addition, superfluous insofar as the unrelinquishable human interest in the question of a future beyond death seemed already satisfied elsewhere by the idea of immortality.

Plato was the first to develop the idea of immortality of the soul in the form of a philosophical demonstration. We do not need to present the reasons in greater detail here. They are associated principally with the unchangeability of the soul, its participation in the universal Logos and thus in the divine. This concept of the undying continuation of the soul while the body perishes has become untenable today. The separation between body and soul that forms the basis of the concept is no longer tenable, at least in this form, in the light of contemporary anthropological insights. What was once distinguished as body and soul is considered today as a unity of human conduct. The peculiarity of this behavior itself explains the emergence of an inner world for our experience of ourselves that is to a certain but limited extent independent. However, even for theories that only assume a very close interrelation between body and soul, the idea of a soul existing without a body is no longer possible. The fundamental relativity and mutual solidarity of all moments of human life make necessary a different way, corresponding better to this situation, of conceiving the eternal destiny of man beyond death. The so-called "life after death" can no longer be thought of as immortality of the soul, but only as another mode of existence of the *whole* man. However, that is the content of the picture of a resurrection of the dead. This expectation also can only be a symbolic concept of man's eternal destiny expressed in the so-called openness in relation to the world of human behavior—but a symbolic concept whose particular form can be justified by what we know about man.

These considerations briefly suggested here reach back from modern anthropological problems to the content of the apocalyptic expectation. In this expectation they uncover a truth that has long remained obscured by the traditional separation between body and soul and the associated philosophical idea of immortality. This naturally does not provide wholesale justification for the apocalyptic conceptual world. Also, in what has been said up until now, nothing has yet been decided about the idea of judgment that is connected with the expectation of resurrection in apocalyptic. The same is true for the question as to whether the resurrection of the dead is to be thought of as an event that will be experienced at the same time by all who are to be raised, as well as for the question about the relation between the resurrection of the dead and the end of the world.

In some form, to be sure, the assumption of a relation between the resurrection of the dead and the end of the world is meaningful, since a universal resurrection of the dead is not imaginable within this present world, but, on the other hand, man cannot be understood without his world. This argument would still permit restricting the concept of the end of the world to the human world, to the space required for human life.

The unity of human destiny for all individuals plays a role in regard to the universality of the resurrection. In spite of what has been said previously about the independence of the individual against his being absorbed into society, on the other hand, the unity of the humanity in terms of its destiny is still to be maintained. Only for this reason do we justifiably speak about "man." The unity of mankind, however, expresses itself in the concept of the resurrection of the dead in that this event is expected as universal fate that will involve all men. Even if the resurrection as a saving event does not happen to every individual, it is still related to the unity of humanity because it is connected with the idea of a universal judgment coming over all men at the end of history in which every individual will be measured in terms of the destiny of man as such.

None of these questions can be discussed more fully in the present context. They belong primarily in a systematic anthropology.[79] It is only necessary to say enough to indicate that the expectation of a resurrection from the dead need not appear meaningless from the presuppositions of modern thought, but rather it is to be established as a philosophically appropriate expression for human destiny. Thus, precisely today a continuity of our thought with the apocalyptic hope again has become possible at a decisive point, and with this also a continuity with the primitive Christian perception of the event of Jesus' resurrection. The question of the historicity of this event, which was perceptible as an encounter with the resurrected Jesus within the horizon of the apocalyptic expectation, will concern us in the following section. In addition to the questions that are related to a critical evaluation of the traditions, additional problems will appear from the perspective of the structure of the concept of the resurrection that we have just discussed.

IV. JESUS' RESURRECTION AS A HISTORICAL PROBLEM[80]

The Easter traditions of primitive Christianity divide into two different strands: the traditions about appearances of the resurrected Lord, and the traditions about the discovery of Jesus' empty grave. In the historical development of the traditions in the Gospels a tendency is at work to draw the two complexes of tradition closer together to an increasing extent. Mark still offers an unadulterated account of the empty tomb; Luke, at any rate, still holds discovery of the grave and the appearance of the resurrected Lord

[79] In a preliminary way, see the lectures by Wolfhart Pannenberg, *Was ist der Mensch? Die Anthropologie der Gegenwart im Lichte der Theologie* (Göttingen: Vandenhoeck & Ruprecht, 1962), esp. pp. 38 f. and 54 ff.
[80] Both of the following works will be cited in this section without reference to the titles: Hans von Campenhausen, *Der Ablauf der Osterereignisse und das leere Grab;* Hans Grass, *Ostergeschehen und Osterberichte* (3d ed.; Göttingen: Vandenhoeck & Ruprecht, 1964).

apart. Matthew connects the discovery of the grave with a report of an appearance; John and the Gospel of Peter then allow appearances to take place at the grave. In the oldest stratum of tradition, however, both strands are still separate: Mark reports only the empty tomb (ch. 16); Paul reports only appearances of the resurrected Lord (I Cor., ch. 15). Historically, then, one must investigate both traditions separately. I will begin with a summary of the tradition of the appearances.

The historical question of the appearances of the resurrected Lord is concentrated completely in the Pauline report, I Cor. 15:1-11. The appearances reported in the Gospels, which are not mentioned by Paul, have such a strongly legendary character that one can scarcely find a historical kernel of their own in them. Even the Gospels' reports that correspond to Paul's statements are heavily colored by legendary elements, particularly by the tendency toward underlining the corporeality of the appearances.[81]

In I Cor., ch. 15, Paul enumerates the basic appearances of the resurrected Jesus: first the resurrected Lord appeared to Peter, then to the Twelve, then to five hundred Christian brethren at once, then to James, the brother of Jesus, then to all the apostles, and finally to Paul himself. The intention of this enumeration is clearly to give proof by means of witnesses for the facticity of Jesus' resurrection.[82] The intent to prove is especially clear in v. 6 where the reference to the appearance to the five hundred brethren at once is supplemented by the notice that some of them have fallen asleep, although most are still alive. Whether that is not supposed to be "a historical proof in the modern sense," as Hans Grass among others asserts (p. 96, n. 1), depends on one's understanding of what the expression "a historical proof in the modern sense" means. If it means a mere "historical curiosity" without personal engagement (so Grass, p. 108), then it is certainly to be admitted that Paul argues differently, namely, from an inner involvement. But does this characteristic really accurately get at the historical interest and the uniqueness of historical proof? Does not the vital interest of the historian already lie at the basis of all historical investigation, even though such an interest certainly cannot be permitted to prejudice the results of the inquiry? If one pays proper attention to these presuppositions of historical inquiry itself which have been discussed for decades under the catchword "preunderstanding" (*Vorverständnis*), one will hardly be able to call into question Paul's intention of giving a convincing historical proof by the standards of that time, in any case, not from the perspective of a historical inquiry that is supposedly disinterested.

81 Grass, pp. 88 and 92 f.

82 R. Bultmann, *Theology of the New Testament*, Vol. I, p. 295; similarly as early as 1926 against Barth in *GuV*, I, 38 ff.; further, W. G. Kümmel in H. Lietzmann, *An die Korinther I/II*, p. 192, in reference to Lietzmann, p. 77, line 42; also, K. H. Rengstorf, *Die Auferstehung Jesu*, p. 47.

In judging the Pauline report one must, in the first place, emphasize that it is very close to the events themselves. This involves, first, the person of Paul and, second, the age of the formula as such. First Corinthians was probably written in the spring of 56 (or 57?) in Ephesus. However, Paul speaks from a still older, personal knowledge. According to Gal. 1:18, he was in Jerusalem three years after his conversion and there visited at least Peter and James. The particular mention of the appearance to James may well go back to this visit (Grass, p. 95). If Paul's conversion is to be dated, from the information in Gal., ch. 1, in the year 33 (35?) and if Jesus' death is to be put in the year 30, then Paul would have been in Jerusalem between six to eight years after the events. From this the statements in I Cor., ch. 15, are very close to the events themselves. This observation is strengthened by a further finding. Not only does the author of this text stand very close to the events, but in addition he uses formulations coined previously. Thus he does not create his statements *ad hoc* from a possibly inaccurate memory, but he appeals to a formulated tradition, for whose formation little time remains between the event and the composition of First Corinthians. For various reasons, one must even suppose that this tradition arose very early, namely, prior to Paul's visit in Jerusalem.

It is questionable whether or not the kernel of Paul's statement involves a unified formula. Generally the first is asserted. According to this view, the kernel of the enumeration in I Cor., ch. 15, consists of an old, originally Aramaic formula that, however, may have included only vs. 3b-5 (Grass, p. 95): "That Christ died for our sins in accordance with the scriptures, that he was buried, that he was raised on the third day in accordance with the scriptures, and that he appeared to Cephas, then to the twelve." Paul himself then would have expanded this old formula with the appearances reported in vs. 6 f., presumably in accordance with the information he received in Jerusalem. The formula itself, if Paul had received it soon after his conversion, must have reached back to the first five years after Jesus' death.

Recently, Ulrich Wilckens has offered a different analysis of the section in I Cor. 15:1-11.[83] In his view, vs. 3b-5 do not involve one single formula, since the connection of the individual parts by *kai hoti* is not otherwise attested within closed formulas and suggests, rather, a free enumeration. To be sure, the parts connected in such a way were already available to Paul as formulated material. Wilckens thinks the same is true for the basic contents of the following sentences as well. The formal elements that Paul has brought to-

---

[83] U. Wilckens first developed his interpretation, differing with the general assumption of a unified core in the formula I Cor. 15:3b-5, in his book *Die Missionsreden der Apostelgeschichte,* pp. 74 ff. Now, however, see his article "Der Ursprung der Überlieferung der Erscheinungen des Auferstandenen," *Dogma und Denkstrukturen,* pp. 56-95, esp. pp. 63-81.

gether involve, according to Wilckens, "legitimation formulas for the justification of the special authority of particular Christians who were honored by an appearance." Although the original intention of such formulas may have been the legitimation of an individual or of a group under presupposition of the reality of Jesus' resurrection, the Christian mission and, in any case, Paul in the text under consideration, collected such formulas in order to prove their presupposition, the resurrection of Jesus.

In view of the age of the formulated traditions used by Paul and of the proximity of Paul to the events, the assumption that appearances of the resurrected Lord were really experienced by a number of members of the primitive Christian community and not perhaps freely invented in the course of later legendary development has good historical foundation. Under such circumstances it is an idle venture to make parallels in the history of religions responsible for the *emergence* of the primitive Christian message about Jesus' resurrection. J. Leipoldt, who has traced the possible importance of motifs from the "history of religions" environment for the primitive Christian message of Jesus' resurrection in detail,[84] has also said this emphatically: "One cannot doubt that the disciples were convinced that they had seen the resurrected Lord. Otherwise the origin of the community in Jerusalem and with it of the church becomes an enigma." The question can only be whether and to what extent the formal language of the religious environment has been used in the *tradition* of the appearances of the resurrected Lord. But here, too, care is demanded as long as Gerhard Kittel's conclusion remains valid that "hardly the slightest traces" of cults of dying and rising gods can be demonstrated in first-century Palestine.[85] This means that at least for the early stage of the primitive Christian tradition such influences may be assumed only in the

[84] Johannes Leipoldt, "Zu den Auferstehungsgeschichten," *ThLZ*, LXXIII (1948), 737-742, quotation, p. 737. According to Leipoldt, the influence of forms in the religious environment on the formation of the primitive Christian Easter tradition is present above all for the expression "on the third day," which is also attested in the Osiris myth (*ibid.*, pp. 738 f.). He thinks that the search of the women for the empty grave is a motif from the account of the search for Osiris (*ibid.*, p. 739). The finding of the open grave—with the stone rolled away—early in the morning agrees with a corresponding account in the Hellenistic Callirrhoë novel by the poet Chariton (*ibid.*, p. 739). Of interest in regard to the world into which the message of Christ entered is the old saga of the ascent of Romulus into heaven, which is attested as early as the second century B.C., and which may well be the origin for the later rite for the deification of the Roman emperors at the time of their cremation. According to Suetonius (100,4), an official present had to make a sworn statement that he had seen the dead Augustus ascend to heaven (*ibid.*, p. 740; cf. also Justin, *Apol.* I, 21,3). At a later time ascension stories were also told about philosophers; thus, e.g., of Apollonius of Tyana by Philostratus in the third century (*ibid.*, pp. 741 f.), as well as of the Cynic Demonax by Lucian of Samosata. But Leipoldt also remarks, "It is astounding to what extent extra-Palestinian traditions are at home in these [Palestinian author] circles" (*ibid.*, p. 742). Just this surprising observation should cause one to be careful before too quickly accepting formal parallels as motifs of the formation of primitive Christian tradition.

[85] See G. Kittel in *Deutsche Theologie*, IV (1937), 159. Kittel mentions only an Adonis grove from the time of Hadrian near Bethlehem.

case of completely unambiguous similarities to motifs from the religious environment that cannot be explained from Palestinian presuppositions. Formal parallels are not to be evaluated without further ado as indications for motives of the formation of Christian tradition, as little as influences of this sort can be excluded in principle.

The conclusion that one must reckon with appearances of the resurrected Jesus actually experienced by the apostles does not yet permit us to say anything about what sort of experiences these may have been. At this point the greatest difficulties begin to arise.

First, the question about the content of the appearances must be posed. Also, here one must begin with Paul, for, on the one hand, the reports of the Gospels with their tendency to underscore the corporeality of the encounters offer no firm basis for historical considerations, especially since in this tendency they stand in contrast to Paul. On the other hand, Paul himself apparently presupposed in I Cor., ch. 15, that the appearance that happened to him had been of the same kind as those imparted to the other apostles.

For the question about the probable nature of the appearance of the resurrected Lord to Paul, the accounts in Acts[86] are usable only insofar as they are in agreement with Paul's own statements in Gal. 1:12 and 16 f. Here five elements can be set forth. First, the relation of the appearance to the man Jesus has been clear to Paul. God has revealed his Son to him (Gal. 1:16); Paul has seen the Lord Jesus Christ (I Cor. 9:1). Second, we have already established that Paul must have seen a spiritual body, a *sōma pneumatikon*, on the road to Damascus, not a person with an earthly body. Third, this did not involve an encounter taking place on earth, but an appearance from on high, from "heaven"; this element in the Damascus narrative in Acts, ch. 9, corresponds completely to the fact that, for the oldest New Testament witnesses, the resurrection and Jesus' departure to heaven coincide.[87] The appearances of the resurrected Lord thus were experienced as appearances coming from heaven. Fourth, if one takes both of the last two elements indicated, the glorious form and the appearance from heaven, together, it becomes probable that the Damascus appearance could have happened as light phenomenon as it is described in Acts 9:3 f. This argument should not, to be sure, be supported with an appeal to Paul's representation of the knowledge of the glory of God in the face of Christ (II Cor. 4:6) as illumination, since there need be no direct play by Paul on his Damascus experience. The terminology of light used here is much rather a general stylistic element.[88]

---

86 Acts 9:1-22; 22:3-21; 26:1-23. Cf. H. Grass, pp. 207-226.

87 Phil. 2:9; Acts 2:36; 5:30 f.; Mark 14:62. Cf. Grass, pp. 229 f.; R. Bultmann, *The History of the Synoptic Tradition*, p. 290.

88 Grass leaves this possibility open (pp. 22 f.; cf. pp. 218 f.). Grass emphasizes (pp. 221 f.) that Luke's account in Acts, ch. 9, must be bound to an old tradition that did not permit its being harmonized with the massiveness of his other resurrection narratives.

Fifth, Paul's Chistophany was certainly connected with an audition;[89] to be sure, here also the content of the audition would hardly go beyond what the appearance of Christ itself must have meant in Paul's situation. This meaning is, however, nothing less than his gospel of freedom from the law (Gal. 1:12).

These five elements, with the possible exception of the fourth, the light phenomenon, may also be presupposed for the other appearances of the resurrected Lord. In any case, all witnesses recognized Jesus of Nazareth in the appearance. That the completely alien reality experienced in these appearances could be understood as an encounter with one who had been raised from the dead can only be explained from the presupposition of a particular form of the apocalyptic expectation of the resurrection of the dead.

With regard to the character and mode of the Easter appearances, the first thing to be considered is that it may have involved an extraordinary vision, not an event that was visible to everyone. This is especially clear with regard to the Damascus event. It is most improbable that Paul traveled to Damascus as the deputy of the Jewish authorities without companions. Consequently, objections can hardly be raised against the picture presented in Acts, ch. 9, that Paul's companions were certainly present at the time of the event that happened to him, but that they did not perceive the appearance or did not understand its meaning.[90] The particular character of the appearance as a Christophany, as Paul experienced it, seems in any case not to have been perceived by his companions. Had it been otherwise, the tradition would scarcely have failed to mention the fact. An event of this sort must be designated as a vision. If someone sees something that others present are not able to see, then it involves a vision. Grass correctly emphasizes that the form of experience in which the appearances of the resurrected Lord were perceived can only be designated by the term "vision" (p. 229). It involves extraordinary sights that were not imparted to all and also (in any event in the case of Paul) were not perceived by all present. These are the characteristics of visions.

89 *Ibid.*, p. 221.
90 According to Acts 22:9; 26:13 f., Paul's companions shared the vision of light but did not hear the voice. Adolf von Harnack held this to be an indication of the historical kernel of the entire tradition, which originally lacked the auditory element (*Die Verklärungsgeschichte Jesu: Der Bericht des Paulus* [*1. Kor. 15,3 ff.*] *und die beiden Christusvisionen des Petrus* [Sitzungsberichte der Preuss. Akademie der Wissenschaft, Philosophisch-historische Klasse, 7; Berlin: Walter de Gruyter & Co., 1922], p. 71). Hans Grass rightly disagrees (p. 221) with regard to Paul himself. For the companions something of the sort is not improbable; on the contrary, it can hardly be assumed that they heard the voice but saw nothing (so Acts 9:7). When Grass points out that according to Acts 10:41a there were appearances only to the witnesses who were chosen by God, this is not necessarily evidence to the contrary, since in this case only Paul would have *understood* the appearance. Seeing and understanding seem to belong just as closely together here with respect to what is seen in particular as do visionary and auditory elements. Grass's assertion that the event "had no neutral witnesses, nor any who were only halfway involved" (p. 222) is a mere postulate.

93

However, this does not necessarily mean that what was seen was imaginary. "At most it may involve giving seeing the resurrected Lord a special place within the category of visionary seeing. Even in form one vision is not the same as another. The New Testament appears to be familiar with several forms: visions in dreams and visions while awake, visions in ecstasy and visions in a peaceful frame of mind." (P. 229.) Also, Paul himself may have distinguished the character and mode of his vision of the resurrected Lord from other visions such as he mentions in II Cor., ch. 12. An encounter with the resurrected Lord was imparted to him only *once,* as the last appearance of all, according to I Cor. 15:8. However, he was also aware of still later revelations of the Lord (II Cor. 12:1). It cannot be gathered from the text that he would have thought of the Lord only as the author and not also as the content of these latter visions (thus Grass, p. 230).[91] This, however, would have been expected if the uniqueness of the resurrection appearances had resided only in their content (Jesus), as Grass would like to think (p. 231). Further, it is not very probable that the visionary experiences of primitive Christian enthusiasm would not have been familiar precisely with visions of Christ. One only needs to think of Stephen's vision (Acts 7:55). If the term "vision" is to be used in connection with the Easter appearances, one must at the same time take into consideration that primitive Christianity itself apparently knew how to distinguish between ecstatic visionary experiences and the fundamental encounters with the resurrected Lord. To be sure, the question about how this distinction was understood in primitive Christianity is difficult to answer. E. Hirsch, in opposition to Althaus, has called attention to the fact that the *ōphthē* of the Easter appearances is not terminologically distinguishable from *optasia* (II Cor., ch. 12, *et al.*).[92] According to Acts 26:19, Paul in Luke's presentation designates his Damascus appearance also as *optasia*. Admittedly, this passage in Acts does not exclude the possibility that Paul himself could have made a terminological distinction, and that Luke simply did not maintain the distinction (cf. also Luke 1:11,22). Also, apart from this, Luke does not give Paul a position equal to the Jerusalem apostles and therefore perhaps also, in contrast to Paul himself, did not presuppose that the appearance to Paul was of a rank equal to that to Peter. What the distinction is supposed to have been for Paul himself is then, as Hirsch points out, still problematical. In this period the character of reality was apparently also conceded to Hellenistic and apocalyptic visions.[93] Does

91 That the Lord was also the content of the visions is asserted by P. Althaus, *Die Wahrheit des kirchlichen Osterglaubens: Einspruch gegen E. Hirsch* (Gütersloh: C. Bertelsmann, 1940), pp. 16 f.; and most recently U. Wilckens, "Der Ursprung der Überlieferung der Erscheinungen des Auferstandenen," *Dogma und Denkstrukturen,* pp. 85 f., in dependence on W. Michaelis.

92 Emanuel Hirsch, "Zum Problem des Osterglaubens," *ThLZ,* LXV (1940), 295-302.

93 In regard to the psychiatric concept of vision, see the article by W. Schulte in *EKL,* Vol. III, pp. 1668 f. The genuine illusion (hallucination) is the extreme phe-

there then exist a distinction with respect to the character of reality—or is the uniqueness of the Damascus event for Paul given only by the missionary commission connected with it, by his authorization as an apostle?

The latter is not probable, however, because in I Cor., ch. 15, where Paul emphatically sets forth the appearance imparted to him as the last such appearance, he is not thinking about his commission as an apostle but about attesting the reality of the resurrected Lord. May one assume that Paul was conscious of a difference between the appearances of the resurrected Lord understood as apocalyptic visions and the experiences of the Hellenistic spiritual experiences in II Cor., ch. 12? Also, in this case, however, it probably would have involved an apocalyptic vision *sui generis* for Paul, the uniqueness of which may have been conditioned by its content.

At any rate, in our context the term "vision" can only express something about the subjective mode of experience, not something about the reality of an event experienced in this form. The psychiatric concept of vision, which is primarily derived from the investigation of mentally ill persons, cannot be applied without further ado to phenomena in the history of religions. If by "vision" one understands a psychological event that is without a corresponding extrasubjective reality, then one can certainly not presuppose such a "subjective" concept of vision for the resurrection appearances as self-evident. Only if the corresponding psychiatric point of contact can be inferred from the texts could this understanding of vision be used.

Recent studies in the field of parapsychology (extrasensory perception),[94] including such things as prophetic intuition (precognition), clairvoyance, and telepathy, have reopened the question of the objective reality of unusual occurrences. One should be on guard against drawing direct conclusions for our question about the reality of the Easter appearances from such investigations. Up to now they show nothing more than the possibility of visionary experiences that are not merely to be judged as subjective projections but—in statistically demonstrable numbers—involve something to which they coincide, that is, they lay hold of extrasubjective reality. Nevertheless, in any case one conclusion may be drawn: precisely in the area of the history of religions, where only exceptional phenomena are handed down, the psychiatric concept of "vision" may not be postulated unless a more specific point of contact for it is given by the tradition.

Since David Friedrich Strauss, repeated attempts have been made to explain the experiences of the resurrection appearances on the part of Jesus' disciples in terms of mental and historical presuppositions on the side of the

nomenon and appears rarely. It is related, for example, to epilepsy. A hallucination always presupposes morbid alterations. On the other hand, there are also visions resulting from psychoses. They can have either endogenous causes (mental illness, especially schizophrenia) or exogenous causes (toxic drugs).

[94] On this subject, see esp. Joseph Banks Rhine, *New World of the Mind* (2d ed.; William Sloane Associates, Inc., 1953).

disciples with the exclusion of the reality of the resurrection. These explanations have failed to date.[95]

To maintain, first, that the appearances were produced by the enthusiastically excited imagination of the disciples does not hold, at least for the first and most fundamental appearances. The Easter appearances are not to be explained from the Easter faith of the disciples; rather, conversely, the Easter faith of the disciples is to be explained from the appearances. All the attempted constructions as to how the faith of the disciples could have survived the crisis of Jesus' death remain problematic precisely in psychological terms, even when one takes into account the firm expectation of the imminent end of the world with which Jesus presumably died and in which his disciples lived. It cannot be disputed that, in spite of all this, Jesus' death exposed the faith of his disciples to the most severe stress. One could hardly expect the production of confirmatory experiences from the faith of the disciples that stood under such a burden. Certainly such psychological considerations by themselves are as little suited to support any conclusions as to support the criticism of the New Testament traditions. They only acquire importance in connection with findings in the history of traditions, in this case the improbability of the assumption that people who came from the Jewish tradition would have conceived of the beginning of the events connected with the end of history for Jesus alone without compelling reasons. The primitive Christian news about the eschatological resurrection of Jesus—with a temporal interval separating it from the universal resurrection of the dead—is, considered from the point of view of the history of religions, something new, precisely also in the framework of the apocalyptic tradition.[96] Primitive Christianity required a long time to learn that with Jesus' resurrection the end had not yet begun in general, and still would not arrive for an indefinite time. One observes how the Easter message as an account of an event that happened to Jesus alone only gradually took shape in the horizon of apocalyptic tradition. Something like this did not arise as the mental reaction to Jesus' catastrophe.

The second principal difficulty of the "subjective vision hypothesis" consists in the number of the appearances and their temporal distribution. It has been

95 In detail, Grass, pp. 235 ff.

96 See also G. Ebeling, *Theology and Proclamation*, pp. 92 f. and 67 (literature). Ebeling concludes from this observation that the early Christian Easter message by preaching "the present *eschaton*" must be judged as having "burst the bonds of the apocalyptic" (*ibid.*, p. 92). This conclusion seems to be too hasty insofar as it suggests that the apocalyptic horizon of expectation "borrow," says Ebeling—as if it involved one arbitrary means of expression among others) is now irrelevant, after it has been "burst." Against this position it is to be maintained that this significance of the event, even if it "bursts" the apocalyptic expectation, can be expressed only in the language of the apocalyptic tradition and thus precisely in its uniqueness it remains related to the apocalyptic horizon of expectation.

asserted[97] that Jesus' disciples were especially prone to visions and that the manifoldness of the appearances may be explained through a sort of chain reaction resulting from the first appearance to Peter. But now, with regard to the first part of the argument, insofar as the traditions permit a judgment, the enthusiastic manifestations in primitive Christianity were primarily a result of the appearances of the resurrected Lord. The second part of the argument, the assumption of a mental chain reaction, is questionable because "the individual appearances did not follow one another so quickly."[98] In the sequence of the appearances at least three stages that are temporally separated from one another to an extent that is not insignificant must be distinguished: first, the appearance to Peter, which probably took place soon after his return to Galilee; second, the appearance to James, who apparently did not belong to the first group of Jesus' followers to return to Jerusalem but only later joined the Jerusalem community, as is suggested by the few things we know about the events in the primitive community; third and finally, the appearance to Paul, three years after Jesus' earthly end in Jerusalem. The appearances to the "Twelve," to "all the apostles," and the "five hundred brethren" are to be put in between, should they also be accepted as historical. There is no more specific basis for fixing them more precisely in time. Among them the appearance "to all the apostles" parallel to that to the Twelve is perhaps the most questionable, since here the legitimation of James as the leader of the primitive community is simply connected with his relation to a circle of disciples corresponding to that of Peter. One most easily would suspect a secondary formulation in this statement, the content of which may be identical with the appearance to the Twelve. The appearance to five hundred brethren at once cannot be a secondary construction to be explained by the development of the history of traditions, because Paul calls attention precisely here to the possibility of checking his assertion by saying that most of the five hundred are still alive.

Although the attempts at a purely psychological explanation of the Easter appearances as imaginations of the disciples thus fail, because, on the one hand, positive points of contact for the application of the psychiatric concept of vision are lacking and, on the other, serious difficulties that argue against this are present in the tradition, the historian still remains obligated to reconstruct the historical correlation of the events that has led to the emergence of primitive Christianity. Certainly the possibilities that he can consider in this will depend upon the understanding of reality that he brings with him to the task. If the historian approaches his work with the conviction that "the dead do not rise," then it has already been decided that Jesus also has not risen (cf. I Cor. 15:16). If, on the other hand, an element of truth is to

[97] So esp. Emanuel Hirsch, *Die Auferstehungsgeschichten und der christliche Glaube* (Tübingen: J. C. B. Mohr [Paul Siebeck], 1940), pp. 38 f. (for Peter).
[98] Grass, p. 241.

be granted to the apocalyptic expectation with regard to the hope of resurrection, then the historian must also consider this possibility for the reconstruction of the course of events as long as no special circumstances in the tradition suggest another explanation. We have seen that the latter is not the case. Therefore, the possibility exists in reconstructing the course of events of speaking not only of visions of Jesus' disciples but also of appearances of the resurrected Jesus. In doing so, one speaks, then, just as the disciples themselves, in metaphorical language. However, that need not hinder us, just as it did not hinder them, from understanding the course of events with the help of what is designated by such language when other possibilities for explanation remain unsatisfactory.

Thus the resurrection of Jesus would be designated as a historical event in this sense: If the emergence of primitive Christianity, which, apart from other traditions, is also traced back by Paul to appearances of the resurrected Jesus, can be understood in spite of all critical examination of the tradition only if one examines it in the light of the eschatological hope for a resurrection from the dead, then that which is so designated is a historical event, even if we do not know anything more particular about it.[99] Then an event that is expressible only in the language of the eschatological expectation is to be asserted as a historical occurrence.

The possibility of the historicity of Jesus' resurrection has been opposed on the grounds that the resurrection of a dead person even in the sense of the resurrection to imperishable life would be an event that violates the laws of nature. Therefore, resurrection as a historical event is impossible. Yet it appears that from the perspective of the presuppositions of modern physics judgments must be made much more carefully. First, only a part of the laws of nature are ever known. Further, in a world that as a whole represents a singular, irreversible process, an individual event is never completely determined by natural laws. Conformity to law embraces only one aspect of what happens. From another perspective, everything that happens is contingent, and the validity of the laws of nature is itself contingent. Therefore, natural science expresses the general validity of the laws of nature but must at the same time declare its own inability to make definitive judgments about the possibility or impossibility of an individual event, regardless of how certainly it is able, at least in principle, to measure the probability of an event's occurrence. The judgment about whether an event, however unfamiliar, has happened or not is in the final analysis a matter for the historian and cannot be prejudged by the knowledge of natural science.

One customarily objects theologically to the possibility that the resurrection

99 H. Conzelmann's assertion (*RGG*, III [3d ed.], 650) that as soon as reflection takes place "the result is that history cannot establish the facticity of the resurrection" is not established more precisely. For criticism of this prejudgment, see also Richard R. Niebuhr, *Resurrection and Historical Reason* (Charles Scribner's Sons, 1957).

of Jesus could be a historical event, that the resurrection from the dead has to do with the beginning of a new aeon. However, it is self-evident that the reality of the new aeon cannot be perceived with the eyes of the old aeon. The historian, however, must make judgments within the standards of the old aeon and can, therefore, say nothing about the resurrection of the dead. There is something quite correct about this argument. Because the life of the resurrected Lord involves the reality of a new creation, the resurrected Lord is in fact not perceptible as one object among others in this world; therefore, he could only be experienced and designated by an extraordinary mode of experience, the vision, and only in metaphorical language. In this way, however, he made himself known in the midst of our reality at a very definite time, in a limited number of events, and to men who are particularly designated. Consequently, these events are to be affirmed or denied also as historical events, as occurrences that actually happened at a definite time in the past. If we would forgo the concept of a historical event here, then it is no longer possible at all to affirm that the resurrection of Jesus or that the appearances of the resurrected Jesus really happened at a definite time in our world. There is no justification for affirming Jesus' resurrection as an event that really happened, if it is not to be affirmed as a historical event as such. Whether or not a particular event happened two thousand years ago is not made certain by faith but only by historical research, to the extent that certainty can be attained at all about questions of this kind.

Some theologians seek deliverance from their plight brought about by historical criticism by asserting that alongside the historical certainty of past events there is an intuitive certainty as well.[100] An intuitive perception of past events should not be denied in principle. But such intuition can never be sure whether it meets its object or misses it. Intuition always requires confirmation through detailed historical observation, through the totality of the historical evidence that comes in question. Intuition does not open an "immediate, prescientific relationship to past history, across centuries and millennia, which *bears within itself unconditional certainty about this past life*" (so Althaus; italics by the author). The danger of such an illusion is shown, for example, when Walter Künneth, in dependence on Althaus' ideas and going even farther, asserts that the certainty of faith as "unconditional certainty also involves the perception of historical facts."[101] The only method of achieving at least approximate certainty with regard to the events of a past time is historical research. If one claims to possess other means in addition to the instruments of historical criticism which are given priority over historical criticism in case of conflict, then one is led to contest the right of the historical method in principle.

So far we have spoken only about the appearances of the resurrected Lord

100 So P. Althaus, *Fact and Faith in the Kerygma Today*, p. 69.
101 K. Künneth, *Glauben an Jesus?*, p. 285.

to his apostles. The second strand of the tradition of Easter reports, the tradition of Jesus' empty tomb, has not yet been touched. This means that the results reached in the preceding discussion are valid independently of the judgment made about the tradition concerning the tomb. Nevertheless, the decision about the question of the historicity of Jesus' empty tomb is not without significance for the final conclusion.

The trustworthiness of this report is not necessarily shaken by the fact that Paul nowhere mentions Jesus' empty tomb, since the empty tomb does not affect the parallel between the Christ event and the destiny of the believers, which Paul explains again and again in his letters. Jesus' empty tomb, if it should be a historical fact, belongs to the singularity of Jesus' fate. He precisely had not lain many years in his grave or decayed as the other dead had, but after a short time he was "transformed" to another life, whatever such an expression may mean. This singularity, which applies only to Jesus because of the shortness of the time between his death and resurrection, was not necessarily of interest for Paul's proclamation of Christ, even if he—as is probably doubtful—should have known the Jerusalem tradition of the discovery of Jesus' grave. For the primitive community in Jerusalem, the situation was completely different. How could Jesus' disciples in Jerusalem have proclaimed his resurrection if they could be constantly refuted merely by viewing the grave in which his body was interred?

Paul Althaus has rightly seen this point: "In Jerusalem, the place of Jesus' execution and grave, it was proclaimed not long after his death that he had been raised. The situation *demands* that within the circle of the first community one had a reliable testimony for the fact that the grave had been found empty."[102] The resurrection kerygma "could not have been maintained in Jerusalem for a single day, for a single hour, if the emptiness of the tomb had not been established as a fact for all concerned."[103] E. Hirsch has objected that this postulate of Althaus' seems "to rest upon the inability to think oneself into a situation in which the grave and corpse are surrounded by taboolike fear, in which, therefore, no one can think about opening grave chambers in order to take the bodies out and to identify them through scientific examination."[104] Remarkably, the traditions of the discovery of the grave, the origin of which must most probably be sought in the Jerusalem community, suggest nothing of the idea that such a search would meet with basic objections. Had they existed, they would certainly also have had to be presupposed on the part of the original hearers of such a story, whom the narrative, therefore, would have had to set at ease in some way. Moreover, it is hardly conceivable that the "taboolike awe" about the grave and corpse could not have been abrogated by the Jewish authorities as an exception, at

102 P. Althaus, *Die Wahrheit des kirchlichen Osterglaubens,* p. 25.
103 *Ibid.,* pp. 22 f.
104 E. Hirsch in *ThLZ,* LXV (1940), 298.

least to the extent that one could be persuaded that Jesus' grave was still intact—in case one knew where it was to be sought. It was not even necessary to consider exhuming the body. If such a step were possible, even only as an exception, under special conditions, it surely would have had to be done by the Jewish authorities in view of the primitive Christian proclamation of Jesus' resurrection in the place where he was executed. Likewise, the Christians must have attached great interest to this question. The assumption that the "taboolike awe" about the grave and corpse could not have been suspended at all at this time is probably already excluded by the fact that in the early period of the Empire the Roman authorities found themselves obliged to take steps against grave robbery that was apparently getting the upper hand in Palestine.[105]

Among the general historical arguments that speak for the trustworthiness of the report about the discovery of Jesus' empty tomb is, above all, the fact that the early Jewish polemic against the Christian message about Jesus' resurrection, traces of which have already been left in the Gospels,[106] does not offer any suggestion that Jesus' grave had remained untouched. The Jewish polemic would have had to have every interest in the preservation of such a report. However, quite to the contrary, it shared the conviction with its Christian opponents that Jesus' grave was empty. It limited itself to explaining this fact in its own way, which was detrimental to the Christian message.

Thus general historical considerations already show that the proclamation of the news of Jesus' resurrection in Jerusalem, which had established the Christian community, is hardly understandable except under the assumption that Jesus' tomb was empty. A judgment in this question does not depend primarily on an analysis of Mark, ch. 16. Even if the account of the discovery of Jesus' grave which has been reserved for us should be shown to be a late legend conceived in the Hellenistic community, the weight of the arguments presented here would remain. Only when one restricts oneself one-sidedly to the analysis of the textual tradition for the basis of the historical judgment, as Grass still has done, can one really come to a negative result in the question of Jesus' empty tomb. Grass thinks that the existing traditions in themselves provide no argument for the historicity of the empty tomb that is "unconditionally conclusive" (p. 183). For all that, even Grass concedes in his discussion with von Campenhausen "that the gap in the historical proof for the empty tomb is very small" (p. 184), although he does not pose the question in view of the situation of the Easter kerygma in Jerusalem but limits him-

105 On this point, see J. Irmscher, "Zum Diatagma Kaisaros von Nazareth," ZNW, XLII (1949), 172-184. It is surely false to connect this inscription directly with what happened at the grave of Jesus (so Grass, pp. 139 f.); nonetheless, it shows that one has to be cautious when speaking about a "taboolike awe" about the grave and corpse.

106 On the beginnings of Jewish polemic against the Christians, see H. v. Campenhausen, Der Ablauf der Osterereignisse und das leere Grab, pp. 31 ff.

self only to the analysis of the textual tradition. If one begins with the historical consideration of the situation of the resurrection kerygma in the first Jerusalem community, then, however, the existing tradition confirms what is already to be presupposed as historically probable, for other reasons, namely, that in Jerusalem it was known that the grave was empty. Only if the existing text virtually forced one to make the opposite judgment could the weight of the historical argument from the relation between the resurrection proclamation in Jerusalem and Jesus' empty tomb, which this proclamation presupposes, be countered at all. In this matter, Grass apparently permits himself to be led by particular theological points of view. "If the proof for the empty tomb could be strictly carried through in every respect, one could . . . almost prove the fact of the resurrection historically. By God's will, that is apparently not possible. It is supposed to remain something unheard of that is not to be attained by human proofs." (Pp. 184 f.) Where does Grass obtain his information about what is possible by God's will and what is not? Does not all striving toward historical certainty with regard to the Easter event pale to a comparatively insignificant undertaking beside such apodictic knowledge?

The tradition about the tomb, which is the only Easter account common to all the Synoptics, appears in its most original form preserved in Mark, ch. 16. The deviations in Matthew and Luke are all understandable from dogmatical or redactional motives and, therefore, can be left out of consideration for a historical inquiry. The two most difficult questions posed by the text in Mark are: Is Mark 16:8 the original conclusion to the Gospel? And what is the relation between v. 7 and v. 8? These two questions are connected: If the word of the angel in v. 7 that points to appearances of the resurrected Lord in Galilee[107] originally belonged to the tradition, one would have to reckon with a missing Easter account. Then v. 8 would not have formed the original conclusion of the Gospel. However, the unmotivated *alla* ("but") with which v. 7 begins shows that material has been added here that did not originally belong to the tradition, perhaps, just like Mark 14:28 (cf. Nestle's critical apparatus), added by Mark himself. Further, ch. 16:8 is probably not a unity: v. 8b offers with "for they were afraid" a materially superfluous repetition of 8a. The narrative originally would have ended then with 8a: "And they went out and fled from the tomb; for trembling and astonishment had come upon them," directly following v. 6, the message of the angel that Jesus, whom they sought, had been raised. The second part of the word of the angel, v. 7, is, like v. 8b, an insertion into the transmitted text. Both contain references to an appearance tradition known to Mark, which he

[107] Willi N. Marxsen, *Der Evangelist Markus: Studien zur Redaktionsgeschichte des Evangeliums* (2d ed.; Göttingen: Vandenhoeck & Ruprecht, 1959), pp. 47 ff., 73 ff., refers the *proagei* to the parousia instead of to Jesus' resurrection. Nevertheless, *proagei* suggests a rather massive conception of the reality of the resurrected Lord and may be late, perhaps coming from Mark; in any case, it does not point to the concept of the second coming.

has nevertheless not included, perhaps because the passion narrative with the discovery of the empty tomb had lain before him as a local Jerusalem tradition that was already complete. This presupposes that the appearance traditions were not originally localized in Jerusalem.[108]

Grass substantiates his skepticism toward the tradition about the discovery of Jesus' tomb with the consideration that Jesus' disciples had returned to Galilee after he was taken prisoner and before his death and then returned to Jerusalem again only after several weeks had passed in order to proclaim Jesus who had appeared to them in Galilee. Grass presupposes that at that time "no certain information about the whereabouts of the body was to be obtained, that inquiry by friend and foe remained fruitless, and in any case it also was not pursued with particular zeal by Jesus' friends, since they were certain of the resurrected Lord through the appearances" (p. 184). The possibility that Jesus' body and his tomb had not been heard of again after such a short time is worth considering only under the presupposition that Jesus was buried as a criminal in just any tomb that happened to be empty or even in a mass grave without anyone having taken the trouble to inform Jesus' followers of its location. Still, such conjectures remain completely fantastic. They are extremely improbable because the tradition does not contain the slightest indication of an unsuccessful search for Jesus' grave, not even—and this again is especially important—in the Jewish polemic. In the latter it was asserted that the disciples themselves had removed the body, but not that Jesus' grave had remained unknown. Thus the possibility advanced by Grass is to be judged as practically irrelevant. Even if the traditions carry a strongly legendary overgrowth, they point in the opposite direction, which had to be assumed historically from the very beginning as the presupposition for the resurrection kerygma in the Jerusalem community: the Jews there, as well as the Christians, were familiar with the fact of the empty tomb.

The considerations presented by Grass rest on the presupposition that the account of the burial in Mark 15:42-47 constitutes a pure legend without any historical value (Grass, pp. 173-183). But the strange way in which one would have to conceive the growth of the burial legend as described by Grass (p. 180) is in itself an argument against his thesis. The burial itself is tied to the name of Joseph of Arimathaea. This can hardly have been invented secondarily, since the entire tradition about Jesus' burial hangs on this name. The passage in Acts 13:27-29 according to which "the Jews," thus Jesus' enemies, had buried him can claim no historical value because the removal from the cross was the responsibility of the Roman authorities. In addition the terminology "the Jews" points to the Lucan schema of the

---

[108] Against Conzelmann (RGG, I [3d ed.], 699), this assumption results from the verse added by Mark (ch. 16:7). Both this verse and ch. 14:28 are presumably additions by Mark (with R. Bultmann, The History of the Synoptic Tradition, p. 285), not old sayings, as Marxsen, Der Evangelist Markus, pp. 73 ff., assumes.

speeches in Acts.[109] The account of the burial, as well as that of the discovery of the grave, seems to have a firm place in the pre-Marcan Jerusalem passion tradition. Also, the Pauline "he was buried" in I Cor. 15:4 gives an indication of the age of the tradition about the grave.[110] Even if one decides that no sufficiently great probability can be attained for the historical kernel of the burial tradition, it is not possible to take the legendary character of the story of the burial as given in order to base further hypotheses upon this about the impossibility of discovering Jesus' corpse after his disciples returned from Galilee.

The question upon which we have just touched, namely, that of the relation between the discovery of the empty tomb and the appearances of the resurrected Lord, is extraordinarily difficult. Contemporary scholarship is in extensive agreement that the basic appearances took place in Galilee; the grave, on the other hand, was naturally discovered in Jerusalem. For the relation between the two events the solution of the question whether the disciples returned to Galilee immediately after Jesus was taken prisoner—in which case they need not necessarily have left Jerusalem in flight—or whether they at first still remained in Jerusalem is decisive. If the disciples began their return to Galilee immediately, then the empty tomb would have been discovered without them, and the Easter appearances would then be independent of the discovery of the empty tomb.

However, the assumption of a "disciples' flight" to Galilee is now rejected by von Campenhausen as a "legend of the critics."[111] In his opinion the disciples remained in Jerusalem and were first given cause to go to Galilee by the discovery of the empty tomb: "Where was Jesus now supposed to be found? . . . He must have gone back to his home territory, to Galilee, where he had worked, where he possessed his following, where he and all the disciples were at home."[112] Thus von Campenhausen materially follows Mark's conception of the disciples' journey to Galilee; but he replaces with Peter's reflection the instructions of the angel whom the women, according to Mark

109 See H. v. Campenhausen, *Der Ablauf der Osterereignisse und das leere Grab*, pp. 32 ff.

110 On I Cor. 15:4a, see U. Wilckens, "Der Ursprung der Überlieferung der Erscheinungen des Auferstandenen," *Dogma und Denkstrukturen*, pp. 74 f. The argument of Grass, pp. 180 f., is peculiar. In the first place, Grass says in reference to I Cor. 15:4 that the fact that Jesus was properly buried "is strongly suggested, but not made unconditionally necessary by the 'he was buried.' " However, he then continues with a reference to the silence of the rest of the oldest tradition in Paul and in Acts about the empty tomb and thinks that this finding "makes the assumption difficult that primitive Christianity knew about the tomb." However, to have this result, one must not only have excluded the account of the burial with Grass, but also the "strongly suggested" interpretation of I Cor. 15:4. Nonetheless, Grass assesses the alleged *argumentum e silentio* as "a very significant, not to say decisive" argument.

111 H. v. Campenhausen, *Der Ablauf der Osterereignisse und das leere Grab*, p. 44, n. 174, the formulation by M. Albertz.

112 *Ibid.*, p. 44, n. 175 (p. 45). *Ibid.*, p. 49.

16:1-8, met at the tomb. Grass objects to this conception: "The concept of a Jesus who had departed from Jerusalem and whom his disciples, full of presentiment, followed in the hope of a reunion in Galilee—even though Galilee is a big place—is less believable than the most massive Easter legends of the tradition in the Gospels" (p. 119). The psychological motivation suggested by von Campenhausen for the return to Galilee is, in fact, hardly tenable. His remark in the second edition of his study is much more convincing: "Some time or other the pilgrims to Jerusalem had to depart for home."[113] However, for this the discovery of the empty tomb need not be presupposed; it is even questionable whether the disciples would not have remained in Jerusalem after such a discovery in order to await the end of the world there, just as they did in fact return to Jerusalem after the appearances granted to them in Galilee. Thus the conclusion suggests itself that the return of the disciples to Galilee took place independently of the discovery of the empty tomb. The disciples may have come to know about the grave only after their return to Jerusalem. This is supported, as Grass (p. 119) rightly emphasized, by the situation in the history of the traditions, that is, by the original independence of the two strands of tradition, the appearance tradition and the tomb tradition. In addition, in view of a series of individual elements in the passion tradition, difficulties emerge if one begins with the assumption that the disciples had remained in Jerusalem until the discovery of the empty grave (Grass, p. 116): "If the disciples still stayed in Jerusalem, why do we not hear that they were witnesses of Jesus' execution at least from afar?" Only with regard to John does Grass establish a "tendency of the tradition to bring the disciples into connection with the cross." And further: "Why do the disciples play no role in the burial?" In addition, according to the oldest strata of the tradition, the disciples did not show any concern for the empty tomb. All these observations help support the assumption that the tomb tradition and the appearance tradition had come into existence independently of each other.

These last considerations possess great importance for the entire question about the historicity of Jesus' resurrection. If the appearance tradition and the grave tradition came into existence independently, then by their mutually complementing each other they let the assertion of the reality of Jesus' resurrection, in the sense explained above, appear as historically very probable, and that always means in historical inquiry that it is to be presupposed until contrary evidence appears. The so-called subjective-vision hypothesis then becomes even more questionable than it already seemed to us above. The

[113] Mark 16:7 (the angel's instruction to go to Galilee) is then perhaps to be judged as an early attempt to connect the two traditions, which already is prepared for by the Marcan addition ch. 14:28. That both additions speak against the assertion recently defended again by Conzelmann (*RGG,* I [3d ed.], 699), that all appearances took place in Jerusalem, was brought out above (n. 108). A return to Galilee, the mention of which is missed by Conzelmann, is presupposed precisely in these verses.

situation would be very different, however, if the discovery of the empty tomb had been the cause of the disciples' journey to Galilee, as the matter appears in von Campenhausen. For then we would have to consider the possibility of spontaneous visionary experiences as more likely in view of the eschatological expectation of the nearness of the end in which Jesus' disciples lived before the events in Jerusalem, even though the problem of the broad temporal distribution of the appearances would still remain a difficulty burdening the subjective-vision hypothesis.

V. THE DELAY OF THE PAROUSIA AND THE MEANING OF JESUS' RESURRECTION

The significance of Jesus' resurrection was originally bound to the fact that it constituted only the beginning of the universal resurrection of the dead and the end of the world. Only under this presupposition is the end present in Jesus' resurrection. Only as the beginning of the end, of the judgment through the Son of Man, as whom Jesus himself is now expected, could Jesus' resurrection be understood as the confirmation of his pre-Easter claim to authority, in particular as the confirmation of his words about the coming Son of Man and his judgment on the basis of men's relationship to Jesus. Only as the One who had been exalted by God himself to be the executor of the end was Jesus the one of whom it could be said that in him the glory of God was revealed or—in the language of Hellenism—that in him God himself or God's revealer had appeared. All these statements about the meaning of Jesus' resurrection are bound to the connection of this event with the imminent end of the world and the general resurrection of the dead.

In contrast to the expectation of the oldest community and even of Paul, however, the end of the world and the resurrection of all the dead did not take place in the first generation of primitive Christianity. The interval between Jesus' resurrection and the present time of the community became increasingly larger. It was soon to be measured in centuries and finally in millennia.

What is to be concluded from this? For us, but already for the second generation of the New Testament witnesses themselves—as, for example, for Luke—Jesus' resurrection and his return for judgment have become widely separated in time, in distinction from the earliest community, which understood both events as directly connected in one event. The oldest community counted on the speedy conclusion of the series of end events that had already begun in Jesus' resurrection; for us, in contrast, the conclusion of the end events still will not arrive for an uncertain period of time. For the oldest community, it was immediately necessary to say everything about Jesus that was appropriate to him as the one provided to be the eschatological judge, whose appearance for judgment had already been announced by his appearances to the disciples. However, it no longer presses itself upon us so irresistibly that the resurrected Jesus is the eschatological judge. If we did not have the witness of primitive Christianity, we would hardly arrive by ourselves at the idea that the One who was crucified almost two thousand years ago had introduced the end of the world through his resurrection from the dead. However, since we do have primitive Christianity's witness, which has arisen from the evidence existing in the situation then, we do not stand before the question at all of what we are supposed to make of that two thousand years, but before the other question whether, in spite of the increasing temporal interval between ourselves and the event of Jesus' resurrection, we are still able to hold on to the tension that binds this past event with the end of the world which has not yet arrived. This relation of the Christ event to the end of the world in the sense of an anthropologically interpreted apocalyptic expectation is not bound to the length of the interval between both events. It is bound only to the material analogy of what has already happened in and with Jesus and that for which the apocalyptic expectation hopes from the ultimate future. In this we presuppose that this expectation can be justified as true for us in its fundamental elements, even if from a different horizon of interpretation than that of apocalyptic itself. Neither the two-thousand-year interval from the time of Jesus' earthly appearance nor its continuing quantitative growth is sufficient in itself to let the connection between the activity and fate of Jesus and the expected end of all things discovered then to become untenable; for this connection depends only upon the material correspondence of what happened in Jesus with the content of the eschatological expectation. So also for the "Son of Man" saying in Mark 8:38 the question as to how much time might elapse between the appearance of Jesus and the coming of the Son of Man is completely irrelevant. The important thing in it is the material correspondence of the coming judgment with the present attitude of men toward Jesus. Only such a material correspondence is involved in the question about the truth of seeing the fate of Jesus in association with the eschatological expectation as it took place in primitive Christianity.

Only in connection with the end of the world that still remains to come can what has happened in Jesus through his resurrection from the dead possess and retain the character of revelation for us also. The question continually arises anew whether what had been evidently true at that time in the past still holds good as truth in the present also. There is no answer to this question that can be formulated in a single sentence; it is answered at any particular time by theology as a whole, and not only by theology, but also by the way in which the faith of Christians, which is grounded upon the truth known in the past, stands the test today in the decisions of life.

The delay of the end events, which now amounts to almost two thousand years, is not a refutation of the Christian hope and of the Christian perception of revelation as long as the unity between what happened in Jesus and the eschatological future is maintained. However, the Christian perception of what happened in Jesus will always retain an openness to the future. The ultimate divine confirmation of Jesus will take place only in the occurrence of his return. Only then will the revelation of God in Jesus become manifest in its ultimate, irresistible glory. When we speak today of God's revelation in Jesus and of his exaltation accomplished in the resurrection from the dead, our statements always contain a proleptic element. The fulfillment, which had begun for the disciples, which was almost in their grasp, in the appearances of the resurrected Lord, has become promise once again for us. The unique significance of the apostles' witness for all subsequent church history, however, is connected with the fact that at that time Jesus' resurrection and the end of the world could be seen together as a single event under the impression of the imminent expectation of the end. To that extent the eschatological future was nearer then than at any time since. All subsequent church history lives from that, even though the truth of seeing the resurrection and the end together has become more problematic again in the meantime than it was for the first community, and will be completely confirmed only in the future.

APPENDIX: THE EVALUATION OF JESUS' RESURRECTION IN MODERN DOGMATICS

The thesis presented in this paragraph that Jesus' resurrection is the basis for the perception of his divinity, that it means above all God's revelation in him, stands in contrast to the way in which a Christology "from below" is set up elsewhere in contemporary theological work. In the first section we have seen that from Elert and Althaus through the modern research about Jesus Christology builds on Jesus' claim to authority. It remains now to examine the evaluation that Jesus' resurrection receives in such a context. Is the fundamental significance of Jesus' resurrection for the primitive Christian proclamation of Christ then not even seen?

One cannot say that in this way. Elert, for example, certainly has seen that Jesus' pre-Easter work was called into question with his death on the cross and that, therefore, only Jesus' resurrection has become the basis of faith in Christ.[114] Nevertheless, Elert bases the assertion of Jesus' divinity on his pre-Easter "claim" to be the Son of God (p. 303). Elert says nothing further about the significance that then still remains for Jesus' resurrection. Jesus' resurrection appears to be only a repetitious confirmation of what was also already adequately established before Easter.

[114] W. Elert, *Der christliche Glaube,* p. 300.

The problem that arises here is expressed more clearly in Althaus. He sees that "Jesus' death calls the validity of his claim into question."[115] Therefore, "faith lives from Easter" (p. 432). Althaus maintains this point expressly against Wilhelm Herrmann, for whom only the person of the earthly Jesus was the ground of faith. But in what sense does Jesus' resurrection belong, for Althaus, to the ground of faith? Certainly not as a proof of one sort or another. "Faith must be *dared*. For this reason dogmatic Christology also cannot desire to prove the presence of God in Jesus Christ." (P. 425.) With regard to Jesus' resurrection such a proof is not possible, according to Althaus, because it is "not a demonstrable historical fact" (p. 426). "The experiences of the disciples, the 'appearances' of Jesus after his death and probably the fact of the empty tomb as well are historically perceptible. But historiography as such is not capable of saying how these facts are to be understood, what actually happened on Easter. That is a matter of religious judgment, of faith, which comes into existence in the total witness about Jesus."

To this it must be said that primitive Christianity did not make such a distinction between fact and meaning, that, rather, there the occurrence and meaning of Jesus' resurrection belong most closely together. The distinction between the two is at home philosophically in Kantianism.[116] It has often been connected with the positivistic understanding of the historical method, according to which history establishes only "facts." However, within the discussion of the historical method itself this understanding has been shown to be inadequate: historical inquiry always takes place from an already given context of meaning, out of a preunderstanding of the object of inquiry, which, however, is modified and corrected in the process of research on the basis of the phenomena examined. As long as historiography does not begin dogmatically with a narrow concept of reality according to which "dead men do not rise," it is not clear why historiography should not in principle be able to speak about Jesus' resurrection as the explanation that is best established of such events as the disciples' experiences of the appearances and the discovery of the empty tomb. If, however, historical study declares itself unable to establish what "really" happened on Easter, then all the more, faith is not able to do so; for faith cannot ascertain anything certain about events of the past that would perhaps be inaccessible to the historian.

In Althaus' argument, however, not only is the assertion that Jesus' resurrection cannot be a historical fact problematic, but also the motif that faith must remain a risk is problematic. This motif is widespread in contemporary theology. Thus Ebeling also constantly differentiates himself sharply from efforts toward a "proof" of the ground of faith, without giving further rea-

---

115 P. Althaus, *Die christliche Wahrheit*, p. 431. The following quotations refer to this work.

116 On this, see R. R. Niebuhr, *Resurrection and Historical Reason*, pp. 62-81, 109 f., 115 f.

sons for this.[117] Apparently he is afraid that the essence of faith will be destroyed by the attempt at a proof. However, the essence of faith is preserved by the eschatological tension of the "not yet" in which the believer lives on the basis of the Christ event. In contrast the essence of faith is destroyed where it appears as an unfounded risk. The ground of faith must be as certain as possible. Certainly the presentation of the basis of faith in God's revelation through Jesus' resurrection still always retains an openness to the eschatological future, an openness into which the person is also drawn who enters into this event, and that is the element of truth in speaking about the character of faith as risk.

For Althaus, faith is not only established by the event of Easter, but this event has the significance of showing Jesus' authority "as present and valid" only for those who believe his claim to authority (p. 432). Through the Easter event the crucified Lord gives his action "continuing presence" (p. 433). How is this related to the fact that according to the primitive Christian witnesses the presence of the resurrected Lord on earth, the period of his appearances, had been a limited, closed period?

Althaus' idea corresponds to the formulation encountered, for example, in Käsemann and Bornkamm that through Jesus' resurrection the "once" of his pre-Easter claim has become a "once for all." So also according to Emil Brunner the knowledge of the Easter event already presupposes faith in Jesus' authority: "Only when they understood Him as this absolute Lord, to whom the full divine sovereignty belongs, did Easter as victory, and Good Friday as a saving Fact, become intelligible."[118] Tillich, too, is of the opinion that "the experience of the New Being in Jesus must precede the experience of the Resurrected."[119] Similarly, Ebeling declares that the ground of faith "according to Biblical witness is not the isolated and objectified fact of the resurrection but Jesus as the witness of the faith."[120] In this it is certainly

---

117 G. Ebeling, *Theology and Proclamation*, pp. 49, 56f., 63, 71. Naturally, in theology there can be no talk of proof in the exact mathematical, scientific sense. It neither has to do with deductions from apparent principles nor is an empirical verification of theological statements possible (or even meaningful) in the sense that they can be explained by recorded statements about intersubjective sensorial perception. That is true for the whole field of the humanities. However, "proof" in a broader sense that has also been adopted by theology since the patristic period can also mean that argument which appeals to a reasonable judgment and makes possible at least a provisional decision between contrasting assertions. Understood in this broader sense, a "proof" for the truth of faith does not need to stand in contradiction to its essence, for not every argument means having its "object" at its disposal. It need not displace the mysterious depth of the subject matter of faith, but it can precisely lead into it. Precisely the openness for what has not yet appeared in the history of Jesus of Nazareth, on which faith depends, could be decisive for the "proof" of the truth of faith.

118 E. Brunner, *The Christian Doctrine of Creation and Redemption*, p. 339. See also p. 370: "We believe in the Resurrection of Jesus because through the whole witness of the Scriptures He attests Himself to us as the Christ and as the Living Lord."

119 Paul Tillich, *Systematic Theology*, Vol. II, pp. 157 f.

120 G. Ebeling, *The Nature of Faith*, p. 71.

correct, and that will concern us below,[121] that Jesus' resurrection cannot be the ground of faith as an isolated individual fact. It must be understood in the context of the Jewish expectation and above all of the appearance of Jesus on earth. However, with the justified rejection of a substantiation of faith by the "isolated" fact of the resurrection, Ebeling turns away altogether from understanding Jesus' resurrection as the decisive basis of faith and seeks this basis in the message and conduct of the pre-Easter Jesus. He designates it as "misinterpretation: as if the additional fact of Jesus' resurrection had accomplished what he was not able to do, and as if post-Easter faith were something different than the consequence of Jesus' certainty."[122] This "misinterpretation," at any rate, characterizes the entire primitive Christian history of traditions, for which Jesus' resurrection constitutes the actual point of departure.

Also, according to Karl Barth, Jesus' resurrection is not a completely new event with its own decisive importance, but still only the "revelation" of Jesus' history consummated on the cross.[123] Barth expressed this idea most clearly in 1922 in the second edition of his *The Epistle to the Romans*,[124] namely, "that the raising of Jesus from the dead is not an event in history elongated so as still to remain an event in the midst of other events. The Resurrection is the nonhistorical (iv. 17b) relating of the whole historical life of Jesus to its origin in God" (p. 195). This calls to mind Bultmann's controversial thesis that Jesus' resurrection is only "the expression of the significance of the cross."[125] However, Barth's position in the *Church Dogmatics* is distinguished from his own earlier position and from that of Bultmann in that he permits the event of revelation, the nonhistorical relation of Jesus' whole life to its origin in God, to be a particular event in the temporal course of Jesus' history.[126]

[121] The observation that the fact of Jesus' resurrection cannot be the ground of faith "in isolation" is completely correct. Cf. what has been said above, pp. 66 ff., about the relation of Jesus' resurrection to his pre-Easter activity on the one hand and the Jewish expectation of resurrection on the other.

[122] G. Ebeling, *Theology and Proclamation*, p. 91.

[123] Karl Barth, *CD*, IV/2, pp. 122 ff., 140 ff.

[124] Karl Barth, *The Epistle to the Romans*, tr. from the 6th ed. by Edwyn C. Hoskyns (London: Oxford University Press, 1933).

[125] R. Bultmann in *Kerygma and Myth*, Vol. I, p. 38.

[126] Thus K. Barth can stress against Bultmann "the priority of the personal resurrection of Jesus Christ over every other resurrection there may be in the kerygma, in faith, in the Church or in the sacraments" (Karl Barth, "Rudolf Bultmann: An Attempt to Understand Him," *Kerygma and Myth*, Vol. II, ed. by Hans Werner Bartsch [London: S.P.C.K., 1962], p. 101). To be sure, apparently all that makes him uneasy is that Jesus' resurrection on the third day is not, in Bultmann's view, "the basic fact of Christianity" for knowledge of the history of Jesus Christ, "but only an explanation of the kerygma and of faith, and one which could be dispensed with if necessary" (*ibid.*). Even Barth does not seem to find the ontic (or even ontological) foundation of Christology in the statement of Jesus' resurrection. Is this perhaps a consequence of the fact that for Barth, the doctrine of the incarnation takes the place of this foundation?

Karl Rahner comes to a similar result from a different point of departure. For him the death of Christ is "the total act of Christ's life, the ultimate act of his freedom, the full integration of his whole time into his human eternity." Therefore, according to Rahner, "the resurrection of Jesus" is "not another event after his suffering and after his death, but the appearance of that which has happened in Christ's death." Thus Good Friday and Easter appear as "two essentially mutually interrelated aspects of an event that is strictly unified."[127]

The previously considered positions fail to appreciate the relatedness to the future and therefore the dependence on the future of Jesus' whole pre-Easter appearance, especially the dependence of his claim on a confirmation by God himself in the beginning of the end of history. The fact remains unnoticed that Jesus' claim after his crucifixion could no longer be accepted, as previously, simply in the trusting anticipation of a future confirmation. Rather, if the cross is the last thing we know about Jesus, then—at least for Jewish judgment—he was a failure, and it is not understandable what he is supposed to have to say to non-Jews that would basically go beyond the area of their other experience. After his crucifixion Jesus' claim is no longer simply open, but it either has miscarried on the cross or has been ultimately established and justified through the resurrection.

Although the theological judgments about the significance of the message of the resurrection considered above do not adequately bring to bear the fact that for primitive Christianity only this event cast a new and proper light on everything that was to be said about Jesus, nevertheless, they all do still have Jesus' resurrection in view as the confirmation that came to him from God, even though they do not allow it its full significance for the establishment of faith. However, Ernst Fuchs goes still farther in rejecting a substantiation of faith on the basis of the fact of Jesus' resurrection. He thinks that basing faith on the experience of the Easter appearances is characteristic for Peter, who thereby has lapsed into a mere *fides historica*. With Paul, on the contrary, the cross moves into the center of the proclamation.[128] In taking this position Fuchs overlooks the fact that also for Paul the cross received saving significance only in the light of Jesus' resurrection.[129] Hence, Fuchs comes to the amazing conclusion that the first preachers of the message of Jesus "had to believe not because but in spite of their having seen."[130]

The steps toward a "theology of the resurrection" in Walter Künneth and Gerhard Koch stand in diametrical opposition to this kind of deprecation of the primitive Christian Easter message. Both have worked out clearly the

127 Karl Rahner, "Dogmatische Fragen zur Osterfrömmigkeit," *Schriften zur Theologie* (Zurich-Köln: Benziger Verlag Einsiedeln, 1960), Vol. IV, pp. 165ff.

128 Ernst Fuchs, *Gesammelte Aufsätze* (Tübingen: J. C. B. Mohr [Paul Siebeck], 1959), Vol. I, pp. 302 f. Fuchs agrees with Bultmann that the resurrection of Jesus still only expresses the significance of the cross (*ibid.*, p. 297, cf. p. 299).

129 See K. H. Rengstorf, *Die Auferstehung Jesu*, p. 26.

130 E. Fuchs, *Gesammelte Aufsätze*, Vol. I, p. 304.

fundamental significance of Jesus' resurrection for primitive Christianity and for all Christian theology. However, both fail to do justice to the radical sense of the past character of the Christ event. The same is true also of Jesus' resurrection. To be sure, the life of the resurrected Jesus, which is no longer limited by death, cannot be designated as past, but surely the event of his resurrection, which has taken place once at a definite time, can be so characterized. For this reason we must inquire about the historicity of this event. Künneth, however, emphasizes very strongly the nonhistoricity of the resurrection. It is an event that "essentially breaks the limits of the merely historical."[131] The question is why then can one still talk about an event that really happened at a definite time? For Künneth, that is apparently something which is supernaturally given, a "reality of revelation having unconditional character" (p. 24). The freedom "from the paralyzing spell of scholarly historical methods" (p. 25) for which Künneth strives—a wish that is certainly understandable—surely may not be achieved so simply if one does not want to allow the reality of Jesus' resurrection to shrivel to a mere affirmation. To be sure, for Künneth the reality of Jesus' resurrection does not depend on what has happened in the past. He thinks, rather, that one can become certain of the reality of the resurrected Jesus in the church as "the existential community of the believers with the present Lord" (p. 170). Naturally, this is expressed particularly in the Sacraments.[132]

This line of thought has been continued in a somewhat different way by Gerhard Koch's book *Die Auferstehung Jesu Christi*. This book reaches its climax in the thesis, "Worship is Easter event." "In it the confrontation of the Lord in his reality with his community in the world takes place"; worship is even the "repetition" of the Lord (p. 330).

We have already taken a position above with regard to the assertion about a present experience of the reality of Jesus' resurrection.[133] Apart from the question of the criterion by which experiences of this sort might be protected against resting on mere illusions, in contrast to such assertions, attention must be called to the hiddenness of the reality of the resurrected Lord between the conclusion of his appearances to the disciples and his return. In this sense

131 W. Künneth, *The Theology of the Resurrection* (London: SCM Press, Ltd., 1965), p. 31.

132 *Ibid.*, pp. 200 ff. Also, in Künneth's new book, *Glauben an Jesus?*, the "sacramental presence of Christ" (Sec. 2 of the chapter "Der aktuelle Vollzug des Glaubens") appears as the concretion of that which "faith as personal communication (Sec. 1) is and as the foundation for the "certainty of faith" (Sec. 3). For "Jesus, the Lord, is as one who is present as the sole initiator, center, and goal of this certainty of faith" (*ibid.*, p. 285). The latter is awakened by the witness to the revelation (*ibid.*, p. 284); the point of "encounter" with the living Lord, however, apparently is especially the Sacrament for Künneth (*ibid.*, p. 261; cf. p. 273 in reference to the Lord's Supper: "The encounter with the Lord who is present occurs in the association at the table, which is both spatial and temporal, physical and historical").

133 See above, pp. 27 f.

Paul attacked the assertions by the Corinthian Gnostics of a present experience of the glory of the exalted Lord and of the participation in this glory. Paul conducted his ardent battle against such assertions under the banner of the theology of the cross. Paul's theology of the cross certainly does not intend, as Fuchs thinks, to contradict the significance of Jesus' resurrection as the basis for faith. However, it does emphasize that the reality of Jesus' resurrection as a past event cannot be experienced at present without further ado. In the present, one can experience the cross of Christ only in baptism (Rom., ch. 6) and in the Lord's Supper (I Cor., ch. 11). The experience of the glory of the resurrected Christ is not something that occurs in the present in a mystery cult, as the Gnostics asserted, but constitutes the future hope of Christians.[134]

[134] To that extent the presence of the Spirit in the Christian community is not to be confused with the experience of the resurrection reality itself, which has appeared first only in Jesus, even though the latter is very closely connected with the Spirit. According to Paul, the resurrection life is the creation of God's Spirit, which dwells in the believers. Nevertheless, the resurrection is not yet the content of present experience. At most, one could designate the Spirit with E. Käsemann as "basis of the post-Easter imminent expectation" (*ZThK*, LIX [1962], 264, n. 2). However, possession of the Spirit is certainly not the only and ultimate ground of the imminent expectation. This is rather to be sought in the unity of Jesus' resurrection with the universal resurrection that still remains to come, and the reception of the Spirit is itself to be understood as an effect of the message of the resurrection of the crucified.

JESUS' DIVINITY IN RELATION TO THE FATHER'S DIVINITY

In his revelational unity with God, which constitutes Jesus' own divinity, Jesus at the same time still remains distinct from God as his Father. The beginning of the doctrine of the Trinity lies in this.

I. THE MODE OF GOD'S PRESENCE IN JESUS

It is the task of this chapter to examine the Christologies of the church on the basis of the foundation outlined in the preceding chapter. That involves showing the extent to which the Christological tradition becomes understandable from the perspective of Jesus' resurrection as an explication of the historical Jesus, insofar as the Easter event reveals Jesus' activity and fate as a unified complex of meaning. In this connection, Jesus' relation to God implied in the Easter event, which has already been described in the thesis of the preceding chapter as "Jesus' unity with God," must first be developed more precisely. We have already seen that the revelatory character of the Christ event, originally understood within the horizon of eschatology, and translated into Hellenistic categories as the epiphany of God in Jesus, constitutes the key to the clarification of Jesus' unity with God.

Before this can be done more precisely, we must obtain a general view of the diverse paths that have been taken in the course of the history of theology in order to express God's presence in Jesus. Not all these paths imply Jesus' unity with God. God's presence in Jesus has not always been understood as Jesus' unity with God. The difficult debates of the ancient church about Jesus' divinity were necessary for the understanding of God's presence in Jesus as Jesus' unity with God to prevail. And still in later periods, God's presence in Jesus was understood in ways other than in the sense of unity with him, partially in spite of a formal recognition of the patristic dogma.

When God's presence in Jesus is spoken of in this connection as the extension of the question about Jesus' unity with God, it means that Jesus' relation to God cannot be ascertained by itself apart from the question of how God

115

appears to other men through Jesus. Jesus' relation to other men is the sphere in which the question of his relation to God arises, namely, insofar as he alone exercises God's authority toward the rest of humanity. Thus, from the very beginning the question of Jesus' unity with God involves the presence of God *for us* in Jesus. We must inquire about the way in which God is present to us, to the whole of humanity, in Jesus. Otherwise, the question of Jesus' unity with God cannot be posed at all if this unity is supposed to be found in God's revelation.

The types that will be presented in the following discussion again have the purpose of providing a preliminary survey and a consciousness of the variety of the elements of meaning oriented toward the systematic approach that have been worked out in the history of theology. In the following discussion I will distinguish five different conceptions of God's presence in Jesus.

1. The Presence of the Spirit

Probably the oldest attempt to express God's presence in Jesus was characterized by the concept of the Spirit. Through the Spirit, Jesus is not only connected with particular figures of Jewish expectation, with the prophet of the last times, the Son of Man, the Servant of God, or the Messiah, but directly with God himself. Naturally, no competition is asserted thereby between the concept of the Spirit and these titles; rather, the eschatological figures named were themselves understood as bearers of the Spirit in a special way.

The significance of God's Spirit in primitive Christianity is to be understood primarily from the perspective of the Old Testament and Jewish tradition and only secondarily from the perspective of Hellenistic ideas that modified the Old Testament and Jewish terminology. The Spirit of God had been bestowed upon the charismatic leaders and the prophets in ancient Israel, as well as upon others who received a special commission from Yahweh. According to the predominant Jewish conception, the Spirit no longer worked in the present after the end of the exile, but has been absent since the last prophets in order to be poured out "on all flesh" only in the *eschaton*.[1] Since the time of the prophets, the bringers of eschatological salvation in the future were expected as distinctive bearers of the Spirit of God: the Messiah of the last time (Isa. 11:1 ff.; Ps. of Sol. 17:37; Test. Levi, ch. 18), the Servant of Yahweh (Isa. 42:1 ff.), the Son of Man (Eth. Enoch 49:3; 62:2), and, of course, the eschatological prophet. That is to be understood in the sense that the special capacity and function of the bearer of salvation at the end of time is the effect of the Spirit of God, of whom he will constantly partake.

[1] Corresponding to the promise of Joel 2:28-32 (ch. 3:1-5 in the Hebrew text); cf. Zech. 6:1-8. In Deutero-Isaiah (Isa. 44:3) and Ezekiel (chs. 36:27; 39:29) the promise is referred only to Israel.

Coming from expectations of this kind, primitive Christianity understood Jesus as the bearer of the Spirit. To what extent there were beginnings in this direction in the self-understanding of the historical Jesus, thus to what extent Jesus had understood himself as a charismatic figure, is difficult to ascertain. In any case, the early Palestinian community had recognized in the activity of the pre-Easter Jesus the eschatological prophet whom one found promised in Deut. 18:15 ff., the New Moses who, like the first Moses, was supposed to be not only the mediator of the law but also above all the miracle-working savior.[2] "Because Jesus has appeared as an authoritative teacher and interpreter of the law, but also as a worker of miracles, this concept may even have suggested itself" (p. 382). The tradition of Jesus' baptism and anointment with the Spirit is also originally rooted in this circle of tradition (pp. 396 f.; cf. also pp. 345 f.). The tradition of Jesus' anointment with the Spirit of God, which took place at his baptism, later became the connecting link between the concept of Jesus as the eschatological prophet and the title *Christos*, which at first had only been used eschatologically for the function of the one who would return in power, but which was soon also connected with the earthly Jesus through the passion tradition and could designate his whole activity.[3] Because of his charismatic activity, Jesus was understood in Hellenistic Jewish Christianity as a "divine man," in which the Old Testament designation for the charismatic figures of ancient Israel fused with the Hellenistic evaluation of extraordinary men as "divine," as *theioi anthrōpoi*. In this sense the title "Son of God," which had been used for the resurrected Lord, was also applied to the pre-Easter Jesus. Also for this the Spirit that was given by God was decisive (pp. 297, 299 ff.). At first the "Son of God" concept did not express a participation in the divine essence (pp. 293 f.). Only in Gentile Christianity was the divine Sonship understood physically as participation in the divine essence. In the Jewish, also in the Hellenistic-Jewish, sphere, in contrast, the expression "Son of God" still retained the old meaning of adoption and of God's presence through his Spirit which was bestowed upon Jesus for a long time. In Mark's Gospel the basic concept of Jesus as the epiphany of the Son of God begins, but represents a conversion into the Hellenistic way of thinking. The special "two-stage Christology" of the formula quoted by Paul in Rom. 1:3 f. stands closer to the Jewish way of thinking: Jesus Christ, "who was descended from David according to the flesh and designated Son of God in power according to the Spirit of holiness by his resurrection from the dead." Here the divine Sonship that is established by the divine Spirit has not yet been accorded to the earthly Jesus (although as the Son of David

[2] F. Hahn, *Christologische Hoheitstitel,* pp. 356-371, esp. pp. 360 f. and 380-404. The following page numbers in the text refer to this work.

[3] *Ibid.,* pp. 221 f. on Matt. 11:2-6. On the Messiah's endowment with the Spirit, cf. also Robert Koch, *Geist und Messias* (Vienna: Verlag Herder, 1950), pp. 71-127; esp. about anointing with the Spirit, pp. 124 f.

he already has been chosen for it), only to the exalted Lord. The connection of the Spirit with the resurrection from the dead, which is present here, is inherited from Jewish eschatology, so that "the resurrection of the *Kyrios* and his being equipped with the Spirit belong together."[4] In this way Paul has brought to expression God's presence in Jesus Christ and through him in the believers in connection with Jesus' resurrection and the Christians' hope of resurrection. To be sure, for Paul himself, in distinction from the formula quoted in Rom. 1:3 f., Jesus was already preexistent as the Son of God. This is expressed in the Pauline phrase that "God has sent his Son" (Gal. 4:4; Rom. 8:3). In the Christ hymn quoted by Paul in Phil. 2:5 ff., such a two-stage Christology is connected with the concept of preexistence at the beginning.[5]

The pattern of a double assessment of Jesus, according to the flesh and according to the Spirit, also occurs in the New Testament apart from the Pauline writings in such a way that the Spirit is connected with Jesus' resurrection (I Tim. 3:16; I Peter 3:18). These two passages show, however, that the contrast made in this schema can give expression to different Christological conceptions. In First Peter it does not involve the contrast between the Davidic sonship and the divine Sonship in the sense of the two-stage Christology, but the contrast between Jesus' dying and becoming alive, thus an idea that belongs in the context of the passion tradition. In First Timothy the contrast is that between a path from above to below and, in reverse, from below to above, between the epiphany in the flesh and the justification in the Spirit. Thus, the idea of preexistence lies at its basis, and it involves the descent and the ascent again of the Revealer. The contrast of Davidic sonship and the divine Sonship according to the Spirit-flesh schema, which is suggested in II Tim. 2:8 only with regard to the Davidic sonship, appears in the second century several times in Ignatius of Antioch. Characteristically, however, not only the Davidic sonship but also the divine Sonship, the existence from the Spirit, is related to Jesus' birth here instead of to his resurrection (Ignatius, *Eph.* 18:2; *Smyrn.* 1:1). In place of a two-stage Christology, the double origin of Jesus from God and from man is the center of attention. The Davidic sonship is no longer a preliminary stage along Jesus' path to the full Messianic office, but only an expression for Jesus' concrete humanity. Therefore, Ignatius can also apply the Spirit-flesh schema very generally to the imperishable

[4] I. Hermann, *Kyrios und Pneuma: Studien zur Christologie der paulinischen Hauptbriefe*, p. 62; on the two-stage Christology of Rom. 1:3 f., see G. Bornkamm, *Jesus of Nazareth*, p. 228; Eduard Schweizer, "Der Glaube an Jesus den 'Herren' in seiner Entwicklung von den ersten Nachfolgern bis zur hellenistischen Gemeinde," *EvTh*, XVII (1957), esp. p. 11; F. Hahn, *Christologische Hoheitstitel*, p. 25.

[5] On Phil. 2:6-11, see Günther Bornkamm, "Zum Verständnis des Christushymnus Phil. 2:6-11," *Studien zu Antike und Urchristentum: Gesammelte Aufsätze*, Band II (Beiträge zur evangelischen Theologie, 28; Munich: Chr. Kaiser Verlag, 1959), pp. 177-187. References to further literature will be found there.

divinity and the perishable humanity which taken together constitute the existence of the one Lord Jesus (Ignatius, *Eph.* 7:2).

Loofs has rightly pointed out that the double assessment of Jesus according to the flesh and according to the Spirit provides the root for the doctrine of the two natures in later dogma.[6] This development has been initiated in Ignatius. In Tertullian at the end of the second century the double assessment of Jesus according to the flesh and according to the Spirit has clearly passed over into a doctrine of two "states" or natures. According to Tertullian, the Spirit also has accomplished his work, namely, the demonstrations of power, deeds, signs, just as the flesh did, which has borne his suffering (*Adv. Prax.* 27; *De carne Christi* 13:4).

Still, elsewhere at this time the double assessment of the historical Jesus according to the flesh and according to the Spirit receded behind a way of thinking that started from the concept of the Logos, in order to trace his path into the flesh. The change, in which Christological thought was derived more from John 1:14 than from Rom. 1:3 f., has come about particularly under the influence of the Logos doctrine of the Apologists.[7] This perspective was already the dominant one in Irenaeus' argument for the unity of God and man in Jesus (*Adv. haer.* III, 16 ff.), although the dual point of view is still echoed in the way in which Irenaeus can say of "the gospel": "It knew Jesus Christ, who was born, as the Son of God . . ." (III, 16, 5). Again, in the famous phrase *vere homo, vere Deus* one must still see an expression of the older viewpoint, for immediately before it says: "Thus it was no one else who showed himself to men and no one else who said, 'No one knows the Father,' but it was one and the same" (IV, 6, 7).

Originally, the schema said that Jesus had been installed as the Son of God through the resurrection from the dead. However, even as early as Paul, that did not exclude the concept of a preexistence of the Son of God. The term "adoptionism" has been used for this ancient Christology. However, this designation is not correct for Paul's Christology, which was able to speak about the sending of the preexistent Son of God into the flesh, nor is the Jewish-Christian formula quoted by Paul in Rom. 1:3 f. adoptionistic in the sense of the second century, because the alternative of full divinity for Jesus which arose later could not be in view at that early stage of the tradition.

A tradition that is different from the two-stage Christology, but perhaps even older, in which the concept of the earthly Jesus as the New Moses has been joined to the idea of the Messiah, has connected the gift of the Spirit to

[6] F. Loofs, *Leitfaden zum Studium der Dogmengeschichte,* § 14, 5a, p. 70. See also II Clement 9:5.

[7] A. Grillmeier, "Die theologische und sprachliche Vorbereitung der christologischen Formel von Chalkedon," *Das Konzil von Chalkedon: Geschichte und Gegenwart,* Vol. I, pp. 5-202, esp. p. 31. See also Grillmeier's article "Jesus Christ," *LThK,* V (1960), 941.

Jesus and his installation as the "Son of God" with his baptism by John, not with his resurrection. This concept is present in the Synoptics' account of Jesus' baptism (Mark 1:11 and parallels): the descent of the Spirit upon Jesus is accompanied by the Voice, "Thou art my beloved Son; with thee I am well pleased."

Jesus' endowment with the Spirit is placed even earlier by the Synoptics' stories of his childhood in the legend of his birth. While in Luke the divine Sonship is established by the almighty activity of the divine Spirit upon Mary (Luke 1:35), in Matthew it is apparently thought of even more emphatically in the sense of a supernatural procreation (Matt. 1:18).[8]

All these conceptions—whether the Spirit is associated with Jesus at the resurrection, at the baptism, or at his birth—may presuppose the concept that the Spirit of God is himself preexistent, as is stated expressly in the Shepherd of Hermas by identifying the preexistent Son of God with the Spirit (Sim. 9, 12, 2; cf. Sim. 9, 1, 1; Sim. 5, 6, 5).

Neither are the various early concepts of the way in which the divine Spirit was associated with Jesus to be understood as adoptionistic in the sense of the second-century problem because the question whether the divine Spirit is an independent being, a separate hypostasis, or only a divine power had not yet been raised at all. Only in this question, however, was there opposition between the patristic adoptionism and the doctrine that was established as orthodox that the divine element in Jesus had been a preexistent hypostasis. That Jesus *according to his humanity* had been the Son of God only by adoption had been considered self-evident for a long time in the patristic church.[9] Only in the so-called second adoptionistic controversy in Spain at the end of the eighth century was this understanding definitively repudiated by reference to the virgin birth.

The patristic adoptionism first arose in the second half of the second century from the idea of the divine monarchy and in opposition to the Logos doctrine.[10] In order to preserve the monotheistic character of the Christian faith, theologians did not want to designate Jesus as God alongside the Father. If Jesus were designated God, it seemed that then there must be two Gods, and this idea was rejected with abhorrence. Thus, an abstract, philosophically determined monotheism was the basis for contesting the special divinity of Jesus. Theodotus the tanner[11] acknowledged completely the birth of Jesus of

[8] On this point, see Martin Dibelius, *Jungfrauensohn und Krippenkind* (Sitzungsberichte der Heidelberger Akademie der Wissenschaften, Philosophisch-historische Klasse; Heidelberg: Karl Winters Universitätsbuchhandlung, 1932). In Luke (ch. 1:35c), Jesus' divine Sonship is explicitly established by his miraculous birth. To be sure, as Dibelius stresses (p. 30), it is not thereby conceived as a mythological procreation by the Deity, but as the omnipotent effect of the creative divine Spirit. Cf. pp. 142 f., below.

[9] Hermas, Sim. 5,6,7; 5,2. See F. Loofs, *Dogmengeschichte,* § 14, 5b, p. 71.

[10] See *RGG*, I (3d ed.), 98-100.

[11] F. Loofs, *Dogmengeschichte,* § 17, 2a, pp. 142 f.

the virgin through the Spirit. However, he refused to designate Jesus as a divine being, as "God"; Jesus is only a man filled by the Spirit of God. The older adoptionism is, therefore, the doctrine that the divine Spirit present in Jesus had merely been an impersonal power, not a particular hypostasis alongside the Father.

Barely a century later and in the framework of a more thoroughly elaborated system this doctrine was advocated once again by Paul of Samosata and was condemned at Antioch in 268. Paul of Samosata also emphasized the impersonal essence of the Spirit of God, which had been breathed into Jesus at the baptism. Otherwise, he thought of Jesus' path in the schema of the *homoiōsis theōi* as a progressive assimilation to God, with whom Jesus finally became one through his continual progress toward the good. For Paul of Samosata, Jesus had been different from Moses and the prophets as a bearer of the Spirit only in degree.

In the following centuries the doctrine that Jesus was not a divine person but only a man filled with the Spirit of God could no longer be advocated as long as the Trinitarian dogma remained in force. Nevertheless, the concern of Paul of Samosata had its aftereffect in the subsequent Antiochene Christology, when the doctrine of the Trinity had been formally accepted and the process of the *homoiōsis theōi* was understood as the path of the unification of Jesus with the Logos. Only when the authority of the Trinitarian doctrine disappeared in the modern period, first with the Italian heretics of the late Renaissance in the sixteenth century,[12] was adoptionism advocated again. Concepts very similar to patristic adoptionism have appeared in the eighteenth and nineteenth centuries in Kant, Schleiermacher, Ritschl, Adolf von Harnack, and others. That even here nothing more than an analogy is present follows from the fact that these theologians did not make the Spirit the decisive Christological concept terminologically as was done in the second century.

2. Substantial Presence

With this expression, I designate the dominant understanding of God's presence in Jesus in the patristic doctrine of the incarnation, above all in its Alexandrian strand. According to this, God himself is fully and completely present in Jesus; Jesus Christ is not a mere man, but a divine person. Therefore, whoever participates in Jesus participates in the life of God himself, in his immortal "nature."

The first impulses in the direction of the presence of the divine essence in Jesus are found in primitive Christianity where Jesus' divine Sonship is understood in a Hellenistic way in the sense that a divine being has appeared in the figure of Jesus—a concept that is present wherever one speaks of the

[12] D. Cantimori, *Italienische Häretiker der Spätrenaissance* (1939; German Basel: B. Schwabe & Co., 1949), pp. 8, 27 f., 32 ff., 49, 166 f., 229 f., 233 ff.

sending of the Son of God into the flesh, thus in Paul, but also in Mark's concept of the hidden epiphany of Jesus' divine Sonship in his actions. A second starting point is the Greek translation of the polite form of addressing Jesus as "Lord" (Aramaic, *maranah*) with *Kyrios,* a word that was common in the mystery religions as a divine designation and that also is used in the Greek translation of the Old Testament for the divine name "Yahweh." In this way it became possible to apply Old Testament words that spoke of God to the *Kyrios* of the Christian community.[13] The combined effect of these two impulses has led to the conception of the essential divinity of Jesus. Within the New Testament, John's Gospel probably comes closest to this understanding with the fundamental statement in the Prologue (John 1:1), with the proclamation of Jesus' unity with the Father (ch. 10:30), and with the confession of Thomas (ch. 20:28). However, while even here the Jewish manner of thought about a functional connection of Jesus with God as the Revealer is still perceptible,[14] Ignatius has placed the emphasis clearly on the immortal divine nature of Jesus.[15]

A precise distinction between the substantial presence of the divine nature and the mode of God's presence that we have designated as the presence of the Spirit is difficult to carry out, for the Spirit also is conceived as a divine substance, as essentially divine, even by the adoptionists of the second century. Yet for them the person of Jesus Christ is not essentially "God," but God is present in Jesus only as the power of the Spirit that fills this man. One sees that the adoptionistic concept was close to the old functional understanding of Jesus' unity with God in the event of God's revelation. However, these ideas acquired a different significance by being turned against the assertion of Jesus' essential divinity.

The impression that the divine Spirit, the power of God, was only temporarily, accidentally connected with Jesus, or that its lasting connection with this man had only been something accidental because the one God in the sense of Monarchianism still remained essentially a reality beyond the man Jesus, was only to be overcome if the man Jesus himself was at the same time a divine person and thus substantially divine. With this step, which was made possible by the Logos Christology of the Apologists, naturally, the assumption of more than one divine person necessarily arose, and thus the appearance of having two Gods.

The opposition between substantial presence and mere presence of the Spirit first arose in the adoptionistic controversy. The older Spirit Christology could also have had in mind a preexistent hypostasis that took on flesh in Jesus, as the Shepherd of Hermas and the so-called Second Clement show.

13 References in F. Hahn, *Christologische Hoheitstitel,* pp. 117 ff., as well as generally in all of par. 2, pp. 67-132.
14 O. Cullmann, *The Christology of the New Testament,* pp. 306 ff.
15 Ignatius, *Trall.* 7:1; *Eph.* 15:3; *Smyrn.* 1:1; *Ep. to Polycarp* 3:2.

Here the presence of the Spirit is thought of as the presence of a preexistent Spirit in a thoroughly substantial way.

Interest in the essential presence of God in Jesus led not only to the problem of a plurality of divine persons, but it also had a certain tendency toward Monophysitism. The Monophysite picture of Christ bears most clearly the elements of the deified man. This concept had to become obtrusive when Jesus was understood substantially as God. Yet one of the greatest accomplishments of the patristic Christology was that it confronted the Monophysite deification of the man Jesus. Precisely God's presence in Jesus for humanity, which required the statement of Jesus' unity with God, would be curtailed from the other side if Jesus was not fully and completely man, if the presence of God in him had extinguished his humanity.

3. Mediator Christology

There are Christologies that have no interest at all in the immediate presence of God himself in Jesus—neither accidentally nor substantially—but are simply interested in Jesus' mid-position between God and man. It can be that such Christologies presuppose the doctrine of the unity of God and man in Jesus Christ, but are nevertheless primarily concerned with the independent mid-position of Jesus and less interested in the coincidence of the divine and the human spheres in Jesus. Rather, a third thing, the figure of the mediator, is inserted between these two spheres.

The simplest form of a mediator Christology is that in which the preexistent heavenly being incorporated in Jesus is not God himself but a being that is subordinated to God but which stands higher than man.

Such a concept probably lies at the basis of the Jewish-Christian angel Christology of the postapostolic period.[16] Here the strict Jewish monotheism was steadfastly maintained at the price of not granting full divinity to Jesus. This could be maintained only as long as the principal emphasis was placed on his *mediating function* in the sense, for example, of Philo's hierarchal cosmology. As a being standing between God and man, Jesus was then able to connect God and man, to build a bridge between them.

Also, the Logos Christology had retained a similar structure from Philo for a long time: the structure of a subordination of the Logos under the Father in the sense that the Logos is a being less than the Father in being and essence. Philo characterized the Logos, the world reason, as inferior to God (*De. som.* 7: II, 188; III, 289, 6) because the Logos is not without beginning like God, but has gone forth out of God. In a similar sense the Apologists

---

[16] In addition to M. Werner, G. Kretschmar, *Studien zur frühchristlichen Trinitätstheologie* (1956), pp. 64-124, 161 ff., 220 ff., also designates early Christian concepts that think subordinationally of a hypostasis that is different from God himself as embodied in Jesus by the concept of angel Christology.

called the Logos the first of God's creatures (Justin, *Apol.* I, 21, 1), originating by the will of the Father (Justin, *Dial.* 61, 1 f.; Tatian, *Or.* 5, 1). Origen also thought the same, designating the Logos as the first of God's creatures,[17] while the later church doctrine distinguished sharply between the Trinitarian persons resulting from the nature of God and the creation called into existence through his free will.[18] Origen spoke expressly of a middle position of the Logos between the one and the many, between the God who transcends all becoming and the created things.[19]

This kind of mediator Christology found its classical expression in Arianism, which developed Origen's ideas just mentioned in a one-sided way, abandoning Origen's idea of the eternal generation of the Logos. The rejection of Arianism was primarily motivated by the soteriological interest of the substantial Christology: we can have full community with God through Christ, we can achieve deification, only if he is God in the fullest sense.[20] In this way Athanasius had overcome the understanding of the Logos as a mediate nature (*mesiteuousa physis*) between unbegotten (*agennētos*) and begotten (*genēta*).[21]

The mediator concept was developed in a different form on the basis of the doctrine of the two natures. Although the basic ideas of these doctrines essentially conflict, the concept of the mediator, when connected to the doctrine of the two natures, could come to the fore so strongly that the Christological concept was really determined by it. Medieval Christologies were oriented very strongly to the office of Christ the Mediator.[22] In the Protestant doctrinal tradition, the concept of the mediator came to have central significance especially for Calvin's Christology. However, in distinction from Scholasticism, Calvin understood Jesus' divine-human person, not his human nature, as the bearer of his office as mediator, and in this way he interpreted the doctrine of the two natures itself through the mediator concept.[23]

---

17 Origen, *De princ.* IV, 4, 1 (*GCS* 22, p. 349, 13, with appeal to Prov. 8:22); *Contra Celsum* 5,39; 8,12 (*GCS* [*Origen's Works,* Vol. 2], 19, pp. 43, 22 f., and 239, 10 ff.).

18 Athanasius, *Adv. Arian.,* Or. 3, n. 61 (*MPG* 26, 452 A-C).

19 Origen, *Contra Celsum* 3, 34 (*GCS* [*Origen's Works,* Vol. 1], pp. 230 f.).

20 Athanasius, *De syn.* 51, B (*MPG* 26, 784).

21 See Athanasius, *Adv. Arian.,* Or. 2, 24 ff. (*MPG* 26, 197 ff.); on this, see F. Loofs, *RE,* II (3d ed.), 18, 23 ff.; further, Loofs, *Dogmengeschichte,* § 32, 3b, p. 187.

22 In Thomas Aquinas, *Summa theologica* III, q. 26, the concept "Mediator" appears certainly more in the form of an appendix; on the position of early Scholasticism regarding the concept of the Mediator, see A. M. Landgraf, *Dogmengeschichte der Frühscholastik* (8 vols.; Regensburg: F. Pustat, 1952-1956), Vol. II/2, pp. 288-328.

23 *Calvin: Institutes of the Christian Religion* (1559), 2 vols., ed. by John T. McNeill, tr. and indexed by Ford Lewis Battles (The Library of Christian Classics, Vol. XX; The Westminster Press, 1960), II. xiv. 3: "Those things which apply to the office of the Mediator are not spoken simply either of the divine nature or of the human." How strongly the doctrine of the two natures is molded by the idea of the Mediator in Calvin is seen in the formulations at II. xii, where he says that Christ "coupled human nature with divine"

From this point let us look back again at the language of the New Testament. In primitive Christian writings the concept of the mediator was judged in different ways. Paul had set it in opposition to the Christ event as characteristic for the office of Moses (Gal. 3:20). Hebrews and First Timothy, on the other hand, transferred the mediator concept typologically to Jesus (Heb. 9:15; cf. 8:6; 12:24; I Tim. 2:5).

4. Presence as Appearance

One can speak of God's presence in Jesus Christ as an appearance, or better, as a *mere* appearance, where one finds in Jesus an epiphany of God or of a divine being without, however, accepting as a consequence an identity in essence of this with Jesus. The structural difference from the adoptionistic understanding of the presence of the Spirit clearly consists in the fact that here one finds present in Jesus not only an impersonal power but a hypostasis that belongs to the divine sphere without, however, the idea of an identity with the man Jesus.

The idea of the epiphany of a divine being in Jesus that emerged in primitive Christianity (for example, in the Gospel of Mark) in connection with the Hellenization of the title "Son of God" and other concepts connected with the idea of preexistence had not yet developed into the alternative between essential presence and mere presence as appearance. Only with the Christian Gnosticism was this alternative posed, corresponding to the Gnostic dualism between the heavenly world beyond and the remoteness of this world from God. This dualism, which could not be bridged for Gnosticism, permitted the notion, to be sure, that the heavenly Revealer appears in the earthly figure of the man Jesus, but not in such a way that he had been united with this earthly figure, with a material body, in an indissoluble way. In the Gnostic Christology the divine Revealer was connected only temporarily with a human body and left it again before Jesus' death. Therefore, Gnostic Christology has borne the designation "Docetism" since Irenaeus, because in his judgment it asserted a connection of the Revealer with the man Jesus that was only apparent.

John's Gospel had already developed the concept of the incarnation in opposition to a similar Gnostic Christology: the divine Revealer, God himself, has really become flesh, has also become united bodily with a man. On the same front, Ignatius of Antioch later coined his formulations of the paradoxical unity of the contrasts, of the imperishable and the perishable, of life

(II. xii. 3) or that the incarnation happened "that his divinity and our human nature might by mutual connection grow together" (II. xii. 1). Cf. also II. xiv. 4, where "person" parallels "office of the Mediator."

and death, of inability to suffer and suffering in Jesus. Thus the idea of the substantial presence of God in Jesus, which found its first clear expression in Ignatius, was originally directed against the Gnostic Docetism in which God's presence was that of a mere appearance. Only later was it also directed against the Jewish-Christian Monarchian understanding that only the power of an impersonal Spirit, not God himself, had been present in Jesus.

Gnostic Christology will always be the primary example of the presence of God in Jesus as a mere appearance. A second form of this type, which admittedly has little more in common with the structure of Gnostic Christology than the notion of a unity of Jesus with God that is only temporary, is to be found at the beginning of the third century in the so-called modalism of Sabellius. The modalists desired to preserve monotheism, the oneness, of God under all circumstances. Therefore, they rejected the doctrine of the Logos. Therefore, they could not find the presence of a particular divine hypostasis in Jesus that is permanently different from the Father. Instead of this, Sabellius thought Jesus constituted a particular mode of the efficacy of the one Deity in saving history. The one God worked as Creator until the birth of Jesus, from then until the ascension as the Savior, and since then as the Holy Spirit.[24] This solution has made an impact again and again. In more modern theology it found agreement especially in Schleiermacher. In its *heilsgeschichtliche* character Sabellius' theology certainly shows itself to be Biblically rooted. Its difficulty is that the particularity of the form of the divine activity, of the *oikonomia,* here hides rather than reveals God's essence. According to this view, the particularity of Jesus' figure would be God's veiling, not his revelation.

A third form of the appearance Christology interpreted the Christological formulas as symbols or ciphers for a presence of God in Jesus which, nevertheless, was not conceived strictly as unity of essence. Such conceptions are represented today by Paul Tillich and Fritz Buri.[25] Tillich speaks of "manifestations" of the New Being in Jesus, but rejects the idea of the incarnation, of the substantial unity of Jesus with God (pp. 94 f.). God's revelation in Christ is for Tillich only the high point of the "revelations" of God that are also found everywhere in the history of religions.[26] This means that God becomes transparent through the most varied media, but none of these media adequately expresses his essence, but every medium of revelation at the same time conceals him. Will not the perception of God then necessarily also lead one beyond the figure of the earthly Jesus? For Tillich, Jesus thus is not himself God, but only a symbol for the perception of God.

[24] F. Loofs, *Dogmengeschichte,* § 27, 3b f., pp. 144 f.
[25] P. Tillich, *Systematic Theology,* Vol. II, pp. 95, 121 ff.; Fritz Buri, *Theologie der Existenz* (Bern: Paul Haupt, 1954), pp. 84-93, esp. pp. 89 and 90 f.
[26] P. Tillich, *Systematic Theology,* Vol. I, pp. 106 ff.

5. Revelational Presence

This term indicates a presence as appearance that is not—as is presence as *mere* appearance—set in contrast to the identity of essence, but rather includes the idea of substantial presence, of an essential identity of Jesus with God. However, Jesus' identity in essence with God in the revelatory event is thereby to be understood from the perspective of the functional unity of Jesus with God, which stood in the foreground in the history of the transmission of the Christological titles in primitive Christianity, to the extent that Jesus' relation to God was explicitly reflected upon at all at that time.[27]

That appearance and essence belong together is expressed by the concept of "revelation" as self-revelation. The concept of revelation is predominantly understood in this way in contemporary theology: revelation is not the communication of some "truths" by supernatural means, by inspiration, for example, but it is essentially God's "self-disclosure," as Karl Barth says.[28] The exclusive use of the concept of revelation for God's self-disclosure goes back to German Idealism, especially to Hegel. As I have shown elsewhere, Hegel's concept of revelation may well have been mediated to Barth particularly through Marheineke.[29]

Thus the restriction of the concept "revelation" to the strict sense of self-revelation is modern. It is to be noted above all that the Old Testament and

[27] See O. Cullmann, *The Christology of the New Testament*, p. 306; also, F. Hahn, *Christologische Hoheitstitel*, p. 120.

[28] K. Barth, *CD*, I/1, pp. 362 f. The understanding of God's revelation as self-disclosure, self-revelation, is almost universal in contemporary Protestant theology. Cf. Emil Brunner, *The Christian Doctrine of God* (*Dogmatics*, Vol. I), tr. by Olive Wyon (The Westminster Press, 1950), p. 15; P. Althaus, *Die christliche Wahrheit*, p. 21; O. Weber, *Grundlagen der Dogmatik*, Vol. I, pp. 184, 187 ff.; H. Vogel, *Gott in Christo*, pp. 126 f., 159 f.; Hendrick van Oyen, *Theologische Erkenntnislehre* (Zurich: Zwingli-Verlag, 1955), p. 117. Among British and American writings on the subject, see William Temple, *Nature, Man and God* (London: Macmillan & Co., Ltd., 1949), pp. 299 f., 301-325; Herbert Henry Farmer, *Revelation and Religion* (London: James Nisbet & Co., Ltd., 1954), pp. 27 ff., 51; H. Richard Niebuhr, *The Meaning of Revelation* (The Macmillan Company, 1946, reprinted 1960), pp. 138-156, esp. p. 152 with reference to Wilhelm Herrmann, *Der Begriff der Offenbarung* (Giessen: J. Ricker, 1887), p. 11, and to Albrecht Oepke, *ThD*, III, 573; D. W. Richardson, *The Revelation of Jesus Christ* (4th ed.; John Knox Press, 1957). Only occasionally has the concept of self-revelation been discounted because it does not appear terminologically expressed in Scripture (thus W. Elert, *Der christliche Glaube*, pp. 133 ff.; see also G. Gloege, art. "Offenbarung" in *RGG*, III [3d ed.], 1609-1613, esp. p. 1611).

[29] In more detail, *OaG*, pp. 8 f. Of course, this does not mean that Barth's concept of revelation should be understood exclusively on the basis of Marheineke. It is primarily the motif of God's "self" revelation, that God reveals "himself," in Barth that is derived from Marheineke. Following Barth's own statement for the understanding of other aspects of his idea of revelation, we shall have to think in the first place of W. Herrmann ("Die dogmatische Prinzipienlehre bei Wilhelm Herrmann," *Zwischen den Zeiten*, III [1925], 246-280, esp. pp. 256 f., 263 ff.). Barth had also encountered the motif of "self" revelation in Herrmann (in addition to the writing mentioned in n. 28, cf. Herrmann's *Systematic Theology* [The Macmillan Company, 1927], § 12-14, pp. 34 ff.

the New Testament expressions that are translated by "to reveal" and "revelation" do not have this meaning at all, but were meant as the making known of the most varied sorts of information through inspiration or as the "appearance" of God or of Jesus. Nevertheless, the Old and New Testaments do speak about the subject matter of a self-revelation of God, although it is not terminologically so designated. In the Old Testament this involves especially the so-called *Erweiswort* ("word of demonstration"), formulas that designate the knowledge of Yahweh's divinity as the purpose of the divine activity in history.[30] The more all happenings were perceived in Israel as a single great historical unity, the more the full knowledge of Yahweh became an event that would be possible only at the end of all happenings. Yahweh would complete the entire course of world events, world history, in order that man might thereby know his divinity. Only at the end of history is he ultimately revealed from his deeds as the one God who accomplishes everything.

Correspondingly, Jewish apocalyptic expected God's full revelation as an event of the end time. Terminologically, apocalyptic spoke of the future appearance of God's glory.[31] The concept of the glory of God in the Old

[30] Walter Zimmerli in a series of studies is the first to have pursued these formulas. See esp. *Erkenntnis Gottes nach dem Buch Ezechiel* (Zurich: Zwingli-Verlag, 1954), and "Das Wort des göttlichen Selbsterweises (Erweiswort), eine prophetische Gattung," *Mélanges Bibliques: rédigés en l'honneur de André Robert* (Paris: Bloud & Gay, 1955), pp. 154-164. However, Zimmerli himself finds the idea of God's revelation, God's self-disclosure, expressed not so much in this formula of recognition as in the expression "I am Yahweh," which constitutes the principal part of the formula, but also appears independently (W. Zimmerli, "'Offenbarung' im Alten Testament," *EvTh*, XXII (1962), 15-31; see also his earlier essay, "Ich bin Jahwe," *Geschichte und Altes Testament; Festschrift für A. Alt* (Tübingen: J. C. B. Mohr [Paul Siebeck], 1953), pp. 179-209. Zimmerli's interpretation depends upon his form-critical thesis that the "short form" "I am Yahweh" is more original than the longer formula of recognition and that the former must be understood in its original independence as a "formula of self-presentation" (Selbstvorstellungsformel). This has been questioned by Rolf Rendtorff (*OaG*, pp. 35 ff.). In the short form "I am Jahweh," which "appears without additions only in the strict sacral-law style of the late Priestly Pentateuchal texts and Ezekiel," he does not see the original basic form, but conversely "a reduction of the statement to an expression of the utmost pregnancy" (p. 34). Zimmerli thinks he can challenge this by referring to older texts that contain the short form "so that in any case the argument for a late emergence of the short form is untenable" (*EvTh*, XXII [1962], 20). But on what kind of texts does he rest this argument? They are without exception examples of the formula of recognition "and they will know that I am Yahweh" (e.g., I Kings 20:13, 28). It is very doubtful whether these texts can prove the age of the short form "without additions" in the sense of the "formula of self-presentation," i.e., whether an *originally independent* formula "I am Yahweh" is already presupposed by them. Is it not more probable that these texts represent concisely formulated references to the longer form of the statement that characterizes the name Yahweh more precisely through the use of additional predications? In any case, only statements of the latter type are to be found in the earlier period as *independent formulas*.

[31] See, for example, IV Ezra 7:42: That day will have a special light, "not luster, not brightness, not glow, but only the radiance of the *glory* of the Most High in which all will be able to see that which is determined for them." In Syr. Baruch 21:22 ff., Baruch prays: "Restrain mortality from this mortal nature and threaten therefore the angel of death. May thy *glory* be revealed and thy sublime majesty be known . . . and now quickly make known thy *glory* and delay not with that which thou hast promised." Correspondingly, the

Testament was the only one that designated a revealedness of Yahweh's own essence. In apocalyptic the self-revelation of God and in the New Testament its anticipation in the Christ event is expressed by the concept of the glory of God. To be sure, the concept of the glory of God slips over from the apocalyptic into a dualistic, Gnostic sense in some of the New Testament writings, particularly in the Johannine corpus.

The path should now be indicated in three steps that lead materially from the concept of revelation to the knowledge of Jesus' divinity.

1. The Christ event is God's revelation—the appearance of the glory of God in the face of Jesus (II Cor. 4:6)—only to the extent that it brings the beginning of the end of all things. Therefore, Jesus' resurrection from the dead, in which the end that stands before all men has happened before its time, is the actual event of revelation. Only because of Jesus' resurrection, namely, because this event is the beginning of the end facing all men, can one speak of God's self-revelation in Jesus Christ. Without the event of Jesus' resurrection the ground would be pulled out from under theological statements about God's self-revelation in Jesus Christ.

2. The concept of self-revelation includes the fact that there can be only a single revelation. God cannot disclose himself in two or more different ways as the one who is the same from eternity to eternity. When someone has disclosed himself ultimately in a definite, particular event, he cannot again disclose himself in the same sense in another event different from the first. Otherwise, he has not disclosed himself fully and completely in the first event, but at most partially. Thus either there is always only a partial self-disclosure of God that is perceived under one-sided aspects, or there is in one instance a revelation that certainly is unique by definition, because a plurality again would abrogate its character as revelation.

3. The third factor is closely related to the essential uniqueness of God's self-revelation: the concept of God's self-revelation contains the idea that the Revealer and what is revealed are identical. God is as much the subject, the author of his self-revelation, as he is its content. Thus to speak of a self-revelation of God in the Christ event means that the Christ event, that Jesus, belongs to the essence of God himself. If this were not so, then the human event of Jesus' life would veil the God who is active therein and thus exclude his full revelation. Self-revelation in the strict sense is only present where the medium through which God makes himself known is not something alien to

just will be radiant with glory, i.e., they will be revealed in their alliance with God: Syr. Baruch, ch. 51, esp. vs. 10 and 12; but also Enoch 49:1; 50:1; 62:15. On the prehistory of the ḳābōd concept in Israel, cf. R. Rendtorff in OaG, pp. 28-32, and the literature mentioned there. The finest summary of the apocalyptic idea of God's revelation in the end time, related at the same time to the prophetic word preceding and announcing it, is found in IV Ezra: *Sicut omne quod in mundo fit: initium in verbo et consummatio in manifestatione; sic et mundus altissimi: initium in sermone et in signis et in potentia, et consummatio in actione et in miraculo* (ch. 9: 5). See below, n. 1 to Chapter 5.

himself, brings with it no dimming of the divine light, but, on the contrary, results in the knowledge of the divinity of God for the first time. That happens when the distinction of the revealing medium from God himself disappears with the coming of a more precise understanding. How this can happen without ending in a disastrous alloy of God and man certainly cannot be described in mere abstract conceptions but only in reflection on the concrete relation of Jesus to the Father. The following discussions will be directed to this task (especially Chapter 4, Sec. III, 7).

To begin with, only the identity of God with the event that reveals him claimed in the concept of self-revelation is maintained. If God is revealed through Jesus Christ, then who or what God is becomes defined only by the Christ event. Then Jesus belongs to the definition of God and thus to his divinity, to his essence. The essence of God is not accessible at all without Jesus Christ. God is essentially "the God . . . who gives life to the dead" (Rom. 4:17)[32] because he is the one "who raised Jesus from the dead" (Rom. 8:11). We do not first know who God is and then also something about Jesus, but only in connection with Jesus do we know that the ground of all reality about whom every man inquires, openly or concealed, consciously or unconsciously, is in its real essence identical with the God of Israel. We know this—to repeat it once again—because the end that stands before us and all things has already happened in Jesus as an event produced by Israel's God. The destiny of all that is has already been fulfilled in him.

The identity of the essence of Jesus with God claimed in the concept of God's self-revelation through Jesus has been worked out especially by Karl Barth and has been made the basis of his theology. The demonstration of the connection of Jesus' divinity with the concept of revelation constitutes one of Barth's greatest theological contributions. "If we have to do with his revelation, then we have to do with himself and not, as the modalists of all times think, with an entity distinguished from himself."[33] That is the basis upon which Barth deduces God's eternal essence from the way God appears in his revelation.[34] Barth quite rightly has built the doctrine of Jesus' divinity and the doctrine of the Trinity on the concept of God's revelation in Jesus. To be sure, that has not affected the methodology of his Christology.

The uniqueness of the revelation in Christ which allows no competition beside itself—through a "natural theology," for example—is connected for Barth with the thesis that revelation means the full disclosure of God's essence through this particular, revealing event. Heinrich Vogel was the first

---

[32] Paul here immediately combines creation with the resurrection of the dead: "And calls into existence the things that do not exist." If the creation is in a special way the expression of God's divinity, its true nature is revealed only in the light of the resurrection of the dead, and the latter is revealed in the light of Jesus' resurrection.

[33] K. Barth, *CD,* I/1, pp. 358, cf. pp. 134, 349, 362 f.

[34] *Ibid.,* p. 448; cf. pp. 472, 474, 488, 530.

to represent explicitly the uniqueness of the revelation as a consequence of the concept of self-revelation.[35]

That the entire problem of the concept of revelation and especially of the connection between Revealer and what is revealed in God's self-revelation has been thought through only in more modern theology—indeed, fully only in the present—is probably connected with the fact that the existence of a God in general was self-evident in earlier periods and appeared to be secured by the philosophical proofs for God. One began with such a given concept of God and simply asked how this God could have come into the flesh. Thereby one was already stuck in the middle of insoluble difficulties. Since the destruction of the old theistic picture of the world by the Enlightenment and by Kant, such a procedure is no longer possible.

Even if we maintain, against all atheistic opposition, that man as man can never cease to ask about God and thus to think the idea "God"—regardless of the word by which it may be designated—that still does not mean that one already knows who God is in this way. The idea of God has the character of a question, which man, certainly, cannot escape. It still constitutes no answer such as natural theology repeatedly tried to obtain from it. The answer to man's question about God is received, rather, only through the particular experience of the reality about which the question asks. This always involves an experience of the whole of reality, but it involves this as it appears from the perspective of a definite occasion that produces it, from a definite point of view. Only through the particular experience of reality as a whole is the answer to the question about God, to the question about the origin of my own and all of reality, received. Only in this way does the particular conviction result about who God is, whether this takes place in an appropriate or inappropriate way. Only within the framework of the total experience of reality derived from historical occurrences does the further question pose itself as to whether it is a *correct* knowledge of who God is. And only if God himself is *revealed* in one of the occurrences from which a total understanding of reality is disclosed from time to time is a correct knowledge of God possible at all. For this reason, the problem of revelation has become the fundamental question in modern theology, that is, the only possible basis for speaking about God himself. Therefore, today one must give a precise account of what this step, so characteristic for Barth's theology among others, really means, especially for Christology.

Thus for contemporary theology the central significance of the concept of revelation is closely related to its specific situation in the history of ideas. However, certain Biblical facts only come to view at all from the perspective of this historically conditioned way of putting the question. Primitive Christianity could, of course, presuppose the Old Testament concept of God as

[35] H. Vogel, *Gott in Christo*, p. 204.

self-evident. But for the first Christians it was in no sense self-evident that God was in Jesus. Nonetheless, in the course of the historical development of the primitive Christian traditions it constantly became clearer that the first Christians understood who God is from the perspective of Jesus' history in a new way and really for the first time. Because of this, the Old Testament idea of God became something preliminary, not in the sense that something was added to it, nor in the sense that something completely different had taken its place, but in the sense that in view of Jesus everything previously thought about God appeared in a new light. In this way the reality of God was experienced in Jesus in early Christianity. The consciousness of this went hand in hand with the knowledge of Jesus' own divinity.

The primitive Christian impulses to Christological thought arose "from below," that is, from Jesus' claim to authority confirmed by the Easter event, although the conceptuality of the Son of Man Christology, as well as that oriented to the Hellenistic idea of epiphany, moves "from above to below." The investigation of the development of the primitive Christian Christological traditions shows that the statements presenting Jesus' path "from above to below" have as a basis a motivational context that runs from below to above counter to the sense appropriate to its conceptions. This situation gains special theological importance in the contemporary intellectual situation when the self-evidentness of talking about God has been lost and for which, therefore, the idea of revelation has become even more central than it was in earlier times.

The idea of the revelatory presence of God in Jesus, of a revelatory identity of Jesus with God, which includes identity of essence, will prove more and more clearly in the course of our discussions to be the only appropriate understanding of the presence of God in Jesus. This does not exclude the other types for understanding God's presence in Jesus, but it takes away their significance as guiding points of view for understanding the presence of God in Jesus and permits them to have validity only as aspects of the idea of the revelatory unity of Jesus with God. And even that is the case in different ways for the particular aspects.

The patristic idea of a substantial presence of God in Jesus has become accessible in our century from the perspective of the problem of revelation, insofar as revelation implies identity of essence. In contrast, a mere presence of the Spirit remains just as inadequate as the mere presence of an appearance of a being who is still to be distinguished from his appearance. Revelational identity combines the presence as an appearance and a substantial presence. So far as the revelation of God is perceived in Jesus' human life, however, the presence of the Spirit also retains its right. The mediator Christology remains particularly problematic. Taken independently, it leads to the concept of Jesus as a sort of half God or it lets him become an inconceivable mythological middle being between God and the rest of mankind as a God-man. Therefore, the mediator concept cannot be the leading idea of Christology; it can only receive its meaning within a Christology built on God's revelatory presence in Jesus as an identity of essence, inasmuch as Jesus as the Revealer of God is in fact also the mediator of salvation and of the knowledge of God.

II. JESUS' ESSENTIAL UNITY WITH GOD

In the first section the various possibilities for thinking of the mode of God's presence in Jesus were discussed. This question will be clarified still further when we now turn to the question of the "scope" of God's presence in Jesus' life. If Jesus is God's revelation through a particular event in his life, then did he only become one with God after this event or was he one with God from the very beginning? As we pursue this question, the meaning of God's revelatory presence in Jesus and how it includes Jesus' essential unity with God will become clear.

1. Revelatory Identity and Adoption

Jesus' unity with God himself was expressed in very different ways in primitive Christianity, not only in a multiplicity of traditional titles, among which "Son of God" and *Kyrios* stand out, but also in such a way that these titles were connected with definite events in Jesus' life. This is to be seen especially in the usage of the title "Son of God." One finds the concept of Jesus' destiny to be the future, eschatological Son of God (Luke 1:32 f.; Mark 14:61 f.; I Thess. 1:9 f.), that of an exaltation to be the Son of God in connection with the resurrection (Rom. 1:3 f. and elsewhere), the idea of an adoption as the Son of God at the baptism (Mark 1:9-11), that of a deification at the transfiguration (Mark 9:2-8), the physical basis of the divine Sonship through the generation by the divine Spirit (Luke 1:35), and finally, the idea of preexistence. Do these various conceptions exclude one another in the sense that Jesus either *became* the Son of God only at his baptism, through the particular event of transfiguration, or through his resurrection, or that he already was the Son of God from the beginning, from his birth or even as a preexistent being before his earthly birth? Or can a material relationship among all these conceptions be shown? Certainly, purely on the basis of the various conceptions one may scarcely bring the various statements together into an overall picture. Otherwise, one would misunderstand the varied intentions of the individual texts. Tensions exist between the physical basis of the divine Sonship through Jesus' divine procreation and the idea of the installation as the Son of God through the resurrection, for example, but also between the latter and the corresponding statement about Jesus' baptism, that can hardly be resolved into a unified conception without exegetical violence. But perhaps it is possible to discover a relationship in another way, namely, in the unity of the primitive Christian history of traditions out of which all these Christological concepts have grown. Is it possible to discover in the historical development of the primitive Christian Christological traditions a definite theme that connects the varied conceptions with one another and in which an intrinsic logic that is also apparent to us asserts itself?

Without a doubt the oldest Christian community understood Jesus' resurrection from the dead as the decisive point in the history of his relation to God. Because of his resurrection, Jesus himself was now expected to come again as the Son of Man who would come in the near future.[36] The call "*Maranatha*" (I Cor. 16:22; Didache 10:6) could now ring out at the celebration of the Lord's Supper. This call entered into the character of the original community at table as an anticipation of the *eschaton* in the community with Jesus and now summoned the resurrected Lord for the ultimate, eschatological community.[37] So also, beginning with the inscription on the cross, Jesus was understood after his resurrection as the one destined to be the future Messiah,[38] although he may have rejected the title "Messiah" on earth.[39] In contrast to this strictly eschatological aspect, the concept that Jesus now has already been exalted to be the Lord and Messiah probably belongs only to a later stage of the tradition.[40] However, both conceptions have been formulated from the perspective of Jesus' resurrection, whether one now saw the resurrection as the basis of Jesus' destiny to be the *future* judge of the world and Messiah, or as the basis of the exaltation to Lordship that has already occurred even though it is still hidden in heaven, as is the case in Phil. 2:9 ff. and elsewhere. The incisive significance of Jesus' resurrection for the Christological understanding of his life was expressed especially sharply in the so-called two-stage Christology of Rom. 1:3 f. Here the titles "Son of David" and "Son of God" are related to each other in order in this way to characterize the relation of the pre-Easter Jesus to the resurrected Jesus. The earthly Jesus was not yet designated as "Son of God," but this title was, rather, attributed to him only on the basis of the resurrection and exaltation.

[36] On this, see H. E. Tödt, *The Son of Man in the Synoptic Tradition*, pp. 230, 250 ff., 273, 293 f.

[37] F. Hahn, *Christologische Hoheitstitel*, pp. 95-112, presents the meaning of the call convincingly in this way. Of course, the title *Kyrios* here does not yet have the meaning of a divine predicate.

[38] With this limitation, F. Hahn, *ibid.*, pp. 174 ff., has adopted O. Cullmann's statements with respect to Mark 8:27-33 (*The Christology of the New Testament*, pp. 124 ff.).

[39] Mark 14:61 f.; Acts 3:20 f.; Rev. 11:15; 12:10; Matt. 15:31-46; on this see Hahn, *Christologische Hoheitstitel*, pp. 179-189.

[40] Hahn, *ibid.*, pp. 112 ff. (esp. with reference to Mark 12:35-37a), assigns the conception of exaltation to Hellenistic Jewish-Christianity (cf. also pp. 189 ff.). It is possible, however, that a difficulty for such a sharp separation of this conception from the older layers of the tradition may be found in the fact that, on the basis of Jewish ways of thinking, it must have been at least plausible to imagine that which would be revealed only in the *eschaton* as already a present reality in heaven (in a hidden way).

However, this "adoption" to be the Son of God was preceded by another stage that was distinguished in a particular way, the Davidic sonship. As Son of David, Jesus at the same time had already been designated for the future reception of the honor of the divine Sonship.[41]

To be sure, the expression "adoption" here must not be taken in the sense of the Christological controversies of the second century, because no contrast to a "physical" Christology was intended. To begin with, one was interested only in Jesus' function, not in statements about his nature.[42] In addition, the interest precisely of the two-stage Christology of Rom. 1:3 f. is that even before his resurrection Jesus was already set apart from the multitude of other men by the Davidic sonship. Thus a continuity of the pre-Easter Jesus with the exalted Lord was perceived. With this the theme that dominated the further development of Christology in primitive Christianity has been touched, and certainly—as we shall still see—for reasons that lie in the subject matter itself.

In his *Theology of the Resurrection,* Walter Künneth takes the position that divinity was conferred upon Jesus only through his resurrection, since only through the resurrection was he exalted to be the *Kyrios* (pp. 114 ff.). In doing this, Künneth distinguishes rather arbitrarily between Jesus' divinity and his Sonship. Jesus was already the Son of God previously. However, this title means only "a middle position of Jesus between God and humanity." This distinction between the divinity received through the resurrection (*kyriotēs*)[43] and Sonship is strange, since, according to Rom. 1:4, Jesus receives precisely Sonship through the resurrection.

The emphasis on the significance the resurrection has for Jesus' relation to God is certainly justified. That is the merit due to Künneth's argumentation, especially at a time when this point of view is usually neglected. Nevertheless, the idea that Jesus had received divinity only as a consequence of his resurrection is not tenable. We have seen in our discussion of the meaning of the resurrection event that the character of the confirmation of Jesus' pre-Easter claim is connected with the resurrection. To this extent the resurrection event has retroactive power. Jesus did not simply become something that he previously had not been, but his pre-Easter claim was confirmed by God. This confirmation, the manifestation of Jesus' "divine Sonship" by God, is the new thing brought by the Easter event. However, as confirmation, the resurrection has retroactive force for Jesus' pre-Easter activity, which taken by itself was not yet recognizable as being divinely authorized and its authorization was also not yet definitively settled. However, this has been revealed in its divine legitimation in the light of Jesus' resurrection.

The idea that an event has retroactive force is familiar from legal terminology. Ordinances or laws can be said to have retroactive force. Such a con-

---

41 Cf. F. Hahn, *ibid.*, pp. 259 ff. and 262 ff. on Mark 10:46-52 and 12:35-37.
42 Hahn, *ibid.*, pp. 117, 120, and 294.
43 In his new book *Glauben an Jesus?* Künneth no longer takes up this question.

ception is foreign, however, to the usual ontological thought. Nevertheless, what is said above does not involve something unique about the Christ event that would be ontologically incomprehensible and thus reduced to an empty assertion, but it involves a matter of universal ontological relevance. To be sure, for the concept of essence in the Greek philosophical tradition this aspect remained hidden, because for Greek thought everything has always been in its essence what it is. However, for thought that does not proceed from a concept of essence that transcends time, for which the essence of a thing is not what persists in the succession of change, for which, rather, the future is open in the sense that it will bring unpredictably new things that nothing can resist as absolutely unchangeable—for such thought only the future decides what something is. Then the essence of a man, of a situation, or even of the world in general is not yet to be perceived from what is now visible. Only the future will decide it. It is still to be shown what will become of man and of the world's situation in the future.[44] To that extent it is not a special case that Jesus' essence is established retroactively from the perspective of the end of his life, from his resurrection, not only for our knowledge but in its being. Had Jesus not been raised from the dead, it would have been decided that he also had not been one with God previously. But through his resurrection it is decided, not only so far as our knowledge is concerned, but with respect to reality, that Jesus is one with God and retroactively that he was also already one with God previously.

The character of Jesus' resurrection in its retroactive significance as confirmation has not been considered by those who reject the establishment of Christology on Jesus' resurrection because it would imply that through his resurrection Jesus became something that he previously was not. Thus Ebeling explains a theology that derives "everything from the fact of the resurrection" to be "pseudo-orthodox," since it "conceals the decisive point of view of true Christological orthodoxy: that Jesus did not become the Son of God after his death, but that he, the historical Jesus, was and is God's son."[45] Ebeling may be justified over against the position of Walter Künneth, who has expressly defended the view that Jesus first *became* God through the resurrection. Nevertheless, Ebeling's criticism suffers from the same one-sidedness as the thesis he attacks. Both fail to appreciate the confirmatory character of Jesus' resurrection and thus its retroactive meaning. Ebeling's criticism does not at all affect a Christology that takes its point of departure from Jesus' resurrection, as did the primitive Christian formation of traditions, in such a way that it recognizes the confirmatory character of the resurrection and thus knows *from the perspective of the resurrection* that Jesus was previously one

44 In greater detail, see my treatment of the Israelite concept of truth, "Was ist Wahrheit?" *Vom Herrengeheimnis der Wahrheit; Festschrift für H. Vogel* (Berlin: Lettner-Verlag, 1962), pp. 214-239, esp. pp. 216 ff.
45 G. Ebeling, *Theology and Proclamation,* p. 63, n.39.

with God. Such a Christology is likewise untouched by W. Lohff's objection that a Christology which views Jesus' resurrection as a decisive turning point must understand "the divine Sonship as something imparted to Jesus in stages."[46] On the other hand, Otto Weber has correctly seen the retroactive significance of Jesus' resurrection, at least insofar as it concerns the perception of him: "What becomes evident in the resurrection (Rom. 1:4) has been on the stage from the very beginning."[47] To this one must only add that it had only been on the stage from the very beginning because Jesus has been raised from the dead.

The idea that Jesus' exaltation to participation in the divinity of God was accomplished only through the resurrection is not appropriate because of the confirmatory character that belongs to the Easter event and through which it points back to the pre-Easter life of Jesus. Rather, from the perspective of his resurrection, Jesus is recognized as the one who he was previously. He was not only unrecognizable before Easter, but he would not have been who he was without the Easter event.

The Easter event points back to the pre-Easter Jesus insofar as it has confirmed his pre-Easter claim to authority. Jesus' unity with God, established in the Easter event, does not begin only with this event—it comes into force retroactively from the perspective of this event for the claim to authority in the activity of the earthly Jesus. Conversely, the pre-Easter Jesus' claim to authority is to be understood as an anticipation of his unity with God that was shown by the Easter event. From this point it can appear at first that the origin of Jesus' unity with God is to be sought where his claim to authority arises. This leads to the idea, which is understandable in terms of the history of traditions although it was quickly overtaken by the pre-existence Christology, that Jesus was installed as Son of God through baptism.

Mark's Gospel understood Jesus' baptism in this sense as an act of adoption (Mark 1:9 ff., cf. esp. v. 11). The tradition of Jesus' baptism by John the Baptist, already in a Hellenized form here, was probably originally connected with the ancient Christology that understood Jesus' activity as that of the "prophet like Moses" expected by contemporary Judaism in accordance with Deut. 18:15.[48]

To this extent the tradition involves a prophetic consecration rather than the "Messianic consecration" of Jesus which Bultmann finds described in this piece of tradition.[49] A Messianic note can be heard only in the title

---

[46] W. Lohff, art. "Sohn Gottes," RGG, V (3d ed.), 123.

[47] O. Weber, Grundlagen der Dogmatik, Vol. II, p. 120.

[48] F. Hahn, Christologische Hoheitstitel, pp. 340-346, 396; see also H. Kraft, "Die Anfänge der christlichen Taufe," ThZ, XVII (1961), 399-412.

[49] R. Bultmann, The History of the Synoptic Tradition, pp. 245-254; H. Braun, "Entscheidende Motive in der Berichten über die Taufe Jesu," ZThK, L (1953), 41 (now

"Son of God," which, however, may have in Mark a more general, Hellenistic character, designating Jesus as a Hellenistic miracle worker (*theios anēr*). Matthew, on the other hand, "by the other formulation given to the heavenly voice makes a proclamation of Messiahship out of the consecration of the Messiah," as Bultmann says.[50] That is, in Matthew the Voice from heaven is no longer directed to Jesus but to the bystanders (Matt. 3:17).

If we balance the Christology expressed in the tradition of Jesus' baptism against the two-stage Christology of Rom. 1:3 f., the first thing to catch our eye is that the former seems to be an extension of the tendency to be observed in the latter to see the certainty derived from Jesus' resurrection in continuity with the activity of the pre-Easter Jesus. With more precise observation we must differentiate this impression more exactly. The baptismal tradition probably did not arise initially out of such a projection back into Jesus' earthly life of the knowledge of the divine legitimation of Jesus acquired from his resurrection. If this unit of tradition is connected with the conceptual complex that dealt with Jesus as the eschatological prophet, then it is quite possible that it may have its roots in the pre-Easter period. In this case, after Easter the primitive Christian community simply would have fallen back upon a recollection or a tradition that had already been connected with the question of the origin of Jesus' authority prior to Easter. The decisive significance of Jesus' resurrection only becomes apparent here when one asks how the first Christians could return to such a pre-Easter explanation of the origin of Jesus' authority as still valid in spite of Jesus' failure on the cross. This can be understood only from the character of Jesus' resurrection as the confirmation of his pre-Easter activity, which the crucifixion had radically called into question.

However, the baptismal tradition itself obscures the motif in the history of traditions that made its further transmission in the Christian community possible. It does not speak explicitly of the significance of Jesus' resurrection, but sees Jesus' authority as already established in the reception of the Spirit at the baptism by John. If one takes this tradition as a theological starting point, then cross and resurrection appear as an appendix of only secondary significance. On the other hand, in this way Jesus' unity with God, which is established in his resurrection and its retroactive character, can fall from view. The understanding of Jesus as a "mere man," adopted by God through the bestowal of the Spirit, could have been developed and consolidated in this way in Jewish Christianity.[51] This was the presupposition for the adoptionism of the second century whose specific character was derived from a

also in *Gesammelte Studien zum NT und seiner Umwelt* [Tübingen: J. C. B. Mohr (Paul Siebeck), 1962], pp. 168-172).

[50] Bultmann, *The History of the Synoptic Tradition,* p. 253.

[51] J. Schoeps, *Theologie und Geschichte des Judenchristentums* (Tübingen: J. C. B. Mohr [Paul Siebeck], 1949), pp. 71-116, describes the Christology of the Jewish Christians in its contrast to the belief in preexistence (cf. esp. p. 72). On adoption at baptism, pp. 73 ff.

rejection of an essential unity of Jesus with God. It is understandable that one could fall into this dead end by beginning with the baptismal tradition in isolation, since the motif of the resurrection event which would have led past this impasse remains obscured—in spite of the fact that only the resurrection event made it possible for primitive Christianity to take up the event of Jesus' baptism again as a part of their tradition.

In recent times Reinhold Seeberg wanted to find the "moment of incarnation" in Jesus' baptismal experience: "Under the strong impression of John the Baptist's preaching" Jesus had experienced "in the enormous excitement the breakthrough of the divine Spirit in his soul." "The Spirit of God comes upon him, and he thereby attains the consciousness that he is the elected mediator of the saving Lordship of God for his people."[52] In this thesis we must distinguish two elements that Seeberg combines without further consideration. On the one hand, was Jesus' conviction that he had received the Holy Spirit connected with his baptism by John? On the other, is this proceeding to be designated as the "moment of incarnation"?

The first question not only involves whether Jesus was baptized by John. This is generally regarded as a historical fact. Rather, at issue is whether in receiving John's baptism, Jesus had the experience of an impartation of the Spirit, of an endowment with the Spirit of the end time—in contrast to the normal character of John's baptism. This latter is overwhelmingly contested by critical scholarship. This criticism is at any rate correct insofar as Mark's account of Jesus' baptism in fact may be a legend stemming from the Hellenistic community.[53] The decisive evidence for this judgment is the absolute use of Spirit ("*pneuma*," Mark 1:11). Mark apparently understood Jesus' baptism from the perspective of the Hellenistic community's baptismal practice and its experience of the Spirit and projected the combination of these two moments back into Jesus' baptism. In spite of this, it is not to be excluded that Jesus had known himself to be the bearer of the Spirit of the end time, even though the Synoptic tradition makes remarkably little mention of such a fact. Bultmann says that this idea reaches back at least to the primitive community.[54] According to Käsemann, Jesus also "without doubt" understood himself as the bearer of the Spirit of the end time.[55]

However, where is Jesus supposed to have attained this consciousness? This question cannot be ignored, precisely because the pouring out of the Spirit was expected only at the end of history. Jesus' reception of the Spirit before the beginning of the general event of the end of time can only be connected

---

[52] Reinhold Seeberg, *Christliche Dogmatik* (Erlangen: A. Deichert'sche, 1925), Vol. II, p. 159.

[53] So Bultmann, *The History of the Synoptic Tradition*, pp. 250 f.

[54] *Ibid.*, p. 250.

[55] E. Käsemann, art. "Geist und Geistesgaben im NT," *RGG*, II (3d ed.), 1272-1279, esp. pp. 1273 f.

with a particular occurrence. Can it be connected with Jesus' baptism by John? This assumption has been defended by Johannes Schniewind.[56] More recently the same opinion has been expressed by H. Kraft and Gerhard Gloege.[57] But this assumption is open to the objection that according to Acts 19:2 John's baptism did not involve an impartation of the Spirit. There is hardly reason to doubt that John actually would have understood the baptism that he practiced as a symbolic action pointing forward to the eschatological baptism of the Spirit, as expressed in Mark 1:8 and parallels.[58] Just such a typological relation to the *eschaton* would underscore once again that John's baptism was not generally connected with an impartation of the Spirit.

Must Jesus' baptism by John correspond, however, to baptism otherwise practiced by John? Can it not constitute a special case? One is led to the thought that Jesus' baptism may have been a special matter when one inquires about the relation between the tradition about Jesus as the eschatological prophet and the life of Jesus himself. Did Jesus have anything to do with circles in which such ideas were alive? This is not necessarily contradicted by Jesus' evaluation of John as "more than a prophet" (Matt. 11:9).[59] Rather, such a contrast of the figure of John with the series of the older prophets can be meaningful precisely within the horizon of the prophetic tradition. Jesus' baptism by John could thus be understood in analogy to a prophetic consecration. It would then be distinguished from the Baptist's normal baptismal practice and could have been experienced by Jesus with the consciousness of receiving the Spirit.[60]

To be sure, the idea that John is supposed to have designated someone unknown as his successor causes problems. But this assumption can hardly be avoided if one wants to assign such a special status to Jesus' baptism. Is it thinkable, for example, that Jesus belonged to the circle of John's disciples before he received the general baptism? Or is one supposed to assume that John had baptized him twice, once in the sense of the general baptism and

[56] J. Schniewind, *Das Evangelium nach Markus,* pp. 46 f. Schniewind thinks of some kind of visionary call at the baptism.

[57] Gerhard Gloege, *The Day of His Coming* (Fortress Press, 1963), pp. 124 f. On H. Kraft's interpretation, see n. 60 below.

[58] H. Kraft, "Die Anfänge der christlichen Taufe," *ThZ,* XVII (1961), 401 ff.

[59] R. Bultmann has called attention to the fact that lifting the Baptist out of the series of the old prophets implies a distinction between him and them which makes it appear improbable that the identification of the Baptist with Elijah in Matt. 11:14 derives from Jesus himself. (*The History of the Synoptic Tradition,* pp. 164 ff., and the supplementary remarks.) See also F. Hahn, *Christologische Hoheitstitel,* p. 375.

[60] So H. Kraft, "Die Anfänge der christlichen Taufe," *ThZ,* XVII (1961), 404 f. That Jesus experienced the impartation of the divine Spirit of the end time in connection with his baptism by John can be reconciled with the old tradition that Jesus was installed as Son of God in power through the Spirit only through his resurrection and not before only under the condition that the impartation of the Spirit (experience of the Spirit) and the declaration of "Sonship" in the tradition of Jesus' baptism are to be distinguished, and the latter attributed to the legend.

the second time in the sense of a prophetic consecration? One thus returns to the idea that the event which must be presupposed as the origin of Jesus' spiritual self-consciousness was connected with a "prophetic consecration," to be sure, but still was different from Jesus' baptism and was only seen together with it as a single event under the influence of the Christian baptism with the Spirit.

Even if Jesus had experienced his baptism by John as an endowment with the eschatological Spirit of God, it would not be correct to designate Jesus' baptismal experience as the "moment of the incarnation," as does Seeberg. Even Jesus' being filled by the eschatological Spirit at his baptism or in connection with another event would not be able to justify the conviction that God is revealed in him and thus to form "the moment of the incarnation" of God. That God is revealed in Jesus can only be asserted on the basis of his resurrection from the dead. Judged from this angle, this assertion is valid not only for the period after Jesus' baptism, but prior to that. For the light that falls back on the pre-Easter Jesus from the resurrection involves his person as a whole. Jesus' claim to authority, confirmed by the resurrection—although perhaps originating in the baptism of John—is related to men's attitude toward his person and not to a commission distinguishable from his person. Therefore, Jesus' baptism cannot be understood as the origin of his unity with God, but at most as its first anticipatory unveiling for Jesus himself, and preceding any question about Christological titles. If Jesus as a person is "the Son of God," as becomes clear retroactively from his resurrection, then he has always been the Son of God. Measured by Jesus' revelational identity with God, which is constituted by the Easter event and which implies Jesus' partnership with God's essence, the idea of Jesus' adoption by God says too little. This idea can only express the concept that after a definite point in time it has fallen to Jesus to be God's representative for the world. That may be correct, but it is not enough. For, as Jesus' claim at least implicitly concerned his own person, the resurrection establishes retroactively that Jesus as a person is not to be separated from God in any way and at any time. "Jesus was what he is before he knew about it."[61]

2. Virgin Birth and Incarnation[62]

However one may theologically judge the legend of Jesus' virgin birth from the Spirit of God, one must maintain its concern that Jesus was God's Son from the beginning, that he is therefore the Son of God in person. The light of Jesus' resurrection had to fall back beyond the beginnings of his public

---

[61] P. Althaus, *Die christliche Wahrheit*, p. 440.

[62] On the following, see esp. Martin Dibelius, *Jungfrauensohn und Krippenkind*, and Hans von Campenhausen, *The Virgin Birth in the Theology of the Ancient Church*, tr. by Frank Clarke (Studies in Historical Theology, 2, Alec R. Allenson, Inc., 1964).

activity, beyond his baptism by John, to the very origin of his earthly life as a whole. In distinction from the tradition of Jesus' baptism by John, the legend of his virgin birth may have come into existence at all only out of this interest in the history of the development of traditions. How could Jesus have been inferior to the election from birth that the Old Testament reports for Samson (Judg. 13:5), for Jeremiah (Jer. 1:5), and for the Servant of the Lord (Isa. 49:5)? And had not Isaiah announced the birth of the Messiah from a virgin (Isa. 7:14, LXX, quoted by Matt. 1:23)? The legend probably emerged relatively late in circles of the Hellenistic Jewish community. Paul and Mark were as little familiar with it as was John. Paul even designated Jesus as the one born of a woman in order to express his equality with other men.[63] The concept of the virgin birth tends in exactly the opposite direction; it attempts to find precisely Jesus' uniqueness expressed in the mode of his birth.[64]

Paul, to be sure, is familiar with the notion of a birth without masculine assistance. He mentions it with respect to Sarah.[65] However, he does not apply it typologically to Jesus, but rather to the Christians as heirs of the promise (Gal. 4:28). With John, we perhaps even meet a "polemical allusion" to the concept of Jesus' birth from a virgin.[66]

The legend of the virgin birth is preserved by Luke in an old, originally Aramaic, form and has been only slightly changed by him (Luke 1:26-38).[67]

[63] Gal. 4:4. The birth from woman, like the parallel expression "born under the law," designates the situation common to all men. See von Campenhausen, *ibid.*, pp. 17 f.

[64] The proximity to the motif, known especially from Egypt, that gods customarily practice intercourse only with virgins is clear (Dibelius, *Jungfrauensohn und Krippenkind*, pp. 42 ff., with reference to Philo, *De Cherub.* 49 f.). But Dibelius has rightly called attention to the fine distinction that resides in the fact that the conception of Jesus is attributed to the free, omnipotent activity of the divine creative Spirit (*ibid.*, p. 30, on Luke 1:35, against H. Leisegang). This element removes the Christian legend from the conceptual world of the *hieros gamos*. See H. von Campenhausen, *The Virgin Birth*, pp. 26 f.; on the more recent criticism of Dibelius' differentiation, see the literature cited there, p. 27, n.2.

[65] Gal. 4:23 and 27c,d, 29; on this, see Dibelius, *Jungfrauensohn und Krippenkind*, pp. 29 f.

[66] Thus H. von Campenhausen, *The Virgin Birth*, p. 16, on John 1:13: "A virgin birth in the literal sense, as others had asserted it as regards Jesus, is rather, through the extension of the idea to Christians as a whole, robbed of its meaning and repudiated." Von Campenhausen, however, holds that the problem cannot be decided with certainty. In any case, the conception of Jesus' virgin birth is alien to John's Gospel. The author of the Gospel agrees completely with Philip's greeting of Jesus as "Joseph's son" from Nazareth (*ibid.*, pp. 13 f. on John 1:45).

[67] According to Dibelius, the change affects primarily the comment in Luke 1:27 that Mary was engaged to Joseph: by means of this comment, which does not fit in the context (the tension to the question in v. 34), Luke connects our legend with the other of Jesus' birth in Bethlehem. The latter, however, presupposes that Mary and Joseph traveled together as man and wife (Luke 2:4 f.). Thus here, too, the inserted reference to Mary's status of betrothal makes the impression of being out of place (v.5). Dibelius also holds v. 36 to be an addition with the function of connecting the narrative of Jesus' infancy with that of the Baptist's infancy by means of a reference to Elizabeth, as well as the entire scene of the meeting of Mary and Elizabeth, ch. 1:34-45, 56.

It explains the divine Sonship literally in such a way that Jesus was creatively begotten by the Spirit of God (Luke 1:35). Matthew defends this idea against obvious objections by reporting a special revelation to Joseph about the origin of Mary's pregnancy (Matt. 1:18-25). "Here the opponents' suspicion is refuted by refuting Joseph's suspicion."[68] Besides this, Matthew is primarily interested in the fulfillment of the Old Testament prophecy (Isa. 7:14) in Jesus.[69]

In its content, the legend of Jesus' virgin birth stands in an irreconcilable contradiction to the Christology of the incarnation of the preexistent Son of God found in Paul and John. For, according to this legend, Jesus first *became* God's Son through Mary's conception.[70] According to Paul and John, on the contrary, the Son of God was already preexistent and then as a preexistent being had bound himself to the man Jesus. "When the time had fully come, God sent forth his Son, born of woman, born under the law" (Gal. 4:4).[71]

This is not yet the place to evaluate the idea of the preexistence of the Son itself. That will be the concern of the next section. Here it only involves the relation between preexistence and virgin birth. The significance of the idea of a preexistence of the Son of God for Paul (cf. also Phil. 2:6 ff.) shows that Paul had sensed no opposition between the preexistence of the Son and his public installation into the function of Sonship through the resurrection (Rom. 1:4). On the other hand, the contrast between the idea of the Son's preexistence and the explanation of the divine Sonship by means of the virgin birth is much sharper. It is indeed compatible with the idea of a sonship existing formerly that it only became effective and was revealed at a particular, definite point in the life of Jesus. However, it is irreconcilable with this that the divine Sonship as such was first established in time. Sonship cannot at the same time consist in preexistence and still have its origin only in the divine procreation of Jesus in Mary.

Therefore, it is impossible to conceive, with Karl Barth, the two different ways of understanding the origin of Jesus' divine Sonship as the unity between the secret of the incarnation and the "sign" that points toward it.[72] The virgin birth is precisely not the sign of the secret of the incarnation of the preexistent Son of God (p. 212, *passim*). It does not point toward this secret, but stands in contrast to it in its conceptual structure.

According to Barth, the sign of the virgin birth means "that in the midst of the continuity of the creaturely world, but independently of it, God begins

[68] Dibelius, *Jungfrauensohn und Krippenkind*, p. 25.

[69] H. von Campenhausen, *The Virgin Birth*, p. 26.

[70] F. Hahn, *Christologische Hoheitstitel*, pp. 306 f., emphasizes, however, the adoptionist character of v. 35b. Even Jesus' creation by the Spirit was at first a mode of adoption.

[71] On the conception of the "mission" of the Son, cf. also Rom. 8:3; John 3:13 ff.; I John 4:9 f.

[72] K. Barth, *CD*, I/2, § 15,3: "The Miracle of Christmas" (pp. 172-202). The following page numbers in the text refer to this volume.

with himself with regard to our understanding of his deed as well as with regard to his deed itself" (p. 199). Only God himself is the author of his revelation. "Mary's virginity in the birth of the Lord is the negation—not of man before God, but of his possibility, of his aptitude, of his capacity for God" (p. 206). Man participates here "only in the form of the unwilling, nonaccomplishing, noncreative, nonsovereign man, only in the form of the man who can only receive, who can only be ready, who can merely allow something to happen to and with him" (p. 209). Therefore precisely the man had to "be eliminated here" (p. 212). With such an argument does not Barth find himself already on the path of Roman Mariolatry? This question should be considered with calmness, without thinking that thereby one would be finished with the evaluation of Barth's presentation. Even Mariolatry can, of course, contain intentions that must be taken seriously by one who stands critically over against the dogmas of Mary in the Roman Church. One can hardly ignore the fact that Barth's understanding of the virgin birth moves along the line of Mariological thought. Indeed, he speaks expressly of a special "aptitude of the woman" for the symbol of the "man who merely receives" (p. 213). One should note that this intention does not appear in the Biblical legend of the conception of Jesus by a virgin. The Biblical legend seeks to express that from his birth onward Jesus has been God's Son because *through* his birth he is God's Son. It is, thus, directed toward Jesus, not toward Mary. In Luke it is still completely "open to what extent it was necessary or appropriate for the birth of God's Son to exclude precisely the man and to elect an untouched virgin."[73]

Except for a phrase in Justin (*Dial.* 100, 4), Irenaeus was the first to elevate the figure of Mary in this connection by seeing her as the representative of the whole of humanity. The believing obedience of Mary stands over against the disobedience of Eve.[74] The comparison between Eve and Mary became the principal source of Mariological speculation in the following period. In this comparison an element of meaning is to be recognized beyond and independent of the somewhat schematic-sounding typological antithesis: here Mary attains independent significance as the symbol of the new humanity dedicated to God in faith. In the following period, the more Jesus was seen at the side of God as the representative of the divine redemptive will toward men and the less he was seen at the same time as the representative of man before God, the stronger the accent had to be that fell upon the figure of Mary as

[73] Hans von Campenhausen, *KuD,* VIII (1962), 3, continues: "This appears in the New Testament rather as a simple given, receiving no further theological penetration."

[74] On Irenaeus, *Adv. haer.* V, 19, 1, and III, 22, 4, see H. von Campenhausen, *The Virgin Birth,* pp. 38 f.: "It goes without saying that Irenaeus did not take Mary into account for her own sake in discussions such as these, and had no wish to attribute to her anything like active participation in the work of redemption. The whole range of ideas is oriented Christologically; it is Mary's first-born who has alone compensated for the ancestor's guilt." On Justin, see *ibid.,* pp. 41 f.

the personification of believing humanity. Conversely, the more Jesus himself in his humanity was seen as simply man before God, the less the figure of Mary needed to appear as the bearer of a fully independent principle.[75]

Nevertheless, believing humanity, the church, is to be perceived precisely in its distinction from Jesus Christ also, and here a particular possibility for its symbolic representation in the figure of Mary remains open. Because Mary, in distinction from Jesus, is not one with God, she can be understood in a particular way as the prototype of man under the free grace of God, as Luther has presented her in his exegesis of the Magnificat.[76]

Here we have to recognize an element of truth in the Roman veneration of Mary and Mariological speculation, in spite of all our bewilderment at the exotic growths that have flowered here and there. Mary can be the symbol of humanity receiving the grace of God in faith in contrast to the old humanity symbolized by Eve, and thus also the symbol of the church in its relation to God. From this point of view we follow with some understanding the efforts in contemporary Catholic theology that seek to understand the figure of Mary, from the perspective of her relation to the church against the background of the typological relation to Eve, as the representation of the church, of the new humanity, in Mary.[77]

It would be a very helpful contribution toward the clarification of the question of Mary and of the objections repeatedly raised from the Protestant side against the increasingly developed parallelism of Mary with Christ that stands between the confessions if the fundamental formal distinction between

[75] In this light it is especially questionable to declare that the idea of motherhood is the fundamental principle of Mariology as has been done by G. Roschini (*Mariologia*, 4 vols. [Rome, 1947-1948]; quoted from the 2d ed., Vol. I, p. 337, according to A. Müller, "Fragen und Aussichten der heutigen Mariologie," *Fragen der Theologie heute*, ed. by J. Feiner, J. Trütsch, F. Böckle [Einsiedeln: Benziger Verlag, 1957], p. 310).

[76] *WA* 7, pp. 544 ff. In this connection Luther emphasizes that one should not present and honor Mary for her own sake, but let her call attention to God and his grace, because precisely Mary "still is supposed and gladly wants above all to be an example of God's grace, to attract the whole world to divine grace, confidence, love and praise" (*WA* 7, p. 569, 18-20). At the end of this text, Luther does not hesitate to petition from Christ the right understanding of the Magnificat "through the intercession and will of your dear mother Mary" (*WA* 7, p. 601, 11).

[77] Thus A. Müller in the essay cited in n. 75, esp. pp. 308 ff., with references to similar efforts by O. Semmelroth, H. Köster, H. Rahner, K. Rahner, as well as in French Mariology ("Marie et l'Église, I-III," *Bulletin de la Société Française d'Études Mariales,* Paris, 1951-1953). K. Rahner says, "Mary is the one consummately redeemed through grace, the one who most perfectly realizes and represents what the grace of God effects in humanity and in the church" (*Rech. Sc. Rel.,* XLII (1954), 503, quoted by Müller in the essay cited above, p. 311). See also the volume of essays, *Die heilsgeschichtliche Stellvertretung der Menschheit durch Maria,* ed. by C. Feckes (1954), esp. H. M. Köster, "Die Stellvertretung der Menschheit durch Maria: Ein Systemversuch," pp. 323-359, esp. pp. 341 ff. In opposition to a *mediatorial* substitution that applies only to Jesus, Köster wants to affirm a *membral* substitution for Mary, by which the representative is himself "a member of the whole," i.e., of the community which he represents (p. 335). However, this distinction remains questionable because one must also assert of Jesus primarily this membral substitution, as will be shown in the second part of this Christology.

Christological statements and Mariological statements would be worked out clearly. What A. Müller says about the coredemptive suffering of Mary under the cross is probably valid of Mariological thoughts as a whole: they belong "more to symbolic than to scholastic-conceptual thinking."[78] The statements about Mary have essentially symbolic significance, insofar as the humanity favored by God with grace, the church, finds itself represented in the figure of Mary. What is to be said about the church in its relation to God cannot thereby be understood as *mediated* through Mary. To do so does violence to the uniqueness of the position of Jesus Christ. The relation of the church to God can at most be symbolized by means of an individual person in the figure of Mary.

The Mariological statements—independent of the question whether they are to be judged as true or false—are not the interpretation of a historical event in terms of its inherent significance, as Christological statements are. In Christology the statements about Jesus as the representative of man before God are the consequences of the fact that Jesus is the revelation of God because of his resurrection from the dead. Also, the statements about the universal significance of Jesus' humanity, as we will deal with them in Part Two, involve unfolding the historical particularity of Jesus. It is not accidental, on the contrary, that the root of the Mariological statements is a legend, the legend of the virginal conception of Jesus, even though this legend originally did not have a Mariological but a Christological scope, as we have seen. Christologically, the legend of the virgin birth has only the significance of a preliminary expression for a fundamental element of the revelatory event, namely, that Jesus was the "Son of God" from the very beginning. It is preliminary because the ultimate expression of this interest is found in the conception of preexistence, which cannot be connected without contradiction conceptually with the original motif of the virgin birth. The significance that later accrued to the birth from a virgin, in the struggle against the Gnostics of giving witness to the reality of the incarnation, does not depend upon its character as a virgin birth but would be even better preserved by a normal birth.

Thus the legend is Christologically justified only as the expression of a passing stage in the primitive Christian development of tradition. It has, however, become the permanent point of departure for the formation of Mariological ideas. This point of departure, the attitude taken by Mary toward the announcement of the angel, is symbolic in nature from the beginning. The connection of Mary with Eve and with the church, which determines the further course of Mariological thinking, also bears a symbolic stamp. Only in view of this basically symbolic structure of the Marian doctrine can its defenders regard the silence of the New Testament about this matter as

[78] A. Müller, in *Fragen der Theologie heute,* p. 315.

146

tolerable. This silence would be intolerable if Mariolatry involved the historical ground of salvation itself, for then the ground of salvation would not be completely accessible in the primitive Christian witnesses. Indeed, it would have been even insufficiently known to the primitive Christian witnesses, who certainly intended to point again and again to the events that are fundamental for human salvation. If one notes the symbolic character of the conceptions about Mary, then one can assert that primitive Christianity has in fact witnessed to the subject matter itself, even where it did not know its symbolic expression through the figure of Mary. Furthermore, from our point of view, it is understandable that Mariolatry has worked with unparalleled productivity in the history of piety without a sufficient historical basis and even to a great extent without an old tradition. In Mariolatry the church has not, as in Christology, pursued the inner logic of a historically given starting point, but has sought repeatedly to express its own essence in the figure of Mary. This distinction should certainly suggest the fact that there can be no Marian dogmas in the sense that there are Christological dogmas upon whose acceptance or rejection the salvation of the individual depends. For the same reasons, no dogmatic necessity can be ascribed to Mariological statements. To place them parallel to and on an equal level with Christological statements, which in their structure are grounded differently, remains theologically objectionable, because the uniqueness of the history of Jesus Christ, which is decisive for the saving significance of the revelation, is thereby prejudiced.

We have shown that Karl Barth finds himself on the path of Mariological reflection[79] with his explanation of the virgin birth as a sign that God grants man a share in his revelation only in the form of one who "merely receives" (p. 209). Barth in no way avoids this tendency with the stipulation that human virginity becomes "a sign not by virtue of its nature, not from itself, but only through divine grace itself" (p. 210). For, naturally, the Roman Mariolatry also understands Mary's election as an effect of God's unmerited grace, and for Barth also human virginity as such in distinction from the masculine nature apparently possesses an "aptitude" (p. 213) for serving as a sign of unmerited grace.

Barth's train of thought is meaningful in its basic intention if one understands the figure of Mary and her attitude in the legend as a symbol, as a "sign" for the man who receives God's revelation. But his formulations never-

---

[79] Thus, in addition to H. Asmussen (*Maria: Die Mutter Gottes* [Stuttgart: Evangelisches Verlagswerk, 1950], pp. 16 ff., 33 f.) and W. Stählin (*Maria die Mutter des Herrn: Ihr biblisches Bild* [1951]), Köster can also name Karl Barth (*CD*, I/2, pp. 194-195) as Protestant witnesses in support of the assertion that the idea of ("membral") substitution for humanity by Mary expresses a matter which "resides inescapably in the preaching situation pictured in Scripture," even though it is not expressly formulated in Scripture (p. 357). This can be conceded, but one must emphasize the legendary character of this "preaching situation" of the angel in confrontation with the mother of Jesus without harming the symbolic content of this scene.

theless become unacceptable where they appear as arguments for Jesus' coming into existence without male assistance, for example, where for dogmatic reasons historical reality is supposed to be ascribed to the individual elements of a legend that is to be interpreted from its scope.

One may say that the receptivity accepted in the traditional stylization of the behavior of the sexes as characteristic for the behavior of the woman "fits" better as a parable of man's situation in relation to God's saving activity than the "masculine" behavior in the creative organization of the world. However, the latter can with good reason be seen as the expression of man as created in the image of God. But in no case can it be asserted that the path of divine grace in actual history was, so to say, shorter to woman than to man. However, such a conclusion could hardly be avoided if a virginal conception of Jesus is presented as necessary with ideas of the sort that Barth offers. This conclusion would turn the Reformation's *sola gratia,* whose personification Mary can represent symbolically, as she did for Luther, into its exact opposite. That man, whether male or female, is equally dependent upon God's grace can be upheld only if one sees all men in the same way destined for God, but also fallen into God's judgment upon sin, no less in their receptivity than in their creative activity. Thus one cannot and may not say that in the reality of the divine work of revelation the masculine "must be eliminated."

It is another question whether the conventional, typical picture of feminine behavior is more appropriate as a symbolic expression for man's reception of the divine work of revelation than that of masculine behavior. Even Barth speaks of a "sign." He does not, however, consider sufficiently that this does not directly involve a sign established by God but a sign shaped by men in the form of a legend. Consequently, he also does not see the distinction between the symbolic power of the picture and the question about the real course of events. This distinction is, however, constitutive for the purity of the picture of Mary itself, that is, for the picture of Mary as the example of man who can only accept the grace of God, who can do nothing about it on his own initiative. As soon as one attempts to establish by dogmatic arguments why Jesus could only have been born of a virgin, the purity of just this picture is spoiled.

Paul Althaus has rightly rejected three paths of dogmatic legitimation of the virgin birth as theologically unusable. First, it is "absolutely forbidden to conceive the human fatherhood as competition for the divine."[80] Second, the virgin birth may not "be treated as the condition for the sinlessness of Jesus."[81] Barth, who defends this connection against Schleiermacher, Althaus, and Emil

[80] P. Althaus, *Die christliche Wahrheit,* pp. 442 f.

[81] H. von Campenhausen has called attention to the fact that Ambrose was the first to relate the virgin birth to original sin so that for him Mary "becomes the means of guarding Christ himself from all defilement by original sin" (*The Virgin Birth,* p. 79).

148

Brunner (p. 207), would logically have to accept the Roman dogma of the immaculate conception of Mary. For, otherwise, Jesus would have had a share in the sin of humanity through Mary just as he would have through a human father.[82] Third, Althaus correctly turns against placing the virgin birth on the same level with Jesus' resurrection. Unfortunately, Barth is also incorrect on this score (p. 199). Against this it must be said in the first place that the basis for the historical evaluation of these two "miracles" at the "entrance" and "exit" of Jesus' life, as Barth calls them, are totally different. The story of the virgin birth bears all the marks of a legend that has been constructed out of an etiological interest, namely, in order to illustrate the title "Son of God." It is therefore highly probable that the story is to be judged as non-historical. On the other hand, the traditions of the resurrection, as well as that of Jesus' empty tomb, are of a completely different sort: where they have undergone legendary influence, something recognizably historical has been expanded in a legendary way. In the second place, the legend of his virgin birth is scarcely comparable in significance to the message of Jesus' resurrection in primitive Christianity. "There has never been a message about the Christ that was not an Easter message, certainly, however, there can be witness to Christ and faith in Christ without the virgin birth."[83]

Emil Brunner goes even farther than Althaus in the rejection of the virgin birth: "If it be true that Matthew and Luke are simply dealing with the question: how did the Person of the Redeemer come into existence? and not with the Incarnation of the Eternal Son of God, this is a Christological view which the Church cannot accept."[84] In fact, the patristic confession also picked up the legend only in a new interpretation, in connection with the concept of the incarnation. This connection, however, does not correspond to the intention of the texts in Luke and Matthew. Therefore, here, beyond the historical assessment of these texts as legends, an alternative may be established between the virgin birth and the concept of incarnation.

Theology cannot maintain the idea of Jesus' virgin birth as a miraculous fact to be postulated at the origin of his earthly life. To that extent it is problematic that the virgin birth found entry into the Apostles' Creed. Certainly, the concept has in the creed as well as in the Christological conflicts of the patristic church two functions that dogmatically cannot be given up but that can be handled more adequately in another way.

In the first place, we have the antiadoptionistic thought that Jesus had been what he is from the beginning as God's work alone. This is expressed in the phrase "conceived by the Holy Spirit" in the Apostles' Creed. Equally un-

82 It is difficult to understand how, under these conditions, the virgin birth is nevertheless supposed to be meaningful as the *designation* of Jesus' sinlessness, although not as the *reason* for it.

83 Althaus, *Die christliche Wahrheit*, p. 443.

84 E. Brunner, *The Christian Doctrine of Creation and Redemption*, p. 353.

relinquishable is the antidocetic point of view in the phrase "of the Virgin Mary" that Jesus' origin, his birth, was a truly human event. This latter interest, along with the concern for the proof from Scripture for Jesus' birth, dominated the theological presentations in the first centuries after Ignatius.[85] Only for the sake of this twofold antidocetic and antiadoptionistic tendency is it tolerable for our contemporary judgment that the virgin birth has its place in the liturgical confession of the church. As a theologoumenon it cannot, however, be counted as an ultimate expression of the theological concern safeguarded in it, for historical as well as for dogmatic reasons. There is the contradiction of preexistence which the patristic church apparently did not notice. In addition, the interest of patristic theology in the virgin birth as an especially "conclusive" proof for the validity of the Old Testament prophecy no longer has any weight for us, since we know that the concept has nothing to do with the literal meaning of the Hebrew text, Isa. 7:14. Nevertheless, because the intention of the creed's formulations is to be sought precisely in their antidocetic and antiadoptionistic function, the creed, even with the formulation "conceived by the Holy Spirit, born of the Virgin Mary," can be confessed in worship without abandoning truthfulness. The repetition of a confession of the church is certainly something different from the statement of faith of an individual. Whoever joins in the confession of the church confesses the unity of Christianity through time by placing himself in the context of the intentions expressed in the formulations, even where the mode of expression must be perceived as inappropriate. We must also maintain the continuity with the antidocetic and antiadoptionistic function of the formulation in the Apostles' Creed. Nevertheless, theologically we shall find this intention expressed better by the concept of the incarnation than through that of the virgin birth.

3. The Truth of the Concept of Incarnation

As we have seen, Jesus' unity with God in the revelatory event of his resurrection from the dead can be understood only as his unity with God's eternal essence, so that the eternal divinity of God cannot be appropriately conceived except in relation to Jesus of Nazareth. Jesus' unity with God, insofar as it belongs to God's eternal essence, precedes, however, the time of Jesus' earthly life.

From the idea of revelation we attain access to the understanding of the old concept of Jesus' preexistence. At least this concept appears as a meaningful *expression* for a material concern that we, too, must retain, namely, for Jesus' full and complete affiliation with the eternal God. Jesus' revelational unity with the God who is from eternity to eternity forces us conceptually to

[85] See von Campenhausen, *The Virgin Birth*, pp. 29 f., 34 f., 47.

the thought that Jesus as the "Son of God" is preexistent. This is true even if we must characterize the idea of preexistence taken by itself as a mythical concept.

We have mentioned that Paul presupposed the preexistence of the Son (Gal. 4:4; Rom. 8:3). With the help of this idea, Paul conceived the destiny of Jesus as a path of the Redeemer from heaven as the dwelling place of God downward to the earth and back again to heaven. This Christological pattern of descent and ascent was current in the pre-Pauline Hellenistic community. The Christ hymn in Phil. 2:6-11 shows that.[86]

But how was such a transformation of the original faith in Christ possible? How did Jesus, exalted through the resurrection from the dead, become the preexistent divine being descending from heaven? This remains to the present a chief problem of the history of primitive Christian traditions.

This question can no longer be simply answered with a reference to the influence of the "Gnostic redeemer myth."[87] After Carsten Colpe's book *Die religionsgeschichtliche Schule: Darstellung und Kritik ihres Bildes vom gnostischen Erlösermythos,* it must be considered very questionable whether in the pre-Christian period there had been a complete redeemer myth that was then merely transferred to Jesus. Although the later Christian, Egyptian, Mandaean, Manichaean, and Islamic forms of Gnosticism undoubtedly possess pre-Christian roots, it is nevertheless possible that the figure of the Redeemer within primitive Christianity came into existence from genuinely Christian motives and within the conceptual horizon of the Jewish sphere of tradition. One may not, however, think that all non-Christian Gnosticism was influenced by Christianity but must reckon with the possibility of multiple origins of the Gnostic idea of the Redeemer that are independent of one another. Under these circumstances we may not answer the question about the origin of the primitive Christian concept of the descent and return of the Son of God to heaven simply with parallels in the history of religions, but must seek the basis for the development of this concept in the tradition about Jesus itself. The Hellenistic concept of a divine being active from time to time on earth may have offered no more than a point of contact that secured an understanding of the Christian message, which originated independently in the Hellenistic world—while admittedly leaving it open to misunderstanding as well. Here, too, in the ascent of Jesus to the Father, we will seek the

---

[86] Among the many exegetical studies of Phil. 2:6-11, Ernst Käsemann, "Kritische Analyse von Phil. 2:5-11," *ZThK,* XLVII (1950), 313 ff., now *Exegetische Versuche und Besinnungen,* Vol. I (Göttingen: Vandenhoeck & Ruprecht, 1960), pp. 51-95, and G. Bornkamm, "Zum Verständnis des Christushymnus Phil. 2:6-11," *Studien zu Antike und Urchristentum,* pp. 177-187, deserve special attention.

[87] This idea is normative for R. Bultmann's picture of the comparative religious environment of primitive Christianity. See, for example, *Theology of the New Testament,* Vol. I, § 15, pp. 175 ff. Against the assumption of a fully developed pre-Christian Gnosticism, cf. also the brief remarks in Carsten Colpe's article "Gnosis I. Religionsgeschichtlich," *RGG,* II (3d ed.), 1648-1652.

point of departure for the emergence of our Christological concept in his resurrection from the dead. The concept that this ascent was preceded by a descent was close at hand as soon as one was convinced of the preexistence of Jesus' person.

The idea of preexistence was close at hand in the Jewish sphere of tradition in the various titles of the divine envoy expected for the end of history. Thus the Son of Man was thought of here and there in apocalyptic as a preexistent heavenly being (Enoch 39:6; 40:5; 48:3,6; 62:7; IV Ezra 13:26,52). A descent of the Messiah from heaven and his return seems to have been thought of similarly in Syr. Baruch, ch. 29 f. A different strand of the idea of preexistence is associated with the Wisdom speculation (Prov. 8:22 ff.; Sirach 24:3 ff.; Enoch 42:1-3).[88] But the origin of the New Testament idea of preexistence seems to have had little to do with either of these two starting points. In the Synoptic tradition the Son of Man does not appear as a preexistent being.[89] Nor did the Wisdom interpretation of Jesus' activity (Matt. 11:25 ff.) lead at once to the concept of preexistence. This happened only with the Logos concept in the Gospel of John (John 1:1 f.), which comes close to the idea of preexistent Wisdom and is perhaps related to Philo.[90] Alongside this, the understanding of Jesus, stamped by Wisdom, as the image of God probably contributed to the idea of preexistence.[91] In any case, the idea of preexistence was primarily connected with the idea of the Son of God by relating the concept of Jesus' being "sent," which may have had at first only the sense of a commissioning,[92] to Jesus' birth. This is the case in the Pauline texts Gal. 4:4 and Rom. 8:3.[93]

How is the development of the concept of preexistence to be judged, especially in the light of the designation of Jesus as the Son of God? We have seen that this title was originally used after Jesus' resurrection for the One who was to come again in Messianic Lordship. Then it was used also for the present, hidden Lordship in heaven, and finally also for the earthly activity of Jesus in connection with the baptismal tradition, and even for the entirety of his earthly life from birth onward. In this process in the history of traditions the recognition of the fact that Jesus belongs to the sphere of

[88] On this, see Ulrich Wilckens, *Weisheit und Torheit: Eine exegetisch-religionsgeschichtliche Untersuchung zu I. Kor. 1 und 2* (Beiträge zur historischen Theologie, 26; Tübingen: J. C. B. Mohr [Paul Siebeck], 1959), pp. 160 ff., 180 ff.

[89] H. E. Tödt, *The Son of Man in the Synoptic Tradition*, pp. 284 ff.

[90] C. Colpe has convinced me of the probability that, now that the theory of Gnosticism in the form in which it appears in Bultmann must be held to be severely shaken (cf. Colpe's criticism of Reitzenstein in *Die religionsgeschichtliche Schule: Darstellung und Kritik ihres Bildes vom gnostischen Erlösermythos* [Göttingen: Vandenhoeck & Ruprecht, 1961]), the question of the relation of the Johannine Logos to Philo must be reopened under a new point of view.

[91] Col. 1:15. Cf. Wisd. of Sol. 7:26. See also J. Jervell, *Imago Dei* (1960), pp. 171 ff.

[92] See the presentation by Karl Heinrich Rengstorf in *ThW*, I, 397 ff.; *ThD*, I, 398 ff.

[93] Cf. also Heb. 1:2 f. and Mark 12:37. On this, see most recently F. Hahn, *Christologische Hoheitstitel*, pp. 260-262.

God, which was established through the revelatory character of his resurrection, expresses itself. Viewed from the confirmation of Jesus' claim by his resurrection, the inner logic of the matter dictates that Jesus was always one with God, not just after a certain date in his life. And in view of God's eternity, the revelatory character of Jesus' resurrection means that God was always one with Jesus, even before his earthly birth. Jesus is from all eternity the representative of God in the creation. Were it otherwise, Jesus would not be in person the one revelation of the eternal God. We can no longer think of God in his eternal deity without Jesus. That is, indeed, the meaning of Jesus' resurrection.

In the transmission history of the title "Son of God" in primitive Christianity it becomes especially clear how the idea of preexistence was developed from Jesus' resurrection and the understanding established by this that Jesus was the coming Messiah, the Son of God.[94] The idea of a "sending" of the Son, which we meet in Paul, was probably originally implied in the idea of preexistence. Since the "descent" of the preexistent Son of God from heaven always stood in relation to an "ascent" in the form of the message about Jesus' resurrection and ascension to God, we have the picture of the descent and ascent of the Redeemer that is familiar from later Gnosticism, as well as from the church's doctrine of the incarnation.

Thus even the remolding of the Christian message into a form that was understandable and attractive to Hellenistic thought may not be attributed only to a Hellenistic "influence," to an infiltration of alien elements into what was originally Christian. In the history of ideas absolutely nothing is clarified and understood by the phrase: this or that has "influenced" something or other. The history of ideas is not a chemistry of concepts that have been arbitrarily stirred together and are then neatly separated again by the modern historian. In order for an "influence" of alien concepts to be absorbed, a situation must have previously emerged within which these concepts could be greeted as an aid for the expression of a problem already present. This preceding situation that first made an "influence" possible must be ferreted out if one wants to understand the change of a concept in the course of history. It is also certainly possible that as the result of the superficial illumination of one's own intellectual situation, alien concepts that are only half understood can be haphazardly taken over. In this case there is often a grave loss of the substance of the original heritage. But such is hardly the case in the matter at hand.

The representation of the Christ event as the descent and reascent of the Redeemer hardly involves a Gnosticizing reinterpretation that misconstrued the Jewish tradition and that would be explained as a lack of understanding for the original meaning of the Christian message. Rather, the resurrected

---

[94] For the relation between the titles "Son of God" and "Messiah," see *ibid.*, pp. 284 ff.

Lord's essential unity with God leads to the idea of preexistence through its own intrinsic logic. This idea, whose emergence is understandable from the course of primitive Christian history of traditions itself, nevertheless came in contact with various currents in the atmosphere of the Hellenistic world. It was equally in the air for the Jewish *anthrōpos* doctrine, for the Jewish-Hellenistic Wisdom speculation, for the Hellenistic notion of outstanding men as appearances of a deity, and for the Oriental cults transformed into a doctrine of salvation for individuals as fostered in the mysteries. The unique persuasive power of the Christian concept of incarnation in the late classical world is explained by this situation. That the inner problematic of the Christ event pressed for an explication that simultaneously met the sense of truth and the desire for salvation in its environment reveals not the weakness but the strength of the primitive Christian message and constitutes its missionary power.

But can these concepts be anything more for us today than mythical pictures? In the age of technology can we speak seriously of the descent and ascent of a heavenly divine being?

Let us attempt to approach this question from the idea of God's revelation in the Christ event. We have already seen that in this concept the kernel of our contemporary theological problematic coincides with the keynote of the primitive Christian history of traditions. If God has revealed himself in Jesus, then Jesus' community with God, his Sonship, belongs to eternity.

But what have we said when we say this? Taken exactly, we affirm only the indivisibility of Jesus with God, but not the distinction between Jesus' community with God as something eternal and his temporal and transitory human person. The concept of preexistence stands under the suspicion of conceptually separating Jesus' community with God as a special *being* (the preexistent Son of God) and his temporal appearance. The two distinct things are then reunited through the idea that the divine being has, in the incarnation, joined himself at a particular point in time with the earthly corporeality of the man Jesus. Thus the distinction between a preexistent divine being and the man Jesus or his earthly appearance conceptually divides precisely that which belongs together in Jesus' existence. This constitutes the mythical element of the incarnational Christology: it conceptually divides the eternal Son of God and the earthly, human appearance of Jesus, which together constitute the concrete existence of Jesus, into two separate beings. Therefore, what is thus divided must be subsequently brought together again. But the dramatic concept of the uniting of the eternal Son of God with the earthly, human appearance of Jesus also has a mythical character, insofar as it presupposes that conceptual division of the elements that belong together in Jesus' activity and fate, in order to link them together again in this concept.

One can understand the conceptual division of the elements of eternal Sonship and earthly human existence that belong together in the concrete figure of Jesus (the latter is not given up through the resurrection, but is transformed into another mode of life) as an example of an intellectual bent that likes to find the prototypal eternal occasionally effective in the flux of things and events and also in other ways. Indeed, the uniqueness of mythical thinking in general is that it separates the essence of reality as a special, prototypal essence from the appearance in order to reunite the two through a dramatic process especially conceived for the purpose.

However that may be, we too cannot escape distinguishing the *eternal Son* from the *man Jesus*. Certainly, in so doing we always remember that this involves nothing more than two different aspects of the one Jesus Christ.[95] But the eternity of Jesus' Sonship, which is the reason that all things come from him and are directed toward him, as they come from God and are directed toward God, even today cannot be combined without difficulty with the individuality of this one man living in his own time and at his own place. Christology involves precisely the conjunction of these two elements. The patristic doctrine of the descent and ascent of the Redeemer did justice in its own way to this requirement by emphasizing as resolutely as possible the unification of the Son of God with the human, earthly existence of Jesus against Gnosticism. All Christology must keep in view that the two aspects distinguished here, the eternity of the Sonship and the earthly, human mode of Jesus' existence, are a part of a single, concrete life. This must be seen even when Christology no longer conceives those two moments as two independent substances—a concept that was also finally excluded by patristic Christology through the doctrine of the personal unity of divinity and humanity in Jesus Christ.

However, it is not only the unity of the two elements that are necessarily distinguished, namely, the divine Sonship and the manner of Jesus' earthly existence, which must be maintained in the sense of the incarnational Christology. The movement from God to man expressed in the concept of the incarnation also affirms a truth that cannot be abandoned.

---

[95] In this light it becomes understandable in present-day Christology both that some theologians assert the concept of Jesus' preexistence (according to his divinity) to be essential (W. Elert, *Der christliche Glaube*, pp. 306 ff.; E. Brunner, *The Christian Doctrine of Creation and Redemption*, p. 347) and that others want to restrict themselves to the formulation of statements about the historical Jesus in his relation to God (F. Gogarten, *Die Verkündigung Jesu Christi*, pp. 496 ff.; P. Tillich, *Systematic Theology*, Vol. II, pp. 147 f.). However, it is necessary to see both aspects. Precisely the relation of the historical Jesus to his God leads, when properly understood, to the concept of preexistence; but the latter can be retained only in critical reference to this root. The paradox of the preexistence problem, that Jesus' unity with God is supposed to precede temporally his own human existence, has been avoided by K. Barth through the assertion that also Jesus' humanity was preexistent in the divine elective decree (*CD*, III/2, pp. 484 f.; IV/1, pp. 49 f., 53, in substance already in II/2, pp. 179 f.). Even though this idea, which is well grounded in the logic of the act of election, is very tempting, it cannot solve the difficulties of the preexistence problem because one has to speak of the preexistence of Jesus' divinity in a sense that is qualitatively different because of God's eternity from the ideal preexistence of the man Jesus in the divine elective "intention."

We will clarify this again from the concept of revelation. God has been revealed at all times. Also, for the time following the Christ event until the *eschaton* he is not directly revealed but only indirectly through the historical connection of any particular epoch with the history of Jesus of Nazareth. For this reason, no other event and no other man either before or after Jesus is united with God's essence in the same way as the Christ event. That unity of the divine essence with the man Jesus which is brought to expression in the concept of revelation did not exist before Jesus appeared. To that extent one must say that in Jesus, God himself has come out of his otherness into our world, into human form, and in such a way that the Father-Son relation that—as we know in retrospect—always belonged to God's essence now acquired corporeal form.

Thus from the perspective of the concept of revelation, it is quite legitimate to speak of God's having become man. That and to what extent this involves the incarnation of the Son in particular and not the incarnation of God's essence in general—as has just been indicated provisionally—must occupy us in the next section when we will consider more closely the distinction within the Godhead that is also contained in the concept of revelation.

Finally, a look should be taken at the relation of the incarnational Christology to the apocalyptically determined exaltation Christology of the earliest Christian community.[96] Through its contact with Hellenistic conceptions the concept of incarnation had a tendency to emancipate itself from the basis of Old Testament apocalyptic expectations. Patristic Christology moved in the pattern of the incarnation idea and to a large extent lost the connection with the Old Testament theology of history which survived through primitive Christian apocalyptic. One must be clear that a loss of substance took place in this. We have a criterion by which this process can be judged, since we have the connecting link between apocalyptic theology of history and incarnation theology at hand in the concept of revelation.

The essential connection of Christology with the Old Testament was brought into extreme jeopardy through the disengagement of the concept of incarnation from its original background. This disengagement began under the influence of the Logos Christology in the second century. Often the connection was retained only for the sake of the proof from prophecy or for reasons of piety. Certainly, this danger has become acute only very recently when piety toward the Old Testament lost its self-evident validity and proof from Old Testament prophecy was shown, in the light of historical con-

---

[96] The concept of an "exaltation Christology" is used here in the broader sense of the old Protestant dogmaticians. It is not intended to designate especially the conception of an already present Lordship of the resurrected Jesus, which was surely far from the intention of the earliest stage of tradition, but is supposed to indicate the movement of Christological thinking "from below to above," which characterized the *process* that formed the Christological tradition in primitive Christianity (though not always of the structure of the various conceptions employed in this process).

sciousness, to be a questionable undertaking. To the extent that the concept of the incarnation cuts itself loose from the Old Testament and Jewish theology of history, it becomes a mere myth, a myth of a divine being descending from heaven and ascending again. The process in the history of traditions that led to the development of the idea of incarnation is here obscured and remains unintelligible. Then it easily appears that there is a rift between the incarnational Christology and the historical Jesus.

On the other hand, within the horizon of the Old Testament and apocalyptic idea of history the formation of the Christological tradition in primitive Christianity becomes understandable. It becomes clear that the talk of God's becoming man in Jesus Christ involves a final result, final affirmations of theology that are necessary from the perspective of God's eschatological revelation in Jesus. These affirmations do not have their meaning in themselves—then they become mythological—but are justified only as the expression, but certainly the indispensable expression, of God's eschatological revelation in the destiny of Jesus of Nazareth. In addition, they bring us to the limit of what can be said at all, that is, to peculiarly paradoxical formulations. The more sharply one sees this, the more clearly one will learn to distinguish these statements from the harmless vividness of myth. That in the eternal God himself a becoming takes place, a path to incarnation; which took shape only in the career of the man Jesus (indeed only at the end of that career), yet precedes the earthly beginning of his life as unity with the eternal God—these are the most important of the paradoxes that emerge here. They can be tolerated only when one perceives the necessity of their emergence from the circumstances of the proleptic appearance of the *eschaton* in Jesus' history. But this concept of the prolepsis of the *eschaton* is itself paradoxical. The word "paradox" does not mean here, as in Kierkegaard, a contradiction that thought cannot supersede. The assumption of such a contradiction misunderstands the nature of thought, which transcends a contradiction in the act of establishing that the contradiction exists. Paradox means something that is contrary to appearance (*doxa*), by exceeding its capacity. Thus to speak of the end of everything that happens as having already happened in Jesus is contrary to the apparent literal sense. Nevertheless, this way of speaking can be justified, and only then is it meaningful.[97]

[97] An absolutely "not synthesizable paradox" in the sense of a logical contradiction that can be in no way resolved (W. Joest, "Zur Frage des Paradoxon in der Theologie," *Dogma und Denkstrukturen; Festschrift für E. Schlink,* pp. 116-151, esp. pp. 118 f.) must probably be judged with Scholz, Schilder, Kiesow, Schröer, and others (literature cited in Joest's article) as meaningless. The theological examples that Joest gives for such insoluble paradoxes all contain a logical mediation of the contradiction by *establishing why,* in certain questions, theology arrives at contradictory statements that are at the same time true. We have treated the preexistence problem in this latter sense. The process of such an establishment represents in itself a logical mediation of the logical contradiction residing in the paradoxical assertion. It is another question whether such a legitimation for the unavoidability of a logically paradoxical theological assertion can be given in an exhaustive and

The loss of substance that threatens to take place when the concept of incarnation is loosed from its original context becomes apparent in the increasing concentration of such an independent incarnational theology on the birth of Jesus, while the resurrection is reduced to a mere illustration of the significance of the birth. In general, the significance of the unique historical life of Jesus recedes. In consequence, the horizon of history, the eschatological expectation, pales for the believer. The content of the event of incarnation itself becomes insecure. From this point on, the significance of God's becoming man changes in accordance with the kind of concept of God one presupposes. The real significance of the incarnation is established only from the Old Testament, from the apocalyptic expectation, from the earthly path of Jesus. Only so long as the perception of Jesus' resurrection remains precedent to the concept of incarnation is the Biblical meaning of the idea of God preserved in Christology and only so long does Christology also remain related to the Biblical understanding of man and of the world as history.

III. THE ORIGIN OF THE DOCTRINE OF THE TRINITY AND THE PROBLEM OF THE LOGOS CHRISTOLOGY

In the preceding section we considered the unity of the man Jesus with God as it is contained in the concept of God's revelation in Jesus. Now we turn our attention to the same subject matter as seen from another side. This involves the distinction between Jesus' divinity and the Father's divinity.

1. The Distinction Between Father and Son

It has been shown—and this remains the point of departure for all further considerations—that Jesus' person cannot be separated from God's essence if Jesus in person is God's self-revelation. However, Jesus understood himself as set over against the God whom he called Father. He distinguished the Father from himself. Even though Jesus may not have spoken of himself as Son,[98] the Palestinian community may have designated Jesus with this title

conclusive way. It is perhaps here that we encounter the intention of Joest's argument. By seeking to reflect upon and formulate the significance of the history of Jesus that reveals God, at certain points theology really does find itself forced to make contradictory assertions that once more give cause for further reflection, for wrestling for a deeper understanding of their "why." The very question about this "why" already presupposes the anticipation that the contradiction "is 'apprehended,' 'interpreted,' that is, in essence *believed* as belonging together in a hidden unity" (Joest, in *Dogma und Denkstrukturen*, p. 127). Even if this hidden unity in and behind the contradiction can never be expressed exhaustively and conclusively, neither does it remain even logically a mere contradiction (on p. 127, n. 38, Joest speaks of "antinomy") to the extent that a justification is sought for the fact and the reason that in the matter under consideration a paradoxical assertion is unavoidable and meaningful.

[98] Cf. F. Hahn, *Christologische Hoheitstitel*, pp. 319-333, who there follows G. Born-

in correspondence to the mode in which he himself had spoken of his Father. If Jesus' history and his person now belong to the essence, to the divinity of God, *then the distinction that Jesus maintained between himself and the Father also belongs to the divinity of God*. The relation of Jesus as Son to the Father may be summarized with primitive Christianity as "obedience."[99] It is therefore a relation proper to the essence of God himself. God is not only "Father," but as the God who is revealed through Jesus' resurrection he is in his eternal essence also "Son." Thereby the expressions "Father" and "Son" are to be strictly applied to the relation to God of the historical man Jesus of Nazareth. Here the word "Father" means the God of Jesus, who was the God of the Old Testament, to whom Jesus directed his prayers and from whose hand he accepted his fate. The word "Son" here does not designate, as it does in other places in the New Testament, Jesus' place of honor in contrast to humanity and the cosmos, but primarily his relation to the Father, a relation of obedience and "mission" (Rom. 8:3; Gal. 4:4; John 3:17, *passim;* I John 4:9), but also of trust.[100] The latter term may well be taken as a more appropriate expression for that which Jesus' addressing God as Father implied in his own understanding.

We have been speaking of "Father" and "Son" in a figurative sense. Likewise, to speak of a contrast between Father and Son within the Godhead has a figurative, symbolic sense. It is justified only in the fact that Jesus' relation to the God of Israel as his "Father" belongs to the essence of this God himself, just as does the person of Jesus of Nazareth, insofar as he is revealed in Jesus.

God's essence as it is revealed in the Christ event thus contains within itself the twofoldness, the tension, and the relation of Father and Son. The

---

kamm, *Jesus of Nazareth*, pp. 226 f. O. Cullmann, *The Christology of the New Testament*, pp. 281 ff., wants to derive the use of the name "Son" from Jesus himself. Against this attempt, see W. G. Kümmel, *Promise and Fulfillment* (Studies in Biblical Theology; London: SCM Press, Ltd., 1961), p. 42, whom Bornkamm follows, *Jesus of Nazareth*, p. 226.

[99] The idea of obedience is, to be sure, expressly mentioned first in Hebrews (ch. 5:8) and connected directly with the title of Son, but in Paul the obedience of Christ is "the characteristic of his way and activity as a whole" (Günther Bornkamm, *Das Ende des Gesetzes, Paulusstudien: Gesammelte Aufsätze*, Band I [Beiträge zur evangelischen Theologie, 16; Munich: Chr. Kaiser Verlag, 1952], p. 88 on Rom. 5:19 with a reference to Phil. 2:8). With Cullmann, *The Christology of the New Testament*, pp. 283 ff., it is probably correct to suppose an original affinity between Sonship and the motif of obedience that goes beyond the paucity of explicit New Testament references.

[100] It is not permissible to question that Jesus' relationship to the Father was characterized by trust by referring to the fact that the New Testament witnesses do not apply the concept of faith to that relationship. Thus G. Ebeling probably is right in substance when he says that it is "impossible to except him himself from faith" ("Jesus and Faith," *Word and Faith*, p. 234). It is, however, another question whether this statement can be justified on purely exegetical grounds. Thus, in later publications, Ebeling also speaks of Jesus as the "witness of faith," but not, so far as I can see, of Jesus' own faith (cf., e.g., *The Nature of Faith*, pp. 55 ff.).

deity of Jesus Christ cannot therefore have the sense of undifferentiated identity with the divine nature, as if in Jesus, God the Father himself had appeared in human form and had suffered on the cross. This was the opinion of modalism concerning Jesus' divinity. The modalists thought they could save God's unity only by identifying Jesus with God without differentiation. Therefore, Tertullian designated the modalists as "Patripassians" in his tract against Praxeas.[101] In contrast to the modalists' position, the differentiation of Father and Son in God himself must be maintained, because this differentiation, which is characteristic of the relation of the historical Jesus to God, must be characteristic of the essence of God himself if Jesus as a person is God's revelation.

2. The Classical Logos Christology

The merit of the so-called Logos Christology, which had its origin with the Apologists of the second century and which prevailed against modalism, not only in fact but also with the inner rightness of its position, is that it asserted the differentiation of Father and Son within the Godhead. The Logos doctrine of the Apologists, subsequently taken over by the whole of patristic theology, was able—at least in embryonic form—to show how the Son could be thought of as different from the Father and yet together with him as a single God. This intention distinguishes the Logos Christology of the Apologists from the older application of the Logos concept to Jesus Christ in John or Ignatius. For in the latter theologians the question that the Apologists clarified at least in an initial way with the help of the Logos concept remains obscure: how the Son of God can be distinguished from the Creator and still be one and the same God with him.

The concept of the divine Logos in the Johannine Prologue is probably to be understood within the context of the hypostatized wisdom (cf. n. 89 above) and the *anthrōpos* speculations of Judaism, as they are found similarly combined with the Logos concept in Philo (cf. n. 91 above), rather than from the perspective of a pre-Christian Gnostic redeemer myth that is entirely too hypothetical. The Johannine Logos is not, however, a middle thing between God and the world, but he himself is simply God (John 1:1c). Just like the Logos in Philo and in the Psalms of Solomon (chs. 12 and 16), the Johannine Logos simultaneously has cosmological (as Mediator of the creation of the world) and soteriological (as Redeemer through revelation) functions. The apparent contradiction that the Logos is with God, thus is another being next to God, and still is designated simply as "God" corresponds to the fact that throughout John's Gospel the Son is designated, on the one hand, as one with the Father (ch. 10:30), as having equal power and glory with the Father

101 See F. Loofs, *Dogmengeschichte*, § 27, 3b-d, pp. 144-146.

(ch. 5:21 ff.), but, on the other hand, the Father is called greater than the Son (ch. 14:28) and the Son is obedient to the Father in the execution of the Father's will (chs. 5:30; 6:38).[102] The difficulty presented by such statements standing side by side is not removed by John.

In one passage Ignatius of Antioch called Jesus "the Logos" in a somewhat different sense, namely, as "the Word in which God broke his silence" (*Magn.* 8:2). In the background of this statement we probably have to assume a Gnosticism in which the Logos has the function not of Creator but only of Revealer. This was probably a dualistic Gnosticism that did not believe in creation, but for which, rather, the Logos comes into an alien world made by the evil Demiurge. This is naturally not Ignatius' conception, but it can be clearly seen behind his formulation. Here the word is understood wholly and completely as communicative speech, while the Johannine Prologue thinks rather of the Word of creation.

In contrast to Ignatius, the Apologists of the second century understood the Logos concept primarily cosmologically but in the sense of Hellenistic philosophy rather than in reliance upon Gnostic conceptions. The Logos as the world reason, as the natural law holding the cosmos together, was a well-known concept in the educated Hellenistic world, above all in the form of the Stoic Logos concept. For the Stoics, the Logos orders the world into the unity of a system (*systēma*) by setting matter in motion and giving it form, just as the Logos in man establishes the unity of the soul.[103]

Heraclitus' concept of the Logos from which the Stoic Logos concept is derived meant in a similar way the law that reigns supreme over what happens in the world and which consolidates the world into a unity.[104] The Platonic understanding of the Logos as the guide to true being[105] was quite different. In the Platonic school the Logos was not conceived pantheistically as the law holding the cosmos together, but as a middle being between the transcendent God and the world. The same is true in Philo and in the Apologists. However, in the Logos concept of the Apologists, as in the philosophy of that time, the Platonic concept is combined with certain Stoic elements. On the one hand, the Logos occupies a middle position between the Most

---

[102] Cf. R. Bultmann, *Das Evangelium des Johannes* (10th ed.; Göttingen: Vandenhoeck & Ruprecht, 1941), p. 18.

[103] This parallelism between cosmology and psychology in Stoic thought is extensively treated by U. Wilckens, *Weisheit und Torheit,* pp. 225 ff. See also M. Pohlenz, *Die Stoa: Geschichte einer geistigen Bewegung* (2 vols.; Göttingen: Vandenhoeck & Ruprecht, 1948-1949).

[104] On Heraclitus' Logos concept, see O. Gigon, *Untersuchungen zu Heraklit* (1935), pp. 18 and 43 ff.; esp. also, H. Fränkel, "Eine heraklitische Denkform" (1938, now in *Wege und Formen frühgriechischen Denkens* [1955], pp. 253-283. In this light one sees how misleading is the remark about Heraclitus made by E. Fuchs, *RGG,* IV (3d ed.), 437, art. "Logos." According to Fuchs, Heraclitus was a thinker who "cast forth" the Logos "powerfully now and again as a saying."

[105] See E. Hoffmann, *Platon* (1950), pp. 65 ff.

High God and the world—this is the Platonic element. On the other, the Logos' coming from God and his historical appearance in Jesus are described through thought patterns of Stoic origin.

Thus for the Apologists the relation of the Logos to God had to be closely connected with the creation of the world, as was already the case for Greek philosophy and for the ancient Oriental religions.[106] Thus, the relation between God and the Logos was thought through primarily in the context of the philosophical problem of the world's origin, rather than in view of God's historical revelation. What was learned in this way was merely applied to the revelation in Christ. Such a procedure has to involve the danger that theology would be enveloped by substantially alien philosophical presuppositions.

In accordance with the statement about Wisdom in Prov. 8:22 f., the Logos was characterized as the first creature of God.[107] Thus, it went forth only at the time of the creation of the world by the divine will.[108] Justin and his pupil Tatian began with the assumption that a power of reason (*dynamis logikē*) belongs to God's essence.[109] This power of reason, originally an essential constituent of the divine omnipotence, became distinguished from God as an independent being for the purpose of the creation of the world, namely, in order that through it a multiplicity of creatures might come to be: "Out of the *dynamis logikē* of the Father the independent *dynamis logou* has arisen."[110] This emergence is not to be thought of as though a piece of the Father's essence had been separated off.[111] Such division would violate the simplicity and unchangeability that characterize God's essence for the Apologists.[112] Just for that reason they defined the bringing forth of the Logos through God as an act of his will, as an intellectual act.

Theophilus of Antioch characterized the bringing forth of the Logos with the help of the Stoic distinction between the "word" of thought spoken internally, in the mind, and the word spoken externally, orally.[113] In substance this distinction stands quite close to Tatian's distinction between the *dynamis*

106 For the particular character and distribution of the ancient Near Eastern concept of the power of the word, in particular, naturally, the divine word, and especially of creation through the divine word, cf. L. Dürr, *Die Wertung des göttlichen Wortes im AT und im antiken Orient* (Leipzig: J. C. Hinrichs Verlag, 1938).

107 Justin, *Apol.* I, 21, 1: *Prōton gennēma tou theou* (E. J. Goodspeed, *Die ältesten Apologeten,* p. 40).

108 Justin, *Dial.* 61, 1 f. (Goodspeed, p. 166).

109 Justin, *Dial.* 61, 1; Tatian, *Or.* 5, 1, and 7, 1 (Goodspeed, pp. 272 f.).

110 Martin Elze, *Tatian und seine Theologie* (Göttingen: Vandenhoeck & Ruprecht, 1960), p. 74.

111 Justin, *Dial.* 128, 4: *ou kata apotomēn* (Goodspeed, p. 250); Tatian, *Or.* 5, 1: *ou kata apokopēn* (Goodspeed, pp. 272f). On the relation of both expressions, cf. Elze, *Tatian und seine Theologie,* p. 77.

112 M. Elze, *ibid.,* pp. 73 ff.

113 *Logos endiathetos* and *Logos prophorikos.* Theophilus, *Ad Autol.* II, 10 and 22. Tatian avoided this distinction. Cf. Elze, *ibid.,* p. 76.

logikē held in the unity of God and the *dynamis logou* that has gone forth from it. The differentiation of the thought from the thinker makes it possible to express the distinction between Father and Son within the deity more sharply.

For Tatian, the Logos concept was not merely a means for conceiving the unity of the Son with the Father without surrendering philosophical monotheism; it was at the same time the key to the solution of an old problem characteristic for the tradition of the Platonic school, namely, overcoming the antithesis between unity and plurality. Tatian overcame this antithesis through the idea of a "real self-unfolding of the one God."[114] God distinguishes his logical power from himself in such a way that it remains at the same time united with him; thus begins the creation of a world, whose multiplicity is embraced by the one, transcendent God through the Logos in order to be present in the world in spite of his transcendence.

The Logos is the prototype of the world, or more precisely the essence of the prototypes of all things in the world, just as it itself is the image of the Father.[115] Just as with Philo, the Logos especially appears in men as rational beings, to be sure in varied degrees. The seeds of the Logos are effective in the whole of humanity.[116] But only in Jesus Christ has the whole Logos, *to logikon to holon,* appeared.[117]

3. Advantages and Dangers of the Logos Theory

The first advantage of the Logos theory is to be seen above all in the fact that it could make Jesus' unity with the Father and at the same time his differentiation from him understandable. This contrasts with the various positions which spoke of God's sovereignty but defined the relation of the Son to God inappropriately in one way or another. The Logos that appeared "totally" in Jesus was always contained in the eternal unity of God as the power of reason or as his eternal thought; even after he became independent at the creation, he remains joined to the Father with respect to his essence (*ousia*), as well as through power and mind (*gnōmē*).[118] The Logos is different from the Father as a being only in number. The distinction of Jesus' divinity from that of the Father is thus brought to expression without surrender of monotheism. Tatian even recognized that only through the unity of the Logos with God can the old problem of the antithesis of unity (of

114 *Ibid.*, p. 78.
115 Elze, *ibid.*, pp. 79 f.
116 But only as *logos spermatikos:* Justin, *Apol.* II, 8,1; 13,3. For the meaning of this conception, see A. Grillmeier, "Zur dogmatischen Vorgeschichte des Konzils von Chalkedon," in *Chalkedon,* Vol. I, esp. pp. 56 ff. For Tatian, see Elze, *Tatian und seine Theologie,* pp. 94 f.
117 Justin, *Apol.* II, 10, 1; cf. 8, 3 (Goodspeed, *Die ältesten Apologeten,* pp. 84 f.).
118 Justin, *Dial.* 128, 4, and 56, 11 (Goodspeed, pp. 250, 157).

origin) and multiplicity (of the appearances) be solved: because God's unity embraces the many through the Logos, only through the Logos doctrine is monotheism realized in pure form.[119]

The second advantage of the Logos doctrine of the Apologists consists in the fact that it made the divinity present in Jesus familiar to Hellenistic society as a power that was decisive for its conception of the world. The Logos theory succeeded impressively in explaining the role of the preexistent Son of God in mediating creation, to which the New Testament testifies, within a different sphere of tradition. The universal significance of God's revelation in Jesus is the natural consequence when the Logos, the foundation of the world's being, has appeared in his fullness in Jesus.

However, the dogmatic weaknesses of the Logos Christology are closely related to these advantages. In the first place, the unity of the Logos with God cannot be so strictly conceived in the categories of the Platonic cosmology as is required by the Christian interest in salvation and the idea of revelation. As one who has gone forth from God, the Logos remains a being of subordinate rank in comparison to the Father who has no beginning. This subordinationism is closely related to the concept that the Logos was not independent alongside the Father from eternity but went forth from him only at a definite time, namely, at the beginning of the creation of the world. Patristic Christology through the time of the Arian controversy was occupied with the problem of how to establish the equality of the Logos' deity with that of the Father and thus to counteract the subordinationist tendency of the Logos doctrine. Indeed, this problem constituted the real kernel of the Arian controversy. For soteriological reasons the fathers were extremely concerned that the Logos revealed in Jesus possess equal divinity with the Father. Athanasius especially expressed this concern: if the Most High God himself is not present in Jesus, then we also do not gain a share in the divine life through Jesus nor are we reconciled with God himself through Jesus. But there was little possibility of doing justice to this soteriological concern within the framework of the Logos doctrine.[120] The inner logic of the Logos doctrine supported Arius rather than Athanasius. Because the procession of the Logos means the first step of creation and the Logos is thus the first creature, a subordinationist tendency belonged to the Platonically conceived Logos doctrine from the very beginning. The Nicene dogma, which established the identity of the divinity of the Son with that of the Father, therefore meant a breakthrough out of the conceptual structure of the Logos Christology. This is why it had such difficulty gaining acceptance. This breakthrough is Bibli-

119 Cf. Elze, *Tatian und seine Theologie,* pp. 74 f.

120 A starting point for this development was given by Origen's idea of an eternal, not merely temporally accomplished, generation of the Logos (*De princ.* I, 2, 4 [*GCS* 22, p. 33]). Characteristically, however, for Origen himself the Logos was still a *ktisma* (*De princ.* IV, 4, 1 [*GCS* 22, p. 349]); a second, subordinated God (*Contra Celsum* 5, 39 [*GCS* (*Origen's Works,* Vol. 2), 19, p. 43]).

cally justified, however, even though Athanasius had argued more from the soteriological concern for full participation in divinity through Jesus than from the concept of revelation. His thesis is still taken care of through the idea of revelation. Jesus' essential unity with God in the sense of the *homoousios* is inherent in the concept of God's revelation, in contrast to the subordinationist tendency of the Logos Christology.

A second weakness of the Logos Christology is the precarious loosening of the connection of the Son's divinity with Jesus of Nazareth, God's historical revelation. Tatian, for example, could develop his whole Logos doctrine without saying anything at all about Jesus Christ. In contrast, we established in the preceding section that one can speak theologically of Jesus' preexistent divinity only in view of his concrete fate. Only in this way is Jesus' unity with God apparent. We have seen that the necessity of asserting Jesus' divinity as preexistent over against his earthly path leads to peculiarly paradoxical concepts if the theological assertion is to avoid drifting into a false, mythological simplicity. There is not much trace of such paradox in the Apologists, as in patristic Logos Christology as a whole. One is often astounded at the way these theologians know how to say everything about Jesus' divinity without reference to the historical Jesus. This results from their taking a point of departure primarily from a philosophical theme in order to develop the concept of the Logos as a middle being between God and the world, with rather superficial appeals to New Testament assertions about Christ as the Son of God, the image of God, the Mediator of creation, and the Logos.

A third problem is closely associated, namely, the problem of the unbroken influence that the philosophical concept of God, the conception of an unchangeable and simple origin (*archē*) of the world at hand, attained in the center of Christian theology through the Logos doctrine. One cannot object without qualifications to the acceptance of the philosophical concept of God. It is justified by the task of proclaiming God's act in Jesus Christ as universal truth for all men, as the revelation of the one God of all men. Such a message could not prove credible in the Hellenistic world for any length of time if it did not enter into the philosophical question about the true form of the divine in some way. The thrust of the Christian message and the Biblical God stood the test for the men of late antiquity who were not Jews precisely through utilizing the philosophical question about God. However, the one God is revealed in the person and history of Jesus differently than he had been conceived by philosophy. He is revealed, not as the unchangeable ultimate ground of the phenomenal order, but as the free origin of the contingent events of the world, whose interrelations are also contingent and constitute no eternal order but a history moving forward from event to event. This difference between the Biblical God, fully revealed in the history of Jesus, and Greek philosophy's concept of God, did not achieve decisive significance in the Logos Christology. Rather, the Logos Christology contributed to the obscuring of this problem because its thought structure was borrowed from philosophical question patterns.[121]

4. Renewal of the Logos Christology?

The theological positions constructed after World War I have largely been concerned with a renewal of patristic Christology in general and the Logos doctrine in particular. But can the concept of the Logos fulfill the functions that it had in the patristic church in a contemporary Christology? Can it still express the divinity of Jesus for us in the way that was possible at that time?

This is a difficult question. An affirmative answer can certainly not be given without qualification, for the presupposition that provided the basis for the introduction of the Logos into patristic theology has disappeared today: the figure of a Logos mediating between the transcendent God and the world no longer belongs to today's scientific perception of the world. A contemporary analogy to the Apologists' Logos Christology perhaps would have to look something like this: Jesus Christ would be conceived as the embodiment of Einstein's theory or of some other inclusive physical law. But even if that were successful, it would be only an analogy to the Stoic not the Platonic concept of the Logos. The laws of contemporary physics are inherent in the processes they describe; they do not transcend them and are hardly mediators of divinity! Thus an incarnation of such a natural law would be completely superfluous and would not, in any case, be anything very extraordinary because such a natural law comes to expression equally in everything that happens. If one wished to reproduce an analogy to the patristic Logos Christology, namely, in connection with the contemporary thought of natural science, one would have to begin by understanding the laws of nature, contrary to the self-understanding of natural science, as prototypes existing beyond and not fully expressed in the natural processes. The whole experimental methodology of our modern understanding of nature resists such an interpretation. Further, the totality of the laws of nature would have to be conceived as an image of God. After all of this, one would only have put back together the Logos concept, laden with all the previous theological objections.

Thus it is hardly possible—and in any case meaningless—to renew the patristic idea of the Logos in this form. Does the possibility, nevertheless, perhaps remain to repeat the intention of the Logos doctrine in another form less closely oriented to the patristic relationship to Hellenistic thought? The renewal of the doctrine of the Logos in the Christology of the last decades has not understood the Logos in the sense of the Apologists' Logos Christology. In Emil Brunner's book *The Mediator*, the first systematic presentation

121 On the details of the necessity of the ancient philosophical doctrine of God in theology, see my article "Die Aufnahme des philosophischen Gottesbegriffs als dogmatisches Problem der frühchristlichen Theologie," *ZKG*, LXX (1959), 1-45.

of Christology from the ranks of dialectical theology, the doctrine of the "divinity of the Mediator" begins with a chapter about the "divine word."[122] Here, however, "word" is understood not as prototypal world law but as "address" (p. 177). Behind this understanding stands the personalistic understanding of man as "I and Thou" in the sense of Ferdinand Ebner and Martin Buber.[123]

Brunner thinks that Jesus did not proclaim, as did the prophets, a "word of God," a *dābār,* only from time to time, but that he was in his person *the* Word of God (p. 189; pp. 199 f.), the "personal communication of God" (p. 185). The concept of "word of God" here, as well as in Karl Barth's dogmatics,[124] does not attach itself to the mainstream of the patristic Logos Christology that followed the Apologists of the second century, but to the Logos concept of Ignatius (*Magn.* 8:2), to the concept of the Word "in which God broke his silence."

This understanding of the divine Word has, however, hardly any other value than that of a metaphor. It is only figuratively possible to say that the invisible God speaks. In this sense one may, of course, say that God seeks to communicate something through certain events, just as in other situations events have a "language." Certainly, with respect to Jesus a peculiarity is to be noted. Jesus' resurrection means that God has claimed as his own the promise of salvation made by the pre-Easter Jesus and thus recognized Jesus' word in a definite sense as his own word. Nevertheless, it is still only a figurative expression when the event of God's revelation in Jesus' fate is designated as God's "Word," an expression that—in order to be true—presupposes a substantiation outside itself for the fact that God is revealed in the person of Jesus. However, this concept of the Word does not have the ontological significance of an independent hypostasis beside God the Father, and thus does not have the significance of the patristic Logos concept, even though Brunner[125] and Barth think they can take up without further ado the accomplishments of patristic Logos Christology, especially the differentia-

[122] E. Brunner, *The Mediator,* 7, pp. 201 ff.

[123] *Ibid.,* pp. 208-209. For Ebner, cf. T. Schleiermacher, "Ich und Du: Grundzüge der Anthropologie Ferdinand Ebners," *KuD,* III (1957), 208-229, and *idem, Das Heil des Menschen und sein Traum vom Geist: Ferd. Ebner: Ein Denker in der Kategorie der Begegnung,* 1962. Besides Ebner, of course the writings of Martin Buber are to be seen as the source of Brunner's personalistic idea.

[124] Nevertheless, in spite of all its similarities to the personal concept of word, a different intention is dominant in Barth's concept of the Word of God, and this intention is presumably not bound to the personal understanding of word. This intention is the idea of God's superiority to all human experience. J. Moltmann has rightly called attention to this in his introduction to the collection of early essays from the circle of dialectic theology that he edited, *Anfänge der dialektischen Theologie* I (Theologische Bücherei 17; Munich: Chr. Kaiser Verlag, 1962), p. XVII.

[125] Brunner, *The Mediator,* pp. 247-248, esp. with reference to Irenaeus, pp. 249 ff. Cf. also pp. 280 f.

tion of Jesus' divinity from that of the Father, for their theology by their personal concept of word.[126]

Today the idea of revelation must take the place of the Logos concept as the point of departure for Christology. This is largely also the case where one pursues a Christology of the word, insofar as the concept of word here is used as a figurative expression for the revelatory event. The insight into Jesus' unity with God's essence and into the differentiation between Father and Son within the essence of God himself, which remains in spite of this unity, can be substantiated only through the perception of Jesus as God's revelation. The unity with God's essence and the differentiation of Jesus' divinity from the Father's are elements that are implicitly established already in the recognition of Jesus as God's revelation. Their explicit formulation only unfolds the content of the perception of revelation.

5. The Problem of the Mediation of Creation by Jesus Christ

For a Christology that begins with the idea of revelation, an open problem remains at the point where the patristic Logos Christology was most effective. The idea that Jesus is not only preexistent as the Son of God but was also actively involved in creation, indeed, that everything was made "in him" and through him, is related to the full divinity of Jesus and to the fact that the relation of God to the world and so also to the creation of the world is focused in the Revealer. The Apologists' Logos theory was able to make the mediation of creation by the Son testified in the New Testament understandable. Also, in the opinion of the philosophy of that time-view as well, the cosmos was held together as a unified whole through the Logos. The designation of Jesus as the incarnation of the divine Logos was, therefore, understandable to every educated person without lengthy explanations; in this title, Jesus' significance was clear without further ado. Today, in contrast, the Son's mediation of creation must be strictly established through the concept of revelation; it is not established as something given in the philosophy of nature. We can only ask subsequently whether our understanding of the world permits us to perceive something of the relation of the Son to the Father, thus whether the world may be understood as aimed at the relation of the Son to the Father that is revealed in Jesus Christ. Certainly, to fuse in such a way the modern understanding of the world into an understanding of reality derived from the revelation in Christ demands an extraordinary effort on the part of theological thinking. But this method would probably correspond

[126] When Irenaeus, and later especially Augustine in his doctrine of the Trinity, understood the Logos as *verbum*, as the word that is at first spoken inwardly (as idea) and only then outwardly (as Theophilus of Antioch had already done), they all conceived this anthropological phenomenon in the context of the cosmological Logos concept.

more closely to the way in which the faith in creation emerged—or better, was appropriated[127]—from the perspective of the concrete experience of salvation in ancient Israel than did the patristic identification of the Son of God with a definite concept available in the philosophical understanding of the world at that time. The statement that all things and beings are created through Jesus Christ means that the *eschaton* that has appeared beforehand in Jesus represents the time and point from which the creation took place. According to the Biblical understanding, the essence of things will be decided only in the future. What they are is decided by what they will become. Thus the creation happens from the end, from the ultimate future. (For greater detail, see below, Chapter 10, Sec. III.)

6. *The Holy Spirit*

That the distinctiveness of Father and Son is a distinction in the essence of God himself is the beginning point for the doctrine of the Trinity systematically as well as historically. In order to make the connection with the doctrine of the Trinity somewhat clearer, it is necessary to look now at the concept of the Holy Spirit and his relation to Jesus Christ. Why should one speak of a "Trinity" and not of a "Duality" of the Son with the Father? With what right does the Holy Spirit belong to the Trinity, to the divinity of God, as an independent, differentiated "person"?

The Spirit was an eschatological reality for primitive Christianity. Israelite prophecy had promised that the Spirit would be poured out at the end of history, and the primitive Christian community experienced just this eschatological reality as already present in the gift of the Spirit.[128] "Through the *pneuma* the *doxa* [glory] promised for the eschatological consummation is already poured out now on the Christians."[129] The eschatological character of the primitive Christian understanding of the Spirit has recently been given attention in dogmatics also, especially by Karl Barth and Otto Weber.[130] In order to understand the unique character of the Spirit's reality in primitive

127 On this, see Gerhard von Rad, *Old Testament Theology*, tr. by D. M. G. Stalker (2 vols.; Harper & Row, Publishers, Inc., 1962, 1965), Vol. I, pp. 136 ff. This process, however, did not take place as a sort of conclusion drawn from faith in salvation but probably in the course of a blending of elements in the history of religions, as an identification of the gods of the patriarchs and Yahweh with the common Semitic God of heaven, El, who was held to be the creator god. But apparently just this process of identification was made possible by the particularity of the figure of Yahweh.

128 Cf. R. Bultmann, *Theology of the New Testament*, Vol. I, p. 41; see also pp. 153 ff., 335.

129 I. Hermann, *Kyrios und Pneuma*, p. 33. For the relation between the Pauline idea of *pneuma* and primitive Christian eschatology, see also Eduard Schweizer, art. *"Pneuma,"* *ThW*, VI, esp. pp. 414, 417. Presumably the connection between *pneuma* and *doxa* is rooted in apocalyptic (cf. also I Peter 4:14 and Eph. 1:13 f., 17) and is not specifically Hellenistic (against E. Käsemann, *RGG*, II [3d ed.], 1273).

130 K. Barth, *CD*, I/1, pp. 530 f.; O. Weber, *Dogmatik*, Vol. II, p. 268.

Christianity, one must go back to the significance of the Spirit of God in the Old Testament.

The Spirit of God was not primarily a source of supernatural knowledge in the Old Testament, but the ground of life in the most inclusive sense.[131] The conceptual association of spirit, wind, air, and breath must be noted in this connection. Psalm 104 describes, perhaps most impressively of all, the vitalizing effect of the Spirit of God. There it is said about creatures in their dependence on the Creator: "When thou hidest thy face, they are dismayed; when thou takest away their breath, they die and return to their dust. When thou sendest forth thy Spirit, they are created; and thou renewest the face of the ground" (Ps. 104:29-30; cf. Gen. 1:2; 2:7; Ezek. 37:5 ff.). The extraordinary works of power of God's Spirit, which provided the basis for the Israelite charismatic phenomena, are to be understood from this perspective. A special endowment with God's creative Spirit is necessary for especially outstanding activities, as in the case of the heroes and—at least in the early period—of the prophets, as well as for singers and artists. This always involves a special working of that power of God in which all life has its origin.

At the end of history, according to Israelite expectation, the Spirit of God will become effective in a special way. According to Isa. 11:2, the Messiah not only will be filled and driven by the Spirit but the Spirit will be continually joined with him, will rest upon him. Third Isaiah (Isa. 61:1) also understood the Messiah as the bearer of the Spirit: the Spirit rests upon him. According to Second Isaiah (Isa. 42:1), not only the Messiah but all Israel will share in God's Spirit in a new way at the end of history (cf. also Ezek. 36:27; Isa. 44:3). In his last vision in the night Zechariah saw the Spirit of Yahweh come over all peoples; the wagons of the winds bear *ruach Yahweh* into the four corners of the world (Zech. 6:1-8). Finally, Joel also promises the pouring out of God's Spirit on "all flesh" for the end time (ch. 2:28). Luke understood this prophecy as fulfilled in primitive Christianity (Acts 2:17 ff.).

The Spirit of God was understood in all this as power of life, not primarily as the source for knowledge which could not otherwise be attained. This remained true in postexilic Judaism. Wisdom and insight, called effects of the Spirit in Isa. 11:2, were also understood in Judaism only as one effect of the divine Spirit of life among others (Wisd. of Sol. 7:22 ff.). If one begins with the question of knowledge rather than with the broad area of the Spirit's creative working, one obscures the Biblical understanding of the Spirit. Wisdom and knowledge are, to be sure, possible only through God's Spirit. But this is nothing supernaturally special, for it is true for all life.

---

[131] On this, see O. Procksch, *Theologie des Alten Testaments* (Gütersloh: C. Bertelsman, 1950), pp. 459-468; G. von Rad, *Old Testament Theology,* Vol. I, pp. 323 f. See also Hans Walter Wolff, *Dodekapropheten: Joel* (Biblischer Kommentar, XIV/2; Neukirchen: Menkirchener Verlag, 1963), pp. 78 ff. on Joel 3:1.

For Israel the distinction between the eschatological and the present work-ing of the Spirit consisted in the fact that in the *eschaton* the Spirit is poured out, that he will rest upon men, that he will be imparted to them intrinsically —in short, that he will be completely given to them. Therefore, we can ex-pect that life in the *eschaton* will be a higher life in comparison to the earthly condition in which men do not really have the Spirit of God but can only be driven by him.

Contemporary theology lacks a doctrine of the Holy Spirit that corresponds in breadth to the Biblical concept of the Spirit. Such a doctrine would require a treatment of our present knowledge of the causes of life. Can we still speak today of a "spiritual" origin of all life?[132] What sense would such talk have with respect to the phenomena and structures of life that have been explored by biology? Can one show that certain statements analogous to the Israelite language about God's Spirit as the creative origin of all life are necessary for the understanding of such phenomena? The Christian statements about the Holy Spirit can again receive full weight only through answering such ques-tions. Otherwise, they remain a dead piece of tradition or in any case—es-pecially where the Holy Spirit is restricted to the function of a supernatural principle of knowledge—do not correspond to the Biblical idea of the Spirit. This task of a doctrine of the Holy Spirit cannot be solved here in passing. We must bypass these presuppositions of our talk about the Holy Spirit here and limit ourselves to following the connection of the Spirit with Jesus Christ, as it is conceived in the literature of primitive Christianity.

The close connection that existed for Paul between the *pneuma* and the reality of the resurrection that appeared in Jesus and is hoped for by Chris-tians is demonstrated by the Old Testament understanding of the Spirit as the power of life. It was not accidental that Jesus was raised through the Spirit (Rom. 1:4; 8:2, 11; cf. I Peter 3:18). Further, the life-creating prin-ciple of the Spirit of God has not only produced the resurrection life, but it is one with that life in distinction from the present, temporal life, and corre-sponding to the Israelite expectation that in the end of time the Spirit will remain upon men. Thus in I Cor. 15:44 f. Paul can speak of a spiritual body (*sōma pneumatikon*) when he wants to describe the uniqueness of the resur-rection life: the Last Adam became a life-giving Spirit (v.45).[133] From here it is understandable that "all 'genuine,' theologically pregnant statements about the Spirit in the principal Pauline letters are Christologically stamped."[134]

132 Paul Tillich in Part IV of his *Systematic Theology* ("Life and the Spirit," *Systematic Theology,* Vol. III, pp. 11-161).

133 I. Hermann, *Kyrios und Pneuma,* p. 63.

134 *Ibid.,* p. 144. See also II Cor. 3:17. In view of the parallel idea in I Cor. 15:45, the identification of *Kyrios* and *pneuma* in II Cor. 3:17 can hardly be held "un-Pauline" (thus W. Schmithals, "Zwei gnostische Glossen im 2. Korintherbrief," *EvTh,* XVIII [1959], 552-573, esp. p. 567). In any case, this argument will have to be excluded from the dis-cussion about whether II Cor. 3:17 is a gloss.

Conversely, too, *Kyrios* and *pneuma* belong together. Wherever there is a reference in any way to the reality of the resurrected Lord, as it is established through hearing the message of Jesus' resurrection, there one is already in the sphere of the Spirit's activity. Whoever believes the message of Jesus' resurrection has thereby already received the Spirit who guarantees to the believer the future resurrection from death because he has already raised Jesus: "If the Spirit of him who raised Jesus from the dead dwells in you, he who raised Jesus Christ from the dead will give life to your mortal bodies also through his Spirit which dwells in you" (Rom. 8:2-11, v.11). Thus the Spirit is the pledge of the Christian resurrection hope (II Cor. 1:22), the firstfruits of the coming salvation (Rom. 8:23).

Everything that stands in relation to the reality of the resurrected Lord is filled with the power of life of the divine Spirit. This is true to begin with for the apostolic message, but also for the special tasks and services of the individual members of the community, insofar as they are grounded in the eschatological reality of Christ and contribute to the edification of the community. In the Spirit "the resurrected Lord" manifests himself "with his resurrection power, which is more than mere power of ecstasy and of miracle, which reaches for the world and leads in the new creation. The Spirit incorporates men into the worldwide body of Christ; he himself is the unity of the body composed of the bearers of the gift of the Spirit (I Cor., ch. 12) and finally brings about the resurrection of the dead."[135]

The Spirit guarantees the participation of the believers in the living Jesus Christ. The significance of this guarantee (Rom. 8:9 f.) is illuminated by the fact that the resurrected Lord himself is absent from his community and stays in heaven. We will come back to this later. First it should be noted that community with God himself is made accessible by community with Christ. Christians are "sons of God" because they are filled with the Spirit (Gal. 4:6; Rom. 8:14).[136] Because the Spirit is the Spirit of God himself, he unites with God himself. Paul expresses this in describing the believers' knowledge of God (I Cor. 2:10 ff.). Basil of Caesarea considered this the greatest witness for the Holy Spirit's belonging together with Father and Son in one Divinity.[137] Paul's statement, in fact, presupposes the Spirit's belonging to the

135 E. Käsemann, art. "Heiliger Geist," *RGG,* II (3d ed.), 1274.

136 In any case, the title "Son" designates a particularly close community with the "Father." Although at first in ancient Israel, analogous to a patriarchal social order, the people as a whole was viewed as standing in a relationship of sonship to Yahweh, though later this idea was pushed into the background by the idea of the covenant, and the father-son relationship was used to designate the special proximity of the king to Yahweh (Fr. Horst, "Recht und Religion im Bereich des Alten Testaments," *EvTh,* XVI [1956], 49-75, esp. p. 68), through Jesus' addressing of God as the Father of all men, the close community with God characterized therein is extended to all men. Jesus' community corresponded to this attitude by, in the first place, designating Jesus himself as "the Son," and then, as Paul does here, applying the term to Christians as "sons" of God.

137 See H. Dörries, *De Spiritu Sancto: Der Beitrag des Basilius zum Abschluss des*

divinity of God and its significance for the believers. If the Spirit who enters into the hearts of those who hear and believe with the message of Jesus' resurrection were not the Spirit of God himself, then the believer would have no true community with God through this message. This is the soteriological argument for the true divinity of the Spirit, which is to be found in Athanasius.[138]

Certainly, it is not sufficient to postulate the divinity of the Spirit by referring to the interest in salvation involved. Nevertheless, this reference makes clear the importance of the question to be decided here. The Scriptural texts to which one appeals, even the reference to the baptismal formula and to the inclusion of the Spirit in the doxology of the community, which played such a large role for Basil,[139] also leave the question open as to the inner reasons why the Holy Spirit who is present in believers should be regarded as God in the full sense as identical in essence with the Father and the Son. Basil answered this question by saying that the Spirit frees, while every creature is dependent and subservient.[140] As a theological argumentation from the perspective of the divinity of Jesus Christ, this suggestion is thoroughly illuminating, but it already presupposes *that* the Spirit makes free. If the latter is understood in the sense of an experience of faith through which the divinity of the Spirit would be first established, then the burden of proof expected of such experience is surely greater than it can bear. Erich Schaeder has recently attempted to substantiate the divinity of the Spirit in this sort of way.[141] He thinks that it is a matter of the experience of faith that the Christian possesses God's Spirit (p. 54). To the extent that the word of the gospel produces "the effect of an unconditional bond . . . , that becomes at the same time our absolute liberation" we experience here "a Spirit, . . . that does not belong to our natural status of being, that is radically different from what we are" (p. 64). Thus for Schaeder, as so often before him, it is really the ethical experience of guilt and forgiveness which causes us to believe that we "encounter the reality of God or of his Spirit in this experience" (p. 70).

Karl Barth has rightly rejected this argumentation for the divinity of the Spirit. Not experience, not even the experience of faith, establishes the divinity of the Spirit, according to Barth. "Who, then, can examine his consciousness for its God-content, following Schaeder's directions, without already knowing

---

trinitarischen Dogmas (Göttingen: Vandenhoeck & Ruprecht, 1956), pp. 62 and 160 on *De Spiritu sancto* XVI, 40. Of the other Scripture references in Basil, John 14:23 should be mentioned particularly.

[138] M. A. Schmidt, *RGG*, II (3d ed.), 1280, calls attention to Athanasius' letter to Serapion in 359 and to the position he took at the Synod of Alexandria in 362.

[139] H. Dörries, *De Spiritu Sancto*, pp. 132 ff., 146 f., 154 ff., 180, 183.

[140] Basil, *De Spiritu sancto* XXIV and XIII (Dörries, *De Spiritu Sancto*, pp. 59 and 69; cf. p. 88).

[141] E. Schaeder, *Das Geistproblem der Theologie* (Leipzig: A. Deichert, 1924). The following page numbers in the text are to this work.

from somewhere else what he is looking for?"[142] According to Barth, he knows what he is looking for through the word. But to believe that the word of the message about Christ itself is true, thus in order to believe that Jesus is the Lord, one needs the Holy Spirit, according to Barth.[143] That God's revelation becomes really revealed to man "is not a human possibility. It can only be God's own reality if that happens."[144] That Jesus' divinity cannot be known through any sort of experiences apparently makes the way clear, in Barth's thinking, for the particular reality of the Holy Spirit as a power who effects our knowledge of Jesus' divinity in spite of such human incapacity.

This argument for the reality of the Holy Spirit through whom the believer knows Jesus and is united with him is not convincing for us. To be sure, Barth is quite correct when he says that it is "not a human possibility" that God's revelation becomes known to man. However, it is precisely the power *of* the word that points back to the uniqueness of Jesus' history, thus to the uniqueness of this particular history, which penetrates into the ears and understanding of men through the word of the proclamation. This word brings with it the Spirit, through whom we perceive God's revelation in the history of Jesus recounted by the word. A Spirit *added to* the word—and where should it really come from?—is unnecessary. In this argument we intend to follow even farther Barth's argument against Schaeder which sets the word of the message about Christ in opposition to the experience of the Spirit that Schaeder insisted upon. The Holy Spirit is to be found in this word alone. He does not come to it additionally as a sort of appendix.

In view of this situation we must follow a different path to the knowledge of the Spirit's divinity than that taken by Barth. We must proceed from the knowledge of Jesus' divinity attained from the message about Christ if we want to understand the divinity of the Spirit.

As has been shown, the Christ event is, as an eschatological event, itself spiritual: it is—in the language of apocalyptic—the reality of the new aeon. For this reason, Christians have a share in the Holy Spirit to the extent that they share in the Christ event—in their confession to Jesus as the *Kyrios* (I Cor. 12:3), in the active verification of their belonging to him, in trust in him, and in the hope in one's own future participation in the life that has appeared in Jesus' resurrection from the dead. Because Jesus Christ, as the revelation of God, is one with the essence of God himself, the Spirit of Christ dwelling in Christians and going out from Jesus is the Spirit of God himself.

[142] K. Barth, *Christliche Dogmatik* (1927), p. 107.
[143] *Ibid.*, pp. 112 and 200 f. "The revealedness of the revelation" must be added to it from God "as a second, special factor that first makes the revelation revealed" (*ibid.*, p. 201). Cf. *CD*, I/1, pp. 470 f.; IV/1, p. 721. We will have to take over the sentence quoted positively in a specified sense later; it is questionable only in its assertion of an activity of the Spirit *externally added to the word* (in distinction from such an activity brought by the word itself) as a supplementary presupposition for its perception.
[144] K. Barth, *CD*, I/1, p. 473.

Only through the Spirit who unites with Jesus and thus with the revealed God do Christians know of God; for to the extent that men really know of God in Christ they are already bound to him through the confession, they already have the Spirit of Christ. The Christian consciousness of possessing the Spirit of Christ only expresses a reflection upon that which already happens in the knowledge of Jesus' divinity insofar as it is *my* perception. No knowledge, not even the knowledge of God's revelation in Jesus, is imparted to me in any other way than that *I* have the knowledge. Therefore, the Spirit belongs essentially to the event of God's revelation and thus to the divinity of God himself. For what belongs to God's revelation also belongs to the essence of God, if the revelation reveals God himself. Karl Barth has rightly emphasized that it belongs to the revelation that God really becomes revealed to *us* and that therefore God's becoming revealed in us must be understood as God's own reality.[145] Thus the divinity of the Spirit is dependent upon the divinity of Jesus. Because and only because Jesus is the Son of God and as such is God himself can the question of the criterion as to which Spirit is the Spirit of God (I Cor. 12:1 ff.) be answered: therefore, the confession to Christ is this criterion.

Because God is not only Father and Son but Spirit as well, he is not only the *object* of our consciousness but takes us up into his own reality. Thus he is beyond the subject-object dichotomy, not by excluding both but by uniting both. That is the true "nonobjectivity" of God.[146] The differentiation of

---

[145] *Ibid.*, pp. 473 and 478.

[146] The slogan heard so often today of God's "nonobjectivity" because he cannot be manipulated usually appears in the form of a simple alternative to objective consciousness, as if there were, in addition to objective experience and language, a particular nonobjective experience and language that are then usually related to an "existential" or "personal" sphere. However, the assertion of an immediate, nonobjective experience of nonetheless definite content (God, for example, in distinction from the world) is self-contradictory, since every definite content is grasped in distinction from one's own subjectivity and other contents. Thus it is "objective" in one degree or another (on this, see my statement in *ThLZ*, LXXXIII [1958], 327 f.). Only by going through the objective experience of God's actuality—through the ultimate suspension and absorption of its objectivity—is a nonobjectivity possible that is not merely general indefiniteness, but God's nonobjectivity. Thus this latter is itself mediated through an objective knowledge of God, which, because of its particular content, tends toward the suspension and absorption of its objective form. So, too, in R. Bultmann's famous essay, "Welchen Sinn hat es, von Gott zu reden?" of 1925 (*GuV*, I, 26-37), the critique of all objectifying language about God (p. 26) is derived from a specific concept of God, which, formally, is equally objectifying, namely, from the traditional idea of God's omnipotence (*passim*). The latter implies that there can be no place where man could escape God's claim, as is implied in the form of objectifying statements (p. 27). Thus in Bultmann's case, too, the thesis of God's nonobjectivity is in fact mediated by means of objective statements and only so can it be recognized as language about *God's* nonobjectivity. Admittedly, Bultmann himself does not reflect upon this structure of his argument. The proper form of being of this objectively mediated nonobjectivity of God is to be seen in the Trinity, its appropriate formulation in the Trinitarian doctrine, for the divinity of the Father and the Son, experienced as distinguished from the believer and thus as "objective," springs over through the Holy Spirit to embrace the subjectivity of the believer himself.

the Spirit from Father and Son thereby prevents our taking the wrong path, pantheism, which appears to lie close at hand. The Spirit of the knowledge of God in Jesus is the Spirit of God only insofar as believers distinguish themselves in such knowledge from God as creatures and from Jesus Christ as "servants" of the Lord: precisely in the humility of this self-differentiation from God that avoids all mystical exuberance, believers prove themselves to possess God's Spirit and thus to participate in God himself.

Through Jesus, the Spirit opens the way to community with God. Therefore, the Spirit of Christ demonstrates himself as the Spirit of community with God. That means the Spirit makes Christians the sons of God, just as Jesus has been designated to be the Son of God through the Spirit (cf. Rom. 1:4 with 8:23; Gal. 4:6). The difference is only that Christians become sons of God not immediately but through participation in the Sonship of Jesus— not by nature, but by adoption, as later dogmatics said. In that the Spirit is essentially the Spirit of Sonship, even as he is imparted to Christians, in that the Spirit is the Spirit who joins the Son with the Father, so the Holy Spirit of God is here recognizable as the Spirit of the community of Father and Son. This is the most inclusive concept of the Spirit in the revelation of God and thus in his eternal essence as well.

The patristic church attributed the character of an acting person to the Spirit, not merely that of an impersonally working power.[147] It expressed thereby an essential element of the Christian experience of faith. The believer who lives out of the power of Jesus Christ is not himself master of his behavior. He does not do the deeds of faith, hope, and love, which happen through him, on his own initiative but as one who has been overwhelmed by a power that works through him. "It is no longer I who live, but Christ who lives in me," says Paul (Gal. 2:20). In place of "Christ" one could also say "the Spirit."

We have seen how closely Christ and the Spirit belong together for Paul. The Spirit of Christ is the real subject of Christian action, insofar as such action happens out of trust in Jesus and the Father. The Spirit works in believers through the gifts especially distributed to each: "All these are inspired by one and the same Spirit, who apportions to each one individually as he wills" (I Cor. 12:11). Through the Spirit, the love of God is poured into hearts (Rom. 5:5; 15:30) and hope has been received (Gal. 5:5; Rom. 15:13), just as the Spirit has been received through faith (Gal. 5:5; 3:5, 14). The believers are "led" by the Spirit (Rom. 8:14; Gal. 5:18). The leading of the Spirit is not, however, the leading of a blind force of nature, but is of a personal sort. In this sense Paul can speak of a "mind" of the Spirit (Rom. 8:6,

147 Toward the end of the fourth century, in the controversy over the full divinity of the Spirit, his participation in personality, in the sense of hypostatic independence, was no longer contested. Cf. H. Dörries, *De Spiritu Sancto,* pp. 66 f. on Basil, *De Spiritu sancto* XX f., XXVIII.

27, *phronēma*). The Spirit shows himself to be a personal reality by not extinguishing the personal character of human action through his activity but by letting personal life come to consummation through willing dedication. A "serving" on the part of Christians (Rom. 7:6; cf. II Cor. 3:6; Phil. 3:3), the "walking according to the Spirit" (Rom. 8:4; II Cor. 12:18; Gal. 5:16) corresponds to the "mind" of the Spirit. However, this does not involve only a new ethical standard to which the individual would have to adjust his behavior. The Christian has rather been transplanted into a sphere of power in which his behavior is no longer subject to his own decision,[148] but which is nevertheless experienced as freedom, not compulsion. Through the Spirit the Christian has been transplanted into the freedom of sonship (Gal. 4:6 f.; Rom. 8:15; cf. II Cor. 3:17b).

The confession that the Holy Spirit is "person" thus expresses primarily the experience that the Christian is not his own lord. Insofar as he lives out of faith in Christ, the center of his person that determines his behavior lies outside himself. The personal center of Christian action is the Holy Spirit.[149]

That the Spirit is the personal center of Christian action residing outside the individual makes it understandable that in Paul, as elsewhere in primitive Christianity, the Spirit is characterized both as person distinguished from the Christians and also as a power that they possess internally. The Spirit comes to our aid (Rom. 8:26), gives witness to our spirit (v. 16), and claims our service (ch. 7:6); but he is also given to us, received by us, dwells in the believers, rests upon them. That both series of statements belong together is made clear by the insight that the Christian exists outside himself to the extent that he lives in faith in the resurrected Jesus and thus "in the Spirit." The immanence of the Spirit in believers exists only through the fact that as believers they have found the ground of their life *extra se,* beyond themselves.[150]

The most difficult problem of a doctrine of the Holy Spirit, namely, the question of his personal independence within the Trinity, can be approached only from the perspective of the personal manner that belongs to the working of the Spirit in believers. To be sure, we are now concerned with the personal character of the Spirit in relation to the Father and above all in relation to the Son, not in relation to the believer as previously. It has already been shown that Jesus as the Son remains distinct from the Father, even and

---

148 E. Käsemann, art. "Heiliger Geist," *RGG,* II (3d ed.), 1272-1279, esp. p. 1275.

149 To this extent the reality of the Holy Spirit is to be understood personally, even though the Holy Spirit apparently cannot be "person" in the same sense that we are, namely, not as an individual beside and confronting other individuals. We have omitted consideration of the designation of the Spirit as *Kyrios* (II Cor. 3:17) in our treatment of the personality of the Spirit because there the Spirit is apparently identified with the *Kyrios* Jesus Christ (see n. 134, above).

150 Therefore we cannot be satisfied with the distinction made by P. Althaus, *Die christliche Wahrheit,* pp. 497 f., between the two groups of assertions about the immanence and transcendence of the Spirit in relation to the believers.

precisely insofar as he belongs as Son to the essence of the Father, to the divinity of God. But what is the situation in this regard with the Spirit? The patristic doctrine of the Trinity apparently sometimes all too rashly inferred a similar personal uniqueness for the Spirit from the personal uniqueness of the Son.[151]

For us, however, a difficulty arises at this point that apparently played no role in the development of the patristic dogma. Precisely the close association of the Spirit with the resurrected Lord, as is seen in Paul, makes a personal distinction of the Spirit from the Son appear problematic. The Second Adam is himself the life-giving Spirit (I Cor. 15:45b). The Lord is the Spirit (II Cor. 3:17). In the conviction that the Spirit is identical with the resurrected Jesus, John too seems to have a point of contact with Paul (John 14:16, 18 ff.).[152] To be sure, both distinguish, though in different ways, between the Son and the Spirit. In John the Spirit is distinguished from the earthly Jesus and his way until the resurrection precisely by referring the Spirit back to the way of Jesus, binding them together (John 16:14). It was not without good reason that John wrote a Gospel describing the earthly life of Jesus. Paul, in contrast, distinguishes the Spirit as a reality already present from the coming revelation of the returning Christ (Rom. 8:23; cf. II Cor. 1:22). However, the expressions "earnest" and "firstfruits" imply that the difference between present and future with respect to the reality of the Spirit is only quantitative, so to speak, because believers will bear the image of the Second Adam who is the life-giving Spirit. Here Paul does not make any basic qualitative distinction between the present reality of the Spirit and that of the resurrected Lord, just as elsewhere he can speak almost promiscuously of the dwelling of the Spirit and of Christ in the believers (Rom. 8:9 f.).

The question here is whether the personal character of the Spirit who leads the believers is not perhaps identical with that of the exalted Lord. In any case in Paul the most one finds are beginning points for a distinction between the present reality of the Spirit who already "dwells" in the believers now and the Lord who will return only in the future (see I Thess. 4:16). The question that these texts pose for subsequent Christian thought is whether the distinction between the present time of the Spirit and the future of Jesus of Nazareth is so deep that Christian thought must go beyond the statements made by Paul and John. Perhaps one might say that primitive Christianity still lived so close to the Easter event and so much in the expectation of Jesus' imminent Parousia that its own present was wholly saturated by this. That the time of the church between the departure of the resurrected Lord and his

151 Cf. Basil's argument against Marcellus of Ancyra in Dörries, *De Spiritu Sancto*, pp. 166 ff. In general, the "breathing" of the Spirit and the "generation" of the Son were distinguished in the well-known way. On this distinction it is to be noted that in contrast to the Father-Son relationship, "breathing" as such does not reveal any personal difference.

152 On this, see R. Bultmann, *Das Evangelium des Johannes*, pp. 475 f., 477 ff.

future Parousia is characterized by his absence from the community is an insight that only begins to develop in Paul's debate with the Corinthians. And that the Spirit has already been given to the church in this interim period, precisely *in place of* the presence of Jesus himself only begins to come into view in Luke and John, once again in very different ways. The independence of the Spirit, which became increasingly clear with increasing distance from the Easter event and with the decreasing expectation of the nearness of the *eschaton,* can be taken as an indication that a third independent moment in God's essence is to be assumed only when a personal relation and thus also a difference of the Spirit from the Son can be demonstrated. The breathing of the Holy Spirit (cf. John 20:22), which played such an essential role in distinguishing the Spirit from the Son in the old doctrine of the Trinity, is not sufficient for such a demonstration. It would be preferable to refer to the glorification of the Son, which is not only mentioned by John as a work of the Spirit (John 16:14), but which has to do with the Spirit insofar as the Spirit is the driving force toward the confession of Christ (I Cor. 12:3).

Was Jesus not the recipient partner with regard to his glorification as it was granted to him by the Father in the exaltation of the crucified and resurrected Lord? And is he not the recipient partner in his glorification through his believers' confession? Is not the glorification something that happened to Jesus from outside himself? If this notion proves itself sound, then one can perhaps justify the step to the dogma of the Trinity in 381 that called the Holy Spirit the third "Person" in God alongside the Father and the Son. But even then one must clearly understand that this step leads beyond the concepts expressed by Paul and probably by John too.

The doxology of the church had been for Basil a decisive basis for knowledge of the Spirit's divinity insofar as the believing community in prayer knows how to distinguish the Spirit from itself and on the side of the Father and the Son. Similarly, it is the basis for our knowledge of the independence of the Spirit as a person over against the Son and the Father, because he leads us to glorify the Son and the Father and thus demonstrates himself to be distinct from both. On the other hand, the unity of the Spirit with the exalted Lord, which comes so clearly to the fore in Paul and John, reminds us of the unity of God in all the difference of his three modes of being which diverge in the revelatory event. Of what sort is this unity in difference?

7. The Unity in the Trinity (The Trinitarian Mediation of Monotheism)

For full understanding of Jesus' unity with God in the concept of revelation, we were led to the doctrine of the Holy Spirit. It is likewise indispensable for understanding the mode of Jesus' unity with the Father to consider the possibilities usually discussed within the doctrine of the Trinity for conceiving the unity of the divine Persons distinguished. It has already been shown that the concept of God's revelation in Jesus Christ contains within itself the Trinity of the Father, Son, and Spirit. Jesus, one with the Father, remains at the same time distinguished from him as the Son. Whoever perceives the divinity of Jesus, his unity with the Father, is thereby already engaged in the confession of Jesus as the Lord and thus is in possession of the Spirit. If Father, Son, and Spirit are distinct but coordinate moments in the accomplishment of God's revelation, then they are so in God's eternal essence as well. But how are they one single God in spite of such differentiation? The history of the doctrine of the Trinity shows an incessant wrestling with this problem. The unity of God is the presupposition of the concept of revelation and cannot be relinquished as a consequence of it. Otherwise, the concept of revelation would abrogate itself. How could an absurdity like that express the sense of Jesus' history?

The three most important paths toward solution of the problem of the unity in the Trinity are the doctrine of procession in the Eastern Church, the Western relational theory, and finally the theory of the self-sublimation of the three Persons in the unity of God.

The Eastern Church understands God's unity along the lines of the Logos Christology as a unity of origin, a unity of source (*pēgē theotētos*). This source of divinity is the Father. From him proceed Son and Spirit, not through a temporal process and not through a voluntary act but in eternal movement. Origen spoke of an eternal begetting. The commonness of origin establishes the unity of Father, Son, and Spirit with one another and with the origin.

It is easy to see that the Platonic or Neoplatonic idea of an emanation of the many out of the one stands in the background of this form of the Trinitarian doctrine, whose definitive formulation goes back to the great Cappadocian theologians toward the end of the fourth century, Gregory of Nazianzus, Gregory of Nyssa, and Basil of Caesarea. To be sure, the Neoplatonic pattern has been broken through by the thesis of the equal divinity of the three hypostases. Their continuing differentiation in spite of their identity of essence, the difference of *ousia* and *hypostasis,* seems to have been clarified with the help of Stoic ideas.[153] The background, nevertheless, remains Platonic. The subordinationist tendency of the Logos doctrine also can still be sensed when the Father is called the "source of divinity" and as such establishes the unity of the Three Persons.

In the Western Church the unity of the Trinity has been understood as a relational unity since Augustine. The relations of the divine Persons among

---

[153] See A. Grillmeier, "Das Scandalum oecumenicum des Nestorius in kirchlich-dogmatischer und theologiegeschichtlicher Sicht," *Scholastik* XXXVI (1961), 321-356, esp. pp. 339 ff., on the Stoic background of the Cappadocian doctrine of the Trinity, esp. of the thirty-eighth epistle of Basil.

themselves were seen as constitutive for their distinctiveness. This idea appears occasionally in the Eastern doctrine of the Trinity as well (e.g., Basil, *Ep.* 38, 7), but only through Augustine does it receive fundamental significance for the formation of Trinitarian doctrine. The Father is Father only vis-à-vis the Son; the Son is Son only vis-à-vis the Father; the Spirit is Spirit only as the bond of the community of Father and Son. No one of the Trinitarian Persons is who he is without the others; each exists only in reference to the others.

The weakness of this theory consists in its tendency toward dissolving the personal character of Father, Son, and Spirit. The designation of Father, and Son, and Spirit as "Persons" has been contested repeatedly since Augustine (*De trin.* V, 9; VII, 4) because it appeared to express too great an individual independence of the three. Karl Barth has called particular attention to this fact in his doctrine of the Trinity (*CD*, I/1, pp. 375 ff.). This Western tendency reaches its climax in Barth, namely, in his suggestion that one should speak of three "modes of being" instead of "persons" (pp. 378 ff.).

In the twelfth century Richard of St.-Victor pointed a way out of this difficulty by defining the very concept of "person" by means of that of "relation." To him personality seemed to be essentially a standing opposite, which is characterized by the inexchangeability of the relation of origin (*ex-sistentia*).[154] The antinomy between the personal independence of Father, Son, and Spirit, on the one hand, and the unity of the divine essence, on the other, is resolved in such a way that the personal independence consists precisely in the relation of origin through which the persons are bound together in the unity of the divine essence. But even in Richard the apparent limitation of the unity of the divine essence in the plurality of persons is not overcome. Richard does not conceive the unity of God himself from the reciprocity of the persons, even though he deduced the inner-Trinitarian confrontation from the essence of God as love.

In his treatment of the doctrine of the Trinity in his *Philosophy of Religion*, Hegel was the first to so elaborate the concept of "person" in such a way that God's unity becomes understandable precisely from the reciprocity of the divine Persons. Here we shall not go into the broader horizon of this argumentation, namely, Hegel's defense of the personal character of God against Fichte's denial of it.[155] His personality, God's being as subject over against

154 Richard of St.-Victor, *De trin.* IV, 12 (*MPL* 196, 937 f.). Here Richard sharpens the definition of "person" in Boethius as *naturae rationalis individua substantia* (*MPL* 64, 1343C).

155 J. G. Fichte, "Über den Grund unseres Glaubens an eine göttliche Weltregierung," *Philos. Journal* VIII (1798), 16 f., *idem, Gerichtliche Verantwortungsschrift* (1799), Vols. I, II, 3 (H. Lindau, *Die Schriften zu J. G. Fichtes Atheismus-Streit*, 1912, pp. 225 ff.). By contrast, Hegel's untiring emphasis that God as Spirit is not substance but subject signifies a defense of the personality of God (not only against Spinoza, but also against the Fichte of the atheism controversy), which forms the context for Hegel's statements about

the world, displays in Hegel the same structure as the personality of the Trinitarian Persons. And indeed for the perception of the Trinity from God's revelation both are associated in the closest way. The God who reveals himself is essentially person. He shows himself to be such in his revelation as Father in relation to the Son, who as the Son of the Father belongs indissolubly to the divinity of God. Thus the personality of the divine essence is also the presupposition for the differentiation of persons within the divinity. Here Father, Son, and Spirit confront one another as three distinguished subjects, three Persons. But, as Hegel says, it is "the character of the person, of the subject, to relinquish its isolation. Morality, love, is just this: to relinquish its particularity, its particular personality, to extend it to universality—friendship is the same. . . . The truth of personality is just this: to win it through immersion, through being immersed in the other."[156] Through this profound thought that the essence of the person is to exist in self-dedication to another person, Hegel understood the unity in the Trinity as the unity of reciprocal self-dedication, thus, as a unity that only comes into existence through the process of reciprocal dedication. Thereby he conceived God's unity in an intensity and vitality never before achieved, not by striking off the threeness of persons, but precisely by means of the sharpest accentuation of the concept of the personality of Father, Son, and Spirit. After Hegel this idea was no longer fully realized and was soon forgotten. Nonetheless it constituted the high point up to now of the conceptual clarification of the doctrine of the Trinity with respect to the relation between unity and threeness. With the exception of the problematic derivation of the Trinity from the concept of

God's inner-trinitarian Trinity of persons. The personal community of the three divine Persons is the living subjectivity of the one, personal God.

[156] Georg Wilhelm Friedrich Hegel, *Lectures on the Philosophy of Religion* (Humanities Press, Inc., 1962), Vol. III, pp. 24 f. D. F. Strauss objected to this defense of God's Trinitarian personality (*Die christliche Glaubenslehre* [2 vols.; Tübingen: C. F. Osiander, 1840 and 1841], Vol. I, pp. 493 f.) because it could not be harmonized with his young-Hegelian, pantheistic interpretation of Hegel, which, like the theistic critique of the younger Fichte, had to deny the element of personality to Hegel's concept of God (*ibid.*, pp. 512 ff.).

[157] The first steps toward a derivation of the divine Trinity from the concept of the Spirit are found in the West as early as Augustine, even though in his case this probably must be understood as mere explication of the existing dogma (M. Schmaus, *Die psychologische Trinitätslehre des hl. Augustinus* [1927], pp. 186 ff.). On the other hand, Anselm of Canterbury properly constructed the content of the Trinitarian dogma on the basis of the essence of God as Spirit (*Monol.* 27 ff.; cf. R. Perino, *La dottrina trinitaria di S. Anselmo nel quadro del suo metodo teologico e del suo concetto di Dio* [Rome, 1952]). Even in Thomas Aquinas, who in the doctrine of the Trinity attributes to the *ratio* only the ability to bring proofs of congruence (*Summa theologica* I, 32, 1c and *ad* 2), the psychological argument forms the real guideline for the development of the Trinitarian doctrine (*ibid.*, I, q. 27 ff.). A legitimation of the doctrine on the basis of the particular character of God's historical revelation, as it would have to be worked out in contrast to Hegel, was alien to the traditional doctrine of the Trinity in the church as it was developed in the line begun by Augustine. But the same is also true of the origins of the Trinitarian problem in the Logos Christology of the Greek Apologists.

Spirit that Hegel shared with tradition,[157] his idea is especially suited to the relation of Jesus to the Father and of the Father to him, as well as to that of the Spirit, who glorifies both, to the Father and the Son, as it is expressed in the New Testament. The relation of Jesus to the Father is entirely characterized by the dedication of the Son to the Father, that of the Father to Jesus by his acknowledgment of the Son in his raising Jesus from the dead. The Holy Spirit moves the believer to dedication to Jesus through believing trust and through praise in the confession of him. Conversely, the dedication of the Son to men constitutes the content of this confession. Jesus is dedicated to men in obedience to the will of the Father who invites all men to trust in him, so that in Jesus' dedication to his mission the love of the Father to men as his children has appeared. Correspondingly, the Holy Spirit mediates not only participation in Jesus through dedication to him, but also the community of the Son—and of the sons—with the Father. In the vital movement of such reciprocal dedication, the unity of Father, Son, and Spirit consummates itself in the historical process of the revelatory event. An intimation of this perception of the unity of the three persons grounded in complete reciprocal dedication is already to be seen in the patristic doctrine of the perichoresis, the reciprocal indwelling of the Three Persons in one another. But because of the influence of the abstract theism of the classical philosophical school, it was not then understood that this reciprocal indwelling of Father, Son, and Spirit constitutes the specifically Christian perception of God's unity.

Excursus: The Structure of Statements About Jesus' Divinity

As we have seen, anyone who thinks about God's revelation in the person and history of Jesus of Nazareth arrives necessarily at statements that contain apparently contradictory concepts, paradoxes: Jesus' unity with God, his divinity, is supposed to precede his own earthly existence as preexistent; the eternal God possesses in his essence a becoming that leads to the incarnation; the divinity of Jesus, which we confess to express Jesus' unity with the Father, is still distinguished as the Son from the Father and nevertheless is one with the Father. Such concepts, contradictory when taken for themselves, are meaningful only when they are *not* taken for themselves but are understood in their connection with their basis in the event of God's revelation in Jesus. The doctrine of the Trinity formulates the concept held by finite men of the God who is revealed in Jesus.

The conceptions of a preexistent divinity of Jesus and the ideas of the doctrine of the Trinity become contradictory when taken for themselves, because here we do not have finite objects that can be neatly defined over against one another and over against the one who is speaking about them. The contradictory character of the conceptions calls attention to God's infinity, which remains a mystery to finite understanding, even though our thought experiences God's infinity in its movement through the interrelated aspects of the revelatory event that leads to the doctrine of the Trinity. Our thought experiences the infinity of God, but does not comprehend it.

The structure of the conceptions that are formed in such a movement of reflection upon God's revelation in Jesus may be designated as doxological. In using this expression we follow Edmund Schlink's distinction between kerygmatic and doxological forms of expression. Kerygmatic statements speak of definite earthly events that are understood as events that come from God, and in this sense they speak of "God's acts." Doxological statements, on the other hand, intend primarily to speak of God's eternal essence. They are the praise of the eternal God on the basis of his deeds.[158] All theological language about God has such doxological character; it is essentially characterized by the structure of devotion and worship. In such doxological statements "God's eternal, all-inclusive sameness is praised." While in kerygmatic statements the "I" of the witness expressly appears and vouches for the truth that is witnessed to (p. 257), in the doxological statement the "I" who speaks disappears. For such a statement only the divine content comes into view. This "objectivity" is associated with the fact that doxology is essentially worship: "In the doxology the 'I' is sacrificed" (p. 256). To this extent Schlink's concept of the doxological statement is peculiarly related to Hegel's understanding of cult as faith and sacrifice, as devotion of the finite "I" in elevation to the absolute.[159] But unlike Hegel, Schlink does not overemphasize the sacrifice of the conceptions and of their consistency through the concept. He keeps more closely to the structure, which Hegel also recognized, of the sacrifice of one's own "I" in elevation to God.[160] "Doxological statements are final statements, beyond which nothing more can be said by man—statements in which the believer presents himself, his word, the logical consistency of his thought, to God as an offering of praise" (p. 271).

The distinction between kerygmatic and doxological statements only partially coincides with the form-critical usage of the corresponding terms.[161] In the sense here intended, doxological statements are statements about God on

158 Edmund Schlink, "Die Struktur der dogmatischen Aussage als ökumenisches Problem," KuD, III (1957), 251-306, esp. p. 255. The following page numbers in the text refer to this article.

159 Hegel, Philosophie der Religion, Teil I (Phil. Bibl. 59; Leipzig: Verlag von Felix Memor, 1925), p. 236; cf. pp. 141 f.

160 On this, see my article "Analogie und Doxologie," Dogma und Denkstrukturen; Festschrift für E. Schlink, pp. 96-115, esp. pp. 102 f. To show that and how, in spite of such sacrifice of the tendency proper to thinking to come to rest in the concept, the vitality of thought is not sapped but rather emancipated (in other words, how openness to a never exhaustively conceptualized infinity does not destroy thinking) would be the task of a theology of reason.

161 On this distinction, cf. my article "Was ist eine dogmatische Aussage?" KuD, VIII (1962), 81-100, esp. p. 94.

the basis of events that have been experienced as having occurred from him. They speak of the way in which God has shown himself in specific occurrences. Thereby human conceptualization sacrifices itself in adoration. Since designations and relations drawn from the finite realm are transferred to the eternal and infinite God, contradictory conceptions inescapably result. Thus in the act of praising adoration of God's eternity, the finite conceptions in which the praise takes place on the basis of definite finite occurrences are broken.

For this reason, doxological statements cannot be used as premises from which conclusions can be drawn without further ado. That is, only ideas that are in themselves unequivocal can be used for drawing conclusions. Conclusions can be drawn in an unequivocal and controllable way only from unequivocal concepts. In statements about God, however, the conceptual clarity of the ideas used disappears. Since they are transferred to God, they are consigned to God's infinity in an act of adoration. Conclusions can be drawn only from reflection upon the acts that lead to specific statements about God for specific reasons, but not from such statements by themselves. Therefore, for example, God's historical activity cannot be deduced from the doctrine of the Trinity and from the doctrine of the divinity of Jesus.

These statements cannot be used as "logical premises." "The historic way of the humiliation and exaltation of Jesus Christ can be neither inferred nor theoretically explained from the confession 'true God and true man.' "[162] Also, in this sense doxological statements are "final" statements.

The doxological element of Christological statements is founded upon their proleptic character which has already been touched upon (pp. 106 ff.).[163] Only an integrated view of the Easter event together with the coming end, a view originally based on the expectation of the eschatological imminent end, made it possible to understand Jesus' activity and fate as God's revelation. An individual event can say something about the one God only when it has in view the totality of reality. In the Biblical sense, however, this totality as the totality of history is accessible only through the anticipation of the end of all events. For this reason, the integrated view of the end toward which the expectations originally formulated in the apocalyptic literature were directed together with Jesus' fate was, therefore, the basis for the subsequent statements about Jesus' divinity. If these statements possess doxological structure, then the doxologi-

162 Edmund Schlink, "Die Christologie von Chalkedon im ökumenischen Gespräch," *Der kommende Christus und die kirchlichen Traditionen* (Göttingen: Vandenhoeck & Ruprecht, 1961), p. 85 (cf. *KuD* [1957], p. 271).

163 In greater detail in "Was ist eine dogmatische Aussage?" *KuD,* VIII (1962), 94 ff. The following could also be treated as interpretation of the expression "doxology," provided attention were paid to the Biblical meaning of *doxa* as the designation of the coming, eschatological revelation of God. In these terms it is clear, even from the designation "doxology," that this term has to do with an anticipation of God's future, which will first bring the full perception of his essence.

cal element of Christological statements is based on the proleptic element, since statements about God can only be made with a view to the totality of reality, which for its part comes into view only through anticipation of the end of history.

The doxological and proleptic structure distinguishes Christological statements about Jesus' divinity from mythological expressions that sound similar. While myth conceives a prototypal, divine reality as the origin of everything earthly and human, Christology finds God *in* the man Jesus. Where mythical thought focuses on the relation of the deity to man and to the world, this corresponds to its structure of thinking from the perspective of the prototypal divine, from "above" to "below." In contrast, Christological statements take their departure not only psychologically (as is, of course, also the case in mythical language) but also logically from the man Jesus, from what happened in Jesus to which the confession of faith answers. This distinction was not seen as sharply in primitive Christianity as it must be emphasized today. Primitive Christianity had the power to put forward without embarrassment conceptions that moved from above to below, from God to man. This is especially clear in the concept of the sending of the preexistent Son of God into the world. But even such statements intend to unfold the significance of what happened in the earthly history of Jesus. Even they have their beginning in historical occurrences. Here Christian theology quickly found its contrast to the mythical thinking of its religious environment. On the other hand, the concept of preexistence and hence that of the incarnation appeared inescapably in the line of thought taken from the historical Jesus and his resurrection. With this an element of truth in mythical thinking comes into view; it makes the points of contact perceived by the primitive Christian witnesses to mythological concepts of their environment understandable not only historically but substantively as well. However, in the Christian message this element is integrated into a context in which it attains a function different from that possessed in the myth. There exists, admittedly, the danger of remythologization, and it was certainly not always avoided in the patristic church. But the growth of mythical thought in theology became dangerous at that time only when the historical kernel of the Christian tradition was dissolved into supposedly timeless truths. In the modern period, the mythological way of thinking as such has come increasingly into conflict with the scientific understanding of the world and has thereby become a dead weight hindering the Christian message. Even the element of truth in the myth can be made valid today only in a way of thinking that is, in principle, unmythological. For this reason the old self-understanding of Christian theology, that its point of departure resides not in mythical divinations but in historical events, achieves new significance and a previously unknown radicality. However, as exegesis of the inherent significance of these events, theology must also accentuate those features that enabled early Christianity to establish contact with the mythical

186

thinking of its environment and permitted the recognition of an element of truth in the language of myth.

Occasionally the concept of "myth" is so broadly understood that the point of departure of this chapter, Jesus' resurrection from the dead, also appears as mythical language. If this judgment were justified, then the claim of Christology merely to unfold the significance inherent in the historical events of Jesus' history and of Jesus' person characterized by these events would be untenable. However, the expectation of a resurrection from the dead does not have the same character as the information provided by myths concerning prototypal events in the divine sphere. The expectation of the resurrection of the dead, which lies at the basis of the Christian Easter message, and such mythical information have only a metaphorical structure in common.

Its distinction from mythological language lies in the fact that the expectation of a future resurrection of the dead represents the adequate expression—precisely again in the contemporary situation in anthropological research—of the question beyond death which is inalienably a part of human existence. It is metaphorical, and, to be sure, in the sense of the "absolute metaphor"[104] which is the sole appropriate expression for a definite subject matter, and is neither interchangeable with other images nor reducible to a separate, rational kernel. The Christian Easter message itself rests on the absolute metaphor of the resurrection of the dead, as well as the proleptic element that provides the basis of doxological statements about the God revealed in Jesus, which are metaphorical in structure in their own way. The diverse metaphorical patterns of such statements and their involved connections of their establishment require more exact investigation, instead of the gross oversimplification that throws all metaphorical expressions into the pot labeled "mythological."

[104] On the concept of the "absolute metaphor," see H. Blumenberg, *Paradigmen zu einer Metaphorologie* (1961), esp. pp. 84 f.

Part Two
Jesus the Man Before God

In the contemporary scene it no longer seems particularly remarkable that Jesus was a real man. This is rather the self-evident presupposition of all statements about Jesus, both within and outside the church. In theology itself this presupposition becomes problematic only secondarily, from the perspective of Jesus' divinity; and perhaps with regard to the Jesus who has been raised and transformed into a new life, one may ask whether he can be called man in the full sense of the word. In contrast, there can hardly be any doubt about the fact with regard to Jesus' earthly life that one has to do with a man whose behavior is more or less to be understood in analogy to what we know as human behavior in ourselves and in others. Where the statement that Jesus is God would contradict his real humanity, one would probably rather surrender the confession of his divinity than to doubt that he was really a man. The strange ideas of Gnosticism and of Monophysitism are scarcely still accessible to even mere understanding, not to mention the truth claimed by them. The concept of man in appearance only and the Monophysite concept of a being who was completely permeated by divine immortality and glory on earth belong for us to the realm of fable and myth. If Jesus lived at all, if his existence is not to be counted as a matter of spiritistic mysticism, then he was a man like us. The only question is where the uniqueness of this man in distinction from other men is to be seen.

The historical uniqueness and individuality of Jesus does not interest us in dogmatic Christology for its own sake, but only insofar as it has *universal significance* at the same time. Certainly it involves the unique, the individual, in Jesus—not merely the universal human characteristics which Jesus of course shared. However, Christology involves Jesus' uniqueness only under a certain perspective, namely, to the extent that it has universal significance, to the extent that this particularity possesses saving significance for all other men. The saving significance indeed implies universality, namely, a relation to the universality of human destiny, which is valid for individuals as men and thus for all of them in common. This saving significance means the emancipation of men for their common destiny as men. The destiny of men is not present all along in the internal structure of individuals as what is common to them, but, so to speak, it comes upon them from outside as their future. Therefore, it can constitute Jesus' uniqueness that in him that which is man's destiny as man has appeared for the first time in an individual and thus has become accessible to all others only through this individual.

Undoubtedly one must seek Jesus' uniqueness first of all in his relation to God: then the uniqueness of the man Jesus consists precisely in his divinity, thus in what we considered in Part One. However, what Jesus' unity with God means for man as such is still to be considered in what follows. To that extent the reflections to which we now turn involve the soteriological power of Jesus' humanity, not only the fact that Jesus simply was a human being. That soteriological power is not an expression of human nature as such; it is not attributed to him by his community in the sense that the community projected its own desires and experiences back onto Jesus, that it merely became conscious through him only of the powers slumbering within itself. The soteriological power of Jesus' humanity follows, rather, from his particular relation to God. To be sure, the God of Jesus always shows himself anew at every time as our God, as the God of all men. He shows this in the power that proceeds from him to illuminate the humanity of man, his destiny, in a way that is always new and cannot be derived from the average empirical content of human existence or from its universal structure. Thus the question about the universal significance of Jesus' human uniqueness is associated with the fact that Christology does not consider Jesus from just any point of view, but rather as the Christ, the "Son of God," and thus in terms of God's revelation in him. The confession of Jesus' divinity finds its confirmation in Jesus' soteriological significance, and that means in the universal significance of his particular humanity.

CHAPTER

5

THE TRUE MAN

As God's revelation, Jesus is at the same time the revelation
of the human nature and of the destiny of man.

I. THE REVELATION OF MAN'S DESTINY IN
JESUS' DEEDS AND DESTINY

God's divinity is revealed in Jesus of Nazareth insofar as the relationship to Jesus determines men's ultimate destiny. It had been Jesus' claim that survival or failure of the men who confronted him was decided on the basis of their relation to him: "Everyone who acknowledges me before men, the Son of man also will acknowledge before the angels of God; but he who denies me before men will be denied before the angels of God" (Luke 12:8 f.; cf. Mark 8:38 and parallels). "And blessed is he who takes no offense at me." (Matt. 11:6.) Through the resurrection this claim of Jesus' was confirmed by God. Thus his relationship to Jesus reveals what a man is in God's eyes. The ultimate unveiling in the coming judgment is decided in advance by the relationship of Jesus to men and their relationship to him.

As we have seen earlier, Jesus' claim implied an identity with God insofar as he chose on his own authority those men whom he would accept into community with himself, into his community at table, and whom he would reject. By going beyond the traditional norm of the future participation in salvation, beyond the law, by interpreting the wording of the law on his own authority and taking sinners into the community of the eschatological meal with himself, Jesus made himself equal to God. Jesus knew that he was commissioned to carry out the ultimate decision about the men whom he met in the name of God himself. That had been in fact Jesus' office, for he was confirmed therein by his resurrection from the dead.

Through the event of Easter, Jesus' followers and all those who accepted the news of this event recognized that Jesus himself was identical with the eschatological judge, the Son of Man. He was now recognized as the bearer

191

of the office whose function he had already exercised on earth. How did this happen? In Jesus himself the ultimate destiny of man for God, man's destiny to be raised from the dead to a new life, had been fulfilled. Thus the revelation in Jesus of man's ultimate destiny in Jesus himself became the basis for the perception of his divine authority. The disclosure of God in Jesus and the revelation of the human destiny in him are thus closely associated.

In a certain sense this association was already clear in the apocalyptic eschatological expectation. Apocalyptic expected the universal unveiling in the eschatological event of everything that is now hidden. The unveiling of the riddles of existence, of the whole cosmos and of history, will take place in the end events because they will happen in the light of the glory of God himself: the Day of Judgment will "have neither radiance nor brightness nor light, but only the radiance of the glory of the Most High alone, by which all can see what is determined for them" (IV Ezra 7:24; cf. Rev. 21:23). Thus the revelation of God brings with it the revelation of all occurrences. For apocalyptic the glorification of the righteous and the making known of God's glory especially belong together.[1] So, too, the revelation of salvation for men may not be separated from God's revelation in Jesus. By creating eschatological salvation and by the fact that whoever he whom Jesus rejects incurs eschatological judgment, Jesus shows himself to be the executor of the end.

"Salvation" means nothing else than the fulfillment of the ultimate destiny toward which man is aimed, for which he seeks in his entire behavior. Salvation is the wholeness of his life for which he longs but never finally achieves in the course of his earthly existence. No one on his own initiative can make life complete, "whole," since the slightest discrepancy must destroy the whole. Where a life rounds itself out to a whole, it receives a reflection of its fulfillment; this can happen despite the deep contradictions that sever a man's existence. Only through the granting of salvation, however, is the essence of man realized; for the essence of man is not to be sought in what is already realized in man, but it still comes to him from his future. The essence of man

---

[1] Thus in the second Similitude of Ethopian Enoch, the throne of God is called the "throne of his glory" (ch. 45:3) and his name "glorious." Correspondingly, "glory does not cease" (ch. 49:1) before the Son of Man, and his glory is from eternity to eternity (ch. 49:2b). But even the just and the saints in the Final Judgment will "turn to glory and honor" (ch. 50:1), while unrighteousness will not be able to stand before the glory of the Lord of the spirits and in his judgment (v. 4). In Syr. Baruch, Baruch prays to God for the coming of the end in these words: "May thy glory be revealed and thy sublime majesty be known" (ch. 21:22); "and now quickly make known Thy glory and delay not with that which thou hast promised" (v. 25). Here, too, it is said that "glory" is prepared for the just (ch. 48:49). They will be transformed into glory (ch. 51:10, 12). Similarly, in IV Ezra the "glory of the Most High" (ch. 7:87) is the "glory of him who takes them [the just] unto himself" (v. 91); at the same time, however, it is "the glory that finally still awaits them" (v. 95). On this, cf. Rev. 21:23 and further in particular the mutual glorification of Father and Son in John (chs. 12:28; 13:31 f.; 17:1 ff.), the glorification of the Son through the Spirit (ch. 16:14), and the passing on of the *doxa* to the believers (ch. 17:22). See also above, n. 31 in Chapter 4.

is the destiny that still lies beyond the empirical content of man's present and that always lures man beyond everything at hand for man. Salvation is obtained when the destiny of man becomes identical with his present existence, when man is united in his present with his past and his future. It is surely clear that such unity with oneself is not possible without concurrence with the world and without community with other men. Anyone who correctly considers what such a wholeness of life means will recognize that in the life of the individual man, it finds no ultimate realization this side of death. The question about the fulfillment of man's destiny remains open beyond the death of the individual. The wholeness of his life in unity with himself, the world, his fellowmen, and God can come only in the resurrection from the dead, which is hoped for.

It is thus shown that the essence of man becomes revealed through Jesus, the Son of God, in a twofold way: first, through Jesus' deeds in that Jesus grants or promises community with himself and thus participation in eschatological salvation; second, in Jesus' fate insofar as man's destiny in the resurrection life has been revealed in Jesus himself.

The close association of God's revelation through the anticipation of the *eschaton* and the revelation of man is finally established in the fact that the essence of man, like his salvation, the fulfillment of his destiny, consists in openness for God. Openness for God is the real meaning of the fundamental structure of being human, which is designated as openness to the world in contemporary anthropology, although this designation means an openness beyond the momentary horizon of the world. Man's question about his destiny expresses itself in this openness. Only when man lives in the openness of this question, when he is completely open toward God, does he find himself on the way leading toward his destiny. Conversely, God's revelation means at the same time essentially the opening of men for God. Therefore, God's revelation means the salvation of men, fulfillment of their destiny, of their essence.

This connection is to be seen in Jesus' life and work. It was Jesus' vocation, his office confirmed through the resurrection, to call men into the Kingdom of God. Precisely for this reason he could impart salvation to them. Through this particular office Jesus distinguishes himself from all other men on whom he exercises this office. Jesus' disciples acquired a share in his office only from him, through the historical connection of a commissioning by him. On the other hand, through his office, calling men into the Kingdom of God, Jesus stood with his people in the history of Israel's God. Jesus' activity is understandable only from this history, for Jesus called Israel back into the nearness of the God who was Israel's God from Egypt on and for whose coming the pious Jew prayed daily. The election of this people by God and the expectation of the future revelation of his glory and majesty was the presupposition for Jesus' work. His office consisted in granting God's elected people a share in their election, by placing them under the Lordship of God. The next chapter will show how Jesus' whole work was determined by this office. Meanwhile, the concept of "office" itself must be more precisely clarified.

The way in which we have just spoken of Jesus' office is closely related to Albrecht Ritschl's concept of the "ethical vocation" of Jesus.[2] Ritschl saw the individual and the society closely connected in the concept of vocation, in much the same way as has been here asserted for Jesus' office: "The civil vocation designates the particular field of work in human society in whose regular exercise every individual realized simultaneously his own personal ends and the common ends of the society" (p. 420). Ritschl saw Jesus' vocation expressed in the title "Christ" (p. 421), since the content of this title is the Kingship exercised in God's name. Jesus "made the binding together of men through love or the Kingdom of God the goal for his disciples" (p. 391, § 45).

To be sure, when Ritschl called the "establishing of the Kingdom of God" (p. 425) as the ethical community of love the object of Jesus' vocation, he misunderstood the eschatological character of the language about the Kingdom of God in Jesus' proclamation. Jesus' office was not the establishing of the Kingdom of God, but rather calling men into the "soon" to set in, "near" approaching Lordship of God. Therefore, the "binding together of men through love" (p. 391) is not identical with the Kingdom of God nor with its establishment. Rather, Jesus' interpretation of the law that is summarized in the commandment to love is surely to be understood as the proclamation of that form of life which is appropriate to the impending Lordship of God. Only when its meaning is altered in this way, can we retain Ritschl's concept of Jesus' "vocation." Nevertheless, we still prefer to speak of "office" rather than "vocation." Ritschl wanted to substitute the expression "vocation" for the old Protestant term "office" (§ 46, pp. 409 f.), because in his opinion the concept of office had a too strongly legal character. However, Ritschl's contrast between love and justice, which constitutes the background of this argument, must be judged to be wrong. Love is not opposed to justice, but rather constitutes the kernel of justice itself.[3] In addition, the concept of office is important because it contains the aspect of a commissioning; Jesus' conduct is to be understood as activity in the service of an employer, not as a "free religious vocation" (p. 409). This aspect has, to be sure, roots in the literal sense of vocation as "calling." However, since we usually connect the notion of the "free choice of vocation" with the word "vocation," the concept of office is more appropriate for expressing the fact that Jesus understood himself entirely from God.

Man's destiny to openness for God constitutes not only the object of Jesus'

[2] A. Ritschl, *The Christian Doctrine of Justification and Reconciliation,* § 48, pp. 445 f. Cf. F. Schleiermacher, *The Christian Faith,* § 100,2.

[3] On this, see the preliminary suggestions in my essay "Zur Theologie des Rechts," *ZEE,* VII (1963), 1-23, esp. pp. 20 ff.

office, but it is at the same time fulfilled by Jesus' own conduct in his office and in his destiny. In the exclusive dedication to the office he received from God, Jesus lived as the man completely dedicated to God. If the concept of Jesus' office leads us to see him as God's authorized representative to men, then in his own conduct, precisely in the exercise of his office, he simultaneously represented the human situation over against God.

II. JESUS AS REPRESENTATIVE OF MEN BEFORE GOD

In his person, Jesus has become the fulfillment of the human destiny to community with God. While it was to be said with regard to Jesus' divinity, looking backward from his resurrection from the dead, that it always existed even before the beginning of his earthly existence, the effect of his unity with God upon the human course of Jesus' life went through a process of development. Even a rough consideration of Jesus' path lets three periods be distinguished, in spite of certain overlapping, in which Jesus' relation to God had different forms: the dedication to his office, the acceptance of his fate, and his glorification by God.

Through his resurrection, Jesus' earthly conduct was legitimated by God as dedication to an office conferred upon him by God. Here orthodox Protestant dogmatics spoke of the active obedience of Jesus; this was not, however, restricted to his office, but was primarily related to Jesus' individual ethical testing. This point of view will be completely omitted here, since Jesus' conduct must be entirely conceived from the point of view of his office. Jesus was not a private citizen alongside and outside of his office.

Jesus' acceptance of his destined death was also understood in primitive Christianity as the expression of dedication to God, of obedience to God. Thus, Paul apparently was thinking of Jesus' death, which is mentioned in Rom. 5:6 ff., when he says that through the obedience of one man God treats the many as righteous (Rom. 5:19). Here the expression "obedience" is clearly related to Jesus' death. This particular relation of Jesus' obedience to the destiny of death that befell him and that he accepted is also expressed in Phil 2:8 and Heb. 5:8: "Although he was a Son, he learned obedience through what he suffered." In orthodox Protestant dogmatics this obedience was designated as Jesus' passive obedience, in distinction from his active dedication to the will of the Father. This distinction acquires new meaning for us in the light of the contrast between the office and the fate of Jesus and it will be presented later in more detail. We must, however, avoid the idea that active obedience is connected with fulfilling the will of the Creator formulated in the law while passive obedience goes beyond this in offering the obedience as satisfaction for sin. We shall see that Jesus' vicarious suffering may not be understood as a work of satisfaction.

The fulfillment of human destiny has been revealed in Jesus through his resurrection from the dead. Jesus did not experience this event only for himself but for all men; Jesus' resurrection allowed the destiny of all men to a life in nearness to God, as Jesus had proclaimed it, to appear in him. Therefore, Paul could speak of the resurrected Lord in the terminology of the Jewish Adam speculation. Jesus is the New Adam, the second heavenly man, the life-giving Spirit in contrast to the first, earthly man (I Cor. 15:45 ff.). We will all bear "the image of the man of heaven" (v. 49); he is the prototype of reconciled humanity. As death came through the first man, so the grace of God (Rom. 5:15), life (vs. 17 f.), and righteousness (v. 18) has come through the second, true man. These ideas of the letter to the Romans are apparently an expansion of the concept of the resurrected Lord as the heavenly man in I Cor., ch. 15. The latter started from the idea of Jesus' resurrection; in Romans the pre-Easter obedience of Jesus is included as well (Rom. 5:19).[4]

[4] The tradition standing in the background of the Pauline Adam typology is still a matter of controversy. To be sure, there is general agreement that in I Cor. 15:45 f. Paul refers to a doctrine that we also find in Philo (*De opif. mundi* 134 ff. and *Leg. all.* I, 31 on Gen. 2:7); according to this the first man was of heavenly origin, the image of God (Gen., ch. 1) and the second of earthly origin (following Gen., ch. 2). Paul inverts this thesis by expressly asserting that not the first but the last Adam is the spiritual man coming from heaven. Up to this point Oscar Cullmann, *The Christology of the New Testament*, pp. 167 ff., and Egon Brandenburger, *Adam und Christus: Exegetisch-religionsgeschichtliche Untersuchung zu Röm. 5:12-21 (I. Kor. 15)* (Neukirchen Kreis Moers: Verlag der Buchhandlung des Erziehungsvereins, 1962), pp. 117-131, are in agreement. Both also assume an influence of extra-Jewish speculation about the primal man. However, Cullmann postulates such an influence of (Iranian?) teaching about the primal man even for the "man" (or Son of Man) coming with the clouds of heaven in Dan., ch. 7 (pp. 142 f.), and views the "original solidarity" of the Son of Man with the separately developed doctrine of the prototypal glory of the first man (Adam) as being based on this influence (p. 144). Brandenburger, ôn the other hand, emphasizes that the apocalyptic Son of Man has nothing to do with the historical first man, nor with the first man in the sense of a prototype of humanity, or even of the creation of the world (*Adam und Christus,* p. 132, against W. Schmithals, *Die Gnosis in Korinth* [Forschungen zur Religion und Literatur des Alten und Neuen Testaments, 47; Göttingen: Vandenhoeck & Ruprecht, 1956], pp. 100-104, who recognizes Reitzenstein's Iranian primal man in the Son of Man). This latter differentiation is to be welcomed; however, it leads Brandenburger, who objects to Cullmann's insufficient distinction between the "incompatible conceptions of the *heavenly* and the *first* historical man" (*ibid.,* p. 138, n. 1; cf. also C. Colpe, *Die religionsgeschichtliche Schule* [Göttingen: Vandenhoeck & Ruprecht, 1959], p. 194, n. 1), to the conclusion that the idea of the "heavenly" man and his glory are foreign to the Jewish tradition (*Adam und Christus,* pp. 114, 138) and derive from Gnostic Adam-*anthrōpos* speculation of extra-Jewish origin (*ibid.,* pp. 130 f.). In this sense he thinks that in Hellenistic Jewish circles the Son of Man title was "virtually of necessity" reinterpreted; correspondingly, here he finds the explanation for the disappearance of the "Son of Man" title in Hellenistic Christianity as dissolution in the related, equally heavenly, "Christian-Gnostic *anthrōpos*- ("Man-") Redeemer" (*ibid.,* p. 156). But against both Brandenburger and Cullmann it is necessary to consider the possibility of a coherent inner-Jewish formation of tradition, a possibility which Brandenburger questions (*ibid.,* p. 114, against J. Jervell, *Imago Dei,* pp. 38 ff.). Brandenburger's presupposition of Gnostic doctrine of the primal man who is the redeemer in the pre-Christian period has been made doubtful by C. Colpe's thorough critique in the work named above of the Gnosticism hypotheses of Reitzenstein and Bousset. The interpretation deriving from

In all three areas Jesus is man's representative before God, bringing the destiny of men to fulfillment in his own person. To this extent Jesus is the representative of humanity before God. The idea of representation[5] does not involve only—and not primarily—Jesus' death. It is already contained in Jesus' realization of man's destiny as such, in his simply becoming the representative of true humanity, as is asserted by the Pauline idea of Jesus as the New Adam. Only because Jesus stands as the representative of man before God as the "Last Adam" in the light of his resurrection, can his death acquire vicarious significance.

Jesus is the man well-pleasing in the eyes of God in the dedication to his office, in the obedient acceptance of his fate, and through his resurrection to a new life. Only for this reason can other men's community with Jesus become the guarantee of their community with God, just as Jesus had claimed for himself.

Bousset's *Religion des Judentums im neutestamentlichen Zeitalter* (Berlin. Reuther & Richard, 1903), that the figure of the "man" in Judaism requires clarification by appeal to extra-Jewish influences (p. 253), needs to be reexamined. If it is true that one has to take into account various, independent starting points for "Gnostic" thinking on the basis of the various religions in the ancient Near East rather than simply a single, unified Gnostic movement, one will also have to seek a special Jewish history of traditions in the case of the "Son of Man" (Adam) complex. This would not have to exclude contacts with extra-Jewish conceptions; the latter, however, do not always provide a sufficient explanation for the emergence of specific ideas within the Jewish tradition. It is often the case that motifs from Jewish tradition may well exercise stronger motivating power than the parallels in comparative religion which may have served as a stimulus but are in many cases very vague. Cullmann himself calls attention to the fact that the connection of the figure of the "Man" with the heavenly sphere, which is characteristic for the Son of Man after Dan. 7:13, and which cannot be explained on the basis of Jewish texts (*The Christology of the New Testament*, p. 142), nevertheless has a "point of contact" in the Old Testament idea of man as created in the image of God (*ibid.*). This has less to do with the idea of "image" than with proximity to the divine sphere: Ps. 8:5 has said that man is made a little lower than the Elohim beings and is endowed with glory and majesty. Even Brandenburger (*Adam und Christus,* pp. 136 ff.) holds the wisdom and beauty of the first, protoypal man praised in Ezek. 28:12 ff.; Job 15: 7 f; Sirach 49:16 to be genuinely Jewish. Should we not perhaps conceive similarly the "initial forms" of the Gnostic-Jewish Adam-speculation of Philo and others, "initial forms" that Brandenburger suspects "as the background of the Son of Man conception" (*ibid.*, p. 134)? Further, is not the concept of Adam as a being like an angel with a *doxa*-body (held to be non-Jewish by Brandenburger) understandable as an exegesis of Ps. 8:5? (Cf. Apoc. Moses 33 and 35; Vita Adae 12-14; Brandenburger, *Adam und Christus,* p. 113.) Presumably the same is true of Enoch, chs. 49 and 71 (against Brandenburger, *ibid.*, pp. 114 f.). Accordingly, the symbol of the "Man" ("Son of Man") in apocalyptic after Dan. 7:13 gave an eschatological turn to the idealized image of the first, archetypal man, making of the latter an image of the promised consummation of humanity in the end time (on Dan. 7: 13, cf. Klaus Koch, "Spätisraelitisches Geschichtsdenken am Beispiel des Buches Daniel," *Historische Zeitschrift,* CXCIII (1961), 1-32, esp. p. 24). Then Paul, by inverting the theologoumenon of the first and the second man, contrasted the eschatological understanding of true humanity to the archetypical one (I Cor. 15.45 ff.); but at the same time he could also describe in archetypical language the eschatological destiny of man as already fulfilled in Jesus Christ (I Cor. 15:49; Rom. 5:15 ff.). Cf. below, n. 13.

[5] O. Cullmann, *The Christology of the New Testament,* pp. 171 ff., has especially brought out the idea of substitution implied in the Adam Christology.

The exemplary significance of Jesus' humanity has quite properly played a large role in the history of Christology. From the beginnings of the patristic church until the present, Jesus has been considered in a variety of conceptual patterns as man's representative before God.[6]

a. Through the incarnation of the Logos, the nature of man as living being having the Logos (*zōion logon echon*) is consummated: Jesus is the man who finds himself in full possession of the Logos. Athanasius expressed the matter in this way in his work about the incarnation of the Logos. Irenaeus expressed it similarly before him, as did the Alexandrian Christology later. Only through the incarnation of the Logos does the true man come into existence.

b. Jesus is the man who brings the universal human striving toward the imitation of God (*homoiōsis theōi*) to its goal. Through his ethical perfection, he achieves perfect participation in the divine unchangeability, in God's permanence in the good. We found this idea developed in Paul of Samosata and later, above all, in the Antiochene Christology.

c. Through the merit of his freely offered striving, Jesus is the man who has fulfilled the duty of obedience incumbent upon all men and the duty, which has burdened humanity since Adam's fall, of satisfaction through a work of supererogation. The penitential thinking of the medieval church, first in Anselm of Canterbury, recognized itself in the image of Jesus.

d. Jesus is the prototype of God's dealings with humanity and thus also the prototype of justification by faith. He is the man who even in the undeserved misfortune on the cross upholds the right of the God who judges and thus is himself righteous before God because he remains in harmony with God's will. This is the idea of Luther whose early period is particularly characterized by this formulation.

e. In Jesus, man's true humanity is realized in that in him the consciousness of God that establishes the unity of human existence is dominant with a prototype strength that has not been exceeded in contrast to the self-consciousness, the object-consciousness that is characteristic of man's inner-worldly relations. With this concept Schleiermacher expressed in a classical way the understanding of Christ in the piety and theology of Pietism as it lives on somewhat altered in the present day. This is true in spite of all later criticism of his idea of the prototype.

f. Jesus is the prototypal man, who as the one completely obedient to God was completely dedicated to his fellowman.[7] This concept of Barth's has made clear the priority of Jesus' relation to God over his significance "for us," so that the latter has its only adequate basis precisely in Jesus' relationship to God.

g. As the Son, Jesus is in a prototypal way what all men ought to be: the reality of the sonship that is intended for all in trusting obedience to the

---

[6] On the following, cf. the survey of types of soteriological motivation in Christology given above, pp. 39 ff.

[7] Karl Barth, *CD*, III/2, § 44, 1, and § 45, 1.

Father and in free responsibility for the inheritance of the creation entrusted to him. With this idea, Gogarten has traced back the sovereign lordship of modern man over the world to Jesus' relation to God as its origin, and discovered in this idea a way to avert the doom of modern self-glorification and enslavement to the world.

h. Jesus is eminently the believer who exposes himself directly to God's future. Jesus is the "essence of faith" and faith is the "essence of what Jesus did."[8] Thus for Ebeling, Jesus is the "witness of faith." Because faith as man's new self-understanding has its support in Jesus himself, in Jesus' relation to the Father, it is protected from the suspicion that it might be "objectless."[9] Ebeling is concerned to bring the structure of Christian faith into relationship with Jesus' message of God's nearness and Lordship as well as with his own conduct. This concern is justified, even if the Synoptic Gospels, which speak of Jesus' demand of faith from his hearers, used the terminology of the Hellenistic-Jewish mission. If faith determines the entire life of the Christian, then it is important that it be, even in its structure, discipleship, participation in Jesus' way, in his behavior.[10] Even if Jesus himself is not supposed to have issued a call to "faith," this expression, precisely as it was stamped by Paul, appropriately designates the conduct of the hearer demanded by Jesus' message of the nearness of God's Lordship. His own activity, especially in his last journey to Jerusalem, expressed this same confidence in the imminent arrival of God's Lordship that Jesus demanded of his hearers.

i. Also, in contemporary Catholic Christology, Jesus Christ as the divine-human person is understood as the highest perfection of the human. Thus Karl Rahner says, "Christology is the beginning and the end of anthropology, and this anthropology in its most radical realization, namely Christology, is in all eternity theology."[11] According to B. Welte, Jesus is the fulfillment of that unlimited openness which is constitutive for being human and whose truth is openness for God.[12] This conception has the advantage of making the insights of modern anthropology about man's openness to the world fruitful for Christology. Among the Protestant proposals, the ideas of Ebeling (and Bultmann) come closest to that suggested here. What Ebeling calls faith is, as openness for the future and thus in its specifically modern character, very closely related to the anthropology of openness to the world. In fact one must

8 G. Ebeling, "Jesus and Faith," *Word and Faith*, pp. 201-246, esp. p. 204. At greater length he says on p. 238, "The communication of faith takes place solely out of the certainty of Jesus, which in turn consists in his obedience, so that this obedience has a vicarious function, viz., as vicarious obedience it becomes the source of faith."
9 G. Ebeling, *The Nature of Faith*, p. 46. On Jesus as the witness of faith, cf. pp. 51 ff.
10 *Ibid.*, p. 56. He no longer speaks expressly of Jesus' own faith; cf. p. 100.
11 Karl Rahner, *Schriften zur Theologie* (1960), Vol. IV, p. 151.
12 Bernhard Welte, "Homoousios hemin," in *Chalkedon*, Vol. III, pp. 51-80, esp. pp. 58, 67, 71. See also Karl Rahner, art. "Jesus Christus," *LThK*, V (1960), 953-961, esp. p. 956, and the studies by Rahner cited there; *idem, Schriften zur Theologie* (1960), Vol. IV, p. 142.

understand Jesus' unity with God as the fulfillment of the openness to the world that is constitutive for man as such, if this openness has its real meaning in an openness extending beyond the world to God.

When one looks at the series of various understandings of Jesus Christ as the fulfillment of human nature, an important suspicion arises: Is the change of Christological conceptions perhaps explained as a change in the image of man? Has one perhaps always simply read into the figure of Jesus the changing ideal images that man projects about himself, as Albert Schweitzer demonstrated was the case in the quest of the historical Jesus? Would this not mean a complete failure to grasp Jesus' uniqueness in these various Christological conceptions? Would not one rather simply have hidden Jesus' uniqueness under the universal ideal images of man?

In order to test this suspicion we must ask: Where do these changing ideal images of man's essence arise? What relationship do the conceptions of man's essence, of the true man, attached to the figure of Jesus have to the historical figure of Jesus himself?

In the first example of the series, in the Jewish Adam speculation that Paul applies to Jesus, a point of contact is present in Jesus' own fate. As the resurrected Lord, as "the first fruits of those who have fallen asleep" (I Cor. 15:20), Jesus is the prototype of the new man. Thus Paul continues: "For as by a man came death, by a man has come also the resurrection of the dead. For as in Adam all die, so also in Christ shall all be made alive" (I Cor. 15:21 f.).

In Paul the transfer of the ideal of the true man to Jesus has an impulse in the fate of Jesus himself. This is, of course, related to the fact that the appearances of the resurrected Lord were experienced within the horizon of the universal human hope for resurrection in apocalyptic. This made it possible for Paul to ascribe universal human significance to what happened to Jesus. In no sense did he simply transfer the notion of the prototypal, heavenly man unthinkingly to Jesus. In a Jewish exegetical tradition, used in the speculation of Philo of Alexandria, the two Old Testament accounts of the creation of man were characterized as that of the heavenly man (Gen. 1:26 ff.) and as the creation of the earthly man (Gen. 2:7) about whom the account of paradise and the Fall is narrated. Paul reversed this sequence, apparently because he thought that life in community with God, in heavenly glory, is represented only by the future human reality expected from the eschatological resurrection of the dead, which has already begun in Jesus Christ. Paul thus shifted the locus of true humanity from the distant past to the future. For mythical orientation to a prototypal distant past, he substituted an eschatologically oriented concept of human history.[13] Although this repeats in a way

13 E. Brandenburger, *Adam und Christus,* pp. 237-245, argues convincingly that Paul "forces" the *anthrōpos* category "from the sphere of the suprahistorical-speculative into that of history" (p. 238), and, in the sense of an eschatological universalism of salvation

what Daniel had already expressed by symbolizing the coming Kingdom of God in the figure of a "man" (the Son of Man), Paul establishes this conception in a different way, namely, with the beginning of the reality of this "new man" that has already occurred in Jesus' resurrection. Only in this way is there a real parallel between Adam and Christ, because the reality of the new, last man is destined to become effective for all men through Jesus, just as sin and death affected every individual through the first Adam.[14] Just as both death and its basis, sin, have been transmitted to all men from the first Adam, so Paul can reckon both the new life that has appeared in Jesus' resurrection and his "obedience," which corresponds negatively to Adam's sin, to the reality of the "Last Adam" that has appeared in Jesus (Rom. 5:15 ff.).

The reinterpretation of traditional, anthropologically relevant concepts and titles in their application to Jesus can also be shown in other New Testament examples. This is true especially of the concept of Jesus as the image of God,[15] and probably also of the Johannine concept of the Logos. Here we have chosen the concept of the heavenly man as an example because it characterized Jesus as the "true man" expressly, not merely by implication. The connection, although it was probably seldom consciously made, in the history of traditions between this concept and the figure of the Son of Man, which was important for Jesus' message and for the earliest Christology, shows that the understanding of Jesus as the eschatological man was by no means merely a peripheral concept in primitive Christianity.

In the patristic Logos Christology a more or less extensive transformation

(p. 244) in which the universality of the forgiveness of sins accomplished by the death of Christ (p. 237), presupposes a corresponding universality of the sin that humanity incurred through the first Adam, which therefore is not to be understood only as violation of the Mosaic law (pp. 203 f.). As Brandenburger stresses, this historical-typological inversion of the doctrine of the first and the second man was possible only in the context and by means of the Jewish apocalyptic traditions (pp. 241, 246). We can add that in the figure of the apocalyptic Son of Man the understanding of the genuine reality of man had already been shifted into the eschatological future. This is true even though this original, symbolic meaning of the future of the Son of Man which appears in Daniel (K. Koch, article cited in n. 4 above) may subsequently have been forgotten in favor of a rather "mythological" understanding of the Son of Man as an individual eschatological figure. Paul, then, with his doctrine of the "Second Adam," restored the original meaning of the idea of the Son of Man as the eschatological realization of the human in its heavenly destiny. But he also "fundamentally restructured" (Brandenburger, *Adam und Christus,* p. 246) this apocalyptic eschatology by means of the archetypal language of the Adam speculation that was on the way to developing into Gnosticism. Apparently this had to happen because for Paul the eschatological destiny of man had already dawned in Jesus Christ, thus raising the question of participation in it. This question could be answered by the archetypal aspect of the *anthrōpos* category. Thus Paul, in the light of the experience of the Christ event, transformed not only the Adam speculation about the first, prototypal man, which we find in Philo, but also the eschatological turn that had already been given to this speculation in apocalyptic.

[14] On the characteristic limits of these parallels, cf. G. Bornkamm, "Paulinische Anakoluthe im Römerbrief," *Das Ende des Gesetzes, Paulusstudien: Gesammelte Aufsätze,* Band I, pp. 80-90; E. Brandenburger, *Adam und Christus,* pp. 219-231.

[15] On this, see J. Jervell, *Imago Dei* (1960), pp. 256 ff.

of the given conceptual material is also to be recognized. In John's Gospel one reads that in Jesus the divine Logos has appeared. The language of the incarnation of the Logos here signified a profound change in the Logos concept in contrast to the mediatorial hypostasis of the Logos found in Philo—perhaps identical with the "heavenly man."[16] One must recognize a similar accomplishment in relation to the Stoic Logos doctrine in Justin's theory that in Jesus the fullness of the Logos has appeared as man in contrast to the seeds of the Logos which are otherwise dispersed in men. With its formula about man as the living being having the Logos (*zōion logon echon*) the Greek philosophical anthropology merely provided the opportunity to connect the general understanding of man with the particularity of Jesus' person. In this process—and this was the danger—the philosophical Logos concept could occasionally assert itself in a rather unbroken form. But it was also possible to understand the rationality of man in general from the perspective of the divine-human unity in Jesus as the dependence of man upon the freely active God of the Bible.

The images of man of the "likeness to God" (*homoiōsis theōi*) type and of penitential thought are relatively alien to the New Testament tradition about Jesus. To be sure, impulses to both conceptions are present in primitive Christianity, although they are of a rather superficial nature. One possibility of interpreting Jesus in the sense of the *homoiōsis theōi* was justified for the patristic exegesis in that he had not only interpreted and reformulated God's law—viewed superficially, similarly to a Hellenistic teacher of virtue who preached the *homoiōsis theōi*—but he also placed himself under the law and was determined to be the fulfiller of the law. This way of thinking seems still more profound than the concept of Jesus in the modern Enlightenment as the ethical teacher and ideal of a virtuous life.

The medieval penitential thought continually took its impulse from Jesus' own call to repentance. Anselm of Canterbury could appeal to fundamental New Testament statements for Jesus' obedience. To be sure, his understanding of Jesus as the representative of the human obligation to bring satisfaction to God found a point of departure only in primitive Christianity's theory of atonement, and even here Jesus' death was hardly understood as a work of satisfaction.

The image of man in the doctrine of justification by faith which we find in Luther, as well as Schleiermacher's conception that there can be no full humanity without a dominating consciousness of God, stands much closer to the real figure of Jesus perceived behind the Synoptic tradition. For us, Schleiermacher's conception has the deficiency that it is so abstract that we gain little information about what concrete form the knowledge of the true God in human existence has. This becomes clearer in the pictures of man expressed in the modern Christologies. They show how man is truly man only

[16] So Carsten Colpe in a lecture, as yet unpublished.

in openness to God, to the future, in the risk of trust, in the responsibility for the world of true sonship, and in loving dedication to the neighbor. These concepts of man's destiny involve throughout an understanding of man that has become possible only within the realm of Christendom. This was true, as well, of Luther's concept of Jesus as the prototype of justifying faith. Here it is not just any handy understanding of man that is projected onto the figure of Jesus. The historical sequence is rather the reverse. Our understanding of man today is deeply stamped by the centuries-long influence of Biblical thought, and especially of the figure and message of Jesus. Therefore it is completely appropriate to bring to light the roots of certain definite, fundamental elements in our general understanding of true humanity in Jesus' behavior and in his message.

To be sure, these relationships are not always obvious at first glance. In the case of the image of man as a person they are mediated by the history of the doctrine of the Trinity and the transformation of the concept of person that has taken place in this history.[17] The sovereignty of modern man over the world has not emerged without express appeal to God's having committed lordship over the earth to man, as found in the Priestly account of creation (Gen. 1:28), but it is probably even more deeply rooted in a particular understanding of man as the image of God, namely, as man's intellectual creativity in analogy to the creativity of the Biblical God.[18] Finally, the classical humanistic tradition, which was already understood more or less in the light of such ideas as expressed by Nicholas of Cusa, contributed to produce a Christian humanism of the active life.

The bases of the concept of man's "openness" are even more multileveled. The Aristotelian notion that the soul is everything, as it were, and the Platonic upward glance toward the divine idea of the good were led beyond the limits of macrocosm-microcosm analogy through the Biblical faith in the divine promise and its transformation in the Thomistic doctrine of the supernatural destiny of man and only thus are transformed to the concept of the openness of man. The justification for tracing this conception back to the figure of Jesus is established by the concentration of the Biblical heritage on his person. This is true even where anthropological insights have been acquired under the influence of the Biblical faith in the divine promise but not directly through Christological argumentation. This is true especially since the correspondence of anthropology and Christology has been operative in the whole history of ideas in Europe since the rise of Christendom. The situation is similar with the concept of the sovereignty of man over the world. The understanding of personality probably reflects even more direct influences from the picture of Jesus himself.

[17] On this, see my article "Person," *RGG*, V (3d ed.), 230-235.
[18] Cf. my article "Wirkungen biblischer Gotteserkenntnis auf das abendländische Menschenbild," *Studium Generale,* XV (1962), 586-593, esp. pp. 589 ff.

The result of our survey is that the ideal of the truly human was not projected onto Jesus' figure at random without any foothold in his historical reality. Rather, everywhere that Jesus has been thought of as the true man, corresponding to the intention of the respective theologians, the concept involves elements of Jesus' own particular individuality which have been recognized in their universal significance. This is surely the task of the church's doctrine of Jesus' humanity: to point out the universally human significance of his particular individuality, of his particular life and work. This significance, because of the uniqueness of Jesus' activity, cannot reside in something distinct from himself, not in a life work that can be separated from his person, but rather only in his person itself.

The formal law of the earliest transmission process of the tradition about Jesus was designed to transmit only the particular elements of Jesus' work and conduct that had general significance for the community and for the world that was to be evangelized. That has remained the formal law of all theological statements about the man Jesus. Therefore, in various individual elements of Jesus' person and work, we can discern a more general significance. It is only important that the beginning point for such consideration always be an element that belonged to Jesus himself. Otherwise, the unique historical reality of Jesus is no longer interpreted, but rather replaced, by anthropological conceptions derived elsewhere. For example, we see today that the ethical ideal of the *homoiōsis theōi* and Anselm's understanding of the task of ethical accomplishment before God have little support in Jesus himself. The impulses that the authors of these interpretations apparently thought to maintain—the ethical teaching of Jesus, his demand to be perfect as the Father in heaven is perfect, the primitive Christian concept of Jesus' expiatory death as an act of obedience—rest extensively on misunderstanding, compared with Jesus himself. The situation is different with the other conceptions mentioned. They have support in Jesus himself to a higher degree.

Theology cannot be satisfied with discovering Jesus' significance for humanity in one or another individual element of Jesus' figure which, when set free from its context and isolated, perhaps acquires a completely inappropriate significance. The sermon can and probably must proceed by bringing near to the hearers definite individual aspects of Jesus' appearance set forth in the Biblical witness in their saving significance. Nevertheless, even the preacher needs the continuous influence of theological reflection in order to preserve his vision for the right proportions. But theology must take into consideration the complex totality of Jesus' historical individuality and seek to formulate his universal significance, even though it is probably only able to perceive that totality as relevant for humanity under one aspect or another that is related to the anthropological problematic of the time.

One ought not to despise the task of considering the universal significance of Jesus' particular individuality, even if it has hardly ever been undertaken in a methodical way. It is not without reason that the material about Jesus was transmitted from the very beginning in such a way that the criterion of universal significance, for example, the Savior motif in the healing narratives, functioned as the principle of selection and formation. Only the universal significance of the particular humanity of Jesus and his message made it possible to have community with him. If Jesus' activity was so unique that it had to be considered as something without any analogy, then no one could have community with him. But having community with Jesus is the basis of being Christian. How we can have community with Jesus is the main problem not only of the church's *doctrine,* but also of her life. Therefore, it is so important in theology to inquire about the universal significance of the particular elements of the life, work, and teaching of Jesus. Only Jesus' universal significance makes it possible for the hearer of the proclamation to find himself in the figure of Jesus, to have community with Jesus. This certainly does not mean that every particular element in Jesus' individuality must have universal significance. Nevertheless, the theological greatness of a Paul is expressed in the fact that he could find and exhibit a fundamental element of Jesus' universal significance precisely in the event that seemed to the Corinthian Gnostics completely inappropriate to divinity, namely, in Jesus' cross.

The saving character of the universal relevance that belongs to Jesus' figure is determined by whether Jesus is to be understood as the *fulfillment* of the hopes and deep longing of humanity. There is no salvation that is not related to the needs of those to whom it is imparted. Certainly the wishes that determine the superficial aspects of men's behavior can be in complete opposition to their deeper needs and their true happiness. It is not seldom that a man does not have the faintest notion of that toward which his deepest need is really directed. Men's self-understanding and desires can stand in contradiction to their real destiny. To that extent, whether an experienced event satisfies a man's *wishes* is no criterion for the saving character of the event. It may be sharply opposed to these wishes, but it must stand in a relation to the true *needs* of the man if it is salvation; it must be the fulfillment of these needs. At least later, seen from the perspective of the fulfillment, the satisfied need, which had previously been expressed in a perhaps more or less inadequate way, must become apparent in its fundamental significance. This is true with regard to the salvation that has appeared in Jesus. Otherwise, it would be meaningless to attribute saving significance to his person, his work, and his fate. When we say that ultimately through his resurrection from the dead the true man, the real human being that is the destiny of us all, has appeared in Jesus, then we can only mean that in him the hopes of men are fulfilled. The hopes of men are always directed toward something through which they hope to come closer to their destiny, through which they think they will achieve happiness. Certainly men often delude themselves in that toward which they direct their hope. Even when what is hoped for is realized

205

or possessed, one is often no nearer one's human destiny than before. But this does not alter the fact that in his hope man is directed toward his real destiny—whether he himself understands the content of his hope rightly or not. If Jesus is the true man through his dedication to God's future, in his message of the nearness of God's Lordship, as well as through the anticipatory fulfillment of human destiny in his own person through his resurrection from the dead so that truly human life becomes possible through community with him, then that realization toward which all human hopes are aimed is already fulfilled in him in an anticipatory way.[19]

In this broader context one must also consider the question, To what extent have the promises that Israel had received from its God been fulfilled in Jesus? The promises from which Israel lived are certainly to be distinguished from the manifold desires and hopes that move all men. They are different because the promises were not invented by men at will, but were proclaimed by Israel's prophets with the claim that through them the God of Israel himself was speaking. In addition, by far the greatest number of these promises were addressed especially to the Israelites. Also, the relation of Jesus to the promises of Israel is closer than to the hopes of other men. Jesus' activity took place within the context of the history of traditions that was determined by the promises of God received by Israel.

Nevertheless, the Old Testament promises are associated with the longing that moves all humanity. This has been indicated by their form. The promises point expressly to the future toward which human longing is turned, so that hope no longer has to be evaluated as deceitful and uncertain,[20] is no longer an empty fancy. In content, too, the promises of Israel touch that toward which the hopes of men in similar situations are directed: possession of land,

19 Schleiermacher expressed this in his famous sentence, "The appearance of Christ and the institution of this new corporate life would have to be regarded as the completion, only now accomplished, of the creation of human nature" (*The Christian Faith,* § 89, thesis sentence). Schleiermacher was right as far as he went, but he did not see that even in Jesus the creation of human nature is completed at first only proleptically, only as the anticipation of what forms man's eschatological destiny. Therefore, the impartation of this new being from Jesus is not to be conceived simply in the schema of the effects that stream outward from a great historical figure, but it always takes its course by way of the expectation of God's future. As throughout the nineteenth century, so also in Schleiermacher's thesis, the eschatological character of the new creation (or consummation of creation) that had begun in Jesus was overlooked and with it the preliminary character of all present participation in and knowledge of this reality, which nevertheless was already present at that time in Jesus.

20 Rudolf Bultmann in *ThD,* II, 517-521, has called the consciousness of the ambiguity of all hope characteristic for the ancient Greek world. It is still alive in Plato's remark that all men are full of hope (*Philebus* 39e,f). Plato did not, however, evaluate hope entirely as injurious to man. Rather, a virtuous life justifies hope even in the face of death: *Phaedo* 67b, 7 ff.; 114c, 6-8; *Apology* 41c, 8; *Republic* 331a, 2, 8; *Laws* 718a; 732c 6 and d 4; *Symposium* 193d 2. To be sure, the hope that Plato thus affirms is not directed toward future happening in its contingency. I am grateful to E. Mühlenberg for these references to a positive evaluation of hope in Plato.

posterity, wise and just government, emancipation from bondage. The prophetic promises did not pass up the hopes of the people, but met these hopes—although neither always nor all of them. They took up definite hopes.

This is particularly true of the promise of the resurrection of the dead (Isa. 26:19). It took up the question of the individual's participation in salvation in view of the postponement of the eschatological salvation in the postexilic period.[21] The promises of a future kingdom of peace spoken of in Isa. 2:2-4 and 11:1-11 take up not only the Israelitic hopes for an ultimate realization of the divine will to justice but also are expressly related to the desire of the nations for a golden age of human society characterized by peace and justice (Isa. 2:4; 11:10). This promise, which continues an old Israelitic tradition of Israel's mission to all humanity (Gen. 12:3), was later renewed in a particularly lofty way by Second Isaiah (Isa. 42:6; 45:5 f.; 49:6; 52:10). In Daniel, finally, this promise takes the form of the prophecy of an empire that is designated by the figure of a man (Dan. 7:13) unlike the earlier world empires following one another after the fall of Jerusalem that were designated by animal symbols. The first three empires had the character of beasts of prey and the fourth was even worse. But the future empire of "man" that comes not from chaos but from the divine sphere will bring that final change "through which men are freed for their real destiny."[22] This exemplary figure of the "man" or of the "Son of Man" lived on into the Jewish apocalyptic, though in part restricted to the function of world judgment. It apparently played a role in Jesus' own message and was seen by the Christian community first as identical with the expected return of Jesus, then with the resurrected Lord, and finally even with the earthly activity of Jesus. Thus not only with respect to the particular form in which this figure of the "man" is encountered in Paul (Rom. 5:5-21; I Cor. 15:21 ff.), but also with respect to the origin of the "Son of Man" tradition, the judgment is justified that Jesus fulfills the hopes of the peoples because with his activity the fulfillment of the promises of Israel begins. Both are essentially associated: only as the fulfillment of the longing of the peoples is Jesus really the fulfillment of Israel's eschatological promises. Conversely, only in the way in which Israel's eschatological promises have been fulfilled in Jesus in an anticipatory way is the longing that moves humanity fulfilled in its real sense.

In still another respect a parallel can be drawn between universal human hopes and the hopes expressly encouraged by the prophetic promises. Hopes are seldom fulfilled in the way in which they were originally imagined. Often they are completely disappointed. Sometimes they are surprisingly fulfilled,

[21] On the question of the participation of the individual in salvation, cf. G. von Rad, *Old Testament Theology,* Vol. I, pp. 383-418: "Israel's Trials and the Consolation of the Individual," esp. pp. 391 ff., 404 ff. On Isa., chs. 24 to 26, see O. Plöger, *Theokratie und Eschatologie,* pp. 69-97, esp. pp. 80-86.

[22] K. Koch, in *Historische Zeitschrift,* CXCIII (1961), 24.

more or less differently than one would have expected. Nevertheless, the person who experiences such a surprising fulfillment perhaps still senses that his real hope was fulfilled beyond expectation in an unpredictable way.

The prophetic promises, too, were seldom fulfilled as they originally had been understood. In any case, they have been fulfilled in Jesus differently than the prophets themselves may have imagined the fulfillment of their words. Nevertheless, one can speak of a fulfillment with far-reaching exclusion of subjective caprice when one can show that the hope that was encouraged by the prophetic promises has been satisfied in a deeper sense in an anticipatory way with the activity and fate of Jesus. Such a deeper fulfillment of the Old Testament promises is present in any case if the true destiny of man has appeared in Jesus. Then the deeper sense of all human hopes is fulfilled in him and thus also the deeper sense of the promises to Israel, even if their wording originally intended something different.

III. THE OFFICE AND PERSON OF JESUS

The Protestant dogmatics of the seventeenth century treated the person and office of Jesus Christ separately in the presentation of Christology. The so-called doctrine of the two natures was unfolded first under the title *de persona Christi*. This was the interpretation of the unification of the natures (*unitio naturarum*) that was accomplished in the incarnation to the point of a mutual interpenetration of their properties (*communicatio idiomatum*). Under the title of the office (*de officio Christi*) the explanations of Jesus' kingly, priestly, and prophetic offices followed. Normally the doctrine of the "states" of his humiliation and exaltation (*de statibus Christi*) followed as the third part of the Christology.

Since Schleiermacher the separation of the doctrines of Christ's person and work has been contested with important arguments, and a close connection between the two doctrinal parts has been sought. In his dogmatics Schleiermacher said, "The characteristic activity and the exclusive dignity of the Redeemer are related to one another and are inseparably one in the self-consciousness of the believer." It is "to no purpose . . . to attribute to the Redeemer a higher dignity than the efficacy attributed to him requires, since from the excess of dignity nothing is explained" (§ 92,2). Albrecht Ritschl, as well, strongly stressed the correlation of the person and work of Christ. With an appeal to Luther, he rejected "confessing the divinity of Christ before it is established in his works."[23] In the first edition of his chief work, Ritschl stated even more clearly why the separation of the doctrines of the person and work of Christ is false: We perceive "the nature and the attributes, i.e., the definite-

[23] A. Ritschl, *The Christian Doctrine of Justification and Reconciliation,* § 44, p. 399. The reference to Luther is found on p. 394.

ness of being, only in the effect a thing has upon us, and we conceive the nature and the extent of its effect upon us as its essence."[24]

The correspondence of Christ's person and work has prevailed generally in contemporary theology. Reference to the assertions of Paul Althaus and Karl Barth provide sufficient examples. Althaus says of Jesus' authority: "This authority is suited to him in *person*. But to the person belongs his *history*."[25] Karl Barth says, "His being as this one is his history."[26] Correspondingly, in the introduction to Barth's doctrine of reconciliation the pattern of the three offices is crossed with the doctrine of the two natures. The division of his doctrine of reconciliation into three parts is oriented to the three offices of Christ, but expresses at the same time the divinity which humbles himself to man (Part 1), the man who is exalted to God (Part 2), and the unity of God and man in the person of Christ (Part 3).

In fact, the office and the person of Christ do belong closely together. In our method this has resulted from the path we had to follow to the knowledge of Jesus' divinity. Perception of Jesus' divinity was possible only from the consideration of his earthly work and of the claim contained in his whole activity on the one hand and of his fate in the cross and resurrection on the other.

The method employed here will have to be fundamentally different from Schleiermacher's. When Schleiermacher spoke of the activity of Christ, he meant his effect on present-day men, on the contemporary Christian community.[27]

This means that the Christ who is experienced in the present formed the basis of Schleiermacher's assertions. But we have already seen that before anything can be said about Jesus' effect on us, Christology must establish its statements about Jesus as person on the basis of his former historical activity in view of the context of his whole life history leading to the crucifixion and resurrection.

While Schleiermacher said nothing about the particular activity of the historical Jesus in his doctrine of the "work" (*Geschäft*) of Christ, Ritschl had made the activity of the historical Jesus in a certain sense the criterion of this doctrine. He thereby revived the old distinction between the states of humiliation and exaltation, for which Schleiermacher could find no better place than the appendix to § 105, "the history unto preservation." For Ritschl, "the persuasive power of the conception of the divinity of the exalted Christ is wholly

---

24 A. Ritschl, *Die christliche Lehre von Rechtfertigung und Versöhnung*, Vol. III, p. 343.

25 P. Althaus, *Die christliche Wahrheit*, § 45, p. 462.

26 K. Barth, *CD*, IV/1, p. 128.

27 For Schleiermacher, the redeeming work of Christ is that he "assumes believers into the power of His God-consciousness" (§ 100, thesis sentence). This, his "act in us," is the "original activity of the Redeemer" that belongs alone to him and precedes any promoting activity on our part (§ 100, 1).

dependent upon whether or not its characteristics can be pointed out in the earthly historical life of the person."[28] If Christ founded the community "through his royally prophetic and priestly offices, one can judge its present-day preservation through the continuation of these functions by the exalted Christ only according to what one perceives to be their content in the historical appearance of his life" (pp. 407 f.). Nevertheless, the doctrine of Christ's offices for Ritschl also stands in the *immediate* service of the task of "comprehending the significance of Christ for the community that believes in him" (p. 408). In so doing, Ritschl could properly appeal to the tradition of the doctrine of the works or offices of Christ. The content of the latter, however, cannot be interpreted simply as an unbroken continuation of Jesus' "historical appearance of his life," of the historical particularity of his activity. The traditional concepts of the works or offices of Jesus do not simply describe the extension of the historical uniqueness of his activity beyond the end of his earthly life, but are interpretations of Jesus' total appearance from the perspective of the post-Easter situation of the Christian community. The basis of all these interpretations is provided not just by Jesus' *works* in the past during his pre-Easter activity, but also by his *fate* carried out in his crucifixion and resurrection, while activity and fate are to be distinguished in the life of the pre-Easter Jesus himself. All effects coming from the total appearance of Jesus on later generations are therefore different in content from his own pre-Easter works because they derive not just from his pre-Easter activity but essentially from his fate as well. In a certain sense one is perhaps justified in speaking of Jesus as the subject of these effects. We will be concerned with this question in connection with Jesus' Kingship (Chapter 10). These effects are in any case to be distinguished from Jesus' pre-Easter works and from the task of giving a theological evaluation of this activity in its uniqueness. In Christology one is not permitted to obscure the difference too quickly between Jesus' work and his fate unless one wants to lose sight of the specific reality of the pre-Easter Jesus in its distinction from all subsequent periods—and thus of the *extra nos* in the basis of salvation.

In the preceding considerations it has been shown that the revelation of human destiny, of man's essence that results from God's revelation in Jesus' fate—and thus from Jesus' resurrection—is shaped very differently in Jesus' activity and in his fate. Jesus' works decided the destiny of the men who confronted him. His fate, on the contrary, reveals the destiny of man in Jesus himself. To that extent one must say that Jesus' works are legitimated materially through what has become revealed in Jesus himself through his fate. Only because the destiny of man is supposed to be revealed in his own fate could Jesus claim for himself in his earthly activity that the meaning of life

---

[28] A. Ritschl, *The Christian Doctrine of Justification and Reconciliation;* the following page numbers in the text also refer to this volume.

for all other men, their human destiny, was decided in the encounter with him.

The difference between fate and activity in the life of the pre-Easter Jesus is thus to be taken into consideration. Jesus' works are to be conceived in the light of this difference as those of Jesus of Nazareth who lived at that past time. In this sense we shall discuss the office of Jesus as the commission under which the historical Jesus knew himself to stand (Chapter 6). Then will follow a treatment of Jesus' fate and its interpretation, especially of Jesus' fate on the cross (Chapter 7), since the significance of Jesus' resurrection has already been handled extensively on its own account. How Jesus' office and fate are mutually interrelated and how both relate to the divinity of Jesus is to be presented in Part Three, which will concern itself with the unity of divinity and humanity in Jesus.

CHAPTER

6

THE OFFICE OF JESUS

The office of Jesus was to call men into the Kingdom of God, which had appeared with him.

I. CRITIQUE OF THE DOCTRINE OF THE THREE OFFICES

The concept of the office first moved into the center of Christology in Protestant theology. Here the concept *officium* has to a great degree taken over the position held by the doctrine of the incarnation in patristic theology and by the concept of the work (*opus*) of Christ as an accomplishment of satisfaction in the Middle Ages. The notion of office in the theology of the Reformers expresses the idea that Jesus' efficacy is to be understood completely from God, as the execution of his divine mission, not so much as a meritorious influence upon God. Quite correctly, Luther's Christology has been called a "Christology of the efficacy of God alone."[1] This is also suggested by the emergence of the concept of office. With the catchphrase "the efficacy of God alone" the connection of Christology with the Reformers' doctrine of justification becomes apparent. As a more subordinated aspect, the Christology of Jesus' office was effective even beyond the area of Protestant theology, probably because of the specific advantages for the systematic organization of the Christological material. In its extensive scope as used by the Reformers, the concept of office includes the entire life of Jesus, while the concept of the work of Christ could really consider only the reconciliation accomplished by his death. This is probably the reason why modern Catholic theology since the eighteenth century has taken over the concept of office and the pattern of the three offices to supplement the traditional conceptions of the work of Christ.

The understanding that three offices—that of Priest, King, and Prophet—

---

[1] Y. M. J. Congar, "Regards et réflections sur la christologie de Luther," in *Chalkedon*, Vol. III, pp. 457-486.

are brought together in the title "Christ" is to be found occasionally in the fathers, but does not appear there very often. It achieved no significance for systematic Christology in the patristic church nor for medieval Scholasticism.[2]

Luther was not the author of the doctrine of the three offices in the Reformation. Luther spoke only of the Kingship and Priesthood of Christ. The figure three seems to go back to Andreas Osiander. In his defense written for the Augsburg *Reichstag* of 1530 he gave the argument, which later became classic, for the necessity of speaking of three offices—or better, of a threefold office—of Christ: "Since Christ thus is called an Anointed One and only the prophets, kings, and high priests were anointed, one notes well that all three of these offices rightly belong to him: the prophetic office, since he alone is our teacher and master, Matt. 23:8 ff.; the authority of the king, since he reigns forever in the house of Jacob, Luke 1:32 ff.; and the priestly office, since he is a priest forever after the order of Melchizedek, Ps. 110:4. Thus it is his office that he is our wisdom, righteousness, sanctification, and redemption, as Paul testifies in I Cor., ch. 1."[3] The threefold character of the offices of Christ achieved general recognition through Calvin, who had used the doctrine after 1536 in the Geneva Confession and in the various versions of the *Institutio Christianae Religionis.*[4] Apparently the subsequent Reformed, as well as Lutheran, orthodoxy took over the doctrine of the three offices from him.[5]

Osiander's statements quoted above have already made clear that the pattern of the threefold office was derived from the literal meaning of the title "Christ." This title originally meant "the Anointed One," and it was thought that according to the Old Testament a particular anointment had been required for the three offices, for those of the prophet, the king, and the priest. This justification was to be found in some of the fathers, for example, Hegesippus (according to Eusebius), Lactantius, Gregory of Nyssa, and John Chrysostom.[6]

For present purposes our examination of the Scriptural passages used to support the derivation of the doctrine of three offices from the title "Christ" will begin with the relation of the prophetic office to the rite of anointment.

---

[2] So also M. Schmaus, art. "Ämter Christi," *LThK*, I (1957), 457-459. Further, E. F. K. Müller, "Jesu Christi dreifaches Amt," *RE*, VIII (3d ed., 1900), 733-741, esp. p. 734.

[3] Quoted according to W. Gussmann, *Quellen und Forschungen zur Geschichte des Augsburgischen Glaubensbekenntnisses* (Leipzig and Berlin: B. G. Teubner, 1911), p. 302. On the priority of Osiander over Calvin on this question, cf. E. Hirsch, *Hilfsbuch zum Studium der Dogmatik* (1951), pp. 65 f.

[4] The final version is found in 1959 in Calvin, *Institutes of the Christian Religion*, II. xv.

[5] See E. F. K. Müller, in *RE*, VIII (1900), 735 ff.

[6] References in M. Schmaus, in *LThK*, I (1957), 457 ff., esp. p. 458, as well as in the significant essay by A. Krauss, "Das Mittlerwerk nach dem Schema des *munus triplex*," *Jahrbücher für deutsche Theologie*, XVII (1872), 595-655.

Calvin[7] found prophetic anointment asserted in Isa. 61:1: "The Spirit of the Lord God is upon me, because the Lord has anointed me." In Qumran, too, prophets, especially the eschatological prophet, were designated as "anointed."[8] Isaiah 61:1 played a significant role in the primitive Christian history of traditions: a logion from Q picks up Isa. 61:1 (Matt. 11:2-6; Luke 7:18-23), as does the Lucan special tradition in Luke 4:16-30 in which the old Christology about Jesus as a prophet like Moses (following Deut. 18:15) can be recognized. Here, as in Acts 10:38a and 4:27, the "anointment" of Jesus by the Spirit is expressly emphasized. This seems to be associated with the conception of Jesus as the eschatological prophet from the perspective of Isa. 61:1. It has, however, no connection at all to the high-priestly anointment, which is not mentioned anywhere in the New Testament, nor to the royal anointment, which occurs only metaphorically in Heb. 1:9. The derivation of the anointment with the Spirit from the title of Christ and especially the view of its threefold occurrence plays no role at all.[9]

Even in substance, the pattern of the three offices cannot be justified from the anointment. In Israel an anointment was hardly required for the office of the prophet (in spite of I Kings 19:16). The language of imparting the divine Spirit to the prophet through an anointment in Isa. 61:1 is to be understood figuratively.[10] In addition, the title of Messiah in the Israelite tradition does not designate any random anointed person, but particularly the king. To be sure, in the postexilic period the title was occasionally attributed to the priest as well, especially to the high priest. Thus Zechariah speaks of the "two anointed ones," the high priest Joshua and the messiah-king Zerubbabel (Zech. 4:14). The Testaments of the Twelve Patriarchs and the Qumran sectarians continued this broadening of the messianic concept. Both spoke of a priestly messiah alongside the royal messiah, with the priority of the former.[11] But there is no attempt to derive the duality from the *concept* of the Anointed One. The expectation of two messiahs, rather, involves the two most distinguished offices of the eschatological time. It is to be mentioned as a curiosity that the three offices were in exceptional cases heaped upon one person in the Judaism of Jesus' time. Thus Josephus[12] describes the Hasmonaean John Hyrcanus as the possessor of the three highest honors of his

---

[7] Calvin, *Institutes,* II. xv. 2.

[8] On this, see F. Hahn, *Christologische Hoheitstitel,* pp. 634 ff., 369 f. (on CD VI, 1; 1QM XI, and CD I, 12); also p. 364, n. 4 on Isa. 61:1.

[9] Cf. Hahn, *Christologische Hoheitstitel,* p. 395, and esp. the article mentioned there in n. 2: J. de la Potterie, "L'Onction du Christ," *Nouvelle Revue Théologique,* LXXX (1958), 225-252.

[10] R. Koch, *Geist und Messias,* p. 125, maintains that the communication of the Spirit "in Old Testament prophecy is never connected with physical anointing." Even I Kings 19:16 is perhaps to be understood as imagery, according to the suggestion of Weinel (*ibid.*).

[11] Test. Levi, ch. 18; Test. Judah, ch. 24; 1QS IX, 11; 1QSa II, 12 ff.

[12] Josephus, *Antiqu.* XIII. x. 7; cf. *De bell. Jud.* I. ii. 8. See also O. Plöger, *Theokratie und Eschatologie,* p. 55.

people, the rulership over his people, the high-priestly honor, and the gift of prophecy. However, the three honors are not brought together here in the Christ title. Only this much can be said: prophecy, kingship, and priesthood were understood and combined occasionally in the time of Jesus as the three highest honors that the Jewish people knew, regardless of whether they were only tradition and expectation or were also institutional actualities. Later we must evaluate this finding as an element of truth in the doctrine of the three offices. Of course, from such an occasional combination it is not to be concluded that Jesus claimed for himself these three honors.

Thus the justification of the threefold character of Jesus' offices from the Christ title is untenable. The title "Christ" designates in the first place only kingship, at best priesthood as well, but hardly the office of the prophet. In this judgment we shall disregard for the time being the question of applying the title "Christ" to the historical Jesus.

Even if it cannot be derived from the "Christ" title that the royal, the priestly, and the prophetic honors properly belong to Jesus, it still remains to be determined whether the functions in fact apprehended by or devolved upon Jesus do demonstrate him to be king, prophet, and priest. From this point of view as well, the concept of the three offices in the dogmatics of Protestant orthodoxy is subject to considerable objection.

a. According to the understanding of the orthodox Protestant dogmaticians, the prophetic office consisted above all in Jesus' teaching activity, in both his interpretation of the law of Moses and his proclamation of the joyful message of the imminent Kingdom of God.[13] This description is to a certain extent accurate for Jesus' activity as a wandering preacher. The designation "teacher" may not, however, be understood in the sense of instruction in and mediation of insights (primarily ethical), because Jesus' message primarily had the character of a call to repentance and the announcement of salvation. Further, Jesus' message must be seen as one with his conduct—the acceptance of sinners, above all into the community at table, and his healing activity. In the sense of contemporary expectation of an eschatological prophet like Moses (following Deut. 18:15), it is thoroughly understandable that these elements belong together. Nevertheless, the entirety of Jesus' activity and his self-understanding cannot be characterized accurately as prophetic, either in the ancient Israelite sense or in the sense of the contemporary Jewish expectation.

First, it is not accurate in the ancient Israelite sense. Precisely the most important characteristic of ancient Israelite prophecy is lacking in Jesus, the prophetic reception of the word. To be sure, we must consider the possibility that Jesus knew himself to be inspired. In the Synoptic tradition is still to

13 Cf., for example, J. A. Quenstedt, *Theologia didactico-polemica* (1685), III, 218; J. Gerhard, *Loci theologici* (1610-1621), III, 578 (quoted in Heinrich Schmid, *The Doctrinal Theology of the Evangelical Lutheran Church* [Augsburg Publishing House, 1899], pp. 341 f.).

be found the indication of an apocalyptic vision of Jesus': "I saw Satan fall like lightning from heaven" (Luke 10:18). Rudolf Bultmann thinks, concerning the singular character of this saying, that perhaps the tradition "could have suppressed other passages reporting visions or auditions."[14] The saying agrees, in any case, exceptionally well with what we otherwise know of the particularity of Jesus' message. The starting point of Jesus' message was surely that the end had already begun and the Kingdom of God was near. But according to apocalyptic conceptions the fall of Satan to earth introduces the end events (cf. Rev. 12:8 f.). Is it permitted to suspect here the possible trigger for Jesus' message?

Even without considering the singular account of the vision of Luke 10:18, there can be no doubt that Jesus knew himself to be inspired in what he did and said. Here we must pay special attention to the use of the expression "amen" at the beginning of many of Jesus' sayings. "Amen" is actually the reply to a received communication.[15] Nevertheless, Jesus did not, like the prophets, proclaim his sayings as words received from God. He never said, "Thus says the Lord . . ." Strictly speaking, Jesus did not exercise the office of a prophet in the ancient Israelite sense. It can hardly be the case, either, that he understood himself as a prophet in the sense of the prophetic traditions and expectations of his own time.

Jesus seems to have reckoned the time of the prophets up to and including John the Baptist (Matt. 11:13). If this formulation goes back to Jesus himself, he distinguished his own activity from that of the prophets. It is even possible that he designated the Baptist as "one greater than a prophet" (Matt. 11:9). It may have been Jesus' community that developed the very old Christology that understands Jesus as the eschatological prophet.[16] Nevertheless, the fact that Jesus probably lived and thought in prophetically stamped traditions remains untouched by this statement. Jesus himself perhaps understood his life in the light of what was generally the fate of "the prophets" (Mark 6:4; Matt. 23:37; Luke 13:32 f.). The contemporary prophetic traditions in whose

[14] R. Bultmann, *The History of the Synoptic Tradition*, p. 109; cf. also p. 161. Bultmann continues, probably correctly, that the suppression of visionary elements of Jesus' activity by the tradition of the community can hardly have taken place to any great extent, "for in late Judaism visions and auditions were features of the apocalyptist, and Jesus was not an apocalyptist in the strict sense." In the proper sense of the term, Jesus certainly was no apocalyptist, being neither the author of apocalyptic writings nor the originator of a specific apocalyptic conception of history. Nevertheless, even though this vision, whose authenticity Bultmann leaves open but does not deny, is an isolated phenomenon, it belongs to those elements in Jesus' activity which show his proximity to apocalyptic.

[15] See above, Chapter 3, n. 13.

[16] So also O. Cullmann, *The Christology of the New Testament*, pp. 23-42. With Hahn, *Christologische Hoheitstitel*, p. 375, one will have to doubt whether the designation of the Baptist as the eschatological prophet in the sense of Elijah (Matt. 11:14) derives from Jesus himself (so Cullmann, pp. 24, 36). On the varied prophet Christologies of the Baptist sects and of Jewish Christianity, see Hahn's treatment, pp. 371-404.

context Jesus knew himself to stand must be seen as apocalyptically influenced. Prophetic tradition and apocalyptic are indeed tightly interlaced in the whole postexilic period.[17] The apocalyptic broadening and transformation of the prophetic expectation for the future into the hope for God's Lordship at the coming judgment of the living and the dead is everywhere presupposed by Jesus. Thus Jesus would have been closer to being an apocalyptic than a prophet in the old sense.

But he also was not an apocalyptic, although the views of the apocalyptic tradition are everywhere the presupposition of what he said and did. Jesus certainly thought in apocalyptic categories.[18] But he wrote no apocalypse; rather, he proclaimed the immediate nearness of that which the apocalyptics described as the end of the course of history and called his people to repentance in view of the imminent end. John the Baptist had already done this, and both materially and temporally Jesus stands closer to John's work than to that of anyone else. The Baptist, too, wrote no apocalypse of his own, but worked as a preacher of repentance under the presupposition of the validity of the apocalyptic views. To this extent the work of both demonstrates prophetic elements, but these are the elements of an apocalyptically stamped prophecy whose call to repentance is related to the content of the general apocalyptic-eschatological expectation, not to special prophetic announcements. What distinguished Jesus from the Baptist breaks at the same time the classification of his activity in the prophetic tradition.

Jesus not only issued a call to repentance, but with full authority he granted to the men he met the salvation expected in the future. He was certain that in his activity the future salvation of God's Kingdom had broken into the present time. This distinguishes Jesus basically from the Baptist as well as from all the prophets.

Thus it may well have been that Jesus lived and thought in close relation to the apocalyptically influenced prophetic tradition. Through this tradition he stood in a living relationship to the old Israelite prophets. But he himself was neither a prophet nor an apocalyptic. Therefore, the specific character of Jesus' earthly mission cannot be adequately described with the concept of the prophet. Nevertheless, Jesus' actual activity stands far closer to the prophetic tradition than to either of the other two "offices."

b. During his earthly activity Jesus neither sought nor practiced the royal office. Many of his disciples may have hoped that Jesus would reestablish the Kingdom of Israel. Apparently something of the sort also played a role in the Jews' accusations against Jesus before the Roman procurator, because in this way—as a messianic pretender—Jesus could have been brought under

[17] On this, see O. Plöger, *Theokratie und Eschatologie*, and esp. K. Koch, "Spätisraelitisches Geschichtsdenken am Beispiel des Buches Daniel," *Historisches Zeitschrift*, CXCIII (1961), 1-32, esp. 28 ff.
[18] See above Chapter 3, n. 30.

suspicion of revolt against the Roman rule. In any case, his disciples understood Jesus' resurrection as his installation as the future Messiah, as the "Son of God." With regard to the resurrected Lord, it is quite meaningful to speak about Jesus' Kingship, even though we must consider that the conceptions of Messiah and Son of Man have been connected with one another in the picture of Jesus as heavenly King from the beginning. On the basis of the inscription on the cross (Mark 15:26), which designated Jesus as the King of the Jews,[19] it lay close at hand to understand the resurrected Lord as the one actually destined to the Messianic office—whether it was in the future at the completion of the eschatological events or already at present in heaven —even though Jesus himself had rejected this title. In any case, after Jesus' resurrection no one else could have been expected as the eschatological king. The one destined to be the Son of Man must, therefore, be one and the same person as the expected Messiah.

The title of King (Christ) thus designates the position that is due to Jesus because of his resurrection, first of all with regard to the eschatological future, but then also as a present reality in heaven.[20] The Kingship of the exalted Lord may be understood in the sense of the orthodox distinction as *regnum potentiae, gratiae,* and *gloriae:* Jesus has been exalted to exercise God's power, his Kingdom is extended on earth in Jesus' commission through the church's means of grace, and Jesus will come again as the eschatological ruler in all the glory of God. Thereby the contrast between theocratic and Messianic hopes[21] is resolved insofar as Jesus is one with God, and the Father exercises his Lordship through Jesus in that Jesus serves the Kingdom of the Father through his unreserved devotion. Nevertheless, before Easter, Jesus had not been king. He neither acted as king nor sought kingship for himself. The latter was the slander of his opponents, while Jesus himself seems to have explicitly rejected the Messianic title.[22] Even looking back from Easter, we

[19] F. Hahn, *Christologische Hoheitstitel,* p. 178 (with Martin Dibelius, *Botschaft und Geschichte* [Tübingen: J. C. B. Mohr (Paul Siebeck), 1954], Vol. I, p. 256, and against R. Bultmann, *The History of the Synoptic Tradition,* p. 293), supports the historicity of the inscription on the cross. In any case, there can probably be no doubt that Jesus was condemned by the Roman authorities as a Messianic pretender.

[20] This was seen in the old Reformed dogmatics by Keckermann and others; on this account they assigned the *munus regium* to the *status exaltationis.* E. F. K. Müller, *RE,* VIII (1900), 735, wrongly misses "systematic consistency" here. A formally consistent, undifferentiated distribution of the three offices, each assigned to both states, is precisely not able to do justice to the Biblical witness in the matter.

[21] On this contrast between the theocratic expectation of the Kingdom of God and the hope for a Messianic Kingdom (not so sharply on the figure of the Son of Man), cf. Hahn, *Christologische Hoheitstitel,* pp. 27 ff.

[22] See Cullmann's statements about the rejection of the Messianic title by Jesus himself, esp. *The Christology of the New Testament,* pp. 122 ff., on Mark 8:33. F. Hahn's analysis of Mark 8:27-33 comes, on this point, to the same result, at any rate for the original tradition standing behind the present text (*Christologische Hoheitstitel,* pp. 226-230, esp. p. 228, n. 3) against Bultmann, *The History of the Synoptic Tradition,* pp. 258 f.

can understand the earthly Jesus at most in the sense of the early Christian "two-stage Christology"[23] as the King already designated by God's secret decision; he cannot, however, be understood as the holder of this office. On the other hand, his pre-Easter office, his special mission understood in relation to the prophetic tradition, cannot automatically be extended beyond his death. In particular the preaching of the church cannot be considered a part of the prophetic office itself. Although the church, in a certain sense, continues Jesus' work, her work still may not be identified with his without distinction.

c. The most difficult problems are presented by the designation of Jesus as priest, the discussion of his priestly office. A tradition of the church that reaches back into the early Christian period designates Jesus' vicarious suffering by the concept of his priesthood. The old Protestant dogmatics distinguished between the priestly functions of *satisfactio* and *intercessio: satisfactio* is produced through Jesus' active fulfillment of the law and through his suffering on the cross; *intercessio* consists in his intercession for us before the Father on the basis of the satisfaction accomplished on the cross. The *intercessio* was understood particularly as the priestly function of the exalted Lord, as making valid his offering on the cross before the Father. But sometimes the supplications of the earthly Jesus were also rightly regarded as pleas for us in the sense of *intercessio*. The act of satisfaction itself, in contrast, belongs entirely to Jesus' earthly life for the dogmatic tradition.

The doctrine of Jesus' priestly office has two New Testament roots, the explicit designation of Jesus as High Priest and the conception of his death on the cross as the atonement for our sins. The designation of Jesus as the High Priest is a specific characteristic of the Christology of The Letter to the Hebrews. Its Alexandrian thought pattern has a unique allegorical character and is not to be compared to other Christological titles in view of its establishment in the history of traditions. The assumption that the Qumran sect's concept of a high-priestly Messiah was applied to Jesus in the Synoptic tradition may not be valid.[24] The basis in the history of traditions for the interpretation of Jesus' death as atonement is much broader. The relation of the atonement idea to the concept of sacrifice is not found in the oldest level of the early Christian understanding of the atoning significance of Jesus'

23 On this, cf. G. Bornkamm, *Jesus of Nazareth*, pp. 227-228, and, in greater detail, F. Hahn, *Christologische Hoheitstitel*, pp. 251-268. According to this conception, Jesus as the Son of David is the one designated to be the *future* Messiah. Hahn, *ibid.*, pp. 219 f., emphasizes that only under the influence of the interpretation of Jesus as the eschatological prophet and of the Hellenistic understanding of divine Sonship could the predicate *Christos* be applied to the whole of Jesus' earthly activity.

24 F. Hahn's argument, *ibid.*, pp. 231-241, against Gerhard Friedrich, "Beobachtungen zur messianischen Hohenpriestererwartung in den Synoptikern," *ZThK*, LIII (1956), 256-311, is convincing. Hahn also denies a relationship between Hebrews and Qumran and in its place assumes with Windisch, Michel, and others a relation to Jewish-Hellenistic ideas (Hahn, *ibid.*, pp. 232 f.).

death, to be sure. It reaches back, nevertheless, into Hellenistic-Jewish Christianity and is already attested by Paul (Rom. 3:25).[25] The sacrificial idea easily carries with it the idea of priesthood. Thereby Hebrews had already developed the unique idea that Jesus in his person was both priest and sacrifice. This idea has only the value of a somewhat baroque picture.[26] The heavenly Father himself who had given Jesus into death could more appropriately be seen as the priest in the sacrificial event. At any rate, Jesus' death on the cross does not involve so much a part of Jesus' *work* as something that befell him, that he had to endure. E. Lohse summarizes the beginnings of the understanding of the atoning power of Jesus' death in the Palestinian community: "Christ's atoning death did not first have to create the gracious God, as was true with the pious of late Judaism who went to death in order to pay off the debts of the people and turn away the wrath of God. Rather, Christ's atoning death presupposes the gracious God who had offered up the Christ in order that he would carry the punishment of sin for us."[27] The fundamental meaning of the early Christian interpretation of Jesus' death as having occurred "for us" is that *God* gave him up to death. Paul expresses it in this way with an earlier formula in Rom. 4:25. (Compare Rom. 5:8-9, as well as II Cor. 5:21.) When Paul in other places speaks of Christ as the subject of the offering unto death (Gal. 1:3 f.; 2:20),[28] he no longer has the pre-Easter Jesus himself in mind, but views his death in the light of his exaltation and even from the sending of God's Son into the flesh (Gal. 4:4). We should judge similarly the stylization of the Synoptic passion stories as a path deliberately thought out and premeditated by Jesus. Here, too, the picture of Jesus as the acting agent results only from transferring the Messianic office of the exalted Lord back into the path of Jesus to the cross. This interpretation may be well founded in and of itself. It does not, however, agree with the character of Jesus' pre-Easter life. In terms of Jesus' pre-Easter situation, his path of suffering as something that occurred to him must be distinguished from his mission which came to expression in his activity. Hence, one probably cannot speak here of an office of Jesus, at least not in the same sense as with reference to his pre-Easter activity. While we

[25] Thus Eduard Lohse, *Märtyrer und Gottesknecht: Untersuchungen zur urchristlichen Verkündigung vom Sühnetod Jesu Christi* (Göttingen: Vandenhoeck & Ruprecht, 1955), pp. 138 ff. (on the blood of Christ) and p. 152 (on Rom. 3:25). See also R. Bultmann, *Theology of the New Testament*, Vol. I, pp. 295 f.

[26] E. Lohse, *Märtyrer und Gottesknecht*, p. 179, also emphasizes the symbolic character of the statements in Hebrews: Hebrews uses "the cultic image of the high priest and his sacrifice . . . in order to present the universal validity of Christ's expiatory death. However, the framework of the picture is broken because it is not able to contain the content poured into it. The sacrifice was slaughtered on earth, and this sacrifice is identical with the high priest, who is supposed to exercise his office in the heavenly holy place." Cf. also p. 169.

[27] *Ibid.*, p. 146.

[28] Cf. further Eph. 5:2, 25; I Tim. 2:6. On these passages, E. Lohse, *ibid.*, pp. 134 f.; R. Bultmann, *Theology of the New Testament*, Vol. II, p. 12.

would rather not speak of a priestly *office* of Jesus, we do not at all deny that through his fate Jesus took the place occupied in Israel and other religions by the priesthood and the sacrificial rituals. It will be shown more precisely that this judgment is quite appropriate.

In contrast to the suffering of Jesus, one can include his intercession for us—particularly in his supplications, but in all of his mission as well—in his office. However, such an intercession does not presuppose, as in the same sense of the older dogmatics, a sacrifice of satisfaction. Further, this function in Israel was in no way considered a special priestly one. Precisely, the Israelite prophets had the task of interceding for the people before God.[29] Especially in Ezekiel, a reproof of the false prophets is that they did not step into the breach on behalf of the people (Ezek. 13:5); the tradition of the vicarious suffering of the prophet seems to take its beginning from this point.[30] Although dogmatics has included this aspect of Jesus' life in his priestly office, we have to conclude that in this respect, too, Jesus belongs in the prophetic tradition. While at this point an aspect was assigned to the priestly office which did not exclusively belong there, in other respects the function of the office of the priest has been too narrowly defined, at least in comparison to the concept of priesthood in ancient Israel. The ancient Israelite understanding of priesthood did not only and not even primarily involve the offering of sacrifices, but above all the mediation of "all kinds of God's decisions" as well as the extensive knowledge of the sacral tradition presupposed for this.[31]

d. As we have seen, only one of the three offices, namely, the "prophetic office," to some extent properly characterizes the earthly work of Jesus. How is this result to be explained? How could the older dogmatics include in the concept of Jesus' office that which we must distinguish from Jesus' earthly mission as his fate, as well as the Messianic office that became his only through his exaltation?

This is connected with the fact that in the older Protestant dogmatics the God-man Jesus Christ, not the man Jesus, was considered the bearer of the office. For Luther, the immediate object of all statements about Jesus was the God-man Jesus Christ. In our approach, on the contrary, Jesus appears first as a human being; the claim of his unity with God requires more exact proof. Luther did not yet sense this difficulty of speaking about the divinity of Jesus. In spite of Luther's emphasis that one must draw Jesus into the flesh, must begin with his humanity,[32] the presupposition of Jesus' divinity still remained self-evident. All of Jesus' humanity had its sense only as the

29 G. von Rad, *Old Testament Theology*, Vol. II, p. 51, with reference to I Sam. 12:19, 23; 15:11; II Kings 19:1 ff.; Jer. 7:16; 42:2.
30 *Ibid.*, pp. 275 f.
31 *Ibid.*, Vol. I, p. 244.
32 Reinhold Seeberg, *Lehrbuch der Dogmengeschichte*, Vol. IV/1, pp. 183 f.

most radical humiliation of the divinity to participation in our suffering, weakness, and temptations. The "person" of Jesus was for Luther the directly visible unity of God and man: he is "combined in one person, true God and man."[33] In Luther's time the visible directness of the concept of the God-man Christ belonged to the contemporary intellectual world; in our time it must be regarded as a mythological concept.

While Luther only seldom used the concept of the mediator,[34] Calvin, as has been previously mentioned, had understood the divine-human person of Jesus as the holder of the mediating office: *Neque de divina natura, neque de humana simpliciter dici, quae ad mediatoris officium spectant.*[35] For Calvin and also later for orthodox Protestant dogmatics, the office of mediator involves something that belongs to the divine-human person, that unites the two natures. In this sense, the event of the incarnation itself stands for Calvin under the heading of the office of mediator: the Son of God became man so that his divinity and human nature could grow into one another through a reciprocal union.[36]

Significantly enough, Catholic Scholastic Christology understood the mediating office of Jesus quite differently. Here Jesus Christ was considered the mediator because of his human nature, not in view of his divine-human person.[37] This was substantiated on grounds that the mediator must be different from God in order to be able to offer him the service of satisfaction.[38] Among the Reformers, Zwingli[39] and later Stancarus took this position. Between the position of the latter that Christ is our mediator because of his humanity and the position of Osiander that only Christ's divinity is our righteousness, Calvin formulated a middle solution that Christ is our mediator through his divine-human person, not through his humanity or through his divinity alone. The Formula of Concord of 1577 followed this position. In its eighth article, *De persona Christi,* it says: "Christ is our mediator, savior, king, high priest, head, shepherd, etc., not because of one nature alone, whether the divine or the human, but because of both natures."[40] In opposition to Stancarus and thereby also to the medieval Scholastics, the Formula says that the human nature alone could not do enough for us; against Osiander, the divine nature alone could not "mediate" between us and God.[41]

33 *WA* 36, p. 60; 40/II, p. 517. Cf. Seeberg, *Dogmengeschichte,* p. 224.
34 See E. Vogelsang, *Die Anfänge der Christologie Luthers nach der 1. Psalmenvorlesung,* p. 162.
35 Calvin, *Institutes,* II. xiv. 3.
36 *Ibid.,* II. xii.1: "That his divinity and our human nature might by natural connection grow together." *Ibid.,* II. xii. 3: "He coupled human nature with divine."
37 Thomas Aquinas, *Summa theologica* III, q. 26, a. 2.
38 *Ibid., ad* 3.
39 Zwingli, *Opera,* Vol. II/2, pp. 163 f.
40 *SD* VIII, § 47, in *The Book of Concord: The Confessions of the Evangelical Lutheran Church,* tr. and ed. by Theodore G. Tappert (Fortress Press, 1959), p. 61.
41 *SD* III, § 56, *ibid.,* p. 549.

Because the orthodox Protestant doctrine of the office of Christ considered the divine-human person the bearer of the office, the historical reality of Jesus was bypassed. Jesus appeared at the beginning not as a God-man but as a man, and as a man he knew himself to be under a mission, an office, and assignment from Israel's God. Can this discovery be unimportant for dogmatic Christology today? Should Christology not rather seek to be true to this in its speaking about the office of Jesus? Jesus was the bearer of an office from God first as simply man; this statement is a presupposition for the discussion of his divinity. Precisely the confirmation of Jesus in his earthly mission through his resurrection was the basis for the confession of his divinity.

A series of further deficiencies in this doctrine become understandable in the light of the observation that the early Protestant dogmaticians conceived the divine-human person of Jesus Christ as the bearer of his office. In the first place, this presupposition had as a consequence that all three offices were related to Jesus' entire life from birth to exaltation. If the office belongs to the divine-human person of Jesus, then he possessed it from the very moment of the incarnation and during his entire life. At this point what Quenstedt says about Jesus' Kingship is very revealing. Of course, Quenstedt sees that Jesus fully exercised (*plenarie exercet*) his Kingship only after his exaltation, but in contrast to the position held by Keckermann, he thinks that Jesus had already possessed royal authority—which properly belongs to the person of the Logos—in the condition of humiliation and merely kept it hidden.[42] With such a presupposition the course of Jesus' life necessarily takes on a superhuman, mythological cast. The conscious life of such a half-god would be inconceivable for us. To be sure, one may not overlook the fact that a conception that tends in this direction is evident already in the Gospel of Mark and even more so in John. Under these conditions, however, it is no longer possible to speak of Jesus' human consciousness.

The excessive emphasis upon the character of Jesus' history as act is closely connected to the association of his earthly activity with his divine-human person. If Jesus as God-man knew beforehand the course of his life, then his passion too becomes an act and the exercise of an office, in the sense of the passion predictions of the Gospels. Thus the uniform treatment of Jesus' passion as the priestly office emerges alongside the prophetic and royal offices. In the treatment of Jesus' passion as an actively executed office, just as in the antedating of his royal office into his pre-Easter life, the concrete conception of his individuality as a divine-human person comes to expression. Thereby that which is known in the light of the Easter event—Jesus' unity with God— is read back into his pre-Easter life as if, independently of the Easter event, it

[42] J. A. Quenstedt, *Theologia Didactico-Polemica,* III, 261, quoted by Schmid, *The Doctrinal Theology of the Evangelical Lutheran Church,* p. 372. Against Quenstedt, cf. the position taken by Keckermann (cited above, n. 20), who expressed himself more reservedly about the relation of the royal office to the earthly Jesus.

had already provided the basis for Jesus' actions in their humanly psychological progression. The beginnings of such a procedure can be seen in the Gospels, and these were regarded by orthodoxy as "historical." However, in contrast to this one must keep clearly in mind today that the divine-human unity of Jesus can never be expressed independently of the Easter event. In retrospect from the perspective of the resurrection, it is true that Jesus in his person was one with God also in his life before Easter. However, when Jesus' pre-Easter life is conceived as having been already divine-human in a direct sense, our conception of Jesus falls back into the mythological realm. Jesus' resurrection is not only constitutive for our perception of his divinity, but it is ontologically constitutive for that divinity. Apart from the resurrection from the dead, Jesus would not be God, even though from the perspective of the resurrection, he is retrospectively one with God in his whole pre-Easter life. Here, then, is a final objection to the traditional dogmaticians' coordination of the history of Jesus with his divine-human person. Whenever the tradition about Jesus is interpreted as the action of a divine-human person without considering the indirectness of the language about God and thus about Jesus' divinity, one overlooks the incisive significance that the crucifixion and then the resurrection have for the whole of Jesus' life. The concept of the divine-human office and its unbroken extension over cross and resurrection smooths over the cleft that the cross designates in Jesus' fate. This is especially clear with respect to the royal office. If Jesus was already the Messiah, independently of the progression of his history, if his unity with God had the character of an accomplished fact, then his crucifixion can hardly be understood as anything but a mere episode or a suffering temporarily assumed by Jesus, but by no means as the catastrophe that it must have signified for Jesus and for his disciples. With this kind of viewpoint, dogmatic Christology bypasses the real depth of meaning of Jesus' crucifixion and resurrection.

e. The merit of the Protestant theology of Jesus' threefold office did not consist exclusively in incorporating in this way the primitive Christian traditions about Jesus into dogmatic Christology, which could represent Jesus' historical life as the history of the one who was sent from God and executed his will. Beyond this, the doctrine of the offices had the particular merit that it expressed the relation of Jesus' activity and fate to ancient Israel. The older dogmaticians stressed that Jesus' three offices constituted the three most important institutions in Israel. Their concentration in Jesus presents him as the fulfillment of God's Old Testament history. First-century support for the position that the concentration of the three offices is not just a later construction and that it really is to be connected with the significance later ascribed to it is provided by the previously mentioned remark of Josephus that John Hyrcanus held the three highest offices of his people, the royal, the priestly, and the prophetic. Thus it is perhaps still possible to say without anachronism that not only the prophetic tradition—to which Jesus' mission gave him the closest affinity—but also the priestly institution and the Messianic hope as the representative elements of the Israelite tradition in general found their fulfillment in Jesus' history. To be sure, the fulfillment is in each case very different, because Jesus did not really exercise the office of priest and king. The pattern of three offices has typological meaning. One may not misuse this schema for an all too formal and unbroken conception of the fulfillment of God's history of the old covenant in Jesus' figure and history. One must consider the changes in the three institutions in the course of Israel's history, as well as the fact that they did not exist side by side throughout the whole of Israel's history. The Davidic Kingdom existed for about 400 years. The series of great canonical prophets is crowded into a significantly shorter period of time. To be sure, prophecy in Israel apparently had a long prehistory from the time before the occupation of Canaan,[43] as well as aftereffects following the end of the canonical prophecy into the time of Jesus. Only the priesthood existed as a stable institution until the time of Jesus. Precisely here in the concentration on sacrificial ritual, a sharp change in function is to be observed over against the early Israelite period. The activity of prophetic circles and the expectation of a new kingdom certainly were decisive in stamping Israel's later history, but apparently no longer in the continuity of an institution as with the priesthood. We have already stressed that the ancient institutions were not simply restored in the person of Jesus. Josephus' characterization of John Hyrcanus probably contains a symbolic component that cannot be overlooked, particularly with respect to the prophetic element. Compared to John Hyrcanus, Jesus gave even less reason in his early appearance for viewing him as the bearer and renewer of these three offices. The typological pattern of the threefold office represents more a symbol for the relation of Jesus' activity to Israel's traditions than a showing of the real context in tradition in which Jesus' activity became possible. The real line of connection is in the apocalyptic transformations of prophetic traditions. Because of the significance of his activity and fate, the figure of Jesus attracted to itself all of Israel's traditions. Here resides the truth of the typological pattern of his threefold office.

II. THE CALL TO THE KINGDOM OF GOD

1. Jesus' Imminent Expectation

Like John the Baptist, Jesus proclaimed the imminent Kingdom of God. This message forced his hearers out of their everyday affairs, made turning back to God urgent for them because the beginning of God's Lordship brings

[43] See Rolf Rendtorff, "Erwägungen zur Frühgeschichte des Prophetentums in Israel," ZThK, LIX (1962), 145-167.

with it the decision for salvation or judgment, for nearness to or distance from God for every individual man. When the ultimate questions can no longer be put off, everything that otherwise keeps us busy becomes inconsequential by comparison.

We are concerned with the question of the universal validity of this message. There is no doubt that Jesus erred when he announced that God's Lordship would begin in his own generation (Matt. 23:36; 16:28; Mark 13:30 and parallels; cf. Matt. 10:23). The end of the world did not begin in Jesus' generation and also not in the generation of his disciples, the witnesses of his resurrection. Here we stand before the notorious problem of the delay of the Parousia, the problem of the two thousand years that have since elapsed without the arrival of the end of the world and God's universal rule.

Jesus' imminent expectation did not, however, remain unfulfilled. It was fulfilled in the only way it is possible to speak of the fulfillment of prophetic proclamations and promises, namely, in such a way that the original sense of the prophecy is revised by an event that corresponds to it but nonetheless has a more or less different character than could be known from the prophecy alone. The Christian Easter message speaks of the mode of fulfillment of Jesus' imminent expectation. It was fulfilled by himself, insofar as the eschatological reality of the resurrection of the dead appeared in Jesus himself. It is not yet universally fulfilled in the way in which Jesus and his contemporaries had expected. In spite of this, Jesus' resurrection justifies the imminent expectation that had moved him and establishes anew the eschatological expectation fulfilled in him for the rest of humanity.

Jesus' imminent expectation has not only been fulfilled in himself, but it has cleared the way for an understanding of man that still holds good as the most profound insight into the human situation in the world. Jesus' message of the nearness of God's Lordship called men out of the securities of their everyday way of life and thereby unmasked the provisional character of all inner-worldly forms and fulfillments of life. What man is destined to be was revealed in the light of the message about the nearness of God's Lordship, regardless of the date of its arrival. Man as man is always something more than and extending beyond his present situation; his destiny is not fulfilled in any given framework of his life. God's reality is not only the ultimate source and guarantee of a present form of life, but points beyond every presently given or possible security and fulfillment of existence. This opening-up of human beings for God's future, through which man's destiny to openness toward the future—even in his relationships to the world—is realized, is independent of *particular* apocalyptic deadlines. This is suggested in Jesus' own message: "The kingdom of God is not coming with signs to be observed; nor will they say, 'Lo, here it is!' or 'There!' for behold, the kingdom of God is in the midst of you" (Luke 17:20 f.). This "in the midst of you" was the sense of the imminent but not definitely dated future, as in the following saying in Luke: "And they will say to you, 'Lo, there!' or 'Lo, here!' Do not go, do not follow them. For as the lightning flashes and lights up the sky from one side to the other, so will the Son of man be in his day" (Luke 17:23 f.). This reference over and beyond the present commitments of human life to God's future, which is not bound to any specific date, retains its validity as the inauguration of the openness to God of human existence independently of the delay of the date of the eschatological events. Of course, this is true only if Jesus' own imminent expectation—as has been previously suggested—can be judged as meaningful with respect to his own resurrection from the dead and thus also as an adequate confirmation of the understanding of existence made possible thereby.

To allow all present human commitments to become irrelevant in the light of God's ultimate future is surely no self-evident style of life. If, however, the understanding of existence as a radical openness to the future were the only element of truth in Jesus' eschatological message, it would have had to carry its own weight after being once originated, independently of Jesus' otherwise erroneous and thus outdated eschatological message. This possibility is all the more to be doubted, since openness for God's future, even though independent of particular calendar dates for the end, is in no way independent of the expectations of the end in general. If the future expectation of a transformation of our world and of the resurrection of the dead should collapse, then the openness for the future of human existence would also lose its decisive impulse. Even though openness for always new possibilities belongs constitutively to the anthropological structure of the human being, it can slacken: as it was once hidden in the bondage of ancient man to a sacral order of the world, so it can once more atrophy, for example, in the conformity of a technically perfectly organized consumer society if it loses its creative power.

2. The Presence of Salvation

The message of John the Baptist apparently connected only the hope for a future salvation with the call to repentance in the face of impending judgment. Jesus directly granted eschatological salvation. *That is, the nearness of the Kingdom of God that he proclaimed is itself salvation for those who take notice of it.* This fundamental insight seems to have distinguished Jesus' activity from that of the Baptist. The nearness of the Kingdom of God signifies a threat of judgment only for those who close themselves to it by seeking to fulfill their lives in striving for riches, in their own righteousness, and in care for their own well-being.[44] The others who direct their vision

---

[44] In his article "Jesus Christ," *RGG*, III (3d ed.), 640, Hans Conzelmann places the accent in the right place when he says on Mark 10:25 and Luke 12:13 ff.: "Possessions are not forbidden, but Jesus shows their *danger* for the one possessing them." "Not the

beyond their own accomplishments and possessions toward God's future have salvation already in this attitude. Therefore those are especially to be called blessed who in their situation have no other hope than God's future: "Blessed are you poor, for yours is the kingdom of God. Blessed are you that hunger now, for you shall be satisfied. Blessed are you that weep now, for you shall laugh" (Luke 6:20 f.). Because salvation, the fulfilled destiny of man, consists in the fulfillment of openness for God, it is already present for those who long for the nearness of God proclaimed by Jesus; it has already come to those who hear and accept Jesus' message of the imminent Kingdom of God. Jesus does not decide whether such hearing and accepting happens in an individual case, but declares it to be a matter for the coming judgment. This is shown by the parables of the weeds among the wheat (Matt. 13:24-30) and of the fish net (Matt. 13:47-50).

Because the future salvation was already present in Jesus' preaching, he did not preach in the desert as the Baptist did, but went to men in their cities and where they lived. It is not essential that men go out from the world in which they ordinarily live into the wilderness, to the locale of Israel's early history, in order to return to the God of Israel. Repentance does not mean to go back to the beginnings but to turn toward God's future. But God's future seeks men where they happen to be at the moment. It is only essential that they accept Jesus with his message of the imminent Kingdom and seek community with him. For this reason, Jesus could promise salvation directly. "Blessed are the eyes which see what you see!" (Luke 10:23). For this reason, he could forgive sins without preconditions and could share the eschatological meal with publicans and sinners.[45] Even the cheating holders of tax-collecting concessions and other notorious wrongdoers have salvation if they only open themselves to Jesus and his message. Therefore, their example makes clear the offer of salvation that is present in the nearness of God, in the imminence of God's Kingdom, in its unconditional character. For this reason community at table with publicans and sinners was intended by Jesus as a demonstration. He did not, however, eat only with such men—he went to Pharisees as well (Luke 7:36).

Like the promise of forgiveness and the assurance of salvation, so too Jesus' healing ministry was closely bound up with his message of the coming of the Kingdom of God. The healing he performed demonstrated concretely

wealth of the 'wheat farmer' is castigated, but rather his *foolishness* for trusting in it." Luke 12:34 shows the reason for this danger: "Where your treasure is, there will your heart be also."

45 That Jesus' community at table had the sense of guaranteeing eschatological salvation has been shown convincingly by Ernst Fuchs, *Das urchristliche Sakramentsverständnis*, p. 38, on Matt. 11:19 and parallels (cf. also Mark 2:16 f.), following Ernst Lohmeyer, *Lord of the Temple: A Study of the Relation Between Cult and Gospel*, tr. by Stewart Todd (Edinburgh: Oliver & Boyd, Ltd., 1961); see Fuchs's reference to Lohmeyer in Beiheft 1 to *ZThK* (1959), 37.

that where the message of God's nearness is grasped completely and in full trust, salvation itself is already effective.[46]

3. The Fatherhood of God

That nearness of God's Kingdom includes salvation in itself establishes the confident nearness of God himself expressed in addressing God as "Father."[47] Taken for itself, the designation of God as Father is not Jesus' invention. It is to be found in many religions. In the Old Testament, Yahweh is regarded as the Father of Israel (Jer. 31:9; Isa. 63:16) and especially of the king (II Sam. 7:14). In Judaism, Yahweh was also designated as the Father of the individual pious person (Ecclus. 4:10; Wisd. of Sol. 2:16 ff.). For Jesus, on the other hand, the relationship of childhood to God is "not the prerogative of the pious."[48] God is Father over the evil and the good, the just and the unjust (Matt. 5:45). On Jesus' tongue the name "Father" expresses God's nearness in a special way. "This is also shown in the expression by which Jesus chooses to address God in prayer, an expression which would have appeared to any Jew as too unceremonious and lacking in respect. Abba— Father, this is the word Jesus uses (Mark 14:36), which the Hellenistic church has taken over in its original Aramaic form from the oldest records about Jesus (Rom. 8:15; Gal. 4:6). It is the child's familiar address to his father here on earth, completely uncommon in religious language."[49] The language of the Lord's Prayer, in distinction from the Jewish Kaddish to which it is otherwise related even in the individual formulation, shows a uniquely everyday immediacy to God expressed precisely in the address "Abba" in contrast to the solemnly liturgical "Abinu" (Matt. 6:9).[50] The address of God as Father must, however, be understood in the context of the first three petitions, all of which have to do with the coming of the Kingdom of God. Thus the nearness to God that is expressed in the address of God as Father is identical with the eschatological nearness of the Kingdom of God. Since the beginning of the Kingdom of God is temporally so near, God has also drawn so near to man in Jesus' preaching in the sense that one can converse with him in the language of everyday familiarity.

Thus in the name of God as Father the unity of two thought complexes in Jesus' preaching that have previously been widely thought to be hardly

[46] To this extent, the connection of the healings with the faith of the person healed, even if the terminology is supposed to come from the later community, calls attention to an essential aspect of Jesus' healing activity; cf. Matt. 8:10, 13; 9:22, 29; 15:28 and, on the other hand, ch. 13:58. See also G. Ebeling, "Jesus and Faith," *Word and Faith*, pp. 230 ff.

[47] G. Bornkamm, *Jesus of Nazareth*, pp. 124-129; cf. also pp. 135 f.

[48] *Ibid.*, p. 126.

[49] *Ibid.*, p. 128.

[50] U. Wilckens in *OaG*, p. 55. Cf. the text of the Kaddish in P. Fiebig, *Jesu Bergpredigt* (Göttingen: Vandenhoeck & Ruprecht, 1924), p. 50.

reconcilable becomes accessible. This involves on the one hand the eschatological message of the imminent beginning of the Kingdom of God and on the other the formally rather uneschatological group of Wisdom sayings and parables drawn from the everyday experience of human life. Hans Conzelmann, for example, thinks "that the statements about God's sovereign rule and those about the coming of His Kingdom stand side by side in a more or less unrelated way." For Conzelmann, the relation between the two different conceptualities results only from the fact that "God is God."[51] "The reference to the administration of the world by the God who lets the sun rise and the rain fall upon the good and the evil and to God's care for the flowers of the field and the birds of the sky stands side by side with the announcement of the imminent end of the world corrupted by evil."[52] That both themes are related is indicated by the use of the name "Father" in both places. When Jesus contrasts God's everyday care for the birds of heaven and the lilies of the field to the anxiety of men and concludes with a view of human necessities of everyday life, "and your Father knows that you need them," the train of thought appears to move wholly in the context of faith in God's providence. But only then does the point come: "Instead, seek his kingdom, and these things shall be yours as well" (Luke 12:30 f.). The trusting commitment to God, also expressed in the petition for daily needs (Matt. 6:8; 7:11), is most closely related to conduct that is completely dedicated to the Kingdom of God. Over against Conzelmann, Ulrich Wilckens has emphasized this connection: "In the view of Jesus, to entrust oneself to God's everyday care and to direct oneself totally with intense expectation toward the approaching Kingdom of God coincide. . . . The immediacy of God that stamps both conceptual complexes in the same way is grounded in Jesus' basic eschatological conception," namely, in his conviction of the nearness of the Kingdom of God.[53]

This means, however, that in Jesus' proclamation the true nature of creation is revealed for the first time in the light of the approaching end. This has fundamental significance also for the understanding of creation itself. Creation is not to be understood as an act that happened one time, ages ago, the results of which involve us in the present. Rather, the creation of all things, even including things that belong to the past, takes place out of the ultimate future, from the *eschaton*, insofar as only from the perspective of the end are all things what they truly are. For their real significance becomes clear only when it becomes apparent what ultimately will become of them. There-

51 *RGG*, III (3d ed.), 641.

52 *ZThK*, LVI (1959), Beiheft 1: "Die Frage nach dem historischen Jesus," pp. 10 f. F. Hahn also takes a critical attitude toward this dualism. When Conzelmann "wants to divide substantially the eschatological and ethical components of Jesus' preaching and does not want the ethics understood on the basis of the eschatology, this raises the strongest doubts" (*Christologische Hoheitstitel*, p. 27).

53 U. Wilckens, in *OaG*, p. 56, n. 35.

fore, the nearness of the imminent Kingdom of God puts all things into that relation to God which belonged to them as God's creatures from the very beginning. It is just this that demonstrates the universal truth of Jesus' eschatological message: it reveals the "natural" essence of men and things with an urgency nowhere achieved outside of this eschatological light. Therefore, Jesus' preaching can use everyday examples in its parables. Even the structure of the parable presupposes the correspondence of creation and *eschaton*. Indeed, the uniqueness of the Kingdom of God is supposed to be made clear in everyday affairs.

Therefore, Jesus can speak in the language of Wisdom teaching and clothe his message in proverbial expressions.[54] Especially the unqualified trust, the unreserved commitment to the imminent Kingdom of God that Jesus demands of his hearers, is nothing else than the childlike trust that man as creature should in any case bring to God. Thus the natural essence of man is revealed in Jesus' eschatological preaching. By promising salvation without preconditions but demanding unconditional trust for this promise, he brings man into his natural relationship to God, corresponding to man's creaturely destiny. Or, expressed in a more modern way, Jesus brings man into the radical openness that constitutes the specific fundamental element of human nature.

From this point we may look back again at the problem of Jesus' relationship to apocalyptic. The immediacy to God that characterizes Jesus' preaching has been strongly emphasized by all contemporary exegetes.[55] This immediacy, expressed in the name "Father" and in the everyday language of Jesus' parables, forms, according to Käsemann, the real contrast between Jesus and apocalyptic. "The situation was surely this: Jesus took his point of departure from the apocalyptically determined message of the Baptist but his own preaching was not constitutively stamped by apocalyptic, but proclaimed the immediacy of the near God."[56] With the "but" Käsemann surely has overlooked that the "immediacy" to God does not arise at all in such an immediate way, but is mediated through and through by Jesus' eschatological message. Precisely the eschatological nearness of the Kingdom of

---

[54] Examples for this are treated by G. Bornkamm, *Jesus of Nazareth*, pp. 117-124, "Creation and World."

[55] H. Conzelmann, *RGG*, III (3d ed.), 633, n. 10; G. Bornkamm, *Jesus of Nazareth*, p. 62, also speaks of "unmediated presence" and he thinks that "to make the reality of God present: this is the essential mystery of Jesus" (*ibid.*). In substance E. Fuchs, *ZThK*, LIII (1956), 228; *ZThK*, LIV (1957), 146 f., comes to the same conclusion by anticipating the idea of Jesus' faith to which our faith corresponds, as subsequently developed by G. Ebeling. Cf. also the following note.

[56] E. Käsemann, "Die Anfänge christlicher Theologie," *ZThK*, LVII (1960), 179. In Käsemann's presentation "Zum Thema der urchristlichen Apokalyptik," *ZThK*, LIX (1962), 257-284, the word "immediacy" is absent and the language about the nearness of God in Jesus' proclamation in the sense that "the proclamation of the imminent *basileia* is the nearness of this *basileia* itself" (p. 270) is no longer subject to the criticism made here against Käsemann's earlier formulation. It appears rather to correspond to what was said above, pp. 227 f., about the presence of salvation in Jesus' message.

God discloses the nearness of God to man as to all creatures in general and thus uncovers the "natural" destiny of human existence. The natural immediacy of all things to God is not something immediately given, but comes into view only through the apocalyptically founded message of the nearness of God's Kingdom.

From this perspective let us return to Jesus' proclamation of the Fatherhood of God. Jesus' God is decisively characterized by the goodness of the father. God's fatherly goodness can, on the one hand, be represented by his rule in creation: No sparrow "will fall to the ground without your Father's will. But even the hairs of your head are all numbered" (Matt. 10:29 f.). But also the eschatological gift of citizenship in the Kingdom of God reveals God's fatherly goodness: "Fear not, little flock, for it is your Father's good pleasure to give you the kingdom" (Luke 12:32). The sayings about God's fatherly goodness again probably have a common core. This is to be sought in the unconditionality with which Jesus can promise salvation to those who accept his promise. To that extent God's fatherly goodness has found its pure expression in the parable of the prodigal son (Luke 15:11-32). The Father's love belongs to the son who, trusting in that love, returns from the misfortunes for which he himself is responsible.

4. The Life in Love

"The radical understanding of God's *demand* follows"[57] precisely from the absoluteness of Jesus' promise of salvation. Whoever accepts Jesus' message of the nearness of the Kingdom with his whole heart and thereby comes into the right, humanly natural relationship to God and receives the forgiveness of sins cannot possibly live other than as one who "seeks first the kingdom of God." He cannot want to serve God and mammon at the same time (Matt. 6:24). He will rather seek his treasure in heaven (Luke 12:33) and will give everything else away in exchange. He will act like the merchant who found the rare pearl and gave up all his possessions for it (Matt. 13:45 f.) and like the man who found a treasure in the field and sold everything else so that he could buy the field (v. 44). Whoever has really understood the message of the nearness of God's Kingdom and the unconditional salvation included in it will stake everything for God's rule, for the fulfillment of God's will.

But to do the will of God means to act as God acts, who lets his sun rise on the evil and the good and—that is what the picture means—directs his salvation to the just and the unjust (Matt. 5:44 f., 48). For this reason, the forgiveness of sins especially is connected with the receiver's forgiving his

---

[57] H. Conzelmann, *RGG*, III (3d ed.), 633.

debtors. This connection comes to expression in the Lord's Prayer (Luke 11:4), as well as in other places: "Forgive, if you have anything against any one; so that your Father also who is in heaven may forgive you your trespasses" (Mark 11:25). This corresponds negatively to the prohibition, "Judge not, that you be not judged" (Matt. 7:1). The parable of the unmerciful servant (Matt. 18:23-35) makes clear that what is involved in the command of forgiveness is to act in agreement with the conduct of God. Even the forgiveness that has already been received is forfeited when it is not passed on in one's own conduct toward others. Here the structure of the "holy law," the *ius talionis,* may have a place in the center of Jesus' message.[58] The divine forgiveness that opens the future to the recipient places him in a position to open up the future for his fellowmen also.

This, however, is the structure of freely giving love. Forgiveness includes the most radical form of love, love for the enemy (Matt. 5:43 ff.). It is decisive for understanding forgiveness that one sees it in this kind of unity with love and does not conceive it only negatively as the renunciation of hostile sentiments. It is common to love and forgiveness that both open the future. Therefore, also, forgiveness always includes the active element of help for life, just as Jesus himself heals by forgiving sins (Mark 2:1-12). The parable of the good Samaritan (Luke 10:25-37) shows love's creative relation to the situation and lack of preconditions, corresponding to the lack of preconditions in Jesus' proclamation of forgiveness and promise of salvation.[59] The sayings about the salt and lamp (Matt. 5:13-16) as well as the parable of the pounds (Luke 19:11-27) make clear the essential connection between the salvation received and its effect on the deeds of the recipients. With all this we have already described the connection between love for God and love for the neighbor that is the norm of Jesus' whole interpretation of the law (cf. Matt. 22:40). The insight into the connection between forgiveness of sins received and love for the neighbor makes understandable both the radicality of Jesus' interpretation of the law as well as his freedom with respect to rules that cannot be derived from this core.

Here also we must inquire once more about the universal validity of Jesus' message. The radicality of his instructions has often been judged as utopian, as not appropriate to the raw reality of life. This judgment is tenable only so long as one sees in the commandment of love a norm to be fulfilled that nevertheless goes beyond every realization. The love about which Jesus speaks is not, however, an ultimate intensification of the law. Rather, Jesus means by love concretely the power imparted to the hearer by the message of forgiveness, by the promise of eschatological salvation, equipping him in turn in

[58] Differently, E. Käsemann, "Säzte heiligen Rechts," *NTS,* I (1954-1955), 248-260; *idem, ZThK,* LVII (1960), 165 f., 171 ff.
[59] In supplement to this, G. Bornkamm, *Jesus of Nazareth,* pp. 109-117.

concrete situations to make the future possible for the neighbor in need of such assistance.

In this sense, not primarily as commandment but as the power emanating from the eschatological promise of salvation, creative love is the source of human community; without forgiveness no community can exist for any length of time. This has not been the case just since the appearance of Jesus; what has always been the basis of possibility of human community in general has moved fully into light only by his message. Love is inventive; in the respective situations it enables the realization of the conditions that make community possible. To this extent, love does not contrast with justice, but is rather itself the origin of positive legislation, not of an ideal natural law but of the creation of new forms of justice appropriate to the respective situation.[60] This concept goes beyond the literal formulation of Jesus' commandment of love; his message did not at all involve the problem of founding a legal form in which men could live together. Nevertheless, such an establishment of justice on the basis of love is a consequence of Jesus' own preaching. It corresponds to the fact that Jesus intended to interpret the Jewish law in what he said about love.

By creating community, love realizes the unity of human destiny. Thus Jesus' commandment of love also reveals the essence of man, his destiny to community. This significance of the commandment of love demonstrates its validity in the question about the relation between love and law. To the extent that all human striving toward community finds its fulfillment in the love Jesus has made possible by his message of eschatological salvation, of God's forgiving goodness, the universal significance of his activity in this respect also becomes apparent.

Precisely in the fact that Jesus' message makes love possible among men, Jesus shows himself to be the fulfillment of Israel's hope for the Messiah. Jesus' activity as helper of the distressed was not designated by the primitive Christian tradition as an expression of his Messiahship, but it was probably connected with the title "Son of David" (Mark 10:46-52). This title was used by the Jewish-Christian community for the earthly Jesus who was designated to receive the Messianic honor. By acting as the helper of the distressed, Jesus assumed his royal duty. It had been the office of the Israelite kings to assist widows and orphans who otherwise had no legal protection and generally to establish and defend justice and righteousness over and above the normal legal procedures.[61] The Messianic hope was especially oriented toward the establishment of peace and justice by the expected eschatological ruler (Isa. 11:3 ff.). But just this happens in Jesus' interpretation of the law.

---

[60] I have dealt with this and the following in greater detail, although still in a rather preliminary way, in my essay "Zur Theologie des Rechts," *ZEE*, VII (1963), 1-23, esp. pp. 18 ff.

[61] G. von Rad, *Old Testament Theology*, Vol. I, p. 322.

The eschatological community of justice is founded by the love that grows out of Jesus' message, and thereby the beginning is realized of that which Israel expected from the coming of the Messiah.

This establishment of Jesus' Messiahship is admittedly not that of primitive Christianity. The latter took its point of departure from the fact that Jesus, even though he himself probably rejected the title "Messiah" (Mark 8:27-33), was accused and executed by the Romans as a messianic pretender. The next step was the understanding of Jesus as the one designated by God as the coming Messiah, and then as the Messiah already ruling in heaven. Only later was Jesus' earthly life interpreted messianically. This final step ran into difficulties because Jesus' earthly behavior showed no explicitly sovereign elements. But from the perspective of Jesus' resurrection, it was clear that no other Messiah was to be expected. On this basis it was finally necessary to bring Jesus' earthly activity into relationship to the Messianic title intended for him. This involved a search for traces of a fulfillment of the Old Testament Messianic hope. The preceding remarks have had the purpose of calling attention to such traces.

III. UNIVERSAL AND HISTORICALLY CONDITIONED ELEMENTS IN JESUS' ACTIVITY

Jesus' divinity and the universal validity of his mission and activity as man are closely related. If one judges Jesus' activity as one-sided, as the expression of a merely partial truth, then it seems that the basis has been destroyed for a confession of faith in his divinity from the very beginning. In fact, Jesus can be the ultimate revelation of the one God only if the true relation of men and of their world to God has been entirely brought to light by his actions and fate. If essential elements of our experience of reality with its ultimate questions do not receive an answer from the figure of Jesus, then we live without Jesus and without the God revealed in him in those areas. This would call into question the universal divinity of the God of the Bible as he is revealed by Jesus as the Father.

By far the most decisive and far-reaching denial of the universal validity of the human figure of Jesus in the nineteenth century was that by Friedrich Nietzsche, especially in his *Antichrist* (1888/1895). Standing on the same plane with the "quest of the historical Jesus" literature, Nietzsche took a position diametrically opposed to its efforts to set forth precisely the man Jesus as the new point of orientation for Christian piety. The bitterness of his attack on the piety that even an increasingly dechristianized Europe continued to offer Jesus' person has hardly been exceeded since. It has, however, been replaced by more sober and therefore more important criticism. We

235

select from the series of such works[62] the presentation and position taken by Karl Jaspers, which is to be found in his work *Die grossen Philosophen,* Vol. I, pp. 186-214. Jaspers' ideas deserve special consideration with regard to his differentiation from Nietzsche as well as because of the importance of his own critical arguments.

In distinction from Nietzsche and many of his followers, Jaspers takes a positive position toward what he calls "Biblical religion." With this concept he designates especially the prophetic movement in Israel whose high point he sees in the figure of Jeremiah. For him, Jesus is "historically the last of the prophets" (p. 202). In the Bible, Jaspers does not find witnesses of a binding divine revelation, but the historical foundation of our cultural existence and of Western civilization generally. Because that implies a certain affinity to Jesus and especially to the Old Testament, his criticism of Jesus is all the more serious.

Without difficulty, Jaspers rejects Nietzsche's attack as a distortion of the figure of Jesus. Nietzsche had attempted to understand the whole of Jesus' actions as the expression of a lack of vital power. "Do not resist evil" was for him the characteristic saying of Jesus. According to Nietzsche, Jesus could not bear conflict with any real power; this was the source of Jesus' ethic of forgiveness. "Denial is for him the completely impossible. He cannot oppose."[63] Against this presentation, Jaspers rightly calls attention to Jesus' words of judgment and to his conflicts with his opponents: "In the Gospels one meets Jesus as an elemental power, no less clear in its hardness and aggressiveness than in those elements of infinite mildness. . . . It does not work to make of Jesus a patient, soft, loving figure, and even less to make of him a nervous, unresisting man" (pp. 200 f.).

In his own criticism, Jaspers takes another approach. He appreciates the penetrating power of Jesus' radical message of the coming Kingdom of God. At the same time, he regards it as the root of Jesus' one-sidedness. "Everything worldly has disappeared, as it were, in the luster of the Kingdom of God. The bonds of piety, justice, and culture are nothing in comparison to this Kingdom" (p. 189). Correspondingly, Jaspers hears in Jesus' teachings "that which is impossible in the world." "These imperatives are imperatives for saints, as if man no longer had any situation of finitude in the world, any

---

[62] See additionally, esp. G. Szczesny, *The Future of Unbelief* (George Braziller, Inc., 1961), esp. pp. 57 ff.

[63] So Jaspers, *Die grossen Philosophen* (Munich: R. Piper, 1957), Vol. I, p. 200. This is not in the English, *The Great Philosophers* (Harcourt, Brace & World, Inc., 1962): *"Negation* is just what is completely impossible to him." On this, cf. Friedrich Nietzsche himself in *The Antichrist* (Alfred A. Knopf, Inc., 1920), Aphorism 32: *"Denial* is precisely the thing that is impossible to him." Aphorism 29: "The very incapacity for resistance is here converted into something moral ("Resist not evil!"—the most profound sentence in the Gospels, perhaps the true key to them)." According to Nietzsche, *ibid.,* the "aggressive fanatic, the mortal enemy of the theologians and ecclesiastics," was first introduced into the picture of Jesus by his disciples.

task of constructive work in the world and of realization." (P. 190.) Jaspers calls such radicality "frightening" (p. 205), even though he says of Jesus as of Buddha (!), they are "of unique importance as a question for us. We only know what we are and do as we see it from the perspective of their shadow" (p. 228). Nevertheless, Jesus' radicality frightens Jaspers: "Jesus has stepped outside the bounds of all real order in the world" (p. 205). Jaspers appeals to Hegel's judgment: "Never has anyone spoken in such a revolutionary way, for everything otherwise valid is made irrelevant and of no account" (p. 205). Thus Jesus' extremism makes known "the chance of human nature itself under all conditions—even in that which is despised, lowly, and ugly when measured by the world's standards" (p. 205). Just this, however, makes of Jesus' appearance a mere corrective: "His shortcoming is that there can no longer be any interest for constructive work in the world" (p. 223). Thereby Jaspers relativizes Jesus' figure to only one among the "definitive men" alongside Socrates, Buddha, and Confucius, all of whom possessed their greatness as revelations of human nature not achieved by others; all, however, had their specific shortcomings as well (p. 226).

Thus Jaspers' critique is directed toward the assertion that for the hearer of Jesus' message about the imminent Kingdom of God "there can no longer be any interest for constructive work in the world," even though he "set everything under the condition of the Kingdom of God at the end of the world, without negation of the world" (p. 223). It is surely correct that in the light of the imminent Kingdom of God in Jesus' message, political and social concerns recede "to the point of disappearing," as is the case in the whole of primitive Christianity. Hans von Campenhausen thinks this: "The determinative vital interests of primitive Christianity were apparently of a fundamentally different sort and offered for the time being no point of contact for participation in civil and political affairs."[64] Of course, Jesus occasionally took a position with respect to political and social questions. He did not allow himself to be drawn into a condemnation of the Roman occupation forces by a question about Galileans murdered by Roman soldiers (Luke 13:1 ff.), but took the occasion to deliver a call to repentance to the morally indignant questioners (p. 183). He affirmed the duty to pay taxes to the Roman Caesar in his saying about tribute money (Mark 12:13 ff. and parallels). But he drew the line at acting as umpire in an inheritance dispute (Luke 12:14). To this extent it is rightly said that one cannot find any interest for "constructive work in the world" in Jesus, even though his message does not encourage flight from the world and affirms the natural life of men as creatures before God.

[64] H. von Campenhausen, "Die Christen und das bürgerliche Leben nach den Aussagen des Neuen Testaments," *Tradition und Leben: Kräfte der Kirchengeschichte* (1960), pp. 180-202; the quoted passage is found on p. 180. The following page numbers in the text refer to this article.

Yet it is a different question whether this lack of interest is to be understood from Jesus' particular situation characterized by imminent eschatological expectation or whether there are in general no points of contact, no motives for constructive work in the world to be found in his message. The difference between the two is great. Jaspers assumes without further question not only that no concern for "constructive work in the world" was effective in Jesus himself but also that from the perspective of his message it is basically impossible for there to be any such effort. If such were the case, all participation of Christianity in the problems of structuring the world—especially since the beginning of the Constantinian period—certainly would be the indication of a break with Jesus' own intention, a compromise with the world. This is, in fact, Jaspers' opinion (p. 212).

In general, Jaspers sees a cleft between Jesus' message and the church's faith in Christ (pp. 209 ff.). This corresponds to the level of exegetical research represented by critical scholarship in Adolf von Harnack's time and with consequences through the work of Rudolf Bultmann. It does not yet have in view the results of the new inquiry of New Testament scholarship into the continuity in the history of traditions between Christian kerygma and Jesus, which began with Bultmann's observation of the Christological implications of Jesus' claim to authority. The assertion of a cleft between Jesus and primitive Christianity is disastrous for Jaspers' picture of Jesus. It hinders his recognition of the context that connects the post-Easter message of God's action in and through Jesus with the activity of Jesus himself, in spite of all differences, namely, the connection between the *implicit* Christology of Jesus' own claim and the *explicit* post-Easter Christologies modified according to the particular conceptual context. Also, with regard to the relationship to the world, one must similarly inquire whether there are implicit starting points in Jesus' message and in primitive Christianity that might not only permit but even motivate the subsequent participation of Christianity in the structuring of the world, up to and including modern man's sovereign authority over the world.

In contrast to Jaspers, von Campenhausen understands the primitive Christian reserve in social and political questions as conditioned by the particular situation. Christians have, to be sure, no definite program, but are "not indifferent or simply neutral" toward the tasks existing for all men in the social and political world, "but are affirmatively disposed toward them. This is in essence self-evident for a community that comes out of the Old Testament. It needs, therefore, no new, specifically Christian or even Christological legitimation for its behavior in this respect. That the extent of civil participation and responsibility remained quite small at first is based, as has been said, on the circumstances and will change with the changes in the social-political situation" (p. 201). The "circumstances" were primarily that Christians "like most subjects of the Roman Empire" possessed "no active political responsibility." Thus, at first they did not come into question as state officials. Therefore, it is not astonishing that one finds in the New Testament only general appeals for peace and obedience, the expression of "a typical subject morality" (p. 198). All of this can likewise be said of Jesus' own conduct. Neither he nor his later community directly evaded the question of the public responsibility; the question did not confront them in that form at all. That happened only later. Then it could be answered affirmatively. For even though—or better, precisely because—there is no such thing as a particular Christian program for structuring the world, the earliest Christianity contains "a tendency of the will and a readiness that are valid under all circumstances" (p. 261), but that are expressed in different ways according to particular circumstances.

The root of this tendency of the will resides in Jesus himself. It becomes apparent, for example, in the parable of the pounds and in the commandment of love. Such sayings on Jesus' tongue were not directed immediately toward an activity of transforming the world, but under changed historical conditions they led to such responsibilities. To this extent, the church acted wisely in not closing itself to the Christian renewal of the Roman Empire accomplished by Constantine. A critique of the church's attitude toward Constantine's successors can only consist in the observation that the church could have taken up the responsibility that it inherited in a more conscientious way, without at the same time permitting the disappearance of the difference between the church's task directed toward God's future and the civil order of the contemporary society. In the light of the future Kingdom of God, the church should have perceived more clearly the provisional character of a political order—and especially of one for which Christians are responsible—thereby at the same time being able to see more concretely the possibilities for the change of that order. The assumption of political responsibility as such, however, cannot be the object of criticism. For this reason, Luther was quite right when he later invoked the commandment to love as the basis of the Christian's participation in "worldly rule." Jaspers' critique of Jesus, "that there *can* no longer be any interest for constructive work in the world" (italics mine) misjudges the scope of Jesus' commandment of love, which does not restrict itself only to an individual ethical horizon but—to speak with von Campenhausen—reveals "a tendency of the will and a readiness that are valid under all circumstances" and that must be expressed very differently according to the situation.

There is a fundamental consequence to be drawn from all of this. What we have established about the universal validity of Jesus' actions does not suggest that we may overlook the differences in situations. Our situation is no longer that of Jesus nor that of primitive Christianity. Therefore, every abstract program for following in Jesus' footsteps is doomed to failure. The Franciscan poverty movement, for example, was something completely different from the procession of Jesus with his disciples through Palestine. When one dismisses the situational differences and then follows Jesus' teachings or example ever so literally, one will certainly have done something completely different from that which Jesus had in mind.

It is not only true for the external circumstances of life and for participation in transforming the world that Jesus' situation is no longer ours. That these tasks were not urgent for Jesus is related not only to his exclusion from political responsibility in the Roman world as a Roman subject, but it is also related to the imminent eschatological expectation that determined his whole activity. Jaspers' critique brings out only one aspect of this situation, which strikingly illuminates the alienation of our whole modern situation from Jesus' conceptual world.

The discovery of the apocalyptically conditioned character of Jesus' message and of the whole of his activity, which was slowly achieved by the quest for the historical Jesus after David Friedrich Strauss and which achieved a breakthrough with Johannes Weiss, presents even today the real problem for the question of the universal validity of the figure of Jesus. While the quest for the historical Jesus in the nineteenth century still sought in Jesus' historical figure the example for its own piety, the discovery of Jesus' thoroughgoing connections with the concept of Jewish apocalyptic signified the end of such efforts. Even critical scholars, even those who belonged to the front line of the "history of religions" approach such as Wilhelm Bousset and Hermann Gunkel, rejected Weiss's results because thereby Jesus' proclamation was "moved into a historical distance no longer accessible to the faith of modern theologians."[65] "The consistent placement of Jesus' proclamation in the conceptual world of late Judaism had all too clearly resulted in the consequence that this proclamation became alien and not understandable to modern man. It could not, therefore, be accepted as necessary so long as the observation of a consistent 'history of religions' approach was not recognized as inescapable."[66] This observation is valid even today as an explanation for the otherwise ununderstandable reserve of some exegetes toward assigning Jesus a place in the context of apocalyptic traditions. For the advocates of the "consistent eschatological" interpretation of Jesus' history, on the other hand, the question is raised about what still has something of permanent value in the figure of Jesus. In this circle, too, it was taken as self-evident, as M. Werner formulated it, that "the conceptions contained in the original imminent eschatological expectation" constitute merely "what is transitory in Chris-

[65] So Werner Georg Kümmel, *Das Neue Testament: Geschichte der Erforschung seiner Probleme* (Freiburg: K. Alber, 1958), p. 294, on Wilhelm Bousset, *Jesu Predigt in ihrem Gegensatz zum Judentum* (Göttingen: Vandenhoeck & Ruprecht, 1892). Cf. also Kümmel, *Das Neue Testament,* pp. 290 f., for Gunkel's attitude and p. 306 for the reaction to A. Schweitzer.

[66] Kümmel, *ibid.,* p. 291.

tianity."[67] Werner understands the whole history of Christian thought to the present day as a process of "de-eschatologization," set off by the failure of the eschatological events to arrive. This development has been progressing by stages and must not be resolutely brought to a conclusion. To be sure, Werner is of the opinion that "Protestantism nevertheless remains in inner agreement with the conscious intention of Jesus' message for all people in the course of the consistent de-eschatologization of Jesus' teaching demanded by the essence of the matter itself."[68] That is, Jesus declared "unambiguously that one's own readiness to forgive others is the only condition for achieving the divine forgiveness of sins." Salvation depends only on "the active demonstration of a particular frame of mind" (p. 906). Thereby Werner forgets the eschatologically conditioned character of the morality Jesus proclaimed. Johannes Weiss has shown that "the nearness of the Kingdom is the *motif* of the new morality."[69] The commandment of love is to be understood only against the background of the forgiving work of God's own love revealed in Jesus' message, and only the nearness of the Kingdom of God lets all inner-worldly considerations melt away. Jesus' interpretation of God's will cannot be separated from his eschatological message. In a de-eschatologized world even the demand of love will not be able to retain the meaning and significance it had in the light of Jesus' eschatological message.

Over against the vain attempt of "consistent eschatology" in Albert Schweitzer and M. Werner to retain Jesus' ethic in spite of rejecting his eschatology, Bultmann's formalization of Jesus' eschatological message clearly has the advantage. Bultmann has tried to divest Jesus' eschatological message of its concrete temporal reference and to establish the validity of the formal attitude of openness for the future in general as its decisive aspect in order thus to save it for modern understanding.[70] Bultmann is able to reach this

67 M. Werner, *Der protestantische Weg des Glaubens* (Bern: P. Haupt, 1955), Vol. I, p. 127. E. Käsemann has recently put his finger on the fact that the "last two generations in the history of theology" are characterized by avoiding the "rediscovery of the significance of primitive Christian apocalyptic for the whole New Testament." It is "M. Werner's merit that in his controversial book, *Die Entstehung des christlichen Dogmas* (1941), he called to mind the unfinished, but more or less deliberately eliminated or pushed aside, problem of primitive Christian apocalyptic, admittedly without leading the New Testament scholar anywhere beyond Schweitzer's theses" (*ZThK*, LIX (1962), 258 f., n. 3).

68 M. Werner, *Der protestantische Weg des Glaubens*, Vol. I, pp. 906 f.

69 Johannes Weiss, *Die Predigt Jesu vom Reiche Gottes* (Göttingen: Vandenhoeck & Ruprecht, 1892), p. 32.

70 Thus Bultmann says in *Theology of the New Testament*, Vol. I: "Both things, the eschatological proclamation and the ethical demand, direct man to the fact that he is thereby brought before God, that God stands before him; both direct him into his Now as the hour of decision for God" (p. 21). Therefore, Bultmann can oppose an overemphasis on the significance of the delay of the Parousia for primitive Christianity: "The essential thing about the eschatological message is the idea of God that operates in it and the idea of human existence that it contains—not that the end of the world is just ahead" (p. 23; cf. pp. 25f.). To the openness to the future of eschatological existence, see also

interpretation of eschatology only by bringing the eschatological movement even in late Judaism into sharp contrast with historical thought. This contrast reaches its high point in primitive Christianity: "In primitive Christianity history has been swallowed up by eschatology."[71] Only in this way can Bultmann think that he has come upon the real meaning of the eschatological element in Jesus' message by cutting it free from all the concrete references to history that still cling to it. But the contrast between eschatology and history cannot be maintained either for the apocalyptic or for Jesus.[72] Without the conviction of the temporal imminence of the transformation of the world with the coming of the Kingdom of God, that openness toward the future which is so characteristic for Jesus' message would never have arisen. Cut loose from every reference to a temporally concrete future, the attitude of unworldly openness in the framework of a noneschatological understanding of the world could hardly endure, apart from the fact that it would mean something other than the conduct to which Jesus calls.

The imminent expectation of the Kingdom of God, which determined the activity and the life of Jesus, is no longer a live option for us in its original sense. Even holding to it literally would no longer succeed in repeating the attitude of Jesus and his first disciples. The two thousand years that lie between him and us make that impossible. The mere process of historical time makes every attitude that can be assumed today different from Jesus' imminent expectation. Thus we can no longer share Jesus' imminent expectation. We can, however, live and think in continuity with it and thus with Jesus' activity if we recognize Jesus' imminent expectation as described above (Sec. II) as having been previously fulfilled in Jesus' own resurrection. We experience this continuity as long as we retain the expectation and hope for its universal consequence that has not happened yet, namely, the universal resurrection of the dead as entrance into the Kingdom of God. In distinction from the imminent expectation of Jesus' time, this general expectation for the end is not related to a particular calendar date (or to a limited period of time) for its fulfillment. Therefore, it does not become outdated with the passage of historical time in the sense just described, but like all traditional ideas is merely set in a different light in every new situation. It is not correct that the Pauline thesis of the "shift in phase" between Jesus' fate and that of the rest of humanity, as a consequence of which the eschatological reality has already appeared in Jesus but still has not happened for other men, is bound to the expectation of the first Christian generation that the eschatological events would take place quickly.[73] Scholars have rightly called attention to the fact

GuV, III, 207 ff.; idem, History and Eschatology (Edinburgh: The University Press, 1958), pp. 278 ff.

[71] Bultmann, History and Eschatology, p. 37; see also the direction of the whole argument, pp. 25-42. Cf. GuV, III, 106.

[72] Cf. my more extensive argument in KuD, V (1959), 223 ff.

[73] M. Werner, Der protestantische Weg des Glaubens, Vol. I, p. 156.

that the dying out of the "entire first generation of believers in the apostolic period" did not at all result in shaking the Christian faith, as would necessarily have happened in consequence of the further delay of the Parousia according to the thesis of "consistent eschatology."[74] On the contrary, the further existence of the Christian hope for the future was the object of discussions ending in retention of the future hope as indispensable, but without any definite temporal determination for its fulfillment. That this hope receded in the later course of the patristic church no longer had a direct relation to the delay of the Parousia, but was the result of the Hellenistic interpretation of the presence of salvation in Jesus Christ and of the related loss of understanding for the apocalyptic connection of the salvation that appeared in Jesus' resurrection with the future universal resurrection.

Today we can still retain Jesus' eschatological message in the Pauline sense of the shift in phase between Jesus' course which is already finished and the course of the Christians which still remains. The temporal interval between Jesus' resurrection and the event of the universal resurrection of the dead that still remains to happen is of no significance here; only the parallelism is important: what has already appeared in Jesus still lies ahead for all those bound to him in faith. As long as the expectation of the coming Kingdom of God in any form can be our expectation, we remain within the framework of Jesus' message. The *imminent* expectation of the eschatological events, however, is not only inaccessible for us, it has become superfluous for all who come after him through Jesus' resurrection. The nearness of God, his salvation and his judgment, is eternally guaranteed by Jesus, since his imminent expectation has been fulfilled in Him. Therefore, since Jesus, mankind has been freed from the question of when the end will come. Nonetheless, humanity still lives unto the end; Christians continue to pray for the coming of the Kingdom of God. Without this future expectation, Jesus' message and the meaning of his fate would not be understandable for us. Thus the imminent expectation constitutes the particular characteristic of Jesus' time, and because it has been fulfilled in him, it has become subsequently unnecessary. The original condition making Jesus' message possible was this particular situation of imminent expectation. A message of this sort could not arise in our contemporary situation. Nevertheless, it remains valid for all time by confronting men in every situation with that which is always the ultimate destiny of man, even though it is often hidden by many other things in everyday life. It confronts men with the coming Kingdom of God, which is nothing else than the nearness of the Creator for whom man inquires in the openness of his existence.

Thus Jesus' particularity is not a law for all times and every situation.

[74] Cf., for example, H. W. Bartsch, "Zum Problem der Parusieverzögerung bei den Synoptikern," *EvTh*, XIX (1959), 116-131; Hans Conzelmann, art. "Parusie," *RGG*, V (3d ed.), 130 f.

Nevertheless, Jesus, in the uniqueness of his activity, which was only possible in that time, and his effectiveness, places every man in every situation through all possible changes of the times before the ultimate decision in the face of the God who is coming, just as he did at that time in his earthly ministry. This constitutes the universal validity of his activity.

CHAPTER

7

THE MEANING OF JESUS' VICARIOUS DEATH ON THE CROSS

Jesus' death on the cross is revealed in the light of his resurrection as the punishment suffered in our place for the blasphemous existence of humanity.

After the discussion of Jesus' activity, we turn to his fate. This concept of "Jesus' fate" is intended to include his crucifixion and resurrection. Both were "sent" to Jesus as an occurrence to be suffered and accepted. Neither the crucifixion nor the resurrection was actively accomplished by Jesus. As already mentioned, it is certainly not improbable that Jesus reckoned with the possibility of his death when he turned his course toward Jerusalem (cf. Luke 13:33). The character of Jesus' death as something that occurred to him need not mean that the catastrophe in Jerusalem had happened to Jesus as a complete surprise. There are indications that Jesus on his own initiative had taken to himself the fate awaiting him. Perhaps he had even more or less provoked the outbreak of the latent conflict. Nonetheless, his passion and death remain something that happened to him and are not to be understood as his own action in the same sense as his activity with its message of the nearness of the Kingdom of God.

In the Gospels, the character of Jesus' passion as something that befell him is pushed into the background by means of the so-called passion predictions (Mark 8:31; 9:31; 10:32-34 and parallels). Critical scholarship since Wrede has judged these predictions to be *vaticinia ex eventu*. The reasons for this judgment have recently been summarized once more by Willi Marxsen:[1] (1) The passion predictions are literarily late. They are not to be found in the source Q, but appear for the first time in Mark. Even the oldest version of Mark probably did not have them in their present form; the other Synoptics vary greatly. (2) The passion predictions presuppose a detailed knowledge of the passion and Easter history. The Easter accounts, however, represent the Easter events as something that came as a surprise. (3) The sayings about the

[1] W. N. Marxsen, *Anfangsprobleme der Christologie*, pp. 22 and 31 f.

passion and resurrection of the Son of Man have nothing in common with the authentic sayings of Jesus about the coming Son of Man (Mark 8:38 and parallels). While the latter are connected with apocalyptic, the former can be understood only in the light of the transformation of the Son of Man concept through the identification of the resurrected Jesus with the Son of Man.

Jesus' fate did not end with his crucifixion, but beyond the cross it included his resurrection by God. We have already extensively treated the significance of the resurrection as the confirmation of Jesus' pre-Easter claim. Therefore, the following is concerned with the significance of the resurrection only as it relates to the crucifixion. While Jesus' resurrection did not become understandable only in connection with the crucifixion, but could be directly connected with his pre-Easter claim as authority as the confirmation of that claim, the crucifixion stood from the very beginning in primitive Christianity in the light of the resurrection. The specific difficulty in understanding Jesus' death on the cross emerged from this situation, and could be resolved only in the light of the Easter event.

I. THE OLDEST INTERPRETATIONS OF JESUS' DEATH

Not every event possesses an immediately clear and unavoidable meaning within its own context. The resurrection of Jesus was an event that spoke an unambiguous language within the context of Jewish tradition and in relation to the pre-Easter life of Jesus. The situation is different with Jesus' crucifixion. Precisely because of Jesus' resurrection, the question had to arise as to why Jesus had to go the way of suffering to the cross if God was subsequently to acknowledge in the resurrection the unheard-of claim with which Jesus appeared. Why did God permit Jesus' rejection by the Jews? Why did he not acknowledge Jesus earlier so unambiguously that Jesus would have been incontrovertibly shown to be God's authorized representative? Why must his path have led to the cross?

The theological question about the significance of Jesus' fate on the cross was early felt to be pressing. This is reflected in the legendary account of the disciples on the Emmaus road (Luke 24:26). The answer was sought in Scripture and answers or at least hints were found. These answers cannot hide the fact, however, that the significance of Jesus' crucifixion was not so clear as that of the resurrection of the crucified. The disciples surely sought more in this event than blind accident, and rightly so.

Perhaps the oldest tradition about Jesus' death saw the crucifixion along the lines of the rejection and murder of the prophets by the stiff-necked people.[2] The Jews had him killed—the Romans appear only as the ones carrying out

---

[2] F. Hahn, *Christologische Hoheitstitel*, p. 49, on Matt. 23:37; Rom. 11:3; 1 Thess. 2:14 f.

the sentence, so to speak[3]—but God raised him from the dead (Acts 2:23; 3:15; 4:10; 10:39 f.). The core of the idea that Jesus must suffer the fate of all prophets (cf. Mark 12:2 ff.)[4] may go back to Jesus himself (Luke 13:33-35), even though Jesus never understood himself as prophet in the strict sense.

The idea connected with this was that the Jewish officials who rejected Jesus did not thereby frustrate the will of God, but that their actions were fore-ordained by God's inscrutable decree (Acts 2:23; 4:28). The divine "must" that stood over Jesus' passion according to Mark 8:31—originally one of the passion summaries out of which the Jerusalem passion tradition grew[5]—implies the same thing. The Palestinian community sought to find this divine "must" intimated in the Old Testament Scriptures: the Scriptures must be fulfilled (Mark 14:49). It was for this reason that the account of the passion was formulated under so strong an influence of proof from prophecy.[6]

From the perspective of the Scriptures, the disciples sought to find not only the necessity for Jesus' having to follow the way to the cross but also the meaning of this event. Thereby, it seems that the notion that Jesus did not die for himself but for us had already taken on fundamental importance. Jesus' resurrection had proved that he though innocent had been rejected, given over to the Romans, and executed. Thus the meaning of his death could only be understood as an expression of service to humanity in the name of the love of God revealed in his message, which determined his whole mission. It could only be understood as dying for us, for our sins. The Palestinian community understood Jesus' death in this sense as expiation—but not yet as expiatory *sacrifice* in the cultic sense.[7] This understanding is expressed in the saying about the ransom (Mark 10:45)[8] as well as in the reference to the blood of

3 The attribution of responsibility for Jesus' death to his Jewish opponents in this pre-Lucan tradition associated with the idea of murder of the prophets stirs skepticism toward the effort made by P. Winter in his perceptive book *On the Trial of Jesus* (Studia Judaica, I; Berlin: Walter de Gruyter & Co., 1961) to present the Evangelists' accounts of Jewish cooperation in Jesus' death so far as possible as late, politically motivated attempts to exonerate Pilate and thus to claim him as a witness for the political harmlessness of Christianity in the Roman state (see esp. pp. 58 ff.).

4 On this, see Joachim Jeremias, *The Parables of Jesus*, tr. by S. H. Hooke (Charles Scribner's Sons, 1963), pp. 70-77; see also Matt. 23:30 ff.

5 Thus R. Bultmann, *The History of the Synoptic Tradition*, pp. 275 ff.

6 On this, see the summary remarks of Bultmann, *ibid.*, pp. 280 ff.

7 Here following E. Lohse, *Märtyrer und Gottesknecht*, pp. 119 and 126. On the later connection with the idea of sacrifice, cf. *ibid.*, pp. 138 f.

8 On the origin of Mark 10:45 in the Palestinian community, not first in Hellenistic Christianity, cf. *ibid.*, pp. 107 ff. against Bultmann, *The History of the Synoptic Tradition*, pp. 143 f. (In the supplementary notes, p. 407, Bultmann reconsidered the question briefly and did not exclude the possibility of Palestinian origin for the logion.) Although Mark 10:45 is transmitted as a saying of Jesus, according to Lohse, *Märtyrer und Gottesknecht*, p. 117, both it and Mark 14:24 are "formal kerygmatic expressions that have their *Sitz im Leben* in the proclamation and activity of the community." A "certain conclusion about Jesus' 'Messianic consciousness' is not possible on the basis of these sayings" (*ibid.*). With Bultmann (*The History of the Synoptic Tradition*, pp. 143 f.), I see an authentic founda-

Jesus poured out "for us" (Luke 22:20) or "for many" (Mark 14:24) in the Last Supper tradition. In both cases, the expression "for many" suggests the possibility of a connection with Isa. 53:12. If so, the notion of expiation had already been connected with the proof from Scripture. First Corinthians 15:3, however, demonstrates that the idea of expiation may not have grown out of the proof from Scripture and thus especially from Isa., ch. 53. When Paul emphasized that Christ died "for our sins in accordance with the scriptures," the plural *graphai* excludes a specific reference to Isa. 53:12. Instead, we must assume that in the formula quoted by Paul two independent motifs have been bound together, namely, the concept of the expiatory power of suffering and death current in Jewish circles[9] and the "fundamental idea of the old account of the passion" of the death of the Son of Man foreordained by God and predicted in Scripture.[10] Only this connection probably "opened the gate for taking over the motif of the expiatory suffering of the Servant of God which, so far as can be seen, was completely avoided in Judaism and in no way had been connected with other statements about vicarious expiation."[11] The connection with Isa., ch. 53, provided the understanding of the expiation accomplished by Jesus' death with its universal significance "for many." This universal significance distinguished it fundamentally from contemporary Jewish concepts of expiation, as the expiation accomplished by Jesus' death is to be understood as ultimate and final, requiring no further supplementation.[12]

In addition to the concept of the Suffering Servant of God and the figure of ransom taken perhaps from Isa. 53:10, other traditional motifs were also present in primitive Christianity for interpreting the expiatory character of Jesus' death. A specialized, more metaphorical form of the expiatory concept is offered by the understanding of Jesus as expiatory *sacrifice,* as in Rom. 3:25 and in Hebrews. This idea takes its point of departure from the language about the "blood" of Christ poured out for us, which is probably rooted in the

tion for this tradition only in the saying of Jesus preserved by Luke: "But I am among you as one who serves" (Luke 22:27b).

[9] See Lohse, *Märtyrer und Gottesknecht,* pp. 31 f., on the expiatory power of the suffering of prophets and martyrs, and pp. 64 ff. on that of death.

[10] F. Hahn, *Christologische Hoheitstitel,* pp. 55 ff. and 201-203 against Lohse, *Märtyrer und Gottesknecht,* pp. 113 ff., who in spite of being otherwise skeptical of the early influence of Isa., ch. 53, nevertheless would like to relate I Cor. 15:3 to Isa. 53:4 ff. Hahn calls attention particularly to the plural *graphas* in I Cor. 15:3, which hardly expresses a reference to a single passage of Scripture.

[11] Hahn, *Christologische Hoheitstitel,* p. 202, with reference to Lohse, *Märtyrer und Gottesknecht,* pp. 108 ff.

[12] Lohse, *ibid.,* pp. 120 f., 124. Thus through the idea of the Suffering Servant of God a result was achieved analogous to that of the Pauline connection of Jesus' obedience in suffering with the *anthrōpos* category (see above, Chapter 5, n. 13, and below, p. 262), namely, the assertion of the universal significance of Jesus' suffering. The difference is that the uniqueness of the Suffering Servant remained bound to the primitive Christian proof from Scripture as its presupposition.

tradition of the Lord's Supper.[13] The interpretation of Jesus as the eschatological Passover Lamb also belongs in the context of this expiatory concept.[14] The notion of the covenant sacrifice leads in another direction. It occurs in the Pauline and Lucan accounts of the words of institution of the Lord's Supper (I Cor. 11:25; Luke 22:20) in the sense that the "new covenant" promised in Jer. 31:31 has been sealed by the shed blood of Jesus. Matthew (ch. 26:28) and Mark (ch. 14:24) speak simply of a "covenant." Even in Mark the notion of covenant may represent an addition by the Hellenistic community.[15] The concept of the covenant sacrifice goes farther than that of the expiatory sacrifice insofar as all the means of expiation, even the expiatory death of a righteous man,[16] never establish a new covenant but are valid only on the basis of an already existing covenant. The concept of expiation is apparently not unconditionally excluded by that of covenant sacrifice, however. This is seen not only in Hebrews, but in the subsequent transmission of both concepts side by side in the Lord's Supper tradition as well. Perhaps one can even agree with Eduard Lohse that the covenant sacrifice of Jesus' death is superior to that of Ex., ch. 24, in that it possesses expiatory power at the same time.[17] If this is true, the concept of covenant sacrifice represents an especially broad interpretation of the expiatory character of Jesus' death.

It is necessary, finally, to mention the Pauline interpretation of Jesus' death because at one point it moves significantly beyond the older ideas which have been here considered. Paul understood the cross of Christ as the end of the law. Jesus has taken upon himself on the cross the indicting power of the law, its curse, and thus removed it from us (Gal. 3:13). The fundamental idea here is the same as in II Cor. 5:21 in the statement that he who knew no sin was made by God to be sin (and expiatory sacrifice) for us (cf. also Rom. 6:10). Unique for Gal. 3:13 is only the idea that Jesus Christ, by taking upon himself the curse of the law as an innocent person, has nullified completely the indicting power of the law. Following Paul, Colossians also expressly emphasizes the significance of Christ's death as setting aside the law (ch. 2:13 f.). In Ephesians the concept is discussed even more extensively (ch. 2:14-16). For Ephesians the relation between the abolition of the law through Jesus' cross and the mission to the Gentiles, toward which Paul's thought in Galatians

13 References, Lohse, *ibid.*, pp. 138 ff. On Rom. 3:25 (also, II Cor. 5:21; I Peter 1:24), see pp. 149-154.

14 On I Cor. 5:7; I Peter 1:18 f.; John 1:29; 19:36, cf. Lohse, *ibid.*, pp. 141 ff., calling attention to the fact that while in Judaism expiatory power was not attributed to the ordinary Passover sacrifice, this probably was held to be the case with the Passover Lamb to be slaughtered in the end time.

15 Lohse, *ibid.*, pp. 123 f., 126 ff. On the distinction of the two covenant formulas, see Günther Bornkamm, "Herrenmahl und Kirche bei Paulus," *Studien zu Antike und Urchristentum: Gesammelte Aufsätze*, Band II, p. 157. Cf. also Heb. 9:18.

16 On this, see Lohse, *Märtyrer und Gottesknecht*, p. 85.

17 *Ibid.*, p. 126.

had been aimed, is also important. According to Paul, Christ has ransomed us from the curse of the law by his death under the curse, in order that the Gentiles might have a share in the blessing of Abraham (Gal. 3:14; cf. Rom. 11:11 ff.).

How are all these assertions related to each other and to the event of Jesus' death on the cross? To what extent is Jesus' crucifixion to be understood with Paul as the consequence of the power of the law's curse against him? Can a relation be demonstrated between Jesus' death and the law that would permit or even demand that we adopt this concept of Paul's? We cannot accept as adequate the basis that Paul himself gives for his concept. The appeal to the statement in Deuteronomy which said that persons hanged for crimes are cursed by God (Deut. 21:23) can provide such a basis only for one who accepts all the statements of the Old Testament as an irrevocable and eternally binding authority that can be cited atomistically, without reference to the context. These were the presuppositions of Jewish exegesis in the time of the early church, but we no longer share them.

For us, Paul's idea that Jesus was brought to the cross by the curse of the law and that the law itself with its curse was thereby nullified requires a verification for us in Jesus' own history, namely, in the relation of his way to the cross to the traditional law. The same is true for the concept of expiation, or for the vicarious element included in the expiatory concept. The primitive Christian proof from Scripture may have illustrative significance today, but we cannot attribute legitimating power to it. The typological relating of Jesus' death to expiatory sacrifice, covenant sacrifice, and the Passover mean something for us only if Jesus' own path to the cross contains a vicarious element and if the common human situation of selfish entanglement in personal concerns designated with the term "sin" is thereby transformed and can be convincingly presented as having been transformed. Of the various ways in which the concept of expiation was connected with Jesus' figure in primitive Christianity, the image of the just man suffering vicariously for his people may be the most easily accessible for us today. This figure avoids the problem of the specifically cultic substitution, and Jesus himself would have been familiar with such ideas through the prophetic-apocalyptic theology of suffering in whose tradition he may have stood.[18] It may even be that Jesus himself approached his fate with such thoughts in mind. Nonetheless, a vicarious-expiatory significance of Jesus' suffering and death cannot be justified merely by transferring the concepts vital in this context of traditions to Jesus' fate, but can only be justified on grounds drawn from the unique character of his own

[18] See text above in the context of n. 2. The treatment of the suffering of the just by Dietrich Rossler, *Gesetz und Geschichte* (Neukirchen Kreis Moers: Verlag der Buchhandlung des Erziehungsvereins, 1960), pp. 88 ff., is fundamental for the idea of suffering in apocalyptic. The correspondences to the New Testament are so broad in all levels of the primitive Christian history of traditions that individual references here seem to be unnecessary.

course. Only a few traces of such a legitimation can be found in primitive Christianity, insofar as reference to his innocence is occasionally connected with the assertion of a vicarious expiatory power of his death to exclude the notion that Jesus died because of guilt he had himself incurred (II Cor. 5:21; I Peter 2:21 ff.; 3:18). We may certainly assume this to be implicating all the statements about Jesus' vicarious expiatory death. However, it is not sufficient to convince us of the substitutionary and expiatory character of Jesus' death. It is clear that we cannot judge every subjectively innocent death as having the character of vicarious expiation. In addition, Paul's assertion that Jesus was under the curse of the law makes it difficult for us to speak of Jesus' sinlessness. Apparently we can speak of Jesus' sinlessness only in a way that does not exclude conflict with God's law. Thus the task of investigating Jesus' conflict with the law to determine its relation to his death and that of inquiring into the question of a substitutionary expiatory significance of his death are closely interrelated. Both can be approached by clarifying the context of meaning of Jesus' path to the cross.

II. JESUS' SELF-UNDERSTANDING AND THE DISASTER OF HIS CONDEMNATION

First we must inquire into the relation of the Jerusalem catastrophe to Jesus' previous activity. The relation between the two cannot be overlooked.

We discussed earlier (Chapter 3, Sec. I) the way Jesus' claim to authority became apparent in the so-called antitheses of the Sermon on the Mount.[19] By placing his "but I say to you" without any further legitimation from the authority of the Torah, against the authority of Moses, Jesus equated his own authority with that of God, since this was the only authority that was higher than that of Moses. In the act of forgiving sins, Jesus likewise claimed for himself an authority that belonged only to God himself. Our examination has shown that the promise of the forgiveness of sins is no arbitrary presumption but stands in a meaningful and indissoluble connection with the content of Jesus' message. Whoever accepts the message of the nearness of God is thereby near to God and as a consequence his sins are forgiven. Nevertheless, through such behavior Jesus placed himself in the position of God. It is for this reason that his community at table with publicans and sinners must have seemed so unbearable and blasphemous to the Jews. What John transmits as the central point of the Jewish accusation against Jesus—he had made himself equal to God (John 5:18), he had made himself the Son of God (ch. 19:7)—may in this case come very close to the historical truth. To be sure, the indictment before the Jewish authorities did not have as its object a title claimed by Jesus,

19 Following Ernst Käsemann, "The Problem of the Historical Jesus," *Essays on New Testament Themes*, pp. 37 f.

251

since Jesus in all probability did not claim himself either as Messiah, Son of God, or as Son of Man. It is more likely that the accusation was brought about by certain concrete incidents, perhaps by a saying of Jesus against the Temple (Mark 14:58) or by his willful activity in the Temple (Mark 11:15-17). We can no longer definitely establish the details. However, the deeper basis of the conflict that led to the indictment is certainly to be sought in the whole of Jesus' activity, especially in the way in which he placed himself above the law and claimed the authority of God himself for his activity.

One can scarcely agree with Otto Weber[20] that Jesus' claim did "not consist in placing himself *over* God's commandment, *over* men, but in taking a position *for* them." The phrase "for them" appears here all too kerygmatic and abrupt. Even in Jesus' community with publicans and sinners, probably the only thing objectionable was that he promised them a share in the Kingdom of God, and that in this way he nullified the law. The objection thus resided precisely in the fact that Jesus placed himself above the law, not as Weber thinks: "Men do not want to expose themselves to being purely and exclusively recipients" (p. 223). How does Weber come to such a judgment about Jewish piety? Jewish piety would rightly protest against an interpretation that attributes to it the opinion that the law was no longer the gift of God, "but rather a protecting wall against righteous doing or receiving" and even a "means for bullying God into bringing his Kingdom" (p. 222).

The reproach of blasphemy (Mark 14:64) through the claim of an authority properly belonging only to God was probably the real reason why the Jewish authorities took action against Jesus, regardless of what the pretexts may have been in detail in the indictment itself. Least of all can the pretext under which Jesus was given over to the Romans, the charge of rebellion by the alleged messianic pretender, be taken into consideration for a more deeply penetrating understanding of the causes of Jesus' rejection.[21] It is even possible that Jesus expressly rejected the designation as Messiah.[22] That pretexts were sought to

20 O. Weber, *Grundlagen der Dogmatik,* Vol. II, p. 224. The following page references in the text are to this work.

21 According to P. Winter, the unrest that Jesus excited among the people was the only reason why the Jewish authorities, who wanted to avoid any suspicion of revolutionary intentions, accused him before the Romans (*On the Trial of Jesus,* p. 41, and esp. p. 135; also, however, p. 146). But because, as Winter concedes (p. 148), Jesus' activity lacked any politically revolutionary accent and Jesus himself left no room for any doubt about this, it is hard to believe that the Jewish authorities are supposed to have accused him merely because of his popular reputation. In fact, they could and would have had to explain their error to the Romans, had the latter taken the initiative in acting against Jesus. The accusation of rebellion would not be understandable, had Jesus not come into conflict with the Jewish authorities. Only this conflict, the character of which is understandable from the nature of Jesus' activity and teaching, provides the motive that permitted Jesus' popularity among the people to serve as a welcome excuse for accusation before Pilate. Thus it is misleading when Winter asserts: "Rather than the content of his teaching, it was the effect which his teaching had on certain sections of the populace that induced the authorities to take action against him" (p. 135).

22 See above, Chapter 6, n. 21.

252

get at him is based on the fact that the offensive thing about Jesus' activity offered no clear facts threatened by the law. Nonetheless, the offense resided in Jesus' conflict with the law, but a conflict not envisioned by the law itself.

Thus the charge of blasphemy against Jesus was not merely a malevolent slander without any basis. Had Jesus' claim to authority not proved itself to be legitimate, if one did not believe with the disciples in its future confirmation but judged it only in the light of what was presently at hand, then Jesus could very easily appear to be a blasphemer, one who placed himself on a par with God. If Jesus' claim to authority did not find the future confirmation for which his disciples waited, it must be understood as the most frightful pretension possible.

To be sure, the claim made in Jesus' explication of the law and his unconditional promise of forgiveness were clearly based on his message of the nearness of the Kingdom of God and thus were the outgrowth of Jewish tradition, so that Jesus could even find faith among the Jews. His message even had universal validity for all men. But at the same time this message brought him inescapably into conflict with the Jewish tradition as it had been formed in the postexilic period. Over against a law understood as the ultimate criterion of salvation, Jesus had to appear as a blasphemer. This conflict had to be resolved before the universal validity of Jesus' message could come unambiguously to the fore.

The judgment of "the Jews" about Jesus was thus not merely the reaction of aroused malice, as it is represented in the pattern of the murder of the prophet, which Luke subsequently adopted (Acts 2:23; 3:13 f.; 4:10; 7:52). The rejection of Jesus was inevitable for the Jew who was loyal to the law so long as he was not prepared to distinguish between the authority of the law and the authority of Israel's God. Jesus certainly did not attack the law formally; but he did place his own authority above that of the words of Moses. It is understandable that this behavior was considered to be blasphemy.

It is another question whether the trial of Jesus before the Jewish authorities[23] was conducted in legally unobjectionable form. The answer to this question is difficult because we cannot achieve the necessary certainty about the nature of the trial and the course of the proceedings. Therefore it must remain open whether, as Otto Weber would like,[24] one can acquit the Jewish authorities of complicity in a "judicial murder," for which the principal responsibility admittedly lies on the Roman governor. But if one disregards the question of a formal legal procedure and concentrates on the real core of Jesus' conflict

---

[23] That something like this did take place in one form or another can probably be assumed with Joachim Jeremias, "Zur Geschichtlichkeit des Verhörs Jesu vor dem Hohen Rat," ZNW, XLIII (1950/1951), 145 ff., against Hans Lietzmann, Der Prozess Jesu (Berlin: Akademie der Wissenschaften im Kommission bei Walter de Gruyter, 1931), pp. 313-322. Cf. also Joseph Blinzler, The Trial of Jesus (The Newman Press, 1959), pp. 117 ff., 157 ff. Differently, P. Winter, On the Trial of Jesus, pp. 87 f.

[24] O. Weber, Grundlagen der Dogmatik, Vol. II, p. 224.

with the Jewish authorities, we must say that Weber is certainly correct. "Anyone who behaved in the way Jesus of Nazareth did found himself in irreparable conflict with the law as it stood. He committed a religious outrage. The law prevailed over him" (p. 224).

The depth of Jesus' conflict with the Jewish tradition, the real, profound ambiguity of the situation in which Jesus had involved himself, and thereby the depth of meaning of his passion itself are obscured when, motivated by rash zeal for the image of Jesus' purity and sinlessness, we see only ill will on the side of his opponents. Jesus was not undone by a few inadequate individuals, but by the Jewish law itself, whose traditional authority was called into question by the mode of his activity. To that extent Paul is right when he says that Jesus came under the curse of the law (Gal. 3:13). This does not involve just the superficial sense that according to Deut. 21:23 every person hanged is cursed by God. Even Paul himself probably did not intend such a superficial meaning, but had in view that the curse expresses the exclusion of the transgressor from the community of God's people. Jesus could come under the curse of the law only if and to the extent that he stood as a transgressor against the law and thereby against God himself who had given the law. That, however, was in fact the case, since he had set himself above the traditional authority of the law through his claim to authority. This action appeared at the same time to question God himself as the one who had made known his will in the law. To that extent Jesus' claim to an authority on a par with God inevitably meant blasphemy in the eyes of the Jew who was faithful to the law (see below, n. 30).

Only from the perspective of Jesus' resurrection is all this seen in a new light. If Jesus' resurrection from the dead could only be understood as an act of God himself upon Jesus and thus as the confirmation of Jesus' pre-Easter activity, the judgment of the Jews is upset. If and only if Jesus has really been raised from the dead, not he but the one who rejected him in the name of the law was the blasphemer. Even more, if the same Jesus who was rejected in the name of the law afterward has been raised by God, then the traditional law itself is revealed to be at least an inadequate expression of God's will. Paul understood this, in distinction from other tendencies in primitive Christianity.

But it was also understood by the Jewish opponents of Jesus and of the first Christians. Therefore, the message of the resurrection of the one who was rejected in the name of the law and delivered up on the cross was for them the offensive thing as such. It was not only that Jews, even the leaders of the Jewish people, were shown thereby to have acted unjustly, but it was that the law itself consequently became invalid. This explains why the Jews took offense at Jesus' cross, that is, at the cross of him who had been raised by God (I Cor. 1:23), or conversely, offense at the resurrection of him who had been rejected in the name of the law as a blasphemer. With this message the foundations of Jewish religion collapsed. This point must be held fast even today in the discussion with Judaism. One may not be taken in by benevolent subsequent statements of liberal Jews about Jesus as a prophet or allow that the conspiracy for Jesus' death was merely a failure of the Jewish authorities. There may be some truth in such explanations. But the conflict with the law in the background of Jesus' collision with the authorities must remain apparent in all its sharpness: either Jesus had been a blasphemer or the law of the Jews—and with it Judaism itself as a religion—is done away with. That the latter is the case became clear from the perspective of Jesus' resurrection. Judged in this light the standards are reversed. What previously was blasphemy is now the expression of the highest authority, or true unity with God himself; what previously seemed to be demanded for the sake of the divine law is now revealed to be blasphemous outrage. Jesus' resurrection cleared away the ambiguity that hung over Jesus' pre-Easter activity. Therefore, the message of freedom from the law results from the perspective of the resurrection.

The removal of the authority of the law, which is included in the significance of the resurrection of the crucified Jesus, was not yet understood by the earliest Palestinian community. Rather, here the activity of Jesus was understood as that of the New Moses whom Judaism had expected as the eschatological prophet in accordance with Deut. 18:15.[25] This picture of Jesus does not appear for the first time in Matthew; the earliest traditions about Jesus show the characteristic picture of the New Moses: the teacher of the Torah on the one side and the miracle worker and "savior" of the people on the other. Therefore, Jesus' resurrection was at first understood, not as an abrogation of the law, but as a confirmation of Jesus' activity in the sense of the New Moses and thus completely in continuity with the Mosaic law.

Paul was the first to recognize the setting aside of the law by the cross of the resurrected Lord. Even he, however, did not understand Jesus as the "end of the law" in the sense that the law was completely abrogated. It is true that his statements in Galatians point in this direction. But the function of the law in the history of salvation (as a custodian—*paidagōgos*) mentioned in Galatians, enables Paul to say in Romans: "Do we then overthrow the law by this faith? By no means! On the contrary, we uphold the law" (Rom. 3:31). As the following chapter about Abraham shows, this "upholding" of the law happens in the sense of an interpretation in terms of salvation history.[26] Now

25 F. Hahn, *Christologische Hoheitstitel*, pp. 380-404.

26 Shown by Ulrich Wilckens, "Die Rechtfertigung Abrahams nach Röm. 4," *Studien zur Theologie der alttestamentlichen Überlieferungen*, ed. by K. Koch and R. Rendtorff (Neukirchen Kreis Moers: Verlag der Buchhandlung des Erziehungsvereins, 1961), pp. 111-127, esp. pp. 117 ff. The objections of G. Klein, "Röm. 4 und die Idee der Heilsgeschichte," *EvTh*, XXIII (1963), 424-447, have been answered by Wilckens (*EvTh*, XXIV [1964], 586-610), and thereby he has established his thesis more thoroughly. Klein's rejoinder (*ibid.*, pp. 276-283) does not bring any new point of view except the

it belongs to the function of the law in the history of salvation that it has reached its goal through Jesus' death. If the law came into human history in order that sin might become even greater (Rom. 5:20), the work of the law in general is accomplished through death. Therefore, the believers are free from the law by virtue of their being united with the death of Christ, since death emancipates from bondage to the law (Rom. 7:4). Whoever has hope in a new life beyond death is free from the law in the realm of this hope. And because believers already live out of that hope in the coming glory, their behavior is no longer subject to the law.

Thus that Christ is the end of the law (Rom. 10:4) means for Paul first of all that those are free from the law who are "in Christ," united with Christ in one body (Rom. 7:4), so that they also share in the fulfillment of the law through Christ in love (cf. Gal. 5:14; 6:2; Rom. 13:10). It is difficult to decide in contrast whether and in what sense Paul also thought that with Jesus' death the period of the law as a historical epoch, as it is presented in Gal. 3:15 to 4:6, came to an end. Paul has not expressed this idea explicitly in this way, even though it is in line with his placement of the law in the history of salvation. This is especially clear in Galatians, where Paul describes the law as given not immediately by God himself but by angels and therefore being only temporarily valid (ch. 3:19). In this text, Paul apparently is thinking about the specifically Israelite law. In Romans, on the contrary, he extends the concept of law in order to demonstrate the inexcusability of the Gentiles also by finding a correspondence to the Israelite law in the conscience (Rom. 2:14). In Romans, he is interested in the universal validity of the law for the sake of the universality of salvation. Since he now understood the law as the "law of God" himself (Rom. 7:21, 25), he could no longer restrict its authority to a limited period of history as he did in Galatians, but called it without reservation "holy and just and good" (v. 12).

There appear here, on the fringe of the Pauline doctrine of the law, problems that Paul did not clarify. Can it be true of the concrete Israelite law—which Paul primarily calls "law"—in its totality that it is the unchangeable, holy will of God himself? If the connection of Jesus with the law in the history of salvation—along the line of Galatians—is to be understood primarily as the concrete Israelite law, must we not say that it has come to an end in Jesus in a different sense than as God's will for justice as such, which Paul has in mind when he speaks of the law in Rom., ch. 7? The theological doctrine of the law has always gone beyond Paul in this question. This is inescapable, because of the unclarity left by Paul, because of his failure to distinguish between God's will for justice and the particular legal tradition of Israel.

Various solutions to this problem that Paul leaves open have been attempted. Some have contrasted the "new law" of Jesus Christ with the "old" law of

information that Klein is able to think of history only in the mode of that which is present at hand (pp. 682 f.).

Moses. Others have abstracted the "moral law" from the Israelite legal tradition and retained it as the immutable expression of God's will, while the greater part of Israel's traditional law that is related to cult and judicial administration is considered to be abrogated. Here it is not necessary to discuss the extent to which these two attempts are inadequate. It is only necessary to establish that they are motivated at least in part by Paul's lack of clarity with respect to the relation between God's eternal will for justice and the concrete Old Testament law.

In line with Galatians, we have taken as our point of departure the position that through the cross of Jesus, the Jewish legal tradition as a whole has been set aside in its claim to contain the eternal will of God in its final formulation. On the other hand, we must look at the interest that caused Paul to adopt his "history of salvation" establishment of the law in Romans. In so doing, it must be considered that the law does not simply end with Jesus Christ, but is consummated, fulfilled in him (cf. Gal. 5:14; in another sense also ch. 4:21). The interpretation in Romans, according to which the law (the Jewish law) is still the valid expression of God's own will, apparently comes closer to the understanding of Palestinian Jewish Christianity regarding the relation of Jesus to the law than does that of Galatians which went so far as to question the Old Testament law's claim to immediate divine origin and authority. Was such a compromise materially legitimated in any way we can understand? I think this question can be answered affirmatively. In the first place, Paul rightly saw in Rom. 2:14 f. that the Jewish law has analogies in the life of other peoples in that it follows norms which are binding on the conscience. In this way it is in a certain sense representative for the situation of man generally. Further, Paul recognized that this universal significance of the Jewish law establishes the possibility for relating the salvation accomplished in Jesus' collision with the law on the cross to all humanity (see below). In addition, the Jewish-Christian position could, after all, claim support in the fact that Jesus himself never turned against the law in general, but merely interpreted it with free authority. This interpretation certainly implied (by its freedom) the break that is supposed to be revealed by the rejection of Jesus and the resurrection of the crucified One. Nonetheless, it also expressed a continuity that is obvious in the concentration of the law on the commandment of love. The commandment of love as the center of Jesus' interpretation of the law indicates the sense in which a continuity between Jesus' message and the traditional law remained. As we have seen, in Romans (ch. 13:10) and even in Galatians (ch. 5:14), Paul also maintained that the love which appeared in Jesus was the fulfillment of the law. Paul does not clearly determine how this continuity is to be tallied with the perception that the Jewish law came to an end on the cross of Jesus.[27] It seems to us that the perception

[27] Here it is not sufficient to say that according to Paul the law has been annulled only as the means to achieve *salvation* but remains valid as a demand for human *behavior*. The

of the fundamental structural difference between love and law within the theme of justice (in the multiplicity of meanings for this word) that includes both love and law must be deepened at this point. Perhaps it can then be understood that on the one hand, the validity of the Jewish legal tradition has come to an end through its conflict with Jesus and that on the other hand, the divine will originally vital in this tradition has been given the new and final form of Jesus' commandment to love, or rather, the power of love revealed in his activity and fate. To be sure, out of this power of love new structures of common life, new systems and traditions of justice, will always emerge.[28] But they will never again be able to claim the unconditionally binding character that belonged to the Jewish law.

Finally, we can now answer the question whether Jesus came into collision with the law itself or merely with the "administration" of the law by sinners, with the law "usurped" by sinful men, as Otto Weber would like to have it.[29] The answer must be that Jesus' conflict was with the law itself, that is, with the positive Israelite legal tradition which had become calcified as "the law" after the exile. Admittedly, the history of Jewish law could hardly have taken any other course than the one it actually took. Until Jesus' activity the law actually was the historical form of the goodwill of God for Israel. That was changed only by Jesus' new legitimation of the commandment of love on the basis of the eschatological nearness of the Kingdom of God. In this way the validity of the law in its traditional form was really fundamentally shaken. Through Jesus' resurrection the emancipation from this law was confirmed by the God of Israel himself.

III. JESUS' DEATH AS SUBSTITUTION

The substitutionary significance of Jesus' suffering and death seems to have been discovered from two starting points in early Christianity. The one was the Lord's Supper tradition and the other was Jesus' saying about his serving in the disciples' midst (Luke 22:27b), which appears in Mark expanded to the saying about ransom (Mark 10:45). In fact, Jesus' having suffered death for our benefit fits in the context of the service to men that stamps his whole activity. But how is his death related to his service for humanity? Is it merely

fact is that Paul does not establish his own ethical instructions by appeal to the authority of the Old Testament law, but derives them—except for appeals to reason and natural propriety—from the meaning of the history of Jesus Christ and his behavior: consider, e.g., Phil. 2:5. Cf. H. von Campenhausen, *Die Begründung kirchlicher Entscheidungen beim Apostel Paulus* (*SHA* [Heidelberg, 1957]), pp. 29 ff. For Paul the Old Testament "is no longer considered—at least not directly—as a normative source of justice" (p. 40).

[28] I have dealt in greater detail with the relation between love and justice, especially in view of the historicity and changeability of the forms of justice, in my article "Zur Theologie des Rechts," *ZEE*, VII (1963), 1-23.

[29] O. Weber, *Grundlagen der Dogmatik*, Vol. II, pp. 224 f.

the consequence of his service, or was it in itself a service? Upon this depends its vicarious significance. That is, every service has vicarious character by recognizing a need in the person served that apart from this service that person would have to satisfy for himself. Such vicarious significance does not, however, belong to the consequences that the service has for the one who served, but only to the service itself. Thus one must ask whether Jesus' death itself had the character of a service. This was unreflectively presupposed in primitive Christianity by understanding Jesus' death in the image of the ransom or of the expiatory sacrifice or typologically in the image of the Suffering Servant of God. However, the appropriateness of this presupposition needs to be examined. Such an examination can be made only after an investigation of the meaning inherent in the events of Jesus' way unto death.

1. Substitution for Israel

Let us begin with the inversion of standards inherent in the resurrection of the crucified One: What meaning does Jesus' death have from this perspective? What really happened there? The resurrection reveals that he died as a righteous man, not as a blasphemer. Rather, those who rejected him as a blasphemer and had complicity in his death were the real blasphemers. His judges rightly deserved the punishment that he received. Thus he bore their punishment.

At first glance there may seem to be a logical error in this statement. If the standard by which Jesus was condemned—the law—is nullified from the perspective of the resurrection as his acquittal, it would seem that his judges cannot themselves be designated as blasphemers, at least they cannot be viewed as deserving the punishment for blasphemy, since to do so would once more presuppose the validity of the law. Two things must be said to this: (1) Jesus' judges are not blasphemers because of the law, but because of the simple fact that they condemned him whom God legitimated. (2) That the blasphemer deserves rejection before God and thus death is not something unique to the Jewish legal tradition, but is an independent consequence of the fact that God as Creator is the source of all life, so anyone who turns against God cuts himself off from life. Tolerance even over against blasphemy has become justifiable only on the basis of the substitutionary significance of Jesus' death.

The inclusive significance of the exchange of roles between Jesus and his judges is a consequence of the insight that the Jewish authorities were not particularly malicious, but acted in accordance with the law,[30] even if their

30 To be sure, J. Blinzler thinks that the blasphemy that is expressly forbidden in Ex. 22:28 and threatened with death by stoning in Lev. 24:16 was interpreted so broadly in the time of Jesus, in distinction from the later Rabbinic period, that these provisions could have been applied to him (LThK, IV, 1117-1119, art. "Gotteslästerung"; The Trial of Jesus, pp. 102-110, 123 ff.). "Whoever spoke impudently against the Torah (SNum 112 on 15:30 f.) or otherwise 'extended his hand toward God' (SDt 221 on 21:22) had al-

259

legal procedure perhaps was not formally irreproachable. They could rest their decision against Jesus on the *intentio legis,* even if not on its express provisions. The latter would contribute to the fact that Jesus was handed over to the Romans to be condemned under threadbare pretexts. In any case, this circumstance is remarkable under the presupposition of a legitimate Jewish criminal jurisdiction at the time. It could be clarified by the assumption that the law contained no clear provisions covering a condemnation of Jesus. However that may be, even if the Jews did have criminal jurisdiction in Jesus' time and even if the case against Jesus could have been grounded on individual provisions of the law, the intention of the law continues to be decisive for Jesus' rejection. That means that every Jew who was faithful to the law would have had to act in the same way or similarly had he been in the position of the Jewish authorities. In the light of Jesus' resurrection not only the circle of his Jewish judges but in principle every Jew who lives under the authority of and is bound to the law thereby is shown to be a blasphemer. The death penalty borne by Jesus is the punishment deserved by the whole people to the extent that it is bound to the authority of the law.

2. Substitution for Humanity

Does Jesus' death have vicarious significance for all humanity beyond Israel? This is possible only under the presupposition that not only the Jews but with them all men are disclosed as blasphemers by Jesus' cross. Is this presupposition correct?

This idea cannot be adequately justified on the basis of the circumstance that in addition to the Jews the Romans also participated in Jesus' crucifixion as representatives of the Gentile world. The participation of the Romans was of a completely different sort, conditioned by slanderous accusations, and not motivated by the essence of Jesus' claim, as was the judgment of the Jews. Nonetheless, one can find a more profound meaning in Pilate's judgment behind its superficially accidental and irresponsible character. To be sure, Jesus did not come into conflict with Roman sovereignty as a nationalistic revolu-

ready committed the crime of blasphemy" (*LThK,* IV, 118). P. Winter has asserted, with considerable reason for doing so, that before A.D. 70 the Sanhedrin "had full jurisdiction over Jews charged with offences against Jewish religious law and had the authority openly to pronounce and carry out (!) sentences of death where such penalty was provided in Jewish legislation" (*On the Trial of Jesus,* p. 74; cf. pp. 75-90). On the other hand, see J. Blinzler, *The Trial of Jesus,* pp. 160 ff. It is necessary either to assume, with Blinzler, that the Jewish authorities had to transfer Jesus to the court of the Roman governor after a formal conviction of religious outrage (p. 160) if they wanted to have him executed, or else to consider special reasons that caused the Sanhedrin to refrain in this case from execution of the death penalty on its own authority. In any case, it is probably not correct to follow Winter in declaring the entire tradition of a hearing before the Sanhedrin to be unhistorical on the basis of the assumption that the Jews had criminal jurisdiction in the time of Jesus.

tionary, as the slander seems to have asserted. The early history of Christianity was to show, however, that Jesus' activity was by far more dangerous to the foundations of the Roman Empire than that of a revolutionary would have been. His eschatological message took away the glitter of ultimacy from every human political order. In the sphere of the influence of Jesus' message, the right of every existing state to bind its subjects to it in the innermost way is contested. The ruler does not assume the place of God. On the face of it, Christianity has rather a positive relation to the political order in its hope for the Kingdom of God, but it has this only where the political order remains conscious of its own provisional character. The conflict with the political power of the Roman Empire which considered itself to be divine occurred only superficially in Jesus' trial as the product of accidents and misunderstandings. Still, the furtive concern for the favor of the people, the reverse side of the supposed identity with God, shows the fundamental nature of the problem. And yet in political power one may see only one form of the delusion of human identity with God, even though it is an especially instructive example. Therefore, the conflict with political power is not yet an adequate legitimation of the universally human significance of Jesus' vicarious death. Only after it is otherwise established that Jesus in his death suffered the abandonment by God in death as the effect of the pride of equality with God, which separates man universally from God, and has taken it away once and for all, might one find non-Jewish humanity represented by the activity of the Roman procurator in Jesus' trial; then Jesus has interceded with his death for non-Jewish humanity as well.

Paul has pointed the way to such a more general legitimation. For Paul, that Jesus has died for all men (II Cor. 5:14 f.) is related in the first place to the significance of the cross as the sign of Jesus' rejection by Israel in the name of the law. This legitimates the abolition of the law as the way to salvation and the turning to the mission to the Gentiles. In this sense, Jesus died for the Gentiles in order to open the way for their participation in Abraham's blessing (cf. Gal. 3:13 f.; also, Rom. 11:11 ff.; and Acts 13:46 f.). Indeed, Jesus' death in fact did become the entrance for the Gentiles into Israel's history of election. By nullifying the law, community with the God of Israel was also made possible for those men who do not accept Israel's traditional divine law, those, therefore, who do not become Jews. The abolition of the law is, however, merely the negative condition for the Gentiles' community with the God of Israel. This also depends upon the fact that community with Israel's God is positively made possible by Jesus and all the more so since the judgment of the law over human sin, the Gentiles' like the Jews', is in no way impugned. How, then, is access to God for the Gentiles, in spite of their entanglement in sin, made possible by Jesus? Paul answered this question with the Jewish "Adam" speculation. This conception enabled him to explain the universal significance of Jesus' death for all men.

261

According to Paul, Jesus' fate is to be related to the fate of all men, including the Gentiles. The death of Christ is to be seen as one with human death in general (II Cor. 5:14; Rom., ch. 5, *passim*). In what way is death understood here? The death that is the fate of all men is the consequence of their sin (Rom. 6:23). Because all have sinned, all are subject to death (Rom. 5:12). This is the universal anthropological presupposition under which it is possible to assert that the vicarious significance of Jesus' death extends to all men, not just to the Jewish people, since the death of one just man (Rom. 5:6 ff.) takes the place of humanity which as a whole has incurred death. The assertion that Jesus died "for our sins," not just for the sins of the Jews, thus depends on the anthropological truth of this interpretation of universal human mortality as the consequence of sin. The Jews, disclosed as blasphemers by Jesus' resurrection, are then only the representatives of all humanity over against Jesus. According to Paul, the Jewish law includes an element that is universally valid (cf. Rom. 2:14 ff.); it formulates explicitly what is valid and effective in the life of the rest of humanity and is made known to all men in their conscience. The law asserts the relation between sin and death which is at work even outside the Jewish law (Rom. 5:13 ff.; 7:8 ff.). In this way Paul links the Jewish law with the general anthropological relation between sin and death, thus making it possible to relate Jesus' death to all humanity.

Paul could express this most vividly by means of the analogy between the death of Jesus and that of a mystery deity.[31] Like a mystery deity, Jesus shared men's fate, the consequence of their sin (Rom. 6:10), and in return men receive a share in his life. That which is experienced by the Savior has validity for those who belong to him; he lives out their fate. In this sense, Paul presented the universal vicarious significance of the death of Jesus Christ for his time. Today such an explanation is no longer possible. The ideas of the mystery religions can no longer be presupposed as universally convincing truth.

In contrast, the Pauline concern to demonstrate the relation between sin and death as holding good for all humanity retains its validity today. This relation can also be developed in modern anthropological conceptuality, since man is subject to death just because of his being closed in upon himself, while his destiny to openness to the world still points beyond death. The way in which Paul connected the Jewish law to universal anthropological conditions is also valid as an explicit example of the relation between sin and death, conduct and consequences, the deed and its issue, which is everywhere at work.

On this basis, we can appropriate Paul's judgment which takes Gentiles and Jews together in their situation before God (cf. Rom. 1:18 to 3:20). When one understands the universal human significance of the Jewish law as the explicit formulation of the universally valid relation between deed and its

[31] R. Bultmann, *Theology of the New Testament,* Vol. I, § 33d (p. 298).

consequences, as one form of the legal structure of social life which is realized everywhere in different ways, then the Jewish people actually represent humanity in general in its rejection of Jesus as a blasphemer in the name of the law. Here, too, belongs in substance Paul's view of Jews and Gentiles as equally rejecting the cross of Jesus Christ. It is not just a scandal to the Jews. We have already considered the special meaning of this expression. The cross is also foolishness to the Gentiles (I Cor. 1:23). Indeed, for the cosmological wisdom of the Stoics just as for Gnostic thinking in the time of Paul, it was completely irrelevant to seek the salvation of the world in the weakness of one crucified and so expelled from all existing order.[32] And anyone who seeks today the meaning of the existing world in the world itself or in man's earthly life would probably not come to a very different conclusion.

3. The Concept of Inclusive Substitution

To what extent does Jesus' death have vicarious significance if it was his in the place of all other men's? Are other men spared anything thereby? Jesus died the death all have incurred, the death of the blasphemer. In this sense he died for us, for our sins. Of course, this does not mean that we no longer have to die. But it does mean that no one else has to die in the complete rejection in which Jesus died. Jesus' death meant his exclusion from community with the God whose coming Kingship he had proclaimed. He died as one expelled, expelled by the entire weight of the legitimate authority of the divine law, excluded from the nearness of the God in whose nearness he had known himself to be in a unique way the messenger of the imminent Kingdom of God. No one else must die this death of eternal damnation, to the extent that he has community with Jesus. Whoever is bound up with Jesus no longer dies alone, excluded from all community, above all no longer as one who is divorced from community with God and his future salvation. Even he who is condemned by the state as a criminal, he who is outlawed by the spiritual and moral powers of society, is no longer wholly forsaken. Society no longer has ultimate power over the self-consciousness of individuals. Whoever is bound up with Jesus dies, to be sure, but he dies in hope of the life of resurrection from the dead that has already appeared in Jesus.

In this sense, Jesus' death has vicarious significance for all humanity. Not in such a way that men no longer have to die, but in such a way that their death is taken into the community of Jesus' dying so that they have a hope beyond death, the hope of the coming resurrection to the life that has already appeared in him. This is the concept of inclusive substitution that was developed by Philip Marheineke: Jesus' dying includes ours in itself and thereby transforms the latter into a dying in hope.[33] Nevertheless, inclusive substi-

[32] Cf. U. Wilckens, *Weisheit und Torheit,* esp. pp. 214 ff., 268 ff.
[33] Philip Marheineke, *Die Grundlehren der christlichen Dogmatik als Wissenschaft* (2d

tution contains an element belonging exclusively to the death of Jesus. Only he died completely forsaken, while the death of all other men can find safety in community with him. In its substance, the concept of inclusive substitution is derived from Paul. It picks up the Pauline—perhaps even pre-Pauline—statement that Christians die with Christ and are raised up with him. In this respect, too, Paul unfolded with particular appropriateness the meaning that is included in the event of Jesus' death.

4. The Universal Horizon of the Concept of Substitution

The concept of substitution, which has been used above, requires a fundamental justification because it is not universally agreed that substitution can take place at all in the sphere of personal life. For the Enlightenment, this was the most offensive thing about the church's doctrine of reconciliation. The Socinians declared "the exchange of the debtor" to be something "unthinkable." "Neither merit nor guilt and punishment in the sense that they are spoken of here is transferable. Not merit, because the law does not demand just good works in general, but also that they be the deed of him who stands under the law. Ethically religious guilt and punishment are not, however, something objective like debts of money—with which the church's orthodox doctrine did not hesitate to compare them—but something personal, bound to the individual. A debt of money is held to be satisfied when paid, whether by the debtor himself or by another. A moral debt, however, is not paid at all unless it is atoned for by the one who has incurred it."[34] Faustus Socinus thought it would be unjust of God to punish the innocent for the guilty, above all because the guilty are in his power and could themselves be punished.[35]

Also, Albrecht Ritschl agreed with the Socinian arguments against the concept of substitution.[36] However, it has as its presupposition, as we will

ed.; Berlin: Duneker und Humbolt, 1827), § 398: "He is not the representative of humanity in that he stands outside it but in that he is himself humanity and represents united in himself what is alike in all individuals." Cf. also Gottfried Thomasius, *Christi Person und Werk* (2 vols.; 3 ed.; Erlangen: A. Deichert, 1886 and 1888), Vol. II, pp. 66 ff. The definition of the concept presented in the text is, however, distinguished from this by the element of overcoming what is alike in all individuals, namely, death, in that the resurrection from the dead followed Jesus' death. Here resides the element of truth in J. Chr. K. von Hofmann's interpretation, although he wrongly rejected the idea of vicarious penal punishment (*Schutzschriften für eine neue Weise, alte Wahrheit zu lehren*, 1856-1859). Karl Barth has also understood the vicarious significance of Christ's death as summation and, at the same time, overcoming of our dying (*CD*, IV/1, pp. 252 ff., 295 ff.).

[34] Thus D. F. Strauss summarizes the Socinians' criticism of the idea of substitution (*Die christliche Glaubenslehre*, Vol. II, pp. 294 f.).

[35] Faustus Socinus asked: *Quid enim iniquius, quam insontem pro sontibus punire, praesertim cum ipsi sontes adsint, qui ipsi puniri possunt?* (*Praelect. theol. c.* 18).

[36] A. Ritschl, *The Christian Doctrine of Justification and Reconciliation*, pp. 268. On this point Ritschl agreed with the Socinians, in spite of the social-ethical intention of his

see more exactly, an extreme ethical individualism that has been characteristic of modern man's self-understanding up to the middle of this century but which may well have been shaken by the crisis of the social transformation of the present day.

In any case, the people of Israel lived with a completely different understanding of the relation beween guilt and punishment.[37] Here the word "punishment" is not entirely appropriate, since this word suggests an arbitrary sanction which—from the point of view of the recipient of punishment and his actions—could just as well not be invoked. For Israelite perception, there was a kind of natural-law relation between the deed and its consequence. Thus Koch, with reference to many examples from Prov., chs. 25 to 29, says that "an evil deed—comparable to the necessity of a natural law—necessarily has as its consequence a painful outcome" (p. 3). Modern thought has normally viewed punishment or reward as the effect of ideal norms that have nothing to do with the natural essence of the doer or his deed. By contrast in Israel, misfortune was always understood as something already built into the evil deed. In this sense Paul thought that death is the "wages" of sin. This means that death is built into the essence of sin as the most extreme consequence of sin's desire for separation from God, the origin of life. Death is not added externally to sin, as an arbitrary "punishment" imposed upon it. It is characteristic for the Israelite way of thinking that Hebrew has a single word for the deed and its result; 'āwōn or ḥaṭṭā't designate the evil deed as well as the misfortune following from it.[38] Paul in II Cor. 5:21 is to be understood in this sense too: God has made Christ to be sin for us, that we might become in him the righteousness of God. That Christ has been made to be sin means that the misfortune following from our sin has fallen upon him. Similarly, the Israelites designated the sin offering by the same word as that for "sin." It may well have a more profound meaning when Paul translates this Hebrew linguistic usage unchanged into Greek. Paul had mastered Greek too well to use such a Hebraicism without a particular intention.

Besides the natural relation between deed and consequence, we must also pay attention to the involvement of the individual in society in the Israelite understanding of guilt and expiation. The merit or fault of an individual has consequences not only for himself but also for the entire society in which he lives. "If a serious violation of the divine law had occurred somewhere, the burden that thereby fell upon the society before God stood wholly in the foreground since nothing less important than its qualification for cultic prac

doctrine of the Kingdom of God, because in his own ethics the individual is the fundamental phenomenon and only secondarily do the individuals join together in community.
[37] Klaus Koch, "Gibt es ein Vergeltungsdogma im Alten Testament?" ZThK, LII (1955), 1-42. To a great extent, G. von Rad has agreed with Koch's theses: Old Testament Theology, Vol. I, pp. 262 ff.; cf., however, the critical reservation, p. 265, n. 183.
[38] Ibid., p. 385.

tice was thereby threatened."[39] The evildoer was "in a completely realistic and direct sense dangerous to society" (p. 265) because the wrong done had to react in one way or another on the society "unless it formally and demonstratively annulled its solidarity with the offender." If the deed were not "turned back" on the guilty party, there was cause to fear that its inherent destructive power could strike somewhere else. This presupposes that the deeds of men, especially the evil deeds, pregnant with impending misfortune, have their effect to a great extent independently of the person of the doer. To be sure, they do have a tendency to fall back upon the head of the doer, but so long as their destructive effect has not found its target, it can involve wider circles of society. Therefore, the evil deed must be turned back upon the doer; if not, it seeks out another victim in the offender's vicinity. This extensive independence of the deed from the doer also makes it possible that the catastrophe inherent in the deed can be directed to some other being and so be annulled. Especially indicative of this attitude is the prescription that a young cow be sacrificed when the originator of the misdeed is unknown (Deut. 21:1-9). The transferability of guilt is the fundamental concept underlying the Israelite institution of the sin offering. It is especially vivid in the ceremony of the great Day of Atonement. The priest laid both hands on the head of the male goat and confessed all transgressions and offenses committed by the Israelites and placed them on the head of the goat, which was then driven into the wilderness by a man standing ready for that purpose. Thus the male goat was supposed to bear away all their offenses into the wilderness (Lev. 16:21 f.). Such a ritual is only understandable on the basis of the general conceptions of the natural relation between the deed and its consequences and of the independence of the deed with respect to the doer, which we have just described. Certainly even within the context of such a way of thinking, the fixation of the consequences of the deed on a sacrificial animal requires an additional cultic authorization; man cannot do such a thing on his own initiative. But even turning the deed back to the doer requires divine action, and this, too, is a demonstration of Yahweh's grace, since through the punishment of the offender guilt is annihilated and can no longer become a threat to society.

Within this conceptual sphere there is thus "substitution." The deed, which is to a great degree independent of the doer, can unload its catastrophic power somewhere else than on the doer himself. This understanding is at the basis for the Israelite concept of expiation and is probably a religious phenomenon which is by no means restricted to Israel. We must now inquire whether the presuppositions of such a way of thinking can still have validity today. In the first place, we must note the decline of this conception in Israel itself: this happened at the moment when the unity of the people was dis-

[39] *Ibid.*, p. 264.

solved. Within a large society, every deed always has, in one way or another, its corresponding consequence. Difficulties appear, however, when it is no longer held to be sufficient that the deeds of the individual produce effects in the doer's clan, perhaps generations later, when it is demanded instead that the relation of the deed to its consequence should come to full effectiveness in the life of every individual. Under the pressure of the Jewish catastrophe in 587 B.C. such a dissolution of the unity of the people occurred. The generation living at the time, having experienced Josiah's cultic reform, did not understand why they had to atone for the sins of earlier generations. This protest refused to accept solidarity with Israel's past. In Jeremiah (ch. 31:29) and Ezekiel (ch. 18:2) we meet the sarcastic saying, "The fathers have eaten sour grapes, and the children's teeth are set on edge." Jeremiah promised that this would no longer be the case in the coming time of salvation. Ezekiel preached for his own day that every individual must bear only the consequences of his own deeds. In the future it shall no longer be said, "The way of the Lord is not just" (Ezek. 18.25, 29). Thus it came to the demand that good and evil deeds should have their corresponding consequences in the life of every individual. But the correspondence did not work. This became the special theme of Job: the godless succeed while the pious are overtaken by misfortune. It had, of course, always occurred that the deed and its consequences did not always fit the pattern they should have. But as long as the individual was an integral part of society, this caused no particular problem. His good or evil deed that did not receive its reward or punishment in his life was left to his descendants, to his people. Only when the individual became independent of the people did the disparity between deed and consequence become unbearable.[40] This is surely one of the motives for the development of the apocalyptic expectation of a future judgment of the dead and of a resurrection of the righteous.[41] That the relation of deed and its consequences no longer worked out in the life of the individual forced one to the notion of an adjustment beyond death.

The threat to the conviction of the connection between the act and its result by the increasing individualism because of the dissolution of the social unity is significant for our problem. The Enlightenment's criticism of the idea of substitution has advanced since the Socinians began with an individualistic conception of guilt and responsibility. It was thought that only the doer could be held responsible, and the deed could only afflict him. Admittedly, there was an essential difference between modern ethical individualism and the comparable, though not nearly so extreme, moral individualism in postexilic Israel. In the latter, the disparity between the deed and its consequence in the life of the individual was felt to be an unbearable problem. In Socinianism it

[40] K. Koch, *ZThK*, LII (1955), 32 f.; G. von Rad, *Old Testament Theology*, Vol. I, pp. 391 ff.
[41] G. von Rad, pp. 402 ff.

was dissipated with the help of the idea that the relation between guilt and punishment is merely external, residing in no way in the nature of the matter and becoming a reality only through the force of the state.

The relation between guilt and the social group is not sufficiently clarified by an extremely individualistic understanding of guilt. It is grounded in the social character of human existence that every person continually deals in responsibilities that include other people to some degree. Every person is involved in the society in which he lives by what he does and by his share in the deeds of others. In social life, substitution is a universal phenomenon, both in conduct and in its outcome. Even the structure of vocation, the division of labor, has substitutionary character. One who has a vocation performs this function for those whom he serves. Especially in extraordinary times one experiences the fact that the condition of good and evil can be borne vicariously by individuals. Much that befalls the society as a whole affects some of its members in particular who, in such a situation, represent the entire society. The individualism of ethical responsibility' can never completely set itself free from these relationships without becoming abstract and unreal in the same measure.

The anthropological problems involved here can only be suggested to the extent necessary to make clear that the decision about the concept of substitution rests on this basis. If substitution is not a universal phenomenon in human social relationships, if the individualistic interpretation of responsibility and recompense need not be rejected as one-sided because it overlooks the social relationships of individual behavior, then it is not possible to speak meaningfully of a vicarious character of the fate of Jesus Christ. Substitution as such cannot be a miraculously supernatural uniqueness of Jesus. The particular vicarious significance of Jesus' fate "for us" can be defended only on the basis of an understanding of human behavior generally which—as in ancient Israel—sees individuals interwoven with one another in their actions and in the results of their actions and certainly also in the ethical problem. Only in the tradition of such an understanding could the New Testament concepts about the vicarious significance of Jesus' fate have been constructed. They all presuppose the fundamental Israelite view of a relation of the deed to its consequence that goes far beyond the individual.

This fundamental view was not lost, in spite of a definite individualization which prevailed in the exile. It remained in tension with individualistic thinking about salvation and judgment, especially in the cultic tradition. The concept of expiation in the Priestly document may well be in the history of traditions a reaction of the old cultic tradition against the religious-ethical individualism. Only in the Priestly document do we encounter the extension of the concept of expiation to the entire cultic tradition.[42] The reaction of

42 Klaus Koch, *Die Priesterschrift von Ex. 24 bis Lev. 16* (Göttingen: Vandenhoeck & Ruprecht, 1959), pp. 100 ff.

the cultic way of thinking was again institutionalized in the restoration of the Israelite cultic community in Jerusalem under the Persians. Later, the idea of the possibilities of vicarious expiation was extended even beyond the cultic sphere.[43] Thus, the primitive Christian traditions could express Jesus' vicarious significance both in cultic and in noncultic concepts. In the figurative usage of sacrificial terminology, Hellenistic Judaism already led the way, since the sacrificial cult itself could not be practiced in the Diaspora.[44]

Under the presupposition that there is an element of substitution active in all social relationships, one is permitted to understand Jesus' death as a vicarious event in view of the unique reversal that the one rejected as a blasphemer is, in the light of his resurrection, the truly just man, and his judges, in contrast, are now the real blasphemers. That this happened is only a matter of human insufficiency but also a matter of divine disposition, since Jesus was rejected and given over to the Romans for the sake of the law given by Israel's God. To that extent the judgment over him is authorized by the God of Israel himself. God himself, who raised Jesus, had laid on him the punishment for blasphemy through the actions of his legitimate officeholders. He subsequently legitimated Jesus as being justified in what he had preached. But before doing so, he let Jesus go to his death in place of the people whose resistance to Jesus is revealed in the light of his resurrection to be rebellion against its God.

In his death, Jesus bore the consequence of separation from God, the punishment for sin, not just in place of his people, but in place of all humanity. Through him, however, the Godforsakenness of death is overcome for all men. No longer must anyone die alone and without hope, for in community with Jesus the hope for one's own future participation in the new life that has already appeared in Jesus and whose content is community with God has been established.

Excursus: Christ's Descent Into Hell

The concept of Jesus' descent into hell calls our attention once again to the special character of his death. To be sure, we can determine absolutely nothing about Jesus' experience of death. Passion theology and crucifixion mysticism said a great deal more about it than a sober judgment will permit. We can, however, consider the situation of Jesus' dying in the context of his life, and the situation of his dying also reveals something of its special character.

[43] E. Lohse, *Märtyrer und Gottesknecht*, pp. 98 ff. That, on the other hand, "in the Old Testament one can find only slight traces of the idea of substitution" (*ibid.*, p. 98) can be asserted only by ignoring the idea of corporate personality and the meaning of expiatory sacrifice; the latter, to be sure, assumed an important place in the Old Testament only at a comparatively late date (Rolf Rendtorff, *EKL*, II [1958], 1693).

[44] Lohse, *Märtyrer und Gottesknecht*, p. 71.

In the first place, it is a part of the uniqueness of Jesus' death that he died the death of one who had been expelled. This is substantiated not only by the mode of execution, crucifixion. In addition, we must also consider the entire course that led to Jesus' crucifixion. In this way results are achieved that do not arise from the crucifixion as the mode of Jesus' death as such. Jesus died not only as one who was condemned by the Roman state, but one rejected by his people in the name of the authority of his God. This can be seen only from the context of the events in Jerusalem, not from the naked "fact" of the cross.

Death, not only as a final biological fact, but also as rejection from God's eternal life—this is the death of the sinner, the seal upon his having closed himself to the creative origin from whom he once received life and whom he has to thank for it from moment to moment. In closing oneself to the origin toward which human life is directed in its openness beyond itself, death is included in the sense in which no animal dies, namely, as a contradiction to human longing and destiny. Jesus died this death of the sinner because his death on the cross sealed his exclusion from God's nearness.

The special character of Jesus' death must, however, be defined even more precisely. It meant the exclusion from God's nearness for a man who consciously lived in this proximity to God as no other had ever done. How can such an assertion be justified? It is substantiated by the fact that Jesus was the proclaimer of the nearness of God. If this man died the death of one rejected by God, then his death must have meant something for him not involved in the death of other men. Of course, the death of every one of us seals our separation from God, but who experiences it so, through the fog of mortality's physical and mental pain? Does it not belong to the most staggering side of dying, that it can be so banal, at least from the point of view of the survivors? The dark depths of human death are perhaps suspected, but not known when it is not experienced as exclusion from God, and the latter can be the case only to the degree that a man is aware of God's nearness. The older dogmaticians saw the torment of hell in the exclusion from God in spite of full consciousness of his nearness. In the usual course of everyday life we human beings do not live in God's nearness, but that nearness is hidden by the involvement with the finite things that surround us, in happiness as in suffering. Therefore, we experience only rarely being closed to God as the real suffering of our life. Yet it should really be our deepest pain, because it means the destruction of our destiny. Only in the light of God's nearness would that closedness, after it has become inescapable, become absolute torment.

In its details the concept of hell is fantastic. One can hardly claim that the imagery of hell belongs essentially to an appropriate human self-understanding. The pictorial value of the conceptions of infernal torment must be judged quite inadequate, since the decisive factor, exclusion from God, does not appear among the images of the bottomless pit. This is precisely the only element of the conceptions of hell that theology must retain and set free from fantastic incrustations. To be excluded from God's nearness in spite of clear consciousness of it would be hell. This element agrees remarkably with the situation of Jesus' death: as the one who proclaimed and lived the eschatological nearness of God, Jesus died the death of one rejected. How this contradiction may have expressed itself in Jesus' consciousness remains hidden to our view. But we can see the situation characterized by this knowledge which must have determined his consciousness.[45]

From this point we can judge the beginnings of the concept of Jesus' descent into hell, which are to be found in primitive Christian literature, as well as the subsequent doctrinal constructions. In the New Testament, only First Peter offers explicit statements tending in this direction. There we find that Christ "preached to the spirits in prison, who formerly did not obey," namely, in the days of Noah (I Peter 3:19 f.). That "spirits" means the shades of disobedient men who died at that time is suggested by ch. 4:6, according to which "the gospel was preached even to the dead."[46] This idea was further expanded in the second century.[47] Only rarely in the New Testament is a

---

[45] Similarly in some of the orthodox Reformed dogmaticians: Olevian, *De substantia foederis gratuiti inter Deum et electos* (1585), pp. 60f.; later, Melchior Leydecker, *Medulla theologica* (1683), pp. 209 f. Cf. Heppe-Bizer, *Reformed Dogmatics* (London: George Allen & Unwin, Ltd., 1950), pp. 490 and 491 ff. Also, the metaphorical character of speaking about the descent into hell was brought out in the dogmatics of Reformed orthodoxy (see *ibid.*, p. 492) in distinction from the position taken by Lutheran orthodoxy (H. Schmid, *The Doctrinal Theology of the Evangelical Lutheran Church*, p. 379).

[46] Differently, W. Bieder, *Die Vorstellung von der Höllenfahrt Jesu Christi* (Zurich: Zwingli-Verlag, 1949), pp. 110 ff. Bieder does not refer the statement about the "dead" to whom the gospel was proclaimed according to I Peter 4:6, to ch. 3:19 f., but interprets it not very convincingly as a mere metaphor for "unbelievers" (pp. 121 f.: "spiritually dead"). On the exegesis of I Peter 3.19, see Gerhard Friedrich in *ThD*, III, 707 f. According to this, it does not involve the preaching of judgment but the joyous message of Jesus' victory, which "the dead and still living Christ" brings not to fallen angels but to the souls of the dead in a special prison in Hades (thus to *phylakē*). The preaching is not for those who already believe, but for the disobedient men of the time of the Flood, who are to be seen as representatives of the Gentiles. Thus it has the character of a missionary witness (B. Reicke in *RGG*, III [3d ed.], 409, with reference to the context of I Peter 3:13 ff. determined by the idea of the missionary witnesses). Rudolf Bultmann ("Bekenntnis- und Liedfragmente im I Petr," in *Coniectanea Neotestamentica XI; Festschrift für A. Fridrichsen*, 1947, pp. 1-14, esp. 4 ff.; *Theology of the New Testament*, Vol. I, p. 176, n.), finds at the basis of I Peter 3:18-22 a Christ hymn understood for the first time in the sense of a descent into hell by the author of I Peter, as ch. 4:6 shows.

[47] On the interpretation of the descent into Hades in the sense of a proclamation of the gospel to the dead, cf. Gospel of Peter 41 f.; Epist. Apost. 27; Justin, *Dial.* 72,4; Hermas, Sim. 9,16,5-7. Probably, however, these passages intend less the conversion of those who were unrighteous while living than the proclamation of Jesus' victory to the Old Testament pious. Thus also Irenaeus, *Adv. haer.* IV, 27, 2 (cf. W. Bieder, *Die Vorstellung von der Höllenfahrt Jesu Christi*, pp. 145 ff.). On the other hand, in *Adv. haer.* I, 27, 3, Irenaeus expressly rejected Marcion's textually correct interpretation of I Peter 3:19 in the sense of a conversion sermon preached to the heathen; to be sure, primarily because Marcion supposedly allowed salvation to be imparted to the heathen at the expense of the Old Testa-

time spent by Jesus in Hades suggested (Rom. 10:7; Eph. 4:8 f.; Acts 2:24 ff.); or it asserts his victory over death, and Rev. 1:18 adds to this assertion that Christ freed the dead in Hades by overcoming death for himself and for them. This idea also remained vital in subsequent theology.[48]

In the following period, the increasingly mythological conception of Jesus' preaching in the realm of the dead or in hell attached itself to the statements in First Peter.[49] This concept must be understood as the expression of the universal significance of Jesus' vicarious death under the curse. This is also its function in First Peter: even those who have already died are given the possibility of salvation in the coming judgment (I Peter 4:6). The proclamation of the missionary message of primitive Christianity by Jesus himself in the realm of the dead is not, like the crucifixion, a historical event. The pictorial character of this concept is not simply a part of the mode of expression, as is the case with the resurrection which still is a specific, historically definable event. The symbolic language about Jesus' descent into hell and his proclamation in the realm of the dead is just what has been falsely asserted about Jesus' resurrection, namely, a statement about the real significance of another event, his death. One can properly assign this significance to Jesus' death only in the light of the resurrection. It involves the efficacy of his substitutionary power even for the dead. The symbolic language of Jesus' descent into hell expresses the extent to which those men who lived before Jesus' activity and those who did not know him have a share in the salvation that has appeared in him. That is an extremely important question for all Christian missions and for the self-understanding of Christianity in the midst of humanity: Does only the person who believes in Jesus with a conscious decision have a share in the nearness of God that he has opened? Or must account be made for an unconscious participation in salvation by men who never or only superficially came into contact with the message of Christ? The concept of Jesus' descent into hell, of his preaching in the realm of the dead, affirms the latter. It asserts that men outside the visible church are not automatically excluded from salvation. Who participates in salvation and who does not remains, to be sure, open.

Can such a universalism in the understanding of Jesus' vicarious death be justified on the basis of the event itself? We cannot decide this question in view of Jesus' death alone, but must take into account his earthly behavior

ment pious. While Clement of Alexandria and Origen referred to the preaching in Hades as conversion preaching to the heathen, the West followed Hippolytus in holding that only those who had previously been believers received the message of salvation (B. Reicke, *RGG*, III [3d ed.], pp. 409 f).

[48] On the expression: possession of the "keys of Death and Hades" in Rev. 1:18, see E. Lohse, *Die Offenbarung des Johannes* (*Neue Testament Deutsch*, Vol. 11 [8th ed.; Göttingen: Vandenhoeck & Ruprecht, 1960]), p. 19. Similar conceptions are found later in Ignatius, *Magn.* 9:2; Melito of Sardis, *De bapt.* 4 (E. J. Goodspeed, *die ältesten Apologeten*, p. 311).

[49] On this, see A. Grillmeier, *LThK*, V, 453.

as well. Jesus himself did not bind the promise of eschatological salvation to the full recognition of the significance of his own mission. While he attributed the character of the eschatological decision for salvation or damnation to men's encounter with him, he could call men blessed who, because of their particular situation, had no hope except in God's future and men in whom he found the power of the Kingdom of God already at work (Luke 6:20 ff.; Matt. 5:3 ff.). This was true independently of whether these men had an express connection with him. It sufficed that by their behavior they were related to the content of his message, to God's future and to his rule. Thus Jesus could take into account in an explicitly universalistic way the participation of many Gentiles in the coming eschatological salvation (Luke 11:31 f.; Matt. 8:11 f.).[50] If we can ascertain the significance of Jesus' death only within the context of his resurrection on the one hand and of his earthly activity on the other—and that is the methodological principle we have followed—the universal element of Jesus' message and behavior also becomes important for understanding the vicarious significance of his death. By considering Jesus' death within the whole context of his activity and fate, the universal understanding of Jesus' substitution expressed in the concept of the preaching in Hades may be correct, in contrast to the occasionally defended restriction of the preaching in Hades to the fathers of Israel.

To conclude this excursus we shall examine the contrast on this question that emerged between the orthodox Lutheran and Reformed dogmaticians. From the sixteenth century on, Reformed dogmaticians understood Christ's descent into hell as a part of his passion, as the deepest point of his humiliation. This question became controversial among the Lutheran dogmaticians of the sixteenth century.[51] Superintendent Johannes Aepinus, of Hamburg, defended in 1549 the same view that was developed by Reformed theology. The resulting controversies were treated, but not decided in the ninth article of the Formula of Concord. But the Lutheran dogmaticians of the seventeenth century took a position emphatically opposed to that of the Reformers. Christ's descent into hell is not the deepest point of his passion and humiliation, but the first act of his exaltation. It took place between the return to life in the grave and the resurrection and signified the triumph of Christ over hell, not the suffering of the torments of hell.[52] Accordingly, these theologians understood the preaching of Jesus before the dead reported in First Peter as the judgment proclaimed by the victor, the conviction of the damned of their guilt. First Peter 4:6 shows plainly that this is bad exegesis.

In this case the Reformed dogmaticians remained not only closer to the

50 J. Jeremias, *Jesus' Promise to the Nations,* pp. 46 ff.

51 F. H. R. Frank, *Theologie der Concordienformel* (Erlangen: Theodore Blaesing, 1863), Vol. III, pp. 435 ff.; R. Seeberg, *Lehrbuch der Dogmengeschichte,* Vol. IV/2, p. 526 n.

52 J. A. Quenstedt, *Theologia didactico-polemica* III, 373; Hollaz, *Examen theol. acroam.* 778.

concept of First Peter but also closer to the subject matter itself, the explication of Jesus' death. Nonetheless, there is some truth in the Lutheran understanding of the descent into hell as victory over Satan and hell: precisely by suffering vicariously the torments of hell and exclusion from the clearly perceived nearness of God, Jesus overcame this torment, the depth of the fate of death, for all men who are bound up with him. The court preacher Johann Parsimonius in Stuttgart understood Christ's descent into hell in this way as early as 1565.

IV. THEORIES OF THE SAVING SIGNIFICANCE OF JESUS' DEATH[53]

Up to now we have examined the assumption of a substitutionary meaning of Jesus' death as it was expressed in the various primitive Christian concepts of its expiatory power. Such an examination had t be executed by inquiring into the meaning inherent in Jesus' historical course unto death. The result of this investigation was that this event does in fact have substitutionary significance. Even if the world of the Jewish cult, for which primitive Christianity still had an affinity, has become foreign to us, the conceptions of Jesus' death as expiatory sacrifice, as covenant sacrifice, as the killing of the Passover Lamb, still remain expressive illustrations for us of the vicarious event that we perceive in Jesus' own life. Above all, the typological relation to the Suffering Servant of God of Second Isaiah, whoever may have been originally intended by this figure,[54] together with the late Jewish tradition of the suffering of the just and especially of the prophets remains the horizon in the

[53] In the following only those soteriological theories are mentioned which attribute a particular saving significance to Jesus' death. For this reason, it is not necessary to treat either the so-called "classical" (G. Aulén) type of soteriology that is stamped by the motif of Christ's victory over death and Satan or the theory of "subjective" reconciliation, the reconciliation of man through God's loving disposition that is illustrated in Jesus, as has been central for Abelard and for a series of neo-Protestant theologians. These two soteriological conceptions see in Jesus' death only a particular example of that which constitutes the saving significance of his entire activity. In the "classical" theory of the atonement this is the deification that is grounded in the incarnation and consummated in Jesus' victory over death. In the subjective theory of reconciliation the death of Jesus is the ultimate consequence of God's love for man, which characterizes the entirety of Jesus' activity and message. Von Hofmann's soteriological theory, too, which is related to the doctrine of "inclusive" substitution and exercises influence even today, is not centered on the question of the significance of Christ's death but on the idea of the new humanity of the Second Adam originated through Christ, which has already occupied our attention.

[54] G. von Rad, Old Testament Theology, Vol. II, pp. 250-262, shows convincingly that Isa., ch. 53, probably involves a paradigmatic concentration of the picture of the prophet that in the seventh century B.C. had already changed to portray the prophet "as a suffering mediator" (p. 259). Whether the intention of Second Isaiah went even farther to include a specific reference to a particular figure—von Rad suspects a connection with the "new Moses" (cf. Deut. 18:18), ibid., pp. 261 f.—can hardly be decided because of the reserved, merely intimating language of the text.

history of traditions within which Jesus' path of suffering is to be understood. In distinction from primitive Christianity, however, we can no longer identify Jesus' path typologically with one of these conceptions from the cultic or prophetic tradition. The special character of Jesus' path of suffering emerges against its horizon in the history of traditions, and we must seek its proper significance in just this special character of his path of suffering. Therefore, the ideas of primitive Christianity can only be for us, as was in part the case for these writings themselves, clarifying illustrations of the meaning inherent in the special character of Jesus' path of suffering. Certainly this meaning is not accessible to us—here as elsewhere—apart from its context in the history of traditions. But in distinction from Jesus' resurrection, the means of expression that were available in the Jewish tradition for interpreting Jesus' death apparently could not fully absorb the concrete circumstances of Jesus' path of suffering accessible to us, particularly his conflict with the law.[55] Therefore, we can only regard them as explication of an event from which they are to be distinguished. In the light of this event, we must now also examine the later doctrinal constructions of the church that have attempted to understand the atoning significance of Jesus' death. We will concentrate our attention particularly upon three outstanding theories.

1. Jesus' Death as Ransom for Sin and the Devil

The conception that believers have been ransomed from the power of sin and death by Jesus' death can be traced, as can the conception of expiatory sacrifice, to the Palestinian community (Mark 10:45). It later became the common property of Hellenistic Christianity. It is found in Paul, in the Deutero-Pauline epistles, in Hebrews, in Revelation, in First and Second Peter, in First Clement, and in Barnabas.[56] Like that of the expiatory sacrifice, the idea of ransom had in primitive Christianity only symbolic meaning as a designation of the vicarious character of Jesus' death. Even though there is no explicit reflection on this distinction between the image and the subject matter, there is no realistic expansion of the content of the image. Such an expansion would have made the concepts of expiatory sacrifice and of ransom mutually exclusive. Because the expressions had only symbolic character, the question of to whom the ransom was paid did not arise. Bultmann remarks correctly in connection with Paul, "The mythological idea of a bargain with the Devil is far from Paul's thought."[57]

---

55 Paul perhaps came closest to this and has pointed the way for our reflection. However, his formulations do not pick up the conflict of the *earthly* Jesus with the law, which must be the point of departure today for any historically responsible evaluation of the significance of his path of suffering.

56 Gal. 3:13; 4:5; I Cor. 6:20; 7:23; cf. also Rom. 3:24. Further, Col. 1:14; Eph. 1:7; I Tim. 2:6; Titus 2:14; Heb. 9:12,15; Rev. 1:5; 5:9; 14:3 f.; I Peter 1:18 f.; II Peter 2:1 f.; I Clem. 12:7; Barn. 14:5 f.

57 R. Bultmann, *Theology of the New Testament*, Vol. I, p. 297.

The realistic mythological interpretation of the idea of ransom that was vouched for by the authority of the apostolic Scriptures appeared only in the second century. It appeared first in Irenaeus, who emphasized the legality of the redemption from the "dominion of apostasy" through the ransom of the blood of Christ, even though that dominion was not legal (*Adv. haer.* V, 1, 1). Tertullian wrote that the Lord redeemed men from the angels who had dominion over the world.[58] Origen explained Matt. 20:28 to mean that ransom was paid to the devil, even though elsewhere he designated Jesus' death as an expiatory sacrifice reconciling God.[59] Augustine, too, could say that Christ has ransomed us from the power of the devil by his blood.[60] Elsewhere he presents the matter in such a way that the devil, by seizing the innocent Christ, forfeited his right to power over humanity in general.[61] This idea has points of contact with the old concept of deceiving the devil: the devil was deceived when he did not notice that the crucified Lord, whom he attacked, was the Son of God over whom he had no power.[62] The deception consists in the fact that this information was concealed from the devil. This idea appears for the first time in Ignatius' *Epistle to the Ephesians.*[63]

Anselm of Canterbury was the first to reject expressly the idea that Jesus' death ransomed men from the power of the devil because this idea conceded to the devil a right to power over humanity.[64] However, one should not over-estimate the significance of the mythological expansion of the ransom idea for the patristic theologians. As Lakner remarks, this involves "essentially not a theory of the inner essence of redemption, but a popular illustrative statement of its reality, the content of which is further testified by Scripture."[65] The real emphasis of most patristic doctrines of redemption rests on the victory over death that results from God's union with Jesus' humanity in the act of the incarnation. This concept was developed differently in detail in the various schools of patristic Christology.[66] We need not pursue this con-

---

58 Tertullian, *De fuga: "Dominus quidem illum [hominem] redemit ab angelis mundi tenentibus potestatem* (MPL 2, 114).

59 Origen, in *Matthaum* on Matt. 20:28 (*Tom.* 16,8, GCS 40, p. 498) and *Contra Celsum* 7,17 (GCS [*Origen's Works,* Vol. 2], p. 169, 3 ff.).

60 Augustine, *De trin.* XIII, 13 (MPL 42, 1026 ff.).

61 *Ibid.,* XIII, 14,18 (MPL 42, 1028); cf. *Sermo* 263,1 (MPL 38, 1210).

62 Cf. I Cor. 2:8.

63 On the motif of tricking the devil in the early patristic literature, cf. P. Th. Camelot, *Ignace d'Antioche, Polykarpe de Smyrne* (Sources Chrétiennes 10; 2d ed.; Paris: Éditions du Cerf, 1951), p. 88, n. 1. The motif also appears repeatedly later. Cf. Gregory of Nyssa, *Orat. cat.* 23 f. (MPG 45, 62 f.), Gregory the Great, *Homil. in Evang.* II, 25,8 (MPL 76, 1194 f.).

64 Anselm of Canterbury, *Cur Deus Homo* I,7 and 8 (MPL 158, 367-370).

65 *LThK,* III, 1021 f.

66 Cf. Chapter 2, Sec. II, above. On the entire doctrine of redemption in the patristic church, see H. E. W. Turner, *The Patristic Doctrine of Redemption* (London: A. R. Mowbray & Company, Ltd., 1952).

cept any further, because it attributes no specific significance to Jesus' death, but only sees in it only the result of what was already established by the incarnation.

2. The Satisfaction Theory

Anselm's satisfaction theory has already been sketched.[67] Here we shall only compare it with the meaning that can be seen in the event of the cross within the context in which it happened in the light of Jesus' resurrection. In distinction from the conceptions of expiatory sacrifice and of ransom, Anselm's statements do not have merely symbolic meaning, but intend to express the essential significance of Jesus' cross. Thereby, however, Anselm overlooked the character of Jesus' death as something that happened to him, and misunderstood it as something that Jesus had actively done. Here Anselm comes amazingly close to Rabbinic Judaism's understanding of the meritorious power of the suffering of the just,[68] while according to Paul, the universal significance of the expiation accomplished through Jesus is based precisely on the fact that God himself gave him up as an expiatory sacrifice.[69] Nor did Anselm see the relation of Jesus' death to his proclamation. He related Jesus' mission immediately to his offering himself as a vicarious sacrifice. This is not tenable, at least not in this form, because Jesus' mission to proclaim the imminent Kingdom of God must be distinguished from his path unto death, at least to begin with. In addition, in spite of Jesus' relation to the tradition of the suffering of the prophets, we must probably assume or at least reckon with the fact that the expiatory character of Jesus' death was not his own idea but one that emerged only in the light of his resurrection. That Anselm overlooked the character of Jesus' death as something that happened to him was suggested by the tendency in the Gospels, especially in the predictions of the passion, to represent Jesus' death not as something that overtook him unexpectedly but as an objective toward which he systematically directed himself. The divine "must," the divine plan, was transposed into Jesus' own consciousness. Anselm took up this line of thought, especially in connection with the concept of ransom (Mark 10:45), which he understood not symbolically but literally in the light of the doctrine of penance.

[67] See above, pp. 42 f. See also J. Rivière, *Le Dogme de la rédemption au début du moyen âge* (Paris, 1934).

[68] E. Lohse, *Märtyrer und Gottesknecht,* pp. 104, 105 ff., 110.

[69] *Ibid.,* p. 153 on Rom. 3:25. In the tradition of the Lord's Supper and in Mark 10:45 the same thing is accomplished by the presupposed understanding of Jesus as the Suffering Servant of God. There, too, the concern is for God's will and activity through Jesus (*ibid.,* pp. 120 f., 124 ff., 116).

3. The Penal Suffering of Christ[70]

Perhaps Luther's ideas come closer to the meaning of the event itself than any of the other theories of atonement in the history of the church. Luther agrees with the main line of the patristic doctrine of reconciliation in seeing the cross as an action of God in and through Jesus, not as an accomplishment of the man Jesus in relation to God. Thus the character of the cross as something that happened to Jesus is maintained. However, Luther goes beyond the patristic doctrine by emphasizing the penal character of Jesus' passion. Paul's formulations in Gal. 3:13, II Cor. 5:21, and Rom. 8:3, which we have already seen to be especially near the heart of the matter, were very important for Luther. As Tiiliä has shown, patristic theology was also familiar with the motif of vicarious penal suffering in the death of Jesus, but only occasionally touched on it because its soteriological interest was too fixed on the problem of the incarnation and approached the cross of Jesus only from this perspective. Luther, however, with his own experience of temptation behind him, found in Jesus the one who had suffered through temptation in such a way that it must lose its terror for all his disciples. Even though Luther also took his point of departure from the question posed by his situation, he still understood more deeply from this perspective the real meaning of the event of the cross. Thus he says in the *Operationes in Psalmos* (1519–1521) to Ps. 22:2, "*A deo se maledictum sentiat in conscientia*" (*WA* 5, pp. 603 f.). In the great commentary on Galatians (1531) he says to Gal. 3:13: "We must think of Jesus as enveloped in our sins, in anathema and death. God the Father speaks as it were to Jesus: '*Tu sis omnium hominum persona, qui feceris omnium hominum peccata*'" (*WA* 40/1, p. 437). "*Non debemus ergo fingere Christum innocentem et privatam personam* (!) (*ut sophistae et fere omnes Patres, Hieronymus et alii fecerunt), quae pro se tantum sit sancta et iusta.*" (*Ibid.*, 448.) According to Luther, this is an abstract point of view. One must see Jesus in his relatedness to the rest of humanity whose guilt he took upon himself in such a way that he bore it as his own guilt and thus suffered for us the punishment of the cross as though he deserved it: "*Ipsum fuisse passum pavorem horroremque conscientiae perturbatae et iram aeternam gustantis*" (*WA* 5, pp. 603 f.).

Luther thus recognized the meaning of Jesus' death in the fact that the punishment for our sin happened to him. To be sure—this must be mentioned in criticism—Luther also justified the substitution not from the human course of the event but on the basis of the incarnation. Further, he did not see Jesus' fate in the cross in the context of his pre-Easter ministry, not as consequence of his pre-Easter claim, at any rate not in connection with his statements about the cross as penal suffering. Thereby the description of the

[70] This idea has been especially treated by O. Tiiliä, *Das Strafleiden Christi* (Helsinki, 1941).

penal suffering as affliction of conscience comes remarkably close to an understanding of Jesus' cross in the context of his human path, even though we have good reason for abstaining from such statements about the psychical aspects of Jesus' path unto death and have restricted ourselves to the description of the "objective" situation of Jesus' death in the context of his fate. Luther did not clearly see that all statements about Jesus' cross are only possible in the light of his resurrection. This is probably again related to the fact that Luther understood the substitutionary character of Jesus' death in the light of the incarnation, not on the basis of the resurrection. In this he shared the perspective of the entire patristic and medieval tradition that was only shaken by the Enlightenment.

Methodological reasons do not permit us to work in this way with the incarnation as a theological presupposition. To do so would make the humanity of Jesus' life problematic from the very beginning. To be sure, all Christological considerations tend toward the idea of the incarnation; it can, however, only constitute the conclusion of Christology. If it is put instead at the beginning, all Christological concepts, including that of penal suffering, are given a mythological tone.

These objections to Luther's doctrine of the penal suffering of Christ do not affect its fundamental insight. Luther was probably the first since Paul and his school to have seen with full clarity that Jesus' death in its genuine sense is to be understood as vicarious penal suffering. Subsequent Protestant theology, unfortunately, did not maintain this insight. Both Melanchthon and Calvin returned to Anselm's theory of satisfaction with the somewhat baroque revision that not the man Jesus, but the divine-human person was the bearer of the accomplishment of satisfaction.

After the destruction of the satisfaction theory by the criticism of the Enlightenment, it is the most important merit of the great supernaturalist Gottlob Christian Storr in Tübingen to have replaced it with the doctrine of penal suffering. This did not prevail in the time of theological reaction in the church's theology in the nineteenth century. The doctrine of satisfaction was renewed by Tholuck as early as 1823. It was generally accepted by confessional theology. Schleiermacher rejected the idea of penal suffering as expression of the wrath of God against Jesus; he recognized, however, the relatedness of Jesus' vicarious suffering to the community of faith.[71] Von Hofmann in Erlangen questioned the vicarious character of Jesus' suffering as such in order to replace it with Jesus' suffering as the highest fulfillment of his "vocation." In this he was followed by Albrecht Ritschl. Ritschl went farther, however, when, with Schleiermacher, he did not want to see any effect of divine wrath against sin in Jesus' death.[72]

[71] F. Schleiermacher, *The Christian Faith*, § 104,4.
[72] For further details, cf. the good survey in Nitzsch-Stephan, *Lehrbuch der Dogmatik*

Dialectical theology understood the cross of Christ primarily as the expression of the contrast between God and the world. The early Barth considered it the sign of the divine judgment over the world: "By the death of Christ, the line of death has passed vertically through our lives."[73] On the other hand, in the cross of Jesus, God's eternal "yes" to man becomes visible (pp. 145, 149 f.). Here as elsewhere Bultmann has perhaps retained most purely the ideas of the early dialectical theology. Barth later extended the concept in his *Church Dogmatics* to say that Jesus is the one man who was rejected[74] for our sake, and thus the one judged by God for our sake.[75] In these statements, Barth has once more developed the doctrine of atonement as interpretation of the incarnation, not of the historical life of Jesus. Nevertheless, our result stands closer to Barth's statements about the comprehensive character of Jesus Christ's vicarious suffering, which takes up and overcomes our death, than to the satisfaction theory or to the doctrine of Jesus' "vocational suffering."

(3d ed.; Tübingen: J. C. B. Mohr [Paul Siebeck], 1912), § 44, 3, "Neuere Lehren von Christi Werk."

[73] K. Barth, *The Epistle to the Romans*, p. 163.

[74] Barth, *CD*, II/2, pp. 161 ff., 315 ff.

[75] *Ibid.*, IV/1, pp. 235 ff., 252 ff., 258 ff.

Part Three
The Divinity of Christ and the Man Jesus

CHAPTER

8

THE IMPASSE OF THE DOCTRINE OF THE TWO NATURES

Jesus' unity with God is not to be conceived as a unification of two substances, but as this man Jesus is God.

The unity of God and man in Jesus Christ is the concluding and crowning theme of Christology. Our first area of consideration led us from Jesus' resurrection to the confession of his divinity. The second part was dedicated to the activity and fate of Jesus in his humanity. Now we must ask how the two are interrelated, how the divinity of Jesus can exist together with the authentic humanity of his activity and his fate. We must be careful to keep in view everything that has been established up to this point about the basis of the recognition of Jesus' divinity and about his human activity and fate. The question of the relation of the divine and the human in Jesus may not be posed apart from the concrete elements and interrelations that provide its basis on both sides. This is not the question about a unity of God and man in general, but only the question about the unity of this particular human life with the God of Israel as he is revealed in Jesus. Therefore, this question can be put only now, at the conclusion of Christology.

From the very beginning Christian theology was forced to say both that Jesus is truly God and, at the same time, truly man. *Vere deus, vere homo* is what the Formula of Chalcedon says. It had already been used by Irenaeus, who emphasized that Christ as God and man is "one and the same."[1] The formula *vere deus, vere homo* is based on the pattern of the double evaluation of Jesus "according to the flesh" and "according to the Spirit," which appears as a fixed formula in Rom. 1:3. F. Loofs has called attention to the significance of this pattern for subsequent theology.[2]

[1] *Vere homo, vere deus* (Irenaeus, *Adv. haer.* IV, 6, 7 [*MPG* 7/1, 990]). Cf. the Formula of Chalcedon, H. Denzinger, *Enchiridion symbolorum definitionum* (31st ed.; Freiburg: Herder & Co., 1960), 301. References for *eis kai ho autos* in A. Grillmeier, "Die theologische und sprachliche Vorbereitung der christologischen Formel von Chalkedon," *Chalkedon*, Vol. I, p. 36.
[2] F. Loofs, *Leitfaden zum Studium der Dogmengeschichte*, § 14, 5a, p. 70; § 21, 2c, p. 109.

The formula of the two natures or substances in Christ, which appeared first in Melito of Sardis[3] and subsequently became characteristic for patristic dogma, affirmed something completely different.[4] Thus the Council of Chalcedon in 451, which brought the Christological conflicts of the fifth century to a preliminary conclusion, was not satisfied with the *vere deus, vere homo*, but added that Christ is "one and the same" in two natures (*en duo physesin*). Christ did not become a single individual "from" two natures (*ek duo physeōn*) as Cyril thought. Divinity and humanity, according to the Chalcedonian decision, are to be conceived as unmixed (*asygchytōs*), unchanged (*atreptōs*), indivisible (*adiairetōs*), inseparable (*achōristōs*) in the one Christ (Denzinger, *Enchiridion symbolorum definitionum*, 302). The uniqueness of both natures is maintained, even though they are united in a single person (*hypostasis*).

What constitutes the real distinction between the two-sided statement *vere deus, vere homo* concerning the one man Jesus and the doctrine of the two natures? The formula of the true divinity and true humanity of Jesus begins with the fact that one describes one and the same person, the man Jesus of Nazareth from different points of view. The unity of the concrete person Jesus of Nazareth is given, and both things are to be said about this one person: he is God and he is man. The formula about the two natures, on the contrary, does not take the concrete unity of the historical man Jesus as its given point of departure, but rather the difference between the divine and the human, creaturely being in general. Certainly the fathers at Chalcedon also were concerned ultimately about true divinity and true humanity with regard to the historical Jesus Christ. To this extent, Edmund Schlink is correct when he calls for a new interpretation of the Chalcedonian statements "not by placing them in contrast to the history of Jesus, but by understanding them as guidance for praise of the historical Christ."[5] This intention, however, did not make itself adequately felt in the Chalcedonian formulation as was the case in the controversies preceding it. Throughout, the contradiction between God and creature is the logical starting point for thought; from this perspective the attempt was made to understand the unity of the two in Jesus, the relation between divinity and humanity in him. The pattern of thought thus moves in the opposite direction from the formula *vere deus, vere homo*. Jesus now appears as a being bearing and uniting two opposed substances in himself. From this conception all the insoluble problems of the doctrine of the two natures result.

It should be mentioned once again that these comments, like the discussion that will follow, contain no objection to the true divinity and true humanity

---

[3] Loofs, *ibid.*, § 21,5, p. 115. Cf. *MPG* 5, 1222 f., fragment 7.
[4] Against A. Gilg, *Weg und Bedeutung der altkirchlichen Christologie*, p. 37.
[5] E. Schlink, "Die Christologie von Chalkedon im ökumenischen Gespräch," *Der kommende Christus und die kirchlichen Traditionen*, p. 87.

of Jesus. *Vere deus, vere homo* is an indispensable statement of Christian theology. Nevertheless, the notion asserted by the two-natures formula of two substances coming together to emerge as one individual is problematic. On this point the Chalcedonian decision merely shared the general problem of its contemporary theological situation. Chalcedon probably did not intend to go beyond the formula of Irenaeus that it wanted to interpret. Schlink, too, emphasizes the distinction between the intention of the decision at Chalcedon and its doctrinal formulation, which was open to misunderstanding even in the discussion of its own time: "The Chalcedonian declaration is not concerned with the two natures as such, but with the completeness of Jesus' divine and human nature without which his substitution would be illusory."[6]

In § 96 of his dogmatics, Schleiermacher undertook a critique of the church's Christology. Here he temperately summarized and augmented the results of the critical dissolution of Christological dogma by the Enlightenment. His criticism had great influence on·subsequent theology.

Schleiermacher takes exception to the uniform application of the term "nature" to God and man. "For how can divine and human be so subsumed under any single concept, as if both could be mutually coordinated as more precise specifications of one and the same universal; as, for example, even divine Spirit and human spirit cannot be compared in this way without confusion" (§ 96, 1). Thus in the interest of God's otherness over against everything creaturely, Schleiermacher rejects using any expression uniformly or in the same way for God and for man. According to Schleiermacher, however, the expression "nature" is especially misleading because it should only be applied to "a limited being existing in opposition to others," only to finite being, and thus it is completely inappropriate to God's infinity. This second argument probably does not meet the patristic doctrine, since its concept of nature is interchangeable with the concept of being, but without implying the distinction from finite beings that Schleiermacher presupposes. But his first argument scores a direct hit: one cannot speak of divine being and human being as though they were on the same plane. To be sure, this was not the intention of the patristic Christologies,[7] but just in this respect the two-natures doctrine is objectionable.[8]

Albrecht Ritschl and the research into the history of doctrine that resulted from his school made a critique of the two-natures doctrine that is much less

[6] *Ibid.*, p. 84; see in general pp. 80 ff.

[7] Werner Elert, *Der Ausgang der altkirchlichen Christologie* (Berlin: Lutherisches Verlagshaus, 1957), pp. 37-70, has correctly emphasized the significance of the superiority the infinite God has over all the finite and creaturely for the history of the problem of patristic Christology. Cf. also p. 240.

[8] Schlink also emphasizes "that 'nature' does not mean the same thing in statements about Jesus' human and his divine nature. . . . The total superiority of the divine nature over the human excludes any complementary dependence of the statements about the divine nature upon those about the human nature" (*Der kommende Christus und die kirchlichen Traditionen,* p. 86).

convincing than Schleiermacher's. Adolf von Harnack thought that there could be no consideration of a "physical" community of God with Jesus, but only of an "ethical" community. This critique was rightly rejected by the so-called dialectical theology. Emil Brunner established the basis for this rejection in 1927.[9] Karl Barth retains the language of the "two natures" in his doctrine of reconciliation, although he expresses reservations similar to those of Schleiermacher about applying the concept of nature uniformly to God and man. He stresses that their unification in Jesus Christ involves the union of what is otherwise ununifiable.[10] Brunner himself, strangely enough, rejects the pattern of the two natures once again in his dogmatics,[11] because it is not appropriate to the personal reality of Jesus' unity with God. Similarly, Friedrich Gogarten says that the identity of Jesus with God in the sense of Phil. 2:6 ff. "is not of a natural or substantial sort, but is demonstrated precisely in the obedience in which he assumes the form of a servant."[12] According to Gogarten, "the problem of personal being can never be explained" in the ontological perspective of Greek thought bound up with the concept of nature.[13]

Such a contrast can probably only be seen as a retrogression to the one-sidedness of Ritschl's and his school's critique of patristic Christology. Today one merely contrasts personal community instead of Ritschl's ethical community to the unity of nature in the patristic dogma. Both cases involve the exclusion of the general ontological problematic from Christology. In contrast to such attenuations it can make good sense to retain the formula "two natures." Thus Paul Althaus in fact affirms the two-natures doctrine as insurance "against the moralistic leveling and dissolution" of the incarnation.[14]

Our discussion has not yet come to the real center of Schleiermacher's critique of the two-natures doctrine. It resides in the question about the relation between nature and person. "In complete opposition to all normal usage, according to which the same nature belongs to many individual beings or persons, here one person is supposed to participate in two wholly different natures" (§ 96, 1). Schleiermacher thinks that a vital unity could not exist here without one nature giving way to the other. For just this reason presentations of Christology have "always wavered between the contrasting false paths," namely, they have either combined the two natures to form a third or split the two natures and oriented the concrete picture of Jesus exclusively to one or the other.

Here Schleiermacher saw with penetrating insight the weakness of the

---

[9] E. Brunner, *The Mediator*, pp. 249-264. Cf. also Gilg's overview of the history of patristic Christology, *Weg und Bedeutung der altkirchlichen Christologie*, pp. 37 ff.

[10] Karl Barth, *CD*, IV/2, pp. 60 ff.; cf. also pp. 25 ff.

[11] E. Brunner, *The Christian Doctrine of Creation and Redemption*, pp. 361 f.

[12] F. Gogarten, *Die Verkündigung Jesu Christi*, p. 500.

[13] *Ibid.*, p. 496, n.

[14] P. Althaus, *Die christliche Wahrheit*, p. 447.

two-natures doctrine. This insight was previously formulated as early as Apollinaris of Laodicea:[15] two beings complete in themselves cannot together form a single whole. In distinction from the formula *vere deus, vere homo,* the effort to conceive the unification of originally independently existing divine and human natures into a single individual in whom both natures nonetheless remain distinct leads inevitably to an impasse from which there is no escape. If divinity and humanity as two substances are supposed to be united in the individuality of Jesus, then either the two will be mixed to form a third or the individuality, Jesus' concrete living unity, will be ruptured. This impasse of the two-natures doctrine is reflected in three stages of the problem: (1) in the antithesis between the Nestorian and the Monophysite understandings of the incarnation; (2) in the problematic of the *communicatio idiomatum;* (3) in the doctrine of the self-emptying (*kenōsis*) of the God-man in the condition of his humiliation or of the Logos in the incarnation.

I. UNIFICATION CHRISTOLOGY AND DISJUNCTION CHRISTOLOGY

1. The Council of Chalcedon and the Contrast Between Alexandrian and Antiochene Christology

The formula of unity produced by Chalcedon in 451 bears the marks of a compromise.[16] It was intended to overcome opposing solutions to the incarnation problem as it had developed in the Alexandrian theology of Egypt on the one side and in Syrian Antioch on the other. The fate of the Chalcedonian dogma was that it was only a compromise formula which did not lift the problem to a new plane, but which tried simply to force together the theological antitheses on their own plane.[17] But these antitheses are necessary results of a Christology that begins with the concept of incarnation and were not, therefore, ultimately overcome by the Chalcedonian formula but broke out again and again in new forms.

The real founder of Alexandrian Christology is Athanasius. This church father's conception of the incarnation was heavily influenced by the world view of Stoicism.[18] The divine Logos rules the whole world, giving it life

[15] Cf. Loofs, *Dogmengeschichte,* § 35, 4c, p. 210. The axiom comes from Aristotle, *Met.* 1039 a 3 ff.

[16] This fact in the history of the church may not be obscured by Otto Weber, *Grundlagen der Dogmatik,* Vol. II, pp. 135f., with the all too easy way out of such cases, that "the paradox is the only appropriate mode of expression" (p. 136). See below, pp. 303 f.

[17] Differently, O. Weber, *ibid.,* p. 139, who evaluates the controversies following the Council of Chalcedon as a mere relapse into "the contradictions that [the Council] had already substantially overcome."

[18] A. Grillmeier, in *Chalkedon,* Vol. I, pp. 5-202, emphasizes the significance of Stoic thought both for Athanasius and for the Cappadocians (on Athanasius, pp. 81 ff., and gen-

and order. It animates the cosmos, so to speak. The power of the Logos can concentrate itself particularly in individual beings, above all in man who is in an exceptional sense the being that has the Logos (*zōion logon echon*). The Logos was incorporated in Jesus Christ in the highest possible concentration so that the Logos has become the bearer of all Jesus' spiritual functions of life. "The human in Christ is borne by the Logos."[19] The dynamic of the Logos provides the background of all Jesus' actions. The flesh is only its tool, its instrument.

This conception of the divine-human unity of Christ in the Logos-*sarx* pattern as the unification of the Logos with the flesh inevitably has a tendency to replace the human spirit-soul in Jesus with the Logos. Since the human spirit was understood in any case as participating in the Logos, this was an easy solution. Nevertheless, this solution was problematic, not least because the Arians also drew the Logos as deeply as possible "into the flesh," in order to extend the assertion of Jesus' true divinity *ad absurdum*. This explains the extreme reaction by Eustathius of Antioch in separating the two natures in order to save the divinity of the Logos. Apollinaris of Laodicea was also concerned with the divinity of the Logos. However, he brought this intention to expression within the Logos-*sarx* pattern by interpreting the unification of the Logos with the flesh as the deification of the *sarx* instead of the dilution of the Logos, as the Arians had done.

With Apollinaris the tendency of the Logos-*sarx* pattern to set the Logos in Jesus in place of the human soul attained its climax. His doctrine was rejected in Alexandria in 362 because the soul and spirit (*nous*) of man, not only the flesh, must be saved through Christ. Against Apollinaris, Gregory of Nazianzus proposed his basic statement that what is not assumed by God is not redeemed.[20] In the same direction Theodore of Mopsuestia maintained that sin did not happen only in the body, but decisively through the soul. "Thus Christ must assume not only a body, but a soul as well; the soul had to be assumed first, and then for its sake the body."[21] Thus in this Christology the pattern Logos-man was substituted for the pattern Logos-*sarx*. A whole man, not only the flesh, was conceived at the opposite of the Logos with which the latter united himself.

Here for the first time the formula of two complete natures became significant. In the Antiochene Christology, the man Jesus became just in this

erally, pp. 77-102). In view of the transcendence of the Biblical God, however, it is self-evident that the relation of patristic theology to Stoic philosophy had to be conflicting. The problem thus raised, how Stoic and Platonic elements were united to form a unity, requires a more exact examination. Cf. also the observation by Grillmeier in *Scholastik*, XXXVI (1961), 355, n. 98. Unless otherwise noted, the following quotations from Grillmeier always refer to *Chalkedon*, Vol. I.

[19] *Hē sarx theophoreitai en tōi Logōi*, Athanasius, *Contra Arianos*, Or. 3, 40 (*MPG* 26, 409C/412A); cf. Grillmeier, pp. 90 f., 101.

[20] Gregory of Nazianzus, *Ep.* 101 (*MPG* 37, 181C): *to aproslēpton atherapeuton*.

[21] *Homil. catech.* V, 11, translation according to Grillmeier, p. 147.

way so independent that the unity of God and man seemed to be threatened. Apollinaris had previously established that two natures complete in themselves could not become one.[22] The Antiochene theologians left unexplained how man and God could be united in the one person of Jesus. Even though Theodore of Mopsuestia spoke of one single person and hypostasis (pp. 153 ff.), the meaning remains obscure within the context of his conception. It appeared to point toward a third hypostasis uniting the divine and the human.

Thus Antiochene Christology did not prevail over the Logos-*sarx* Christology of Athanasius, because the Antiochene theologians, restricted by their conceptuality of the "two natures," did not succeed in making clear the unity of God and man in the man Jesus. Under the presuppositions of this terminology and method, this unity could be made clear only by Alexandrian Christology,[23] for which the Logos was the bearer of Jesus' concrete behavior. Thereby, as we have previously seen, Jesus' full humanity was threatened.

This Alexandrian unification Christology was developed further in the fifth century by Cyril along the lines of Athanasius. Cyril went beyond Athanasius and entered into the anti-Apollinarian argumentation to the extent that he did not connect Logos and *sarx* directly together, but clearly affirmed that Jesus' body possessed its own life and its human soul (pp. 171 ff.). "The natural impartation of life, which Christ's body needs, is no longer attributed to the Logos as Logos, but is appropriated to the soul. The idea of making alive (*zōopoiēsis*), like the organon concept, could have validity for Cyril only in the supernatural sphere of the God-man's life" (p. 174). Nevertheless, I cannot find that the Logos-*sarx* Christology with its dangers really has been overcome in Cyril, as Grillmeier assumes (p. 173). Human nature, even if a soul now belongs to it, was for Cyril as for Athanasius only the "garment" of the Logos (Cyril, *Ep.* 45, 2). Above all, Jesus' human nature possessed no hypostasis of its own and for Cyril, as for a long time after him, this meant that the human nature of Jesus by itself was not individual. Jesus became an individual only through the Logos. The Logos, which already was an independent hypostasis previously, assumed human nature at the incarnation, but not an individual man. Loofs is right when he sees in this point the most profound antithesis of Alexandrian to Antiochene Christology.[24] Precisely in

22 *Duo teleia hen genesthai ou dynatai,* Pseudo-Athanasius, *Contra Apollinaris* 1,2 (*MPG* 26, 1096B).

23 Corresponding to the Reformed tradition, this positive side of the Alexandrian conception is unfortunately underestimated by O. Weber, *Grundlagen der Dogmatik,* Vol. I, pp. 133 ff. The contrast of the Christological schools thus appears in his presentation as an unambiguous, black or white situation. This is paralleled, to be sure, by an inverted version of the same thing in the Lutheran Christological tradition. Neither version, however, corresponds to the historical facts of the matter. Rather, the reasons that made it impossible to achieve a solution acceptable to both sides must be seen.

24 F. Loofs, *Leontios von Byzanz* (Leipzig: J. C. Hinrichs, 1887), p. 43; *idem, Dogmengeschichte,* § 37, 2, p. 232. Adolf von Harnack has found the origin of this tendency of Alex-

this point, in the strength of this Christology, in its understanding of the Logos as the bearer of Jesus' self, its insurmountable weakness also resides: here Jesus could not be conceived as a real, individual man.

The understanding of the divine-human unity in Christ was perhaps advanced the farthest by the heretic Nestorius at that time, as Grillmeier has recently shown.[25] To be sure, Nestorius' efforts were completely submerged by the polemic of the period, and it is ironic that he, the supposed heretic father of the disjunction Christology, wrestled with special intensiveness with the understanding of the unity of God and man in Jesus Christ. In contrast to Cyril, Nestorius still regarded the hypostasis as an element that belongs to the completeness of the particular nature. For him, the hypostasis is the ultimate basis of the individual being. Nestorius conceived the unity in Christ as a unity of outward appearance (*prosōpon*). By the word *prosōpon* he referred to the totality of properties that make a concrete hypostasis, an individual being, out of the universal essence. Because each of the two natures has its own *prosōpon,* the *prosōpon* that unites both must be a third, which emerges as the result of the mutual interpenetration of the two natures and through the "interchange" of their outward appearances. This third *prosōpon* common to both natures appears concretely in the volitional unity of the man Jesus with God. Nestorius is here on the path later taken by Theodore of Pharan (see below). But certainly even he could not overcome the limitations of the two-natures doctrine. Because he construed the concept of nature as a static, isolated substantiality, he could only bring the two natures together

andrian Christology in Gregory of Nyssa, while it is "only slightly suggested" in *Athanasius* (*History of Dogma,* tr. by Neil Buchanan [7 vols.; Russell & Russell, Inc., Publishers, 1958], Vol. III, p. 297, cf. p. 301). For Cyril what is characteristic "is his express rejection of the view that an individual man was present in Christ, although he attributes to Christ all the elements of man's nature" (*ibid.,* Vol. IV, p. 176). Differently, Karl Holl, *Amphilochius von Ikonium in seinem Verhältnis zu den grossen Kappadokiern* (Tübingen: J. C. B. Mohr [Paul Siebeck], 1904), pp. 222 f.; R. Seeberg, *Lehrbuch der Dogmengeschichte,* Vol. II, p. 201, n. 1; most recently W. Elert, *Der Ausgang der altkirchlichen Christologie,* pp. 146ff., cf. pp. 91 f. But even Elert can defend the "historicity" of Cyril's understanding of Christ only with respect to the reality of Jesus' suffering, including a particular spiritual suffering that presupposes, in an anti-Apollinarian way, the existence of a particular human soul for Jesus. However, Elert cannot meet the objection that Jesus' human nature as such was not individual. Even the passage in *MPG* 75, 1324D, which Elert cites (p. 95) against Harnack cannot show this, because here Christ is contrasted to the collective nature of humanity not as a human individual but as the God-man. Cf. also Grillmeier, in *Chalkedon,* Vol. I, pp. 168 f. More weighty are the arguments presented against Loofs by Joseph Lebon, "La Christologie du monophysisme syrien," in *Chalkedon,* Vol. I, pp. 425-580, esp. p. 517 ff. Cyril can present the unification of the two natures as a connection of two *pragmata* (*MPG* 76, 1200C; *MPG* 77, 396C, even speaks of the coming together of two *hypostases;* cf. 401A). Nonetheless, Loofs did not pull his interpretation out of a hat, as shown by the subsequent, explicit discussions of the question (Ch. Moeller, in *Chalkedon,* Vol. I, pp. 694, 698, 701).

25 A. Grillmeier, "Das Scandalum oecumenicum des Nestorius in kirchlich-dogmatischer und theologiegeschichtlicher Sicht," *Scholastik,* XXXVI (1961), 321-356, esp. pp. 336 ff. The following quotations in the text come from this article.

in such a way that the two outward appearances are connected in a third *prosōpon,* neither divine nor human. It is obvious that this also could not be a satisfactory solution.

Thus the Christological conflict of the fifth century resulted in a dilemma. At the incarnation, the Logos on the one hand may have assumed a whole man. Then this complete human being is presupposed as already independent. This was the Antiochene position. Therefore, Nestorius said that Mary was to be designated only as Christotokos, mother of Christ, not as Theotokos, mother of God. The Logos united himself only with the completed man Jesus. Their unity is a third thing beside the divine Logos and the man Jesus, both of whom were previously independent beings. Then, however, the man Jesus is no longer as such one with God so that he could not be conceived of apart from that unity.

The other possibility, which is just as problematic, is that at the incarnation the Logos found only the universal human nature; whether with or without a soul is a secondary question. In any case, human nature was formed into an individual man only through the incarnation itself. Here Jesus as man is in fact what he is only by virtue of his unification with the divine Logos. But then Jesus possessed no specifically human individuality, and human nature without individuality is a mere abstraction. Accordingly, Jesus as an individual was never a man, but from the very beginning was a superman, the God-man. This is the tendency of Alexandrian Christology. The Mono-physite tendency is present here at its root. Whether one can draw such a rash conclusion as did Julian of Halicarnassus in the sixth century that the body of Jesus was already saturated with the imperishable divine life even before the resurrection is a matter for itself.[26] In this thesis the docetic tendency of Alexandrian Christology certainly becomes obvious. But the problem of Monophysitism has its beginning neither here nor with the rejection of the Chalcedonian formulation of the unity of Christ "*in* two natures" instead of Cyril's "*from* two natures." It begins rather with Cyril, and indeed is really present in Athanasius.

The dilemma of these two Christological solutions is insoluble so long as Christology is developed from the concept of the incarnation, instead of culminating in the assertion of the incarnation as its concluding statement. This false point of departure is common to both the Antiochene conception that the Logos assumed a whole man at the incarnation and the Alexandrian conception that the Logos only assumed human nature. Therefore, neither of the two conceptions was simply right in contrast to the other. Each repre-

---

[26] On Julian, cf. W. Elert, *Der Ausgang der altkirchlichen Christologie,* pp. 100 ff. Elert thinks (p. 104) that the Docetism of Julian's followers destroyed the fundmental intention of the Monophysites, the *unity* of the picture of Christ, because the humanity of Jesus was thus lost to view. Julian "is not the final logical extension of Monophysite Christology, but its disintegration" (p. 104).

sented an important element of truth: in the Antiochene position, the idea of the real, individual human being of Jesus; in the Alexandrian, the unlimited unity of Jesus with God. But a solution of the Christological problem would have been possible only if one would have overcome the approach that lies at the basis of both theses, namely, the question of the process of the incarnation, of the coming to be of the unity of God and man in Jesus. This would perhaps have been easier within the Antiochene perspective, but it was not achieved there because of bondage to the pattern of the two natures and fixation on the question of how the two natures are apportioned to the manifestations of Jesus' existence, rather than by seeking the basis of the confession to Jesus' divinity in the historical particularity of his human activity itself.

The Chalcedonian formula expressed correctly the elements of truth of both schools of patristic theology. This constitutes its truth that the church must never lose: neither the unity of God and man in Jesus Christ nor the truth of his humanity and his being God may be lost from view. However, such definitions accomplish no theological solution for the controversies preceding Chalcedon.[27] It only indicates the criteria that must be unconditionally observed in every Christological theory. As the solution of the Christological problem, the Chalcedonian formula was inevitably suspect from both sides. It appeared to the Antiochene followers of Nestorius as a threat to the real humanity of Jesus. To the Monophysites it seemed a sacrifice of Jesus' unity with God himself, especially against the background of Pope Leo I's didactic epistle, which was also declared dogma at Chalcedon.[28] These opposing suspicions resulted from the Chalcedonian formula's inability to overcome the conceptual dilemma of patristic Christology. The formula rather intended to maintain the elements of truth of the two mutually contradictory elaborations of the two-natures doctrine within the terminology of that doctrine, as developed on the model of the concept of incarnation.

The attempt to force acceptance of the Chalcedonian formula, repeatedly undertaken in the subsequent centuries, proved to be historically fatal and generally unsuccessful. Thus the Chalcedonian formula provided the occasion for the first great confessional schism of Christendom. Heretics were not excluded here, as had been the case in the Arian dispute, but the parties separated for ultimate reasons of Christian concern for salvation, believing the opposing side was not capable of preserving a decisive salvation motif. The consequence of the confessional battles following Chalcedon was the weakening of the Christian empire and ultimately the loss to Islam, almost without a fight, of the Monophysite regions of Syria, Palestine, and Egypt. The Mono-

27 Against O. Weber, *loc. cit.*, in n. 16 above.

28 *Agit enim utraque forma cum alterius communione quod proprium est: Verbo scil. operante quod verbi est, et carne exsequente quod carnis est* (Denzinger, *Enchiridion symbolorum*, 294). Cf. Elert, *Der Ausgang der altkirchlichen Christologie*, pp. 152-164, for Monophysite criticism of this formula.

physite native population of these areas, persecuted in the empire, was no longer ready to offer much resistance to the apparently tolerant Islam. This attitude was surely conditioned not only by religious considerations but by advantages in questions of tax policy as well. National particularities, too, played their role, but just these were brought to a head by the confessional antitheses. Thus the loss of the original areas of Christendom in the seventh century is a staggering example of the consequences of a schism of Christians that did not result from the ultimate basis of the truth of the Christian faith, but only from the inability to hold together opposing concerns of faith in the unity of believed truth and to remain together in the unity of faith over and above the antithesis of theologies.

2. Monothelitism and Dyothelitism

The tensions between Antiochene and Alexandrian Christology, between disjunction Christology and unification Christology, appeared in new form in connection with the efforts of the Greek emperor to achieve peace after the Chalcedonian religious struggles, especially the "energy" conflict and the Monothelite controversy in the seventh century. The great Heraclius, who had decisively defeated the Persian empire, wanted to establish confessional peace in Christendom through a formula that made the Chalcedonian unity of person concrete as the unity of a single divine-human efficacy of Christ (operatio, energeia). The formula mia theandrikē energeia was supported by the authority of the Arcopagite.[29] The resistance to this monoenergetic formula caused Heraclius to proclaim another new formulation of the unity of Christ in 638. According to the emperor's Ecthesis, there was only one single will, not two different wills, in Christ. This Monothelite theory has a certain correctness in view of the unity of Jesus' will with the Father's will in the act of obedience. With reference to the act of the will, the Monothelite theory is appropriate to the meaning of Jesus' behavior and corresponds to the New Testament witness to his obedience. Even Nestorius understood the unity in Christ as a unity of will. The matter looks very different, however, when one considers the voluntary capacity as a capability to act inherent in an intelligent being as a function of its nature. In this light it is clear that doubleness of nature requires doubleness of will.[30] This is the element of truth in the Dyothelite defense of the Chalcedonian tradition. The Dyothelites were strongest in Rome where the sympathies for a more Antiochene way of thinking had always been dominant. After an initial condemnation of Monothelitism in Rome in 649, the Dyothelites achieved the final victory at the Council of Constantinople in 681.[31] By this time the Monophysite lands

[29] MPG 3, 1072B; cf. Elert, pp. 227 f.
[30] So Maximus Confessor in his disputation with the Expatriarch Pyrrhus of Constantinople at Carthage in 645; cf. Elert, p. 250.
[31] Denzinger, Enchiridion symbolorum, 553-559; cf. Elert, Der Ausgang der altkirch-

were already lost to Islam. Palestine and Syria were conquered in 638, Egypt in 641. Now one had to seek peace with Rome instead of a settlement with the Monophysites. Thus Dyothelitism became the dogma of the church.

With the doctrine of Christ's two wills, the pattern of the two natures was uncompromisingly carried through, but the perception of the concrete vital unity of Jesus was basically lost. The tendency of the two-natures doctrine to destroy the unity of Jesus Christ became especially clear in the condemnation of Monothelitism, because the basis for affirming Jesus' divinity lies precisely in his unity of will with the Father in the execution of his mission. This actual unity of Jesus' will with the will of the Father had been the concern of the founder of Monothelite Christology, Theodore of Pharan. The singleness or doubleness of the capacity of will in Jesus, toward which the critique of the Dyothelites was directed, was not his concern.[32] To be sure, the Monothelites could not answer the counterquestion as to whether every act of will does not presuppose a voluntary capacity. One can answer this question only when one takes as the point of departure the voluntary relation of Jesus to the Father, rather than the two-natures doctrine, the God-man, of the Monothelites. The decision about Jesus' own divinity as the Son can be made only indirectly, through his unity of obedience and mission with the Father.

In the Monothelite controversy, the antitheses of the unification and disjunction Christologies broke out anew, as was unavoidable from the perspective of the two-natures doctrine. Monothelitism was rejected because two voluntary capacities must belong to two natures. However, Dyothelitism thereby stood in acute danger of completely tearing apart Jesus' unity, since an opposition of two wills was supposed to have taken place in Jesus himself. In the effort to avoid this consequence, the fathers of the Sixth Ecumenical Council proclaimed the determination of the human will in Christ by the almighty divine will.[33] However, taken strictly, this excluded the independence of Jesus' human voluntary capacity, which constituted the real core of the will according to Maximus the Confessor. Only through this independence (*autexousion*) of the human will, which is admittedly not expressly mentioned in the text, does a material antithesis exist between the Council and the Monothelites, who rejected such an independence of the human will because it would have signified splitting the unity of Christ.[34]

lichen Christologie, pp. 185-259. Elert tries to prove that the founder of Monothelitism, Theodore of Pharan, was not a Monophysite but a supporter of Chalcedonian orthodoxy (p. 202) and that his thesis is to be understood in the light of a concern to protect the Chalcedonian formula against the charge of "splitting" Christ (p. 229).

[32] Elert, pp. 222 f. The dogmatic justification of this concern is also emphasized today by H. Vogel, *Gott in Christo,* p. 662; *idem, Christologie,* I (1949), 340 ff.

[33] Denzinger, *Enchiridion symbolorum,* 556: *Humanam voluntatem . . . subiectam divinae eius atque omnipotenti voluntati.*

[34] Elert, *Der Ausgang der altkirchlichen Christologie,* pp. 258 f.; cf. pp. 244 f.

3. Incarnation Theories of Medieval Scholasticism

Medieval Scholastic Christology developed on the basis of Dyothelitism and thus in constant proximity to the disjunctive Antiochene-Nestorian Christology. In particular, Anselm's theory of satisfaction presupposed Dyothelitism in its most dangerous extreme. This theory was intensely interested in the spontaneity with which Jesus' human will offered itself to God, that is, in the independence of the human will in Jesus over against the divine! Jesus' work, according to Anselm, was meritorious only because of this independence, because of this spontaneity.

In the twelfth and thirteenth centuries three theories of the incarnation were discussed: the *assumptus* theory, the *habitus* theory, and the subsistence theory.[35]

The *assumptus* theory, originating with Abelard, followed the Antiochene school in adhering to the pattern of Logos-man. According to this the Logos assumed a complete man at the incarnation, but is a person only together with him. The independent human person is "juristically" dissolved by unification with the divine person. The two persons, belonging really to two natures, count as only one because of the unification from that point on. This one person cannot, however, be any longer identical with the person of the Logos. If that were the case, Jesus' person would be neither divine nor human. We have already encountered this difficulty with Nestorius' *prosōpon* theory.

The *habitus* theory has been attributed to Peter Lombard and probably came originally from his teacher Abelard. It understood the incarnation with the help of the old image of clothing: the Logos puts on body and soul separately, like clothes. But the picture of clothes, rooted in Alexandrian Christology, does not seem to express the divine-human unity accurately enough. One can take clothes off again without effecting any change in one's self. Some supporters of this theory even stated explicitly that the Logos did not take on "anything substantial" in the incarnation. In this case he would have undergone a change. The phrase "nothing substantial" attempted to exclude this assumption. Nevertheless, the theory stands in obvious danger of denying the reality of the incarnation. Therefore, Pope Alexander III expressly condemned this Christological "nihilianism" in 1177 (Denzinger, 393).

The subsistence theory was founded by Gilbert Porreta. It finally prevailed in the thirteenth century, and was also taken over by Thomas Aquinas (*Summa theologica* III, q. 96, art. 5). The "parts" of the human nature, namely, soul and body, were simultaneously taken on by the Logos and united by him; thus they have their common existence, their subsistence, in the Logos. In Christ, body and soul are united only by the Logos. Thus

[35] On the following, see A. M. Landgraf, *Dogmengeschichte der Frühscholastik*, Vol. II/1, pp. 70-137.

only through the Logos did Christ become a human individual. However, this subsistence theory acquires an Alexandrian-Monophysite character, since all activity in the constitution of the human nature originates with the Logos. Is such a man whose body and soul are united by the Logos still a man like us? This question arises completely independently of the fact that such a separation of body and soul is today untenable. At other points in Thomas' anthropology, the soul was the form of the body; thus the uniting of the body with the soul resulted from the soul's own activity.

Thus Scholasticism was unable to achieve a solution to the Christological question on the basis of the idea of the incarnation, even though, in distinction to the patristic discussion, the question of Jesus' human individuality stood explicitly in the field of view. Duns Scotus came closer than anyone else to a solution of this problem. He drew up his Christological theory not on the basis of the idea of the incarnation, but by beginning with a discussion of the concept of person in general. According to Duns Scotus, there resides in created personality the possibility for becoming person either in dedication to God or in rendering one's self independent from God. While the latter possibility is realized in all other men, Jesus actualized being a person in dedication to God, so that the divine person became the element of his existence which was constitutive for his person.[36] This solution retains a shadow of disjunction Christology only because it understands the dedication to God not as the dedication of Jesus to the Father, but in the pattern of the two-natures doctrine as dedication of Jesus' human will to the divine will of the Logos. This was done instead of recognizing Jesus' dedication to the Father as the basis for his identity with the Son or the Logos.

II. MUTUAL INTERPENETRATION OF THE NATURES AS A WAY TOWARD UNDERSTANDING THE UNITY OF CHRIST

From a very early date patristic exegesis was confronted with the fact that the New Testament writings on the one hand attribute divine glory to the man Jesus, especially to the resurrected Jesus, while on the other hand human imperfections are also attributed to the Son of God. This exegetical situation was bound to cause greater difficulties as the distinction between divinity and humanity in Christology was systematically carried out with the increasing recognition of the significance of Jesus' full divinity and full humanity. On the other hand, this situation also pointed the way and rendered help in clarifying the systematic question of how the divine and the human in Christ could be united without damage to the distinctiveness of each. The solu-

[36] Heribert Mühlen, *Sein und Person nach Johannes Duns Scotus* (1954), pp. 95 ff.

tion seemed to be a mutual interpenetration of the two "natures," through the indwelling of the one in the other and through a "communication of attributes" (*communicatio idiomatum*) based on this. Of course, from the beginnings of the formation of Christological doctrine the exaltation of the divine mission and glory was gladly set alongside the humility of Jesus' human way. One thinks only of Mark 9:31; 10:33 ff. (the Son of Man in the hands of men); II Cor. 5:21 (the sinless one made to be sin), or the paradoxical formulas of Ignatius. But apparently only after the Apollinarian controversy did anyone *reflect* upon the extent to which such an exchange of the divine and human attributes expressed the concrete unity of Christ's life without detriment to the integrity of these two natures. This happened in contradiction to Apollinaris' famous dictum that two things complete in themselves can form no unity.

A mutual interpenetration of divine and human attributes in Christ seemed necessary if any kind of unity of God and man were to exist in him. The Cappadocians in the fourth century still conceived this unity rather carelessly as a mixture.[37] The term for mutual interpenetration (*perichōrēsis*) is, however, mentioned incidentally by Gregory of Nazianzus.[38] This term subsequently prevailed because it suggested less strongly the notion of a blending of the two natures to form a third. The Cappadocians explicitly strived to express the distinction between the two natures as well as their unity,[39] but succeeded only in a series of figurative illustrations that later became famous. The divinity saturates Jesus' humanity as fire makes iron glow, and the humanity dissolves itself in the divinity as a drop of vinegar in the infinite sea.[40] The weakness of such figurative expressions is that they were open to completely opposing interpretations.[41] Those who thought along Alexan-

[37] Gregory of Nazianzus, *Ep.* 101 *ad Cledon* (*MPG* 37, 180A); Gregory of Nyssa, *MPG* 45, 1276C. Further references in K. Holl, *Amphilochius von Ikonium*, pp. 189 f. and 226.

[38] Gregory of Nazianzus, *Ep.* 101 (*MPG* 37, 181C): [tōn Physeōn] . . . *kai perichōrousōn eis allēlas tōi logōi tēs symphyias.* On the later doctrinal form in the Eastern Church, cf. John of Damascus, *De fide orth.* 3,3 f. (*MPG* 94, 993-1000).

[39] F. Loofs, *Dogmengeschichte*, § 35, 5c, p. 216, refers to Gregory of Nyssa, *C. Eun.* 3, 3, 63. Here as also in *C. Eun.* 5 (*MPG* 14, 705) a distinction is made between Christ's concrete unity of life and the continuing differentiation for our knowledge of the divine and human natures that are connected by this unity.

[40] The image of glowing iron derives from Origen (*De princ.* II, 6, 6; *MPG* 11, 213 f.). It is found in Gregory of Nyssa (*Orat. cat.* 10) and Pseudo-Basil (*Homil. in sanctam Christi generat.* II; *MPG* 31, 1460C). Gregory of Nyssa used the comparison of Christ's humanity with a drop of vinegar that is dissolved in the sea of divinity (*Adv. Apoll.* 42; *MPG* 45, 1224). Further references in Elert, *Der Ausgang der altkirchlichen Christologie*, p. 48; cf. also Holl, *Amphilochius von Ikonium*, pp. 227 f.

[41] Thus the image of glowing iron could be used not only by Apollinaris (Elert, p. 58, n. 1), but also on the Antiochene side: Theodoret of Cyrrhus used it to illustrate the continuing differentiation of the natures in spite of their unification (*MPG* 83, 156). On the other hand, Theodoret rejected the image of the drop in the sea (here Gregory's drop of vinegar has become a drop of honey: *ibid.*, 153D) because it implies a mixture. Cf. Elert, p. 57.

drian lines thought primarily of the penetration of the human nature by the activity of the divine. So, later, John of Damascus spoke of a perichoresis of the natures whose movement runs from the divine to the human nature. On the other side, the Antiochene theologians allowed validity only to a communication of the attributes from both natures to the person common to them, but not to an exchange of attributes between the natures themselves.[42] In order to justify this distinction, they refined to the greatest extent the Stoic ontology of nature, attributes, and hypostasis that had already been used by the Cappadocians. If the attributes in their totality form the hypostasis, the external appearance of the nature, then in Christ the external appearances of the divine and the human are united in a third, common external appearance.[43] Because thereby no interpenetration of the natures themselves took place, but merely a community of the hypostases adjoined to the natures, Nestorius did not want to designate Mary as mother of God but only as mother of Christ. He wanted to affirm that the concrete, whole person Christ was born of a woman, but not that this had happened to the divine nature of the Son of God. It is unmistakable that the unity of God and man in Christ, about which Nestorius was so concerned, is thus called into doubt again.

We shall pass over the further history of the doctrine of the *communicatio idiomatum* in patristic literature[44] and turn immediately to the controversies of the Reformation. The antithetical positions of the Reformers in the doctrine of the Lord's Supper brought about a revival of the antithesis between Alexandrian and Antiochene Christology. The essential difference from the discussion of the fifth century was that in the Reformation the unity of person of God and man in Christ was presupposed as a result of the patristic dogmatic formation, while the community of the natures and the transfer of their peculiarities, whether to the other nature or to the entire person and his actions, became the object of controversy. In the fifth century the discussion of the *communicatio idiomatum* involved the question of what constituted the unity in Christ. In the sixteenth and seventeenth centuries, as already in high Scholasticism, the discussion involved the consequences of this unity as unity of person for the relation between the natures.[45] Nevertheless, there

---

[42] On Theodore of Mopsuestia, cf. A. Grillmeier, *Chalkedon*, Vol. I, pp. 150 f. Nestorius could even speak of a mutual perichoresis of Christ's divine and human natures, though only with respect to their forms of appearance; cf. Grillmeier, *Scholastik*, XXXVI (1961), 351. Nestorius emphasized that the object of this "exchange" is to be found not in the natures themselves but only in their *prosōpa* (*ibid.*, p. 348). The latter united themselves in a single, higher *prosōpon* (see above in text) while the natures themselves remained separate.

[43] *Ibid.*, pp. 343 ff., esp. pp. 346 ff.

[44] Here we have to take up primarily the *antidosis idiōmatōn* which Leontius of Byzantium developed in connection with his doctrine of the enhypostasis of Christ's humanity in the Logos (see below, Chapter 9, Sec. II, 2).

[45] Therefore, Isaak August Dorner, *A System of Christian Doctrine* (Edinburgh: T. &

is a certain parallel. In spite of the unity of person recognized by all the Reformers, problems and impasses arose on another plane analogous to those that had previously plagued Antiochene and Alexandrian theologians.

While Luther taught the real mutual interpenetration of the two natures and loved the figure of the glowing iron,[46] Zwingli saw in the communication of attributes a mere figure of speech: one can say things about the person that, strictly speaking, are true only for one of the two natures, but any such statement has only figurative sense, it is only a *praedicatio verbalis*.[47] Zwingli said nothing of a real community between Christ's divine and human natures lying at the basis of that figurative speech. The doctrinal antithesis over the Lord's Supper results from this. For Zwingli the body of the exalted Christ, like every human body, is spatially limited. If he is present at a particular place (*in certo loco*) in heaven since the ascension, he cannot be at the same time really present in the Lord's Supper. Luther, on the other hand, ascribed to the exalted humanity of Christ full participation in the attributes of divine being including omnipresence, so that even after the ascension he is present on earth and can communicate his presence in the Lord's Supper.

In distinction from Zwingli, Calvin did not consider the communication of attributes a mere figure of speech. He found its basis in a real transfer of attributes of both natures to the person of the Mediator and to the mediating work or office he performed, but not in a direct exchange of attributes between the natures themselves. Melanchthon expressed himself similarly. In so doing, both followed the conceptions of high Scholasticism, while Luther united certain ideas of Ockham with the teaching of the Greek fathers.[48] In Calvin, too, the understanding of the Lord's Supper corresponds to the Christological position: although the body of the exalted Christ remains in heaven, the recipient of the Lord's Supper has community with Christ through the Holy Spirit and thus spiritually with his body as well.

Within Lutheranism a controversy arose between Melanchthon's disciples represented by Eber, Major, Crell, and Pezel and the stricter Württemberg

T. Clark, 1890), Vol. III, p. 214, rightly emphasizes that "Nestorianism" cannot be charged to Reformed Christology of the sixteenth and seventeenth centuries because here the unity of Christ's person was completely recognized in agreement with the patristic councils.

[46] See *WA* 7, p. 53; 6, p. 510.

[47] Thus the Formula of Concord, *SD* VIII, § 45, characterizes Zwingli's doctrine. Cf. on this, Zwingli's *Opera* (2d ed., 1581), Vol. II/1, p. 449, as well as the presentation of Zwingli's doctrine of the communication of attributes in Otto Ritschl, *Dogmengeschichte des Protestantismus* (Leipzig: J. C. Hinrichs'sche Buchhandlung, 1926), Vol. III, pp. 118 ff. On Luther's idea of the communication of attributes, see Hans Grass, *Die Abendmahlslehre bei Luther und Calvin: Eine kritische Untersuchung* (1940; 2d ed., 1954), pp. 68-86, and G. Thomasius, *Christi Person und Werk*, Vol. I, pp. 520-537; also, R. Seeberg, *Dogmengeschichte*, Vol. IV/1, pp. 466 ff.; also, P. Althaus, *The Theology of Martin Luther* (Fortress Press, 1966), pp. 196 f.

[48] Calvin, *Institutes of the Christian Religion*, II. xiv. 2 f. On Calvin's rejection of a real communication of attributes between the natures, cf. also Wilhelm Niesel, *The Theology of Calvin*, tr. by Harold Knight (The Westminster Press, 1956), pp. 115 f. Melanchthon,

Lutherans. Melanchthon's disciple Martin Chemnitz attempted to mediate the dispute with the formula that the attributes cannot simply be disconnected from their natures so that they could transfer to another nature, but that nevertheless a real perichoresis of natures in the sense of the figure of fire and iron takes place.[49] This thesis prepares the way for the Christology of the Formula of Concord (*Solida declaratio* [hereafter *SD*] VIII).

The Formula of Concord also took over from Chemnitz the famous and, for subsequent Lutheran theology, definitive, three *genera* of the *communicatio idiomatum*.[50] First, according to the *genus idiomaticum* affirmed also by Zwingli, what applies to one or the other nature can be asserted for the person as a whole. Second, the later so-called *genus apotelesmaticum,* which stands in the center of Calvin's thinking, ascribed all actions, including the three offices, not to only one of the two natures, but to the person of the Mediator. Third, the so-called *genus maiestaticum* defended the communication of divine attributes of majesty, as omnipresence, to the human nature itself. It is noteworthy that in this interpretation of the natures, the divine nature as the superior gives to the human nature a share in its attributes, but does not conversely receive a share in the imperfections of the human nature (in the sense of a *genus tapeinoticum*). By the assumption of a communication of attributes between the natures themselves, or more precisely, from the divine to the human nature, the Lutherans separated themselves from the Reformed[51] as well as from Roman Catholic Christology. The latter united and unites the natures only though the habitual grace flowing out of the *gratia unionis*.[52] This doctrine was replaced by the Lutherans with the

---

CR 21, pp. 626 f. (*Loci communes* [1559], *De Filio;* cf. the version of this passage from 1535, *CR* 21, p. 363, where the communication of attributes is designated as *figura sermonis*). Both Melanchthon and Calvin understand the communication of attributes merely as the transfer of the attributes of the natures to the person; they thus followed the high Scholastic tradition. See Thomas Aquinas, *Scriptum super Sent.* III, d. 11, a. 4 *resp.; Summa theologica* III, q. 16, a. 5 *resp.* (but see *ibid., ad* 3; on this, cf. n. 52 below). The statements in early Scholasticism tend predominantly in the same direction (cf. Landgraf, *Dogmengeschichte der Frühscholastik,* Vol. II/2, pp. 138 ff.). Calvin, however, distinguishes himself from this background by his emphatic reference of the communication of attributes to Christ's mediatorial office (cf. J. L. Witte, "Die Christologie Calvins," in *Chalkedon,* Vol. III, pp. 487-529, esp. pp. 503 f.); this was not, however, completely new, but appears at least as early as the doctrinal letter of Leo I in 449 (Denzinger, *Enchiridion symbolorum,* 449): *Agit enim utraque forma* cum alterius communione *quod proprium est.*

49 R. Seeberg, *Dogmengeschichte,* Vol. IV/2, pp. 513-526.

50 *SD* VIII, §§ 36 ff., §§ 46 ff., §§ 48 ff. See Seeberg, pp. 544 ff.

51 Cf. *SD* VIII, §§ 48 ff.

52 *SD* VIII, § 52, is directed polemically against the opponents who deny the divine perfections communicated to the humanity of Christ: who "contend that the gifts with which the human nature in Christ is endowed and adorned are created gifts or finite qualities." The doctrine rejected here, of the gifts of habitual grace to Christ's humanity connected with the *gratia unionis,* is presented in Thomas Aquinas' commentary on the *Sentences* in a particularly revealing way (III, d. 13, q. 13, a. 1). There the *gratia unionis* which is imparted to the human nature means, first, the unmerited divine will to the incarnation; second, the *donum* of the *unio substantialis* itself, and third, *aliqua qualitas*

third *genus* of the *communicatio idiomatum*. They thus removed themselves from the Latin tradition and moved closer to the Alexandrian-inspired thinking of Greek Orthodoxy.

The conflict between Lutherans and Reformed—and within Lutheranism itself—over the communication of attributes shows the inescapable dilemma of every Christology that begins with the statement of the incarnation in order to reproduce the uniting of the Son of God with the humanity of Jesus beginning with his birth rather than moving to the statement of the incarnation as the goal of Christology in order to find Jesus' unity with God retroactively confirmed from his resurrection for the entirety of his existence. If one thinks from the perspective of the incarnation as an event that took place at Jesus' conception and was concluded at his birth, one is forced on the one hand to the consequent deification of Jesus' humanity, in contradiction to the humanity of his earthly life. Or on the other hand one will be subject to the criticism of having conceived the unity of God with the man Jesus only incompletely and with reservations. If the two are joined together in a real unity, the *communicatio idiomatum* is to be maintained not only between the natures and the person but also between the natures themselves, thus the communication of the divine attributes of majesty to the human nature. Of course, such a unity means a blending together; in this process the human nature does not simply remain what it was and is before and outside of it. If the incarnation is identical with the event of Jesus' creation in Mary, if it is concluded with the ending of Jesus' earthly life, Jesus was from the very first moment of his existence not a man in the same sense as all other men, if in fact divine and human are two different things. In this light, the Reformed polemic was right in objecting that the Lutheran doctrine of the communication of divine attributes of majesty to Jesus' human nature called the authenticity of his humanity into question. However, if the consequences of the mutual interpenetration of the natures were not drawn to include the communication of the divine attributes of majesty to Jesus' human nature, one would be left with a juxtaposition of the two natures as a merely superficial

---

ad unionem disponens (*resp.*). In order that the human nature can be oriented to the supernatural divine activity, it requires even in Jesus' case a *habitus* of grace: *Quia ad operationem perfectam non potest natura humana nisi mediante aliquo habitu; ideo oportet esse aliquam habitualem gratiam quae sit principium illius unionis* (*ibid.*, ad 7). In the case of Jesus' personal unity with God, however, this cannot be conceived as its precondition, but only as its subsequent effect: *Neque etiam facit unitatem, sed consequitur unitatem in persona* (*ibid.*, ad 2). In the *Summa theologica*, Thomas no longer described this habitual grace lent to Christ's humanity under the heading of the *gratia unionis* (III, q. 6, a. 6). However, it is characterized as a consequence of the *unio* (*ibid.* and III, d. 7, a. 13). Presumably, Thomas sees the participation of Christ's human nature in the divine attributes, of which he speaks in the *Summa* (III, q. 16, a. 5 *ad* 3) as well as in the commentary on the *Sentences* (III, d. 5, q. 1, a. 2 *ad* 7), as grounded in the *unio*. Thomas is not concerned exclusively about the *dona creata*, but in them about the participation in the divine nature and its attributes. Here the definition of the Formula of Concord over against Scholasticism is in need of correction.

linking up without ultimate unity. Such a juxtaposition is also the case when the unity of person affects the relation between the natures only in such a way that Jesus' humanity is joined to his divinity through gifts of created grace.

One does not escape this dilemma by emphasizing as does Karl Barth "the dynamic of the history" in which the human "became and is one with the divine."[53] Just such a dynamic of the incarnation event as is here intended led the orthodox Lutheran dogmaticians to their doctrine of the penetration of the human nature with the attributes of divinity. This is especially clear when one considers the irreversibility of the movement from the divine to the human nature, emphasized by Lutherans in dependence on John of Damascus.[54] Whatever may be the deficiencies of this Christological conception, Barth's objection that orthodox Lutheran dogmaticians "abstracted" from the incarnation event in order to concentrate instead on the "state" of the human nature in its connectedness with the divine aims too low.[55] The concepts "static" and "dynamic" are not adequate to describe the problem here present.

Since Barth conceives his own Christology on the basis of the incarnation, he is not able to escape the dilemma. When he speaks of the *communicatio gratiarum* (*CD*, IV/2, pp. 91-115), he revives an idea that was developed by Scholasticism and taken over by orthodox Reformed dogmatics that originally asserted a supplementary and thus external bond between two natures. To be sure, Barth intends to say something more, namely, the "complete determination of Christ's human nature by God's grace" (p. 97). The enhypostasia of the human nature of Jesus Christ in the Logos is, according to Barth, "the essence and root of the whole of the divine grace given to him" (p. 100). But that is now supposed to be "event and not state" (p. 110). What does that mean? If without reference to this event there is still a separate condition of the divine and the human natures taken by themselves, this formula moves along the lines of the disjunction Christology. Barth's language of "event," corresponding to the category of the "moment" and similar formulations in his commentary on Romans, must in fact be understood so punctualistically

53 K. Barth, *CD*, IV/2, p. 80. Here "history" (*Geschichte*) means nothing else than the incarnation event, not the earthly *historia* of Jesus.

54 *Ibid.*, p. 78, where Barth himself brings out that according to Quenstedt (*Theologia didactico-polemica* [1685], III/3, sec. 2, q. 12 *ekth.*) there is no *reciprocatio* of communication in the *genus maiestaticum* in distinction from the *genus idiomaticum*, thus that a communication of human attributes to the divine nature does not correspond to the communication of divine attributes of majesty to the human nature.

55 Barth, *CD*, IV/2, pp. 79 f. It must be said of the rather bold connections that Barth draws to the modern apotheosis of the human as such from the Lutheran communication of attributes (pp. 82 f.) that this apotheosis represents a virtual reversal of the direction in which orthodox Lutheran dogmatics ordered its statements. The following quotations in the text refer to *Church Dogmatics*, IV/2.

in the Prolegomena to the *Church Dogmatics*.[56] If, however, as now seems to be the case, the meaning of "event" is identical with "the life of Jesus Christ" and thus includes a continuous temporal duration (p. 110), then it is not clear where the difference between Barth's position and the unification Christology of the orthodox Lutheran *communicatio idiomatum* according to the *genus maiestaticum* lies. Barth's emphasis upon the "dynamic" character of the divine-human unity in Christ does not overcome the dilemma of the orthodox doctrine of the communication of attributes; it avoids it.

Nor is this dilemma overcome by retreating with Paul Althaus or Otto Weber into the "paradoxical" character of the divine-human unity.[57] As long as Christology begins with the assertion of the incarnation in order to attain by argument a theological understanding of the historical Jesus Christ on that basis instead of moving in the opposite direction, the dilemma "disjunction Christology or unification Christology" cannot be avoided in the problematic of the communication of attributes. The difficulties with the communication of attributes result necessarily from this line of thought, whether one faces them or not. "No trespassing" signs against "betrayal of the mystery" (Althaus, p. 448) are of little help. The majority of patristic theologians, with all respect for the mystery of the incarnation, would surely have viewed as presumptuous a demand to stop trying to think through a formulation like "incarnation," which after all only arose from thought about Jesus, and to let it stand as a mystery. True respect for the mystery can express itself, among other ways, just in the attempt to understand it fully. In a certain sense, Althaus is surely right. "The antinomies and negation are the signs of the truth of the old Christology. With both it protects the mystery" (p. 447). It protected the mystery by means of antinomies and negations where the content of Christology, because of the state of the discussion at the time, could not be positively and coherently expressed without decisive abbreviations. But patristic theology was never satisfied with such a situation. It continually made new efforts to transcend the embarrassment of concrete imperfections in its understanding of that which had been laid hold of in faith. Only after the attempt to transcend these imperfections may one greet the difficulties that emerge on a new plane as a sign of the profound mystery of Jesus' reality, which in spite of the most penetrating understanding can never be so ultimately resolved that there would remain no reason for further questioning. To retreat from the problems inescapably bound up with

---

[56] In Barth's *Epistle to the Romans*, one encounters the concept of "event" in this sense only rarely (pp. 203, 303 f.). More decisive here is what is meant by the Kierkegaardian category of the "moment" (pp. 109, 111, 137 f.) and as coming "vertically, from above" (pp. 30, 102, 139). In *CD*, I/1, "event" became the terminological expression for this matter (pp. 104, 127, 161 f., 169, 207, 308).

[57] P. Althaus, *Die christliche Wahrheit*, pp. 448 f. Also, for O. Weber, *Grundlagen der Dogmatik*, Vol. II, p. 136, "the paradox" is "the only appropriate mode of expression."

a particular approach with the explanation that it has to do with a mystery means the abandonment of the effort given to theology to understand critically its own statements. The situation is similar in Otto Weber's critique of the Antiochene theologians who are otherwise quite close to his own position: "They could . . . not think in paradoxes" (p. 133; cf. p. 132). People who are prepared to refuse to continue thinking at specific points are hardly gifted in that particular art. Had the only issue been the "paradox," patristic Christology could have been satisfied with the formulas of Ignatius and saved itself the intellectual wear and tear of the following centuries.

The difficulties of the communication of attributes, as was the case with the doctrine of the unification of the true God with a truly human existence, are connected with the conception of the incarnation as an event that was concluded with the beginning of Jesus' historical existence. If this is true, since in this case—if the incarnation is understood strictly as unification—the character of Jesus' life as human in the sense of all other human lives becomes doubtful, the question arises whether these difficulties might be avoided by a different conception of the idea of incarnation. Could the incarnation perhaps be more appropriately conceived as a process continuing through Jesus' entire life and leading to ever closer unification with God? Thus in modern theology, I. A. Dorner attempted "to conceive the incarnation not as complete all at once but as continuing, ever-growing, in that God as the Logos continually grasps and appropriates each new aspect that emerges from true human development, just as conversely the growing real receptivity of the humanity consciously and voluntarily unites with ever new aspects of the Logos."[58] In support of such a conception, we might mention that the distinction between the conditions of humiliation and exaltation has hardly ever been wholly without influence upon the doctrine of the person of Christ. Just as one cannot separate Jesus' person from his work or office, neither can one separate it from his historical life, expressed in orthodox dogmatics through the distinction between the "states" of humiliation and exaltation. The uniqueness and identity of a person is not constituted by an abstract self-consciousness, even though it may be in relation to the *conception* of a Thou, but only by the particular character and unity of his life history.[59]

The exaltation of the resurrected Jesus, which Dorner certainly does not have foremost in mind, also means something new for the question about

[58] I. A. Dorner, *Christian Doctrine*, Vol. II/1, § 104, p. 328. Cf. Dorner, *History of the Development of the Doctrine of the Person of Christ*, Vol. III/3 (Edinburgh: T. & T. Clark, 1892), pp. 257 f. On the relation between the two versions, see Ernst Günther, *Die Entwicklung der Lehre von der Person Christi im 19. Jahrhundert* (Tübingen: J. C. B. Mohr [Paul Siebeck], 1911), pp. 236-243.

[59] The relation between individuality, including personal individuality, and life history presents an anthropological problem that cannot be adequately discussed in the present context. Personal individuality, which integrates the profusion of life's moments into moral —but also structural—unity, emerges only as it goes through the course of those moments, and thus in the process of a life history.

the unity of God and man in Jesus Christ. That this unity only comes fully to expression in Jesus' exaltation formed something like a counterpoint to the incarnational theme in patristic theology. This was especially the case as long as the unity in Christ was sought in the penetration of the human by the divine and the hypostatic unity did not yet seem to reside in a different plane.[60] Thus Athanasius understood the penetration of Jesus' humanity by the Logos as a process of becoming that was consummated only in his resurrection.[61] Hilary apparently thought similarly that only at Jesus' resurrection was the doubleness of the divine and the human in him consummated in an ultimate unity.[62] Gregory of Nyssa, too, saw the merging of the humanity of Jesus into God as consummated only in the exaltation of Christ.[63] In tension with the incarnational theme, Cyril of Alexandria maintained the Athanasian judgment about Jesus' resurrection, especially in his understanding of Christ as the Second Adam, which grew out of his exegesis of Paul.[64] Severus of Antioch also ascribed the glorification of Jesus' humanity by means of the attributes of the divine nature to Jesus' resurrection, true to the tradition and in opposition to Julian of Halicarnassus. He thought of this glorification as the fulfillment of the unification of the humanity with God, but explicitly not as a disappearance of the human nature.[65] Even a theologian such as Theodore of Mopsuestia, who stood opposite to the tradition of Cyril,

[60] To this extent Dorner, *Christian Doctrine*, Vol. III, § 102, p. 308, rightly distinguished, though too schematically, between the approach of pre-Chalcedonian Christology, which sought to attain "the unity of the God-human Ego as a result of the union of the Divine and human side in him," and that of later theologians, which was centered on the question of the possibility and uniqueness of Jesus' personality as a divine-human personality.

[61] *Contra Arian.* III, 35; *De incarnatione* I, 8 and 9. Cf. Dorner, *History of the Development of the Doctrine of the Person of Christ*, Vol. I/2, pp. 252 and 350 f., pp. 838 and 972. Dorner emphasizes this, p. 510, n. 55, against Baur, who considered only the theme of the incarnation and attributed to Athanasius the concept of a complete deification of Jesus' humanity—which was then no longer like ours—already at his birth.

[62] Hilary even says (*De trin.* 11, 40): *Ut ante in se duos continens, nunc* deus tantum *sit* (*MPL* 10, 425). However, it is probably questionable whether this formulation can be pressed to mean a renunciation of the human nature in the condition of the completion. Cf. Loofs, *Dogmengeschichte,* § 36, 7a, pp. 224f.; also, Dorner, *Person of Christ,* Vol. I/2, pp. 415 ff.

[63] See K. Holl, *Amphilochius von Ikonium,* p. 229. Against W. Elert, *Der Ausgang der altkirchlichen Christologie,* p. 52, it is not correct to attribute a laying off of the human nature at the consummation to Gregory of Nyssa, but one must rather understand his idea in terms of the consummation of the unification of humanity with God. Dorner, *Person of Christ,* Vol. I/2, pp. 530, n. 69, calls attention to the fact that Gregory in *Antirrhet. c.* 57 brought out the progressive character of the deification of the human nature, as a process that reached its goal only at Jesus' resurrection, as an argument against Apollinaris.

[64] On this, see R. Wilken, "Homo Futurus: A Study in the Christology of Cyril of Alexandria" (Dissertation, University of Chicago, 1963). Perhaps one will also be able to interpret the activity of the Logos as *zōopoiēsis,* as is presented by Grillmeier (in *Chalkedon,* Vol. I, p. 174), bearing in mind the connection with the life that has appeared through Jesus' resurrection and not just in the light of the incarnation and mediatorship of creation.

[65] This has been shown by J. Lebon in his studies of Severus' "Monophysitism." Cf. his contribution to *Chalkedon,* Vol. I, pp. 425-580, esp. 559 ff.

asserted an increasingly intense indwelling of the Logos in Jesus, which was consummated only at his resurrection.[66]

Theodore of Mopsuestia makes clear that the concept of a gradual incarnation as such is not capable of making understandable Jesus' unity as person—and thus in the whole of his life—with the divinity. If one follows this conception, Jesus could be one with God at most at the end of his life and thus not in the totality of his person. Then unity with God would be achieved only by the disappearance of that which established his distinctness from God at the beginning of his life. If one recognizes this as a wrong path, it is clear that it is not without reason that in the other aforementioned theologians, the incarnation as an act establishing the beginning of Jesus' life stands in a certain tension to the concept of the consummation of Jesus through the resurrection and exaltation. That which is supposed to be consummated only in Jesus' resurrection has, according to this position, already happened in the incarnation. Logically, these two ideas are hardly reconcilable. But their juxtaposition means that any Christological theory that attempts to find a better solution to this problem must take both elements into consideration. If for the understanding of Jesus' person one neglects the fact that Jesus was completed only at the resurrection, one arrives at a theory of the incarnation that bypasses the real humanity of Jesus. But if one tries to interpret Jesus' unity with God as a process consummated only in the resurrection, one easily loses sight of the necessity for asserting the unity with God of the entire person of Christ, which subsists in just this unity.

Dorner also did not succeed in uniting both points of view. He wanted to conceive the divine-human unity as realized only in a process, but at the same time he emphasized in the final form of his theory—in a distinction modifying its initial form—that in the course of Jesus' human development there never appeared an aspect of human life that was not immediately also united with God. The unity of God with this man and of this man with God was not yet conscious at first, but only because generally consciousness and self-consciousness develop only gradually in men. Nonetheless, in another way divine being could "weave and work even in the beginnings of this human child."[67] Unity with God then also took place increasingly in Jesus' consciousness in proportion to his mental development. "If this is the case, in no moment is there something human in Christ that the divinity had not assumed in order to satisfy his receptivity in the degree to which it was present at any particular time, and so there is no moment in Jesus' life that does not possess divine-human character" (p. 439). Therefore, Dorner could say that the divine-human unity is neither to be conceived as complete from

[66] Fragment from *De inc.* (H. B. Swete: "Theodori episcopi Mopsuestini," *Epistulas B. Pauli Commentarii,* ed. by H. B. Swete, Vol. II [1882], p. 317, 31 ff.); *Confession,* p. 329, 13 ff., quoted by F. Loofs, *Dogmengeschichte,* § 36, 4, p. 222.
[67] I. A. Dorner, *Christian Doctrine,* Vol. III, § 104, p. 336.

the beginning onward, nor is it to be placed only at a later point in the course of Jesus' life (p. 434). But in his own theory, is that preconscious working of God in Jesus already full divine-human unity? If so, then Dorner's theory is not in principle new over against the older incarnation theories that see the divine-human unity consummated at the beginning of Jesus' life. If Jesus' full unity with God is only attained at the stage of its conscious execution, it did not exist in the true sense at the beginning. Dorner surely had the intention of transcending this dilemma, but his theory does not really open up a way for doing so.

The outline of Christology here proposed shares with Dorner the interest in the becoming of the divine-human unity in Jesus' earthly life (although more in the sense of the old doctrine of states than in Dorner's views about the divine-human self-consciousness of Jesus), but it is distinguished from Dorner in understanding the legitimating meaning of Jesus' resurrection with its inherent retroactive power (see above, Chapter 3, Sec. II, pp. 67 f., and Chapter 4, Sec. II, pp. 134 ff.) as the pivotal point for the knowledge of Jesus' person. This makes it possible to evaluate properly the fact that in the history of traditions only Jesus' resurrection is the point of departure for the recognition of his unity with God. On the other hand, however, the retroactive meaning of the resurrection as the confirmation of Jesus' pre-Easter activity and claim makes it possible to conceive what is true from the perspective of the resurrection as true for the totality of Jesus' person from the beginning onward. The retroactive meaning of Jesus' resurrection as divine confirmation of his previous activity and claim thus overcomes the dilemma between a unity with God *either* already consummated in the beginning *or* only realized through a subsequent event in Jesus' life. The assertion of the incarnation is thus not to be exclusively related to the beginning of Jesus' life nor only to a subsequent event, but to the whole of the life and the person of Jesus as both come into view in the light of his resurrection. Admittedly, this raises once more the question of how the beginning of Jesus' life is to be connected with the divinity of his person perceived in the light of the resurrection. This leads us to the problem of the kenosis.

III. THE SELF-EMPTYING OF THE LOGOS AS MEDIATION OF THE DISTINCTION BETWEEN THE NATURES

A way out of the antinomies of the incarnational doctrine and of the communication of attributes seemed to be opened in orthodox Lutheran dogmatics by the idea of Christ's self-emptying and in a different way in the neo-conservative Lutheran dogmatics of the nineteenth century. Following Phil. 2:7, the concept of the kenosis (self-emptying) of the divine Logos had played a role in patristic Christology, but exercised no determining influence in any of the Christological conceptions. As Loofs has shown, Origen, Athanasius, Gregory of Nyssa, Cyril of Alexandria, Augustine, and others who connected Phil. 2:7 to the coming of the Logos in the flesh meant by the term "self-emptying" (*kenōsis, exinanitio*) the assumption of human nature, but not the complete or partial relinquishment of the divine nature or its attributes.[68] Nor did Hilary, whom Thomasius in the nineteenth century claimed as chief witness for his theory, intend any "relinquishment of the *forma dei* on the part of the Logos" when he said: *Evacuavit se ex forma dei*. Rather he expressed thereby only the mode in which the Logos who rules everywhere was *in Jesus*.[69] Because patristic theology was most concerned about the true divinity of Christ for the sake of its understanding of redemption, any relinquishing of divine attributes by the Logos at the incarnation had to be remote from its thought.

This was still the case with the seventeenth- and eighteenth-century Lutheran theologians who for the first time saw the key to Christological difficulties in the concept of the Christ's self-emptying. They also did not think of a voluntary relinquishment of divinity in the incarnation. But by connecting Phil. 2:7 to the Logos after it had already become flesh, they were concerned about the way in which the unity with the divine nature was effective in the concrete, human existence of Jesus after the incarnation. Self-emptying and humiliation—these terms seemed to hold back the fatal consequences of the realistic communication of attributes. They seemed to maintain Jesus' real humanity without docetic abridgment in spite of the provision of Jesus' human nature with the divine attributes of majesty. But the concept of self-emptying itself broke apart into contradictory theories.

The Tübingen theologians under the leadership of Johann Brenz[70] assumed that Jesus Christ had not only possessed the divine attributes of omnipotence, omniscience, and omnipresence in his humanity from his birth onward, but also that he had actually used them in acting as a human being, although not publicly. In opposition to this theory of a mere concealment (*krypsis*), Martin Chemnitz[71] ascribed possession of the divine attributes of majesty to Christ's human nature, but spoke of a partial refusal to use them during Jesus' earthly life. The Formula of Concord did not decide between the two conceptions but formulated alternately, using first one and then the other.[72] Thus in 1619 conflict broke out again over the unresolved question. The Giessen theologians took their positions against the Tübingen heirs of Brenz's ideas. The controversy was ended in 1624 by the *decisio Saxonica*,

[68] F. Loofs, art. "Kenosis," *RE* (3d ed.), X, 246-263, esp. pp. 248 ff.

[69] *Ibid.*, pp. 253 ff. Cf. Hilary on Ps. 68:25 in *CSEL* 22, p. 334, 15. Thomasius' treatment of Hilary is found in *Christi Person und Werk*, § 40, pp. 428-435.

[70] J. Brenz, *De divina maiestate Domini nostri Jesus Christi* (1562).

[71] M. Chemnitz, *De duabus naturis in Christo* (1570).

[72] Chemnitz' ideas are followed, for example, by *SD* VIII, § 26 and § 65; Brenz's ideas by *SD* VIII, § 73 and § 75.

following essentially the Giessen conception in rejecting a mere concealment (*krypsis*) of the possession and use of the divine attributes of majesty in Jesus' human nature during his earthly life and affirming a real renunciation (kenosis) of their use in the state of humiliation.[73] As a consequence of the conception of the Giessen theologians, the distinction between the two states of humiliation and exaltation with regard to the participation of the human in the divine nature was thrown into sharp relief.

This conflict involved, as already mentioned, only the exaltation and humiliation of Christ *according to his human nature,* not a humiliation and self-emptying of the Son of God himself. It involved the concept that the divine attributes of majesty communicated to Jesus' human nature at the incarnation were kept hidden during Jesus' earthly life or even remained latent, in any case were not really used. In this way, the tendency of the doctrine of real communication of attributes was retarded. A place was made for concrete human life in spite of the communication of divine attributes of majesty to Jesus' humanity. Jesus' glorification, which supposedly had to be connected with his birth because of the doctrine of incarnation, could be returned to its rightful place, to Jesus' exaltation, by means of the doctrine of self-emptying. But the God-man of this Christology who merely declined to use his glory remained a sort of fabulous being, more like a mythical redeemer than the historical reality of Jesus of Nazareth.

As we have seen, the antitheses between disjunction Christology and unification theology appeared again within the doctrine of self-emptying.[74] The Tübingen theologians maintained without reservation the Lutheran conception of the unity of divinity and humanity in mutual interpenetration. However, by the assumption of a mere concealment of the divine glory by Jesus during his earthly life, they threatened the reality of his historical human existence. The Giessen theologians were right in countering that in this way Jesus' earthly life was transformed into a series of pseudodeeds. The Giessen theologians were not open to such criticism. They, however, threatened the vital unity of the person. For a general renunciation of the use of the divine attributes of majesty by Jesus' humanity during his earthly life excluded a full living unity of the human with his divine nature. Both natures existed side by side, without a vital unity. If the Logos had exercised his rule of the world during the time of Jesus' earthly life apart from his unity with the man Jesus, then the unity of person was broken. The Giessen theologians thus found themselves confronted by the old argument: separate activities require separate persons.[75]

[73] For the history of the controversy, cf. G. Thomasius, *Christi Person und Werk,* Vol. I, pp. 519-634. A brief overview is also given by Heinrich Schmid, *The Doctrinal Theology of the Evangelical Lutheran Church,* pp. 388-393.

[74] This was also seen by Thomasius, *Christi Person und Werk,* Vol. I, pp. 604 ff.

[75] *Divisis operibus dividitur persona,* quoted in Thomasius, p. 604; cf. p. 590. On the origin of the argument in the Monophysite polemic against the Dyophysite Christology,

The renewal of the kenosis doctrine in the nineteenth century[76] attempted to avoid these traps. Here it is not the God-man who humiliates himself, not the incarnate Logos, but the divine Logos himself. Thereby connection was made with the most widely held exegesis of Phil. 2:7 in the patristic church. But now the self-emptying of the Logos at the incarnation was no longer understood in the merely moral sense of a humble bending down to humanity, imparting to it unification with God. Rather, a physical self-limitation of the Logos in his divinity was conceived. It was supposed that this idea would harmonize the old Christological dogma with the modern, historical picture of the life of Jesus in his mere humanity.

This conception was first presented by Sartori in 1831. Thomasius developed it fully after 1845 when he first defended the self-limitation of the Logos in the incarnation. Through Thomasius the kenosis doctrine became a part of the neo-Lutheran Erlangen theology. With individual modifications, it appeared in the work of von Hofmann, Frank, and Gess.

Thomasius saw the solution for the difficulties of Christology in the assumption of a "self-limitation of the divine"[77] in the incarnation. At the incarnation, the Son gave up the *relative* attributes of divinity, that is, those which characterize the *relation* of God to the world: omnipotence, omniscience, omnipresence. He retained only the *immanent* perfections proper to God independent of his relation to the world: holiness, power, truth, and love. Critics have called attention to the fact that just the so-called relative attributes, according to Thomasius given up by the Son for the time of his humiliation, are the really divine attributes. To be sure, they involve God's relation to the world, but that is also true of the incarnation. Therefore, the full divinity of Jesus is not saved by the idea that God's freedom and love, which determine his absolute nature above all in his relation to the world, find their perfect expression in the act of self-emptying (p. 412). Thomasius believed that in this way he had avoided an "abandonment of the divine essence or life" (pp. 444 f.). If the earthly Jesus was "neither almighty, nor all-knowing, nor omnipresent" (p. 471), then it is "because he did not want to be" (p. 472). Yet apart from the question of how he rules the world as the Logos in the meantime, the opposite objection immediately arises here: a man on whose will it depends to be almighty, omniscient, and omnipresent would be "simply an apparent man, not a real man."[78] Therefore, it caused later representatives of kenosis such as Gess to take the further step of interpreting the incarnation as a transformation of the Logos into a human soul. In this Thomasius saw an "abandonment of his divinity" (pp. 443 ff.). His

cf. F. Loofs, *RE*, IV (3d ed.), 4, 52 (art. "Christologie"). Further, also, J. Ternus, "Das Seelen- und Bewusstseinsleben Jesu," in *Chalkedon*, Vol. III, pp. 81-237, esp. p. 106.

[76] On this, see E. Günther, *Die Entwicklung*, pp. 165-200.

[77] Thomasius, *Christi Person und Werk*, p. 608. The following page references in the text are to Vol. I of the 3d ed. of this work.

[78] So A. E. Biedermann, *Christliche Dogmatik*, Vol. II, p. 231.

own doctrine remained behind the real humanity of the historical Jesus, in spite of every attempt to make room for the idea of a gradually developing of his consciousness of Sonship (pp. 465 ff.); nevertheless he also did not achieve the concept of Jesus' full divinity.

The claim of this neoconservative theology to represent the true tradition of the church was quickly shaken. I. A. Dorner especially, following his essays about "God's Unchangeability,"[79] attacked the kenotic Christology very sharply. Attention was rightly called to the explicit rejection in the Formula of Concord of the conception of self-emptying as relinquishment of the eternal Logos himself of his divine glory. Through this "the way [is] prepared for the condemned Arian heresy, which finally denied Christ's eternal divinity and thus lost both Christ and our salvation."[80] That is in fact the danger, less so of the Calvinistic and Philippist opponents of the Formula of Concord, but surely of the doctrine of kenosis. Relinquishment of the "relative" divine attributes results in a "relative de-deification" of Christ.[81] The *vere homo* is achieved only proportionately to subtractions from the *vere deus*. An incarnation thus understood as incapacitation of the Son necessarily draws the doctrine of the Trinity into difficulties as well. Is not the Son, who had given up his relative divine attributes in the flesh, excluded from the Trinity for this period, since during his humiliation he was apparently not equally God with the Father and the Spirit?

A self-limitation of the divinity at the incarnation results in a transformation in the Trinity. Therefore, the idea of God's unchangeability played an important role in the rejection of a kenosis of the Logos both in orthodox Protestantism[82] and in the nineteenth century. Dorner fought the kenosis doctrine by means of an inquiry into God's unchangeability. Against Dorner one can stress the problem of the idea of God's unchangeability itself, which has often enough had fatal consequences in theology. The God of the Bible is ever the same "in his unshakable faithfulness," but not unchangeable in the sense of a "static neutrality." Nonetheless, Otto Weber[83] cannot save the modern kenosis doctrine with this justified critique of the concept of God's

[79] Isaak August Dorner, "Über die richtige Fassung des dogmatischen Begriffs der Unveränderlichkeit Gottes," *Jahrbücher für deutsche Theologie*, 1856-1858, now in *Gesammelte Schriften* (Berlin: Wilhelm Hertz, 1883), pp. 188-377.

[80] *Epit.* VIII, 39. On this, F. Loofs observed rightly (*RE*, X, 261, in art. "Kenosis"): "The switch is longer than it needed to be—since the Philippists and Calvinists had no intention of teaching a *transmutatio divinae naturae* (p. 773, 49); but for just this reason it is long enough to stretch across the centuries and strike the modern kenotic theologians." Cf. Dorner, *Gesammelte Schriften*, pp. 224 ff.

[81] So P. Althaus, *RGG*, III (3d ed.), 1245, art. "Kenosis." Cf. also K. Barth, *CD*, IV/1, pp. 182 f.

[82] See E. F. K. Müller, *RE*, XVIII, 755 ff.

[83] O. Weber, *Grundlagen der Dogmatik*, Vol. II, p. 161. For the problems connected with the axiom of God's unchangeability and to its consequences in the history of theology, cf. also my article, "Die Aufnahme des philosophischen Gottesbegriffs als dogmatisches Problem der frühchristlichen Theologie," *ZKG*, LXX (1959), 1-45, esp. pp. 30 ff.

unchangeability. Beyond the question of whether God's sameness is to be conceived "statically" or in the historical sense of faithfulness to himself, there remains the question whether in the denial of a self-emptying of God at the incarnation the term *immutabilitas* did not express primarily the concern for the sameness of God as such. Of course, on the basis of Jesus' unity with God revealed and confirmed in his resurrection, one can say of Jesus' life that God has humiliated himself by uniting himself with the life of humanity perverted by sin and death. But even in self-humiliation he did not cease to be himself. Attributes essential to his divinity cannot be absent even in his humiliation unless the humiliated were no longer God. But if they were present in Jesus, then the unity of the divine with the human in him remains as incomprehensible as ever.

Even the kenotic Christology of the nineteenth century was thus unable to overcome the fundamental difficulty of an incarnational Christology. It, too, could only conceive the humanity of Jesus, bound to a limited space, limited in power and knowledge, to the degree it ignored his divinity.

In spite of the crushing critique experienced by the kenotic theories and even though their foundation, the relinquishment of a part of the divine attributes, has been generally rejected, certain aspects of the conception have held on with astounding tenacity. Paul Althaus, in spite of all his criticism of the kenotic theologians, nonetheless adopts their main idea: "Incarnation is a 'self-emptying' of God. Thereby, God comes into contradiction with his majesty, but does so precisely in the power of his divinity."[84] Althaus, too, takes exception to the systematic presupposition of the kenotic theories, that "not the entire divinity has entered the man Jesus" (*ibid.*, p. 1784). What does it then mean to say that with the incarnation God comes into *contradiction* with his majesty? The expression "contradiction" is meaningful only if there were not just a mere self-limitation but a total disappearance of the divine majesty. Or is this just a rhetorically exaggerated expression for the humility of the unification of God (*in* complete majesty) in Jesus with humanity, which exists in contradiction to him? If so, the dialectical language obscures the problem of how such unification is to be conceived. This is the fundamental problem of Christology.

The express kenotic conception that the Creation was an act of condescension and self-limitation of God the Father is represented today by Peter Brunner.[85] Karl Barth has spoken in his doctrine of creation of the condescension of the Creator without kenotic overtones (*CD,* III/1, pp. 436 ff.). In his Christology, Barth treated the condescension of God in the incarnation

---

[84] P. Althaus, *RGG* (3d ed.), I, 1783, art. "Christologie III." Here Althaus gives his own position a stronger kenotic emphasis, above all in the expression "God came into contradiction with himself," than is the case in his dogmatics (*Die christliche Wahrheit,* pp. 452 ff.).

[85] Peter Brunner, "Die Freiheit des Menschen in Gottes Heilsgeschichte," *KuD,* V (1959), 238-257, esp. pp. 241-245.

in the thoroughly patristic sense of the compromising community with men into which he entered (*CD,* IV/1, pp. 172 f.). Barth not only emphasized thereby that God could not cease to be God (p. 173), but also convincingly criticized the idea that God thus brought himself into self-contradiction (pp. 201 ff.). "He appropriates unto himself the being of man in contradiction to himself; but he does not share that contradiction" (p. 202). Nevertheless, some of Barth's formulations that sound kenotic in spite of all stipulations[86] veil the insoluble problems of an incarnational Christology constructed "from above to below." To say of God, "He chooses condescension. He chooses humiliation, humbleness, obedience" does not show how it is thinkable that "the one true God" now "is identical with the existence of the humiliated, humble, obedient man Jesus of Nazareth" (p. 217). On what basis does theology accept responsibility for such assertions? How can the presence of the one true God in Jesus of Nazareth be expressed in such a way that this man at the same time remains understandable in his humanity and one with God in the totality of his existence? The humble course of the life of this man is surely not as such that of God. Barth views it as the consequence of an all too human concept of God when one thinks that it is irreconcilable with the divine nature that God "in full unity with himself" becomes creature also, enters into "our being in contradiction" (p. 203). It is surely correct that we have "to re-form completely" our conceptions of God's being in the light of Jesus Christ, namely, "in view of the fact that he (God) *does* something like that" (*ibid.*). But even Barth distinguishes between God and man in Christ. He also cannot avoid the question of how both can be united in Christ. In his *Church Dogmatics* (IV/2, pp. 42-79), he treats thematically the "Event of the Incarnation." As in his early works, he calls attention to the "irreconcilability" (p. 65) of divine and human being. That God has in Christ nonetheless taken up into unity with himself and his being as God a human being (p. 44) is for Barth here also "the deed of his divine power and divine mercy grounded exclusively in his freedom, in his free love toward the world" (p. 43), which in turn is described as condescension, as "God's humbling himself" (p. 45), as "humble work" and therefore as work of the Son (p. 47). "God's humble work accomplished in his Son is the sole ground of this event" (pp. 49 f.). The question of how the togetherness, the unity

86 Of course, these similarities are of a more superficial nature and the corresponding ideas in Barth belong to a different and original conceptual context. This conceptual context is determined by the idea of the humiliation of the Son of God, which at the same time is the exaltation of man (*CD,* IV/2, pp. 99 ff., 105 ff.). Thus Barth knows of no temporal succession of the two "states" of humiliation and exaltation (*CD,* IV/1, pp. 132 ff.). As we have seen, Jesus' resurrection is only the "revelation" of his history, which was consummated on the cross (*CD,* IV/2, pp. 122 ff., 140 ff.). The exaltation of man occurs already through the incarnation; it is just hidden until the resurrection. To this extent Barth's conception has similarities to the old Tübingen *krypsis* doctrine, except that in Barth the exaltation of man is conversely the humiliation of the Son of God—and this latter connects Barth with the nineteenth century Erlangen kenosis theologians.

of God and man in this man, is comprehensible without exploding the unity of this man's life is not discussed even when this unity as such becomes the explicit theme (pp. 64 ff.). Instead, Barth only refers once more to that deed of God (p. 67). This corresponds to the fact that Barth introduces the unity of God and man in Christ as a "deduction" (p. 65) from the statement about the humble deed of God's condenscension and the resulting existence of God in the human being. We can hardly understand this other than that precisely the reference to the humble deed of God's condescension is Barth's answer to the question about the unity of God and man in Christ.

But how can God become one with man through this act in such a way that both remain distinguished but still form the vital unity of a single person? Is such unity understandable on the basis of God's humble deed? Can it simultaneously make room for man's particular character over against God and consummate his unity with God? Has Barth given any answer at all to the core question of the whole Christological tradition, the question of the living unity of God and man in Christ with continuing differentiation of the two? The descriptions of the determination of the divine nature toward the human and of the latter from the divine nature (CD, IV/2, pp. 74 ff.) appear as a "conclusion" (p. 74) from the statement of the unification of God and man in Christ. Similarly, the subsequent discussion of the two-sided "communication" of the divine and human being, of the *communicatio gratiarum* and the *communicatio operationum,* which unfold the statement of the determination of human nature by the divine, corresponds to the doctrine of the *effects* of the hypostatic union (p. 79) and thus already presupposes this. For Barth the unity in Christ seems to consist only in the "deed," in the "history," in the "event" of that humble condescension which takes on and determines the humanity of Jesus and thereby humanity in general. It is surely understandable that by the act of God's condescension he respects man's particularity and elects him to community with himself. It is also understandable that Jesus as the humble man to a certain extent participates in God's own act of humility. But is such functional community personal unity?

Barth's failure to answer the question of the understanding of the personal unity of God and man in Christ, the central question of the Christological tradition,[87] is veiled by the kenotic appearance of the language about the humble condescension of God. It is as though the transition from God to man

---

[87] In his direct treatment of the *unio hypostatica* (CD, IV/2, pp. 51-60), Barth emphasizes, in critical discussion with a whole series of traditional interpretations, that this unity has no analogy (cf. esp. pp. 58 f.). At the same time, however, he so removes it from any relation to that which is certainly to be distinguished from it, in the context of which it nevertheless could become understandable and assertable, so that there remains as a positive characteristic beside the reference to the divine deed of power only the equally naked assertion of the "direct unity of existence of the Son of God with the man Jesus of Nazareth" (p. 51).

and—since in this movement God does not cease to be God—the binding of man to God lay in this movement, in God's transition from his divinity to the human being, that is "incompatible" with the divine. But the transition to the reality of man that is different from God through the *act of divine humility* would only be really accomplished if this movement were understood kenotically as God's giving up of himself. Barth has repeatedly and rightly rejected this. With God's act of giving up himself, the unity of God and man is immediately lost again. As Barth has seen, God would then no longer be Lord over the contradiction and his entry into what is foreign would no longer be the reconciliation of the contradiction (*CD*, IV/1, p. 202). Does not this situation show once more that the way "from above to below," even though it be God's own way to unity with Jesus of Nazareth, cannot be the path of our knowledge of this unity? Should not we who are "below" rather attempt here below to make this path of God apparent from its end in the historical life of Jesus?

Heinrich Vogel's Christology[88] boldly avoids the problem of kenosis by representing it as a merely special aspect of substitution. The understanding of the incarnation as paradoxical identity of the otherwise unbridgeable contradiction between the eternal God and sinful man, stated by Kierkegaard and especially developed by Barth, is carried to its last extreme by Vogel's idea of substitution. Even Vogel's introductory discussion of the concept of God's incarnation leads to the idea of substitution, which is not supposed to explain the incarnation but to state it as a mystery (p. 664). Jesus Christ's humanity is then defined in every detail as the humanity of God who took our place by becoming man (pp. 652–673). A distinction results between actual humanity whose place God takes by uniting himself with Jesus and true humanity as united with God in Jesus. In particular, the completeness of Jesus' humanity becomes understandable as the totality of the substitution (pp. 659 ff.). The concept of substitution also demands that Christology begin with Christ's humanity because God is encountered in our place, i.e., as man. Jesus' divinity can be perceived only hidden under his real humanity (pp. 674 f.), namely, from the fact that the man Jesus claimed it for himself, that this claim is reflected in the confession of men to him and—also decisive for Vogel—that it was confirmed through Jesus' resurrection by God the Father

---

88 H. Vogel, *Christologie,* I (1949). So far Vogel has offered the entire outline of his position only in a short version in his dogmatics, *Gott in Christo;* we follow the latter in our discussion. Chapter 7, "Das Werk des Sohnes," pp. 601-802, is unfolded in five sections. The central and most important, Sec. III, "The Person," pp. 624-709, follows the two introductory sections, I: "The Question" and II: "The Name." Here Vogel discusses, first, God's incarnation, and second, the mediator. The latter section is subdivided into three parts, treating the humanity, divinity, and divine-humanity of the mediator. This order suggests a Christology "from below," which is, however, built into the context of the pattern of the incarnation moving from above to below. There follows then the treatment of the old doctrine of states, IV: "The Way," and of soteriology, V: "The Work." The page references that follow in the text refer to Vogel's dogmatics.

himself.[89] Here one has to recognize God's essence (Jesus' essential divinity), as (already treated on pp. 664-673) the true essence of this man (Jesus' true humanity), as well as ultimately the unity of God and man in him (pp. 691-709). Vogel intends to designate this unity with the concept of substitution (pp. 694 ff.). "If substitution . . . really asserts not just an exchange of places in an external sense, but that the one lives the life of the other, dies the death of the other, becomes guilty of the other's guilt, if substitution really asserts in the strict sense the existential penetration of the one into the existence of the other, then it may not be conceived in the dualism of a divine and a human person merely connected in one existence" (pp. 696 f.). Clearly, on this basis, the problem of the self-emptying has already been overcome. The doctrine of self-emptying becomes a mere footnote to the concept of substitution. Thus Vogel defines his own position in sharp opposition not only to the orthodox Protestant kenosis doctrine (pp. 715 f.) but to the modern, nineteenth-century version as well (pp. 718 f.). He does this because the kenosis doctrine was intensely concerned about saving Jesus' human self-consciousness and as a consequence had to sacrifice his divinity. In contrast, Vogel thinks that in the event of substitution, Jesus' full humanity is preserved in every respect precisely by virtue of the divine act.

At first glance, the concept of substitution may in fact appear to be the saving word for the difficulties of the incarnational doctrine. It is true that one can share the troubles or incurred guilt of another, or even bear them in his place, without losing one's own identity. This is only the case, however, because one does not simply become the other, but takes the other's existence on oneself and precisely in this remains distinguished from that other person. Thus it is questionable whether the concept of substitution can perform the task Vogel's Christology expects of it. If we inquire about its appropriateness to Jesus' historical reality, we cannot disagree that—insofar as Jesus suffered in our place—God himself suffered in our place, as we are able to say from the perspective of Jesus' resurrection because of his unity with God revealed there. Nonetheless, to extend this idea to the whole course of Jesus' existence is problematic. It is highly questionable whether *everything* that Jesus did was done in our place. Would this not evaporate into an abstraction the unmistakable uniqueness of his historical figure, which surely does not consist exclusively in the total substitution as such? But even if we would

---

[89] *Ibid.*, pp. 675 ff. To be sure, Vogel orders these three modes of expression of the "active divinity" of Jesus Christ simply side by side. He does not examine the relations that exist, above all, between Jesus' claim and his divine legitimation, and therefore he does not see the retroactive power of the latter in its decisive significance for the doctrine of Jesus' divinity. The preceding section about Jesus' humanity essentially presupposes the subsequent treatment of his divinity, since Vogel speaks throughout of the man Jesus in whom God has assumed our place. Therefore, we have proceeded in the opposite order, inquiring about Jesus' divinity on the basis of the historical man Jesus, in order to consider his humanity in the light of his divinity.

concede the extension of the substitutionary concept to the whole of the existence of Jesus Christ, the concept of substitution cannot express the unity of God and man and still preserve intact their respective particularities. How could a man who knew himself to be God, who interceded in our place, still be man as we are? Knowledge of the limit of one's own existence in the open question about the God who is infinitely different from man because of that limit belongs essentially to being human. If Jesus is man in this sense, however, how could this being human be thought of as the result of an act of divine substitution, establishing his existence without this substitution being necessarily understood as at least a partial self-denial on God's part, with all its consequences that Vogel realizes so clearly as "a God who in his revelation ceases to be God" (p. 719)? The concept of substitution merely obscures the problem of self-denial in the act of self-emptying. It does not really embrace the distinctions in such a way that God and man as different are one in Jesus Christ. The self-identity of the one who substitutes rests only on the fact that he never is radically identified with the other whom he represents. For this reason, the extension of the concept of substitution to the Christological problem necessarily hides the radical nature of the difference that is here held together to form a unity. This consequence is contrary to Vogel's own intention, which is directed just toward the radicality of this difference. The failure of the concept lies in the limits of the idea of substitution itself. It is not able to solve the problem of the kenosis because it falls short of the task confronting the kenotic theories and the problem of the incarnational doctrine in general.

Karl Rahner also has attempted to comprehend the incarnation of God from the perspective of his giving of himself. This self-giving in Rahner certainly involves a line from below: the open transcendence of man to God's absolute being that constitutes the particular structure of being human as such and comes to fulfillment in the event of the incarnation of God in man.[90] Rahner sees the basis for characterizing the incarnation from God's side as his self-emptying in the fact that incarnation means a becoming for God, but that a becoming of the unchangeable God cannot take place in himself but only "in the other."[91] Thus, something other than God must first be produced in order for God to become something in this other. This production of the other means first of all that God empties himself. But at the same time he is precisely in this way connected with this other as the result of his self-emptying. Because Rahner sees this dialectic of self-differentiation that implies at the same time both difference and unity within the difference, the term "self-emptying" in his thought signifies no threat to God's identity. On the

[90] K. Rahner, *LThK*, V (1960), 956, art. "Jesus Christus." The essay "Zur Theologie der Menschwerdung," *Schriften zur Theologie* (1960), Vol. IV, pp. 137-155, also begins with anthropological consideration of the openness of human nature.

[91] *Ibid.*, p. 147.

other side, and for just this reason, the radicality of real self-giving is not attributed to this self-emptying. We will see subsequently that this comprises the problem of Rahner's position.

In the first place, Rahner's concept of self-emptying, similar in content to Barth's conception, is superior to all other usage of the term today because of the conceptual clarity in his dialectic of self-differentiation. Apparently, the Hegelian dialectic of the concept, to be identical with itself in the other, is in the background of Rahner's formulations. Thus, he says of God's activity as Creator, "He constitutes the differentiation to himself by retaining it as his and, conversely, because he truly wants to have the other as his own, he constitutes it in its genuine reality" (p. 148). This means that God remains himself precisely in the other, but also that he becomes something, thus "that God establishes the other as his own reality precisely by emptying *himself,* giving *himself* away through this" (p. 148). God, however, is not always *absolutely* identical with himself in the other that he has distinguished from himself. This is true in Hegel's sense only of the immanent Trinity, and Rahner's presentation attains first only God's inner-Trinitarian self-differentiation (to follow for the moment this way of thinking),[92] not, however, the concept of incarnation. Where the direction becomes radical—as is the case with the emergence of finite creatures—the other identity of creaturely reality is no longer *absolutely* God's own reality. It is, of course, possible, from the human point of view, that he may perceive himself in his creature as its Creator, but that is something other than an identity of the creature with God himself. Of course, Rahner knows this also. The decisive question, however, is how "the other" established by God, after it has once become radically other over against God in creation, can again be united to God, reconciled with God. In order to answer this question, Hegel had to go through the whole of intellectual and religious history, thus the history of the elevation of man to God—in Rahner's language: the open transcendence of man to the absolute being—and even then his answer turned out to be inadequate because he had smoothed over the distinction between God and

[92] In our judgment, Hegel's idea of God as the absolute concept or absolute subject, who both lives in himself and produces the world through the dialectic of his self-differentiation, can also have only the value of a parable that is not adequate to the mystery of the divine reality. This is true, since the activity of grasping which includes both the act of differentiation and the synthesis of what is differentiated, like the analogous structure of the self-assertion of the ego in dedication to that which is differentiated from it, always presupposes the reality of an other which the ego and the concept take possession of through the dialectic of self-differentiation—which only comes into play in response to this external stimulus. The self-differentiation of the ego (or of the concept) occurs in the circle of our experience neither in self-satisfied subjectivity (as would have to be presupposed for God's inner-Trinitarian life if the latter were to be appropriately described by means of this conceptuality), nor is it creative in the strict sense of a *creatio ex nihilo* (rather only in the sense of a transcending of the other which is thereby presupposed). Therefore, as Hegel unfortunately did not see, the value of these categories as explanations applied to God is limited.

creation by means of the concept of the Spirit. When Rahner jumps directly from God's "being with himself in the other" to God's unity with the "other" in the figure of the man in the act of the incarnation, he avoids the abyss of the distinction between God and creature, which the incarnation must bridge. To the extent that it shows how God can be one with himself in the other, the dialectic of self-differentiation forms an important aid to the understanding of the incarnation. It does not yet show, however, how God can be one with what is distinguished from him, provided that this difference is to be taken seriously. Thus, from the perspective of the concept of God's self-emptying in the sense of the dialectic of self-differentiation, Rahner is not yet in a position to conceive the incarnation. On the other hand, the idea of the openness of man to God stands remarkably unrelated, though convergent, alongside this train of thought. The theory of the incarnation, however, must involve the connection of the two points of view. Can one attribute more than metaphorical truth to the concept of God's self-emptying? Is it more than an expression for the relation of Jesus' historical reality to God gathered from that historical reality itself, if one wants to avoid Hegel's attempt to contain God in the concept and prefers to speak with Rahner about the divine mystery, always superior to every penetration by means of our thought?

All modern continuations of the nineteenth century kenosis have emphatically excluded even a partial renunciation by God of his divinity, of definite divine attributes, in the execution of the self-emptying. Thereby the idea of self-emptying loses the radicality of self-relinquishment. This became clear once more in the case of Rahner. Only by means of this element, however, did the later kenotic theologians such as Gess arrive finally, by way of the divine self-emptying, at the existence of the historical man Jesus of Nazareth, who was really differentiated from God. The merit of the kenotic theology of the last century consists in its at least approximate grasp of the depth of this difference bridged in the incarnation. With this, certainly, the problem of the entire conception also becomes apparent. It can connect Jesus' historical human existence with the traditional Christology only by the concept of a self-relinquishment of the Logos; but in so doing it loses the possibility of conceiving God as one with this historical man.

If God's self-humiliation to unity with a man is conceived only as manifestation of the divine glory[93] and not as sacrifice of essential elements of the divine being, this expression does not help make the full humanity of Jesus in the incarnation intelligible; for then Jesus would remain an almighty, omniscient, omnipresent man, even though he humbly hides his glory. Or he remains a dual being with two faces in which divine majesty and human lowliness live and work parallel to one another, but without living unity with one another. A human consciousness of Jesus is unthinkable in propor-

93 So also O. Weber, *Grundlagen der Dogmatik*, Vol. II, p. 161.

tion to the degree that a living unity is affirmed. Thus Monophysitism on the one hand and the alternative of disjunctive Christology on the other remains the grievous dilemma. One can attain the goal of kenotic Christology, preservation of Jesus' humanity, only at the price that Gess had to pay for it: at the price of God's identity. But if God remains the same, he is still God even in the deepest humiliation, and the question remains unsolved as to how he can at the same time and in unity with his divinity be a man as we are.

Of course, the problem of the kenotic theologians—how the divinity of the Logos existing from all eternity could be united with the man Jesus without dissolving the humanity of his life in the divinity—is still there. Even though we cannot describe this unity from "above," from God's perspective, but only *a posteriori,* from the perspective of Jesus' human history, it is still necessary to inquire into the conditions under which Jesus' unity with God (see above, Chapter 4, Sec. I, 5; also Sec. II; below, Chapter 9) as the "incarnation" of God is compatible with our understanding of God in general. The first of these conditions is that God in all his eternal identity is still to be understood as a God who is alive in himself, who can become something and precisely in so doing remain true to himself and the same. The discussions of God's self-emptying have contributed to this insight. This has been expressed especially clearly by Rahner. However, God's becoming and his sameness must be considered more exactly in their relatedness. It will hardly suffice to speak only of a becoming "in the other," as if an inner being of God were to be distinguished that remains completely untouched by such becoming.[94] The maker himself is changed by the production and shaping of another being. The change cannot be held remote from God's inner being. But this does not necessarily affect his identity. To be sure, such identity can be conceived together with a becoming in God himself only if time and eternity are not mutually exclusive. This is the critical point for the question of God's sameness if one may reject the idea of a purely conceptual, timeless becoming as a mere chimera. In the context of Christology the problems of the relation between time and eternity cannot be discussed in great detail. Perhaps, however, it is possible to conceive eternity in the Augustinian tradition, which is at this point un-Platonic. Then the presence of eternity is to be thought of as including in itself and uniting what is separated in the succession of temporal events.[95] On this basis a becoming in God, such as is implied by

[94] Rahner apparently intends it this way when he distinguishes: "One who is in himself unchangeable can *himself* become changeable *in the other*" (*Schriften zur Theologie* (1960), Vol. IV, p. 147; cf. *ibid.,* n. 3). The change of God which takes place "in the other" occurs, however, in the same way also "in himself." Cf. only the dialectic of "something and another" in Hegel's *Science of Logic,* tr. by W. H. Johnston and L. G. Struthers (2 vols.; The Muirhead Library of Philosophy; The Macmillan Company, 1951), Vol. I, pp. 129 ff. Rahner himself refers to Hegel at this point.

[95] See, e.g., Augustine, *Conf.* I,10, and XI,13 and 16. In a still very preliminary way,

the act of the incarnation as a new work of God, could be conceived without infringing upon the divine eternity. But the incarnation does not involve a becoming in general, but God's becoming one with something different from himself.

Thus, in the second place, for an understanding of the incarnation, we must presuppose that dialectic of the divine self-differentiation which Rahner has developed. That God can be himself in creating what is differentiated from himself, in devoting himself and emptying himself to it—and not only in exclusion of everything outside himself—is certainly not yet God's unity with what is differentiated from himself, as we saw. But it is the presupposition of such unity from God's side (or in our understanding of God). Perhaps one may even speak in this connection of a tendency in God to such unity.

In the third place, that an element of God's becoming and being in the other, in the reality differentiated from himself, is one with his eternity requires that what newly flashes into view from time to time in the divine life can be understood at the same time as having always been true in God's eternity. This can be expressed in the form of the concept that the "intention" of the incarnation had been determined from all eternity in God's decree. However, the truth of such an assertion is dependent upon the temporal actuality of that thing, thus in this case the incarnation. What is true in God's eternity is decided with retroactive validity only from the perspective of what occurs temporally with the import of the ultimate.[96] Thus, Jesus' unity with God—and thus the truth of the incarnation—is also decided only retroactively from the perspective of Jesus' resurrection for the whole of Jesus' human existence on the one hand (as we have already seen) and thus also for God's eternity, on the other. Apart from Jesus' resurrection, it would not be true that from the very beginning of his earthly way God was one with this man. That is true from all eternity *because* of Jesus' resurrection. Until his resurrection, Jesus' unity with God was hidden not only to other men but above all, which emerges from a critical examination of the tradition, for Jesus himself also. It was hidden because the ultimate decision about it had not been given. One could speak differently only by depriving the event of the resurrection of its contingency, of its element of newness, by means of some sort of theological or physical determinism, or if one wants to deny the

I have discussed the question of the relationship of time and eternity in the chapter "Zeit, Ewigkeit, Gericht," *Was ist der Mensch?*, pp. 49 ff.

[96] The eschatological element could be formulated on the basis of the idea of God itself as a special, fourth condition for the conceivability of the idea of God's incarnation. Only the occurrence of what is ultimate, no longer superseded, is capable of so qualifying that whole of the course of time, beyond the moment of its own occurrence, that it can be strictly conceived as true (permanent) in eternity and thus as united with God's eternity. Here we see once more that the eschatological character of Jesus and his history as a prolepsis of the end is the correlate and, for our perception, the foundation of his unity with God.

significance of Jesus' resurrection in general for the question of Jesus' unity with God. The confirmation of Jesus' unity with God in the retroactive power of his resurrection makes the hiddenness of this unity during Jesus' earthly life comprehensible and thus makes room for the genuine humanity of this life. It accomplishes what the theory of kenosis attempted with the impossible idea of a resignation of certain divine attributes at the incarnation: the reconciliation of the idea of divine-human unity existing from the very beginning of Jesus' life with the genuine humanity of his activity. If these considerations lead us in the right direction, the concept of the incarnation can be paraphrased in terms such as these: out of his eternity, God has through the resurrection of Jesus, which was always present to his eternity, entered into a unity with this one man which was at first hidden. This unity illuminated Jesus' life in advance, but its basis and reality were revealed only by his resurrection. How this unity was effective in advance in Jesus and thus really constitutes the unity of his earthly life still remains to be considered. This consideration takes us, however, beyond the realm of the two-natures doctrine, even though we will characterize this unity as a personal one.

The problem of the two-natures doctrine does not so much lie in the concepts of "nature." This term could be used in a satisfactory sense. The problem results from speaking of "two" natures as if they were on the same plane. This poses the pseudotask of relating the two natures to one another in such a way that their synthesis results in a single individual in spite of the hindrances posed by the idea of a "nature." Thus the real problem of the two-natures doctrine is its attempt to conceive what happened in the incarnation as the synthesis of the human and the divine nature in the same individual. It is not the desire for an explanation (in the broader sense of the word) that must be rejected in the two-natures doctrine—as if one would come too close to the mystery in seeking to understand it. Rather, the point of departure of this explanation is false. The concept of the incarnation, inescapable though it is, cannot explain the unity of God and man in Jesus Christ because it is itself an expression of this unity, which must be explained and established on other grounds. The impasse reached by every attempt to construct Christology by beginning with the incarnational concept demonstrates that all such attempts are doomed to failure. We found repeatedly that either the unity of Jesus Christ as person or else his real humanity or true divinity were lost to view. This was the dilemma beginning with the Christological controversy in the fifth century, then in the Monothelite controversy, in the discussion of Latin Scholasticism, in the contradictory positions over the communication of attributes, and in the struggle about the kenotic theology of the seventeenth and nineteenth centuries.

The unity of Jesus with God, of the concrete historical Jesus of Nazareth, who in many respects is always enigmatic but still so uniquely characteristic, with the God of the Bible, of the Old Testament, whom Jesus called "Father"

—this unity can be found only in the historical particularity of the man Jesus, his message, and his fate. This is not to say that the basis of this unity resides in Jesus' humanity. Of course, the incarnational doctrine is quite right in affirming that the initiative in the event of the incarnation can be sought only on the side of God. However, we can perceive this unity only from the perspective of its result, from the perspective of Jesus' historical reality. Jesus is no synthesis of human and divine of which we can only see the human side in the historical Jesus. Rather, as this man, Jesus is God. What this means must be made more clear in what follows. It does not mean, naturally, that the universal human nature in Jesus was divine. That would be absurd, an impossible thought. But Jesus as *this* man, as man in this particular, unique situation, with this particular historical mission and this particular fate—as this man Jesus is not just man, but from the perspective of his resurrection from the dead (*kata pneuma*—"according to the Spirit") he is one with God and thus is himself God. Thus, it could make good sense—apart from the traditional framework of incarnational theology—that Karl Barth restricts himself to speaking of the "existential unity of the Son of God with the man Jesus of Nazareth" (*CD*, IV/2, p. 55) instead of constructing some kind of hypothesis about the synthesis of the two. Admittedly, the question of what sort Jesus' unity with God really is still remains open. The more exact answer to this question must demonstrate whether the impasse of the two-natures doctrine is really avoidable.

CHAPTER
9

JESUS' PERSONAL UNITY WITH GOD

*Only his personal community with the Father demonstrates
that Jesus is the Son of God.*

The discussion of Jesus' humanity has led us back to the question of his
unity with God, from which this course of Christological reflection took its
point of departure. In Part One we spoke of the revelatory unity of Jesus
with God (Chapter 4, Sec. I, 5). There, however, we could not yet consider
the internal uniqueness of this unity. We dealt only with the structure of
revelation as the route toward the knowledge that, because of the revelation,
the God revealed in it cannot be separated from Jesus through whom he is
revealed, without contradicting the concept of revelation. Thus with respect
to his essential being revealed in Jesus, the God of revelation cannot be
thought about apart from Jesus.

The concept of the essential unity that results from the revelatory unity
only says something negative. It only says that the inseparable togetherness
of God and Jesus not only involves certain aspects, whether they are of the
appearance of God or of Jesus, but also connects the eternal being of God
and the totality of Jesus' person to each other. What really constitutes this
binding unity has not yet been expressly treated, although its content came
to light in the context of the doctrine of the Trinity. Now, this unity connecting Jesus with God will be set forth more precisely as a unity of person.

We have previously recognized that the essential unity of Jesus with God,
which was confirmed in the resurrection, retroactively affected his person as
such. But we have not yet considered the personal character of that unity
itself. In treating the question of Jesus' essential unity with God, Jesus' humanity was not yet the object of special consideration. Thus the mutual inter-
relationship between these two which will now be described as a personal
unity could not come into the field of view. To be sure, everything said subsequently about Jesus' office and fate was basically presupposed when we spoke
of Jesus' essential unity with God. The explicit presentation, however, con-

centrated on the revelatory unity implied by Jesus' resurrection, which in turn implies his essential unity with God. Now, presupposing the two previous parts, we must ask what Jesus' divinity means for his human existence. How does it express itself in his human course of life? We are now concerned to characterize, not the divinity of Jesus, but its relation to his particular human being. It has previously been shown (Chapter 4, Sec. II, 3) that one must unavoidably distinguish between Jesus' eternal Sonship and his human being that began at a particular point in time. The inescapability of this distinction justifies all the efforts in the history of Christian theology to assert the unity of what is so distinguished, without losing the difference between the *vere deus* and the *vere homo*. Now we too must face this task. How is Jesus' divinity, his eternal Sonship, related to the humanity of his mission and fate?

The choice of the concept of personal unity must first be justified by a more exact examination of the unity of the human and the divine in Jesus. It is not yet justified by the mere fact that the Christological tradition has designated the unity of God and man in Jesus as a hypostatic or personal unity. We will also use the concept of person—and thus of personal unity— in a sense that differs from the tradition. Nonetheless, it can be acknowledged that the Christological tradition stemming from the Council of Chalcedon certainly preserved a reference to the actual personal unity of God and man in Christ in the concept of hypostatic or personal union, even though and just because it has been more of a problem than a solution for the time immediately ensuing and for later Christology.

Classical antiquity did not distinguish between personality and spiritual individuality. The modern idea of person as self-consciousness likewise lies along this line. However, even if one does not share the opinion that personality is adequately characterized as self-conscious, consciously reflected individuality, one must still admit that self-consciousness is an inescapable condition of personality. Therefore, it lies close at hand to turn to Jesus' self-consciousness, to the extent that we can know something about it, with the question whether Jesus' unity with God is to be understood as a personal unity. We also are not able to avoid the question of Jesus' self-consciousness at this point in our Christological thought because it is connected with the question remaining open in the impasse of the two-natures doctrine: How was Jesus' unity with God confirmed in his resurrection effective previously in Jesus' earthly existence, and how did it thus really constitute the unity of his earthly life?

I. JESUS' SELF-CONSCIOUSNESS AND THE DIVINE-HUMAN UNITY

If Jesus is essentially one with God as person and thus in the whole of his concrete human life—even though this unity was ultimately decided and came finally to light only in the resurrection—this cannot take place entirely outside Jesus' pre-Easter life and consciousness. If this were the case, one could not properly speak of a unity of his whole existence with God. Because man is essentially by himself in living his life under the determination of transcending openness and thus of a certain distance and reflection even in relation to himself, and because this self-reference takes place in a very complex and multistaged way in his self-consciousness, man normally has some sort of knowledge about what constitutes his being a self. This may happen more or less obscurely and full of anticipation or also in an inadequate mode of expression. Even so it is decisively important for the unity of the personality. Whoever is scarcely or not at all related in his self-consciousness to individual elements and aspects of his actual existence finds himself in self-contradiction that is more or less radical according to the importance of such elements and aspects for his existence. He lives in self-contradiction because it is essentially constitutive for the self that it have consciousness of itself. Such a lack of identity with one's self is hardly restricted to cases of acute mental illness and dissolution of personality. Indeed, the Christian doctrine of sin holds it to be a universal phenomenon that in a certain way all men live in self-contradiction, in contradiction to their destiny but also to their actual reality.

We are concerned here only with the question whether the assumption of such a contradiction in Jesus' life and self-consciousness is compatible with his unity with God, which we presuppose and which is confirmed in his resurrection. The assumption must be denied. If the pre-Easter Jesus had not been related at all to his unity with God in his self-consciousness, then—assuming we may presuppose this unity as confirmed on other grounds—he would not be one with himself and *to that extent* not one with God, with whom he is one corresponding to our presupposition. This presupposition would then be proved to be false. Therefore, Christology cannot avoid the question of Jesus' self-consciousness, however difficult it may be exegetically and historically. Karl Rahner has rightly said: "To the extent and in the mode that the *unio hypostatica* is a real ontological determination of human nature, in fact, its ontologically highest determination (or implying such), and that his human nature is 'with itself' through itself, thus *unio* also must be a datum of the self-consciousness of this nature from the perspective of itself."[1]

1 Karl Rahner, "Chalkedon—Ende oder Anfang?" in *Chalkedon,* Vol. III, p. 22. The continuation of the sentence, "and cannot be merely the content of its objective knowledge given 'from outside,'" can be left out of consideration here because it is concerned with the special Roman Catholic doctrine of a supranatural objective *visio beata* of the divinity (thus of his own divinity too) by Jesus. Apparently, as the above-quoted expression seems to suggest, Rahner would like not only to elaborate this doctrinal tradition but to substitute for it his considerations about the relation of Jesus' humanity to the divinity that is hypostatically united with it.

In the quest for the historical Jesus, Jesus' self-consciousness was long regarded as the root of his claim to authority; at the same time the self-consciousness of Jesus was understood in a very special sense as the objective knowledge of his own place of honor and community with God. In the Gospels such a self-consciousness is attributed to Jesus. This is done the most clearly in the "I" sayings of John's Gospel. The most important of this group of sayings with respect to content and the clearest in its absence of the usual figurative language is John 10:30: "I and the Father are one" (cf. ch. 10:36, 38). After D. F. Strauss and F. C. Baur, John's Gospel could no longer be claimed uncritically as a historical source of authentic words of Jesus. Consequently, other concepts and titles that were more indirectly connected with Jesus' relation to God came into the foreground of the question of Jesus' "Messianic self-consciousness." However, the transfer of these titles to Jesus, as will not be shown here in detail again, has been demonstrated with growing certainty by critical study of the Gospels to be the work of the post-Easter community. Today it must be taken as all but certain that the pre-Easter Jesus neither designated himself as Messiah (or Son of God) nor accepted such a confession to him from others. It is also rather probable that he held neither himself nor John the Baptist to be the eschatological prophet expected by his Jewish contemporaries. In spite of doubts that have been raised, Jesus may indeed have spoken of the future Son of Man arriving on the clouds of heaven for judgment, but if he did, he had in mind a figure different from himself.[2] The title "Servant of God" hardly designated a particular eschatological figure to be distinguished from those previously mentioned, and one does well to abstain from the assumption that Jesus knew himself to be the Servant of God of Isa., ch. 53.[3] Finally, we must reckon with the fact that the predicate "the Son," which is to be distinguished from the title "Son of God," was also not a designation that Jesus applied to himself but rather that only the community named him who had spoken of God as his Father simply "the Son."[4]

We cannot go beyond Conzelmann's conclusion "that Jesus' self-consciousness is not accessible through the Christological titles,"[5] that his "conscious-

[2] See above, pp. 59 f.

[3] See above, p. 248.

[4] Thus H. Conzelmann, *RGG*, III (3d ed.), 632. Most recently F. Hahn, *Christologische Hoheitstitel*, p. 329, after detailed discussion of the absolute concept of the Son, comes to the conclusion that the primitive community derived this designation from Jesus' characteristic address of God as Father. Hahn thus opposes O. Cullmann, *The Christology of the New Testament*, pp. 281 ff., who speaks of Jesus' "Son-consciousness" and holds the title "Son of God," in distinction from that of "Messiah," to be a self-designation of Jesus.

[5] *RGG*, III (3d ed.), 633. Cf. R. Bultmann, *Theology of the New Testament*, Chapter 4, pp. 26 ff., and G. Bornkamm's conclusion that it is a part of the special character of Jesus' activity "that the earthly Jesus did not claim any of these titles for himself" (*Jesus of Nazareth*, p. 174).

ness of a unique unity with God" rather "expresses [itself only] *indirectly*."[6] Nevertheless, in just this sense the question remains about the sort of self-consciousness implied in Jesus' activity, to the extent that it can be ascertained, and about whether and how Jesus' unity with God manifests itself in his activity. We saw previously[7] that Jesus' activity implied the claim of acting and speaking on God's own authority. But what does that really say about Jesus' self-consciousness?

With this question we turn our attention to the heated discussion that has broken out in Roman Catholic dogmatics in recent decades about Jesus' consciousness. Certainly, among Catholic theologians the judgments about the use of Christological titles by Jesus himself are generally more conservative, but on the basis of the critical foundation just sketched, the problems are set up for us in even sharper form. In this sense, Protestant Christology can learn a great deal from that discussion. The difficulties that arise for traditional Christology under more conservative historical-critical presuppositions become even greater in the context of our historical-critical findings about the Christological titles. On the other hand, this discussion gives an example of the way that the question of traditional Christology can be discussed in the light of these historical findings.

At the turn of the century the dogmatician Herman Schell in Würzburg tried to reconcile the psychological aspect of the historical Jesus with the traditional Christological understanding of Jesus as a divine-human person. He stated, "The same divine person lives in both natures and areas of life appropriate to the forms corresponding to both without the emergence of a third divine-human area of life from these two."[8] In the interest of the possibility of an experiential life of Jesus developing in a truly human way, without which the sacrificial character of his suffering would be infringed upon, Schell rejected the assumption of a "relative omniscience" poured into Jesus' soul, which—as he thought—is incompatible with a true development in Jesus' experience. On the other hand, he held firmly to the idea of the presence in Jesus' self-consciousness of a knowledge of his essential divine Sonship that was perfect from the very beginning. Such knowledge came, according to Schell, from a supernatural, divine illumination. Schell himself thus permitted the unity of Jesus' human experiential life to become questionable. How is it possible that certainty of his own divine Sonship, derived from an immediate vision of God, could fail to influence the rest of Jesus' spiritual life as well as his general experience?[9] Schell's limitation of Jesus'

6 Conzelmann, *RGG,* III (3d ed.), 632.

7 See above, pp. 56 f.

8 Herman Schell, *Katholische Dogmatik* 3,1 (1892), p. 107, quoted by J. Ternus, "Das Seelen- und Bewusstseinsleben Jesu," in *Chalkedon,* Vol. III, pp. 180-186, 182.

9 R. Haubst, "Die Gottesanschauung und das natürliche Erkenntniswachstum Christi," *ThQ,* CXXXVII (1957), 385-412, esp. pp. 410f. Haubst thinks (pp. 400 f.) that Schell

knowledge to a purely human experiential knowledge with the rejection of a "relative omniscience" by divine infusion was rejected in 1918 by the Holy Office.[10] However, to attribute to the soul of Jesus a knowledge of all things past, present, and future, and of everything that God knows from the very beginning, in the sense of a supernatural vision, makes the danger more than considerable that the genuine humanity of Jesus' experiential life would be lost. Roman Catholic theologians have also perceived this.

In recent decades the psychological problem of Jesus' knowledge has been discussed in the broader framework of the question about the ontological structure of the divine-human consciousness. Are two psychical ego centers to be assumed in the God-man, corresponding to the duality of the natures or only one because of the unity of person? Following the logic of the Dyothelite decision of 681, one probably would have to speak of a divine ego and a human ego side by side, since will (and consciousness) are not conceivable apart from an ego center. However, the Roman Catholic Church expressly set a limit to this consequence. The Franciscan Déodat de Basly (d. 1937) assumed a human, "autonomous" ego in Christ beside the divine ego and thus, along the lines of Duns Scotus, advocated an extreme Antiochene relaxation of the unity of Christ. To be sure, he went far beyond Duns Scotus in understanding the one person only as the totality relating Christ's divine and human egos. Déodat was condemned in 1951 by Pius XII.[11]

The most extreme position opposite to that of Déodat is taken today by the Thomist, P. Parente. His work on the ego of Christ,[12] which appeared in 1951, assigned consciousness to the person in such a way that the human consciousness of Christ is wholly subordinated to the hegemony of the Logos and the divine ego forms exclusively the effective center of Christ's divine-human inner life. Thereby, Parente achieved a coherent construction of the vital unity of the God-man, but only at the price of the humanity of his conscious life. Over against this unification Christology of the divine-human conscious life, P. Galtier[13] represents a moderately Antiochene posi-

"forces a cleft depicted as unbridgeable" between "the vision of God and the earthly-human spiritual life in its boundness to empirical data."

[10] H. Denzinger, Enchiridion symbolorum, 3645 f.

[11] In the encyclical Sempiternus Rex (cf. Denzinger, Enchiridion symbolorum, 3905). On Déodat de Basly and the present discussion, cf. besides J. Ternus, in Chalkedon, Vol. III, pp. 208-237, esp. A. Grillmeier, "Zum Christusbild der heutigen katholischen Theologie," Fragen der Theologie heute, ed. by J. Feiner, J. Trütsch, F. Böckle (3d ed., 1960; Einsiedeln: Benziger Verlag, 1957), pp. 265-300, esp. pp. 277-298, and the literature there cited.

[12] P. Parente, L'Io di Cristo (1951; 2d ed., 1955).

[13] The principal work by P. Galtier, L'Unité du Christ (Paris, 1939), appeared twelve years before that of Parente. The latter was followed by a discussion between Galtier, Parente, and others in a series of articles (cf. the summary in Karl Rahner, Theological Investigations, tr. by Cornelius Ernst [Helicon Press, Inc., 1966], Vol. V, pp. 196 ff.). The charge made by B. M. Xiberta against Galtier in El Yo de Jesu Christo (Barcelona, 1954), that Galtier held a neo-Antiochene Christological position, was rejected by F. Lakner,

tion. For him, consciousness is a function of nature, not primarily of the person. Only by the supernatural vision of God through which Jesus knows himself to be united with the Logos is Jesus' human consciousness protected from constituting itself as an ontologically (not just psychologically) independent ego, as human person.[14] Here the disjunction Christology is held in check by a shot of the antidote of the hegemony of the Logos. Similar to the case of Haubst against Schell, however, the unity of the divine-human consciousness is missed. Is it not essential to man's conscious life that the authentic selfhood about which he inquires in the openness of his existence is not yet ultimately decided but is always still open to decision? Would not this structure of human existence be completely changed in the case of one who knows that he is God?

Of the various attempts at mediation, we shall examine here only one article by Karl Rahner which carries the discussion a significant step forward.[15] Rahner, as previously J. Ternus,[16] seizes upon the "actuation theory" of M. de la Taille to solve the problem of consciousness. According to this theory, the unification of the Logos with the human nature first of all helps the latter to its highest possible realization instead of taking something away from it. He further picks up Peregro's demand primarily against Galtier that one must distinguish between objective knowledge and the general consciousness.[17] Thus self-consciousness does not necessarily mean for Rahner that one has an objective knowledge about oneself. In distinction from Peregro, to be sure, Rahner does not claim the supernatural *lumen gloriae* as the medium of that nonobjective consciousness, but an *"a priori,* nonobjective knowledge about oneself as a fundamental given of the spiritual subject in which it is by itself and simultaneously aware of its transcendental reference to the totality of possible objects of knowledge and freedom."[18] In the case of Jesus, this has the character of the "immediacy of consciousness of Jesus to God," which precisely does not mean "having God's essence before oneself as an object" (p. 236), but is comparable to the "unthematic, unreflexive, perhaps never reflected, knowledge about oneself" that forms the fundamental given of human spirituality (p. 237). That this fundamental given is essentially relatedness to God is not in every respect something unique about Jesus, even with

"Eine neuantiochenische Christologie?" ZKTh, LXXVII (1955), 212-228, with the observation that Xiberta, following Parente, offered a neo-Eutychian Christology (p. 228).

14 Grillmeier, in *Fragen der Theologie heute,* pp. 287 f., on Galtier, *L'Unité du Christ,* p. 350.

15 K. Rahner, "Dogmatic Reflections on the Knowledge and Self-consciousness of Christ," *Theological Investigations,* Vol. V, pp. 193-215.

16 J. Ternus, in *Chalkedon,* Vol. III, pp. 229 f.

17 A. Perego, "Il 'lumen gloriae' et l'unità psicologica di Cristo," *Divus Thomas,* LVIII (1955), 90-110, 296-310.

18 Rahner, *Theological Investigations,* Vol. V, pp. 200 f.

respect to this immediate vision of God.[19] The hypostatic union is to be understood as the most radical actualization of human spirit generally (p. 235).

A. Grillmeier objected to an initial, less explicit development of these ideas by Rahner[20] that "the human nature of Christ illuminated by itself" could only deduce from that fundamentally given relatedness to oneself "that it is not complete in itself but is the existence and being of a transcendent subject." "The illuminating of this personal subject as such," however, would no longer come from the created objectified reality because it would be transcendent to it and can therefore be perceived only through a supernatural "object-vision."[21] I doubt that Grillmeier has done full justice to the fact that Rahner, in speaking of that fundamentally given immediacy to God in Jesus' soul, always has in mind the humanity of Jesus concretely united with the Logos and determined by him,[22] never his human nature taken by itself and never the question of what this human nature would be capable of in its own power apart from the Logos. On the other hand, it is in fact necessary to ask whether that fundamental given—in the case of man generally—can ever be conscious without mediation of some sort of "objective" content of consciousness. Is the "objectively reflective coming to oneself of that which nonthematically and nonobjectively is always accepted consciously, if not also in a way that involves knowledge," (p. 240) really merely a second, supplemental step? Rahner emphasizes convincingly that this reflective coming to oneself is to be conceived even in the case of Jesus as a personal and intellectual history, as a "history of his self-interpretation for himself" (p. 241). But is not that history from the beginning interwoven with the social situation into which the individual is born—in Jesus' case essentially with the religious tradition of Israel? Is not that fundamental given itself clarified only by man's growing into the contents of the tradition of his environment and in dialogue with them? Over against the *a priori* fundamental given is it really only *a posteriori* and thus relatively insignificant "what concepts provided for Jesus by his religious environment were used by him in order to gradually say what, in the ground of his existence, he always (!) knew about himself," so that dogmatics could without anxiety relinquish this history of Jesus' self-interpretation "to the *a posteriori* life of Jesus research" (p. 241)? If we cannot follow the separation of an *a*

---

19 Rahner, *ibid.,* pp. 202 f., explicitly rejects calling this *visio* unconditionally *"beata,"* because immediacy to God does not always and necessarily make one blessed, and such blessedness could hardly have existed at the same time as Jesus' anxiety before death and foresakenness by God. Rahner wants to understand the terms *beata* (Denzinger, *Enchiridion symbolorum,* 3912) or *beati* (*ibid.,* 3645) only as an open indication of the specific character of that *visio.*

20 In the article already referred to (n. 1) in *Chalkedon,* Vol. III, pp. 21 f.

21 Grillmeier, in *Fragen der Theologie heute,* pp. 294 and 295.

22 Rahner emphasizes, *Theological Investigations,* Vol. V, p. 210, n. 11, against Galtier that that vision of God is the consequence, not the presupposition, of the hypostatic union.

priori fundamental given from the *a posteriori* concrete conditions of Jesus' life, the elements of Israel's religious traditions that were significant for Jesus' clarification of the fundamental frame of mind become dogmatically significant. Was it perhaps just the Christological titles that had been coined by the Jewish expectation? Or must one draw the circle of relevant traditional material much more broadly in order to include especially Israel's understanding of salvation and God, the expectation of the coming Kingdom of God? The exegetical situation apparently indicates that only the second alternative is appropriate and promising. All assumptions that Jesus claimed for himself any one of the traditional Messianic titles must be judged at least very problematic if not exegetically and historically untenable. On the other hand, it is certain that Jesus' self-consciousness was decisively stamped by his message of the nearness of God and his Kingdom. Must not a dogmatic statement take that into account when it inquires about the self-consciousness of Jesus in its fundamental frame of mind as related to God? Of course, we are not concerned here with a reference of Jesus' consciousness to the Logos, but to him whom he called Father. This seems to cause difficulty because the issue is Jesus' unity with the Logos, with the Son. Further, the self-consciousness of Jesus, to the extent that it indicates a fundamental attitude of openness to God on the part of his humanity, does not at all show that he simply made himself conscious relatively of that which he "in the ground of his existence had always known about himself." We must rather assume that even this fundamental framework of his self-consciousness was also involved in the failure of his message. Is not the fundamental knowledge of man about himself always open to the future, to a still unknown future fulfillment? One may not overlook the temporal element in describing that knowledge. Thus even Jesus' nonobjective, fundamentally given immediacy to God, as it is to be presupposed as the background of his historical activity, is not only to be conceived as historically conditioned through objectified traditional material[23] but also as directed toward a still incomplete future. Jesus knew himself to be related to the God whose future, already begun in his message, was the content of this message, to the God whose future, consummated with the coming of the Son of Man, would have to decide the rightness or wrongness of his own activity. In such a relation to God's future, Jesus was in fact subject to that confirmation of his mission by God himself which took place in his resurrection from the dead in an unpredicted way and which ultimately decided his unity with God—ultimately in the sense of the anticipation of the still uncompleted finality of the universal eschatological future. Karl Rahner has stressed that Jesus' immediacy to God does not exclude an absence of knowledge on the level of reflective knowledge (pp. 242 ff.), since ignorance

[23] Immediacy and mediation, as already brought out above, p. 231, are not mutually exclusive. An experience is immediate when its mediation sinks into inexplicitness and lies outside the intention of consciousness.

is not in all respects an imperfection. As awareness of the not yet decided future, the knowledge of one's own ignorance is a condition of human openness and freedom.[24] It is to be understood in this sense that Jesus' lack of knowledge was apparently not only related to the Day of Judgment, but thereby to his own person as well. Precisely this fact of Jesus' perfection in dedication to the God of the eschatological future reaches its consummation.

[24] Rahner, *Theological Investigations,* Vol. V, pp. 201 f. Patristic and medieval Christology probably completely overlooked this side of the question of the extent of Jesus' knowledge. In all questions of Jesus' capacity for suffering and of the mortality of his human nature, of the corruptibility of his flesh, the majority of the patristic theologians vehemently opposed docetic abbreviations (although always with respect to the human nature alone; cf. W. Elert, *Der Ausgang der altkirchlichen Christologie,* pp. 73 ff.). In the doctrine of Jesus' knowledge, however, a docetic-Monophysite threat was continually present and occasionally dominant. Perhaps this is to be understood as a consequence of the fact that the Arians had attempted to cast doubt upon Jesus' divinity especially by emphasizing the imperfection of his knowledge (cf. A. Grillmeier, *LThK,* V, 950). The position that had to be taken against the Arians perhaps explains why, against Apollinaris, patristic Christology could decide only after much hesitation to emphasize certain limits to Jesus' human knowledge. What was designated in abstraction as a limitation of Jesus' knowledge according to his human nature was immediately abrogated concretely—at least in the Alexandrian tradition— by having Jesus' human nature completely penetrated and illuminated by the divine nature and its omniscience (cf. Grillmeier, in *Chalkedon,* Vol. I, p. 87, on Athanasius; J. Ternus, in *Chalkedon,* Vol. III, p. 113). During the Christological controversies, apparently only the Antiochene theologians accepted a genuine ignorance on Jesus' part. Later such an "agnoetic" theory became suspect on the grounds that it was Nestorian (J. Ternus, in *Chalkedon,* Vol. III, pp. 111 f.; Denzinger, *Enchiridion symbolorum,* 476, gives the judgment of Gregory the Great: *"Quisquis Nestorianus non est, Agnoita esse nullatenus potest"*). Thus at an important point the genuine humanity of Jesus' accomplishment of his existence was curtailed (on the agnoetic controversy, cf. also *LThK,* I, 199 f.). Also, in Augustine's sphere of influence a limitation on his knowledge was held unworthy of Jesus because such a limitation was understood as a lack conditioned by sin, which could not be assumed for Jesus because of his sinlessness. Fulgentius of Ruspe in the first purely dogmatic monograph about the knowledge of Christ defended an extent of Jesus' human knowledge similar to that of the divine omniscience, although he held it to be imparted to Jesus' human nature through grace (*MPL* 65, 420CD). J. Ternus has rightly called this a "mono-noetism," which "coming from Fulgentius brought confusion even to the Augustinian wing of early Scholastic thought about Jesus' human psychology" (Ternus, in *Chalkedon,* Vol. III, p. 116). In the Latin Scholasticism of the twelfth century there were extensive controversies over this question (cf. A. M. Landgraf, *Dogmengeschichte der Frühscholastik,* Vol. II/2, pp. 44 f.). The interpretation that there prevailed conceived of Jesus as a man factually in possession of an at least "relative" omniscience (with reference to the economy of salvation).

In such assumptions we can find no legitimate conclusions from the unity of Jesus' person with the Logos, especially since they have to subject the New Testament data relevant to this problem to tedious reinterpretations. An omniscience or even an infallible foreknowledge is not at all necessarily connected with Jesus' dedication to his mission and to the one who sent him, the Father. Rather, as we have suggested in the text above, the limited character of Jesus' knowledge, even with respect to his own relation to God, belongs to the perfection of the dedication of his person to the Father's future. The doctrine of Jesus' "relative" omniscience must be judged as an overgrowth of doctrinal formation, which is understandable in terms of the false conception of the unity of God and man as the penetration of the human nature by the Logos and in the light of specific historical conditions, but which has contributed its share to making of Jesus a half-divine being, the so-called "dogmatic Christ."

This lack of knowledge is actually the condition of Jesus' unity with this God. The extent to which this unity comes to expression in an anticipatory way in the consciousness of the pre-Easter Jesus thus becomes clearer. The extent to which this involves personal unity, also with regard to Jesus' self-consciousness still remains to be clarified.

II. THE DIALECTIC OF JESUS' SONSHIP

1. The Indirectness of Jesus' Identity with the Son of God

Jesus' self-consciousness has shown him to be related to God, to be sure, not directly to "the Logos" as the second Person of the Trinity, but to the heavenly Father. It is difficult, if not impossible, to decide whether the saying of the Johannine Jesus, "I and the Father are one" (John 10:30), is true of the self-consciousness of the pre-Easter Jesus. However, the assumption is close at hand that Jesus knew himself functionally to be one with God's will in pre-actualizing the future full reality of the Kingdom of God and thus to be one with God himself, namely, in the function of his message and his entire activity determined by his message, which made up his public existence. To that extent the future full reality of God's Kingdom was anticipated in this. But to the extent that this assumption is applicable it is still always the Father —not a divine hypostasis differentiated from him—with whom Jesus knew himself to be one. At the same time, there thereby always existed for Jesus a distinction, and to be sure an infinite distinction between his own ego and the Father. One must surely say that this difference is not just the universal difference between the human and the divine, but that it is implied precisely in the special unity of his mission binding Jesus with the Father. There is hardly sufficient reason, however, for attributing this reflection to Jesus' own self-consciousness. The consciousness of distinction from and subordination to him could exist side by side in Jesus' consciousness of his mission, mediated only by the carrying out of his existence itself. Only the post-Easter community, which had to carry on Jesus' message as *his* message and whose own message therefore concentrated on Jesus' person and fate as its fundamental content, called him the "Son" in the light of the Easter confirmation of his mission and thereby expressed accurately the uniqueness of his unity with the Father through subordination, even the sacrifice of his own ego to Him.

Thus one cannot properly understand Jesus' Sonship without taking his relation to God the Father as the point of departure. The question of the unity of the man Jesus with the eternal Son of God cannot be put and answered directly. That is the common mistake of all theories that attempt to conceive the unity of God and man in Jesus on the basis of the concept of the incarnation of the Logos. This concept is certainly an appropriate and indispensable expression for that unity, but it gives no help in understanding its inner structure and how it came to be. The unity of the man Jesus with the eternal Son of God results rather only by the way of a *detour*. In the course of this detour, we must also find the justification for using the conception of a "Son of God" at all. It is a detour by way of Jesus' relation to the "Father," i.e., to the God of Israel whom he called Father. Only the personal community of Jesus with the Father shows that he is himself identical with the Son of this Father.

Jesus' personal community with the Father showed itself concretely in his behavior (Chapter 6) and in his fate (Chapter 7). If Jesus' office, his earthly mission, was to call men into the imminent Kingdom of God, if Jesus' entire activity was determined by this content of his proclamation, and finally, if this mission of Jesus has been confirmed by the resurrection from the dead that he experienced, then Jesus' whole activity is thereby demonstrated to be dedication to God and his will that aims at the establishment of his Kingdom. But then also the fate he experienced is not something alien that came over him, not simply a malicious act of human violence, but an act of God to him and through him. Not in dedication to the mission that he grasped clearly and wholeheartedly and lived, but only in the dedication to God's will in the darkness of his fate on the cross—which meant first of all the failure of his mission—did Jesus' dedication to God take on the character of self-sacrifice. The trust in the God who has been perceived in the clarity of the message of the imminent Kingdom, of the imminent Lordship of God, had to find its vindication precisely in the darkness of the failure of just this message. In the failure of his mission, Jesus' trust in God, the message whose nearness constituted his mission, became self-sacrifice. Hebrews expressed the matter thus: Jesus "learned obedience through what he suffered" (ch. 5:8).

This relation of dedication to the point of self-sacrifice was the personal community of the man Jesus with the God of his message, the heavenly Father. That it was dedication not to a phantom but to the real God is shown by Jesus' resurrection. Only by the resurrection is Jesus' personal community with God confirmed from God's side also: Jesus is raised *as* the one dedicated in this way to God. From the perspective of Easter he is revealed as the one obedient to the Father in his mission and fate, and as such he is the revelation of the Father and as the revelation of the divinity of the Father is himself one with God. Thus Jesus is not confirmed by the resurrection in something which he might have been by himself, but precisely in his having reserved nothing for himself in his human existence, in having lived entirely from God and for the men who must be called into his Kingdom—both in his mission and unheard-of claim, but precisely also in his fate on the cross, which seemed to exclude him from all community with the God of Israel and with men. The being-from-God of his mission and his claim is the content of the legitimation, which the event of Jesus' resurrection includes for him and for the world. Since then his fate on the cross also stands in its light. But because the event of Jesus' resurrection is to be understood as occurrence in advance of the ultimate revelation of the divinity of Israel's God—and also to the extent that it confirms Jesus' pre-Easter activity, namely, the imminence of God's future which he announced—it follows that through the resurrection from the dead that Jesus experienced he is the revealer of God's divinity to the extent that he is confirmed in the resurrection as the one who had been wholly and completely dedicated to God, as he also is henceforth. Just as the one completely obedient to the Father, he is the revealer of God's divinity and thus himself belongs inseparably to the essence of God. Thus is he the Son.

Thus Jesus is one with God through his dedication to the Father that is confirmed as a true dedication by the Father's acknowledgment of him through Jesus' resurrection. Such personal community is at the same time essential community. It is so first of all in the sense that it is the essence of the person itself to exist in dedication. Hegel said that it is "the character of the person . . . to supersede its isolation, its separatedness" through dedication. "In friendship and love I give up my abstract personality and win thereby concrete personality. The truth of personality is just this, to win it through this submerging, being submerged in the other."[25] To be submerged in the "Thou" means at the same time, however, participation in his being. Thus the divinity of Jesus as Son is mediated, established through his dedication to the Father. In the execution of this dedication, Jesus is the Son. Thus he shows himself identical with the correlate Son already implied in the understanding of God as the Father, the Son whose characteristic it is not to exist on the basis of his own resources but wholly from the Father. The mutual dedication of Father and Son to one another, which constitutes the Trinitarian unity of God, also establishes thereby first of all the true divinity of the Son.

Jesus' relationship to the Father as Son has been brought into the center of Christology, indeed of theology generally, after Christian H. Weisse by Friedrich Gogarten especially.[26] We share with Gogarten the concern that Jesus "is the Son of God precisely in his humanity" (p. 242), that the man Jesus is not synthesized out of a divine and a human substance but as this man is the Son of God. However, Gogarten does not distinguish between the Sonship of Jesus (as the divine Sonship of this man) and his earthly course of life as we have done and as is indispensable because of the eternity of the true divinity asserted along with the divine Sonship. At least, this distinction remains remarkably unclear in Gogarten. He treats the man Jesus from the very beginning as the Son, taking his point of departure from Jesus' supposed consciousness of Son-

---

[25] G. W. F. Hegel, *Lectures on the Philosophy of Religion,* Vol. III, pp. 24 f.

[26] F. Gogarten, *Der Mensch zwischen Gott und Welt,* pp. 15-33; cf. further pp. 245 ff., 259 ff., as well as 358 ff., for the sonship of man generally. On Gogarten, see also W. Kreck, "Die Christologie Gogartens," *EvTh,* XXIII (1963), 169-197. Kreck expresses reservations about Gogarten's understanding of Jesus' Sonship (pp. 187 ff.) that touch on and complement what is expressed here. On Chr. H. Weisse's concept of the "Son-man," see E. Günther, *Die Entwicklung der Lehre von der Person Christi im 19. Jahrhundert,* pp. 205 ff.

ship. Thus, for Gogarten, Jesus' being as man is not indirectly, but directly identical with the divine Sonship. This makes all other elements of the historical Jesus peculiarly insignificant for dogmatics, regardless of the extent to which Gogarten treats Jesus' historical activity: the details of his activity are of interest only as illustrations of Jesus' personality, his Sonship. Gogarten does not see that it is not yet Jesus' pre-Easter consciousness (whatever its content may have been with regard to Jesus' own position), but only his resurrection from the dead that establishes his identity with the Son of God, because only the resurrection brings God's own confirmation of the meaning of Jesus' earthly life as dedication to God. Certainly, from this perspective the designation of Jesus as "Son" is justified as a statement about the whole of the course of his existence. But within the course of this life, this fact is apparent only from its end. If one neglects this distinction, the full humanity of Jesus' earthly way is lost from view. Gogarten's language about Jesus as the Son, undifferentiated in this sense, has therefore a peculiarly mythological aspect: his Christology narrates, so to speak, the primordial history of human sonship over against the God who is the Father. But if one cannot be satisfied with finding in the concept of the Son a symbolic correlate to that of the Fatherhood of God, if the usage of this title involves rather the historical reality of Jesus of Nazareth on which the reality of this title (as well as of the language of God's own Fatherhood) depends, then to speak of Jesus as the "Son" of God requires confirmation from the uniqueness of his earthly course of life through his resurrection.

Thereby, the man Jesus indirectly shows himself to be identical with the existence of the Son of God. His humanity is not synthesized with a divine essence, but it involves two complementary total aspects of his existence. These aspects are as different from one another as God and man are different. Nevertheless, with the special relation to the Father in the human historical aspect of Jesus' existence, his identity in the other aspect—that of the eternal Son of the eternal Father—is given. Thus the perception of Jesus' eternal Sonship as dialectically identical with his humanity is based noetically upon the particularity of just this human being in his relation to the divine Father; ontologically, the relation is inverted, for the divine Sonship designates the ontological root in which Jesus' human existence, connected with the Father and nevertheless distinguished from him, has the ground of its unity and of its meaning.

2. The Enhypostasis of Jesus in the Logos

The unity of the man Jesus with the Son of God was expressed in post-Chalcedonian Christology with the formula of the enhypostasis of Jesus in the Logos. According to the Chalcedonian decision, an independent reality (hypostasis) of its own form of manifestation (person)[27] could no longer be attrib-

27 On the history of the word "hypostasis," cf. H. Dörries, ὑπόστασις: *Wort- und*

uted to Jesus' human nature. By itself Jesus' humanity would not only be impersonal in the modern sense of lacking self-conscious personality, but taken by itself Jesus' human being would be nonexistent. Hence, it can be conceived by itself only by abstracting from the actual reality of Jesus' existence. In his concrete reality the man Jesus has the ground of his existence (his hypostasis) not in himself as man but "in" the Logos. The designation "en"-hypostasis attempted to call attention to this aspect.

The concept of enhypostasis comes from Leontius of Byzantium.[28] The idea that Jesus' human nature without its own hypostasis could not exist on its own account but was united with the Logos from the very beginning so that its creation and its unification with the Logos coincide is even older. It goes back to John Grammaticus of Caesarea at the beginning of the sixth century and, peculiarly enough, was adopted by Leontius of Byzantium only with reservations, but otherwise was thoroughly accepted.[29] According to the logic of the matter it forms the real meaning of the concept of enhypostasis.

What is objectionable in this explanation of th: dogma of the hypostatic unity of God and man in Jesus Christ is not so much what it affirms as what it fails to say. The actual event of the unification of God and man in the temporal execution of the course of Jesus' existence is obscured by the perception—in itself correct—that Jesus' human existence in the whole of its historical course has the ground of its unity and meaning (and thus also of its facticity)

Bedeutungsgeschichte, 1955; also, M. Richard, "L'introduction du mot 'hypostase' dans la théologie de l'incarnation," *Mélanges de Science Religieuse*, II (1945), 5-32, 243-270. Further, see also *LThK*, V, 578 f. Theodore of Mopsuestia and Cyril of Alexandria had already identified the hypostasis in the sense of an independently existing nature with the person as the concrete form of appearance (on Cyril, see *MPG* 76, 157C; on Theodore, the quotations and comment by Grillmeier, in *Chalkedon*, Vol. I, pp. 154 f.; on the concept of the *prosōpon, ibid.*, pp. 187 f., and M. Nédoncelle, "Prosopon et Persona dans l'antiquité classique," *Revue des Sciences Religieuses*, XXII [1948], 277-299).

28 *MPG* 86, 1277CD. The interpretation of the hypostasis as an independent existence provides the basis for this formulation (cf. Elert, *Der Ausgang der altkirchlichen Christologie*, pp. 143 f.). Leontius seems to have been the first to distinguish this from individuality as a complex of concrete particularities, even though he himself did not maintain this distinction consistently enough (Ch. Moeller, "Le chalcédonisme et le néochalcédonisme," in *Chalkedon*, Vol. I, pp. 637-720, esp. pp. 700 f.). This distinction first made it possible to attribute individual concreteness to the human nature assumed by Jesus even though his personal being is that of the divine Logos. The difficulties that the question caused, even in this period, over whether the Logos, if Jesus' human nature has no hypostasis of its own, did not assume human nature generally (thus no individual man) can be seen by the tortuous way in which Pamphilus of Jerusalem finally confessed to this conclusion. Cf. Ch. Moeller, in *Chalkedon*, Vol. I, p. 694, and the references, p. 698, n. 8, to John Grammaticus and Leontius of Jerusalem, and n. 9, to Eulogius of Alexandria.

29 On John Grammaticus, cf. Ch. Moeller, *ibid.*, pp. 672 ff., esp. p. 673, and on the consequences in Ephrem, Justinian, Leontius of Jerusalem, pp. 677 f., 681 ff., 686 f., and on Anastasius of Antioch, pp. 690 f. In distinction from these theologians, Leontius of Byzantium considered it to be purely accidental that in fact the human individuality never existed without being connected with the Logos (*ibid.*). Moeller rightly observes, p. 705, that Leontius thereby approached the Antiochene point of view. As Moeller emphasizes, p. 663, against Loofs, Leontius really was not a "neo-" Chalcedonian theologian, but a thoroughgoing dyophysite.

in the fact that Jesus is the eternal Son of God. Jesus' unity with God is mediated through his human dedication to the Father, and this self-sacrifice consummated, which comes to fulfillment only in the crucifixion, must be distinguished from the ontological dependence of the whole of Jesus' human existence on the person of the Logos. Neo-Chalcedonian Christology, however, saw neither this distinction nor in general the special problem of the execution of the divine-human unity in the human course of Jesus' existence.[30] That means that the real theme of Antiochene Christology has simply disappeared. Thus in the doctrine of enhypostasis, the tenacious inclination of the Logos-*sarx* Christology to miss Jesus' true humanity, continued. Nonetheless, the formula retains a truth that appears when we understand it as an ontological judgment summarizing what took place in the course of Jesus' existence—distinguished from and materially subordinated to that.

Even with respect to Jesus' historical existence, we must say that he did not have his existence in his own right but received it from God. This describes the dedication to God in which Jesus lived. In distinction from the ontological dependence of Jesus' human existence on the Logos, however, the dependence that was the reason for Jesus' human dedication to God is dependence upon the *Father*. Precisely in and because of this dedication to the Father, Jesus is identical with the person of the Son. "Person" is a relational concept, and because the relation of Jesus to the Father in his dedication to him is identical with the relation to the Father intended by the designation "the Son," Jesus in his human dedication to the Father is identical with the eternal person of the Son of God.

Thus the man Jesus had his independence (or the center constituting the unity and meaning of his existence) as the Son (in the person of the Son) of his heavenly Father to the extent that he lived in self-sacrifice to the Father and in dependence upon him in the accomplishment of his existence. He did not live in dependence upon the Son; this obvious understanding of the enhypostasis of Jesus in the Logos does not do justice to the historical features of the life of Jesus. Rather, he lived in dependence on the Father, but precisely in so doing showed himself to be one with the Son. On the other hand, he is not identical with the person of the Father to whom he dedicated himself. The execution of Jesus' dedication which (confirmed by his resurrection) mediates his unity with God and is related to the Father, is thus to be distinguished from the fact established therein that Jesus' human being has its existence (its subsistence) in the person of the Son, the Logos. In this way one can avoid missing the human historical existence of Jesus as did the formula of his enhypostasis in the Logos in Neo-Chalcedonian Christology and in the sphere of influence. Yet we may at the same time retain the truth included in that formula.

30 It was decisive for this—as Moeller, *ibid.*, p. 709, brings out—that in the neo-Chalcedonian-Alexandrian tradition the human life of Jesus' soul achieved no particular Christological significance, in distinction from the Antiochene school, even though the existence of a human soul in Jesus had been admitted since Cyril.

The failure to distinguish between the personal community of Jesus with the Father and the identity of person with the Son thereby established is probably also related to the fact that the significance of the concept of person was still very feebly developed in the sixth century and in particular the relational character of personality had not yet been recognized.[31] Person (and hypostasis) were still identified with concrete individual existence. This pressed one toward the questionable conclusion, though it was not always drawn, that Jesus was a human individual not in his human nature, but only in consequence of its unification with the Logos.[32] The absence of individual concreteness in Jesus' human nature as such, apart from its unification with the Logos, would make the completeness of his humanity problematic. This was the motive of the Antiochene criticism, notorious as "Nestorian," of the Alexandrian Christology and of the uniform Logos-hypostasis of the Chalcedonian dogma. There was concern, therefore, to assert that the Logos had assumed a complete man, a concern to which Leontius of Byzantium—as we saw above—had also attempted to do justice. But this line necessarily led to the conclusion of two individuals in Jesus.

Boethius still identified personality and individuality in his well-known formulation of the concept of person.[33] His formula remained definitive for Scholasticism and to a great extent even for the modern understanding of personality. But in the Scholasticism of the twelfth century the basis was laid alongside this for another and deeper understanding of personality. On the basis of the doctrine of the Trinity in the Augustinian pattern, Richard of St.-Victor defined person as *ex-sistentia,* as an existence (*sistere*) that receives itself from another (*ex-*). Only in this contrast of an originating relation is the person nontransferable (*incommunicabilis*): only in relation to the Father is the Son, Son and nothing else.[34] Around the beginning of the fourteenth century, Duns Scotus deepened this concept of person. According to Duns Scotus, the relationship of man to God in its dual possibility, whether as devotion in

[31] In addition to the article by Nédoncelle already mentioned (n. 27 above) and the older literature cited there, cf. my article "Person," *RGG,* V (3d ed.), 230 ff., esp. on the following discussion.

[32] The distinction between the concept of the hypostasis as being-for-itself and individuality in Leontius of Byzantium is an exception, but he also did not consistently maintain the distinction he made, cf. above, n. 28.

[33] Boethius, *De trin.* V,3: *Persona est rationalis naturae individua substantia* (MPL 64, 1343C).

[34] Richard of St.-Victor, *De trin.* IV,12 (MPL 196, 937 f.). As is well known, Augustine had already defined the divine Persons through their relations to one another in his doctrine of the Trinity, even though he did not yet assess the value of this for the definition of the concept of "person" as such. As early as the Cappadocians, the element of relation occasionally appears, if only peripherally, in characterization of the divine Persons. Thus Basil (*Ep.* 38,7) says that it is not possible to speak of the Son without at the same time thinking of the Father, because the designation of "Son" *schetikōs* codesignates the Father (*MPG* 32, 340A).

openness to God or as self-assertive seclusion from God, is the locus of human personality.[35]

In the modern period since Jacobi, Hegel, and Feuerbach the understanding of person as relation has been dissociated from the notion of the relation of origin and understood as purely reciprocal I-Thou relationship. In the twentieth century this has prevailed in the form of "dialogical personalism" (G. Gloege) represented among others by Martin Buber and F. Ebner. Nevertheless, for a long time even in the modern period the understanding of person as relation receded behind the old concept of person as spiritual individuality. On this basis the Neo-Chalcedonian doctrine of the enhypostasis of Jesus' human nature in the Logos was sharply criticized in the nineteenth century. Thus Schleiermacher[36] thought that "the nature common to us all can be called that of an individual only to the extent that it has become personal in him." This is the old Antiochene objection that the impersonality of Jesus' human nature damages his true humanity. In the same way I. A. Dorner[37] rejected the impersonality of Jesus' human nature, demanded individual personality as an indispensable element of full humanity, and condemned the formula of enhypostasis because of its supposedly "pantheistic flavor" (p. 414). This distrust of the enhypostasis also entered the histories of dogma by von Harnack and Loofs, and even today Paul Althaus rejects enhypostasis, as well as the realistic communication of attributes, as a violation of the Christological paradox.[38] This criticism is related to the fact that person is understood as individuality and not as mere independent existence, as was the case with hypostasis in Leontius of Byzantium, and by no means as relation.

Against such criticism, Karl Barth has called attention to the meaning of the old concept of person as "existence." On this basis he has defended the formula of the enhypostasis and found it an appropriate explanation for "the reality of Jesus Christ attested in Holy Scripture as the reality of an act of divine Lordship in its temporal and qualitative uniqueness over against all other events." In this position some of his students have followed him.[39] To be sure, Barth thereby has first of all reinterpreted the formula in an actualistic sense when he says that Christ's human nature has its existence only "in the event of the *unio*" (*CD*, I/2, p. 178). In this way the enhypostasis becomes for Barth the designation of the miraculous invasion of divine Lordship into our world, while quite the contrary to this the Neo-Chalcedonian Christology

35 Heribert Mühlen, *Sein und Person nach Johannes Duns Scotus,* esp. pp. 106 ff.

36 F. Schleiermacher, *The Christian Faith,* § 97, 2.

37 I. A. Dorner, *A System of Christian Doctrine,* Vol. III, § 102, pp. 308 ff.

38 P. Althaus, *Die christliche Wahrheit,* p. 448, says that human personality belongs "essentially" to human nature. Similarly, Donald M. Baillie, *God Was in Christ* (Charles Scribner's Sons, 1948), pp. 98 ff.; E. Brunner, *The Christian Doctrine of Creation and Redemption,* p. 360.

39 *CD,* I/2, pp. 163 ff., quote on p. 165; I/2 (1938), pp. 178 ff.; cf. H. Vogel, *Gott in Christo,* pp. 695 f.; O. Weber, *Grundlagen der Dogmatik,* Vol. II, pp. 142 f.

invented it as an explanation for the mode of coexistence of divinity and humanity in Christ. Later, Barth treated the enhypostasis of Jesus' humanity in the Logos in the context of his doctrine of the relation of the two natures in Jesus Christ and interpreted it as the total determination of Jesus' human existence by the gracious God (*CD*, IV/2, pp. 97 f., 100). Here he has gone beyond the actualistic element, and the relational character of Jesus' personality has come into view. If Barth here moved beyond the meaning of the patristic concept, he has gone in the direction of overcoming its difficulties through a deeper understanding of Jesus' personality. Nontheless, even Barth does not distinguish that Jesus' dependence upon God describes his relation to the *Father,* while precisely in that way his personal identity with the *Son* is established.

In dedication to the Father, Jesus lives his personality as Son. If this statement is correct, Jesus' divinity is not a second "substance" in the man Jesus in addition to his humanity. Then precisely as this man, Jesus is the Son of God and thus himself God. Consequently, he is not to be thought of as a synthesis of the divine and the human. The unity of God and man in him is much more intensive than the concept of a synthesis can express. Nor does something new, a third thing, result from a mixture of the two. Nor is the humanity absorbed in divinity so that it disappears. Precisely *in* his particular humanity Jesus is the Son of God. Thereby not only his divine Sonship constitutes the particularity of this man, but above all the converse is true that the uniqueness of Jesus' humanity in his path of dedication to the Father has established the confession of Jesus as the Son of God—as can be demonstrated in the history of tradition—and establishes it even today, as has been shown in Part One. This does not mean that Jesus' dedication as such, in distinction from other aspects of his existence, was the divine in him. This dedication rather penetrates, surpasses, and envelopes all expressions and elements of his existence as is revealed in the light of his resurrection. A merely general and thus abstract notion of dedication does not work here. Rather, it involves Jesus' concrete life in the unique eschatological situation of his activity with the message of God's imminent Kingdom as the presence of salvation together with the inseparably related—although not repeatable for us—expectation of its temporally immediate consummation within the same generation.[40] This historical uniqueness of Jesus' situation distinguishes him from all other men and his life from all other dedication to God. Only in the situation of his urgent expectation does his dedication to the Father have its eschatological character and show him, in distinction to all others, to be the eternal Son. Thus Jesus' identity with the eternal Son of God is dialectical: the understanding of this man, in his humanity changed into its opposite, leads to the confession of his eternal di-

---

[40] We have already shown above, pp. 225 f., 242 ff., that this unrepeatable element of Jesus' message does not limit its truth, but that through Jesus' resurrection it is fulfilled *in himself* and thus has been cast into another form for us.

vinity. Conversely, anything said about an eternal Son of God can be sufficiently established only by recourse to the particularity of this man, to his unity with God. The synthesis of this dialectic, the unity of God and man in Christ, emerges fully only in the history of his existence. This happens not just in the history of his historical, earthly existence in his isolated individuality, but in the history of his existence to the extent that it embraces all reality from the perspective of his historical particularity. This will concern us more closely in the following chapter.

The peculiarly different relations between person and nature in the doctrine of the Trinity and in Christology were noticed at an early date. While the doctrine of the Trinity has to do with the participation of a plurality of persons in a single nature, Christology has to do with a unification of several natures through a single person. This difficulty is not due to the special problem of the conceptuality of the two-natures doctrine, nor is it to be solved by distinctive interpretations of the concepts of person and nature in the two doctrinal spheres. Even in Christology the common "nature" of the Trinitarian God confronts the sphere of human existence as a single reality, and the one person with whom Christology is concerned is certainly the same as that about whom statements must be made in the doctrine of the Trinity.

Previously we mentioned Schleiermacher's argument that the participation of several individuals in a common nature is certainly conceivable, while the synthesis of separate natures to form a single person without the abrogation of the vital unity of the person is not. This argument cannot be met simply by criticism of Schleiermacher's interpretation of the concepts "nature" and "person"—which is certainly possible—with regard to its difference from the usage in the patristic church. As long as the unification of God and man in Christ is understood as synthesis, Schleiermacher's position that Jesus' vital unity cannot be maintained in this way is convincing. Schleiermacher's objection still holds good even if we distinguish individuality from personality and understand personality as concrete existence and the latter in turn as personal relation. Personal differentiation is possible in spite of a common essence;[41]

41 Here "essence" can mean the common genus or species in a purely conceptional sense or as common "nature" in the concrete sense; in either case, however, it is to be understood in distinction from individuality. But it can also mean the atmosphere of the common spirit of a society, emerging through the reciprocal interaction of the individuals, in which the individuals "pursue" their essence (as W. Maihofer distinguishes Feuerbach's idea of essence from the traditional one in the *Festschrift für Erik Wolf* [1962], esp. pp. 253 ff.) and in which they thus participate. Finally, it can mean this common factor in that it is produced in the course of time and is revealed only at the end of this process. The path through these nuances of meaning signifies a temporalization of the concept of essence in the Platonic-Aristotelian tradition—established from the horizon of the eschatological understanding of truth in the Biblical tradition (see pp. 136 f., above). However, the concept of essence always involves something common to all the individuals that embraces the differences—whether accidental transformations, whether individual differentiation—and that presumably is related to the ontological priority of unity over differentiation (this priority also expresses itself in the unity of truth, which is closely connected with essence).

personal particularity, however, presupposes a unity of essence; at least the essence must be integrated into unity by the person himself. Through personal community one achieves a share in the essence of the other in spite of continuing personal distinctiveness. An "essence" common to both emerges in the course of their interaction. Personal community, not to speak of an individual person, is not thinkable apart from such an integrating function. The ineradicable difference between God and man in Jesus Christ can, therefore, be understood only when one pays attention to the fact that this difference certainly was integrated into a whole in Jesus' personal community with the Father (by which it constantly appears anew accompanying the personal distinction), but this integration cannot be said to belong to his own individual vital unity. A preferable description of the historical reality of Jesus' historical life is that the particular elements of human life in Jesus' existence were integrated in this way to a whole by his person, that the integrating person realized itself precisely thereby as the person of the Son belonging eternally to the divinity of God. One must observe, however, that because of its relational character the person of Jesus in his historical life must be understood as much passively as actively. It should be clear that we have here a degree of complexity in the matter to be expressed that brings us to the limit of what can be expressed at all and which, therefore, even in a systematically coherent succession of statements, can no longer be described with a sufficient degree of concreteness (i.e., in all its aspects).

With this reservation, we can move a step farther. If the history of a person is accomplished in the give-and-take of acting and receiving, the existence of Jesus is integrated into the person of the eternal Son of God precisely through the history of his earthly way in its reference to the Father. In this sense, the person of Jesus is the locus in which God's essence (in which Jesus participates as a person of the Trinity) and the essence of man, integrated through just this person, is united, as is apparent from Jesus' resurrection. This is the case first in the particularity of Jesus' historical life and then extending to all human reality.

3. Jesus' Sonship as the Fulfillment of Human Personality

The openness to God that characterizes Jesus' humanity in his dedication to the Father and shows him to be the Son constitutes his personal identity with the Son. This is not alien to the humanity of man as such. It is in Jesus' Sonship that the destiny which has stood over man and which is intended from all eternity to become his future is fulfilled. Openness to God is the radical meaning of that human "openness in relation to the world" that constitutes man's specific nature in distinction from all animals.[42] If man in his

42 The term "openness to the world" is here somewhat misleading in the sense of the phenomenon described, since the latter is, strictly speaking, openness that is unqualified,

existence is the question about God as the supporting and reconciling origin of everything real, then the unity with God that the Christian community confesses about Jesus cannot be opposed to man's nature as such. In his personal unity with God, Jesus is then the fulfillment of the human destiny, the true man (see Chapter 5). The dogma of Chalcedon possesses in the openness of human being to God an anthropological presupposition without which it would be meaningless. For only under this presupposition is there no deformation of the genuinely human reality of Jesus when Christian theology asserts that he received his personality, which integrated his life into a totality, from the Father, through his personal community with the Father, and that this personality was that of the Son of God. Conversely, through this event it becomes apparent that all human existence is designed to be personalized by its dependence upon God, to be integrated into a person through its relation to God the Father in such a way that men are constituted as persons by the Fatherly God in confrontation with him. We shall return to consider that this does not happen universally in the way it applies to Jesus, that his being as person is constituted as the Son in dependence upon the Father. If, however, Jesus' identity of person with the Son of God were completely alien to human "nature" as such, the nineteenth-century objections to the doctrine of the enhypostasis of Jesus in the Logos would still be justified. It really would be an essentially Monophysite restriction of Jesus' real humanity. Jesus is the true and real man precisely as the "God-man," only because unity with God, "sonship," is man's eternal destiny, even though it became historical reality only in Jesus' activity and fate.[43]

The concept "sonship" was the category with which Paul expressed the universal human significance of Jesus' personality. As the new man who brings the destiny of man in general to a fulfillment superior to the first creation, Jesus is the Son of God. Precisely in his Sonship, in his relation to the Father, all others shall receive a share through him. God has sent his Son that we may receive sonship through him. Because we are sons of God through Jesus, God has also sent the Spirit of sonship into our heart through which we say, "Abba!

that again and again transcends every new mundane horizon. It is the merit of contemporary Catholic theologians to have made this idea of modern behavioral anthropology fruitful for Christology. "If the essence of man generally is understood existentially-ontologically as open . . . transcendence toward God's absolute being, then the incarnation can appear as the (surely free, unmerited, and singular) absolutely highest fulfillment of what 'man' as such means," says Karl Rahner in *LThK*, V, 956 (art. "Jesus Christus"). Cf. also Rahner, in *Chalkedon*, Vol. III, pp. 15 and 17 f., as well as p. 9, n. 6; further, B. Welte, "Homousios hemin," in *ibid.*, pp. 51-80. Admittedly, the attempts by Welte (pp. 71 ff.) and Rahner (*LThK*, V, 956) to find the modern idea of the infinite self-transcendence of man already completely developed in Thomas Aquinas are not convincing. Though in a very general sense the idea is rooted in the Christian tradition, precisely in the Thomistic idea of the *potentia obedientialis* of the humanly natural toward the Creator, the sharp distinction between nature and super-nature stands in the way of the concept of the infinite process of the human execution of existence in openness that step by step transcends itself and its world.

Father!" (Gal. 4:5 f.; cf. Rom. 8:15). The new man lives on the basis of the new relation to God, on the basis of the community with God as the Father that was opened up through Jesus. Thus Christians share Jesus' divine personality as Son *through* Jesus, and this distinguishes them at the same time from Jesus himself. Through him they share his relation of dedication to the Father.

Through the Spirit of sonship, the Son of God wants to become person-building, existence-integrating power in all men. In comparison to the personality that is open to God as the transcendent, Fatherly Creator and that lives in dependence upon him, all other human personality appears as an imperfect experiment. Nevertheless the moving greatness of every individual man stems from the reflected glory of man's destiny to the personality of the Son of God that falls on every experiment of life, no matter how miserably it may fail. Only since the appearance of the Son in human history has genuine personality become undistortedly possible.

Friedrich Gogarten has developed this Pauline idea in a magnificent way. He has connected the modern understanding of man in his free subjectivity over against the world, which no longer stands over him as a sacral order but has become the sphere of his dominion, with the Pauline statement of the freedom of the Son to whom the world is promised as his inheritance. Sonship does not mean immature devotion to the course of the world, but dominion over the world in responsibility before the Father.[44] It is true that Gogarten has represented the concept of sonship all too formally. This is probably the reason why neither the Sonship of Jesus in its historical particularity, as has been previously shown, nor the different concrete form of participation in the

43 Rahner rightly says of the perception of the incarnation as the consummation of the human in general: "Thereby the incarnation would be more easily and more understandably protected against the false appearance of the miraculous-mythological" (*LThK*, V, 956).

44 F. Gogarten, *Der Mensch zwischen Gott und Welt*, pp. 385 ff. Gogarten's thesis that the modern subjectivity of man has its roots in the Christian faith has been subjected to very suggestive criticism by W. Kamlah in his article "Gilt es wirklich die Entscheidung zwischen geschichtlichem und metaphysischem Denken?" *EvTh*, XIV (1954), 171-177, esp. pp. 174 ff.; cf. also W. Kreck, *EvTh*, XXIII (1963), 175; it surely requires more precise definition in connection with historical studies of the share that the Christian tradition has had in the origins of the modern spirit. But such studies will probably not bring out just the "paradoxical cooperation of the Christian in the emergence of the modern period," which Kamlah emphasizes, *EvTh*, XIV (1954), 174, in the sense that the ancient enlightenment could be renewed with incomparable radicality in the sphere of Christian desacralization of the cosmos. Rather, one will also have to recognize positive relationships and motifs that bridge the gap from medieval Christian thought (e.g., from the fourteenth-century Ockhamistic understanding of the world or from Nicholas of Cusa) to the modern period and that are by no means identical with betrayal of the Christian tradition. To be sure, this would not necessarily offer Christian justification for the Cartesian "subject-object split" (*ibid.*, pp. 174 f.), and that Gogarten presents the problem of the difference and relation between historical and metaphysical thought as an alternative between the two may be in fact partially influenced, against Gogarten's intention, by Cartesian dualism (*ibid.*, pp. 175 f.).

Sonship of Jesus in the life of the church have been made sufficiently clear in his presentation. The latter cannot be our subject in the present context. It can only be said that Christian participation in Jesus' Sonship is to be conceived just as indirectly, mediated through the totality of relations to the world and to God, as Jesus' own Sonship is. The formality of sonship as such remains abstract. The difference between its reality in Jesus and in Christians, however, is connected with that indirectness of participation, to the extent that the indirect participation in sonship by Jesus and by Christians is different in structure.

In the light of his resurrection, Jesus is revealed as the Son of God in such a way that not only his behavior is demonstrated to be that of Sonship corresponding to God's Fatherhood, but also in such a way that he himself is shown to be the Son of God in person. This is connected with the particularity of Jesus' eschatological message, which implied a claim for his person, and which brought him to the cross and is retrospectively legitimated by his resurrection. However, because of its eschatological character, Jesus' claim was bound to the historical situation of Jewish imminent expectation and as such is not capable of repetition. Any attempt at repetition would have an anti-Christian character. Therefore, the mode of Jesus' unity with the Son of God so that he is the Son of God in the whole of his human life in the light of his resurrection is equally unrepeatable and unique. None of the men who are connected with him through faith is identical with the person of the Son of God as he was. As an individual man, only Jesus is the Son of God; only in him has the Son of God become an individual man. Christians become sons of God only to the extent that they participate in Jesus' Sonship. They achieve a share in Jesus' Sonship only in proportion to the degree of their community with this one man who as a man is the Son of God. This particular indirectness distinguishes the sonship of Christians from that of Jesus himself. On the other hand, it can also be said of Christians that through sonship they achieve participation in God's essence.[45] However, this participation also has a different character (not merely a different degree) than for Jesus' himself, because while the community with God's essence in our case as in Jesus' is mediated through personal community with the Father, yet in the manner just indicated this is different for him who knew himself to be God's eschatological messenger than for all other men.

[45] Roman Catholic theology supports its statements about a community of essence (not unity of essence) of the recipient of grace with God (so M. Schmaus, *Katholische Dogmatik* [3d ed.; Munich: M. Hueber, 1951], Vol. III/2, p. 138), especially with reference to II Peter 1:4. However, it cannot be denied that the idea of a community of essence of believers with God occurs otherwise in the New Testament also (cf. the references in Ludwig Ott, *Fundamentals of Catholic Dogma,* tr. by Patrick Lynch [B. Herder Book Company, 1955; 6th ed., 1964], pp. 256 f.). There is no reason for denying every element of truth to the patristic idea of *theopoiesis,* as became the general practice under the influence of the ethicism of the Ritschlian school.

The insight going back to Maximus Confessor that the unity of God and man is not simply opposed to the difference between the two; that, rather, increasing differentiation (and above all increasing consciousness of such differentiation) is a condition for increasingly intensive community and unity,[46] holds true of all personal community. To the extent that community of God with men has personal character, the confrontation of men with God and thus their differentiation from him comes ever anew to the fore through the fact that God creates and opens for man an existence before him and that man recognizes the divinity of God over himself. The differentiation in personal community is renewed again and again through the fact that the persons bound together in community receive reciprocal benefits each from the other at constantly new stages. Because the community of Christians with God is not characterized by the uniqueness of Jesus' eschatological mission (precisely their own mission is based on that of Jesus), the personal differentiation of Christians from the Father means at the same time that they remain essentially different from God in their own individual existence. With the personal differentiation, the difference between Creator and creature is here renewed at every stage of community with God. Not in their particular individuality, each one for himself, do Christians receive a share in the divine glory, but only in their community with Jesus and his mission. The openness to God that belongs to the structure of human existence as such (even when it is in fact lived in contradiction to God) and that finds its fulfillment only when human existence is personally integrated in dependence upon God is fulfilled in Jesus by the divine confirmation of his eschatological message (including its claim to authority) through his resurrection from the dead. It is fulfilled in all other men only through their historically mediated relation to and community with Jesus of Nazareth.

The universal human significance of the personal union of God with the man Jesus of Nazareth forms the element of truth in the previously criticized Alexandrian language about the assumption of human nature—not only of a particular man—by the Logos in the act of the incarnation. In this sense Karl Barth also has said, "In Jesus Christ not only *one* man but rather the humanity of *all* men as such has been exalted and placed in unity with God" (*CD*, IV/2, p. 52). In consequence of his "Alexandrian" construction of Christology "from above to below," Barth of course understands the assumption of the human as such by the Son of God to be the very act of the incarnation. Only as the result of this act does the existence of the Son of God become the existence of a definite man as well (pp. 53 f.). Does not Barth thus come closer

[46] *MPG* 91, 97A: For there is apparently a unification of things insofar as their physical difference is preserved. Maximus used this principle as an argument for the possibility of a real unity of will in spite of differing voluntary capacities in Christ. The intensity of that unification is measured by the degree of the differences between those things which are bound together in unity. Maximus did not yet see the specific problem of unity in personal difference.

than necessary to the difficulties of Cyril's Christology that could no longer understand Jesus' humanity assumed by the Logos as an individual humanity?[47] The converse view of the relation between the one man Jesus of Nazareth and the whole of humanity would really seem to correspond better to Barth's own Christocentric thought: only through this one man has God taken humanity in general into community with himself.

III. JESUS' FREEDOM

It has been seen that Jesus is the Son of the eternal Father only in his complete dedication to the will of the Father, in a dedication that corresponded to the unconditionality of his historical mission and that had to assume the form of self-sacrifice to the Father in the face of the earthly failure of his mission.[48] The absolute, real unity of Jesus' will with the Father's, as was confirmed in God's raising him up from the dead, is the medium of his essential unity with God and the basis of all assertions about Jesus' divine Sonship. The totality of Jesus' dedication to the Father in dedication to his eschatological mission excludes any thought of a freedom of choice by the man Jesus over against God, as if there would have been for Jesus "other possibilities" alongside his divine mission that were passed over only in his own unfounded free decision. Jesus' dedication to the Father and to his mission leaves no room for "other possibilities" that Jesus' will could have chosen in independence from God. While such "other possibilities" may seem to be present for a remote observer of Jesus' situation, for Jesus himself they could be present only as possibilities that were excluded from the beginning. Jesus' freedom consisted in doing the will of the Father and pursuing his mission. With respect to the concrete course of Jesus' life, the assumption of Jesus' "free will" in the sense of an indifferent capacity of choice that would permit a decision, coming from an ultimate indifference even over against God, appears as an empty abstraction. Jesus' enhypostasis in the Son of God means precisely that Jesus claimed for himself no independence of any kind from God because his freedom consisted not in independence from God but in unity with him.[49]

47 Thus Barth can say, "What God the Son assumed into unity with Himself and His divine being was and is . . . not merely 'a man' but the humanum" (*CD*, IV/2, p. 48).

48 R. Bultmann's assertion, "One may not repress the possibility that he collapsed" (*Das Verhältnis der urchristlichen Christusbotschaft zum historischen Jesus*, p. 12) recognizes a possibility supported at most by general considerations, not by any particular evidence in our historical knowledge of Jesus. On the contrary, not the judgment of men about him but only the beginning of the imminent *eschaton*, the coming of the Son of Man himself with the clouds of heaven, could bring, according to Jesus' own expectation, the ultimate decision about his mission. But even despair about his own mission could still have the character of Jesus' self-sacrifice in God's eyes, though this escapes every human judgment.

49 In patristic Christology this unique character of Jesus' freedom was seen not only in the tradition determined by Alexandrian thought but also by others; Maximus Confessor,

Here Roman Catholic Christology is confronted with a difficult problem.[50] There it is also felt that Jesus' close connection with God excludes a vacillation of Jesus' will where it involves the fulfillment of the divine will. On the other hand, according to Roman Catholic doctrine, Jesus' human freedom of choice in relation to God's will is the root of the meritorious character of his suffering.[51] Here Jesus has been viewed, as by Anselm of Canterbury, as the representative before God of sinful humanity's obligation of satisfaction and of its striving to achieve merit. The conflict between Jesus' unity of will with God and the traditional concept of Jesus' merit before God based on the presupposition of freedom of choice is made ever more acute for Roman Catholic Christology through the assumption that Jesus possessed as a man on earth the *visio beatifica*, the divine vision of the blessed.[52] How the clarity of Jesus' vision of God in view of the complete boundness of his whole life as a man to God can still leave room for a possibility of choice over against the divine will (especially over against the so-called "death command") is a mystery. Gutwenger (cf. note 50) names six different proposed solutions, all of which succeed only in revealing the insolubility of the problem when put in these terms.

The assumption that Jesus had the possibility of choice over against God's will is not only impossible under the specific presupposition of a *visio beatifica*, but also as a consequence of Jesus' concrete historical existence in dedication to his mission. When a mission has seized a man so unconditionally, he no longer has any choice with respect to that mission. He reserves no inner independence for himself over against his mission. Precisely this constitutes his freedom. Just in this way Jesus is one with God through his dedication to his mission, through his dedication to the Father. *The thesis of a meritorious freedom of choice for Jesus' human will under these presuppositions would*

for example, did not interpret Christ's freedom (in distinction from the Antiochene theologians) as freedom of choice. For him, conformity to the divine will under the influence of the Holy Spirit was in itself already freedom: "The possibility of choice between acts is not essential to the freedom of man, but a consequence of the sinful condition of the natural man" (Ch. Moeller, in *Chalkedon*, Vol. I, p. 714). Cf. also Ternus' presentation of Maximus' rejection of a "gnomic," i.e., proceeding from reflection and choice, will for Christ (in *Chalkedon*, Vol. III, pp. 109 f.). However, the way in which the rejection of choice is here connected with the rejection of reflection (as an expression of a lack of knowledge) shows the difference between our rejection of an indifferent freedom for Christ and that of Maximus.

50 On this, see E. Gutwenger, art. "Freiheit Christi," *LThK*, IV, 337 f.

51 Against Jansen, Innocent X reaffirmed that freedom of choice is always to be presupposed for the meritorious character of a deed (Denzinger, *Enchiridion symbolorum*, 2003). That redemption, however, is based upon a meritorious deed of Jesus is determined for Catholic theology by decisions of the Councils (Denzinger, pp. 1513, 1547, 1560). Thus, however, the Roman Church sharpened considerably the interest in the *autexousion* of Jesus' human will, formulated in the dyothelite decision of the Council of 680-681.

52 Denzinger, 3645-3647 and 3812 explicit; 474, 3009, 3432-3435 implicit. However, see the new interpretation of this theme by K. Rahner which we have dealt with above, pp. 330 ff.

make his unity with God a work of his human will instead of letting that unity be something that happened to him, which he experienced as having come from God.[53]

The answer to the question of the uniqueness of Jesus' human will in relation to the Father is most closely related to the general anthropological problem. This is made especially clear in Karl Rahner's contribution to the understanding of Christ's freedom. Rahner has attempted to solve the problem by means of the idea that "the establishment of Christ's humanity in its free differentiation from God" becomes "itself the act of unification with the *Logos*."[54] He begins with the consideration that the uniqueness of divine creativity consists in "the possibility, by one's self and by *one's own* act as *such* to constitute something that at the same time is both radically dependent (because *totally* constituted) and possesses a real independence, its own reality, and truth (because it is constituted by the one, unique *God*), even relation with the God who constituted it" (p. 182). The supreme case of such unity of the Creator with the creature set free by him is then the hypostatic union (p. 183; cf. p. 204). When Rahner designates the freedom of Jesus' human nature in relation to God in all its "radical nearness" to God as "independence" (p. 183), he surely comes very close to the assumption of an independent hypostasis; for "independence" is indeed the meaning of hypostasis in the fifth- and sixth-century discussions to the extent that hypostasis and nature were distinguished. One can agree with Rahner to the extent that creation in fact means establishing something in differentiation upon God and thus united with him. One must also see the hypostatic unity in this context. The question, however, is whether that free differentiation before God can ever mean the indifferent freedom of decision for or (just as well) against God, or whether the possibility of decision against God must not rather be related to human sin and not to human creatureliness, and even to sin only mediately in the sense of the implicit or even explicit tendency of *amor sui* toward *odium Dei*. To be sure, Rahner also does not assert any indifference of Jesus' human will toward God. What he means concretely by Jesus' "free will" is still open. To understand freedom in the old sense of arbitrariness (*indifferentia ad opposita*) hardly fits into Rahner's anthropology of the infinite self-transcendence of man as a self-transcendence directed toward the absolute being, not just undirected. But without that

[53] The idea of Christ's merit—even though we do not use it here because of its ambiguity—is not necessarily excluded by the critique we have presented of the assumption of an indifferent freedom for Jesus. The saving consequences of the mission and fate of Jesus for all humanity could be understood as merit in the sense of the harvest or result of a specific activity or behavior, without any relation to ultimate authorship in the sense of indifferent freedom.

[54] Karl Rahner, "Current Problems in Christology," *Theological Investigations* (Helicon Press, Inc., 1961), Vol. I, pp. 149-200 (first published in *Chalkedon*, Vol. III). The quotation is from p. 183; the following page references in the text are to this volume.

element of arbitrariness, the concept of merit, at least in the traditional Scholastic sense, can hardly be applied to Jesus' dedication to the Father.

It is possible to reject the assumption of a capacity of decision in Jesus' will that is in any sense indifferent to God only if we also can reject this assumption as a misunderstanding of human behavior in general.[55] Otherwise, Jesus, without such decisional indifference, would not really be man. However, if there is good reason for rejecting the indeterminist theory of the will (as well as the various determinist conceptions) as a false, one-sided representation of the reality of human freedom, then any excuse for its use in Christology disappears.

Certainly a kernel of truth is included in the traditional, indeterminist concept of freedom of choice according to which the human will is free because in every situation it can also choose differently. Man is capable of transcending every situation in which he finds himself by means of the posture he assumes of taking his distance from the impressions that pour in upon him, and of putting questions that go beyond what is offered in the moment. Therefore, in every moment he does in fact have to decide among a plurality of possibilities. However, in the moment of decision the will never really stands indifferently above the possibilities of choice. This is true only before the more exact consideration of the possibilities to choose from. This aspect of the psychic process leading to decision is absolutized by the indeterminist theory. Through the consideration of the possibilities of choice, however, the undecidedness of the will is to be overcome. In the process of consideration it is to be established which of the available possibilities is most appropriate to the destiny of the one who wills and which should for this reason be chosen. Admittedly, the destiny of man itself is always open to decision. It cannot serve as a fixed norm because man is always open to future fulfillments of his life that will surpass his present self-understanding. This openness, however, does not mean indifference toward the possibilities of the present situation, but such openness exists only in the hidden tendency toward something that is able to fulfill the destiny of man more deeply and richly than any present experience. Presumably, the will can refuse this voice calling man to follow his own as yet unthought-of, not ultimately comprehended, destiny only when the voice becomes unclear to him, although such unclarity about one's own destiny (not to be confused with its originaP openness) may be characteristic for normal human behavior. The specific human capacity to keep one's distance from impressions and to transcend them, a capacity that governs men's behavior toward all surrounding finite reality, has no function in the situation of man before God, although in some circumstances it may well function over against certain conceptions of God. From God's always still uncomprehended reality, from beyond all conceptions of God,

55 On the following, cf. also my article, "Christlicher Glaube und menschliche Freiheit," *KuD*, IV (1958), 251-280.

the reply goes forth to that open questioning of human freedom about its destiny above and beyond every environmental situation and every self-made encasement of mind. Therefore, no one can leave God behind in the sense that one can deny other, finite possibilities of choice. As Augustine knew, a man does not come into the animosity of sin toward God directly through a naked decision against God. Atheism only seems to be such a decision against God; it can affect only specific conceptions of God and in general rests on the atheist's misunderstanding with regard to the openness of his own existence.[56] Rather, a man falls into sin and thereby into contradiction against God through his relation to things and men, through his refusal to transcend and *thereby* to affirm his particular finite situation, or, more precisely, through insisting upon a supposed self-interest (or even on a supposed interest in others) that, focused on egocentricity, denies the openness to God of just this self. Men generally do not come to the decision against God as a result of an original, free decision, but as a consequence of their behavior. Here they live in fundamental error about themselves, since their true self-interest is not identical with their self-centeredness which asserts itself even in dedication to a finite person or task, but which could find fulfillment only in the openness of the self to God.

The nature of sin is in no way exhausted by a "theoretical" act of mere error, as, conversely, theoretical insight seldom has dominant significance for human behavior. However, sin and error are not just etymologically related (in the word *hamartia*). Sin is probably always connected with error about the content of one's own destiny. If this is true, it is also clear on the other side that he who lives not only in openness to God but also in clear, resolute dedication to him does not thereby make an arbitrary decision but rather follows the call of his human destiny. The more clearly this destiny is recognized,[57] the less there can be an alternative to it. Thus we can also say about Jesus' mission that the clarity with which Jesus' mission claimed him must have excluded any alternative for him. The clarity of Jesus' mission can be measured by the way in which the single idea of God's eschatological imminence permeated his message and his whole activity. Apparently the choice of his mission of proclaiming the eschatological imminence of God as the beginning of salvation meant for Jesus the content of his freedom to such an extent that no other choice, no other possibility could remain open for his freedom beside it.

This resoluteness does not exclude Jesus' having had to go through temp-

56 I have dealt in greater detail with the problem of atheism in the article "Typen des Atheismus," *Zeitwende* (1963), No. 9.

57 Of course, "clarity" here does not mean that one-sided, abstract clarity which is purchased at the price of ignoring the complexity of experienced reality, so that it contradicts at least some spheres of experience. It involves, rather, the clarity of the sense for one's own destiny in unity with that of reality as a whole, a clarity that is often not at all articulated conceptually.

tation and doubts. However, when one speaks of Jesus' temptations, one is not permitted to lose sight of their relation to his message, especially since we have no detailed knowledge about Jesus' temptations and must depend here, as in this whole section, primarily on suppositions derived from the total picture of his activity. Jesus probably was tempted to adjust his message to the expectation of his people, as the Synoptics' narratives of the temptation depict with symbolic force. Perhaps, too, he was tempted to avoid his mission completely because of the enormous claim that it brought to his own person and that would necessarily bring him into the ambiguities and conflicts in which his earthly path came to destruction. Such temptations, however, could win power over him only if he became uncertain of his message of God's nearness, which was determinative for his entire activity. That the clarity of this message and thus of his mission left no other possibility of freedom open to him than that which he actually seized upon does not contradict a capacity for temptation that would call that clarity itself into question. On the other hand, we have no reason to doubt that Jesus, in the light of the clarity of his message, could resist the temptation to be untrue to his mission.

Besides the temptations which could have led Jesus astray from his path, we must also consider the doubts of Jesus that are indicated in the Synoptic witness to Jesus' prayer on the Mount of Olives, to his praying Ps. 22:1 on the cross, and in various other indications, even though all these passages may well have no immediate historical value. These attacks of doubt, above all during Jesus' passion, could hardly have the sense of pushing him to give up his mission, but they did threaten him with despair concerning it. In our consideration of Christ's descent into hell, we have already noticed the doubts that must have assailed Jesus at the failure of his message. These doubts presuppose Jesus' freedom in the sense of unconditional identification with his mission. The despairing person subjectively refuses or withdraws from his identification with the path that he objectively cannot roll back and on which he may even have to continue. No psychological reflection can tell us how Jesus endured the doubt caused by his people's rejection of him in the name of the God whom he had proclaimed. We know only that he expected the decision about his mission to come from God, not from any human tribunal. Only on this basis, and thus again out of the clarity of his message, which constituted his freedom, could he endure the doubts about the legitimacy of his message, doubts rising about the authority of the God to whom his message appealed.

IV. JESUS' SINLESSNESS

Jesus' personal community and unity with God, his dedication to God to the point that his own freedom became identical with his divine mission and the Father's will for him, includes his freedom from all sin. The assertion

354

of Jesus' sinlessness is only the negative expression for the same reality of Jesus' dedication to God with which we have been concerned until now under the positive aspects of his being the Son of God and his freedom for God. If sin is essentially life in contradiction to God, in self-centered closing of our ego against God, then Jesus' unity with God in his personal community with the Father and in his identity with the person of the Son of God means immediately his separation from all sin. Therefore, the more exact theological understanding of his sinlessness is dependent upon the understanding of his unity with God.

Paul stressed that Jesus was without sin precisely where he emphasized that Jesus was judged, cursed (Gal. 3:13), treated as a sinner by God in our stead. Only because Jesus was himself without sin can it be said that what he suffered was not the consequence of his own guilt, but that he took his suffering upon himself for our sake. Paul implied this idea in II Cor. 5:21 as well: God has made him who knew no sin—that is, had done no sin[58]—to be sin for us, that through him we might become "the righteousness of God." Romans 8:3 states the same in more general terms. Because of sin, God sent his Son in the form of sinful flesh (that is, in our sinful condition of existence) and so condemned sin in its own realm, in the flesh. Hebrews emphasizes that Jesus was tempted as we are, but remained without sin.[59] Similarly, First Peter 2:22 affirms with reference to Isa. 53:9 that Jesus did no sin (cf. I Peter 3:18). Correspondingly, the Johannine Jesus asks his opponents: "Who among you can accuse me of a sin?" (John 8:46; cf. ch. 14:30). First John says of him who was sent to take sin upon himself and thus to remove it from men: "In him there is no sin" (1 John 3:5). This breadth of the primitive Christian tradition of Jesus' sinlessness surely shows that the special importance of this matter had been recognized since the beginning of the Christian community. And indeed, how could the first Christians hold their own against their Jewish opposition without stressing this point?

Corresponding to the unanimous witness in this matter in the New Testament, the Christological confessions of the patristic church also emphasized Jesus' sinlessness: in the Eastern declaration to the Nicene Creed (Denzinger,

[58] Like Rom. 7:7, this involves a Hebraism. "To know" here does not have primarily theoretical but, rather, practical meaning in the sense of "to know how [to do something]" or "to be familiar with [something]"; *ThD*, I, 703. The expression in II Cor. 5:21 was interpreted similarly even before the Ambrosian gloss (*MPL* 17, 298). On the idea of II Cor. 5:21, cf. Bultmann, *Theology of the New Testament*, Vol. I, p. 277. Bultmann convincingly rejects any "as if" in this statement and derives from the Pauline sentence "the paradoxical fact that God made the (ethically) sinless Christ to be a sinner (in the forensic sense)—viz. by letting him die on the cross as one accursed (cf. Gal. 3:13)." The only questionable point in this formulation is whether the distinction between "ethical" and "forensic" does not dull the point of the idea. Does not Paul mean that God let the one whom he later demonstrated to be sinless, thus the one who was in reality sinless, become a sinner before the forum of men?

[59] *Chōris hamartias*: Heb. 4:15; cf. chs. 7:26; 9:14.

Enchiridion symbolorum, 44), in the Chalcedonian confession (Denzinger, 301) with reference to Heb. 4:15, in Cyril's tenth anathema in 431 (Denzinger, 261) with an allusion to II Cor. 5:21. In theological presentations, too, these two texts seem to have played the leading role, together with the prophetic word of Isa. 53:9[60] which was quoted as early as First Peter and whose fulfillment was found in Jesus.

But how is Jesus' sinlessness to be understood more exactly? The New Testament statements are all directed toward establishing that Jesus in fact committed no sin. The first- and second-century Christian theologians were also primarily interested in Jesus' having done no sinful acts, but saw therein no distinction of his nature from ours. Thus Irenaeus said that the flesh assumed by the Lord did not sin, but this does not mean that it was a substance other than our flesh (*Adv. haer.* V, 14, 3). When Irenaeus justified the necessity of the incarnation of the Son of God with the assertion that sin had to be overcome by a man just as it had its origin in a man (*Adv. haer.* III, 18, 7), he made no reservation regarding a sinlessness that would have distinguished the humanity of Jesus by nature from other men, apart from his activity overcoming sin. Similarly, for Tertullian, Jesus is not sinless because of a special disposition of his nature, but because he is one with the sinless God.[61] In *De carne Christi* 16, Tertullian said that just that flesh whose nature is otherwise sinful has been assumed by Christ and in him sin is thus made powerless (cf. Rom. 8:3), that just this flesh was kept sinless by Christ.[62] Origen was apparently the first to go beyond the statement that Jesus in fact did not sin. The soul of Jesus, he said, is so unwaveringly dependent on God in immeasurable love that even the possibility of turning away and of sin no longer exists; through the mood that grew out of long habit, the resolution of will became nature.[63] It is interesting that here the incapacity for sin appears as the result of Jesus' unconditional dedication to God, even though Origen was concerned with the dedication of Jesus' preexistent soul to God, so that the sinlessness of the incarnate is no longer a problem in spite of participation in sinful flesh. In the East the opposition to the Arians seems to have caused a stronger reserve about Jesus' participation in the hu-

---

[60] Origen, in *John* 28,18,160 (*MPG* 12, 720); *Afrahat demonstr.* 7,1 (*Patrologia syriaca,* ed. by J. Parisot, 1, p. 314); Chrysostom, in *Hebr.* 28,2 (*MPG* 63, 194); cf. M. J. Rouet, *Enchiridion Patristicum,* Nos. 482, 684, 1224.

[61] Tertullian, *De anima* 41: "*Solus enim Deus sine peccato, et solus homo sine peccato Christus, quia et Deus Christus*" (*CSEL* 20, 368).

[62] On *homoiōma* (Rom. 8:3): "*Non quod similitudinem carnis acceperit, quasi imaginem corporis, et non veritatem; sed similitudinem peccatricis carnis vult intelligi, quod ipsa non peccatrix caro Christi eius fuit par, cuius erat peccatum, genere, non vitio Adae: quando hinc etiam confirmamus eam fuisse carnem in Christo, cuius natura est in homine peccatrix; et sic in illa peccatum evacuatum, quod in Christo sine peccato habeatur, quae in homine sine peccato non habebatur*" (*MPL* 2, 780 f.).

[63] Origen, *De princ.* II, 6,5: "*Quod in arbitrio erat positum, longi usus affectu iam versum sit in naturam*" (*GCS* 5, 145).

man fleshly nature. The Arians denied the true divinity of Jesus by calling attention to elements inappropriate to divinity. Therefore, in 377, Basil set forth in a letter that the Lord did not assume our sinful flesh but only something analogous to it, since he assumed the natural human failings, but rejected as unworthy of divinity those which soil the purity of the human nature.[64] Apparently this rejection was supposed to have happened at the incarnation. The contrast to the anti-Gnostic emphasis on Jesus' equality with us as found in Tertullian and Irenaeus is obvious. While these early theologians still restricted themselves to the assertion that Jesus had in fact not committed any sin and thereby had overcome the power of sin in sinful flesh itself, subsequently the emphasis was that human nature was not bound to the Logos in the condition spoiled by sin coming from Adam. While Irenaeus and Tertullian emphasized the equality of Jesus with us, following Paul in Rom. 8:3, it was not emphasized—of course without denying this equality and only in the sense of a reservation—that the Logos did not assume sinful flesh, but an undamaged human nature,[65] which was therefore not identical with sinful flesh, but only similar to it. This distinction, erroneously thought to be in the sense of Rom. 8:3,[66] occurs in Augustine too.[67] His characteristic formulation says that Christ alone was *born* without sin.[68]

With Augustine, the emphasis of the concept of Jesus' sinlessness was conclusively shifted in the West from the actual overcoming of sin in the flesh to the concept of a condition of sinlessness and lack of sinfulness that existed from birth.[69] Understandably, the doctrine of original sin especially tended toward such a conception. That Jesus could have kept his human life free from individual sins under the influence of the divine holiness may be conceivable without the assumption of a lack of sinfulness existing from birth. But how could he remain free of original sin, which clings to all men from birth? Apparently this is possible only if Jesus is excepted from the transmission process of original sin. If original sin is transmitted through natural generation, it was obviously necessary to bring Jesus' sinlessness into the context of his miraculous conception and thus of Mary's virginity. This is

[64] Basil, *Ep.* 261,3 (MPG 32, 972). Cf. also how Epiphanius, *Ancor.* 75 (MPG 43, 157 = *Enchiridion Patristicum*, 1086 f.), speaks of the assumption of a perfect *teleion* man through Christ and then in 168 finds any sin excluded by this perfection (now understood in the ethical sense).

[65] So still Pseudo-Athanasius, *Contra Apollinaris* 1,17 (MPG 26, 1140 = *Enchiridion Patristicum*, 798).

[66] The term means "identity of form," not merely "analogy." See G. Bornkamm, *Das Ende des Gesetzes, Paulusstudien*, pp. 42 f., on the comparison of Rom. 8:3 with Phil. 2:7, Rom. 5:14, and 5:5. A. Schlatter came to the same conclusion, *Gottes Gerechtigkeit* (Stuttgart: Calwer Verlag, 1935), p. 256. Differently, however, J. Schneider, *ThW*, V, 191-197.

[67] Augustine, *De Genesi ad litteram* 10,18 (CSEL 28/1, 320). On the legitimation of Jesus' sinlessness by means of the virgin birth, see below, n. 71.

[68] Augustine, *Ench.* 108 (MPL 40, 283).

[69] Augustine, *De pecc. merit.* 2,11,16 (MPL 44, 161): *"Christi iustitiam, in cuius non tantum divinitate, sed nec in anima nec in carne ullum* potuit, *esse peccatum."*

what Augustine, following Ambrose,[70] often said.[71] Against this, the objection was certainly repeatedly raised that the connection with the sinful generation of Adam continued unbroken through Mary too. An answer to this objection was first made possible by the assertion of the immaculate conception of Mary, which, still controversial in the high Scholasticism of the thirteenth century and rejected by the majority of the great Scholastics,[72] was made dogma in the Roman Church in 1854 (Denzinger, 1803). Accordingly, Christ's merit would have been applied in advance to his mother so that she was purified of sin and Jesus himself could be conceived sinlessly—a very artificial construction! But it is only by such artificiality that one can establish Jesus' natural sinlessness with the help of the virgin birth. Because neither the connection of Jesus' sinlessness with the legend of the virgin birth nor the theologoumenon of the immaculate conception of Mary herself comes from primitive Christianity or can be demonstrated as an implication of the saving event that establishes Christian faith, we have no reason to take this course in order to understand Jesus' sinlessness.

Not only the Augustinian doctrine of original sin, but also the concentration of the Christological discussions of the fifth century on the event of the unification of the Logos with Jesus' human nature at the beginning of his earthly existence contributed to transferring the origin of his sinlessness to the event of his human origin and thus to attributing to Jesus a condition of his nature immune to sin from the very beginning. In this respect his human nature is different from that of all other men. We have observed this tendency in Basil and Epiphanius. Cyril of Alexandria did not even understand any longer why some theologians attempted to attribute to Jesus' human nature a capacity for sin because of his equality with other men. As Cyril observed with amazement, Jesus actually did not sin in any case and thus to attribute to him a possibility that he could have sinned was entirely superfluous (*matēn*).[73] Apparently, Cyril did not sense any problem in the fact that Jesus' ability to be tempted and his assailment by doubts is no longer understandable if there was *a priori* no possibility that he could have sinned. By contrast, this question was hotly discussed in twelfth-century Latin Scholas-

---

[70] Hans von Campenhausen, *The Virgin Birth*, pp. 79 f.

[71] Thus Augustine, *C. Jul.* 2,10,33 (*MPL* 44, 697), emphasizes by listing an impressive row of authorities that original sin was transmitted to all men with one exception: *"Unde nemo eruit, nisi quem sine lege peccati repugnante lege mentis virgo concepit"*; cf. *Ench.* 41 (*MPL* 40, 252) and *De Genesi ad litteram* 10,18 (*CSEL* 28/1, 320).

[72] Duns Scotus became its champion; see J. F. Bonnefoys, *Le ven. Jean Duns Scot, Docteur de l'immaculée-conception* (Rome, 1960). In this work, see pp. 23 ff. on Alexander of Hales; pp. 29 ff. on Bonaventura; pp. 53 ff. on Albertus Magnus; pp. 54 ff. on Thomas Aquinas; pp. 92 f. on Henry of Ghent: they all rejected Mary's total freedom from original sin because such freedom was the privilege of Christ and all other men must be conceived as in a state requiring redemption in contrast to him.

[73] Cyril of Alexandria, *Epistula ad Calosyrium* 23 (*MPG* 76, 1120 = *Enchiridion Patristicum*, 2141).

ticism, especially with respect to the meritorious character of Jesus' sinless obedience.[74] The decision was finally made, in the same sense as the Council of Constantinople in 553 (Denzinger, 224), for the assumption of an inability to sin (*impeccabilitas*) in Jesus' human nature that existed from the very beginning. This inability to sin was not attributed to his human nature as such, nor derived directly from the hypostatic union and the hegemony of the divinity over the human nature. In accordance with the developing Scholastic understanding of the community of the natures within the hypostatic union, it was interpreted as a gracious sinlessness (cf. Landgraf, *Dogmengeschichte der Frühscholastik*, Vol. II/1, pp. 366 ff.), which apparently left the ability to be tempted and the meritorious capacity of Jesus' human will untouched—certainly only apparently, namely, with regard to the abstract concept of human nature. In his concrete existence, according to this Scholastic conception, Jesus was so filled with such divine grace from the very beginning that it is still not understandable how a temptation could really have penetrated through his defenses. Nevertheless, in view of the relation between Jesus' unity with God and his sinlessness, we can understand the concern for a sinlessness in Jesus that existed from the very beginning and was not acquired at some later point.

Older Protestant dogmatics retained the doctrine that Jesus was incapable of sin. They did so, at least on the Lutheran side, however, within a different context provided by the new interpretations of the communication of attributes.[75] In the nineteenth century, Jesus' sinlessness was the particular part of traditional Christology that was the least impugned from Schleiermacher to von Harnack and Herrmann. Certainly the assumption of a strict inability to sin was given up. Schleiermacher called Jesus' inability to sin "essential" to the extent that it is rooted in the "connection of the divine and the human in his person." For Schleiermacher, as for the orthodox dogmatics, that meant an inability for Jesus to sin. This implied in turn in Schleiermacher's view that Jesus' ethical development must have taken its course without any struggle. In this consequence, Schleiermacher himself sensed a difficulty because of the tradition's witness to Jesus' ability to be tempted.[76] At this point Bretschneider raised immediate objections. J. Müller admitted validity in the *peccare non potuit* "only to the consummation and end of this life, the result of its development conditioned by self-determination," while the fundamental assertion of Christology regarding Jesus' sinlessness must be that he actually committed no sin.[77] Under Müller's influence, C. Ullmann also restricted himself in the later editions of his monograph on Jesus' sin-

---

[74] A. M. Landgraf, *Dogmengeschichte der Frühscholastik*, Vol. II/1, pp. 320-370.

[75] Thus, for example, Scherzer in H. Schmid, *The Doctrinal Theology of the Evangelical Lutheran Church*, p. 302.

[76] Schleiermacher, *The Christian Faith*, § 98, 1.

[77] Julius Müller, *The Christian Doctrine of Sin* (Edinburgh: T. & T. Clark, 1885), Vol. II, p. 167.

lessness to Jesus' actual freedom from all sin: "Sinlessness . . . does not exclude as such the *possibility* of sinning."[78] Nevertheless, precisely the actual sinlessness of Jesus in the sense of his ethical purity, asserted merely as an experiential fact, won the significance of a basis for the doctrine of Jesus' divinity.[79] The old dogmatics, conversely, had derived Jesus' incapacity for sin from his divinity. Ullmann was aware of this and therefore wanted his argumentation to be understood as apologetical only (p. 185, n. 2). This did not prevent the Ritschlian school from taking Ullmann's ethical legitimation of Jesus' divinity as the only possible dogmatic argument for Jesus' divinity. In substance this idea already can be found in Ullmann himself. "We have the personal living revelation of God in Jesus precisely as the sinlessly holy one" (p. 192). This ethical argument for Jesus' divinity anticipated especially Wilhelm Herrmann's idea that the ethical grandeur of the picture of Jesus' "inner life" becomes for us the revelation of God. Thus Herrmann made the extremely influential apologetic concept of Ullmann the dogmatic heart of his theology. "The shock given us by the vitality of the good life in his (Jesus') person, the judgment over us that we thereby experience, appears to us immediately as a mighty act of the God of whom we have thereby become conscious."[80]

To a Christology taking its point of departure from the man Jesus it must seem reasonable that Jesus' sinlessness is a precondition of our perception of his unity with God. This heightens the force of the question as to where one must seek this sinlessness of Jesus. Both Ullmann and W. Herrmann had Jesus' individual morality in view, and they substituted the appeal to Jesus' morality for the older approach of validating Jesus' divine authority by miracles and prophecies fulfilled in him.[81] But where do we get so much information about Jesus' unbroken and unique ethical grandeur? The New Testament statements that relate to Jesus' sinlessness, none of which is an

[78] Carl Ullmann, *The Sinlessness of Jesus* (Edinburgh: T. & T. Clark, 1870), p. 33. Cf. p. 163: "On the assumption that Jesus was a true, a real man, it cannot of course be denied that it was possible for Him to sin. This possibility is directly involved in human nature, in so far as is to be morally developed." Note also the reference to J. Müller in Ullmann, p. 34, n. 1. Müller, *The Christian Doctrine of Sin*, Vol. II, p. 224, took a position opposing the connection of the *potuit non peccare* with the *peccare non potuit* which Ullmann had still maintained in the third edition of his work.

[79] Ullmann, *The Sinlessness of Jesus*, pp. 199 ff. The following quotation is also taken from this work.

[80] W. Herrmann, *The Communion of the Christian with God*, p. 98; cf. pp. 84 f. and esp. pp. 113 f., where Herrmann also derives Jesus' historical existence from the ethical impression made by the picture of his character, which could not be the product of fantasy. Cf. further, *ZThK*, I (1892), 256 f. In A. Ritschl, *The Christian Doctrine of Justification and Reconciliation*, § 48, the ethical evaluation of Jesus provides the basis for the doctrine of his divinity too (pp. 450 f.), but he nevertheless has in mind Jesus' ethical *vocational activity* in establishing the Kingdom of God and not simply his individual ethical superiority, as was true for Herrmann. E. Günther, *Die Entwicklung*, pp. 59 ff., has accurately seen the anticipation of Herrmann's ideas in Ullmann's presentation of Jesus' sinlessness.

[81] *Ibid.*, p. 58.

authentic saying of Jesus, can in themselves surely not have so much greater authority than other New Testament statements, for example, about miracles performed by Jesus or having happened to him. Why the New Testament statements about Jesus' sinlessness are supposed to be particularly believable must be established on other grounds, especially since the Jews who were his contemporaries seem to have had a quite different opinion about Jesus' sinlessness. If one finds inventing an ideal ethical image less possible than did Herrmann, it becomes very difficult to attain the conviction of the thorough-going moral grandeur of Jesus' personal life through conclusions drawn from the tradition about his individual style of life. Especially the statement that there could have been no isolated exceptions to this overall picture in Jesus' behavior can hardly be justified from this approach. Jesus' sinlessness in the sense of the supposed historical fact of his exemplary moral behavior, without exception, must be considered an extremely insecure foundation for a Christology.[82] Furthermore, an understanding of Jesus' sinlessness merely as an irreproachable moral behavior presupposes an all too superficial concept of sin. In spite of all the justified reserve one may have toward the traditional doctrine of original sin, nevertheless, the indispensable kernel of truth in this doctrine is that sin was understood not merely as an individual deed but as the fundamental condition of the actual existence of man in its ego-centricity and ego-obstructedness to God. If in this way sin characterizes not the essence (the real definition) of human being but its empirical reality— even in the physical basis of our existence—[83] the question of Jesus' sinlessness is raised in a much more radical way. To what extent has Jesus broken through that fundamental condition of actual human existence with which his fall under the power of death is associated?

This problem was at least seen in the older doctrinal position in which Jesus' sinlessness was made possible only by his miraculous birth. However, this reference to the virgin birth does not correspond to the New Testament testimony of Jesus' sinlessness, nor was it intended by the much more tenu-ously asserted legend of the virgin birth itself. Furthermore, such an assumption can justify Jesus exceptional position with respect to the universal human corruption by sin only under the additional, particularly Augustinian, pre-supposition that original sin is transmitted through the libidinous character of human procreation. If we cannot concede to this circumstance such a deep-

---

[82] It was therefore with ample justification that R. Bultmann substituted the concept of the primitive Christian kerygma for his teacher Herrmann's appeal to Jesus' "inner life" (*GuV*, I, 106 f). When today in opposition to Bultmann the foothold of the kerygma in the historical Jesus is sought anew, this necessary question should not lead to reopening the search for Jesus' inwardness, under whatever concepts this might take place. Rather, Jesus' inwardness is accessible to us only in the expression that it found in the external events of his life and in the witness of his community, together with his authentic words and the overall picture that we can derive from his message.

[83] See my preliminary treatment in *Was ist der Mensch?*, pp. 40-49.

seated causality for the entire organic structure of human existence, especially for the centrality and egocentricity of all expressions of human life, then the assumption of the virgin birth cannot accomplish what it was supposed to as an explanation of Jesus' sinlessness. Jesus' breaking through the self-centeredness of human existence cannot be derived from a miraculous birth if the man who thus emerges is to be a man like all others.

If sin is not associated with the essence of the divine destiny of man, but with the structure of present human existence, one cannot conceive of a natural sinlessness of Jesus. It is inconceivable that Jesus was truly man, but that in his corporeality and behavior he was not stamped by the universal structure of centeredness of animal life that is the basis of the self-centeredness of human experience and behavior, but which becomes sin only in man. The conception that at the incarnation God did not assume human nature in its corrupt sinful state but only joined himself with a humanity absolutely purified from all sin contradicts not only the anthropological radicality of sin, but also the testimony of the New Testament and of early Christian theology that the Son of God assumed sinful flesh and in sinful flesh itself overcame sin. The victory over sin had not been attained before Jesus' birth, but only in the entire accomplishment of the course of his existence. Therefore, Karl Barth is right in emphasizing that Jesus "is identical with our nature under the conditions of the fall" (*CD*, I/2, pp. 167 ff.). "Precisely Jesus' sinlessness was in no way a condition of his human being but the *deed* of his life that took this course from its beginning" (*CD*, IV/2, p. 102; cf. IV/1, pp. 284 f.). With this interpretation, Barth follows a doctrinal line that had its nineteenth-century predecessors in Irving, Collenbusch, Menken, Bezzel, Böhl, and above all Hofmann.[84]

But how did Jesus in carrying out the course of his existence overcome the sinful fundamental condition of present human existence? How was the openness to God appropriate to human destiny opened up? For what reason can we speak of a victory of Jesus over sin? That Jesus overcame sin under the conditions of existence of the general bondage to sin, that he lived in openness to God, can only be asserted in the light of the resurrection. It cannot be derived from the dedication to God that Jesus' pre-Easter existence expresses when taken by itself.[85] Jesus' earthly conduct appeared thoroughly ambiguous. He could appear as the man who claimed for himself divine authority. In the light of the egocentricity of the condition of human existence, the claim implied in Jesus' message necessarily made the impression of unlimited pride, of blasphemy. That just this claim to authority was the expression of Jesus' total dedication to God became visible and became reality only through Jesus' resurrection, through the divine confirmation of Jesus

---

84 References in O. Weber, *Grundlagen der Dogmatik*, Vol. II, p. 223; cf. also Dorner's discussion with Irving and Menken, *A System of Christian Doctrine*, Vol. III, pp. 361 ff.
85 Thus O. Weber, *Grundlagen der Dogmatik*, Vol. II, p. 223.

inherent in it. Without Jesus' resurrection, this truth would not only have remained hidden, it would not have become a fact. This is also true in that only the resurrection life is the final, unambiguous victory over the sinful structure of our present life, over the ego locked up inside itself. In Jesus' earthly existence this structure of sin was overcome by the dedication that pulled him beyond his own givenness. But such dedication remained in Jesus' case, as in the life of all other men, ambiguous in the context of his earthly existence until the new life from God, anticipated in Jesus' dedication to the Father, appeared in him. From Jesus' resurrection, light is shed backward upon his earthly life that reveals its true significance. If we recognize in this light God's judgment upon Jesus, the judgment of his sinlessness, we need no longer attempt the impossible task of penetrating into the inner life of the historical Jesus in order to establish there his sinlessness.

God's decision about Jesus' sinlessness has the character of a divine judgment delivered from beyond, as our justification is from beyond ourselves, although in a different way. As our righteousness is not to be sought in the givenness of our earthly existence, so also Jesus' sinlessness is not to be sought in the givenness of his pre-Easter appearance. Jesus' righteousness also lay *extra se* in the hands of the Father, in God's judgment. But in Jesus' case, God's judgment was related back to the unique claim to authority that was implied in Jesus' eschatological message. Thus, Jesus, in the light of the divine judgment delivered in his resurrection, is actually sinless in himself. Christians, on the contrary, achieve righteousness before God only through Jesus. This mediation establishes once more their difference from Jesus: they are not, not even on the basis of God's judgment, righteous and sinless in themselves, but only in Christ, in view of their community with Jesus.

Thus Jesus' sinlessness is not an incapability for evil that belonged naturally to his humanity but results only from his entire process of life. Only through the entire course of Jesus' existence culminating in his resurrection is sin overcome in sinful flesh. In this process the crucifixion of Jesus is the decisive step—in the light of his resurrection. For through the cross of Christ, sinful flesh was condemned and demolished in him who was nonetheless the Son of God, as his resurrection was to prove. Therefore, he was not himself destroyed in this judgment, but emerged the victor. Thus out of the judgment on sin, the new man was raised up in him—and only in him since all other men are destroyed together with their sin.

Thus the victory over sin in Jesus' life is certainly not to be understood in the harmlessness of moral progress, as if Jesus had finally achieved unchangeability in the good—and thus the lack of sinfulness—through moral purification. This interpretation of Theodore of Mopsuestia was rightly rejected by the "three chapters" of the Fifth Ecumenical Council in 553 (Denzinger, 224). By contrast the truth of the formula of the *impeccabilitas Christi* is that in the light of his resurrection, Jesus was without sin from the very beginning, just

363

as he was also the Son of God in the whole of his life and not only after a particular point in time. However, this was decided only by Jesus' resurrection, just as in general only the future event decides the meaning of earthly events. As in the light of his resurrection Jesus is the Son of God in the whole of his existence, so, too, he is sinless, precisely because with the flesh he also took upon himself the sin of humanity and submitted to the death that set the purity of his mission free from all ambiguity.

CHAPTER

10

THE LORDSHIP OF JESUS CHRIST

Shown to be the Son of God by his dedication to the Father,
Jesus is the eschatological ruler toward whom all things are, so
that all things are also through him.

I. JESUS' KINGSHIP

The participation of the man Jesus in the omnipotent Lordship of God
over his creation is the crowning aspect of the unity of God and man in
Jesus Christ. We have found Jesus' unity with God established in his resurrection from the dead with the resulting divine approval of his pre-Easter
activity. Its concrete form as personal unity was seen in the dedication of
Jesus to the Father as Son. The effect, however, and highest expression of
this unity is reached in Jesus' exaltation to participation in God's Lordship.
Once again, a precise understanding of Jesus' Lordship can be acquired only
in the context of the whole of his earthly activity. Certainly in this question
Christology is not restricted to the ministry of the pre-Easter Jesus. Rather,
this involves primarily the present reality of the exalted Lord to be revealed
in the future. But in order to understand that present reality, we must once
again start with the historical Jesus of Nazareth to assure that we do not
speak unknowingly of something quite different under the name of Jesus.
"If the conception of his present Lordship cannot be filled out with definite
characteristics of his earthly ministry, it is either a worthless schema or an
excuse for every possible enthusiasm."[1]

The pre-Easter Jesus did not proclaim his own Lordship, but the coming
kingly rule of the God of Israel whom he called "Father." Thus his activity
stands in the same line with the Old Testament and Jewish hopes of Yahweh's
kingly rule on earth. To be sure, Jesus spoke of the dawn of God's Lordship
in his own activity. But this presence of God's future in Jesus' activity is

[1] A. Ritschl, *The Christian Doctrine of Justification and Reconciliation*, p. 406.

rightly understood only when one has taken seriously the futurity of the Lordship of God whose imminence Jesus proclaimed. Then its "presence" is shown as the overpowering by God's future of all merely present occupations and concerns of men. The future impinges upon the present precisely as future, and thus the future of God's Lordship announced by Jesus remains wholly distinguished from his own activity, as sharply distinguished as the Father himself is distinguished from Jesus, even though the power of God's future is already presently active through its announcement in Jesus' message. If its futurity were forgotten because of this, its present effectiveness would collapse into nothingness.

Thus the pre-Easter Jesus proclaimed the Lordship of another, of the Father. He rejected application of the title of ruler, the Messianic title, to himself, as we have already seen (cf. p. 219, above). Only after his resurrection could his disciples not only identify him with the announced Son of Man, but also relate him to the Messianic expectation, since there was no reason to expect still another one to bring the esch..tological salvation besides Jesus who had been raised from the dead. Thus, the figure of Jesus attracted to himself the traditional eschatological expectations (cf. p. 219, above). The reason for connecting Jesus with the Messianic title in spite of his own explicit refusal was probably offered by the Jewish accusation that he was a messianic pretender, which is preserved in the inscription on the cross (Mark 15:26) and which may well have been the cause of his condemnation by the Roman governor. At first Jesus was probably understood only as the one designated to be the future Messiah, who had been taken away to heaven until the imminent beginning of the end and his appearance as Messiah.[2] Thus the Lordship of Christ as Messiah was originally related to the eschatological future. This future, to be sure, was thought to be immediately near, indeed, to have already begun in Jesus' resurrection. Corresponding to this atmosphere of earliest Christianity, under the influence of the Greek version of Ps. 110:1 (LXX), the Messianic Lordship of Jesus was understood in Hellenistic-Jewish circles as a lordship already taking place in heaven, as Ferdinand Hahn has shown.[3] This conception was found in the pre-Pauline

[2] Thus, for example, Acts 3:19 f.: The Lord (God) will, when the "times of refreshing" come, "send the Christ appointed for you, Jesus, whom heaven must receive until the time for establishing all that God spoke by the mouth of his holy prophets." On this, cf. F. Hahn, *Christologische Hoheitstitel*, pp. 184 f., and the whole section pp. 179-193, for the difference between the removal of Jesus to heaven and the conception of an already accomplished exaltation to Kingship. For the eschatological understanding of the latter, special attention should be paid to Hahn's treatment of Mark 14:61 (identification of Messiah and Son of Man), Matt. 25:31-46 (designation of the Son of Man as *basileus*), and to Rev. 11:15; 12:10.

[3] Whether the transition from the eschatological concept of Jesus' future Messiahship to the concept of exaltation is so abrupt as it appears in Hahn's presentation requires a more precise examination. Apocalyptic also could conceive what is to be revealed in the future as already present in heaven. The transition to the idea of an already present heavenly Lordship of Jesus does not need to be Hellenistically motivated, even though it was sup-

hymn Phil. 2:6 f. (pp. 120 f.). The exaltation mentioned there involves the same act by which Jesus was installed as Son of God in power according to the equally pre-Pauline formulation in Rom. 1:4. In both cases Jesus' resurrection is no longer understood merely as immediate removal to heaven, but at the same time as his installation into the office of the *Kyrios* (Phil. 2:11) or into Sonship (Rom. 1:4), which has already taken place, and thereby as installation into Lordship over the cosmos in place of God himself. The longer the passage of time after the appearances of the resurrected Jesus to his disciples, the clearer it must become that the present Lordship of the resurrected One over the cosmos is a hidden Lordship to be distinguished from the revealed exercise of Lordship by him at his return.[4] In any case, the history of traditions of this theologoumenon shows that the confession of faith in the royal Lordship of Christ himself already present rests on an anticipation of the *eschaton,* similar to the presence of the divine Lordship in Jesus' own activity. It is reality for the time being only in heaven, in a hidden, if superior, mode.

The transition from Jesus' announcement of the imminent Kingdom of God to the confession by his community of Jesus' own kingly rule is to be understood as a materially established step in the primitive Christian history of traditions, not to be judged as an arbitrary leap or even as falling away from Jesus' proclamation. Because Jesus' resurrection confirmed his earthly claim to authority by the fulfillment of the eschatological future in his own person, he no longer just anticipated the judgment of Him with whom the eschatological reality begins as he did in his earthly activity, but he himself has now become in person the reality of the future eschatological salvation. Therefore, it was meaningful to expect his return as the fulfillment of the eschatological saving future and to understand him as the bringer of the eschatological salvation. Differently expressed, through the resurrection, the revealer of God's eschatological will became the incarnation of the eschatological reality itself; the ultimate realization of God's will for humanity and for the whole of creation could therefore be expected from him. Moreover, because Jesus' claim was eschatological in character, no other could be conceived alongside him to bring in the eschatological consummation after the difference between his proclamation and the eschatological reality had been superseded in Jesus' own person. Further, because Jesus as the eschatological revealer of God belongs inseparably to God himself, his eschatologi-

ported by Ps. 110:1 (LXX). The motivation required for this use of Scripture could reside in the apocalyptic idea of the heavenly presence of the one to be revealed in the future in connection with the special situation of the primitive Christian imminent expectation. When the elevation of Enoch to the Son of Man (Eth. Enoch 71:14 ff.) is compared, it corresponds better to the concept of exaltation than to that of Acts 3:20 f.

4 In primitive Christianity, the "revelation of Jesus Christ" at the future end event was expected in this sense: I Cor. 1:7; II Thess. 1:7; I Peter 1:7,13; 4:13. Cf. also the parallel between the eschatological epiphany of Jesus and the coming of his *basileia* in II Tim. 4:1.

cal Lordship could be no longer restricted to the future—even apart from the particular situation of imminent expectation in which the future merged into the present—but was as future Lordship already given in God's eternity and therefore also effective for the present and even for the past, as will be shown more precisely in the next section. Thus Jesus' future eschatological Lordship as such is not only already present for God's eternity—this is true of all future events—but because of his unity with God, Jesus also rules now, from the *eschaton,* out of the course of time, out of the power of God's eternity.[5]

What is the relation between this Lordship of Jesus and the Lordship of the Father whose coming the earthly Jesus had announced? In Jewish eschatology there was apparently a certain tension between the expectation of a messianic kingdom and the expectation of God's own eschatological Kingdom.[6]

Nevertheless, it was possible to bring the two together, as happened in a series of Jewish apocalypses, in such a way that a period of Messianic Lordship preceded the actual eschatological Lordship of God.[7] A combination of this sort is also found in Revelation (ch. 20:1-10). According to this conception, Christ's kingly rule would be a future thousand-year period of history replacing the age of the Roman Empire; only at the end of this period would the Final Judgment come (vs. 11 ff.) and the new creation (ch. 21:1 ff.) with the direct Lordship of God himself (v. 3). Does this "chiliastic" combination of Messianic Kingdom and Lordship of God appropriately express the relation of the Lordship of Jesus Christ to the Lordship of God?

We cannot here evaluate the ecclesiological aspect of chiliasm and its impact on a theology of history. Chiliasm has certainly contributed to keeping alive an aspect of continuity between Christian and Jewish hope and thereby the consciousness in the Christian church that the Kingdom of God is not wholly alien to this earth but will come on this earth and transform it. But the central Christological idea of chiliasm, the chronological succession of the Kingdom of Christ and the Kingdom of God, must be judged false from the perspective of the structure of Sonship that characterizes the unity of Jesus with God and thus his exaltation to participation in God's omnipotent Lordship. There can exist no competition between the Kingdom of the Son

[5] Cf. my preliminary statement about the concept of eternity in *Was ist der Mensch?*, pp. 49 ff.

[6] The heterogeneity of Messianic and theocratic hope has been set forth by Karl Georg Kuhn in *ThD*, I, 574. The extension of the contrast between the Kingdom of God and the expectation of the Messiah to the figure of the Son of Man by P. Vielhauer, "Gottesreich und Menschensohn in der Verkündigung Jesu," *Festschrift für Günter Dehn*, pp. 51-79, has been contradicted by H. E. Tödt, *The Son of Man in the Synoptic Tradition*, pp. 330 ff., and in greater detail by F. Hahn, *Christologische Hoheitstitel*, pp. 27 ff.

[7] Thus in the ten-week apocalypse of Eth. Enoch 91:12 ff.; further, IV Ezra 7:28 f., where a four-hundred-year Lordship of the Messiah is spoken of, and Syr. Baruch, chs. 28 to 30 and 40:3.

and the Kingdom of the Father. For if the Son rules, he rules as the Son, and that means he rules in dedication to the Father and his Lordship. Therefore, the Father establishes his Kingdom precisely through the Son, not apart from him, or beside him, or after his Kingdom. The Kingdom of the Son is also that of the Father and vice versa. When I Cor. 15:28 says that at the end, the Son, after everything is subjugated to him, will subjugate himself to the Father that God may be all in all, this does not simply express for us a limitation of the Lordship of Christ by the Lordship of God, but the fulfillment of the intention constituting the essence of the Lordship of the Son himself, just as the earthly Jesus lived in obedience to his mission totally in dependence upon the Father and in dedication to him. Judged on the basis of Jesus' earthly ministry, the meaning of his own Lordship can only be the establishment of the Lordship of the Father in the world, ultimately and decisively in the coming judgment and renewal of creation. As the Son he brings the entire creation into the obedience of sonship, thereby mediating it into immediacy to the Father. Because the Kingdom of Christ thus finds in the Kingdom of the Father not its limit but rather its fulfillment in dedication to the Lordship of the Father, it does not itself come to an end with the giving over of Lordship to the Father, but will have "no end," as the Confession of Constantinople in 381 says.[8]

Our considerations appear thus to lead to Karl Barth's statement, "Jesus Christ is himself the established Kingdom of God."[9] In a certain sense this statement is undeniable. It requires, however, differentiation. One must pay attention to the peculiar fact that among the patristic theologians only Origen and possibly also Marcion defended this idea with special energy.[10] Did not

[8] H. Denzinger, *Enchiridion symbolorum*, 150; cf. Luke 1:33. Second Peter 1:11 also calls the Lordship of Christ "eternal." But even in Revelation the chiliastic conception is broken by the assertion that the Lordship of the Lamb continues in the consummation: his throne stands beside that of the Father in the New Jerusalem (Rev. 22:3). On the eternity of the Lordship of Christ, cf. also Rev. 11:15. Here, as in Eph. 5:5 and perhaps also II Peter 1:11, the future Kingdom is spoken of explicitly as the Kingdom of God and Christ and thereby the identity of both is expressed. The intention may be similar in the Synoptic expressions that speak of the Kingdom of Christ (Matt. 13:41; 16:28; 20:21; Luke 22:30; 23:42). In his notes to Lietzmann's commentary on Corinthians (*An die Korinther I/II*, p. 193), W. G. Kümmel has convincingly argued that I Cor. 15:28 is not to be interpreted chiliastically, as if after an interim period of Jesus' Kingdom, the Lordship were to be given over to the Father. "Paul merely wants to emphasize here that at the arrival of the *telos* Christ has conquered all spiritual powers and God alone is Lord" (*ibid.*, p. 193). The conception of an interim kingdom is remote from Paul's mind.

[9] Karl Barth, *CD*, II/2, p. 177; cf. *CD*, I/1, pp. 352 f.; IV/2, p. 764.

[10] Origen, in his commentary on Matthew, called Christ the self-lordship (*autobasileia*) of God (on Matt. 18:33: *GCS* 40, p. 289, 20). In Tertullian's writing against Marcion the single sentence is transmitted as his assertion: "In *evangelio est dei regnum Christus ipse* (*Adv. Marc.* IV, 33, 8). According to *CCL*, I, 634, 6 f., however, the last two words (*Christus ipse*) are not original. Against that, R. Frick, *Die Geschichte des Reich-Gottes-Gedankens in der alten Kirche bis zu Origenes und Augustin* (Giessen: A. Töpelmann, 1928), p. 52, n. 1, finds "no adequate basis" to eliminate both words as scribal errors. On

their identification of the Kingdom of God with Jesus Christ himself virtually have the function of eliminating the idea of the Kingdom of God from Jesus' message? Through this identification both theologians suppressed the futurity of the Kingdom of God, which connects Jesus with the Old Testament Jewish expectation. Certainly they had different motives for doing so: Marcion because of his Gnostic dualism, Origen because of his spiritualism.

The necessary differentiations in the assertion of Jesus' unity with the Kingdom of God are already implied in the previous observation that Jesus' Lordship is identical with that of the Father in such a way that Jesus Christ leads all things into obedience to the Lordship of the Father that is distinguished from him because he is the Son. Precisely by distinguishing himself from the Father and his Lordship, by serving the Lordship of the Father as the Lordship of another in dedication of himself, so and only so is Jesus one with the Lordship of the Father. The eschatological tension that characterizes the entire activity and destiny of Jesus may not be ignored. Otherwise, the difference between Father and Son is also lost with the loss of the difference between future and present, between the Lordship of God and Jesus' own historical activity. As the Son is identical with the Father only in the self-dedication of his obedience as the Son through which he lets the Father be wholly and completely God and Father, so God's future is present in Jesus' activity only in that he lets it be wholly and completely future, and certainly God's future, beside which all else pales. Only in the mode of such self-dedication to the point of self-sacrifice does Jesus share as Son in the Lordship of the Father.[11] Revelation speaks very pregnantly of the Lordship and throne of the "Lamb." Only in the absolute sacrifice of himself, dedicated to the will of the Father to reconcile humanity, is Jesus the eschatological ruler. Only thus is his Lordship identical with that of the Father. The expectation of the coming Kingdom of God, the Father in heaven, thus remains the horizon for understanding the Lordship of Jesus Christ himself.

The coming Lordship of Christ that will establish the Kingdom of the Father on earth is still hidden on earth today. To be sure, the powers that rule the world must serve against their will the coming Kingdom of the Father and thus also the Lordship of him who proclaimed this Kingdom. They must already pay homage to the ruler Jesus Christ, as the primitive Christian hymns sing (Phil. 2:10 f.; cf. Eph. 1:21 f.). However, this homage occurs presently only in "heaven," in the dimension of divine eternity hidden

Origen, Frick (p. 11) thinks that precisely in this point Origen understood Jesus correctly. This judgment is shared by Karl Ludwig Schmidt in *ThD*, I, 589.

[11] To this extent, Luther rightly stressed that the Kingdom of Jesus Christ is the Lordship of the crucified: *Rex iste sic regnat, ut omnia, quae in lege sperastis, contemnenda, omnia, quae timuistis, amanda doceat, crucem mortemque proponit (WA* 5, p. 69, 1 f.). Similarly, F. Lau has recently characterized the confession to Jesus' royal Lordship as "paradoxical language" ("Die Königsherrschaft Jesu Christi und die lutherische Zweireichelehre," *KuD*, VI (1960), 306-326, esp. pp. 312 ff.).

to us. On earth only the Christians now confess to Jesus as Lord of the world publicly. Through the message of Christ, the knowledge of Jesus' royal Lordship as the fulfillment of Israel's hope for the Kingdom of its God is now spread abroad among men, and Christian worship resounds with homage to the eschatological ruler, of whom the world as yet knows nothing. The world still knows nothing precisely when it thinks it knows enough to be able to translate this knowledge to the agenda of everyday affairs.

Into what relation does this put the church to the royal Lordship of Jesus? Do Christians hope only for their future participation in the Lordship of Christ when it will be revealed in this world with his return in judgment? Or is the Kingdom of Christ already realized now in the church's proclamation of Jesus' Kingdom and in the Christians' confession of him? The answer to this question is not easy and can hardly be given in the sense of these alternatives. The future hope and the presence of salvation interpenetrate one another in the New Testament witnesses to the Lordship of Christ as was similarly the case in Jesus' proclamation of the Kingdom of God. With respect to the Lordship of Christ, the situation is complicated because the different primitive Christian witnesses stress in part the future aspect, in part the aspect of the presence of salvation.[12] For Paul for whom the Lordship of Christ was an already present fact, it seems that the full participation of Christians in the Kingdom of Christ as in his Sonship (Rom. 8:19 f.) was still a future matter.[13] By contrast, Colossians says that Christians have already been brought out of darkness into the Kingdom of the Son (Col. 1:13), although it also says that the Christians' life is still hidden with Christ in

[12] Here the aspect of the eschatological future is clearly dominant: thus in Matt. 13:41; 16:28; 20:21 (on the futurity of the Kingdom of God in Matthew, cf. the study by G. Bornkamm, "End-expectation and Church in Matthew," *Tradition and Interpretation in Matthew*, Günther Bornkamm, Gerhard Barth, and Heinz Joachim Held [The New Testament Library; The Westminster Press, 1963], pp. 15-51; *Matthäusevangelium*, 1960; first published 1956), and also in Luke 1:33; 22:29 f.; 23:42 (cf. Hans Conzelmann, *The Theology of St. Luke*, tr. by Geoffrey Buswell [Harper & Row, Publishers, Inc., 1961], pp. 118 f.). Conzelmann opposes the application of the concept of an interim kingdom, which has also been attempted for Luke; in general he emphasizes that the realization of the Kingdom is held by Luke to reside in the future, while the image of the Kingdom through Jesus and his proclamation of the Kingdom is present. In Ephesians (ch. 5:5), Second Timothy (ch. 4:1,18), and Second Peter (ch. 1:11), what is said about the Kingdom of Christ is in any case clearly referred to the eschatological future. Only John 18:36 and Col. 1:13 consider the Kingdom of Christ as a present, though transcendent, reality, whereby the presence of the Kingdom of Christ is conceived quite differently in both writings.
[13] In I Cor. 6:2 f., Paul expects Christians to participate as judges in the coming judgment of the world; in ch. 4:8 he charges the Corinthians with thinking they have already attained lordship. Thus it is probable that for his thinking participation in Christ's Lordship belongs still to the future. This is also a consequence of the fact that, according to Paul, Christians' participation in Jesus' resurrection, through which Jesus has been installed as ruler, still lies in the future. He expects the "inheritance" of the Kingdom of God in one way or another in the future, so that from this point of view, too, there is no reason to consider Kingdom of God and Kingdom of Christ as two different things.

God (Col. 3:3 f.). On the other hand, Paul calls the Christians sons of God now (Rom. 8:14; Gal. 4:6 f.). And doubtless Paul's own mission through the *Kyrios* Jesus Christ had for him the character of a sovereign act of the Lord who is now exalted in heaven to the position of the eschatological ruler.

In summary it may be said that the exalted Lord already rules in his church (as also in the world) and is recognized by the Christians (in distinction from the world) as ruler, but that the full participation of Christians in the Kingdom of Christ still belongs to the future. The Lordship of Christ in his church, as Luther said, occurs through the Word of the gospel.[14] This constitutes its unique character as opposed to all political lordship with which we are otherwise familiar. The rule of Jesus Christ in his church consists in the elimination of the distinction between ruler and ruled. Men are incorporated into the Kingdom of the Son by being bound to Jesus through the proclamation that awakens faith, through Baptism and Lord's Supper, by being shaped to the likeness of the Son of God (Rom. 8:29; cf. the futuristic formulation I Cor. 15:49), and thus by being taken up into Jesus' relation of Sonship to the Father (Rom. 8:15b; cf. Gal. 4:5 f.). The more exact examination of the various modes of community with Jesus—through confession of him and through keeping his words, through Baptism and the Lord's Supper, through prayer in Jesus' name, and including all these, through trust in the promise of him who was sent from God and guarantees in his own person participation in God's eschatological future—forms the central task of the doctrine of the church and cannot be undertaken here. We only maintain that in all these forms of community with him, Jesus rules his community by transforming Christians into his likeness and thus by mediating the individual into the relation of sonship to the Father, which is the structure of the coming Kingdom of God.

Because Jesus Christ is already recognized by the Christian community as the eschatological king and because Christians are incorporated into the Kingdom of Christ through the preaching of the church, so that it is possible to speak of an administration of this Kingdom through the proclamation of the gospel, the church itself was easily understood as the Kingdom of Christ. This idea became influential especially through Augustine, who with Tyconius interpreted the thousand-year Kingdom of the Messiah of Rev., ch. 20, as the time of the church between the resurrection and return of

---

14 Luther, *WA* 7, p. 743, 1; also *WA* 10/1/1, p. 176,18; *WA* 11, p. 249, 33-35. In reference to this, Werner Elert, *The Structure of Lutheranism*, tr. by Walter A. Hansen (Concordia Publishing House, 1962), pp. 491 ff. (Section 35: "The Kingdom of Christ"); *idem*, "Regnum Christi," *Zwischen Gnade und Ungnade* (1948), pp. 72-91; and the important book of G. Forck, *Die Königsherrschaft Jesu Christi bei Luther* (Berlin: Evangelische Verlagsanstalt, 1959). One will have to concede that Luther's understanding of the proclamation of the gospel as the act of the Lordship of Christ the King corresponds to Paul's self-understanding as we have just touched upon it. However, Luther did not retain as strictly as Paul the eschatological character of the Christian's participation in the Kingdom of Christ.

Jesus.[15] Even the Reformation did not distinguish in principle between the Kingdom of Christ and the church.[16] Here the loss or at least the loosening of the eschatological tension that was characteristic for the primitive Christian understanding of Jesus' royal Lordship is expressed.[17] To be sure, Jesus Christ rules his church now, publicly and directly, but the church is only a precursory form of the Kingdom of Christ. It belongs to his Kingdom, but it is not yet the whole of this Kingdom and is only its form of weakness. Its form of glory will only be revealed with Jesus' return to earth. The identification of the church with the Kingdom of Christ is thus subject to objections basically similar to those against the Constantinian idea of the Christian empire as the earthly representation of the heavenly royal Lordship of Jesus.[18] The Kingdom of Christ is identical neither with a particular political order of Christendom nor with the church, precisely because it is the reality of the *eschaton*. This eschatological reality certainly affects the present on the basis of Jesus' resurrection through the preaching of God's revelation in Christ. Thereby the church is constituted as a preliminary form of the Kingdom of Christ. In its community it anticipates the coming reality of the Kingdom of God that will bring the fulfillment of the social destiny of man, of the destiny of the individual to community with all other men.[19] But the church is not itself the consummated society under the Lordship of God. Therefore, it must always climb over the barriers of its own earthly form in anticipation of the eschatological Kingdom of God as its own future. This corresponds to the church's own unique task in calling attention to the eschatological future of salvation distinguished from the present and opening up access to it by mediating community with the crucified Jesus of Nazareth who has been exalted to be the eschatological ruler. Only where the difference between the church and the Lordship of Christ remains clear is a traditionalist hardening of the forms of church life at least in principle arrested. Thereby nothing in the church—neither its traditional piety nor its legal order, nor traditional interpretations of the saving truth or of the rule of Christ in the church taking place through preaching—may escape the renewing power of God's future, of Christ's eschatological Lordship. Admittedly, the renewal of the church can never take place other than as reformation. All new impulses transforming the present form of the church must show themselves to be

15 On this, see R. Frick, *Die Geschichte des Reich-Gottes-Gedankens in der alten Kirche bis zu Origenes und Augustin,* pp. 138-152.

16 W. Elert, *The Structure of Lutheranism,* p. 492, on "Apology," IV, 16,52, and pp. 500 f.

17 In this judgment, I agree with G. Gloege, *RGG,* V (3d ed.), 927, art. "Reich Gottes."

18 On this, see E. Peterson, *Der Monotheismus als politisches Problem* (1935), p. 78, and H. Berkhof, *Kirche und Kaiser* (Zollikon-Zurich: Evangelischer Verlag A. G., 1947), pp. 98 ff.

19 I have considered more precisely the relation of hope for the Kingdom of God to the quest for justice and thus to the whole sphere of social life in my article "Zur Theologie des Rechts," *ZEE,* VII (1963), 1-23, esp. pp. 17 ff.

effects of the renewing future of Jesus Christ by revealing the origin of the church, the significance indwelling the historical activity and destiny of Jesus, in a new and more profound way, or can be recognized on the basis of a better perception of the origin of the church. Because eschatological reality has already begun in the historical appearance of Jesus, the church will always expect its future to be opened from the perspective of its historical origin. However, such ever new "interpretation" of the church's origin must not be tacked on externally, but must force itself upon inquiry into the historical reality of Jesus of Nazareth on the basis of established historical findings, such inquiry being always responsible to its own present situation. Just this kind of new interpretation of the Christian origin is the specific effect of the future of Jesus Christ on his church. Thus the church is not itself the Kingdom of Christ, but is ruled by its exalted Lord through his Spirit and lives toward the future revelation of his Kingdom on earth.

The question whether the Lordship of Christ over Christians is restricted to the preaching and life of the church or whether it goes beyond this to include the formation of social life belongs to the most controversial contemporary dogmatic themes. In this discussion it is agreed that the royal Lordship of Christ extends in fact to the whole of creation and so to the whole sphere of political events that must serve it against its knowledge and will. The question is whether on the basis of the confession of faith in Christ's royal Lordship, political life can be directly structured. In particular, Karl Barth and his friends answer this question affirmatively.[20] On the other hand, in the tradition of the Lutheran doctrine of the two Kingdoms, it is emphasized that the political sphere is the place for merely worldly-political considerations in the context of the divine will to preservation and that every argumentation on the basis of the Lordship of Christ for concrete political tasks signifies a legalizing of the gospel.[21] In the context of Christology, this dispute cannot be discussed in all its aspects. We must restrict ourselves to what is directly relevant to the understanding of the royal Lordship of Christ. On the basis of our conclusions about the eschatological character of the Kingship of Jesus Christ, we must first agree with the Lutheran theologians as they bring this character, as well as the hiddenness of the Lordship of Christ in the present world, to the fore.[22] The hiddenness of the Lordship of Jesus Christ

[20] Karl Barth, *Rechtfertigung und Recht* (Zollikon: Verlag der Evangelischen Buchhandlung, 1938), pp. 20 f., 45: In that the church "proclaims the coming Kingdom of Christ and thus also justification through faith alone," it is what "establishes and preserves the state" in the creaturely sphere. See further esp. Ernst Wolf, "Die Königsherrschaft Christi und der Staat," *Theologische Existenz heute,* Neue Folge 64 (1958), 20-61. Further literature there.

[21] Thus, e.g., W. Künneth, *Politik zwischen Dämon und Gott* (Berlin: Lutherisches Verlagshaus, 1954), pp. 77, 534 f.

[22] *Ibid.,* pp. 40, 54, 77, *et al.;* H. Thielicke, *Theologische Ethik* (Tübingen: J. C. B. Mohr [Paul Siebeck], 1958), Vol. II/2, pp. 727 f. (§ 4166 ff.); W. Trillhaas, *Ethik* (Berlin: A. Töpelmann, 1959), p. 428; G. Hillerdal, *Gehorsam gegen Gott und Menschen:*

is not fully expressed in that only Christendom, and not yet the whole world, perceives Jesus as the Lord over all creation. In addition it means that the church itself in all its aspects is only a provisional form of the Kingdom of Christ. Further, it means that life under the Lordship of Christ in this world repeatedly leads Christians to a participation in the cross of Jesus. However, to interpret the Lordship of Christ in the life of Christians primarily on the basis of Jesus' cross would mean to abbreviate the primitive Christian understanding of discipleship. Participation in the cross of Jesus, where it actually happens, is always only the consequence of the Christian's mission, just as the cross of Jesus must be seen not as the content of Jesus' mission but as the consequence of his being sent to preach the imminent Kingdom of God. Jesus' obedience as Son expressed itself first of all in dedication to his divine mission of announcing the Kingdom of God. The community of Jesus Christ now shares in this mission by proclaiming the coming Kingdom of God as the Lordship of Jesus Christ who now exercises Lordship over the whole creation in hidden superiority (in heaven). It is the task of Christian preaching to call the whole world into the obedience of sonship to the Father and his coming Kingdom. This task is not merely restricted to certain definite spheres of life, certainly not to the sphere of private behavior. Such a restriction would simply express, in a rather revealing way, the split between public and private life that has become characteristic for bourgeois society.[23] It is the unquestionable right of those theologians who champion the political consequences of the confession of faith in the royal Lordship of Christ that they oppose with Barmen II the conception "as if there were spheres of our life in which we belonged not to Jesus Christ but to other lords, spheres in which we do not require justification and sanctification through him." Hope in the Kingdom of God is related to the political common life of men in a special way from the perspective of its origin, namely, as the promise of an ultimate political and legal order of human society under the Lordship of Yahweh. By contrast, the church is only the provisional community of those who wait for the coming Kingdom of God proclaimed by Jesus of Nazareth as realization of true community, of the true totality of political life. Therefore, as the advance division of the coming society, the church will call the attention of present society to the future promised to it.

Of course, the proclamation of the royal Lordship of Christ in the sphere

Luthers Lehre von der Obrigkeit und die moderne evangelische Staatsethik (Stockholm: Srenska kyrkams diakonistyrelsis bokforlag, 1954), pp. 276 ff.; P. Althaus, *The Theology of Martin Luther,* p. 31; F. Lau, *KuD,* VI (1960), 320 f.

23 E. Wolf, *Barmen* (Munich: Chr. Kaiser Verlag, 1957), pp. 113 f., has rightly called attention to the contrast between Barmen II and such "privatizing of Christian life." "For the statement that religion is a 'private matter' is a statement which contradicts the gospel." Here is an inescapable tension between the Christian proclamation and a fundamental element in the structure of bourgeois society, as well as to many forms of bourgeois democracy.

of political life can get its content neither through Biblicistic argumentation nor through Christological conclusions by analogy. It must penetrate theologically to the core of the given social situation. This can be done only in the context of the announcement of God's Kingdom, which will bring the fulfillment of justice among men. The Lordship of Christ can lead Christian proclamation in the political sphere only in its orientation toward the coming Kingdom of God the Father. Above all, however, the question of political consequences of the Lordship of Christ cannot lead to the political establishment of the Kingdom of Christ in the form of a Christian state—in the exclusive sense that this state should be the only Christian one. Such theocratic or Christocratic programs ignore the provisional character of all Christian structuring of life in view of the eschatological future of the Kingdom of God and of Jesus Christ, and thus imply a virtually anti-Christian element. In the common life of men to the end of this world there will always be tendencies and circumstances that more or less mark that abstract bringing of the political order into the free obedience of sonship. To the extent that the order of states still requires force because of the willfullness of its members, it cannot become a pure representation of free obedience to God's Lordship. However, if one remains conscious of the provisionalness of all Christian structuring of life and thus also of political life, the decisive consideration becomes the more or less of the nearness of our political order to the Kingdom of God, which will be at the same time and as such the kingdom of fulfilled humanity. Thus, even Luther recognized a ministry of the Christian as official in a society oriented to the Lordship of Christ.[24] As in the private sphere of life, so also in social common life and its concrete structuring, effects of Christian thought, anticipations of the coming Lordship of God, are possible.

In the sense of such a provisionalness that always is to be superseded, the idea of a Christianly determined society, Christian parties (in the plural), and Christian states would be defensible. It is not necessarily reprehensible that political organizations orient themselves to Christian motives and make such orientation in principle the foundation of their program—if they are not simply adding thereby an ideological decoration to interests of a completely different sort. If political activity is concerned with the appropriate mastery of the given social situation, at least the creatively anticipatory view for what is really necessary and possible depends on the mental capacity on the basis of which one makes one's judgments. Christians, through their knowledge of the eschatological Lordship of God and Jesus Christ, as well

[24] This point of view may have been too one-sidedly pushed into the foreground by G. Forck in his work cited in n. 14 above, and esp. in his article in *KuD*, III (1957)—cf. the critique by F. Lau, *KuD*, VI (1960), 321—but his attempt to place obedience to the commandment of love and thus to the Lordship of Christ over the differentiation of the two realms does contain "an element of truth," as Lau, *ibid.*, also concedes.

as of the differentiation between the present and the future to which it is referred, could offer a greater impartiality of view for what is really necessary and possible. To be sure, in this as well as in other things it is also correct to say that Christians often fail to demonstrate such impartiality. Where programs or orders structured on the basis of Christian motives are held to be solely true or unchangeable because of their Christian motivation, that ignorance of the provisional character of a Christian structuring of life would be at work which has given talk about Christian states or parties a justifiably bad reputation.

Because in the light of the *eschaton* all Christian structuring of life in both the public and private spheres remains provisional and therefore ambiguous, the church must continue to exist as an independent institution alongside the state, even if the latter or the society that bears it were wholly determined by the Christian spirit. The separate existence of the church remains necessary in order to open up access for men beyond the provisionalness of present life to the ultimacy of the coming Kingdom of God in which alone human destiny can find its ultimate fulfillment. Thus a church that is permeated by the eschatological future of the Kingdom of God and therefore is also conscious of its own provisional character will by its mere existence be a reminder of the transitoriness of the political order in whose sphere it lives. The separate existence of the church can be useful to society by freeing it for constantly new possibilities of political formation that transcend its present form of existence.

The provisionalness of all present Christian structuring of life, following from the eschatological essence of Christ's Lordship, contributes its share to the hiddenness of the Lordship of Christ in this world. But this hiddenness of the form of the glory of Christ's Kingdom until the *eschaton* does not justify Christians' limiting themselves to their private sphere of an inner-churchly province. Because they wait for the Kingdom of the Father on earth, they cannot divorce themselves from the problems of political life. Even the hiddenness of the Kingdom of God under the cross will be experienced only by those who participate in Jesus' mission of proclamation of the Kingdom of God on this earth.

The eschatological character of Christ's Kingdom in its unity with the Kingdom of God has proved decisive for its relation to the church, as well as for the political structuring of a Christianly determined society. It is no less significant for understanding the cosmic aspect of Christ's Lordship, as will be shown in the next two sections. The rediscovery since the turn of the century of the eschatological character of Jesus' own message as well as of the message of primitive Christianity makes it possible today to bring to bear, even in dogmatics, the fundamental eschatological element of the faith in the Lordship of Christ in new radicality, in contrast to its neglect since the early church. Accordingly, the orthodox Protestant doctrine of the three forms of the Kingdom of Christ as *regnum potentiae, regnum gratiae,* and *regnum gloriae* must be critically revised. There the breadth of eschatological reference was cut short as it became a special theme alongside and following others. *Regnum potentiae* and *regnum gratiae* are not to be understood as independent entities subsequently followed by a *regnum gloriae*. We have already seen that *regnum gratiae* is not an independent province of lordship, perhaps identifiable with the institutional church, alongside the coming Kingdom of Christ. The proclamation of the church, rather, involves the hope for the coming Kingdom of God, which as such—as coming and therefore through faith and hope—is already present in love. The kingdom of power is likewise to be seen wholly at one with the coming kingdom of glory. The kingdom of power is nothing else than the hidden ordering of all things toward the coming Kingdom of God and so toward the preacher of this Kingdom, Jesus of Nazareth. We must now turn our attention especially to this side of the Lordship of Christ.[25]

II. THE SUMMATION OF HUMANITY IN JESUS CHRIST

The participation of the resurrected Jesus in the omnipotent Lordship of God means Lordship not only over his church, but also over the cosmos. In order to achieve an understanding of this idea, we must first examine the place of Jesus in human history. Only in this way is it possible to discover Jesus' relation to creation as a whole by considering the place of humanity in the totality of the world.

Most primitive Christian writers sought to account for the place of Jesus in the history of humanity. The Pauline ideas about the first and Second Adam and about the relation of Jesus' appearance to the era of the law and to God's promise to Abraham belong here, as does the Johannine connection of Jesus' activity with the light from creation illuminating all men. The entire theme of the primitive Christian proof from Scripture is concerned with demonstrating the place of Jesus, first in the history of Israel, then in human history generally. Jesus' history was understood as predicted or interpreted in advance by the words of Scripture. This means that Jesus' history is not a chain of irrelevant accidents, but was anticipated in God's plan for history in the way that it happened. This way of thinking had its roots in the question about Jesus' relation to Jewish expectation of a final salvation in general.

[25] The understanding of the Kingdom of Christ in the light of the *eschaton*, the *regnum gloriae*, which is presented here, contrasts sharply with Schleiermacher's attempt (*The Christian Faith*, § 105) to reduce the three forms of the Kingdom of Christ as customarily distinguished in orthodox Protestant dogmatics to the *regnum gratiae*. To be sure, Schleiermacher's effort shows the much praised churchliness of his theology, but it also shows complete failure to recognize the eschatological essence of the Kingdom of God and of the Lordship of Christ.

His followers may have sought during his earthly life indications in his behavior as to whether he were the Messiah or the eschatological prophet promised by Scripture. This naturally was more than ever the case after Easter. Probably it was first in the Jerusalem passion tradition that the details of Jesus' life were first interpreted point for point as fulfillment of Old Testament predictions. For primitive Christianity, the earthly failure of Jesus' mission was apparently a stumbling block that called with special forcefulness for a detailed explanation of divine necessity. The concern of Matthew's Gospel to confirm as many individual elements in the Jesus tradition as possible as the fulfillment of particular words of Scripture represents a similar way of thinking expanded to the whole of Jesus' life and expressed not in mere allusions to Scripture but in explicit reflection on the fulfillment of certain predictions in Jesus' life.

Luke elaborated the method of proof from Scripture into a carefully considered systematic theology of history.[26] Repeatedly, Luke called attention explicitly to the plan of God that determines the course of history and the activity of Jesus in it down to the last detail.[27] This plan includes not only Israel but world history as well (cf. only Acts 17:26). In this light, Jesus is the predestined Messiah (Acts 3:20), the divinely ordained Judge of the living and the dead (Acts 10:42). In that Jesus' activity in the framework of the divine plan forms the center of gravity toward which everything else is aimed because God's salvation[28] has appeared in him, all that happens is directed toward Jesus by divine plan. Jesus is elected not just for himself, but to a very specific function in the whole of saving history and thus for the whole of humanity.[29] He is the Messiah and Judge who was already characterized during his earthly activity as the bearer of the Spirit of God.[30] Because Jesus' election and God's plan for history that is aimed toward his activity are so closely related that only the election of Jesus to be the coming Messiah and Judge consummates (and thus constitutes as well) God's plan, Jesus is for Luke the ruling center of history by virtue of his divine predestination.

[26] This has been shown by H. Conzelmann, *The Theology of St. Luke*, pp. 149-169, 185 ff. Cf. also U. Wilckens, *Die Missionsreden der Apostelgeschichte*, esp. pp. 200 ff.

[27] H. Conzelmann, *The Theology of St. Luke*, pp. 151 ff. See Acts 1:7 and esp. ch. 20:27 (cf. ch. 20:20) and, for the content, chs. 2:23; 4:24 ff.

[28] For Luke's conception of salvation, Acts 4:12 is especially characteristic; see Wilckens, *Die Missionsreden der Apostelgeschichte*, pp. 44 f., 184 ff. Also, Ernst Haenchen, *Die Apostelgeschichte* (13th ed.; Göttingen: Vandenhoeck & Ruprecht, 1961), p. 176.

[29] Thus Luke clarifies the heavenly Voice that according to the tradition (Mark 1:11 and parallels; 9:7 and parallels; cf. II Peter 1:17) had been heard at Jesus' baptism and transfiguration: "Thou art my beloved Son," in that he substitutes *eklelegmenos* for *agapētos* in his version of the transfiguration (Luke 9:35b).

[30] H. Conzelmann, *The Theology of St. Luke*, pp. 179 ff. Conzelmann calls attention to the fact that Luke no longer understands the Spirit eschatologically, but connects it with the specific activity of the pre-Easter Jesus, as shown in the Lucan connection of Spirit and *dynamis* (pp. 182 f.).

Luke was not the first in primitive Christianity to suggest the idea of demonstrating Jesus' incomparable significance for all humanity on the basis of his function in the divine plan of salvation. Its origin may be sought in the apocalyptic background of the primitive Christian history of traditions. In Luke the apocalyptic concept of the divine plan for history was already deeschatologized and transposed into the picture of a saving history reaching its climax in Jesus Christ as the center of time. In so doing, Luke apparently had some difficulty expressing the uniqueness of Jesus as bringer of salvation within the new context of his overall conception. That had been no problem for Paul because he saw Jesus' significance grounded in the fact that in him the final eschatological destiny of humanity to "sonship" had already appeared. Not only humanity but the whole creation waits, according to Paul, for the revelation of the sonship that has already appeared in Jesus as the Son of God in Christians (Rom. 8:29). Thereby God's plan for history is characterized in one sentence. Paul had this plan of history in mind also in the contrast of the first and Second Adam (Rom. 5:12 ff.; I Cor. 15:21 f., 45 ff.) and its concrete form occupied his attention in Rom., chs. 9 to 11, and Gal. 3:1 to 4:7. While Rom. 8:29 speaks only of a predestination of believers to participation in the sonship that has already appeared in Jesus Christ, an explicit indication of the relation of Jesus' own appearance to the divine plan for history is found in the brief summary of a theology of history in Gal. 4:1-7: "But when the time had fully come, God sent forth his Son . . . so that we [namely, men after the Son had ransomed them from the law] might receive adoption as sons" (Gal. 4:4).[31] Here the fullness of time means the end of the temporal course of human history. In distinction from Luke's conception of history, it still has eschatological meaning. The eschatological fullness of time and the mission of the Son to the fulfillment of humanity through sonship belong materially together. "The arrival of the terminal point of the world, the ending of time, is revealed in the sending of the Son of God as the eternal divine basis, means, and goal of existence" (I Cor. 8:6; Col. 1:13 ff.).[32] What Paul showed in other places in the *content* of the concept of Sonship—or the Second Adam—namely, that it involves the fulfillment of being human, he here indicated by calling attention to the place in God's plan allocated to the mission of the Son. This locus is not unessential. If the "fulness of time" had not come with the appearance of Sonship in Jesus, if the entire creation were not waiting for this event because it is structurally disposed toward it, sonship would not be what it meant for Paul. Here, too, theological reflection on God's plan for history directs attention to the

[31] On the apocalyptic background of the phrase "fulness of time" (cf. also Eph. 1:10), see Heinrich Schlier, *Der Brief an die Galater* (11th ed.; Göttingen: Vandenhoeck & Ruprecht, 1951), pp. 137 f. The substantial relation to Rom., ch. 8, is made certain by the designation of the impartation of sonship as the purpose of Jesus' mission.

[32] *Ibid.*, p. 138.

significance of Jesus' appearance for humanity, namely, that all human history is ordered toward him.

The introduction to Ephesians brought the Pauline idea of the divine plan for history climaxing in the appearance of Sonship in Jesus Christ to its most pregnant expression. Before the foundation of the world, God elected Christians to receive sonship through Jesus Christ (Eph. 1:4 f.). His eternal plan and decision "for the fulness of time"[33] is to "unite all things in him, things in heaven and things on earth" (v. 10). Thus Christians are elected "in" Jesus Christ, in community with him, to the extent that they consciously participate in the summation of the universe in him and in the ordering of all things toward him in that this plan of God is revealed to them (v. 9). Here not only the universal significance of Jesus for the history of humanity is expressed by referring his appearance to God's plan for history, but going even farther, the meaning of his appearance itself is given in the assertion that "everything" with which God's plan for history has to do will be embraced in him.[34] This idea was contained in substance in the Pauline conceptions of Jesus as the Son and as the New Adam. But now this idea is extended along the lines of Rom. 8:19 to include the whole creation. Everything is predestined toward Jesus, and he is predestined to the summation of this whole. Jesus' predestination is his destiny to reconcile the universe in the literal sense that everything will be taken up into sonship.

Primarily, of course, this involves the summation of humanity. Especially in this sense the formulation of Ephesians was influential in early Christianity. According to Irenaeus, Justin had said that the only-begotten Son came to us in order to unite his creatures in himself,[35] and Ignatius spoke of God's plan of salvation directed toward the new man.[36] Irenaeus connected both the idea of the order of salvation directed toward the new man (*Adv. haer.* III, 17, 4; 23,1) and the idea of the recapitulation of humanity in Jesus Christ together. Through the new man, the summation of humanity takes place.

In the sphere of influence of this theological concept of history, Christ's predestination to be the head of humanity is closely connected with the divine plan for history that is fulfilled in the appearance of the Son on earth. The predestination of Christ does not mean just the divine election of this particular man for his own sake, but is related from the very beginning to all humanity to be reconciled. In just this relation, Jesus is the head of humanity

---

[33] Thus O. Michel in *ThW*, V, 155, on Eph. 1:10. *Oikonomia* means both the plan and its execution (administration)—the emphasis here is on the latter. The apocalyptic term *mystērion* (v. 9) also has the sense of "plan of salvation." Cf. the article by G. Bornkamm on this word in *ThW*, IV, 809-834, esp. pp. 826 f.

[34] H. Schlier has rightly emphasized that the idea *anakephalaiōsis* contains on the one hand the element of summation in Christ as the *head* and on the other the summation itself as something new in comparison with what is summed up in it (*ThD*, III, 682, esp. n. 4.).

[35] Irenaeus, *Adv. haer.* IV,6,2: *Suum plasma in semetipsum recapitulans*, MPG 7/1, 987.

[36] Ignatius, *Eph.* 20:1: *Oikonomias eis ton kainon anthrōpon Iēsoun Christon.*

that is embraced in him. In medieval Scholasticism, however, this unified conception of a theology of history was dissolved.

The themes of Christ's predestination and the divine decree of salvation establishing the incarnation split asunder. Thus Thomas Aquinas handles the divine decree as the motive of the incarnation at the beginning of his Christology (*Summa theologica* III, 1); but only toward the end of his Christology does he come to the questions of whether Christ was predestined as a man and whether his predestination is the prototype and cause of our predestination (III, 24). In this disjunction of a theme that belonged together in the New Testament and in primitive Christian theology, one must see, perhaps, a consequence of the abstractness in conceiving the question of the election of the individual as it became characteristic of the Augustinian tradition. In Augustine himself, the understanding of the divine election seems to be embedded in his theology of creation and history. Subsequently, however, certain of his discussions directed toward the election or rejection of a particular individual (picking up the Pauline examples from Rom. 9:9 ff. which have often been used in a similarly isolated way) determined decisively the history of the doctrine of predestination. Thus the theme of divine predestination as election or nonelection of a particular individual to salvation was loosed from the question of God's plan for history. This resulted, on the one hand, in loss of the insight that God's eternal election is decided not in a hidden divine decree outside of history, but within history itself through Jesus Christ, in the relation of men to him. On the other hand, it was no longer seen clearly that Jesus' predestination forms the keystone in the divine plan for history and is thereby the expression of Jesus' Lordship as head of all humanity. Occasionally, as by Albertus Magnus, the election of Jesus to be the head of humanity was presented as a separate element of doctrine.[37] Thomas Aquinas also treated the election of Christ as the cause of our election (*Summa theologica* III, 24, 4). However, he permitted such causality only with reservations: the actual attainment of our salvation is mediated in Christ's execution of the divine decree, but not with respect to the act of election itself which extends to all the elected at the same time. This latter element is very characteristic for the remarkably abstract approach that relates God's eternal election directly to single individuals without any reference to the divine plan for history. Later in the famous controversy between the Thomists and the Scotists about whether Jesus' human nature was predestined to unification with the Logos even apart from Adam's sin, some connection between the ideas about Christ's predestination and the theme of the saving

---

[37] Albertus Magnus, in *I. Sent. dist.* 40 a. 9, posed the question: *An praedestinatio multiplicetur secundum singulos praedestinatos, vel omnes praedestinati sint in uno?* He answered: the *gratia formaliter gratificans* of predestination, to be sure, applies to each individual particularly, to the extent that he is predestined, but it is mediated through a grace that comes from Christ: *Est etiam gratia expediens nostram gratiam ad actum quoad hoc ut possit nobis valere, et quoad hanc praedestinati sumus in Christo.*

history can be seen. Thomas had answered the question negatively in the introduction to his Christology (*Summa theologica* III, 1,3) without reference to the predestination of Christ: without original sin the incarnation of the Son of God would not have taken place. By contrast, Duns Scotus and his followers declared that Jesus as the supreme man would have been united by God with himself even without the sin of Adam because here as everywhere election is logically prior to the divine foreknowledge of the Fall.[38] The Scotists attempted to establish this position, along with other arguments, by the designation of Jesus Christ as the "head" of the church and of the universe as in Ephesians and Colossians. Duns Scotus himself, however, did not have in mind the summation of the universe as the consummation of the divine plan for history in the person of Jesus, but only the difference in rank between the *summus homo* and the rest of humanity. One may omit the entire conflict, which continues to stir Roman Catholic theology even today,[39] because the question is put in a way inappropriate to the substance of the matter. If the predestination of Christ is most closely related to God's whole plan for history, it is just as much an abstraction to conceive a creation without Christ as the head of humanity and of the universe as it is to conceive the order of salvation without reference to the actual situation of humanity, namely, without reference to sin. If one keeps in view the Biblical relation of Jesus' election and that of the rest of humanity to God's plan for history, the dilemma of having to choose between those two abstract solutions can be avoided and one can admit the relative justification of the arguments on both sides.

Through Karl Barth's Christocentric doctrine of election, the election of Jesus has been rediscovered as a separate theme in contemporary Protestant dogmatics. Barth has also made theology conscious anew of the mediation of all other election, both of the community and of the individual, through the election of Jesus Christ. Further, building on the solid heritage of Reformed covenant theology, Barth has grasped the relation between Jesus and the whole of God's history with humanity more profoundly than most contemporary theologians.[40] For him the unity of God with man in Jesus Christ

38 Duns Scotus, *Rep. Par.* I, 41; the text is quoted in my study, *Die Prädestinationslehre des Duns Scotus* (Göttingen: Vandenhoeck & Ruprecht, 1954), pp. 109 f., esp. p. 110, n. 110.

39 In favor of Thomas, in addition to Thomistic dogmatics in the narrower sense, like that of Diekamp-Jüssen, is L. Ott, *Fundamentals of Catholic Dogma*, pp. 175 f.; in favor of the Scotistic solution, M. Schmaus, *Katholische Dogmatik* (5th ed.; Munich: M. Hueber, 1955), Vol. II/2, pp. 65 ff.

40 P. Althaus only says that in Jesus, history is decided "in its vertical dimension, i.e., as an event with God," and to this extent in Jesus, God has "set history's one center of gravity" which is "simultaneous" with all generations (*Die christliche Wahrheit*, p. 107). In W. Trillhaas, *Dogmatik* (Berlin: A. Töpelmann, 1962), there is complete absence of any explicit reflection on the position of Jesus in the history of mankind. This may be related to Trillhaas' negative judgment respecting Jesus' relation to the Old Testament (pp. 84-96). Werner Elert takes a more positive position when he remarks in his doctrine

is the fulfillment of the community with man which God had always planned in his covenant.[41] Nonetheless, Barth does not unite together the two themes of divine history and the election of Jesus Christ in the way demanded by the New Testament witnesses we have considered. In Barth the election of Jesus Christ does not appear in itself as the summation of God's history with humanity. Rather, Barth's doctrine of the election of and in Jesus Christ precedes the doctrine of creation and covenant and forms its presupposition. Certainly, Barth wants to formulate in this way the Trinitarian foundation for the entire relation of God to the world he was to create. But must not one see an effect of the traditional isolation of the doctrine of predestination from God's concrete plan for history in Barth's having been able to discuss the election of Jesus Christ in itself first apart from the rest of humanity? Through his Christocentric theology, on the one hand, Barth overcomes the abstract doctrine of predestination in the dogmatic tradition that attributed the decision about election or rejection of men to a hidden decree of the eternal God without involving his historical revelation in Jesus Christ. According to Barth, the election of the individual occurs exclusively through Jesus Christ, on the basis of his election, and even then not without the mediation of the election of the community. While the election of the individual is thus assigned a place in divine elective activity including all humanity, the election of Jesus Christ on the other hand still is not so clearly ordered toward the election and consummation of humanity. To be sure, Barth speaks of God's having elected "man" as such in electing Jesus Christ (e.g., *CD*,

---

of providence that saving history "from the limited time and place of Christ's earthly life, draws the whole of history into its train, so to speak," and grounds faith in history's teleological character (*Der christliche Glaube*, p. 283). For Elert as for Althaus, however, this significance of Jesus Christ for the history of mankind is apparently not properly a Christological theme, essential for understanding Jesus Christ himself. At the beginning of his Christology, H. Vogel speaks of the "directedness of the history testified in the Old Testament" toward the history of Jesus Christ (*Gott in Christo*, pp. 613 f.; cf. *Christologie*, I [1949] 41-52), but he, too, does not find that Jesus Christ himself is characterized by this fact in such a way that this relationship would have to become the object of a particular Christological statement. Even a Reformed dogmatician such as Otto Weber, who, like K. Barth, stands in the tradition of the Reformed concept of covenant and strongly emphasizes this idea in various contexts (*Grundlagen der Dogmatik*, Vol. I, pp. 323-334 and 629-639), deals only in his anthropology, not in his Christology, with Christ as the "new man," in whom God's covenant with humanity is fulfilled (p. 637). His Christological considerations of the position of Jesus in history are determined by the contrast of God's revelation in Jesus as "eschatological" history (in which, to be sure, God's Old Testament covenant activity is included: Vol. II, p. 116) to the general "history of death" (Vol. II, pp. 110-117, esp. pp. 115 ff.). E. Brunner, along the lines of Irenaeus, has worked out much more strongly the significance of Jesus in God's history with humanity. (See below, n. 51.)

[41] Barth has extensively developed this idea in the introduction to his doctrine of reconciliation (*CD*, IV/1, § 57), while even Emil Brunner (*The Christian Doctrine of Creation and Redemption*, pp. 214 ff.) connects the covenant only with the law. The relation to the covenant concept remains fundamental for the development of Barth's Christology: *CD*, IV/1, pp. 173 f., 279 ff., 307 ff.; IV/2, p. 167; IV/3, pp. 3 f., 70 f.

II/2, pp. 184 f.). On occasion, in connection with the obedience of suffering to which God has destined this one elected man, he can say, "Not for his own sake but for theirs, for the sake of man in himself and as such, is he elected."[42] Such a teleological reference of Jesus' election to the election of humanity as a whole nevertheless does not determine in Barth's presentation the systematic structure of the relation between Jesus Christ's election and the election of other men. Rather, Barth assigns this task to the idea of the analogy of the election of the community (*CD*, II/2, pp. 216 ff.) and of the individual (pp. 382 f., 457) to that of Jesus. Barth understands the expression that other men are elected "in" Christ in the sense of a prototypal significance of the election (and rejection) of Jesus Christ for all other election. The foundation of the relation between Christ and Christians in Barth's doctrine of election is provided by the idea of the prototypal character of Jesus Christ, not by his being ordered toward God's plan for humanity, toward God's Lordship over humanity. The latter is, however, decisive, both in the historical activity of Jesus of Nazareth, in Jesus' dedication to his divine mission of preaching the Kingdom of God on earth among men, and for the New Testament assertions about Jesus' election and predestination. They always have in view the totality of the divine decree for humanity, indeed for the whole creation. The election of Jesus Christ is just as inaccessible to an isolated examination as is that of individuals generally, as if it could be constructed independently following the pattern of the concept of the incarnation apart from the whole of God's election history, and God's election history with humanity would then be derived from it as a postscript, an analogous reflection. Jesus Christ is "the elected Son" of the Father (Luke 9:35) with regard to those to whom he is sent. He is called the elected cornerstone (I Peter 2:4 ff.) in view of the spiritual house that is to be built on him. His election certainly applies to his person. He was not merely elected to the execution of a particular function so that he would be interchangeable with any other who executed the same function. The unique character of Jesus' historical mission was that it was completely amalgamated with his person. But only in the function of his historical mission of service to humanity toward the coming Kingdom of the Father is he as a person God's elect, on whom is decided the election or rejection of all other men. He is not God's elect in his own right, but in his service to the people of God who are elected by the Father through him. When one notes this involvement of the election of Jesus Christ with that of the people of God, from among the Jews and then out of the Gentiles, one can hardly make the prototypal character of Jesus' election conceived first by itself the decisive point of view for the relation of Jesus' election to that of his community.

[42] *CD*, II/2, 123; cf. p. 195: "Jesus Christ is the eternally living beginning of man and of the whole creation," and God's self-dedication in the election of Jesus seen "teleologically . . . concerns man in himself and as such created by and fallen away from God."

We have already seen that even Barth occasionally mentions another teleological relation of Jesus Christ's election to that of other men, the central significance of which, however, demands a more determinative role. On the other hand, Paul also spoke of the "image" of the Second Adam that we will bear (I Cor. 15:49) and of the "image" of the Son (Rom. 8:29) into which we will be conformed through receiving sonship. The idea of the prototypal character of what has appeared in Jesus has an important and probably irreplaceable function in presenting the universally valid significance of Jesus. This exemplary aspect, however, should be subordinated to that of saving history. This was presumably what Paul also had in mind. The significance of Jesus' person and destiny is rooted in the "history of salvation" context of his activity, in his position in God's plan. Its universality can then be shown by considering its exemplary character. In any case, in Paul, history of salvation and exemplary thinking are so closely related that neither alone could be called Pauline. Here, too, the breaking of the idea of the prototype, which as such is not specifically Biblical, by means of historical thinking stamped by the experience of contingent divine activity and by the eschatological expectation (cf. pp. 200 f., n. 13, above) remains decisive. If Jesus' election is conceived from the beginning in its being ordered toward the rest of humanity, it cannot be understood as the prototype of our election subsisting in itself. Instead, it must be understood with Eph. 1:10 as the summation of the whole creation and in this way as the eschatological decision about the election or rejection of every individual creature. Jesus' election does not establish our election because it precedes the election of all other men, but because of its eschatological character, because it is the summation of humanity and of all creation from the perspective of the end. From this point of view, even Barth's often criticized doctrine of Jesus' rejection[43] would be given the Biblical character of a vicarious assumption and reconciliation of our—thereby already presupposed—rejection, instead of suggesting the misleading conception that Jesus, taken by himself and seen in the same isolation as in the case of his election, is the only one rejected.

The relation of the election of the community and of the individual through Christ with divine predestination was presented with remarkable clarity by Schleiermacher by making the doctrine of election the point of departure for his doctrine of the church. He amalgamated the realization of redemption through Christ and the accomplishment of the divine world order into a single theme.[44] Admittedly, Schleiermacher's construction has more the character of a religious doctrine of progress oriented to Christ's redemptive effects than that of the eschatological summation of creation through the Messiah Jesus. This lack, however, can be excused to a great extent by the absence in

43 Cf. esp. the critique by E. Brunner, *The Christian Doctrine of God*, pp. 346-352.
44 Schleiermacher, *The Christian Faith*, § 119.

the whole nineteenth century of exegetical historical knowledge of the dominant significance of imminent eschatological expectation for primitive Christianity.

Karl Rahner, among contemporary theologians, has most impressively introduced the connection of the old doctrine of Christ's predestination with an eschatologically oriented theology of history. "The old question of Christ's predestination is raised today anew as the question of a cosmic Christocentricity."[45] By raising the question in this way, Rahner has overcome the split between the two themes and reasserted their New Testament and primitive Christian unity, which made it possible to express Jesus' decisive significance for the whole creation. "The essential uniqueness, underivability, and mysterious character of Christ's reality do not exclude seeing it in a perspective in which it appears as the climax and conclusion, as the secret goal of divine activity in creation planned by God from the very beginning."[46] In this way "the 'development' of the world *toward Christ* [would be] conceived"; not, however, as the "upward striving under its own power by that which is below,"[47] but in such a way that Christ as the fullness of time "ultimately embraces the eons as head, recapitulates them, and brings them to their end."[48] Thus the power of God's self-communication bears "from the very beginning the development of the whole history of the cosmos" in such a way that it "becomes manifest [only] in the existence and life of Christ as itself capable of being grasped historically and achieving its own objective."[49] As "objective and end" of the reality of the world, the incarnation is essentially an "inner moment and condition for the universal blessing of the spiritual creation by God himself" (p. 208). Hence, precisely by virtue of its eschatological character, the incarnation establishes the gracious blessing and thus the election of the rest of mankind. As eschatological, Jesus' activity has

[45] *LThK*, V, 955 (art. "Jesus Christus"). Cf. the earlier demand for closer coordination of Christology and saving history in contrast to the "static categories of formal ontology" of classical Christology in Rahner's article, "Current Problems in Christology," *Theological Investigations*, Vol. I, pp. 149-200, esp. pp. 163-168. The quotation is found on p. 166.

[46] Rahner, *ibid.*, Vol. I, p. 164.

[47] *Ibid.*, p. 165. Rahner thus opposes an application of the evolutionary concept to Christology, which he himself approaches in another place (p. 167), by designating Christ as "prospective entelechy" of the whole of history. However, the decisive point of an eschatologically conceived theology of history is that God's saving acts, and thus the incarnation as recapitulation (pp. 167 f.), are precisely not a real, entelechic "development" but rather the contingent, each time unmerited, consummation of the preceding process.

[48] *Ibid.*, p. 167. The idea is formulated as a question whether the divine-human unity of Christ, known from the Chalcedonian formula, is not already expressed in this way in another language, that of the theology of history. This question can be affirmed without qualification. The Christological formulas of traditional Christology merely define in Greek conceptual language what is implied in the more inclusive assertion of the theology of history.

[49] K. Rahner, "Christology Within an Evolution View of the World," *Theological Investigations*, Vol. V (1966), pp. 157-192, quotation, p. 186.

"already surpassed" all subsequent history (p. 220), but in so doing establishes openness for an inner-worldly future in an epoch following the appearance of Jesus (pp. 219 f.).

We perhaps have emphasized the eschatological point of view in Rahner's conception of the entire history of creation toward Jesus Christ more strongly than is immediately evident in reading Rahner's essays. Indeed, the ontologically constitutive significance of the *eschaton* for the totality of history must be brought more closely to the fore than Rahner has as yet done. It is repeatedly obscured by expressions suggesting the contradictory idea of an evolution through self-unfolding of an entelechy.[50] However, the Christ event is not the goal of history in the sense that all events are tending toward Jesus Christ by their own intrinsic nature. He is their consummation in the sense of something contingent but ultimate from which everything happening before—as well as the history following Jesus' historical activity, in that it is already surpassed by him as the eschatological event—is illuminated and receives its true significance and thus its essence. The eschatological event of the appearance of Christ is the summation of the universe from its end in that this event has consummating power in the fullness of time. Only from the perspective of the Christ event as eschatological event is human history to be understood as a unity.[51] Its eschatological character makes it the common point of reference for the meaning of all other events, whether this is understandable for us now or not.

The summation of all events to unity through Jesus Christ is the meaning of the designation of Jesus as the "central individual" of humanity and of the cosmos generally, which was temporarily popular in the last century.[52] This idea asserts that the individuals of a class have their unity not just in the abstract idea of the class, but rather that the unity of the class must show itself in the concrete relation of all individuals to a central member. Even

---

[50] See n. 47, above. The ambiguity here is similar to that which is characteristic of the cosmological outline of Teilhard de Chardin, which is related to Rahner's conception.

[51] Rightly brought out by E. Brunner, *The Christian Doctrine of Creation and Redemption*, p. 196; cf. pp. 197-198. Brunner deals—between the doctrine of creation and Christology—in greater detail than most contemporary Protestant dogmaticians with God's history with humanity (*ibid.*, pp. 193-238). This corresponds to his conscious proximity to the theology of Irenaeus (pp. 199 f.). He regards the history of mankind as "the correlate of the message of Christ," from which it receives its unity (p. 196). The coming of the Son "when the time was fulfilled" (Gal. 4:4) is interpreted by Brunner in the original sense of this formulation as a reference to the "eternal divine decree" (p. 236). "All historical time, regarded from the standpoint of Jesus Christ, tends towards Him" (p. 237).

[52] The term plays a role in G. W. F. Hegel's *Science of Logic*, Vol. II, pp. 361 ff. It then seems to have been introduced as the central idea of Christology by Göschel and Dorner, more or less simultaneously, into the debate around D. F. Strauss's life of Jesus as a substitute for Schleiermacher's "prototype" and the Hegelian "idea," the exclusive and complete incarnation of which in a single individual had been denied by Strauss. Cf. E. Günther, *Die Entwicklung*, pp. 152 ff. Later the idea appears above all in R. Rothe, *Theologische Ethik* (2d ed.; Wittenberg: Zimmermann, 1869/1871), § 555 f., in addition to I. A. Dorner, *A System of Christian Doctrine*, Vol. III, § 103, n. 4 (pp. 323 f.).

though this idea was often associated with the idea that this central member by himself is nothing other than the individual embodiment of the class itself (as the "primal man"), so that the opportunity was given critics of the theory to doubt the true individuality of this central individual, this interpretation of the idea of the central individual is not essential. It can be thought of purely as the relatedness of all members to a single one who thereby in his particularity becomes the crystallizing point of the class. The significance properly belonging to this often misjudged[53] theory does not reside only in the fact that it inaugurated a new understanding of Jesus' significance for the whole of mankind independent of the idea of Jesus' prototypal character, taken as the realization of the idea of a single individual, which was rightly criticized by Strauss. The theory of Jesus as central individual of the human race is especially important because of the way in which it was adequate to this task by renewing, in distinction from the conception of the prototype, the Biblical idea of the summation of all things in Christ. The origins of this theory in the nineteenth century and its original form are almost forgotten in the present day, but the concept of Jesus as the unifying "middle" of human history has not disappeared. On occasion Paul Tillich has designated as the meaning of Christology the understanding of Jesus as the Christ and thus as the middle of history.[54] D. M. Baillie appropriated this concept and brought its significance explicitly to the fore.[55] We must also mention in this connection Oscar Cullmann and his book *Christ und Time* because its intention is not merely exegetical, but also systematic.[56] G. Kaufman has given the idea an interesting twist by saying that every doctrine of the unity of history in reference to its asserted unifying center is to be characterized in the formal sense as "Christology," so that the Christian Christology, which understands Jesus as the center of history, has to debate with other "Christologies" at just this point.[57] In so doing and in

[53] The antispeculative reaction of the second half of the nineteenth century, which today appears in many respects as intellectual superficiality, is responsible for the repression of this concept, without providing a critical clarification that would have led beyond it. Cf. A. Ritschl's uncomprehending judgment, *The Christian Doctrine of Justification and Reconciliation*, pp. 411 f., which is also adopted by Günther, *Die Entwicklung*, pp. 153 f., 221 f.

[54] Paul Tillich, *The Interpretation of History* (Charles Scribner's Sons, 1936), p. 32. However, in the Christological position developed in Tillich's *Systematic Theology*, this idea plays no role at all. The appearance of the New Being in Christ is substituted for it. It stands all the more clearly in the center in the theology of history in the third volume (*Systematic Theology*, Vol. III, pp. 232, 336, 364-369).

[55] *God Was in Christ*, pp. 71-79, esp. pp. 74 f. In addition to Tillich, Baillie also refers to Barth, Wendland, and others.

[56] Oscar Cullmann, *Christ and Time: The Primitive Christian Conception of Time and History*, tr. by Floyd V. Filson (rev. ed.; The Westminster Press, 1964), esp. pp. 70 f. and 107-153.

[57] Gordon D. Kaufman, *Relativism, Knowledge, and Faith* (The University of Chicago Press, 1960), pp. 108 f.: "Every position is actually immersed in history and draws its meaning from some (implicit or explicit) center of history, or, as we might now say, from some 'Christ.'"

distinction from the old theory of Christ as the central figure of humanity, Kaufman sees that the task of establishing a frame of reference is not solved simply by the presence of a center, but that it presupposes power over the future and thus is essentially an eschatological problem (*ibid.*, pp. 111 f.). Here lies the chief weakness of the concept of Jesus as the central individual of humanity as well as of the Lucan conception of Jesus' activity as "the middle of time." The idea of the middle can have only subordinate significance in the context of a Christian, Biblically grounded understanding of time.[58] Only because in Jesus the eschatological destiny and future of humanity has begun can he be humanity's unifying, all-embracing middle without detriment to its open future.

As one eschatological summation, as the reconciliation of humanity across all dividing chasms, the Christ event establishes not only the unity of human history, but thereby also establishes the unity of the universe. This assertion presupposes that the totality of the material world does not possess its unity in itself apart from man, but that this unity is only structured through man. The cosmos is not in itself a unity, as the majority of the ancient Greek thinkers held, which is given prior to man and merely copied in him as the microcosmos. Rather, the multiplicity of things in nature is first united to form the world through men. By means of his thought and his technical skill, man rules the multiplicity of cosmic events and makes of them his world. Precisely when he creates the world out of the things he finds, man is God's image, God's viceroy in the world. The lordship of man over nature is essentially—like the form of all lordship—activity that establishes unity. It finds its fulfillment only in the unity of humanity itself. In this sense, the history of Jesus, on the basis of which humanity is embraced into the unity of a single history, is at the same time the consummation of the unity of the world. As humanity in its history, so too the material universe is only brought together to the unity of a world through its relation to Jesus.

III. THE CREATION OF THE WORLD THROUGH JESUS CHRIST

The question of Jesus' election in the full sense of the divine predestination of Jesus' activity and destiny within the whole of the divine plan for history can only be stated here, not yet adequately answered. The answer could

---

58 O. Piper has rightly called attention to the constitutive function of the idea of the "middle" for a cyclic way of thinking (*God in History* [The Macmillan Company, 1939], p. 19). To this extent it is not fitted to serve as the dominant point of reference for an eschatological conception of history. Nevertheless, as a subordinate element, defined in the horizon of eschatological expectation, it can also find a place even in a Biblically founded understanding of history, in order to designate the unique anticipation of the *eschaton* in Jesus' activity and fate.

consist only in a concrete perception of the divine plan for history including all its details. But even for a fully developed theology of history, which cannot be presented here, such perception can always be achieved only in a provisional and comparatively unconcrete way. If such perception were completely denied to us, however, we would not be able to achieve any perception at all of the universal truth of the person and history of Jesus. In the light of the *eschaton* that has already begun in Jesus' resurrection, a certain preliminary perception of the divine plan for history really seems to be possible. The primitive Christian witnesses, each in his own way, attempted to achieve such perception. It can always consist only in more or less summary, and therefore often one-sided, anticipations of the ultimate perception that will be given in the eschatological future.

The formulations of Ephesians and the Pauline or Lucan theologies of history have already given such answers to the question of the divine plan for history leading to Jesus Christ. These responses to the question about the predestination of Jesus build the bridge to the perception of the Lordship of Jesus over the cosmos, as is expressed in the formula of the creation of all things, not just "toward him," but also "through him."

On the basis of the eschatologically oriented Israelite understanding of truth, according to which the essence of a thing has not always existed—even though hiddenly—but is decided only by what becomes of it, the predestination of all things toward Jesus, their eschatological summation through Jesus, is identical with their creation through Jesus. Every creature receives through him as the eschatological judge its ultimate illumination, its ultimate place, its ultimate definition in the context of the whole creation. The essence of all events and figures is to be ultimately defined in the light of him because their essence is decided on the basis of their orientation to him. To that extent, creation of all things is mediated through Jesus. Christ's mediation of creation is not to be thought of primarily in terms of the temporal beginning of the world. It is rather to be understood in terms of the whole of the world process that receives its unity and meaning in the light of its end that has appeared in advance in the history of Jesus, so that the essence of every individual occurrence, whose meaning is relative to the whole to which it belongs, is first decided in the light of this end. To be sure, the cosmos with which we are familiar can be supposed to have had a temporal beginning, but to speak of the creation of the world does not refer just to this beginning but to the world process as a whole. This is conceivable, because the creation must be understood as an act of God's eternity, even though what is created by this eternal act has a temporal beginning and a temporal becoming. However, God's eternal act of creation will be entirely unfolded in time first in the *eschaton*. Only at the *eschaton* will what is created out of God's eternity be consummated in the accomplishment of its own temporal becoming. Thus, the temporal unfolding of the divine act of

391

creation is to be understood from the perspective of its eschatological fulfill-ment, not from the perspective of the beginning of the world. Certainly the beginning of the world is to be conceived as established by God, not, however, taken by itself in isolation but seen with the totality of the world from the perspective of its end. If the *eschaton* toward which all things have their being has already appeared in an anticipatory way in Jesus, he is, as the one exalted to be the eschatological Judge, also the one from whom all things come. Only from him, through him, do all things have their essential nature (I Cor. 8:6).

That Jesus Christ's predestination and mediatorship of creation belong so closely together is confirmed by the correspondence of the formula in Eph. 1:9 f. about the predestination of Christ to be the "summation" of the universe to the hymnal confessions of faith in Christ's mediation of creation in Colossians (ch. 1:15-20) and Hebrews (ch. 1:2 f.). All these formulations assert essentially the same thing in that they attempt to express the reference of all things to Jesus Christ. The substantial content of this matter does, indeed, have the two sides designated by the terms predestination of Jesus and "mediation of creation" by him. Thereby, however, as we have concluded above, Jesus' predestination in the divine plan for history as its eschatological fulfillment is the material basis for his designation as the mediator of creation. Primitive Christianity apparently did not explicitly reflect upon this relation-ship, perhaps because at that time the concept of a mediator of creation required no special legitimation, but was already accepted in Hellenistic Judaism and only had to be connected with the figure of Jesus.

In the second stanza of the hymn quoted in Col. 1:15-20, the Hellenistic assertions of the first stanza about the "image" of God, the "first-born" (v. 15), the "head" of creation (v. 18a)[59] are applied eschatologically to the resurrection of the dead that has begun in Jesus' resurrection (v. 18b) and soteriologically to the reconciliation of the universe that he has accomplished (vs. 19 f.). This latter motif appears again in Eph. 1:9 f. The tension between the two stanzas has been rightly emphasized recently.[60] The Christian con-

---

[59] According to Harold Hegermann, *Die Vorstellung vom Schöpfungsmittler im hel-lenistischen Judentum und Urchristentum* (Berlin: Akademie-Verlag, 1961), p. 170, *tēs ekklēsias* in v. 18a is a "Pauline" interpolation. The expression *kephalē* in the hymn originally designated Christ as the head of the cosmos, as is still the case in Col. 2:10. Thus, thinks Hegermann, through his interpretation the author of Colossians prepared the way for the ecclesiological conception of Ephesians. There Christ is repeatedly designated as head of the church (Eph. 1:22; 4:15; 5:23).

[60] *Ibid.*, p. 106: "How can the universe, which *par nature* already had the mediator of creation as *kephalē tou sōmatos*, be at all in need of redemption, and how the mediator of creation be exalted in the time of the power of divine election to his cosmic position as head, which he possesses eternally *par nature*? Here the cosmic thought pattern of the hymn is noticeably broken by conceptions of another sort." On the second strophe of the hymn, see pp. 101-109; on the tension between its soteriological content and the first strophe, see also pp. 108 f. and 123 f. That Hegermann, in distinction from E. Käsemann ("A Primitive Christian Baptismal Liturgy," *Essays on New Testament Themes*, pp. 149-

fession of faith in the Lordship of the exalted Jesus over the universe could adopt the Jewish-Alexandrian speculation about the Logos as the bearer of the activity of God dominating the world, conceived in analogy to the Stoic doctrine of God. In distinction from the Stoa, however, Alexandrian Judaism conceived God as transcendent over the world.[61] Even so, primitive Christianity had to break through the cosmological intention of this Logos speculation, oriented to the question of the origin and enduring order of the world, in order that the eschatological turning point in world history that occurred in Jesus Christ could be brought to bear in its incisive newness over against everything that had gone before.[62] The reconstruction demanded here would have been carried out with the necessary radicality if it had succeeded in understanding the assertions about the creation eschatologically in the sense of a creation occurring and being fulfilled from the *eschaton*. Neither Col. 1:15 ff. nor Heb. 1:2 f. succeeded in doing this. Therefore, in both texts the tension remains unresolved between the eschatological turning point of the world accomplished in Jesus' exaltation (cf. Col. 1:18 f. with Heb. 1:3b) and the preceding cosmological conception. Their universality cannot be surpassed by Jesus' exaltation, and so the significance of the exaltation as the turning point for the world[63] is not properly sketched. This comes closest to achieving success in Eph. 1:10 through the idea of the summation of the universe in Christ, but does so only at the price of not speaking explicitly of the creation of the universe.

The unresolved tension between eschatological-soteriological and archetypal-cosmological elements in the New Testament assertions about Jesus Christ as mediator of creation remained characteristic for the subsequent church's Logos doctrine, to which we now briefly return (cf. above, Chapter 4, Sec. III). In John's Gospel and Ignatius the appearance of the Logos in Jesus of Nazareth has only revelatory significance. Its implicit ontological relevance, which is at least clear in John's Gospel, as the consummation of the creation

168), holds the hymn to be of Christian origin (*Die Vorstellung vom Schöpfungsmittler*, pp. 109 f.), is convincing because of the specifically Christian character of the second strophe (so also W. Schmithals in his review, *Thl Z*, LXXXVIII (1963), 593).

[61] Hegermann, *Die Vorstellung vom Schöpfungsmittler*, pp. 63 ff., has pointed out Philo's relation to Stoic thought in this point. The Philonic exegesis of the cosmic interpretation of the high priest's robe, as described in Ex., ch. 28, no longer has in view Yahweh as the prototypal High Priest, but the power of the "Logos as an epiphany-bearer" (pp. 67-87), subordinated to the Most High God—thus breaking with the original meaning of the cosmic interpretation (p. 51).

[62] As Hegermann has shown, the emphasis on the exaltation of the Redeemer and the therein accomplished reconciliation and satisfaction of the universe in the second strophe of the hymn, Col. 1:15-20, points back to the influence of the Palestinian kerygma (*ibid.*, p. 126, cf. also p. 132). This is made even stronger by several of the author's Pauline additions, esp. *tou staurou autou* in v. 20b (p. 171).

[63] There can be no doubt that this is the real intention of the hymn, Col. 1:15-20 (*ibid.*, p. 132), especially in the present context in Colossians, where the remarks in ch. 3:1 ff., which conclude the doctrinal presentation, repeat once more the decisive significance of the Christ event and stress its eschatological character (p. 178).

itself that only now occurs is not consciously reflected upon. Justin and Irenaeus, on the other hand, connected the Logos doctrine with the Pauline concept of the Second Adam and the idea in Ephesians of the summation of creation through Jesus Christ (cf. pp. 381 f., above) in such a way that the appearance of Jesus and his exaltation are brought to bear in their ontological breadth as consummation of creation. Even later the concept of the creation of man as fulfilled only through the appearance of the Logos in Jesus of Nazareth remained alive where the mediation of immortality to men through the incarnate Logos was conceived not merely as restoration of an original condition, but also as divine fulfillment of the destiny intended for man in the beginning, but not imparted to him because of man's sin.[64] Nonetheless, the idea that the creation is fulfilled only in the light of the appearance of Jesus— an idea which is necessary on the basis of the significance of the Christ event as the world's eschatological turning point—never became fully effective in its relevance for understanding creation itself nor, in consequence, for the concept of the divine Logos. For this reason, speculations about the Logos apart from the flesh (*asarkos*) about a divine world law working as creator and ruler of the world apart from the historical Jesus, analogous to the Jewish-Hellenistic philosophy and its Stoic and Platonic sources and parallels, could infiltrate Christian theology. One saw Jesus of Nazareth only as the earthly appearance of this divine Logos instead of seeking in the historical and resurrected Jesus himself the power in which the world intrinsically coheres.[65]

The Greek concept of the Logos as the divine world law as developed by Heraclitus and Stoic philosophy (cf. pp. 161 f.) is transformed on the basis of the perception that Jesus has been installed in the creative omnipotence of God as the one exalted to be the eschatological ruler over the universe so that in eternity God acts creatively only through him as is disclosed in the ordering of all things unto the historical appearance of Jesus. As in other areas, it must be shown whether the Christian transformation can be subsequently justified by its opening up of the understanding of the whole of reality that we experience in common with all other men more profoundly than every philosophical point of departure.

Justin has asserted that the Logos does not realize himself everywhere equally, but enters into the history of creation and only appears at a particular moment in this history, in the historical figure of Jesus, in order from this point to illuminate the whole course of creation. The revolution which this

---

64 Athanasius, *De incarnatione* I, 4 f. (*MPG* 25, 104 f.), 8 (*MPG* 25, 109D). On this, cf. the contradictions in the question among the patristic theologians whether or not Adam possessed immortality in the beginning.

65 K. Barth has rightly rejected the idea of the *logos asarkos* (*CD*, IV/1, pp. 52 f., 66). O. Weber, *Grundlagen der Dogmatik*, Vol. II, p. 143, has agreed with Barth in this. In fact the conception of the *logos asarkos* must be judged as an expression of the fact that the assimilation of Hellenistic and Hellenistic-Jewish cosmology by Christian theology did not lead to a total melting down of the alien substance.

idea implies for the concept of the Logos as world law was apparently never carried to its conclusion. Neither with respect to the whole of events nor to their details does the universality of Jesus' significance have the character of a law that gives the world and its events their form in definite proportions. As the presence of the eschatological reality and—closely related—of God's Lordship, Jesus' history is the point of reference in world events, with reference to which all other events are bound together to form the totality of a single world process. This is true first of the history of humanity, which is a unity only through its reference to the eschatological revelation of God. It is also true for the nonhuman world, mediated through humanity, which is called to Lordship over the cosmos. Thus as the eschatological summation of the world process to a unity, Jesus is the mediator of creation. As such, however, he is *not the law, but the reconciler of the cosmos.*

A law always requires[66] a multiplicity of individual cases in which it is realized. It brings to expression the typical element of analogous cases in distinction from their variant particularities. For this reason, a law or a system of laws can never embrace all sides of the whole of reality. It always embraces only one side of the real event, the side that repeats itself, the typical, and neglects the other side, the contingent particularities.[67] The world process as a whole, however, is a unique succession of events. Its entire set of interrelationships cannot, therefore, be understood in terms of law, no matter how great the role the typical that conforms to law may play as a subordinate element in its course. Because the total process of the world is a unique and irreversible course of events, even contemporary natural science does not speak of this total process as the test case of a law embracing the whole, but speaks of a history of nature. Admittedly, this terminology is laden with the difficulty that the specifically historical continuity is essentially related to the consciousness of history, to the reception of the historical heritage that must take place anew in every generation and that means at the same time the transformation of that heritage. Therefore, one can probably speak of a history of nature only with reference to man—who belongs to nature himself, after all—but hardly apart from man. However, because the history of mankind achieves unity only in the light of the eschatological revelation of God in Jesus Christ, in the final analysis it is Jesus who embraces the world process into the unity of a history.

At the same time, Jesus in his dedication to the Father and to his mission for humanity is also in some sense exemplary for the structure of every individual event. Everything is what it is only in transition to something other than itself; nothing exists for itself. Every particularity possesses its truth in its limit, through which it is not only independent but is also taken up into a

---

[66] Like the Platonic Idea. Cf. the critique mentioned above (n. 52) by Strauss of the prototype Christology of Schleiermacher and Hegel.

[67] See H. Siedentopf, *Gesetze und Geschichte des Weltalls* (1961), pp. 5 f., 20 f.

greater whole. Through giving up its particularity, everything is mediated with the whole and, transcending its finitude, with God, who nevertheless wanted this particularity to exist within the whole of his creation. That which lives must go outside itself in order to maintain itself; it finds its existence outside itself. At the highest level the same is true of human subjectivity, namely, it must empty itself to the world and the "Thou" in order to win itself in the other. Jesus' saying about losing and finding life (Mark 8:35 and parallels) has universal ontological relevance. Whoever will preserve his life must lose it. Only he who gives it up will win it. He will find it again in that to which he has given it up. Therefore, only he who gives up his life for the ultimate, eschatological reality of the Kingdom of God that has appeared in Jesus will find his life ultimately saved.[68] In that such dedication is not just demanded but has been lived by Jesus in supreme resoluteness as dedication to God and to his mission in the world for proclamation to men of God's Lordship, Jesus himself can appear as the incarnation of that "law." But then he would be a law that simultaneously abrogates itself, since in his dedication he sacrifices himself. By virtue of his self-sacrifice, Jesus has made room for other men and forms of life in the uniqueness of their situations instead of making his particularity a universal law.

The concept of Jesus' mediation of creation resulted from our examination of his royal Kingship. Thus the idea of mediation of creation is recognized as the unfolding of the confession of faith in the eschatological Lordship of Jesus as the Christ. The mediatorship of creation is itself the royal Lordship of Jesus Christ, the exercise of God's omnipotence in the world by the exalted Lord. Only in this light can we intimate what the incarnation of God in Jesus of Nazareth means: only in Jesus, indeed, only in the light of the eschatological event of his resurrection, is the eternal Son of God present in time. Only through Jesus is creation mediated into sonship, i.e., into its appropriate relation to God, and thus reconciled with God. Thereby the whole world process receives its structure and meaning. This is asserted by the ideas of Jesus' royal Lordship and mediatorship of creation. Both refer to the world process as a whole. Both express the participation of Jesus in the eternal divinity of God. The incarnation of God in Jesus of Nazareth forms the point of reference in relation to which the world's course has its unity and on the basis of which every event and every figure in creation is what it is. Because Jesus' unity with God is first decided by his resurrection, only through Jesus' resurrection is the creation of the world fulfilled. Jesus' resurrection from the dead and thus the incarnation of the Son of God in Jesus is that event in time through which the Son mediates the creation

[68] On the priority in the history of traditions of the term "for the sake of the Kingdom of God" over "for my sake" (or "for the sake of the Son of Man" or "for the sake of the gospel") in Mark 8:35 and related sayings, cf. R. Bultmann, *The History of the Synoptic Tradition*, pp. 110 f., 93.

of the world and executes God's royal Lordship. Through the power of this historical event that at the same time remains the eschatological future of the world, Jesus exercises his Lordship over the whole of the world process.

It is obvious that these last sentences come to a special degree under the eschatological reservation that applies to all Christological conclusions drawn from Jesus' resurrection—and in a certain sense even to the talk about this event itself as the first case of eschatological resurrection of the dead. All such statements anticipate something that will be shown to be real before the eyes of all only in the eschatological future, even though it has already happened to Jesus. This proleptic structure constitutes the inadequateness, the provisionalness of all Christological statements. After all, we derive the words with which we speak of the eschatological reality that has appeared in Jesus from the experience of a reality that is not yet the reality of the *eschaton*. For this reason, all statements of Christology have only metaphorical meaning. They are valid only to the extent that they are motivated by thinking through the history of Jesus. They are always only exegesis of the history of Jesus and remain in need of expansion and correction in the light of the eschatological future. Only the *eschaton* will ultimately disclose what really happened in Jesus' resurrection from the dead. Until then we must speak favorably in thoroughly legitimate, but still only metaphorical and symbolic, form about Jesus' resurrection and the significance inherent in it.

Scripture Index

Subject Index

of Jesus, 35-37, 48 f., 55, 89, 111, 146, 149, 156-160, 162, 165, 174, 180, 183, 185, 187, 200, 203 f., 210, 292, 303 f., 309, 315, 319 f., 327, 337, 342 f., 350, 374, 382, 390, 395; of traditions, 73, 137, 275, 367

Homoiōsis theōi, 121, 154, 202, 204

Hope, anthropological, 84 f., 205-208

Humiliation and exaltation, 34, 208 f., 297, 308 f.

Hypostasis, 120 f., 180, 289 f., 305, 337 n27, 338-342, 349, 351

Idea of the good, 40 f., 198, 203

Immediacy and mediation, 231, 332n23

Immortality of the soul, 86 f.

Incarnation, 33-36, 39-42, 69, 119, 121, 125 f., 146, 149 f., 153-158, 166, 168, 186, 198, 202, 208, 212, 274n53, 276, 278-280, 286-289, 291, 292, 295 f., 301-313, 315-323, 334, 345n42, 348, 356, 362, 383, 385, 387, 388n52, 396

Individuality. *See* Person, idea of

Influence, Hellenistic, 153 f.

Intercessio, 219, 222

Israel, 31 f., 35, 70, 72, 169, 171, 206 f., 223-225, 234, 256-258, 261, 265-269, 371, 378, 391. *See also* Old Testament; Judaism

Jesus: connection with Israel's apocalyptic present, 32, 58; eschatological character of, 49, 192, 242; quest for the historical, 22-26, 36, 55-57, 200

Jesus' activity and destiny (fate), 32 f., 117, 191, 193, 195, 197, 199 f., 209-211, 215, 217, 221, 223-225, 235, 239, 244, 250, 252, 258, 273, 274n53, 283, 322-324, 335, 342, 353, 365, 370, 374, 379, 385-387, 390. *See also* History: of Jesus; Jesus' significance; Soteriology

Jesus and the history of mankind, 378-397

Jesus and the law, 49, 117, 191, 194, 202, 215, 233 f., 252-263, 275

Jesus as bearer of the Spirit, 116-121, 125, 137-141

Jesus as example, 41, 202, 239

Jesus as representative of man before God, 42 f., 49, 144, 189-191, 197, 201, 204-206, 345, 350, 380, 385 f., 388. *See also* Jesus and the history of mankind

Jesus' baptism, 117, 120 f., 137-142

Jesus' birth, 41, 118-120, 152, 158, 223, 301, 308. *See also* Virgin birth

Jesus' conduct, 57 f., 194 f., 198 f., 204, 215, 235 f., 239, 252, 335, 361, 363

Jesus' consciousness, 223, 306, 311, 316, 319, 325-334, 336

Jesus' death, 35, 65, 96, 125, 195, 197, 202, 204, 220, 245-251, 255, 258-264, 269-280; as expiatory sacrifice, 202, 247-251, 274-277; as ransom, 35, 247, 258, 275-277. *See also* Cross; Passion; Suffering: of Jesus

Jesus' deeds, 63-65, 191, 193, 361

Jesus' divinity, 31, 34-37, 41 f., 46, 69, 108, 115, 117, 119-123, 125, 129 f., 132, 135, 137, 150 f., 156, 160, 163-168, 172-175, 180-186, 189-191, 195, 209, 211, 221-224, 235, 283, 292, 294, 296-299, 301, 306-313, 315 f., 318-320, 325, 335-337, 342, 357, 360; distinction from God as Father, 115, 121-123, 158-160, 163, 168 f., 178 f., 183, 334 f., 366, 370. *See also* Unity of God and man; Son of God

Jesus' eschatological (apocalyptical) presence, 61 f., 64n36, 194, 206n19, 226

Jesus' ethic, 44, 49, 204, 241

Jesus' humanity, 117-121, 142, 146, 154 f., 189-191, 222-224, 278, 283, 289 f., 291 f., 296-302, 304-310, 312, 314, 316, 319 f., 322 f., 331, 333n24, 336-342

Jesus' journey to Jerusalem, 65, 199, 245

Jesus' knowledge. *See* Jesus' consciousness

Jesus' message, 56 f., 61, 64n36, 199, 201, 203, 205, 207, 215 f., 228-238, 243, 253 f., 257, 261, 272 f., 323, 334 f., 342, 347, 354, 361n82, 362, 370 f., 377

Jesus' mission, 32, 183, 224, 235, 277, 297, 323, 333n24, 333-335, 348, 350, 364, 375, 380, 386, 396

Jesus' obedience, 49, 159, 183, 195-198, 202, 204, 293 f., 335, 359, 369 f., 375, 385

Jesus' parables, 60, 230-233

Jesus' presence, 26 f., 39, 299, 365. *See also* Soteriology

Jesus' relation to God as Father, 49, 133-

407

135, 141, 153n94, 156, 158-161, 183, 190, 195, 198 f., 218, 296, 327n4, 342, 344-352, 354 f., 363, 368-370. *See also* Jesus' obedience

Jesus' relation to the state, 237-240

Jesus' return, 108 f., 113, 117, 178, 218, 367, 371

Jesus' revelation, 26-28, 107, 115, 127-133, 156 f., 159, 165, 235. *See also* Revelation of God

Jesus' significance, 38n1, 48, 198. *See also* History: of Jesus

Jesus' sinlessness, 42, 148, 251, 254, 333 n24

Jesus' temptation and doubt, 278, 358

Jesus' title, 31 ff., 54, 56, 142, 190, 249, 251, 255, 274, 327, 335, 355, 366; confirmation of, 63-67, 112, 132, 135-137, 141, 191, 246, 253, 307, 362, 367; proleptic character of, 58, 60, 65-67, 134, 367

Jesus' unity with God. *See* Jesus' divinity; Revelation of God; Unity of God and man

Jesus' vocation, 45, 194, 280

John the Baptist, 61-63, 137-141, 216 f., 225, 227 f.

Judaism, postexilic, 34 f., 70, 116, 160, 170, 214, 221, 248, 253, 258, 269, 274, 277. *See also* Apocalyptic

Judgment, eschatological, 58-60, 64-67, 69, 71, 83, 87, 88, 106, 107, 191, 192, 227, 278, 369, 391

Justification, 198, 202, 212, 363

Kenosis, 307-323

Kerygma, 22 f., 25-27, 53, 57n14; Hellenistic, 82, 117, 199; Jewish-Christian, 32, 119, 123, 138, 257; primitive Christian, 82, 154, 172, 272, 334, 377; relation to Jesus, 56, 67, 238, 334, 361n82

Kingdom of God, 45, 61 f., 64n36, 193, 212, 218n21, 230-232, 237, 239, 241-243, 245, 332, 334, 367-378, 385, 396

Knowledge of God, 170, 174-176, 179. *See also* Revelation of God

Kyrios, 26-29, 32, 69n49, 122, 133, 135, 172, 367

Last Supper, 134, 248 f., 258, 298-299, 372

Law, 195, 254-265, 374; *abrogatio legis,* 71, 249-251, 253-262; conception of, 394 f. *See also* State and church

Logos, 34 f., 40 f., 69, 87, 119-124, 156, 160-168, 180, 198, 201 f., 287-289, 295 f., 302, 306, 307-311, 319 f., 329-332, 334, 337-342, 349, 351, 357, 393 f.

Logos-man pattern, 288, 291, 295 f.

Logos-*sarx* pattern, 288 f., 339

Lordship of Christ, 71, 134, 152, 207, 218, 255, 378 f., 393, 396 f.

Lordship of God. *See* Kingdom of God

Love, love command, 194, 232-235, 239, 256-258, 378

Man: and world, 148, 198, 203, 237-240, 346, 390, 394; as the image of God, 148, 196, 201, 392; body and soul, 87, 295; definition of, 83-88, 199-204, 226 f., 262, 329, 346, 352 f., 390; individual and community, 83 ff., 193, 234, 264-269, 331; openness, 86, 193, 203, 228, 231, 243, 262, 270, 317, 388, 390

Mankind, new. *See* Church

Mary, Mariology, 143-150, 357 f.

Meal, eschatological, 57, 60, 134, 191, 228

Merit of Christ, 42, 264, 295, 350, 352, 359

Messiah, 31, 116, 119, 134, 137, 152, 153, 170, 214, 217-221, 224 f., 234, 235, 327, 366, 379, 386

Metaphor, metaphorical, 74, 159, 187, 271n45, 319

Middle, concept of, 123, 124, 135, 161 f., 165, 222, 297

Miracles of Jesus. *See* Jesus' deeds

Mission. *See* Gentile mission

Modalism, 126, 160

Monarchianism, 120, 122, 126

Monophysitism, 40, 123, 189, 291-294, 296, 309n75, 320

Monothelite dispute, 293-294, 322

Mystery, 303, 319; cults, 154, 262

Myth, mythical, 154 f., 157, 186-189, 200, 224, 279, 309

Natural law, 98, 166, 395

Natural theology, 130

Nature, concept of, 283 ff., 290, 325 f., 345. *See also* Two-nature doctrine
Nihilianism, 295

Office, offices of Christ, 35, 44, 191, 193-195, 208-225, 300, 324, 335
Old Testament, 32, 35, 116, 142 f., 156 f., 170, 200, 206, 208, 213, 224, 229, 238, 250, 257, 322, 365, 370, 383n40
Ontology. *See* Essence
Openness to the future, 108, 110, 193, 199, 203, 227, 233, 243, 332
Original sin, 358, 361, 383. *See also* Sin

Pantheism, 176
Paradoxical, paradox, 157, 165, 183, 304
Parapsychology, 95
Parousia. *See* Expectation; Jesus' return
Passion, predictions of, 65, 245, 277
Passion tradition, 31, 104, 105, 117, 220, 245, 379. *See also* Cross of Jesus; Jesus' death
Penance, 42, 198, 202
Perichoresis (mutual interpenetration), 296-302, 309
Person, idea of, 177n149, 181, 203, 295, 306, 325, 335, 339-348, 395 f.
Personalism, 46, 167, 177, 286, 340-342
Platonic middle, 40, 161 f., 165 f., 180, 390
Potentia obedientialis, 345n42
Prayer, 28, 159, 372
Predestination, 379-387. *See also* Jesus and the history of mankind
Preexistence of Christ, 118-121, 123, 133, 146, 150-154, 165, 168, 186, 356
Present and future: in faith, 108, 203, 370 f., 375, 377 (*see also* Ch. 10); in Jesus, 58, 61-68, 134n40, 217, 228 f., 278, 365, 369
Projection, 47, 190, 200, 203
Prolepsis, 108, 157, 183, 187, 321n96, 374, 391, 397. *See also* Present and future
Pro me, 48. *See also* Soteriology
Promise and fulfillment, 205-208, 377 f.
Prophet of the last times, 116, 137 f., 140, 214-217, 219n23, 255, 327, 379
Prophets, Israelite, 61, 66, 68n46, 70, 116, 137, 140-142, 170, 206-208, 215-217, 225, 247, 250, 274, 277

Prosōpon, 290 f., 295
Prototype, Jesus as. *See* Jesus as representative
Prototype and image, 44, 166, 186, 200

Redeemer myth, 34, 151, 160
Religion, 20, 221
Resurrection, 45, 64, 83, 86-103, 105-115, 171-174, 187, 191 f., 195 f., 200, 207, 224, 242, 391 f.; apocalyptical expectation, 58, 67, 107, 185; appearances, 72 f., 77, 88-99, 102, 104, 367; of Jesus, 53, 63n34, 64n37, 66-78, 91, 94-102, 105-115, 118, 129, 136-138, 141, 146, 149 f., 152 f., 158 f., 167, 171, 177 f., 186 f., 191, 195-197, 200, 206, 210, 218, 223 f., 226, 235, 242 f., 245-247, 254, 257-260, 262, 269, 272 f., 275, 277, 296, 301, 304-307, 312, 316 f., 321 f., 332, 335 339, 344, 347-349, 362 367, 372, 391 f., 394; presence of the resurrected Lord, 110, 113
Retroactive, 135-138, 141, 322, 324, 363
Revelation of God, Revealer, 19, 69, 83, 106-108, 110, 115, 118, 122, 125-133, 144, 146-148, 150, 154, 156-160, 162, 164 f., 167, 175, 179, 183-185, 187, 190-193, 210, 235, 316, 324, 335, 365, 384, 395. *See also* Jesus' revelation

Satisfaction, 42, 195, 198, 202 f., 212, 219, 222, 277, 279 f., 295, 350
Self-consciousness. *See* Jesus' consciousness; Person, idea of
Sermon, 67, 204, 219. *See also* Kerygma
Sermon on the Mount, 56, 60, 251
Servant of God, 116, 248, 259, 274, 327, Sin, 40, 42, 148, 201, 247-251, 263, 270, 275, 288, 315, 326, 351, 353-363, 394; forgiveness of, 45, 228, 234, 278
Son of David (title), 31, 59n22, 117, 134, 219n23, 234. *See also* Two-stage Christology
Son of God, 31, 53, 59n22, 69n49, 117-120, 151-156, 168 f., 172n136, 173, 175, 178-183, 190, 193, 220, 294, 298, 301, 309, 323, 327, 334-337, 339, 342, 344-349, 355, 362, 364 f., 367, 369-372, 380 f., 385, 396
Son of Man, 31 f., 56, 62, 64-66, 68 f., 106 f., 116, 132, 134, 152, 191, 196n4,

201, 207, 218, 246, 248, 332, 349n48, 368n6

Sonship of Christ, 172 f., 175 f., 198, 219 n23, 229, 342-347, 370 f., 380, 385

Soteriology, 38 f., 48, 124, 164, 190, 205, 228, 256, 274n53, 351n53, 380. *See also* Jesus; Man: definition of

Spirit of God, 67, 76n63, 114n134, 116-123, 132, 138-141, 170-183, 346, 379n30

State and church, 238 f., 261, 372-378

Stoic, 161 f., 180, 202, 263, 287n18, 298, 394

Subordinationism, 123, 165, 180

Substitution of Christ, 250, 258-269, 274 f., 315-317, 355

Suffering, 68n46, 247 f., 275; of Jesus, 31, 45, 220, 224, 245-248, 258, 278, 289n24, 328; penal (substitutionary), 44, 49, 195, 219, 221, 245, 277-280

Symbolic concepts, 86 f., 148, 159, 397

Theology and philosophy, 161, 165, 394

Theopoiesis, 347n45

Time and eternity, 320 f., 368

Title, Christological. *See* Jesus' title

Tomb, empty, 88, 91n84, 100-106, 109, 149

Trial of Jesus, 253, 261

Trinity, doctrine of, 34, 115, 124, 130, 158, 169, 177-184, 311, 318, 324, 336, 340, 343 f., 384

Truth, 136n44, 391

Two-nature doctrine, 33, 124, 208, 284-302, 329

Two-stage Christology, 59n22, 117-120, 135, 138, 219

Unio hypostatica, 326, 337 f., 341. *See also* Two-nature doctrine

Universal salvation (in Old Testament), 70 f., 79

Universal significance of Jesus. *See* Soteriology

Unity of God and man in Jesus, 283-288, 290-294, 296-298, 301, 313 f., 331, 334-340, 342-347, 365, 383. *See also* Jesus' divinity; Two-nature doctrine

Virgin birth, 141-150, 357 f., 361 f. *See also* Jesus' birth

Visio beata, 326n1, 330 f., 350

Vision, 93-99, 105 f.

Wisdom speculation, 152-154, 162

Word of God, 162n106, 167

Work of Christ, 44, 212; person and work, 38, 208-210. *See also* Soteriology

World, end of. *See* Fulfillment, eschatological

Name Index

Colpe, C., 151, 152, 196, 202
Congar, Y. M. J., 43, 212
Constantine, 239
Conzelmann, H., 57, 58, 59, 61, 62, 98, 103, 105, 227, 230, 231, 232, 243, 327, 328, 371, 379
Crell, N., 299
Cullmann, O., 29, 30, 31, 32, 122, 127, 134, 159, 196, 197, 216, 218, 327, 389
Cyril of Alexandria, 40, 284, 289, 290, 291, 305, 308, 338, 339, 349, 356, 358

Dell, T. C., 78
Denzinger, H., 283, 284, 293, 294, 295, 300, 329, 331, 333, 350, 355, 356, 358, 359, 363, 369
Dibelius, M., 120, 141, 142, 143, 218
Diekamp-Jüssen, 383
Diem, H., 55
Dionysius Aeropagita, 293
Dorner, I. A., 42, 298, 304, 305, 306, 307, 311, 341, 362, 388
Dörries, H., 172, 176, 178, 337
Duns Scotus, J., 296, 329, 340, 358, 383
Dürr, L., 162

Ebeling, G., 19, 24, 25, 27, 37, 45, 47, 57, 96, 109, 110, 111, 136, 159, 199, 229, 231
Eber, P., 299
Ebner, F., 167, 341
Einstein, A., 166
Elert, W., 37, 53, 54, 55, 108, 127, 155, 285, 290, 291, 292, 293, 294, 297, 305, 333, 338, 372, 373, 383, 384
Elze, M., 162, 163, 164
Ephrem, 338
Epiphanius, 357, 358
Eulogios of Alexandria, 338
Eusebius, 213
Eustathius of Antioch, 288

Farmer, H. H., 127
Feuerbach, L., 47, 341, 343
Fichte, J. G., 181, 182
Fiebig, P., 229
Fincke, E., 38
Forck, G., 372, 376
Frank, F. H. R., 273, 310
Fränkel, H., 161
Frick, R., 369, 370, 373

Friedrich, G., 219, 271
Fuchs, E., 24, 57, 112, 161, 228, 231
Fulgentius of Ruspe, 333

Galtier, P., 329, 330, 331
Gerhard, J., 215
Gess, W. F., 310, 320
Gigon, O., 161
Gilg, A., 39, 284
Gloege, G., 46, 127, 140, 341, 373
Gogarten, F., 26, 37, 46, 47, 55, 63, 155, 199, 286, 336, 337, 346
Göschel, K. F., 388
Grass, H., 88, 89, 92, 93, 94, 96, 97, 101, 102, 103, 105, 299
Gregory of Nazianzus, 40, 180, 288, 297
Gregory of Nyssa, 41, 180, 213, 276, 290, 297, 305, 308
Gregory the Great, 276, 333
Grillmeier, A., 39, 40, 41, 119, 163, 180, 272, 283, 287, 288, 289, 290, 298, 305, 329, 330, 331, 333, 338
Gunkel, H., 240
Günther, E., 304, 310, 336, 360, 388, 389
Gussmann, W., 213
Gutwenger, E., 350

Haenchen, E., 379
Hahn, F., 29, 31, 60, 69, 71, 72, 117, 118, 122, 127, 134, 135, 137, 140, 143, 152, 158, 214, 216, 218, 219, 230, 246, 248, 255, 327, 366, 368
Harnack, A. von, 22, 93, 121, 238, 286, 289, 290, 341, 359
Harvey, V. A., 24, 57
Haubst, R., 328, 330
Hegel, G. W. F., 48, 127, 181, 182, 183, 184, 237, 318, 319, 320, 336, 341, 388, 395
Hegermann, H., 392, 393
Hegesippus, 213
Heim, K., 39
Henry of Ghent, 358
Heppe-Bizer, 271
Heraclitus, 161, 394
Heraclius, 293
Hermann, I., 76, 118, 169, 171
Herrmann, W., 23, 24, 25, 27, 37, 53, 109, 127, 359, 360, 361
Hilary, 305, 308
Hillerdal, G., 374

413

Maximus Confessor, 293, 294, 348, 349, 350
Melanchthon, P., 38, 39, 48, 279, 299, 300
Melito of Sardis, 272, 284
Menken, G., 362
Merki, H., 41
Methodius of Olympus, 78
Michaelis, W., 77, 94
Michel, O., 219, 381
Mildenberger, F., 68
Moeller, Ch., 290, 338, 339, 350
Moltmann, J., 167
Mühlen, H., 296, 341
Mühlenberg, E., 206
Müller, A., 145, 146
Müller, E. F. K., 213, 218, 311
Müller, J., 359, 360

Nédoncelle, M., 338, 340
Nestorius, 290, 291, 292, 293, 295, 298
Nicholas of Cusa, 203, 346
Niebuhr, H. R., 127
Niebuhr, R. R., 98, 109
Niesel, W., 299
Nietzsche, F., 235, 236
Nikolainen, A. T., 78
Nitzsch-Stephan, 279

Ockham, W., 299
Oepke, A., 127
Ogden, S. M., 24, 57
Olevian, C., 271
Origen, 40, 41, 78, 124, 164, 272, 276, 297, 308, 356, 369, 370
Osiander, A., 213, 222
Ott, L., 347, 383
Otto, R., 60
Oyen, H. van, 127

Pamphilus of Jerusalem, 338
Parente, P., 329, 330
Parsimonius, J., 274
Paul of Samosata, 121, 198
Peregro, A., 330
Perino, R., 182
Peter Lombard, 295
Peterson, E., 373
Pezel, Chr., 299
Philo, 123, 142, 152, 160, 161, 163, 196, 197, 200, 202, 393
Philostratus, 91

Piper, O., 390
Pius XII, 329
Plato, 41, 87, 206
Plöger, O., 78, 207, 214, 217
Plügge, H., 85
Pohlenz, M., 161
Porreta, G., 295
Potterie, J. de la, 214
Praxeas, 160
Procksch, O., 170
Pseudo-Athanasius, 357
Pseudo-Basil, 297
Pyrrhus of Constantinople, 293

Quenstedt, J. A., 215, 223, 273, 302

Rad, G. von, 169, 170, 207, 221, 234, 265, 267, 274
Rahner, H., 145
Rahner, K., 112, 145, 199, 317, 318, 319, 320, 321, 326, 329, 330, 331, 332, 333, 345, 346, 350, 351, 387, 388
Ratschow, C. H., 37, 55
Rau, E., 79
Reicke, B., 271, 272
Reitzenstein, R., 152, 196
Rendtorff, R., 70, 128, 129, 225, 269
Rengstorf, K. H., 74, 77, 80, 89, 112, 152
Rhine, J. B., 95
Richard, M., 338
Richard of St.-Victor, 181, 340
Richardson, D. W., 127
Ritschl, A., 22, 36, 37, 39, 44, 45, 48, 49, 53, 121, 194, 208, 209, 210, 264, 279, 285, 286, 360, 365, 389
Ritschl, O., 299
Rivière, J., 277
Robinson, J. M., 24, 55, 57
Roschini, G., 145
Rossler, D., 250
Rothe, R., 388
Rouet, M. J., 356

Sabellius, 126
Sartori, E., 310
Schaeder, E., 173, 174
Schell, H., 328, 330
Scherzer, J., 359
Scheurer, G., 78
Schilder, K., 157
Schlatter, A., 60, 357